D0848437

ORCHESTRATION OF THE GLOBAL NETWORK ORGANIZATION

ADVANCES IN INTERNATIONAL MANAGEMENT

Series Editors: (To Volume 22) Joseph L. C. Cheng, Michael A. Hitt
(Volume 23–) Timothy M. Devinney, Torben Pedersen and Laszlo Tihanyi

Recent Volumes:

Volume 12: Edited by J. L. C. Cheng and R. B. Peterson

Volume 13: Edited by J. L. C. Cheng and R. B. Peterson

Volume 14: Edited by M. A. Hitt and J. L. C. Cheng

Volume 15: Edited by J. L. C. Cheng and M. A. Hitt

Volume 16: Edited by M. A. Hitt and J. L. C. Cheng

Volume 17: Edited by Thomas Roehl and Allan Bird

Volume 18: Edited by D. L. Shapiro, M. A. Von Glinow and J. L. C. Cheng

Volume 19: Edited by M. Javidan, R. M. Steers and M. A. Hitt

Volume 20: Edited by José Antonio Rosa and Madhu Viswanathan

Volume 21: Edited by John J. Lawler and Gregory S. Hundley

Volume 22: Edited by Joseph L. C. Cheng, Elizabeth Maitland and Stephen Nicholas

Volume 23: Edited by Timothy M. Devinney, Torben Pedersen and Laszlo Tihanyi

Volume 24: Edited by Christian Geisler Asmussen, Torben Pedersen, Timothy M. Devinney and Laszlo Tihanyi

Volume 25: Edited by Laszlo Tihanyi, Timothy M. Devinney and Torben Pedersen

Volume 26: Edited by Timothy M. Devinney, Torben Pedersen and Laszlo Tihanyi

ADVANCES IN INTERNATIONAL MANAGEMENT
VOLUME 27

ORCHESTRATION OF THE GLOBAL NETWORK ORGANIZATION

EDITED BY

TORBEN PEDERSEN
Università Bocconi, Milan, Italy

MARKUS VENZIN
Università Bocconi, Milan, Italy

TIMOTHY M. DEVINNEY
Leeds University Business School, University of Leeds, UK

LASZLO TIHANYI
Texas A&M University, USA

Emerald

United Kingdom − North America − Japan
India − Malaysia − China

Emerald Group Publishing Limited
Howard House, Wagon Lane, Bingley BD16 1WA, UK

First edition 2014

Copyright © 2014 Emerald Group Publishing Limited

Reprints and permission service
Contact: permissions@emeraldinsight.com

British Library Cataloguing in Publication Data
A catalogue record for this book is available from the British Library

ISBN: 978-1-78350-953-9
ISSN: 1571-5027 (Series)

ISOQAR certified
Management System,
awarded to Emerald
for adherence to
Environmental
standard
ISO 14001:2004.

Certificate Number 1985
ISO 14001

INVESTOR IN PEOPLE

CONTENTS

LIST OF CONTRIBUTORS ix

EDITORS' BIOGRAPHIES xiii

EDITORS' INTRODUCTION xv

PART I

INTRODUCTION TO PART I: BOOZ & CO./
STRATEGY + BUSINESS EMINENT SCHOLAR IN
INTERNATIONAL MANAGEMENT 2013
Timothy M. Devinney 3

THE ORGANIZATIONAL ARCHITECTURE OF
THE MULTINATIONAL CORPORATION
D. Eleanor Westney 5

PROFESSOR D. ELEANOR WESTNEY AND JAPANESE
BUSINESS STUDIES
Kazuhiro Asakawa 23

PART II

INTRODUCTION TO PART II: ORCHESTRATION OF
THE GLOBAL NETWORK ORGANIZATION
Torben Pedersen, Markus Venzin, Timothy M. Devinney 37
and Laszlo Tihanyi

THE DIFFUSION OF LEAN OPERATIONS PRACTICES
IN MNCs: A KNOWLEDGE-BASED, PLANT LEVEL,
CROSS-FIRM STUDY
Arnaldo Camuffo, Raffaele Secchi and Chiara Paolino   *43*

THE VIRTUE OF IN-BETWEEN PRAGMATISM – A
BALANCING ACT BETWEEN RESPONSIVENESS AND
INTEGRATION IN A MULTINATIONAL COMPANY
Gabriel R. G. Benito, Randi Lunnan and Sverre Tomassen   *75*

FUNCTIONAL-LEVEL TRANSFORMATION IN
MULTI-DOMESTIC MNCs: TRANSFORMING LOCAL
PURCHASING INTO GLOBALLY INTEGRATED
PURCHASING
Frank Elter, Paul N. Gooderham and Svein Ulset   *99*

NETWORK ORCHESTRATION: VODAFONE'S
JOURNEY TO GLOBALIZATION
Ayse Saka-Helmhout and Christopher J. Ibbott   *121*

RE-THINKING A MNC: THE ROLE OF COGNITIVE
INTERVENTIONS IN ORGANIZATIONAL DESIGN
Elizabeth Maitland and André Sammartino   *149*

"THE MOST PUBLIC SECRET": CONCEALING AND
SILENCING ETHNOCENTRISM IN THE MNC
Marianne Storgaard, Janne Tienari and Rebecca Piekkari   *191*

THE OMNIPOTENT MNC – A REVIEW AND
DISCUSSION
Håkan Pihl and Alexander Paulsson   *213*

COMPLEMENTARITY VERSUS SUBSTITUTION
AMONG POLITICAL STRATEGIES
Stefan Heidenreich, Jonas F. Puck and Igor Filatotchev   *235*

THE DARK SIDE OF MULTI-UNIT FRANCHISING:
THE DRAWBACKS OF LOCAL RESPONSIVENESS
Andrey Kretinin, Todd Morgan and Sergey Anokhin   *263*

ORGANIZING EXPORT STRATEGIES
Gabriella Lojacono and Markus Venzin 283

MNC HEADQUARTERS AS GLOBAL NETWORK
ORCHESTRATORS: INSIGHTS FROM
HEADQUARTERS RELOCATION PATTERNS IN
EUROPE
Alfredo Valentino, Phillip C. Nell and Jasper J. Hotho 299

STRATEGIC ARCHETYPES OF EMERGING MARKET
MULTINATIONALS: ANALYSIS OF OUTWARD FDI
OF INDIAN FIRMS
Amit Karna, Rajesh Upadhyayula and Vikas Kumar 325

ORGANIZING MNC INTERNAL NETWORKS TO
MANAGE GLOBAL CUSTOMERS: STRATEGIES OF
POLITICAL COMPROMISING
Elina Pernu, Tuija Mainela and Vesa Puhakka 349

TO ORCHESTRATE MNC INTRA-FIRM
RELATIONSHIPS, ONE NEEDS TO UNDERSTAND
THEM
Snejina Michailova and Smita Paul 377

ORGANIZATIONAL RECONFIGURATION AND
STRATEGIC RESPONSE: THE CASE OF OFFSHORING
Marcus M. Larsen and Torben Pedersen 403

EXPERIENTIAL LEARNING AND INNOVATION IN
OFFSHORE OUTSOURCING TRANSITIONS
Christopher Williams and Maya Kumar 433

MULTINATIONAL FIRMS AND THE MANAGEMENT
OF GLOBAL NETWORKS: INSIGHTS FROM GLOBAL
VALUE CHAIN STUDIES
Valentina De Marchi, Eleonora Di Maria and 463
Stefano Ponte

DISINTEGRATION AND
DE-INTERNATIONALIZATION: CHANGING
VERTICAL AND INTERNATIONAL SCOPE
AND THE CASE OF THE OIL AND GAS INDUSTRY
   Colin Dale, Thomas Osegowitsch and Simon Collinson   *487*

AUTHORS' BIOGRAPHIES   *517*

LIST OF CONTRIBUTORS

Sergey Anokhin	Kent State University, Kent, OH, USA
Kazuhiro Asakawa	Keio University, Tokyo, Japan
Gabriel R. G. Benito	BI Norwegian Business School, Oslo, Norway
Arnaldo Camuffo	Bocconi University, Milan, Italy
Simon Collinson	Birmingham Business School — University of Birmingham, Birmingham, UK
Colin Dale	Henley Business School — University of Reading, Reading, UK
Valentina De Marchi	University of Padova, Padova, Italy
Timothy M. Devinney	Leeds University Business School, University of Leeds, UK
Eleonora Di Maria	University of Padova, Padova, Italy
Frank Elter	Telenor Research, Fornebu, Norway
Igor Filatotchev	WU Vienna University, Vienna, Austria
Paul N. Gooderham	NHH — Norwegian School of Economics, Bergen, Norway
Stefan Heidenreich	GfK Austria, Vienna, Austria
Jasper J. Hotho	Copenhagen Business School, Frederiksberg, Denmark
Christopher J. Ibbott	Surrey Business School — University of Surrey, Guildford, UK
Amit Karna	EBS Business School — EBS Universität für Wirtschaft und Recht, Oestrich-Winkel, Germany

Andrey Kretinin	Kent State University, Kent, OH, USA
Maya Kumar	Ivey School of Business – Western University, London, ON, Canada
Vikas Kumar	University of Sydney, Sydney, Australia
Marcus M. Larsen	Copenhagen Business School, Frederiksberg, Denmark
Gabriella Lojacono	Bocconi University, Milan, Italy
Randi Lunnan	BI Norwegian Business School, Oslo, Norway
Tuija Mainela	Oulu Business School – University of Oulu, Oulu, Finland
Elizabeth Maitland	University of New South Wales, Kensington (NSW), Australia
Snejina Michailova	The University of Auckland Business School, Auckland, New Zealand
Todd Morgan	Kent State University, Kent, OH, USA
Phillip C. Nell	Copenhagen Business School, Frederiksberg, Denmark
Thomas Osegowitsch	University of Melbourne, Parkville, VIC, Australia
Chiara Paolino	Università Cattolica del Sacro Cuore, Milan, Italy
Smita Paul	The University of Auckland Business School, Auckland, New Zealand
Alexander Paulsson	Lund University, Lund, Sweden
Torben Pedersen	Università Bocconi, Milan, Italy
Elina Pernu	Oulu Business School – University of Oulu, Oulu, Finland
Rebecca Piekkari	Aalto University School of Business, Helsinki, Finland

Håkan Pihl	Lund University, Lund, Sweden
Stefano Ponte	Copenhagen Business School, Frederiksberg, Denmark
Jonas F. Puck	WU Vienna University, Vienna, Austria
Vesa Puhakka	Oulu Business School – University of Oulu, Oulu, Finland
Ayse Saka-Helmhout	Nijmegen School of Management – Radboud University, Nijmegen, The Netherlands
André Sammartino	University of Melbourne, Parkville, VIC, Australia
Raffaele Secchi	Bocconi University, Milan, Italy
Marianne Storgaard	University of Southern Denmark, Kolding, Denmark
Janne Tienari	Aalto University School of Business, Helsinki, Finland
Laszlo Tihanyi	Texas A&M University, College Station, TX, USA
Sverre Tomassen	BI Norwegian Business School, Oslo, Norway
Svein Ulset	NHH – Norwegian School of Economics, Bergen, Norway
Rajesh Upadhyayula	Indian Institute of Management, Kozhikode, India
Alfredo Valentino	Luiss Guido Carli University, Rome, Italy
Markus Venzin	Università Bocconi, Milan, Italy
D. Eleanor Westney	Schulich School of Business – York University, Toronto, ON, Canada
Christopher Williams	Ivey School of Business – Western University, London, ON, Canada

EDITORS' BIOGRAPHIES

Timothy M. Devinney is a Professor of International Business and University Leadership Chair at the University of Leeds. He has published 10 books and more than 90 articles in leading journals. In 2008, he was the first recipient in management of an Alexander von Humboldt Research Award and was Rockefeller Foundation Bellagio Fellow. He is a Fellow of the Academy of International Business, an International Fellow under the auspices of the AIM Initiative in the UK and a Fellow of ANZAM (Australia New Zealand Academy of Management). He served as Chair of the International Management Division of the Academy of Management. He is Co-Editor of Academy of Management Perspectives and the head of the International Business & Management Network of SSRN. He is on the editorial board of more than 10 of the leading international journals.

Torben Pedersen is Professor of International Business at Bocconi University. His research interests are in the interface between strategy and international management and he has published over 100 articles and books in this area. His research has appeared in prominent journals such as Academy of Management Journal, Strategic Management Journal, Journal of Management, Journal of International Business Studies and Organization Science. In addition, he has written more than 25 teaching cases published at IVEY case clearing house or in teaching-oriented books. He is currently Co-Editor of Global Strategy Journal and on the editorial boards of numerous journals. He is a Fellow of the Academy of International Business and has previously served as Vice-president for both AIB and EIBA.

Laszlo Tihanyi is the B. Marie Oth Professor in Business Administration in the Mays Business School at Texas A&M University, USA. His main research areas are internationalization, corporate governance in multinational firms, and organizational adaptation in emerging economies. His papers have been published in the Academy of Management Journal, Academy of Management Review, Strategic Management Journal, Organization Science, Journal of International Business Studies, and others. He presently serves as Chair of the Corporate Strategy Interest Group of the

Strategic Management Society. He is an Associate Editor of the Academy of Management Journal.

Markus Venzin, Swiss, Full Professor of Global Strategy at the Management and Technology Department of Bocconi University and the Director of the "Claudio Dematté" Research Division at SDA Bocconi. He has held visiting positions and teaching assignments at the University of Michigan, Fudan University (Shanghai), Copenhagen Business School, Essec (Paris), ESADE (Barcelona) and St. Gallen University. He obtained his PhD in Strategy and Organization from the University of St. Gallen and has since worked as a strategist in the manufacturing industry, founded his own consulting firm and has served as a member of supervisory and advisory boards of several multinational firms. Markus is actively involved in executive development, the facilitation of strategy workshops and consulting to senior executives in a wide range of industries. He is a frequent speaker at corporate or industry events on topics such as internationalization strategies, strategic decision making dynamics, global knowledge management systems, and the development of formal planning and control processes in large multinational firms. His latest books are: *Internationalization of Financial Services Firms: How Successful Firms Design and Execute Cross-Border Strategies* (Oxford University Press) and *Resilience: Sette Principi per una Gestione Aziendale Sana e Prudente* (con Guia Pirotti, Egea, 2014).

EDITORS' INTRODUCTION

This is the fifth volume of *Advances in International Management* under the editorial team consisting of Timothy M. Devinney, Torben Pedersen and Laszlo Tihanyi plus Markus Venzin who has been added as a special co-editor on this particular volume. Previous volumes have focused on topics from the general state of research in International Management over location aspects, institutional factors to meta-analysis in IM research.

The main body of this volume focuses on organizational design of the MNC. It tries to create a bridge to the early literature on different organizational models for the MNC – largely captured in the powerful integration-responsiveness framework – and extend this literature by applying insights from other fields and theories. We hope this volume will help bring back organizational design of the MNC as an important research area in International Management.

OVERVIEW OF VOLUME 27

The first part of Volume 27 contains our annual feature from a leading scholar. Professor D. Eleanor Westney was the recipient of the 2013 Booz & Co./strategy + business Eminent Scholar in International Management Award, given by the International Management Division of the Academy of Management, and in the acceptance speech gives us her very inspiring view on the organizational architecture of the MNC. This is a particular salient introduction to this volume as Professor Westney presents her personal journey into the literature on organizational architecture and specific suggestions on how we can take this research further. Kaz Asakawa provides a commentary that places Westney's work very well in the context.

The second part of Volume 27 presents 18 articles focused on the theme of the volume: *Orchestration of the Global Network Organization*. The process of compiling this volume of unique articles on organizational design of the MNC has lasted for a year and has been a somewhat bumpy road. It has involved intensive reviewing and revision of the papers (with at least two rounds of revision) as well as a two-day workshop (held in Milan) where all authors had a change to discuss each other's contributions and the broader theme that are captured in this volume.

The result of this process is 18 great and insightful articles that together provide a strong message on how vibrant is the research on organizational design of the MNC. Many different perspectives, empirical angels, frameworks are tested in these papers. All papers scrutinize different aspects of organizational design, but the exact focus can vary. In fact, the articles can be divided into three groups. Some of the papers look at organization design as a more internal exercise of socially engineering the organizational system. These are typically case-based studies where you are able to follow the process of socially engineering the organizational architecture. Other papers take a more strategic perspective where organizational design is a matter of choosing the governance form that is most suitable given firm and competitive conditions. These studies do on the other hand often include statistical tests and comparison of the different governance forms on large scale data. The last group of papers is looking more at organizational design as an outside-in occurrence where the organizational design most matches the industry, customers, or other stakeholders.

In closing, we would like to thank Bocconi University for their support of the workshop in Milan and all the Emerald editorial team for their patience and support. In addition, Sara Mitterhofer provided critical editorial and administrative assistance in completing the volume on time. Without this invaluable support, the volume would still be in process!

Timothy M. Devinney
Torben Pedersen
Laszlo Tihanyi
Series Editors

PART I

INTRODUCTION TO PART I: BOOZ & CO./STRATEGY+ BUSINESS EMINENT SCHOLAR IN INTERNATIONAL MANAGEMENT 2013

Timothy M. Devinney

The Booz & Co./strategy+business Eminent Scholar in International Management is an annual award given by the International Management Division of the Academy of Management and Sponsored by Booz & Co./strategy+business.

The 2013 awardee was Professor D. Eleanor Westney, Scotiabank Professor in International Business and Professor of Organization Studies at the Schulich School of Business at York University in Canada. Professor Westney was recognized for her contribution to the field of international business and management based upon her long-standing and well-respected work addressing the application of sociological models to international business and to her unique and innovative work on Japan and the Japanese multinational corporation.

Professor Westney received her B.A. and M.A. in Sociology from the University of Toronto. She received a Ph.D. in Sociology in 1978 from

Orchestration of the Global Network Organization
Advances in International Management, Volume 27, 3–4
Copyright © 2014 by Emerald Group Publishing Limited
All rights of reproduction in any form reserved
ISSN: 1571-5027/doi:10.1108/S1571-502720140000027031

Princeton University and began her teaching career in the Department of Sociology at Yale University. She moved to M.I.T. and into the International Business field in 1982, spending the next 25 years at M.I.T. where she held the Sloan Fellows Chair. Her first book, *Imitation and Innovation: The Adoption of Western Organizational Forms in Meiji Japan* (Harvard University Press, 1987), explored the patterns of cross-border organizational learning, a theme that has continued to be a major focus of her interests. The book remains a classic to this day. She has written extensively on Japanese organizations, on the internationalization of R&D, and on institutional theory and multinational enterprise. She has been a visiting researcher at Hitotsubashi University and the University of Tokyo in Japan, and a visiting professor at the University of Michigan, and is a Fellow of the Academy of International Business.

Professor Westney has been a tireless advocate of the International Business field and been a major contributor in terms of both scholarship and active service to the community, including a stint as the head of the International Management Division of the Academy of Management (2002–2007). In addition, she has left (and continues to expand) a legacy of doctoral students who have become leaders in the field. A short list of those she has led by example and served as a mentor includes: Sumantra Ghoshal (who received his Ph.D. in 1985), Nitin Nohria (1988), Srilata Zaheer (1992), Anthony Frost (1998), Annique Un (2001), Christopher Voisey and Rafel Lucea (both in 2007).

Following Professor Westney's paper, we have a cogent commentary from Professor Kazuhiro Asakawa from Keio University in Japan. Professor Asakawa is a leading international business scholar and an expert on Japan. He provides not just a broad academic perspective on Professor Westney's work, but her role as mentor, colleague, and role model. He makes this distinctly personal by not only linking it to his own research and writing, but also to the deep understanding of Japan that Professor Westney's work has instilled in other scholars.

THE ORGANIZATIONAL ARCHITECTURE OF THE MULTINATIONAL CORPORATION

D. Eleanor Westney

Receiving the Eminent Scholar Award from the International Management Division is an unexpected honor, and I am most grateful to the division and to the two distinguished speakers who are providing commentaries, Sri Zaheer and Kaz Asakawa. An award like provides a somewhat unnerving opportunity to look back over past years in the field and to look forward to future challenges. I am going to take this opportunity to address some unfinished business — a theme that has run through much of my work in the IM field over the past three decades but which I feel I have not adequately tackled — and perhaps to persuade some of you to connect this to your own thinking and research. That theme is the organizational architecture of the multinational corporation.

When I was recruited to the International Business field in 1982 as a sociologist whose research focused on Japan, I quickly realized that MNCs would be an important area of my future research agenda. In the early 1980s, the Japanese were changing the rules of the competitive game in international business, in ways that their Western competitors and an array of academic researchers were striving to understand. The MIT Sloan School of Management recruited a Japan specialist to address the increasingly

Orchestration of the Global Network Organization
Advances in International Management, Volume 27, 5–22
Copyright © 2014 by Emerald Group Publishing Limited
All rights of reproduction in any form reserved
ISSN: 1571-5027/doi:10.1108/S1571-502720140000027026

important impact of Japanese MNCs on international competition, and more specifically, to investigate how Japanese firms were internationalizing and how they were building capabilities abroad. As an organizational sociologist happily teaching comparative organizations and social change in a Sociology Department, I had not actually conducted any research on Japanese MNCs, nor did I know much about MNCs in general. Indeed, my research seemed far removed from the early 1980s competitive battles of international business: it focused on the adoption and adaptation of Western organizational forms into Japan in the Meiji period. However, the MIT Sloan School recognized the potential relevance of the theme of cross-border learning to the contemporary context, and I wound up on the MIT Sloan faculty in the International Management group, with the great good fortune to have as colleagues Richard Robinson, one of the founders of the IB field, and Don Lessard, one of the most creative thinkers in the field, and with close colleagues in Organization Studies that included Ed Schein, Lotte Bailyn, and John Van Maanen, who helped me enormously as my research moved from the historical to the contemporary business context.

REDISCOVERING THE ROOTS OF IM: IDENTIFYING THE MNC AS AN ORGANIZATIONAL FORM

When I entered the International Business field in 1982, I did not realize how recently the term "multinational corporation" had been coined to identify a distinctive organizational form. Multinational companies have existed for over a century (after all, Japanese trading companies had set up offices abroad in the Meiji period, and Japanese manufacturing firms had operated in Korea and China in the early 20th century), but until the 1960s, and indeed well beyond, there was no generally accepted label for firms that owned and operated subunits outside their home countries. Economists treated their activities in terms of cross-border capital flows, as symbolized by the term "foreign direct investment." John Dunning's pioneering 1958 study of the effects of US investment in Britain, for example, moved well beyond the topics then current in FDI research — the effects of inward FDI on local capital formation, employment, and prices — to include an examination of the influence of the US-based managerial practices and organizational patterns of their British subsidiaries on UK suppliers and competitors and on changing British models of management. However, constrained by the standard terminology (even in his title, *American Investment in British Manufacturing Industry*), he was driven to such awkward locutions as "US-affiliated companies engaged in British manufacturing" and "American-financed firms" to refer to US MNCs.

The earliest use of the term "multinational corporation" has been traced to 1960 − and the first use was *not* in Stephen Hymer's 1960 dissertation, which is now widely regarded as the foundation stone of the economic theory of the MNC but which never actually used the term. Indeed, Hymer did not seem to regard such firms as constituting a distinctive category, as his dissertation title, *The International Operations of National Firms*, demonstrated. He aspired to develop not a theory of the multinational corporation, with which he is now widely credited, but "a theory of international operations" as part of the general theory of the firm.

The label "multinational corporation" was first used to identify a distinctive category of firms in a nearly-forgotten paper by David Lilienthal, the first director of the TVA under Franklin Roosevelt and subsequently an international investment banker and consultant. The paper, titled "Management of the Multinational Corporation," was written for a 1960 conference at Carnegie Institute of Technology on the challenges facing American managers in the coming quarter-century.[1] Lilienthal opened with the following definition:

> Many large and even medium-sized American corporations are already operating in other countries ... By *operating* I have particularly in mind industrial or commercial operations which directly involve managerial responsibility. Such corporations − which have their home in one country but which operate and live under the laws and customs of other countries as well − I would like to define here as *multinational corporations*. (Lilienthal, 1960, p. 119)

Lilienthal saw the multinational corporation as a distinctive kind of firm because it faced distinctive managerial challenges, and because its responses to those challenges would, he believed, transform the modern world. Among these managerial challenges were those involving relationships with the different governments under which it operated. The MNC also faced different local customs and institutions, to which MNC managers had to adjust (and Lilienthal distinguished between institutions such as Anglo-Saxon common law or the Napoleonic Code, to which managers had to adapt, and specific regulations, which they could work to change). And the MNC faced the problem of being perceived as foreign not only by local governments but also by local employees and other local constituencies (a problem also emphasized by Hymer).

Lilienthal saw the MNC as dealing with the variety of its host institutional environments in two ways. One was adapting the organization and managerial behavior of its foreign subsidiaries to the local patterns. However, Lilienthal also predicted that MNCs would respond by actively transforming the institutional environments in which they operated: supporting the development of regional trading blocs, working to reduce the differences across countries in the regulations governing their activities, and developing international "protectors and servicers" including marketing and advertising firms and financial and information services (1960, pp. 129, 153). Moreover, they would generate a new multinational class of technicians, production managers, administrators, and financial experts who would move with their families across international postings. Lilienthal was among the first to argue that these encounters with a growing number and diversity of institutional environments would reduce the effects of home country imprinting by exposing managers to different institutional environments, thereby weakening the taken-for-granted nature of their home country patterns (or to use the terminology of Scott's organizational institutionalism rather than Lilienthal's own, weakening both the cognitive and normative pillars of home country institutionalization). MNCs would also need to engage in cross-border learning, which would foster "two-way trade in social and cultural values" between home and host countries (1960, pp. 156−157), and they would "give us the beginnings of a world-wide system of business ethics" (1960, p. 155). In other words, he portrayed the MNC as an agent of institutional change at three levels: the local host environments in which it operated, its own home country, and the new international order (or "field" as we would now call it) for cross-border business, which MNCs were engaged in creating. These activities would enable the MNC to operate in similar ways, with similar structures and routines, in many different locations, and to increase its ability to do so over time.

Perhaps because it was delivered in a forum of executives rather than an academic conference, Lilienthal's paper seems to have gone largely unnoticed and unread by the emerging community of International Business scholars. However, his label of "multinational corporation," was quickly picked up by the business press and by firms such as IBM, perhaps because he portrayed the MNC as a force for positive transformation in the world (and because a number of corporate leaders were present at the Carnegie presentation). In fact, IBM embraced the label of the multinational corporation to such effect that it has in some sources been credited with originating the term (Strange, 1996, p. xv). In the IB field, however, the 1960s and 1970s witnessed a number of terms for the organizational phenomenon of the border-crossing company. Many American economists tended to follow Charles Kindleberger, Hymer's advisor and the scholar credited with disseminating Hymer's work through his widely used textbook in international economics, in calling these firms "international companies," although critics pointed out that not all companies with an international reach owned and controlled operations outside their home countries. Ray Vernon adopted part of Lilienthal's term for his influential research project at Harvard collecting data on what he called "multinational enterprises." Critics like Richard Barnett preferred the (then) somewhat threatening term, "global corporations" (Barnet & Müller, 1974). When the United Nations established a center in 1974 to study the role of such companies in economic and social development processes, it eschewed both "international" and "multinational" and instead called it the UN Centre on Transnational Corporations. It took two decades before Lilienthal's term became the most widely used.

However, Lilienthal's paper deserves to be regarded as a pioneering contribution to the subfield of International Management, as Hymer's is for International Business. This is not simply because of his coining of the term "multinational corporation" but also because of his early identification of one of the core premises of the IM field: that the managerial and organizational challenges of coping with the MNC's external variety of environments and its internal dispersion and variety of subunits are distinctive, and that the MNC's responses to those challenges make it a distinctive organizational form and a potential source of institutional change and organizational innovation.

One aspect of those organizational innovations lies in the strategic design — the architecture — of the MNC. When a firm extends its operations across borders, how does it fit those operations into its organizational architecture, and how does its structure change as its operations abroad expand? Geography and location become unavoidable design variables, but how are they incorporated into the formal structure? These questions were a major topic in the early years of the international business field and well into the 1980s, but drew diminishing attention in the 1990s and in recent years. Although key issues of IM research in those decades, such as HQ-subsidiary relations, cross-unit networks, and global teams, involved formal structure, the design of the MNC that provided the structural context into which they fit was rarely explicated. The architecture of the MNC is, however, an issue of too much importance to be left to the consultants.

RECOGNIZING THE IMPORTANCE OF ORGANIZATIONAL ARCHITECTURE: A PERSONAL JOURNEY

Throughout my research career, the importance of organizational architecture has been unavoidable, although it was rarely central to my inquiries (one exception is Westney, 2003). In my sociological study of the transfer of Western organizational patterns to Meiji Japan (Westney, 1987), it became clear that the easiest aspect for the Japanese to emulate was the formal organization design: the structure of departments (the "org chart"), the formal definition of roles and responsibilities, the rules and procedures, and so on. When I turned to the study of Japanese MNCs after joining the Sloan School, it was quickly evident that their distinctive organizational architecture – separate subsidiaries for each function, manufacturing, marketing and sales, and R&D in each country, and numerous structures and processes for cross-border communications between the functions in Japan and those in each country, but relatively few cross-functional linking mechanisms within each count – was a key to understanding both their successes and their challenges (see Westney, 1999). As organization design specialists such as Jay Galbraith have long told us, the strength of functional organization is its focus on capability development and learning, but it has disadvantages in terms of integrating and managing complete value chains and developing effective general managers.

In studying the internationalization of R&D, I learned, sometimes rather painfully, that not paying enough attention to the larger organizational architecture in which the R&D units were embedded was dangerous. For example, through the MIT-Japan Program, I worked with Eastman-Kodak as they set up their R&D Laboratory in Tokyo. In our focus on helping the laboratory become an insider in the complex Japanese R&D system and the distinctive local technical labor markets, and in building networks between the lab and the research community in Rochester, I later realized that I did not pay enough attention to the implications of Kodak's reorganization into smaller and more focused business units and the increasing shift of R&D funding into the hands of the Business Units. This change in organization structure was a development that made funding an increasing challenge for the lab, which had been a corporate initiative, and it was, I believe, a factor in its rather dramatic shutdown in the early 1990s.

Finally, in two arenas in which I am now conducting research, the internationalization of services (with Beth Rose, Kaz Asakawa, and Kiyohiko Ito) and mining (in conjunction with Schulich's new MBA concentration in mining and minerals), I can see some unanticipated similarities between the two sectors in terms of design challenges, despite their very obvious differences. Both demand a high degree of geographic dispersion of subunits: services to be close to the customer, and mining to be at the site of the resource. However, they have more choice about where they locate the support activities for the front-line units, and for how they cluster both the front-line and support units.

The design choices they make will both reflect and subsequently shape their strategies and their capabilities. For service sector multinationals, some form of geographic grouping seems an obvious architectural choice — but some customers and customer segments span borders, and therefore require an architecture that presents one face to the multi-location customer in everyone location (such as the much-researched global customer account teams) while maintaining their ability to present a local face to local customers. Others deal with multinational suppliers — but architectures that present one face to the supplier have been much less developed in the management literature. Few mining companies, on the other hand, interact with customers: they are in commodity businesses, and only a few have begun developing strategies to differentiate their products for specific customers. However, they increasingly have multinational stakeholders, such as NGOs, which are increasingly demanding consistency in performance on environmental and social factors across multiple locations, and therefore mining companies too face the challenges of building organizational architectures that can present "one face" to certain stakeholders while tailoring local responses to others. And mining companies share with service companies the challenges of developing organizational architectures to interact consistently across locations with global suppliers while interacting effectively and differently with the local suppliers that are so important in maintaining their "license to operate" within a particular country.

Recognizing the importance of MNC organizational architecture for understanding a range of issues is only a first step; however, actually doing research faces some formidable challenges. One is the growing complexity of MNC architectures. One time-honored way of determining organizational structure is to look at the titles of the top management team. Today, they can be bewildering. In the past one could usually identify whether the basic structure was functional, business unit, or geographic from the titles of the executives below the CEO. Today, all three aspects (function, business unit, and geography) are likely to be represented, with equivalent titles, on the top management team, plus a number of corporate officers responsible for a wider range of support functions (such as Corporate

Social Responsibility and IT) than was traditionally the case, when the principal corporate support functions were Finance, Legal, and Corporate Relations. How these different architectural dimensions interact cannot be determined arm's length, and companies can be extremely wary of describing their architectures in detail to researchers, as I have found. Even targeted studies that gain access to a set of companies can face challenges in interpreting these "multidimensional" architectures (see for example Strikwerda & Stoelhorst, 2009).

Another challenge is clearly identifying − to academic colleagues and to MNC executives − why understanding organizational architecture is important. In fact, justifying it to colleagues may well be the more difficult. MNC executives have, in the last few years, increasingly struggled with how to develop effective organizational architectures, and the major consulting firms, McKinsey in particular, have identified organizational complexity as one of the most difficult challenges facing global firms − and have undoubtedly built lucrative practices in helping companies map and address the complexities of their architectures. For colleagues, however, the challenge is different. It centers on the question frequently posed to one of my mentors in my graduate days in the Princeton Sociology Department, Marion J. Levy, Jr., whose preoccupation with building comprehensive grand theory was the target of considerable teasing within the department: "That's all very well in practice, but will it work in theory?"

BROADENING THE THEORETICAL FOUNDATIONS FOR STUDYING MNC ARCHITECTURE

One of the reasons, I believe, for the fact that the organization design of the MNC has become a topic of somewhat narrow scope and interest in IB has been its rather specialized theoretical grounding. Addressing the organization design of the MNC as a central topic of research today demands a broader framing than the information-processing approach that has dominated work on the topic for decades, valuable as it contributions have been and continue to be.

The information-processing paradigm can be complemented by drawing on work over the past decade and a half on evolutionary perspectives on organizations. I have expanded on this at some length in a chapter for Simon Collinson and Glenn Morgan's 2009 book, *Images of the Multinational*, and shall only touch the surface here (Westney, 2009).

Briefly, the view of the MNC as itself an evolutionary system with a set of subsystems that evolve in interaction with each other, as well as with their differentiated environments, is one approach to addressing the complexity of the MNC and providing a framework for integrating the analysis of organizational architecture with some of the key issues in international management today. An evolutionary approach looks at the MNC in terms of internal processes of variation, selection, and retention, and regards MNC organizational design as shaping the selection regime. By "selection regime" I mean the *agents* doing the selection, the selection *target* (what is being selected, such as a particular architecture, product, or practice), the *criteria* for selection (efficiency and short-term performance in a business unit structure, for example, versus responsiveness to local stakeholders in a geographic structure), and the selection *outcome* (strong or weak selection).

The most obvious impact of MNC architecture is its formal identification of selection *agents*. The formal hierarchy assigns decision rights to certain positions (Executive Vice-President of Business Unit X, for example) or structures (such as management committees, technology councils, or the top management committee). The selection *targets* vary by selection agent, and one of the features that makes MNC organization complex is the proliferation of selection agents with different targets and criteria. Global Customer Teams, for example, target routines and organizational patterns that affect a certain subset of customers; stage-gate review forums target development projects. Much of the IM research on innovation processes in MNCs over the last two decades has focused on product innovations as selection targets.

Less obviously, but even more important, the architecture strongly influences the selection *criteria*. One of the most detailed analyses of selection criteria in MNCs is provided by Chris Bartlett and Sumantra Ghoshal in *Managing across Borders* (1989), where they portray the classic parameters of organization design – function, business, geography – as, in effect, creating very distinct selection regimes, in large part because of the selection *criteria* each prioritizes. They contrast the focus of geographic structures on promoting local responsiveness and on maintaining and improving relationships with local customers and stakeholders with the focus of business unit structures on improving efficiency and short-term performance and of functional structures with maintaining and expanding functional expertise and learning. The formal architecture shapes selection criteria not only because it privileges certain kinds of information to selection agents (information on French operations to the country head of France in a geographic structure, for example, versus data on the performance of the French operations in a particular business segment in an array of data from many countries flowing to a global business unit head), but also because the "boxes" of the organization chart also draw political and cultural boundaries around subunits. Those boundaries shape the interests and influence patterns within those subunits and also shape the identity and modes of framing and interpretation of members of the subunit — and hence, shape the criteria used in selection processes.

The justification for the matrix organization is that it balances two sets of selection criteria, by formally incorporating two design parameters (such as product and geography, as in ABB's famous matrix of the 1990s). But Bartlett and Ghoshal strongly resisted advocating any particular design for their model of the transnational, because each of the selection criteria (local responsiveness, efficiency, and learning) should dominate consistently, since the transnational faced all three pressures. No single architecture could do this consistently, in their view: it was the corporate headquarters that functioned as the selection agent for the MNC system as a whole, balancing the three selection subsystems over time and across issues, in order to enable the MNC system as a whole to succeed in the external environment.

The fourth element of the selection regime, *outcome* (strong vs. weak selection), has particular value in the study of MNCs. Strong selection means that "species" — organizations or organizational patterns — that do not fit the selection criteria are "selected out" and eliminated (the stance of early population ecology). "Weak selection" means that local variations are not selected *for*, but neither are they selected *out*: that is, they are allowed to persist locally, albeit with constrained resources. Weak selection is often a characteristic of complex, multi-unit and multi-level structures like MNCs, because one cannot assume that the selection regime at each level of the hierarchy mirrors that of the level above it or that units in one location face the same selection regime as those in other settings. Weak selection means that organizational patterns that do not fit the selection criteria can continue to survive, often in protected niches within the organization. This is often seen as a problem for organizations, because at least some resources continue to be diverted to the maintenance of the "de-selected" variation; however, it can also be a source of strength in the long term, because it can lead to further variation or be available as an adaptive variation to which the organization may turn when conditions change.

One way to interpret the changing architecture of MNCs in the last three and a half decades is to see it in terms of efforts to construct a selection regime that balances the demands of local responsiveness — to local customers and stakeholders and to modes of taking advantage of resources specific to a particular location – with other selection criteria, including efficiency, cross-border consistency for a growing set of international customers and suppliers, and cross-border learning. The early evolutionary model of Stopford and Wells (1972) predicted that MNCs would move towards the geography/product matrix as their international operations expanded and diversified. In fact, by the late 1980s and early 1990s, most MNCs were instead moving to global business unit structures, dividing their activities in a country into highly focused functional subunits and distributing these across business units, often burying the geographic parameter of architecture in the third or even fourth levels of the company. The pursuit of efficiency was a major factor in this change in many MNEs, but so too was the effort of MNE top management to eliminate the power of the country managers to block corporate change initiatives that top management believed were necessitated by the external competitive environment. Lew Gerstner of IBM articulated the perception of many CEOs in the early 1990s when he describes what he found on arriving at IBM as CEO in 1993 as "powerful geographic fiefdoms with duplicate infrastructure in each country" (Gerstner, 2003, p. 42), and characterizes his subsequent actions as "declaring war" on those geographic fiefdoms.

An explicitly evolutionary framing of this structural change to disaggregated focused subunits might be as follows: MNE top management (the primary selection agents of the corporate system) came to believe that shifts in the external competitive environment demanded internal changes to improve the fit between the MNE organization and that environment. The changes they selected at the corporate/system level were being blocked ("selected out") by a powerful subsystem, the national subsidiaries, and so the corporate selection regime selected out the national subsidiaries. It thereby eliminated this subsystem level within the MNE, and focused instead on what had been the lower-level subsystems of the "discrete value-adding activities (a sales operation, a manufacturing plant, an R&D centre)" (Birkinshaw, 2001, p. 381). The corporate selection agents (top management) expected to be able to align the selection regimes at this subsystem level more quickly with the selection processes of the HQ, because the smaller, more focused units were less buffered from HQ influence. They controlled fewer resources, and had less individual power and less visibility at the national level in their local environments. This change in the structure of the MNE subsystems also facilitated the absorption of acquired companies, which, whatever their formal structure, could relatively quickly be disaggregated into focused operating units. This structure also made it much easier to sell non-core businesses. Both processes were increasingly common in MNEs during the 1990s.

By the early 2000s, however, many MNC executives were experiencing growing fears that the geographic fiefdoms of the older MNC model had been replaced by business unit siloes that were too focused on the pursuit of efficiency and short-term solutions within the boundaries of their own subunits. It also proved more difficult than anticipated to align the numerous subunits into a consistent and strong selection regime. One of the very few detailed organizational studies of an MNC in this period has been provided by the remarkable study by Peer Hull Kristensen and Jonathan Zeitlin (2005) of a British MNC producing equipment for the food-processing industry, which had been formed by mergers and acquisitions – an extremely insightful and informative work too little read by North American IM scholars. They provide some useful insights onto the problems faced by the Global Business Unit MNC, in which, contrary to expectations, creating larger numbers of smaller and more focused subsidiaries below the country level did not make it easier for corporate HQ to align the locally differentiated evolutionary processes of these subsystems with its own evolutionary processes. The larger number of subsidiaries, widely dispersed geographically, made it difficult for the selection agents at HQ to understand the capabilities and selection processes of each of them well, a problem exacerbated in many MNEs today by the relatively brief length of any assignment of high-potential managers sent to the subsidiaries on their route to the corporate offices.

Moreover, Kristensen and Zeitlin portray the HQ as a subsystem embedded in its own local environment, London's financial center, with a selection regime strongly shaped by that environment, which applied strong pressure to the company to deliver greater profitability. However, those financial markets interpreted announcements of new programs and the replacement of corporate leaders with new "change agents" at the top as signals of improving prospects for profitability and rewarded them with a rise in the share price. This led to rapidly changing and inconsistent targets and criteria in the corporate selection regime, as each successive change program failed to "meet expectations." In Kristensen and Zeitlin's portrayal, this pressure for repeated change combined with the relatively uninformed higher-level selection agents, led to arbitrary targets and unforeseen negative consequences. This in turn undermined the legitimacy of the corporate selection regime and stimulated resistance from the subunits. In fact, in this description of a global BU structure, the subunits, which are local but not "national," constitute the level of the organizational architecture trying to balance the competing selection criteria of business, geography, and function, not the HQ, which Bartlett and Ghoshal saw as the key balancing level. The system level, in this model, is not defined by the corporate system but by the emergent "interactive game" among subsidiaries, which is beginning to constitute a network-level evolutionary system. It is not completely clear who the key selection agents at this level are, but the account suggests that they are the middle-level managers directly in charge of the numerous front-line business subunits focused on one line of products.

Kristensen and Zeitlin's case study highlights the importance of expanding the scope of inquiry on MNC organizational architecture beyond the focus on the first-order structural parameter (whether the design is a functional, business unit, geographic, matrix, or front-back structure) that has dominated much of the research on MNC organization design. It also demonstrates the value of empirical research that instead of studying MNC architecture from the top-down begins with the front-line units and works up.

EXPANDING THE SCOPE OF ORGANIZATIONAL ARCHITECTURE

The term "organizational architecture" conjures up the image of the organization chart – as indeed it should, since the formal reporting structure of the firm is a fundamental aspect of the organization design. All too often, however, analysis of the organization design of MNCs has focused exclusively on the first-order design parameter. An evolutionary approach to design suggests, however, that going deeper in the organization hierarchy, even simply to the next level of the design, can be extremely useful in understanding similarities and differences across companies with the same first-order structure. Take, for example, a global business unit structure. Each global business unit can itself be organized into global product units, thereby replicating the selection regime of the top level. Alternatively, each can be organized by geography. This was apparently the case with most of the MNCs in Bartlett and Ghoshal's famous study. ABB's Global Business Units in the 1990s were also subdivided by geography, thereby constructing the building blocks of its famous geography/product matrix. A third alternative is to divide the Global Business Units into functional subunits. A structure whose first- and second-order design parameters differ will have different selection regimes at different subsystem levels and therefore likely weaker selection and greater internal variation than one in which the first- and second-order design criteria are the same.

Going below the second-order level to investigate the third-order design parameter can be difficult but revealing. Each of the basic design criteria — function, product, geography — is employed in the organization design of the MNC (which may not be the case for the domestic firm, which may eschew geography). A key question in analyzing the architecture of the MNC is: at what level of the structure does geography become a design parameter. Kristensen and Zeitlin's study indicates that when geography is relegated to a third or even fourth level design parameter, the selection regime can make it challenging for operating units to maintain the locally-embedded capabilities and networks necessary to sustain their performance over time.

Organization design involves far more than the organization chart, however. The conventional categorization of organization design is "structure and processes" — but a more useful model has been proposed by David Nadler and Mike Tushman in their 1997 book, *Competing by Design*. They provide a three-fold categorization of design that I have found extremely helpful: *grouping* (clustering activities into subunits and allocating reporting accountability), *linking* (providing formal roles, structures, and processes such as integrator roles, committees, and IT systems to provide regular horizontal communication across subunits whose activities have some interdependence but which are not directly connected in the grouping structure), and *aligning* (ensuring that people and subunits have the resources to carry out the activities assigned by grouping and linking, through aligning systems such as performance metrics, incentives and rewards, human resource development, budgeting and resource allocation, and so on). This approach divides "structures and processes" into distinct categories: the vertical architecture of grouping, with formally allocated roles and reporting lines; the horizontal architecture of linking, with structures and processes that connect the organizational subunits across the formal reporting structure; and the structures and processes that support the allocation of the necessary resources — and in the case of Human Resource Management systems, generate and maintain resources — for both the vertical and the horizontal architectures.

This distinction between the vertical and horizontal architectures and of their support systems is invaluable in understanding the architecture of today's complex multidimensional MNCs, where the horizontal architecture connecting formally separated subunits with different vertical reporting lines can be even more significant for some evolutionary processes (such as those involving innovation and Corporate Social Responsibility) than the vertical architecture, and may indeed constitute an alternative selection regime. The horizontal architecture can be the vehicle for what Bartlett and Ghoshal call "matrixing the minds of the managers" – which they saw as a solution to the limitations of the inability of the vertical architecture to balance more than two dimensions. However, it is important to remember that the nature and role of the horizontal architecture complements (and indeed is shaped by) the vertical architecture – and studying the former without the latter can lead to ambiguous or even erroneous conclusions. A Corporate Social Responsibility Council or a Global Sourcing Programme in one MNC which has Business Unit structures at the first and second levels of the vertical architecture, for example, may well face very different challenges and need different kinds of aligning and support systems than a seemingly identical structure in another MNC with a first-order business unit and a second-order geographic structure.

Studying linking and aligning as well as the vertical grouping structure in today's large MNCs, however, can be as complex and challenging a process as managing them, and probably requires a different approach to empirical research.

STARTING AT THE FOUNDATION: "ARCHITECTING UP"

One major challenge for empirical research on MNCs is that the horizontal architecture of linking mechanisms can be extremely difficult to map. Even at the very top of the organization, few of the linking mechanisms of standing committees appear on any organization chart, and many of the most significant are at the middle and lower levels of the organization design. Many of them are temporary cross-unit groups, set up to address specific issues or challenges and dissolved when their work is done. These linking mechanisms have proliferated in many MNCs and are often the principal source of the much-lamented "complexity" of today's MNC organization.

One way to deal with this system-level complexity is to complement the top-down approach to analyses of MNC design by "architecting up" – that is, by starting the analysis not with the top level of the organization but with the front-line unit (the lab, the office, the plant, the mine) and working up and out to identify the key grouping, linking, and aligning systems that connect the subunit to others in the MNC and to key external organizations such as suppliers and stakeholders. This last point is extremely important. Examining the organizational architecture of the interfaces with external organizations can be an extremely useful complement to the research on the network architecture of today's MNC subunits. The "network architecture" maps the social actors with whom MNCs and/or their subunits maintain ongoing relationships. The organizational architecture maps how those relationships are managed. Because today's MNCs have such a complex set of internal linking mechanisms and external relationships that must be managed through some kind of formal structure, mapping the connections at the subunit level can provide a much more useful picture of MNC architecture than simply mapping the first-order design criteria.

An evolutionary approach to the MNC combines extremely well with an "architecting up" methodology, because the selection regime at the level of the most basic subunit reveals how the complex "multidimensional" selection processes of today's MNCs really work – and how they vary (or are consistent) across different subunits. It also fits with a lengthy tradition in the international management field: the subsidiary-focused study. Because we have not tended to keep using the traditional terminology (the "subsidiary") while the phenomenon to which it refers has significantly changed in its design, its role, and its place in the MNC system architecture, we have tended not to explore as we should how the changing architecture of the MNCs over the last two decades has affected the organizational and management challenges of operating and support unit managers at the front lines of the MNC. Indeed, perhaps we could benefit by changing our terminology to refer to "operating units" or even "operating subunits." Perhaps we need to adopt "Bottom-of-the-Pyramid" approaches beyond the realm of innovation strategies and employ them in MNC organizational research.

The drawback of research using this approach is that it is virtually impossible to conduct using secondary data. The researcher has to go to the site, and that usually involves getting access from the gatekeepers of the MNC (usually in the legal department), who are often extremely reluctant to admit researchers to the local units. It has, however, been done, and might actually induce researchers to move beyond analyses of the very largest and best-known brand-name U.S. MNCs, which tend to be the most cautious about granting research access (see for example the value of focusing on organizational design for R&D units in Andersson & Pedersen's, 2010 study of Vestas). MNCs in the middle of industry food chains may be more accessible, and certainly MNCs in many service sectors must have their front-line units accessible to the public.

CLOSING

In short, we have an array of concepts and tools for analyzing the architecture of the MNC that could well be a significant contribution to understanding better the nature and challenges of this complex structure that is the central focus of much of what we do in the IM field. Seeing the MNC as an evolutionary system and set of subsystems that co-evolve in interaction with each other and with their differentiated environments can provide a way of turning the complexity of today's MNCs into an advantage in terms of theory-building and theory testing. Conducting empirical research that starts with the operating units of the MNCs and maps not just their interactions with other units, with the higher levels of the organization, and with their key external networks but also the organizational design by which those interactions are managed can provide useful and perhaps novel insights into how the complex organizational systems of today's MNCs work – or don't work – in practice. Finally, paying at least some attention to organizational architecture in the course of research on the MNC, whatever its principal focus, can provide the building blocks for more robust theory and more understanding of the complex phenomenon that is the multinational corporation.

NOTE

1. I am indebted for the trail that led to the original source to Steve Kobrin (2001, pp. 181–182). Interestingly enough, Kobrin cites not Lilienthal directly but a discussion by D. K. Fieldhouse (1986), which for some reason does not quote Lilienthal's initial definition but one that comes in a later section of the paper which describes MNCs as corporations which operate and live under the laws of other countries, eliminating the more expansive phrase "and customs."

REFERENCES

Andersson, U., & Pedersen, T. (2010). Organizational design criteria for the R&D function in a world of outsourcing. *Scandinavian Journal of Management, 26*, 431–438.

Barnet, R. J., & Müller, R. E. (1974). *Global reach: The power of the multinational corporation.* New York, NY: Simon & Schuster.

Bartlett, C. A., & Ghoshal, S. (1989). *Managing across borders: The transnational solution.* Boston, MA: Harvard Business School Press.

Birkinshaw, J. (2001). Strategy and management in MNE subsidiaries. In A. M. Rugman & T. L. Brewer (Eds.), *The oxford handbook of international business* (pp. 380–401). Oxford: Oxford University Press.

Fieldhouse, D. K. (1986). The multinational: A critique of a concept. In A. Teichova, M. Levy-Leboyer & H. Nussbaum (Eds.), *The multinational enterprise in historical perspective* (pp. 9–29). Cambridge: Cambridge University Press.

Gerstner, L. V. Jr. (2003). *Who says elephants can't dance? Leading a great enterprise through corporate change.* New York, NY: HarperBusiness.

Kobrin, S. J. (2001). Sovereignty@Bay: Globalization, multinational enterprise, and the international political system. In A. M. Rugman & T. L. Brewer (Eds.), *The oxford handbook of international business* (pp. 181–205). Oxford: Oxford University Press.

Kristensen, P. H., & Zeitlin, J. (2005). *Local players in global games: The strategic constitution of a multinational corporation.* Oxford: Oxford University Press.

Lilienthal, D. (1960). Management of the multinational corporation. In M. Anshen & G. L. Bach (Eds.), *Management and corporations 1985: A symposium held on the occasion of the tenth anniversary of the graduate school of industrial administration, Carnegie institute of technology.* New York, NY: McGraw Hill.

Nadler, D. A., & Tushman, M. L. (1997). *Competing by design: The power of organizational architecture.* New York, NY: Oxford University Press.

Stopford, J. M., & Wells, L. T. Jr. (1972). *Managing the multinational enterprise.* New York, NY: Basic Books.

Strange, S. (1996). *The retreat of the state: The diffusion of power in the world economy.* New York, NY: Cambridge University Press.

Strikwerda, J., & Stoelhorst, J. W. (2009). The emergence and evolution of the multidimensional organization. *California Management Review, 51–54*(Summer), 11–31.

Westney, D. E. (1987). *Imitation and innovation: The transfer of western organizational patterns to Meiji Japan.* Cambridge, MA: Harvard University Press.

Westney, D. E. (1999). Changing perspectives on the organization of Japanese multinational enterprises. In A. Bird & S. Beechler (Eds.), *Japanese multinationals abroad: Individual and organizational learning* (pp. 11–29). New York, NY: Oxford University Press.

Westney, D. E. (2003). Geography as a design variable. In J. Birkinshaw, S. Ghoshal, C. C. Markides, J. Stopford & G. Yip (Eds.), *The future of the multinational corporation* (pp. 128–142). New York, NY: John Wiley and Sons.

Westney, D. E. (2008). The multinational enterprise as an evolutionary system. In S. Collinson & G. Morgan (Eds.), *Images of the multinational enterprise* (pp. 117–144). Oxford: Blackwell.

PROFESSOR D. ELEANOR WESTNEY AND JAPANESE BUSINESS STUDIES

Kazuhiro Asakawa

ABSTRACT

I discuss Eleanor Westney's significant contributions to the field of Japanese business studies in four regards. First, her genuine interest in Japan and her deep knowledge of Japan and its language drove her thorough investigation of Japanese business and management. Second, her disciplinary approach to Japanese business and society has added value to the studies of Japanese businesses by linking idiosyncratic phenomena to general sociological perspectives. Third, she played a bridging role, facilitating interactions between the Western and Japanese academic communities. Finally, she has been extremely positive, encouraging, and inspiring to people worldwide working in the field. Westney's contribution to academia clearly reaches beyond the field of Japanese business studies and extends to the entire field of international business and R&D/innovation management.

Orchestration of the Global Network Organization
Advances in International Management, Volume 27, 23–34
Copyright © 2014 by Emerald Group Publishing Limited
All rights of reproduction in any form reserved
ISSN: 1571-5027/doi:10.1108/S1571-502720140000027017

DEEP UNDERSTANDING OF JAPAN AS
A RESEARCH CONTEXT

Nobody would question Eleanor Westney's deep understanding of Japan, her working knowledge of the Japanese language, or her enthusiasm for the study of Japanese business, and it is already common knowledge that she studies international business through a sociological lens. What may be less obvious is how she ended up applying this perspective to the study of Japan. It may be appropriate for me to begin this short note from this point because it is precisely this blend of her phenomena-driven and discipline-based approaches that has made Eleanor who she is today.

Eleanor Westney's history with Japan dates back to her undergraduate years at the University of Toronto, where she specialized in sociology and Japanese studies. In her undergraduate program, where she started in East Asian Studies, a four-year honors curriculum, she was devoted to her Japanese language learning – both Modern and Classical. Intensive translation exercises of texts from the original Japanese to English helped her to grasp the deeper, complex, and nuanced meaning of Japanese writing, which is often tacit and contextual. In her senior year in the undergraduate program, she had already read *Okina Mondo* (Dialogue with an Old Man), which is arguably the most famous book written by Nakae Toju, a 17th century Neo-Confucian philosopher. Needless to say, reading and translating this 17th century Japanese classic requires significant knowledge and mastery of the language.

Her knowledge of written Japanese language and Japanese society was further deepened and broadened by her extensive exposure to Japanese culture. Altogether, she has spent over four years in Japan. Her residential record in Japan includes six months in 1970 working for the Canadian pavilion at Expo 70 in Osaka; another six months in 1972 working for the Canadian government; a year and a half in 1975–1976 at Hitotsubashi University carrying out the dissertation research that led toward her Ph.D. in Sociology from Princeton University, using prefectural data to study regional variations in Japan's modernization; six months at the University of Tokyo on an NSF grant conducting research on R&D in the construction industry; six months in 1989 and another six months in 1996–1997, both as a visiting researcher at Hitotsubashi; as well as several shorter visits in the 1990s.

She has demonstrated her thorough understanding of Japan as a research subject, and she has investigated various organizational and management issues in the context of Japanese society. Her expertise on Japan and the way she has built her academic career on it convincingly demonstrate the importance of having a solid understanding of a particular institutional context in which international business takes place. After receiving a Ph.D. in Sociology from Princeton and initially teaching Sociology at Yale, she joined the Sloan School of Management at MIT as the Japan expert teaching IB, and her career evolved into a nice blend of IB, Sociology, and Japanese business studies. While such a move may have been a major leap for a disciplinary-based sociologist, this move has obviously paid dividends in her career. For many of us in the IB field who pick up particular regions as our new research sites without any deep understanding of the society or a good command of local language, Westney clearly shows how powerful it is for IB scholars to have a solid understanding of the particular institutional environments we investigate. In a sense, Japan is much more than a mere research context of her investigation but rather is an important subject on its own.

Her enthusiasm for Japan has enhanced the level of her commitment and loyalty to this country. Westney stuck with Japan during the so-called lost decade of the Japanese economy in the 1990s, when many overseas observers of Japanese business shifted their attention away from Japan to emerging countries such as China and India. This is not surprising, given her continuing enthusiasm toward the study of Japanese language, history, and society since her undergraduate and graduate studies. Because the IB field covers multinational, cross-border issues, it is not surprising to see that many of us are more interested in the theory and practice of the "crossing" of national and cultural boundaries. What Westney reminds us of is the relevance of country (or area) studies in IB research. Her continuing and consistent interest in Japan has brought about abundant opportunities for her to apply and extend her insights from her 1987 book to various issues, including a cross-border US–Japan comparison of R&D organizations (Sakakibara & Westney, 1997; Westney & Sakakibara, 1988), evolutionary perspectives on R&D internationalization (Asakawa & Westney, 2013), the internationalization of the Japanese service industry (Asakawa, Ito, Rose, & Westney, 2013), and the longevity of Japanese corporations (Ito, Rose, & Westney, 2007, 2008).

TAKING A SOCIOLOGICAL LENS TO THE STUDY OF JAPAN

Although Westney is known for her deep understanding of Japan from a sociologist's perspective, little is known about the way she came to blend her understanding of Japan with her sociologically driven approach.

While she began her studies as an undergraduate in East Asian Studies with a concentration on Japan, her studies covered broad topics in Japan and Asia, including introductory Chinese, Japanese history, and East Asian Civilization. Her exposure to such broad subjects eventually stoked her interest in Sociology and led her to switch into the four-year honors curriculum in Sociology. Because she realized the exciting possibility of applying a sociological lens to the study of Japan, she decided to specialize in both Sociology and Japanese during her undergraduate studies. This decision allowed her to build a solid intellectual base as a scholar of Japanese business with a strong disciplinary background. Needless to say, what distinguishes Westney from many other Japan observers includes her sharp sociological lens, which she has applied to the study of Japanese business.

It is no surprise that Westney has written an important book, *Imitation and Innovation: The Transfer of Western Organizational Patterns to Meiji Japan*, which was published in 1987. I believe that only Eleanor Westney could have written this book. It describes the most remarkable social transformation in Japan's Meiji period (1868–1912), when the country adopted a series of new institutions and social systems from the advanced Western nations and transformed them to suit its own institutional context. Westney shed light on the processes of imitation and innovation Japan experienced when the three Western institutions – the police, the postal system, and the newspaper – were built into the Japanese social environment. Her main concern in this scholarly monograph was to illustrate meticulously the process of "selective emulation," that is, the way in which Japan initially adopted a set of Western organizational models and subsequently departed from these patterns to create its own. Westney argues that the distinction between imitation and innovation is a false dichotomy, as the successful imitation of foreign organizational patterns requires innovation (Westney, 1987, p. 6). Applying the insights of organizational sociology, Westney notes that cross-societal emulation must be examined in the broader context of the mutual conditioning of organizations and their environment (Kelly, 1989).

Westney shows the importance of digging deeper into a particular institutional context to make a universal impact. While it may sound contradictory, making an important contribution to theory often requires us to delve deeper into a particular context. She demonstrated that the process of social change in Meiji Japan offers a deeper understanding of the general processes of cross-societal organizational transfers as well as the processes of organizational development (1987, p. 27). She applied the insights from organizational sociology to her analysis of cross-societal emulation

(Kelly, 1989, p. 706). Rather than illustrating Japanese cases for the sake of showing uniqueness and peculiarity, she used the Japanese case as a building block to establish a more generalizable understanding across time and location. Although every country has its own heritage, there is always an opportunity to extract insights that can be applied elsewhere at another time period. Nonaka (1989) also comments, "This book has a unique focus and makes an important contribution to theories of social change and organizational theory" (Nonaka, 1989, p. 267). The following passage from Westney's work represents such a stance:

> The analysis of these transfers of organizational patterns from Western societies to Meiji japan is more than a vehicle for understanding the development of particular institutions, or even for illuminating the more general processes of Japanese social change. All industrializing societies have emulated organizational forms that originated outside their borders, from the earliest modernizers such as Britain to the developing countries of today's Third World. But despite the ubiquity of such emulation, our understanding of the process and our ability to enhance its effectiveness are still painfully inadequate. Interestingly enough, it has been the Japanese case that has in recent years revealed the poverty of our thinking on the subject. (Westney, 1987, p. 7).

What intrigues me is the tremendous foresight she had in the late 1980s. While studying Japan's history of modernization in the 19th century, she discussed some of today's most relevant issues, such as knowledge transfer, learning across borders, and cross-societal emulation. Her insights remain novel and relevant even in the most modern settings. The whole series of case studies powerfully illustrates the meticulous processes of social innovation. Her concrete examples and her insights gained from the analysis of these cases clearly transcend the boundaries of a specific field (i.e., Japan) and period (i.e., the Meiji period in the 19th century). She succeeded in generating universally applicable insights on innovation and change by seriously considering the field and period effects of a social phenomenon.

Her more recent works in the field of Japanese business studies have continued to build on her sociological insights (Westney, 2006). Westney proposes evolutionary theory "as one vehicle for understanding and assessing the basic assumptions of many of the critiques of Japan's business system produced over the last decade." She further suggests that "the concepts of variation, selection and retention can provide fruitful guides to research topics" and proposes that "the field of Japanese business studies should work to re-establish Japan's long-standing role as a "critical case" in social science (Westney, 2006, p. 167). The following quote captures such a view:

> Making explicit the evolutionary thinking that underlies much of the current debate on Japan and contrasting it with how evolutionary theory currently understands

organizational change processes makes Japan much more interesting. ... It provides a potentially valuable arena for advancing our understanding of evolutionary processes in modern society: a case of a large, complex modern society grappling with the problems of responding to a rapidly changing environment where the established criteria for success seem to have changed very swiftly and suddenly. (Westney, 2006, p. 178)

Westney's underlying orientation toward balancing *distinctiveness* and *generalizability* in conducting research in the applied field extends the domain of Japanese studies to cover other fields, such as IB and international R&D management. She writes:

To over-simplify considerably, the focus in Japanese Studies on explaining Japanese success and in IB on identifying ideal types and exemplars of the new forms of the MNC and of cross-border business meant giving less weight to long-standing traditions of critical theory in both fields. This left both at a disadvantage when new critical agendas emerged in the 1990s: explaining the sudden and prolonged downturn in Japan's economy in the post-Bubble era in Japanese Studies, and the explosion of interest in globalization in the social sciences, in which IB experts were conspicuous by their absence. (Westney, 2005, p. 6)

In a similar vein, Westney considers that much more theory development is necessary for research on international R&D management, which has been fairly phenomenon-driven in the past several decades. What she calls for is to strike an optimal balance between the phenomena-driven distinctiveness and theory-driven generalizability. Her main approaches are applying institutional theory and evolutionary theory to the organization and innovation of MNCs' global R&D activities (Westney, 1993a, 1993b). Indeed, her organizational sociology approach to the study of global R&D contrasts with many other works in this field, which have a strong emphasis on managerial solutions.

In all of these applied fields, such as IB, Japanese business studies, and international R&D management, Westney shows her sympathy for phenomenon-driven research, as well as her emphasis on using a sociological lens to interpret the phenomena. Such a balanced view is consistent with the volume that she edited along with Sumantra Ghoshal, *Institutional Theory and Multinational Corporations*, which was published in 1993. IM scholars are primarily interested in complex phenomena pertinent to international business, whereas OT scholars are mostly interested in generalizable theory and pay little attention to phenomena. Their project was to learn from the best of both fields and to synthesize their results (Ghoshal & Westney, 1993).

BRIDGING A GAP BETWEEN JAPANESE AND FOREIGN ENVIRONMENTS

Japan's management research community has had a long tendency of publishing the scholarly works mainly in Japanese language, and such a tradition has prevented many high-quality works from being visible to the rest of the world. Westney has played a critical role as the bridge between the Japanese and the Western academic communities. Through her intensive interactions with Japan's most prominent scholars, including Professors Kenichi Imai, Hiroyuki Itami, and Ikujiro Nonaka, throughout the 1980s and 1990s, she obtained a deep knowledge of the state-of-the-art research conducted by Japanese management scholars.

Westney played a significant role in identifying core management researchers active in the Japanese academic community and in promoting their work to an international audience. For example, Westney greatly appreciated a book entitled *Strategic vs. Evolutionary Management: A U.S.-Japan Comparison of Strategy and Organization* authored by Tadao Kagono, Ikujiro Nonaka, Kiyonori Sakakibara, and Akihiro Okumura (1989), and actively introduced it to her colleagues in the West as an empirically grounded, theory-based research conducted by the Japanese management scholars.[1]

Many prominent Japanese academics have also actively interacted with her during their sabbaticals or research visits to the United States. Kiyonori Sakakibara has engaged in extensive collaboration with Eleanor since his visit to MIT/Harvard regarding the United States/Japan comparison of engineers and R&D organizations, which has led to several joint publications (Sakakibara & Westney, 1997; Westney & Sakakibara, 1988). Sakakibara recalls that it was fruitful and rewarding to work with her as a trusted research partner. He found it intellectually stimulating to work with Eleanor, who brought a broad, comparative, socio-cultural perspective to the study of Japanese business and international R&D.[2] Ikujiro Nonaka acknowledges Eleanor's bridging role for allowing him to engage in intellectual exchanges with Gunnar Hedlund, Yves Doz, C. K. Prahalad, Sumantra Ghoshal, and Bruce Kogut, among others. Such encounters eventually led to his joint publication with Gunnar Hedlund for example (Hedlund & Nonaka, 1993, chapter 5).[3]

Westney kept Japan on the radar of Western management scholars through her writing. Her scholarly review on Japan has promoted non-Japanese audiences' understanding of Japanese business firms and their surrounding social environment (Westney, 1980, 1990). For example, her book chapter on Japan (Westney, 2001) continues to be an invaluable source of knowledge about and insights into Japanese business and its society. This chapter offers an overview of Japan's foreign direct investment, a summary of the research on Japanese MNCs since the 1970s, and the characteristics of Japan as a host country for foreign MNCs. This chapter is a particularly invaluable source of information and insights for readers who seek to understand research on Japan and Japanese MNCs, especially for her extensive coverage of literature by local authors written in Japanese language. As Jesper Edman succinctly says, "Thanks to her, Japan is better known."[4]

INSPIRING PEOPLE

Westney is known for encouraging and inspiring many young scholars throughout the world. While her record of training excellent Ph.D. students at MIT is well known, her mentoring role has transcended national boundaries, and she and her work have inspired quite a few scholars around the world.

What is less known, at least to Western audiences, is her immense intellectual contribution to Japanese academia over the last several decades. She has reminded Japanese scholars of the importance of balancing the generalizability and uniqueness of Japanese management practices at a moment when Japanese management has attracted attention among Western academics and practitioners and the uniqueness of Japanese management has been widely praised. Westney stressed the importance of accounting for the nature of the Japanese management system and practices from an academic disciplinary perspective instead of mystifying Japan and hastily selling this model to the rest of the world. During her research visits in Japan, Westney participated in several research workshops held in Japan to inspire Japanese junior faculty.[5] Her presence encouraged young Japanese scholars to go global, beyond Japanese domestic circles. Nonaka acknowledges Westney's important role in encouraging and inspiring Japanese academics to become more globally visible scholars. Nonaka recalls Westney made him realize the importance of making his own work even more visible globally as he was a mid-career faculty member when he first met her.[6]

Westney also opened the door for and inspired foreign scholars of Japanese business to study Japanese business in a much more scholarly way.

Her work is appealing to many non-Japanese scholars on Japan because it is deeply embedded in Japan's historical, cultural, and institutional context, and at the same time, her insights can clearly be applied to contexts outside of Japan. Her work has inspired foreign scholars of Japan both directly and indirectly because it suggested a huge window of opportunity for them to provide alternative explanations to make sense of Japan's uniqueness, thereby making Japan better understood by the non-Japanese audience. Today, quite a few foreign scholars of Japanese business are directly or indirectly following her lead, approaching the study of Japanese management from more general, disciplinary perspectives. Examples include Mary Yoko Brannen, who is taking a cultural anthropological/linguistic approach, Christina Ahmadjian, who is taking an organizational sociology approach, and Jesper Edman, who is taking the institutional theory approach, to name a few. Westney played a pioneering role in pushing the field in this direction.

CONCLUSION

I discussed Westney's significant contributions to the field of Japanese business studies in four regards. First, her genuine interest in Japan and her deep knowledge of Japan and its language drove her thorough investigation of Japanese business and management. Second, her disciplinary approach to Japanese business and society has added value to the studies of Japanese businesses by linking idiosyncratic phenomena to general sociological perspectives. Third, she played a bridging role, facilitating interactions between the Western and Japanese academic communities. Finally, she has been extremely positive, encouraging, and inspiring to people worldwide working in the field.

Westney's continued enthusiasm toward the studies of Japanese business and society seems endless. This passion has led her to initiate a series of new projects with multiple collaborators. One notable development of her recent research interest includes her joint work with Kiyohiko Ito and Elizabeth Rose on a study of millennium organizations in Japan (Ito et al., 2007, 2008). Studying Japanese business organizations with at least 500 years of continuous operations, they explore factors that support these organizations' extraordinary longevity, influenced by ancestral governance, and they present a model to represent how millennium organizations' resources, structures, businesses, and strategies meet to achieve longevity.

Another line of her recent interest in Japan lies in the internationalization of Japanese service firms (Asakawa et al., 2013). The study sheds light on the relatively low level of internationalization in Japan's service industries, which is a cause for real concern among policymakers and service industry executives. Explanations have focused on distinctive features of Japan's service culture and idiosyncratically demanding customers. Two additional factors are also of significance: the complexity of the customer interface and process embeddedness in the home country.

Another topic of her recent interest is the R&D globalization process of Japanese multinational corporations by drawing on evolutionary perspectives (Asakawa & Westney, 2013). Here, she and I revisit the long-accepted sequential model of internationalization of value-added activities by shedding light on anomalies defying established wisdom. Building on a set of case studies of Japanese firms in the electronics and pharmaceutical industries, we draw theoretical implications for evolutionary perspectives on internationalization.

I was privileged to work on a project with Eleanor as a visiting scholar at MIT during 2004/2005. I am honored to be a co-author of several of her published articles, and I was fortunate enough to learn from her the power of intellectual elegance on top of intellectual rigor. I am grateful to Eleanor for treating me, a significantly more junior researcher, as an independent scholar throughout the entire collaboration process. Such an attitude taught me the importance of maintaining intellectual modesty, no matter how prominent a scholar you are. It is my honor to contribute this article to the Special Issue of *the Advances in International Management* celebrating Eleanor's Booz Eminent Scholar's Award. Congratulations, Eleanor.

NOTES

1. The author's telephone interview with Professor Ikujiro Nonaka on August 7, 2013.

2. The author's email interview with Professor Kiyonori Sakakibara on August 19, 2013.

3. The author's telephone interview with Professor Ikujiro Nonaka on August 7, 2013.

4. The author's telephone interview with Professor Jesper Edman on Augus 6, 2013.

5. For instance, she attended the Mitsubishi Conference, a prestigious research workshop in Japan sponsored by Mitsubishi Foundation, twice in the 1980s,

when promising Japanese junior faculty members had opportunities to interact with her.

6. The author's telephone interview with Professor Ikujiro Nonaka on August 7, 2013.

ACKNOWLEDGMENT

I would like to thank Jesper Edman, Kiyohiko Ito, Ikujiro Nonaka, Elizabeth Rose, and Kiyonori Sakakibara for their insights and information necessary for the preparation of the manuscript.

REFERENCES

Asakawa, K., Ito, K., Rose, E. L., & Westney, D. E. (2013). Internationalization in Japan's service industries. *Asia Pacific Journal of Management, 30*(4), 1155–1168.

Asakawa, K., & Westney, D. E. (2013). Evolutionary perspectives on the internationalization of R&D in Japan's multinational corporations. *Asian Business & Management, 12*(1), 115–141.

Ghoshal, S., & Westney, D. E. (Eds.). (1993). *Organization theory and the multinational corporation.* New York, NY: St. Martin's Press.

Hedlund, G., & Nonaka, I. (1993). Models of knowledge management in the west and Japan. In P. Lorange, et al. (Eds.), *Implementing strategic processes: Change, learning and co-operation* (pp. 117–144). Oxford, UK: Basil Blackwell.

Ito, K., Rose, E. L., & Westney, D. E. (2007). A study of millennium organizations in Japan. *Association of Japanese Business Studies Proceedings*, Indianapolis, July 2007.

Ito, K., Rose, E. L., & Westney, D. E. (2008). A study of millennium organizations in Japan. *Academy of Management*, Anaheim, August 2008.

Kagono, T., Nonaka, I., Sakakibara, K., & Okumura, A. (1989). *Strategic vs. evolutionary management: A U.S.–Japan comparison of strategy and organization* (p. 328). Amsterdam: North Holland.

Kelly, W. W. (1989). Imitation and innovation: The transfer of western organizational patterns to Meiji Japan, By D. Eleanor Westney (Book Review). *Journal of Interdisciplinary History, 19*(4), 705–707.

Nonaka, I. (1989). D. Eleanor Westney: Imitation and innovation. The transfer of western organizational patterns to Meiji Japan (Book Review). *Organization Studies, 10*(2), 265–267.

Sakakibara, K., & Westney, D. E. (1997). Japan's management of global innovation: Technology management crossing borders (chapter 22). In M. Tushuman & P. Anderson (Eds.), *Managing strategic innovation and change* (pp. 331–341). New York, NY: Oxford University Press.

Westney, D. E. (1980). Japan as number one: Lesson for America. By Ezra F. Vogel (Book review). *Contemporary Sociology, 9*(5), 685–686.

Westney, D. E. (1987). *Imitation and innovation: The transfer of western organizational patterns to Meiji Japan.* Cambridge, MA: Harvard University Press.

Westney, D. E. (1990). The state and labor in modern Japan, by Sheldon Garon (Book Review). *Contemporary Sociology, 19*(1), 51–52.

Westney, D. E. (1993a). Cross-pacific internationalization of R&D by U.S. and Japanese firms. *R&D Management, 23*(2), 171–181.

Westney, D. E. (1993b). Institutional theory and the multinational corporation (chapter 3). In S. Ghoshal & D. E. Westney (Eds.), *Organization theory and the multinational corporation.* New York, NY: St. Martin's Press.

Westney, D. E. (2001). Chapter 22, Japan. In A. Rugman & T. Brewer (Eds.), *The Oxford handbook of international business* (pp. 591–622). Oxford, UK: Oxford University Press.

Westney, D. E. (2005). What is international business? A sociological view. In P. Buckley (Ed.), *What is international business?* London: Palgrave Macmillan.

Westney, D. E. (2006). The "Lost Dacade" and Japanese business studies. *Asian Business & Management, 5*, 167–185.

Westney, D. E., & Sakakibara, K. (1988). The role of Japan-based R&D in global technology strategy. In M. Tushman & W. Moore (Eds.), *Readings in the management of innovation* (2nd ed., pp. 327–342). New York, NY: HarperBusiness, A Division of HarperCollins Publishers.

PART II

INTRODUCTION TO PART II: ORCHESTRATION OF THE GLOBAL NETWORK ORGANIZATION

Torben Pedersen, Markus Venzin, Timothy M. Devinney and Laszlo Tihanyi

The organizational design of the Multinational Corporation (MNC) was a vibrant area of research in the field of International Business and Management during the 1970–1990 period. However, since that time this area has largely faded from our scholarship. Our intention with this volume is to spark new life into the research on the organizational design of the MNC. MNCs are meeting new challenges in the forms of focusing on core activities, value chain disaggregation, relocation of activities to emerging markets, industry consolidation, technological change, and market volatility. In this volume we will scrutinize different models for how MNCs can cope with these challenges and orchestrate a global network organization that is able to structure, coordinate, and integrate activities across the globe.

For the study of the MNC as an organization, the 1980s was a particular fertile period. The formulation of the integration-responsiveness (IR) framework spurred research on the organizational design of MNCs. The IR framework was initially proposed by Prahalad (1975) and subsequently developed in a stream of papers by Bartlett, Doz, Ghoshal, and Prahalad. The basic argument of this framework is that MNCs are facing two

Orchestration of the Global Network Organization
Advances in International Management, Volume 27, 37–41
Copyright © 2014 by Emerald Group Publishing Limited
All rights of reproduction in any form reserved
ISSN: 1571-5027/doi:10.1108/S1571-502720140000027033

orthogonal sets of environmental forces − global forces for integration and local forces for responsiveness − that create a need for an organizational design that fits with the firm strategy and the competitive environment.

Many attempts has been made to extend the original framework and conceptualize a new type of MNC organization that were capable of managing the many tensions facing MNCs, for example, between local and global forces, exploitation and exploration, headquarter and subsidiary. The chapter by Pihl and Paulsson in this volume of *Advances in International Management* (AIM) include a long list of conceptualization of this vision that span from the Heterarchic MNC over the Holographic MNC to the Transnational MNC. In fact, the Transactional MNC turned out to become the more popular term for the visionary organization of the MNC.

The fertile period for research on organizational design of the MNC is not just reflected in the many attempts to conceptualize the organizationally fit MNC, but also in the fact that the most significant contributions on the organizational design of the MNC was published some decades ago. However, this line of research seemed to fall out of favor in the subsequent decades. From the second half of the 1980s research on international management switched its focus away from the more outside perspective of studying the fit between the environment and firm choices in terms of strategy and organization to a more inside perspective with a focus on firm's internal structure, resources, and capabilities. The latter focus is associated with transaction cost theory, the resource-based view that obviously changed the unit of analysis and re-directed attention away from the overall fit with the environment. In the organizational design view, the attention is not on the optimization of each individual activity, but rather on how the total configuration of the firm can be optimized. The pendulum was swinging toward an emphasis on more disaggregated activities and the strategic choices related to these activities (like choice of entry-mode, location of individual activities, transfer of specific knowledge) and away from the organizational design view that focus on the organizational architecture and configuration (with an exception of the discussion on subsidiary roles that is linked to organizational design perspective).

One can obviously ask the question of why the organization design literature lost its momentum, as a number of the contributors do in this volume. Was it because the theoretical foundation of the organizational design literature was too weak after all? Many of the key contributions are building on anecdotes or small N-research (with few but very prolific firms) rather than theoretical grounding. The theoretical grounding of the literature on organizational design of the MNC has, for example, been based on

Information-Processing theory and (interorganizational) Network theory. The focus of the Information-Processing theory is on how the information-processing capabilities of agents and business units affect organizational design choices (e.g., Egelhoff, 1991), while the applied Network theory draw on the concepts of within density (local network) and across density (total external network) to explain organizational design and power structures in the MNC (e.g., Ghoshal & Bartlett, 1990). However, none of these theories have really been able to carry the research very far. The result has been that the study of organizational design of the MNC has largely been left to consultants as the research community has given it rather limited attention.

This volume of AIM is an attempt to get back on track and allocate more attention to the study of organizational design in MNC. There are many good reasons for connecting back to this important literature and focus more on organizational design issues again. Here, we will just highlight a few of these reasons:

— The competitive environment has dramatically changed in the last decades which forces firms to reconsider their current global organizational architecture.
— Theoretical developments in related fields like organization theory, learning theory etc.
— Many firms are really struggling with their organizational architecture and need better tools/frameworks for optimizing the organization.

Research is often mirroring the general societal changes as these are affecting the focus of research. The major societal changes all over the world in the last decades are associated with globalization. The world – and competitive environment – has changed substantially in the last decades placing new constrains on the MNCs. External shocks have increased and MNCs need to learn how to live with this increased market volatility. Integrating value chains makes MNCs more efficient but vulnerable at the same time. So, what are the organizational mechanisms that make MNCs more resilient – better able to successfully adjust and thrive in conditions of adversity? The relentless forces of competition and globalization are forcing MNCs to divide their activities and reach for foreign inputs, markets, and partners. By dividing their value chain into discrete pieces – some to be performed in-house, while others to be outsourced to partner organizations – MNCs hope to reduce their overall costs and risks, while possibly also reaping the benefits of ideas from their contractors or alliance partners worldwide. These forces for more division and relocation of the value chain activities infuse new organizational complexity and a need for developing organizational design mechanism in the forms of standardized interfaces, network structures, modularization, delegation, etc.

We have seen a significant development in related fields of organization theory, network theory, learning theory, etc., that can be applied in order to establish a stronger theoretical grounding for the organizational design perspective. We have seen a few attempts in this direction like the paper by Devinney, Midgley, and Venaik (2000), but much more can be done. This volume of AIM includes a number of papers that go in this direction, for example, by drawing on a managerial cognition lens (Maitland & Sammartino), global value chain studies (Marchi, Di Maria, & Ponte), theory on knowledge transfer (Camuffo, Secchi, & Paolino), and modularization literature (Larsen & Pedersen). We trust that some of these contributions will open new paths for theoretical grounding of the organizational design perspective on the MNC.

Finally, but not least, most firms all over the world continue to struggle with this issue. As Garten (2002) put it in his bestseller business book: "How to organize a company for global operations? Even the most internationally experienced business leaders continue to experiment for no one has the right formula" (Garten, 2002, p. 91). In the box below we present a specific example from a company operating in B2B markets on how firms experiment with organizational design issues. These design issues remind us as researchers that we need to develop better tools/frameworks on organizational design that can be applied by managers in today's world.

Examples of organizational design issues pertinent in a company operating in B2B markets:

- What is the optimal span of control? Can CEOs effectively lead more than 10 direct reports?
- How can the span of control be reduced? Are large product divisions and/or regional headquarters the solution?
- The "best" organizational solution depends on the desired level of adaptation, aggregation and arbitrage that firms want to achieve. This however depends on the nature of the businesses firms own. What if the businesses have completely different needs in terms of adaptation, aggregation and arbitrage?
- To facilitate cross-border sales, the responsibility for local factories is often taken away from local CEOs and given to regional/global production heads. Is this the best solution?

- And if regional headquarters are created and production is given to central functions, how do we make sure country CEOs don't get frustrated?
- If local CEOs are responsible for sales, how do we make sure that product businesses are further developed in all regions? How do central product unit heads convince local CEOs to invest time in business development that has a return in the long run? More general, how can decentralized corporate entrepreneurship be fostered without losing cost efficiency?
- To obtain this, firms probably need to align their objectives and incentive systems accordingly. But how does this work in practice?
- What is the role of central functions? How much power should they have and how should they interact with the decentralized units? How often should they meet, or report?
- ... to be continued ...

The cases unfolded in this volume of AIM highlight similar and additional organizational design issues that are very present for companies today.

We hope with this volume of AIM to help bring back organization design of the MNC on the researcher's agenda in order to develop new theoretical models, tools, and frameworks for design of the MNC organization.

REFERENCES

Devinney, T. M., Midgley, D. F., & Venaik, S. (2000). The optimal performance of the global firm: Formalizing and extending the integration-responsiveness framework. *Organization Science, 11*(6), 674−695.

Egelhoff, W. G. (1991). Information-processing theory and the multinational enterprise. *Journal of International Business Studies, 22*, 341−368.

Garten, J. E. (2002). *The politics of fortune: A new Agenda for business leaders.* Boston, MA: Harvard Business School Press.

Ghoshal, S., & Bartlett, C. A. (1990). The multinational corporation as an interorganizational network. *Academy of Management Review, 15*(4), 603−625.

Prahalad, C. K. (1975). *The strategic process in a multinational corporation.* Unpublished Doctoral dissertation. School of Business Administration, Harvard University.

THE DIFFUSION OF LEAN OPERATIONS PRACTICES IN MNCs: A KNOWLEDGE-BASED, PLANT LEVEL, CROSS-FIRM STUDY

Arnaldo Camuffo, Raffaele Secchi and Chiara Paolino

ABSTRACT

Rolling out lean operations practices in MNCs' plants is a complex knowledge transfer process whose design and implementation, though critical to operations performance, to date has not been investigated by operations management, international business, strategy, and organizational design research. Applying conceptual tools drawn from various theoretical approaches to knowledge management, transfer and diffusion, this exploratory study: (a) classifies and interprets lean roll-out processes in MNCs, framing them in terms of (i) knowledge replication strategies (template vs. principles-based), (ii) decentralization of decision making (degree of plant autonomy), and (iii) type of organizational ambidexterity (structural vs. contextual) underlying the process; (b) develops, through seven case studies of lean roll-outs in MNCs' plants, three testable propositions about what might enhance the lean roll-out process

Orchestration of the Global Network Organization
Advances in International Management, Volume 27, 43−74
ISSN: 1571-5027/doi:10.1108/S1571-502720140000027004

performance, arguing about the individual and combined effect of the three above mentioned dimensions on lean roll-out effectiveness and efficiency. We posit that an approach characterized by principles-based knowledge replication, larger decentralization, and prevalence of contextual ambidexterity positively impacts on roll-out process performance.

Keywords: Lean operations; MNCs' organizational design; knowledge transfer; absorptive capacity; ambidexterity

INTRODUCTION

During the last two decades, an increasing number of multinational companies (MNCs henceforth) have embraced lean thinking as operations management philosophy, designed their own adapted version of the Toyota Production System and undertaken the roll-out of such systems in their production facilities around the world. This trend has accelerated during the last few years, when the need to improve operational performance has been exacerbated by the competitive pressure posed by the financial crisis.

The roll-out of lean production systems is a complex organizational process, through which companies decide how to articulate and structure the resources, capabilities, and processes aimed at continuous improvement in their operations.

From a theoretical standpoint, a lean roll-out can be conceived as the organizational process through which an MNC decides to create, disseminate, and store lean knowledge within and throughout its international organization and to foster continuous learning about operational improvements in its dispersed production facilities. More specifically, in MNCs, this is the process through which the headquarter organizes the transfer of newly acquired or previously developed knowledge about continuous improvement to the subsidiary plants and sets up a system of knowledge creation, combination and diffusion, and of continuous learning within (and among) them. The importance of the knowledge dimension underlying lean roll-out processes is to be directly found in the ultimate aim of lean production systems: develop a dynamic capability (Anand, Ward, Tatikonda, & Schilling, 2009) that allows systematic problem solving and continuous improvement within organizations, in order to better serve the customers (Shah & Ward, 2007).

So far, international operations and lean operations research — both that rooted in mainstream operations management literature and that rooted in strategy, organization, and knowledge management literatures (Anand et al., 2009; Camuffo & Comacchio, 1999; Fujimoto, 1999; Staats, Brunner, & Upton, 2011) — have neglected how such within-organization processes of knowledge transfer and learning might affect the implementation of lean operations (with relevant exceptions, such as Letmathe, Schweitzer, & Zielinski, 2012). Similarly, this topic is under-investigated within the fields of international business, strategy, and knowledge management, especially when lean roll-outs take place in MNCs. Here, the current theory and practice of such processes often assume that the roll-out is designed and will take place linearly, "cascading" a predefined, codified lean production system from the headquarter to the subsidiary plants and following a predetermined sequence of steps typically including corporate communication, senior and middle management training, internal and/or external consulting, etc.

Thus, objective of this study is to question and challenge such implicit assumptions, exploring possible alternative ways to conceive the lean roll-out process as well as the very nature of the underlying knowledge transfer process from the center to the periphery of the organization (Friel, 2005). Framing lean roll-outs as a process of knowledge creation, transfer and dissemination, this study aims at exploring the dimensions that might enhance or hinder lean roll-out processes' performance in MNCs and, hence, contribute to the lean operations management literature by both starting to fill the above highlighted gap and addressing an important strategic/international operations management issue for many MNCs. More specifically, this paper defines a framework to interpret lean roll-out processes and their performance, identifies a set of research dimensions/constructs that allow classifying and interpreting lean roll-out processes and develops three testable propositions about how to conduct successful lean roll-outs. Drawing upon a variety of theoretical approaches, we argue that three dimensions might significantly affect the effectiveness and efficiency of lean roll-out processes: (a) the knowledge replication strategy underlying the lean roll-out process (and the associated degree of codification of the knowledge transferred from the headquarters (HQ henceforth) to the subsidiary plants) (Baden-Fuller & Winter, 2007; Letmathe et al., 2012); (b) the degree of decentralization in the decision-making process entailed by the lean roll-out process (and the associated degree of autonomy and absorptive capacity of the subsidiary plants in managing the roll-out process itself (Gupta & Govindarajan, 2000; Tu, Vonderembse, Ragu-Nathan, & Sharkey, 2006)); (c) the way in which the knowledge exploration (introduction of innovative lean operations practices) and exploitation (daily plant operations management) are structured and co-exist at the plant level in the lean roll-out process (the prevalent type of ambidexterity − structural vs. contextual) (March, 1991; Patel, Terjesen, & Li, 2012; Tushman & O'Reilly, 1996, 2004).

From a methodological perspective, our exploratory study consists in the detailed analysis of seven cases of lean roll-out in local plants of MNCs. We believe that a multiple case study approach is particularly suitable to investigate this topic, since MNCs' plants represent a unique opportunity not only to observe the lean roll-out process per se, but also to study how knowledge inflows and outflows take place from the parent corporation to its plants (Baden-Fuller & Winter, 2007).

The paper is organized as follows. We will first review the literature about knowledge management and knowledge transfer, with a focus on MNCs, and show how it applies to our study of lean roll-out processes. Based on this review, we will develop our theoretical framework, identifying the interpretative dimensions and performance criteria of lean roll-outs as knowledge transfer processes. Then, we will illustrate the case study research strategy applied, including company sampling criteria and data gathering procedures. After that, we will proceed with the cross-case analysis comparing and contrasting the seven lean roll-out processes according to the interpretative dimensions identified in the following paragraph. The analysis will lead to the development of three propositions. In the final section, we will highlight some study limitations and suggest directions for future research.

THEORETICAL BACKGROUND AND RESEARCH GOALS

The extensive literature on lean operations has widely explored the core components required to effectively manage the transition toward a lean system (Byrne, 2012; Deflorina & Scherrer-Rathjeb, 2012; Emiliani, Stec, Grasso, & Stodder, 2007; Hartwell & Roth, 2010; Koenigsaecker, 2009; Losonci, Demeter, & Jenei, 2011). Bundling lean practices (Cua, McKone, & Schroeder, 2001; Shah & Ward, 2003) along with top management commitment and people involvement (Bamber & Dale, 2000; Womack & Jones, 1996) have been often indicated as antecedents of successful lean implementation. Nonetheless, to date, there is no explicit theory and no empirical study about the diffusion of lean operations practices and lean production systems throughout business settings, like MNCs, where such process is frequent and often formalized.

In such complex organizational environments, the effectiveness of lean roll-outs is strongly affected by several factors embedded in both headquarter and plant management systems and culture. Given the lack of specific literature on this topic, we set out to look into different research streams and borrowed from them the conceptual tools necessary to develop a comprehensive framework to interpret and investigate lean roll-out processes. Since the adoption of lean operations practices is ultimately a process of knowledge generation, combination, selection and diffusion, as well as a process of learning, we deemed that it would be appropriate to start our theoretical effort from the knowledge-based view of the firm (Grant, 1996), that is, from the broad stream of literature concerning knowledge management and its creation cycle (Nonaka & Takeuchi, 1995) and, more specifically, knowledge inflows and outflows in MNCs from the parent corporation to its subsidiaries.

Given this theoretical premise, the dimensions constituting our framework of analysis and discussion follow. First, we refer to the knowledge transfer literature (Kostova, 1999; Szulanski, 1996) in order to clarify: (a) the performance criteria against which we measure lean roll-outs; (b) the dimensions according to which we classify and discuss lean roll-out processes. Second, we illustrate, building on the above defined literature, the three dimensions, their interplay, and their relationship with the lean operations practices literature.

Lean Roll-Out (Knowledge Transfer) Performance

Knowledge transfer success is related to efficiency as well as effectiveness of knowledge usage in the recipient unit (Argote & Ingram, 2000; Ciabuschi, Dellestrand, & Kappen, 2011; Minbaeva, Pedersen, Björkman, Fey, & Park, 2003; Pérez-Nordtvedt, Kedia, Datta, & Rasheed, 2008; Szulanski, 1996). Efficiency refers to the relative expenditure of resources and time in the transfer process. Effectiveness concerns the extent to which knowledge is actually accepted and adopted by the subsidiary's employees. In other words, this means that, in a successful knowledge transfer process, the recipient unit must incorporate the transferred knowledge into its operations (Kostova, 1999). This aspect is substantial since, sometimes, the adoption of new organizational practices ensuing from the knowledge transfer may be superficial or appear purely mimetic and ceremonial (Kostova & Roth, 2002). Finally, as pointed out by Lin (2007) and Szulanski (1996), effectiveness also implies recipients' overall satisfaction with the knowledge transfer, both in terms of content and process. This study analyzes lean roll-outs performance in terms of both knowledge transfer efficiency and effectiveness. Seven case studies will allow us to understand the typical issues MNCs face with lean roll-outs, to comparatively analyze such cases according to the dimensions of knowledge replication strategy, decentralization, and organizational ambidexterity, and to hypothesize what combinations of such dimensions might be associated to more or less successful knowledge transfer/lean roll-outs.

Knowledge Replication Strategy

Firms can replicate knowledge embedded in practices by following both templates and principles. Nelson and Winter (1982, pp. 119−120) use the term template to refer to working examples of organizational routines. In their conception, templates provide the details of how the work has to be done, which is the right sequence of activities, and which are the links among various components and subroutines. The replication of routines (Szulanski & Winter, 2001, 2002) allows the recipient unit to recreate knowledge developed at the source site. Therefore, using original routines as a template may facilitate knowledge transfer within the firm in the form of easier, quicker and more accurate learning and adoption by the recipient units (Letmathe et al., 2012, offer a comprehensive operations management perspective on this view).

Nevertheless, many international business scholars suggested that adopting a template decreases transfer effectiveness by inhibiting local adaptation (Bartlett & Ghoshal, 1989; Prahalad & Doz, 1987) and increasing local resistance to adoption (Kostova & Zaheer, 1999). Baden-Fuller and Winter (2007) offer several examples where principles, that is, more general and flexible references for knowledge replication, result more effective than templates in promoting knowledge transfer. The underlying line of reasoning is the following: while templates, characterized by knowledge codification, allow for easier and more precise replication at the cost of oversimplification and lack of contextualization, principles, being less codified guides for behavior, imply more complex and costly replication but provides − thanks to the ambiguity built in the replication process − room for local adaptation and learning.

At the organizational level, both template and principles-based replication require that recipients have some type and degree of background knowledge or capability, or absorptive capacity (Cohen & Levinthal, 1990; Patel et al., 2012; Tu et al., 2006). This is even more specifically true in international business studies with regard to the relationships between headquarters and subsidiaries (Schleimer & Pedersen, 2013). Here, the parent-subsidiary knowledge flows might positively affect individual MNC subsidiaries: valuable knowledge received from the MNC parent facilitates subsidiaries' operations and increase their ability to respond successfully to the challenges they deal with in their local environments.

The roll-out of lean operations practices throughout the MNC's plants can be assimilated to the process of replication of the knowledge embedded in practices or routines. Indeed, such knowledge is often incorporated in documents, blueprints, or other artifacts, developed as the result of previous experience and learning processes, and available to the HQ for internal diffusion. Contingent on the extent to which the replication process and the system of lean operations practices that HQ wish to transfer to subsidiary plants are codified, detailed, and standardized, the lean roll-out will be alternatively closer to a template or a principles-based approach.

This dichotomy, based on the degree of knowledge codification, represents the first dimension of our interpretative framework. Our analysis will investigate if and under which conditions a template or principle-based approach might lead to more effective and efficient lean roll-outs.

Decentralization

Several studies point out and even find empirical evidence of a positive relationship between decentralized decision-making rights and corporate knowledge transfer (Gupta & Govindarajan, 2000; Van Wijk, Jansen, & Lyles, 2008). In MNCs, decentralization involves delegating the locus of authority and decision making to improve the quality and quantity of knowledge that can be shared (Van Wijk et al., 2008). Moreover, when decision-making rights are allocated to a decentralized unit, for example to a plant, its perception of autonomy as well as its willingness to be involved in a knowledge transfer process definitely raise (Gupta & Govindarajan, 2000).

The degree of decentralization mirrors the amount of operational absorptive capacity (Patel et al., 2012; Tu et al., 2006) of the receiving unit, which, in our case is the extent to which a plant "can acquire, assimilate, and transform external information" (Tu et al., 2006, p. 203).

The subsidiary's degree of autonomy also refers to the nature and amount of the resources allocated as well as to the subsidiary's ability to access additional knowledge from alternative external sources. Subsidiaries typically rely on a combination of knowledge autonomously sourced from their local environments and knowledge deriving from knowledge inputs from corporate headquarters. A good balance in such combination positively impacts the parent-subsidiary knowledge transfer (Asmussen, Foss, & Pedersen, 2011). Headquarters can support lean roll-outs, and the corresponding knowledge transfer activities, by allocating specific resource budgets to subsidiaries, or by setting aside funds to support the knowledge transfer process. The availability of adequate resources should facilitate knowledge adoption by involving more people from both headquarters and subsidiaries, by providing more local support through internal or external specialists, by delivering additional training, or by encouraging more extensive adaptation in the receiving unit. However, beyond the positive effect of decentralization of decision making and resource administration, simply allowing more autonomy and discretion to the recipient organizational units has not always been proved to be the best option for effective and efficient knowledge transfer. Indeed, research also shows that centralization could positively affect knowledge transfer processes through simpler decision making, better coordination and overall alignment (Puranam, Singh, & Zollo, 2006).

The degree of plant autonomy and the correlated aspects of degree of decision making centralization, resource allocation, and plant absorptive capacity (Patel et al., 2012; Schleimer & Pedersen, 2013; Tu et al., 2006) represent the second dimension of our interpretative framework. Our analysis will investigate the relationship between HQ and subsidiary plants exploring if and under which conditions more discretion at the plant level in selecting alternative courses of action and administrating resources might improve the lean roll-out process.

Organizational Ambidexterity

The notion of organizational ambidexterity, originally developed to describe organizations that are able to both exploit and explore (March, 1991), has been widely used in the knowledge-based approach to conceptualize organizations' ability to simultaneously perform opposed and often contradictory actions (Tushman & O'Reilly, 1996, 2004). It has also been used in operations management research. Patel et al. (2012, p. 204) define it as "pursuing both exploration and exploitation activities" and as "[an] important learning capability that may enhance a firm's response to environmental uncertainty." Ambidexterity might refer to several dichotomous issues such as search and stability (Rivkin & Siggelkow, 2003), manufacturing efficiency and flexibility (Adler, Goldoftas, & Levine, 1999), global integration and local responsiveness (Bartlett & Ghoshal, 1989), exploitative and explorative learning (Kang & Snell, 2009), alignment and adaptability (Gibson & Birkinshaw, 2004), incremental and discontinuous innovations (Benner & Tushman, 2003; Smith & Tushman, 2005), exploratory knowledge sharing and exploitative knowledge sharing (Im & Rai, 2008).

For some researchers ambidexterity is a bi-polar construct since exploitation and exploration lie on the opposite ends of a single continuum. Therefore, the trade-off between them is unavoidable and ambidexterity consequently requires the management of this trade-off (Lavie & Rosenkopf, 2006). However, following March's (1991) seminal contribution, some other researchers implicitly support a multidimensional approach by emphasizing the necessity of pursuing both types of activities. In particular, they argue that too much emphasis on exploitation leads to competency (or success) traps, while too much focus on exploration leads to a failure trap where organizations are not able to leverage on their knowledge and gain returns from it. Having said that, the prevailing view on ambidexterity considers the exploitation − exploration trade-off as an undeniable starting point, but also maintains that successful organizations think and act "ambidextrously" by addressing high levels of both exploration and exploitation simultaneously (Gibson & Birkinshaw, 2004; He & Wong, 2004; Tushman & O'Reilly, 1996).

Recent empirical research highlights various approaches that facilitate firms' ambidexterity (Raisch & Birkinshaw, 2008). From a structural perspective, ambidexterity is gained by putting in place dual organizational structures: certain business, organizational units or teams focus on exploration, while others focus on exploitation (Duncan, 1976; Tushman & O'Reilly, 1996, 2004). The ability to simultaneously pursue both exploitation and exploration ensues from developing and managing multiple contradictory structures that embody distinct strategic and operating logics, cultures, and incentive systems. For instance, a manufacturing plant may become ambidextrous by creating different teams, responsible for exploration and for exploitation, respectively (Adler et al., 1999). Furthermore, ambidexterity has to be also addressed at the next organizational level down by allocating different roles to each individual within the diverse teams (Jansen, George, Van den Bosch, & Volberda, 2008).

Another stream of literature proposes an alternative way to balance exploration and exploitation, different from structural ambidexterity, called contextual ambidexterity, which is grounded in organizational micro processes, collective and individual behaviors and therefore driven, ultimately, by the creation of systems and processes that collectively define organizational members' behavioral context. Organizations can develop contextual ambidexterity "by building a set of processes or systems that enable and encourage individuals to make their own judgments about how to divide their time between conflicting demands for alignment and adaptability" (Gibson & Birkinshaw, 2004, p. 211). Birkinshaw and Gibson (2004) find support for the two opposite ways to achieve ambidexterity (dual structures vs. organizational context). Moreover, they also show that in the structural approach the split between alignment and adaptability is made at the top of the organization while in the contextual approach it is made at the front line − by plant supervisors or front-line workers. Furthermore, in the case of structural ambidexterity the responsibility for defining the structure and making the trade-off between alignment and adaptability is in the responsibility of top management, whereas in contextual ambidexterity top management is in charge of developing the organizational context where the individuals act. With structural ambidexterity the organizational roles are relatively clearly defined in comparison with the relatively flexible roles required to foster the contextual ambidexterity. Finally, skills and knowledge are deeply different in the two cases as in the former case task specialization is higher than in the latter case, where more generalist employees prevail.

The prevalent type of ambidexterity represents the third dimension of our interpretative framework. We will investigate it focusing on the comparative importance, both at HQ and plant level, of: (a) the configuration of LPOs (Lean Promoting Offices) and (b) middle management and workers' involvement and responsibilities in the lean roll-out process. A prevalent role of LPOs in the lean roll-out process, with a clear structural split between who introduces the lean operations practices and who operates the plant represents a proxy for structural ambidexterity. In fact, in this case, LPOs, composed by lean experts, drive the lean roll-out process, here intended as a process of innovation and, hence, of exploration, leaving to line managers and workers the mere application of lean operations practices and the corresponding exploitation of the associated knowledge base.

A prevalent role of line managers and workers in the lean roll-out process, with a blurred distinction between the roles and people introducing the lean operations practices (LPOs) and those operating the plant represents a proxy for contextual ambidexterity. The more plant-level management and workers are involved in the lean roll-out process, actively collaborating with LPOs, the more prevalent is contextual ambidexterity, with line managers and workers actively introducing lean operations practices (i.e., innovating or exploring) while at the same time running the plant and coping with the daily operational challenges.

RESEARCH METHODOLOGY AND STUDY DESIGN

Exploratory studies aimed at theory building or at developing research hypotheses and testable propositions on under-investigated or innovative topics are typically considered as the best settings for applying the case study research method (Barratt, Choi, & Mei, 2011; Eisenhardt, 1989; Ellram, 1996; Meredith, 1998; Voss, Tsikriktsis, & Frohlich, 2002). Since our research setting does reflect such conditions, a multiple case study represents the most appropriate research method (DeHoratius & Rabinovich, 2011; Eisenhardt & Graebner, 2007; Meredith, 1998).

Case Selection

Case study methodology literature suggests theoretical sampling as a prerequisite for rigorous case study research (Eisenhardt, 1989; Meredith, 1998). Accordingly, we proceeded with theoretical case sampling using the selection methodology suggested by Miles and Huberman (1984). First, we established the boundaries of the phenomenon object of the study to ensure that the case selection was appropriate. Then, we framed our literature review within our interpretative model, which also underlies the purposely designed field research protocol described further in this section. The field research protocol was tested in a pilot case study and subsequently refined together with the research constructs. In the meantime, we identified a sample of 15 possible firms/plants/case study candidates and then selected, among them, 7 firms/plants/case studies on which conducting the analysis. These seven cases represent polar types in which different approaches were observable (Eisenhardt, 1989; Yin, 1989) and which represent, simultaneously, somewhat extreme situations and critical incidents with regards to the lean roll-out process (Pettigrew, 1990).

Table 1 summarizes some relevant data of the seven selected case studies.

All the cases represent lean roll-out projects carried out in multinational plants located in Italy. Limiting the research to roll-out processes that took place within Italian operations/plants of MNCs allows to control for several critical variables related to the diversity of national contexts (i.e., labor cost, plant unionization, cultural traits).

Besides, in order to get a more thorough understanding of the different industrial settings and in order to better isolate the effect of the approach to the lean roll-out process, we also checked for other variables that, according to extant literature (Shah & Ward, 2003), could preliminarily explain the cross-case variation. Among them: the MNC's home country, industry, plant origin, field status, plant age, plant size, relative size of plant compared to the rest of the corporation and share of expatriates in the plant management.

Furthermore, we selected the case studies so that there was no significant difference among them in terms of previous exposition to lean knowledge or experimentation with lean operations practices, that is, all the analyzed plants, at the time of the lean roll-out, had not had any previous experience of lean operations practices implementation.

Finally, since most of the lean operations literature indicates top management commitment, plant management capabilities and leadership style, level of employees' involvement, labor relations, and investment in training and consulting as potential explanatory variables of the performance of the lean roll-out process, we also checked for cross-plant differences regarding these variables in the attempt to better isolate the effects related to lean systems characteristics and roll-out strategies.

Research Dimensions' Operationalization, Data Collection, and Method of Analysis

In each of the selected case/firm/plant all data were gathered through two rounds of plant visits and structured interviews. In the first round (3–4 hrs on average) plant managers and other managers from the LPOs responsible for the Lean roll-out were directly interviewed. Data and opinions gathered through the interviews were cross-checked to avoid single respondent bias and data distortion. The interviews were audio taped and the transcripts

Table 1. Summary Information of the Seven Analyzed Plants.

	MT	EX	HK	HV	LW	MS	PX
Industry	Automotive	Household appliances	Chemicals	Motorcycles	Valves and Pipe Fittings	Pharmaceutical	Chemicals
HQ Home country	U.S.	E.U.	E.U.	E.U.	U.S.	U.S.	U.S.
HQ Employees	17,000	n.a.	40,000	105,000	12,000	95,000	26,000
Plant main products	Engine timing systems	Dishwashers	Silicon products	Motorcycles	Water pumps	Drugs	Fluor polymer coatings
Plant turnover (M€)	110	250	50	90	n.a.	n.a.	16
Plant Origin	JV with Italian company and then acquisition	Acquisition from another MNC	Acquisition from another MNC	Acquisition from Italian company	Acquisition from another MNC	Acquisition from Italian company	Acquisition from Italian company
Plant age (years)	16	42	38	14	44	51	27
Plant total employees	430	1,100	60	262	600	250	85
Plant blue collars	280	650	42	48	290	125	45
% expatriates (in the plant)	1	0	0	4	0.5	0	0

were sent back to the interviewees to check for correctness and accuracy. The write-ups (available upon request) were then analyzed independently by the authors. Subsequently, the authors held face-to-face discussions to compare their individual assessments of the cases, to analyze the preliminary findings deriving from the case study data, and to develop additional protocols for further clarifying specific issues through a second round of interviews. In the second round, most of the questions were case-specific, as they were intended to clarify issues and gather additional insights for the development of a framework useful in explaining efficiency and effectiveness of the lean roll-out process. The second round of interviews accounted for an additional 2–3 hrs. As in the first round, all informants of each firm were involved also in the second round, when the research team replicated the approach for data gathering and analysis used in the first round. After completing the analysis, the findings were shared with the key informants for validation. They suggested minor modifications to the analysis.

As above mentioned, the interpretative framework and the three research dimensions were applied to the seven case studies. During the interviews across all the cases a purposely designed field research protocol was adopted. The interview protocol included a specific set of questions referring to the three research dimensions (knowledge replication strategy, decentralization, prevalent type of ambidexterity) and other aspects we considered relevant to describe and explain the lean roll-out process and its performance. The operationalization of the three research dimensions into specific research constructs follows.

Lean Roll-Out (Knowledge Transfer) Success
Having defined knowledge transfer performance in terms of resource efficiency in the transfer itself and effectiveness of the process (Kostova, 1999; Lin, 2007), our interview protocol includes three dimensions to understand cost and time efficiency of the lean roll-out process (length of the process, whether it was on budget, and whether it was on time) and three dimensions to understand effectiveness (in terms of time effectiveness, that is, achievement of the key milestones of the roll-out itself and employees' satisfaction with the process).

Knowledge Replication Strategy
In order to operationalize this dimension, we focus on the degree of knowledge codification and more specifically on the dichotomy template versus principles-based replication strategy (Baden-Fuller & Winter, 2007; Letmathe et al., 2012). Based on this, we included four core sub-dimensions

in the interview protocol: (a) the presence of a formalized and detailed template for lean operations practices plant-level implementation (what in the company jargon is typically referred to as a "lean model" or a "House of Lean"); (b) the presence of codified manuals for lean operations practices implementation and training; (c) the presence of a specified sequence (or of formalized criteria to decide it) regarding the plant-level processes/value streams interested by the lean operations practices implementation; and (d) the presence of a specified sequence (or of formalized criteria to decide it) regarding the various lean operations practices implementation.

Decentralization

In order to operationalize this dimension, we defined the degree of plant autonomy in the lean roll-out process in terms of plant management discretion both in the decision making process and in managing resources (Gupta & Govindarajan, 2000). Thus, our interview protocol includes six dimensions related to the extent of decentralization of the lean roll-out as concerns: (a) HQ involvement in the plant lean roll-out; (b) lean roll-out auditing (level of advancement in adopting the lean operations practices at the plant level); (c) lean implementation results accountability; (d) lean roll-out planning; (e) lean roll-out budgeting; and (f) definition of an assessment tool to audit the level of advancement of lean operations practices implementation in the plant.

Prevalent Type of Ambidexterity

In order to operationalize this dimension we focused on the dichotomy structural versus contextual ambidexterity and tried to assess empirically the prevalent type of ambidexterity in the lean roll-out process. We characterized the lean roll-out process according to the extent to which the diffusion of lean operations practices (a process of exploration/innovation) was led by a dedicated organizational structure (at the plant level) different from the plant organizational structure in charge of managing daily operations (Patel et al., 2012).

The larger (smaller) is the role of LPOs (HQ and/or plant level) compared to the role of plant-level management and workers in leading the lean roll-out process, the more prevalent is structural (contextual). In order to investigate this aspect, we included seven core dimensions in the interview protocol: (a) Presence of a LPO structure (HQ level); (b) LPO role & Responsibility (HQ level); (c) LPO structure (plant level); (d) LPO role & responsibility (plant level); (e) Time allocation of LPO staff to lean roll-out (plant level); (f) management involvement in continuous improvement activities; (g) workers involvement in continuous improvement activities.

CROSS-CASE ANALYSIS AND DISCUSSION

Coherently with qualitative research standards (Ellram, 1996), we carried out the within-case analysis in order to describe the lean roll-out processes for each of the seven firms. Afterwards, we conducted cross-case analysis comparing and contrasting the seven roll-outs.

As a result of the comparative assessment, we ranked the seven cases according to their performance as reported in Table 2, where MT is the best performing case (i.e., most effective and efficient case of lean roll-out process) while EX is the worst.

Then, we classified the seven cases according to the three research dimensions of analysis derived from the literature and the operationalization of the associated sub-dimensions/constructs.

Template- versus Principles-Based Knowledge Replication Strategy

As illustrated in the literature review, one of the most relevant dimensions affecting the roll-out process, when conceived as knowledge transfer, is the degree of codification of knowledge (Letmathe et al., 2012). The seven cases were analyzed according to the four sub-dimensions that, in our model and field research protocol, characterize and distinguish a principles-based versus a template-based approach. The seven cases vary greatly contingent on the presence of a clear, detailed and codified "lean model," including the

Table 2.   Ranking of the Seven Lean Roll-Out Process Performance.

Company	Roll-Out Effectiveness and Efficiency (Ranking)
MT	1
HK	2
HV	3
LW	4
MS	5
PX	6
EX	7

set of lean operations practices that the analyzed MNC wished to roll-out in the plants (something similar to the worldwide famous "House of Lean" codified by the Toyota Motor Company in 2001). On the one side, when providing a detailed template, the HQ offered a well specified and comprehensive description of the lean operations practices that the plants should adopt, as it happened for the PX case.

On the other side, in cases like MT and HK, plants received from HQ just a conceptual description of lean thinking, a set of general principles and some general guidelines about the roll-out process. In this case, each plant had to make sense out of these and elaborate their own locally customized version of the set of Lean operations practices to be adopted.

Moreover cases vary in the extent to which the path (sequence of steps, timing, etc.) they needed to follow in the roll-out process and the lean operations practices they had to implement were codified and predefined by the HQ. Indeed, there are cases, where the sequence and the path were clearly codified and decided at the HQ level and situations where the process was more ambiguous and subjected to interpretation and local decisions. For example, in the MS case it was the value stream mapping exercise, conducted autonomously within the plant by the local management team and workforce (and not decided by the HQ or included as a formal step of a codified roll-out procedure), that led the plant management team to decide in which part of the plant to start with the implementation of the lean operations practices and, even more interestingly, which lean operations practices should be applied first.

Degree of Plant Autonomy

As previously summarized, this dimension is influenced by the degree of the decentralization of decision making rights, HQ's involvement in leading the roll-out process, the earmarking of fund to run the roll-out and the extent to which the implementation plan is defined locally.

The cross-case analysis built on the data gathered though the interviews and site visits shows that cases vary significantly. For example, in the MT case the plant was mostly in charge of the lean roll-out process, with resources, planning activities, and accountability for the process full in the plant management team's hands.

In other cases, the process was heavily driven by the HQ (and more specifically by the central LPO). However, even in cases that were apparently more characterized by decentralized decision-making, the HQ (central LPO) kept a strong grip on the lean roll-out process leaving de facto little possibility to the plant management team and workers to steer the lean roll-out process.

The cross-case analysis also shows that the degree of plant autonomy was associated with the plant absorptive capacity (Tu et al., 2006), that is, the extent to which the analyzed plants were able to acquire, assimilate, and transform external information.

Prevalent Type of Ambidexterity (Structural vs. Contextual)

The introduction of a set of lean operations practices in a subsidiary plant of an MNC represents per se a process of exploration/innovation, since while such lean operations practices are grounded on knowledge that has been (or has to be) generated, selected, and codified (at least to some extent) at the parent level, the process of diffusion (company perspective) or adoption (plant perspective) of such lean operations practices represents a process of organizational discovery, innovation, and change. At the plant level, this raises the problem of how such process has to be led, organized, and conducted while, at the same time, the plant continues to perform daily tasks according to existing processes and routines and the plant management team pursue the given operational targets (exploitation of existing knowledge) (Patel et al., 2012).

Taking into consideration this perspective, we compared the cases according to the seven sub-dimensions we used in our field research protocol to operationalize and investigate the prevalent type of ambidexterity that characterize the lean roll-out process.

There are cases, like EX, where structural ambidexterity prevails. The central LPO office's (HQ) task was to design, lead, and execute the lean roll-out process, especially at the initial stage. The plant management team and workers play a minor role in this innovation/change/exploration process, role that became slightly larger later during the roll-out. Overall, plant staff remained prevalently focused on operating the plant, receiving and trying to integrate in their daily activities the changes brought about by the lean roll-out process driven by the central LPO. In the end, a dual organizational structure underlay the lean roll-out at the plant level: one constituted by the staff and resources of the central LPO (HQ) (assisted by a dedicated plant-level team) driving the process of introduction of the lean operations practices and the other, constituted by the plant management team and organizational structure operating the plant which passively adopted (and adapted to) the new lean operations practices introduced.

Instead, in other cases, like MS, the arrangement was completely different. The central LPO was neither dedicated to the roll-out process in the plants nor directly involved in the analyzed case. Rather, its main task was that of spreading general knowledge about lean thinking, creating a shared mindset, coaching plant managers about the roll-out process and providing directions about how the introduction of the lean operations practices might impact the achievement of the plant operational and performance improvement targets. In this case, there was no clear organizational boundary between the role of lean specialists and line managers. Indeed, the boundaries between the roles of the LPO staff (both HQ and plant level) and of the plant management team were blurred.

Integrating the Cross-Case Analysis Findings

Eventually, the above analysis allow us to classify the seven analyzed cases as virtually located somewhere in a three-dimensional space and lying, for each dimension, within a continuum at the extreme of which there are opposite characteristics with regard to the three dimensions of the interpretative framework (knowledge replication strategy, decentralization of decision making and organizational ambidexterity type entailed by the lean roll-out process). Table 3 summarizes how the seven cases are virtually located in the three-dimensional space defined by our interpretative framework, and shows how each analyzed case of lean roll-out is characterized by a different combination of the dimensions. More specifically, we

Table 3. Summary Configuration of the Lean Roll-Out Process of the Seven Analyzed Cases.

Company	Knowledge Replication Strategy	Degree of Decentralization	Type of Organizational Ambidexterity
MT	Principles-based	Plant management-driven	Contextual
HK	Principles-based	Plant management-driven	Contextual
HV	Principles-based	HQ-driven	Contextual
LW	Principles-based	Plant management-driven	Structural
MS	Template-based	HQ-driven	Structural
PX	Template-based	HQ-driven	Structural
EX	Template-based	Plant management-driven	Structural

classified the seven analyzed lean roll-out processes as either: (a) mainly focused on a template- or on a principles-based knowledge replication strategy; (b) prevalently plant management-driven versus HQ-driven; (c) prevalently characterized by structural or contextual ambidexterity.

In order to understand the influence of the three analyzed dimensions on the comparative roll-out process performance, we associated the performance ranking reported in Table 2 with the results of the cross-case analysis illustrated in Table 3. The empirical evidence provided by the seven cases seems to suggest that a less-codified principles-based knowledge strategy replication, more decentralization and plant autonomy, and contextual ambidexterity might be associated with better lean roll-out process performance.

FINDINGS DISCUSSION AND PROPOSITIONS

On the basis of the analysis presented in the previous sections, three propositions regarding the determinants of lean roll-out processes performance in MNCs follow.

Knowledge Replication Strategy and Lean Roll-Out Performance

As reported in the previous analysis of the literature about the replication of organizational knowledge, there is no unanimous consensus about the direction and intensity of the effect, on lean roll-out performance, of template-based approaches versus principle-based approaches. In many cases, lean experts and practitioners complain about the non-smoothness of most of lean roll-outs, observing that organizations experience serious difficulties in spreading new knowledge and practices and getting recipient units to adopt them effectively and efficiently. And they would try to reduce that risk and increase the likelihood of successful knowledge transfer to plants by codifying the lean model and operations practices and by formalizing the process of transfer. In most of the cases this makes things worse with potential recipients often questioning the appropriateness of the introduction of the lean operations practices, their efficacy or the efficiency of the suggested implementation plan.

As previously highlighted, on the one hand the use of templates helps overcome resistance by demonstrating results (supporting appropriateness), simplifying the adoption process (Swink & Jacobs, 2012) offering working examples of organizational routines, and often providing evidence that someone else in the organizational has already done it (supporting efficacy) (Letmathe et al., 2012). While the replication of organizational routines requires change in the recipient units, templates contain data on the potential outcome. Such tangible proof may well persuade re-use of the knowledge contained in the template. In contrast, without a template there is no data on potential results and the recipients have to rely on faith rather than proof when making the decision to implement, thus lowering the incentive to adopt.

However, on the other hand, the complexity of knowledge transfer processes in international operations always generates potential causal ambiguity about the replicative power of the routines embedded in the lean operations practices HQ wishes to roll-out in the plants, so that even the most careful efforts to replicate organizational practices may miss important details or incorrectly implement essential aspects of the routine. Indeed, the existence of causal ambiguity implies that the factors explaining the template's performance cannot be precisely determined (not even ex post), and that it is therefore impossible to produce an unambiguous conception of how the template works. Under this condition, and we maintain that lean roll-outs in international and disperse operations networks refer exactly to it, research has shown that the use of principles could be more effective for the transfer. Moreover, the adoption of a template could decrease transfer effectiveness by inhibiting local adaptation and innovation and increasing local resistance to adoption (Swink & Jacobs, 2012; Zollo, Reurer, & Singh, 2002). In fact, while templates could in theory assure better coordination with the recipient organization, they can also cause disruption within it, changing the organizational processes and procedures of the recipient and, in such a way, also altering recipient's absorptive capacity (Tu et al., 2006) and innovative capabilities (Benner & Tushman, 2003; Ranft & Lord, 2002). Finally, templates might inhibit the enactment of a self-learning loop within the recipients and the activation of an "experimenting" approach to the transfer, prohibiting, in such a way, a long term behavioral change (Brown & Duguid, 1991; Letmathe et al., 2012; Nelson & Winter, 1982).

Contrary to templates, and especially in case of high complexity in the knowledge transfer (Azadegan, Patel, Zangoueinezhad, & Linderman, 2013), the more general and ambiguous nature of principles oblige the recipients unit to engage in a process of learning and knowledge absorption which, in the end, is the only guarantee that lean operations practices will be really adopted, understood, plant customized, applied effectively and geared toward the improvements of the various plant performance dimensions. Paradoxically, the fact that principles are more general and ambiguous than codified routines, allow plants to capture knowledge related to lean thinking at a deeper level and, making mandatory to the recipients units to explore the principles (and reflect on their meaning), so that the recipient units develops the needed understanding by discovery (Baden-Fuller & Winter, 2007).

Our plant case studies show that a principles-based roll-out process creates the conditions for a self-directed learning process within the plant, characterized by a more active approach to experimentation and self-discovery which is the ultimate meaning of lean thinking (Rother, 2009). This approach led the relevant plants to a better understanding of how to apply lean logics to their contexts, to grasp possible problems and anticipate solutions, ending up with a faster and more satisfying roll-out.

This evidence is, in some ways, consistent with what maintained by the most recent research on the nature of lean systems (Shah & Ward, 2007), whose complexity asks for a conceptualization that goes beyond the idea of a system of practices (Azadegan et al., 2013; Furlan, Vinelli, & Dal Pont, 2011), toward the idea of a management system which includes organizational routines, learning routines, organizational culture, and leadership. Contrary to conventional wisdom, which suggests that the more codified the knowledge to be transferred the easier and better the transfer process, we argue that some level of ambiguity is functional to allow and trigger local processes of learning and adaptation. This conceptualization is consistent with studies that theorize lean systems as a dynamic capability (Fujimoto, 1999) or an organizational capability to systematically question, renovate and improve its routines, remaining engaged in unceasing loops of organizational learning (Anand et al., 2009; Patel et al., 2012). Applied to lean roll-out processes, this approach to knowledge generation and change postulates room for experimenting, trials and errors (Anand et al., 2009; Staats et al., 2011) and sees the diffusion of lean operations practices in MNCs as a process of knowledge creation about both operational processes and how to change them (Linderman, Schroeder, Zaheer, Liedtke, & Choo, 2004; Patel et al., 2012). On the basis of our evidence and of this conceptualization of the lean system as complex, causal ambiguous and more oriented to a dynamic approach to learning and knowledge creation rather than to simple replication, we argue that lean roll-out processes are likely to be more effective and efficient when they are principles-driven rather than template-driven. To formulate our proposition, we conceive a principles-driven roll-out as a process in which the degree of codification of the knowledge associated with the lean operations practices to be diffused and with the process itself is lower.

Proposition 1. The lower the degree of lean knowledge codification, the higher the effectiveness and efficiency of the lean roll-out process.

Decentralization of Decision Making and Lean Roll-Out Performance

In the theoretical background section we showed that, in general, there is some evidence that decision making centralization operates as a facilitator of within-organization knowledge transfer activities, especially between parent and subsidiaries in MNCs. Indeed, direct involvement and control from the Headquarter has been proved to be an effective strategy for successful parent-subsidiary knowledge transfer (see, e.g., Ambos & Schlegelmilch, 2007). The availability of specialized resources (in this case, e.g., a team of lean specialists) at the corporate level, as well as of clear directions and coordinated efforts based on centralized decision making could directly sustain the lean roll-out process by providing top notch expertise and commitment. Through the HQ engagement, the lean roll-out process gains visibility and increases the likelihood of stronger subsidiary plants' participation and commitment. Moreover, in cases of plant management team's resistance to the changes brought about by the lean roll-out process, the headquarter can provide specific rewards and sanctions to pave the way for smoother implementation of the lean operations practices. Finally, when a lean roll-out process is carried out through a centralized structure, it could be perceived or considered as more credible and likely to generate the expected outcomes.

However, another substantial body of empirical evidence suggests that knowledge transfer processes tightly driven and controlled by the headquarters may inhibit recipients' absorptive capacity (Tu et al., 2006), reduce the level of engagement of the subsidiary plants' and frustrate plant management team's propensity to make a consistent and coordinated use of local resources to facilitate the lean roll-out process. Naturally, this renders the parent-subsidiary knowledge transfer process more costly and time consuming. Another aspect of complexity, often underestimated especially when the lean roll-out process takes place simultaneously in several plants or involves not only vertical parent-subsidiary knowledge transfers but also horizontal subsidiary-subsidiary knowledge transfers, is the fact that stronger headquarters' involvement in the lean roll-out process increases the number of actors involved in the knowledge transfer process, potentially making planning, execution and coordination more complicated. Consequently, the lean roll-out process efficiency is likely to decrease with strong HQ involvement because it increases factors like decision-making complexity, project visibility and reporting requirements, which adds to the cost and time required to introduce lean operations practices locally (Birkinshaw, Bouquet, & Ambos, 2007; Björkman, Barner-Rasmussen, & Li, 2004). Moreover, lean roll-out processes characterized by more decentralization, that is, more recipient plant's autonomy, could motivate the plant management team to make independent decisions that best serve the plant task requirements and objectives. More autonomy helps building a greater sense of responsibility and accountability in the plant management team (e.g., Cohen & Ledford, 1994; Cordery, Mueller, & Smith, 1991; Janz, Colquitt, & Noe, 1997) and it fosters, given the plant management team's capabilities, the plant's absorptive capacity (Tu et al., 2006) especially if lean knowledge flows from the HQ are complemented by local sourcing of lean knowledge (Schleimer & Pedersen, 2013). Finally, more plant autonomy in the lean roll-out process fosters local capability development and stimulates active learning through explorative behavior, including activities such as searching, experimentation, playing, discovering, varying and innovating in the recipient organization (March, 1991). Even from the HQ/parent's perspective, more plant autonomy in the lean roll-out process provides learning effects, positive externalities and higher potential cross-plant/subsidiary knowledge flows, by generating the opportunity to compare the effects of diverse local lean roll-outs and to see which one fits the lean roll-out process goals best (Taris & Kompier, 2005).

The anecdotal evidence emerging from multiple case analyses suggests that the benefits of decentralization and plant autonomy in the lean roll-out process more than offset the supposed advantages of a tighter control by the HQ in the knowledge transfer performance. Decentralization not only facilitates local adaptation, but also fosters absorptive capacity development (Patel et al., 2012; Tu et al., 2006) and obliges the plant not to adopt the lean operations practices as a "foreign body" of "things to do on top of the rest," but to make sense of them and of their implementation in the light of the plant's strategic goals, objectives, problems, and priorities.

A more decentralized approach to lean roll-outs is also consistent with the organizational approach and management philosophy underlying lean thinking. Most of the lean literature, both scholarly and practitioner-oriented, underlines that lean management systems constitute a dynamic capability based on multiple-level, collective problem solving, tapping into people ingenuity at all levels and management behaviors geared toward supporting rather than directing others' behaviors, stimulating self-discovery, exploring new knowledge and continuous learning (Hines, Holweg, & Rich, 2004; Holweg, 2007; Womack & Jones, 1996).

Overall, the evidence emerging from our case studies and the comparative performance of the lean roll-outs lead us to argue that decentralization, in the form of more plant management autonomy, is beneficial to the success of lean roll-out process. Thus, we formulate the following proposition:

Proposition 2. The higher the degree of autonomy of the plant, the higher the effectiveness and efficiency of the lean roll-out process.

Prevalent Type of Ambidexterity and Lean Roll-Out Performance

As illustrated in the relevant theory section, lean roll-outs can be conceptualized as processes that imply at least some level of ambidexterity. Plants involved in lean roll-out processes engage themselves in processes of exploration, innovation and change (the introduction of the new lean operations practices, often never experimented and unknown) while, at the same time, performing the daily operations to achieve the current objectives (Patel et al., 2012). Also in the analyzed cases plant management teams simultaneously pursued both the exploitation of existing operational capabilities and the exploration of new operational capabilities. An ambidextrous plant-level organization is a key enabler of lean roll-outs and our case studies, consistently with the outstanding literature, suggest that this goal can be achieved in two different ways, through either structural or contextual ambidexterity.

Although in all the analyzed cases some type of duality in the organizational structure at the plant level does emerge (either through a massive but temporary intervention of the HQ LPO or through the constitution of a permanent local team of lean specialists), the most efficient and effective roll-outs seem to be characterized by a more contextual approach. Contextually ambidextrous plant organizations seem to enable a better process of introduction of lean operations practices, a process of percolation that, although posing all the way down to the employee level the challenge to integrate explorative and exploitative activities, connects the new routines directly to the plant management problems, objectives, and priorities and embed them in individual and collective behaviors.

A more contextual approach seems to generate more opportunities for proactive cognition and behavior (Gibson & Birkinshaw, 2004), as well increased energy and self-efficacy (Schudy & Bruch, 2010) at the plant level.

Our cross-case analysis shows that the comparatively most effective and efficient lean roll-out processes are associated with plant organizations in which, via contextual ambidexterity, there was more room for diffused experimentation and unplanned learning with regard to the introduction of lean operations practices.

In such environments, lean knowledge is engendered and enacted by the everyday actions of plant managers and employees, rather than through top-down, HQ or lean specialist-driven knowledge transfer. Contextual ambidexterity really renders lean roll-outs a plant learning process which occurs not in parallel but integrated with ongoing activities. This view of lean roll-outs as open ended, discovery and learning processes (Letmathe et al., 2012) and the related necessity to adopt a more contextual approach in the organization of the knowledge transfer process at the plant level, is also aligned with lean thinking philosophy and with the conceptualization of lean systems as a dynamic capability (Anand et al., 2009; Fujimoto, 1999; Zollo & Winter, 2002). Our third proposition follows:

Proposition 3. The more the lean roll-out process is based on contextual ambidexterity, the higher the effectiveness and efficiency of the lean roll-out process.

IMPLICATIONS, STUDY LIMITATIONS AND DIRECTIONS FOR FUTURE RESEARCH

From a theoretical standpoint, the contribution of this study is threefold. First, we contribute to research on the determinants of the effects of lean operations on performance (Cua et al., 2001; Shah & Ward, 2003), by pointing out that lean roll-out processes are necessarily the logical and chronological antecedents of any lean production system in place. So far, lean operations management research has prevalently focused on the effects of lean operations practices and other situational factors on performance (Stone, 2012a, 2012b) paying less attention to the analysis of the process through which a lean production system comes into place.

Second, our study bridges several research streams showing how lean and international operations, knowledge management, dynamic capabilities and organizational configurations literatures can be integrated to model lean roll-out processes. So far, extant studies have focused on interpreting lean production and management systems as a dynamic capability of the firm a sort of meta routine that allows on the one hand performance improvement and, on the other, capability development (Anand et al., 2009; Fujimoto, 1999; Spear & Bowen, 1999). Our study argues that the extent to which this double learning loop becomes active, for example at the plant level, is contingent on the upstream knowledge transfer process and on the nature of such knowledge flows (Letmathe et al., 2012; Staats et al., 2011).

Finally, this study offers a counterintuitive view about the effectiveness and efficiency of lean roll-out processes. Conventional wisdom (both scholars and practitioners) would assume that the more codified the set of lean operations practices to be introduced, the more structured and centrally directed the process and the clearer the division of roles in the organization (with a strong LPO and team of lean specialists) the higher the likelihood of a successful roll-out. Instead, we point to the hidden virtues of ambiguity and complexity arguing that lean roll-outs are learning and discovery processes where, paradoxically, codification control and structural differentiation are not necessarily conducive of better outcomes.

Our study suffers from several limitations. We decided to explore our research goals in MNCs, where the knowledge dynamics between the HQ and the plants was more visible. However, a similar analysis could be replicated within a plant, by exploring the dynamics between the top management, in charge of designing the lean roll-out, and the workers, in charge of implementing it. This would bring further validity to our findings. Moreover, we selected seven cases out of fifteen in order to cope with a strategy able to get the most informative cases, due to the very seminal development of the theory we were building. Nonetheless, it could be interesting, in future steps, to go back to the other cases and to check whether they could shed further lights on the combination of these three dimensions and of their effects. This would allow us enriching our theoretical framework and having a further source of triangulation of our evidence. Finally, testing the posited relationships and validating the theoretical framework would be a logical direction for future research. For this purpose, we would like to enlarge the sample and adopt set-theoretic methods such as qualitative comparative analysis (QCA) that offer a rigorous way of assessing the complex ways in which causes combine to create outcomes, and provide a viable alternative much better suited to the configurational nature of the case study approach.

ACKNOWLEDGMENTS

The authors thank participants at the International EurOMA-POM 2012 annual meeting, and at the Academy of Management 2013 annual meeting for comments and suggestions at various stages of the research on which this paper is based. The usual disclaimers apply. This research was funded by the Claudio Dematté Research Division – SDA Bocconi School of Management.

REFERENCES

Adler, P. S., Goldoftas, B., & Levine, D. I. (1999). Flexibility versus efficiency: A case study of model changeovers in the Toyota production system. *Organization Science, 10*(1), 43–68.

Ambos, B., & Schlegelmilch, B. (2007). Innovation and control in the multinational firm: A comparison of political and contingency approaches. *Strategic Management Journal, 28*(5), 473–486.

Anand, G., Ward, P. T., Tatikonda, M. V., & Schilling, D. A. (2009). Dynamic capabilities through continuous improvement infrastructure. *Journal of Operations Management, 27*(6), 444–461.

Argote, L., & Ingram, P. (2000). Knowledge transfer: A basis for competitive advantage in firms. *Organizational Behavior and Human Decision Processes, 82*(1), 150–169.

Asmussen, C. G., Foss, N. J., & Pedersen, T. (2011). Knowledge transfer and accommodation effects in multinational corporations: Evidence from European subsidiaries. *Journal of Management*, first published on October 14, 2011, doi:10.1177/0149206311424316

Azadegan, A., Patel, P. C., Zangoueinezhad, A., & Linderman, K. (2013). The effect of environmental complexity and environmental dynamism on lean practices. *Journal of Operations Management, 31*(4), 193–212.

Baden-Fuller, C., & Winter, S. (2007). *Replicating knowledge practices: Principles or templates?* Working paper, Cass Business School, City University, London, UK.

Bamber, L., & Dale, B. G. (2000). Lean production: A study of application in a traditional manufacturing environment. *Production Planning and Control, 11*(3), 291–298.

Barratt, M., Choi, T. Y., & Mei, L. (2011). Qualitative case studies in operations management: Trends, research outcomes and future research implications. *Journal of Operations Management, 29*(4), 329–342.

Bartlett, C. A., & Ghoshal, S. (1989). *Managing across borders: The transnational solution.* Cambridge, MA: Harvard Business School Press.

Benner, M. J., & Tushman, M. L. (2003). Exploitation, exploration, and process management: The productivity dilemma revisited. *Academy of Management Review, 28*(2), 238–256.

Birkinshaw, J., Bouquet, C., & Ambos, T. (2007). Managing executive attention in the global company. *MIT Sloan Management Review, 48*(4), 39–45.

Birkinshaw, J., & Gibson, C. B. (2004). Building an ambidextrous organization. *MIT Sloan Management Review*, (Summer), 47–55.

Björkman, I., Barner-Rasmussen, W., & Li, L. (2004). Managing knowledge transfers in MNCs: The impact of headquarters control mechanisms. *Journal of International Business Studies, 35*(5), 443–455.

Brown, J. S., & Duguid, P. (1991). Organizational learning and communities-of-practice: Toward a unified view of working, learning, and innovation. *Organization Science, 2*(1), 40–57.

Byrne, A. (2012). *The lean turnaround: How business leaders use lean principles to create value and transform their company.* New York, NY: McGraw-Hill.

Camuffo, A., & Comacchio, A. (1999). Diffusion patterns of lean practices: Lessons from the European auto industry. In A. Comacchio, G. Volpato, & A. Camuffo (Eds.), *Automation in automotive industries. Recent developments.* Berlin: Springer Verlag.

Ciabuschi, F., Dellestrand, H., & Kappen, P. (2011). Exploring the effects of vertical and lateral mechanisms in international knowledge transfer projects. *Management International Review, 5*, 129–155.

Cohen, S. G., & Ledford, G. E. (1994). The effectiveness of self-managing teams: A quasi-experiment. *Human Relations, 47*(1), 13–43.

Cohen, W., & Levinthal, D. (1990). Absorptive capacity: New perspectives on learning and innovation. *Administrative Science Quarterly, 35*(1), 128–152.

Cordery, J. L., Mueller, W. S., & Smith, L. M. (1991). Attitudinal and behavioral effects of autonomous group working: A longitudinal field study. *Academy of Management Journal, 34*(2), 464–476.

Cua, K. O., McKone, K. E., & Schroeder, R. G. (2001). Relationships between implementation of TQM, JIT, and TPM and manufacturing performance. *Journal of Operations Management, 19*(2), 675–694.

Deflorina, P., & Scherrer-Rathjeb, M. (2012). Challenges in the transformation to lean production from different manufacturing-process choices: A path-dependent perspective. *International Journal of Production Research, 50*(14), 3956–3973.

DeHoratius, N., & Rabinovich, E. (2011). Field research in operations and supply chain management. *Journal of Operations Management, 29*(5), 371–375.

Duncan, R. (1976). The ambidextrous organization: Designing dual structures for innovation. In R. H. Killman, L. R. Pondy, & D. Sleven (Eds.), *The management of organization* (p. 167–188). New York, NY: North Holland.

Eisenhardt, K. M. (1989). Building theories from case studies. *Academy of Management Review, 14*(4), 532–550.

Eisenhardt, K. M., & Graebner, M. E. (2007). Theory building from cases: Opportunities and challenges. *Academy of Management Journal, 50*(1), 25–32.

Ellram, L. M. (1996). The use of the case study method in logistics research. *Journal of Business Logistics, 17*(2), 93–138.

Emiliani, B., Stec, D., Grasso, L., & Stodder, J. (2007). *Better thinking, better results: Case study and analysis of an enterprise-wide lean transformation* (2nd ed.). Kensington, CT: Center for Lean Business Management.

Friel, D. (2005). Transferring a lean production concept from Germany to the United States: The impact of labor laws and training systems. *Academy of Management Executive, 19*(2), 50–58.

Fujimoto, T. (1999). *The evolution of a manufacturing system at Toyota.* Oxford: Oxford University Press.

Furlan, A., Vinelli, A., & Dal Pont, G. (2011). Complementarity and lean manufacturing bundles: An empirical analysis. *International Journal of Operations & Production Management*, *31*(8), 835–850.

Gibson, C. B., & Birkinshaw, J. (2004). The antecedents, consequences, and mediating role of organizational ambidexterity. *Academy of Management Journal*, *47*(2), 209–226.

Grant, R. M. (1996). Toward a knowledge-based theory of the firm. *Strategic Management Journal*, *17*, 109–122.

Gupta, A. K., & Govindarajan, V. (2000). Knowledge flows within multinational corporations. *Strategic Management Journal*, *21*(4), 473–496.

Hartwell, J. K., & Roth, G. (2010). Doing more with less at Ariens: A leadership and transformation case study. *Organization Management Journal*, *7*(2), 89–109.

He, Z., & Wong, P. (2004). Exploration and exploitation: An empirical test of the ambidexterity hypothesis. *Organization Science*, *15*(4), 481–494.

Hines, P., Holweg, M., & Rich, N. (2004). Learning to evolve: A review of contemporary lean thinking. *International Journal of Operations & Production Management*, *24*(10), 994–1011.

Holweg, M. (2007). The genealogy of lean production. *Journal of Operations Management*, *25*(2), 420–437.

Im, G., & Rai, A. (2008). Knowledge sharing ambidexterity in long-term interorganizational relationships. *Management Science*, *54*(7), 1281–1296.

Jansen, J. J., George, G., Van den Bosch, F. A. J., & Volberda, H. W. (2008). Senior team attributes and organizational ambidexterity: The moderating role of transformational leadership. *Journal of Management Studies*, *45*(5), 982–1007.

Janz, B. D., Colquitt, J. A., & Noe, R. A. (1997). Knowledge worker team effectiveness: The role of autonomy, interdependence, team development, and contextual support variables. *Personnel Psychology*, *50*(4), 877–904.

Kang, S.-C., & Snell, S. A. (2009). Intellectual capital architectures and ambidextrous learning: A framework for human resource management. *Journal of Management Studies*, *46*(1), 65–92.

Kenney, M., & Florida, R. (1993). *Beyond mass production: The Japanese system and its transfer to the United States*. New York, NY: Oxford University Press.

Koenigsaecker, G. (2009). *Leading the lean enterprise transformation*. New York, NY: Productivity Press.

Kostova, T. (1999). Transnational transfer of strategic organizational practices: A contextual perspective. *Academy of Management Review*, *24*(2), 308–324.

Kostova, T., & Roth, K. (2002). Adoption of an organizational practice by subsidiaries of multinational corporations: Institutional and relational effects. *Academy of Management Journal*, *45*(1), 215–233.

Kostova, T., & Zaheer, S. (1999). Organizational legitimacy under conditions of complexity: The case of the multinational enterprise. *Academy of Management Review*, *45*(1), 215–233.

Lavie, D., & Rosenkopf, L. (2006). Balancing exploration and exploitation in alliance formation. *Academy of Management Journal*, *49*(4), 797–818.

Letmathe, P., Schweitzer, M., & Zielinski, M. (2012). How to learn new tasks: Shop floor performance effects of knowledge transfer and performance feedback, *Journal of Operations Management*, *30*(3), 221–236.

Lin, H. F. (2007). A stage model of knowledge management: An empirical investigation of process and effectiveness. *Journal of Information Science*, *33*(6), 643–659.

Linderman, K., Schroeder, R. G., Zaheer, S., Liedtke, C., & Choo, A. S. (2004). Integrating quality management practices with knowledge creation processes. *Journal of Operations Management, 22*(6), 589–607.

Losonci, D., Demeter, K., & Jenei, I. (2011). Factors influencing employee perceptions in lean transformations. *International Journal of Production Economics, 131*(1), 30–43.

March, J. (1991). Exploration and exploitation in the organizational learning. *Organization Science, 2*(1), 71–87.

Meredith, J. R. (1998). Building operations management theory through case and field research. *Journal of Operations Management, 16*(4), 441–454.

Miles, M. B., & Huberman, A. M. (1984). *Qualitative data analysis: A sourcebook of new methods.* Beverly Hills, CA: Sage.

Minbaeva, D., Pedersen, T., Björkman, I., Fey, C. F., & Park, H. J. (2003). MNC knowledge transfer, subsidiary absorptive capacity and HRM. *Journal of International Business Studies, 34*(6), 586–599.

Nelson, R., & Winter, S. (1982). *An evolutionary theory of economic change.* Cambridge, MA: Belknap Press.

Nonaka, I., & Takeuchi, H. (1995). *The knowledge creating company.* Oxford: University Press.

Patel, P. C., Terjesen, S., & Li, D. (2012). Enhancing effects of manufacturing flexibility through operational absorptive capacity and operational ambidexterity. *Journal of Operations Management, 30*(3), 201–220.

Pérez-Nordtvedt, L., Kedia, B. L., Datta, D. K., & Rasheed, A. A. (2008). Effectiveness and efficiency of cross-border knowledge transfer: An empirical examination. *Journal of Management Studies, 45*(4), 714–744.

Pettigrew, A. (1990). Longitudinal field research on change: Theory and practice. *Organization Science, 1*(3), 267–292.

Prahalad, C. K., & Doz, Y. L. (1987). *The multinational mission: Balancing local demands and global vision.* New York, NY: Free Press.

Puranam, P., Singh, H., & Zollo, M. (2006). Organizing for innovation: Managing the coordination-autonomy dilemma in technology acquisitions. *Academy of Management Journal, 49*(2), 263–280.

Raisch, S., & Birkinshaw, J. (2008). Organizational ambidexterity: Antecedents, outcomes, and moderators. *Journal of Management, 34*(3), 375–409.

Ranft, A. L., & Lord, M. D. (2002). Acquiring new technologies and capabilities: A grounded model of acquisition implementation. *Organization Science, 13*(4), 420–441.

Rivkin, J. W., & Siggelkow, N. (2003). Balancing search and stability: Interdependencies among elements of organizational design. *Management Science, 49*(3), 290–311.

Rother, M. (2009). *Toyota Kata: Managing people for improvement, adaptiveness and superior results.* New York, NY: McGraw-Hill.

Schleimer, S. C., & Pedersen, T. (2013). The driving forces of subsidiary absorptive capacity. *Journal of Management Studies, 50*(4), 646–672.

Schudy, C., & Bruch, H. (2010). Productive organizational energy as a mediator in the contextual ambidexterity-performance relation. *Academy of Management Proceedings, 1*, 1–6.

Shah, R., & Ward, P. T. (2003). Lean manufacturing: Context, practice bundles, and performance. *Journal of Operations Management, 21*(2), 129–150.

Shah, R., & Ward, P. T. (2007). Defining and developing measures of lean production. *Journal of Operations Management, 25*(4), 785–805.

Smith, W. K., & Tushman, M. L. (2005). Managing strategic contradictions: A top management model for managing innovation streams. *Organization Science, 16*(5), 522–536.

Spear, S., & Bowen, H. K. (1999). Decoding the DNA of the Toyota production system. *Harvard Business Review, 77*(9), 97–106.

Staats, B. R., Brunner, D. J., & Upton, D. M. (2011). Lean principles, learning, and knowledge work: Evidence from a software services provider. *Journal of Operations Management, 29*(5), 376–390.

Stone, K. B. (2012a). Four decades of lean: A systematic literature review. *International Journal of Lean Six Sigma, 3*(2), 112–132.

Stone, K. B. (2012b). Lean transformation: Organizational performance factors that influence firms' leanness. *Journal of Enterprise Transformation, 2*(4), 229–249.

Swink, M., & Jacobs, B. W. (2012). Six sigma adoption: Operating performance impacts and contextual drivers of success. *Journal of Operations Management, 30*(6), 437–453.

Szulanski, G. (1996). Exploring internal stickiness: Impediments to the transfer of best practice within the firm. *Strategic Management Journal, 17*(Winter Special Issue), 27–43.

Szulanski, G., & Winter, S. (2001). Replication as strategy. *Organization Science, 12*(6), 730–743.

Szulanski, G., & Winter, S. (2002). Replication of organizational routines: Conceptualizing the exploitation of knowledge assets. In C. W. Choo & N. Bontis (Eds.), *The strategic management of intellectual capital and organizational knowledge* (pp. 207–221). Oxford: Oxford University Press.

Taris, T. W., & Kompier, M. (2005). Job demands, job control, strain and learning behavior: Review and research agenda. In A. Antonio & C. Cooper (Eds.), *Research companion to organisational health psychology* (pp.132–150). Cheltenham: Edward Elgar.

Tu, Q., Vonderembse, M. A., Ragu-Nathan, T. S., & Sharkey, T. W. (2006). Absorptive capacity: Enhancing the assimilation of time-based manufacturing practices. *Journal of Operations Management, 24*(5), 692–710.

Tushman, M. L., & O'Reilly, C. A. (1996). Ambidextrous organizations: Managing evolutionary and revolutionary change. *California Management Review, 38*(4), 8–30.

Tushman, M. L., & O'Reilly, C. A. (2004). The ambidextrous organization. *Harvard Business Review, 82*(4), 74–81.

Van Wijk, R., Jansen, J. P., & Lyles, M. A. (2008). Inter- and intra-organizational knowledge transfer: A meta-analytic review and assessment of its antecedent and consequences. *Journal of Management Studies, 45*(4), 830–853.

Voss, C., Tsikriktsis, N., & Frohlich, M. (2002). Case research in operations management. *International Journal of Operations & Production Management, 22*(2), 195–219.

Womack, J. P., & Jones, D. T. (1996). *Lean thinking: Banish waste and create wealth in your corporation.* New York, NY: Simon & Schuster.

Yin, R. K. (1989). *Case study research: Design and methods.* Newbury Park, CA: Sage Publications.

Zollo, M., Reurer, J. J., & Singh, H. (2002). Inter-organizational routines and performance in strategic alliances. *Organization Science, 13*(6), 701–713.

Zollo, M., & Winter, S. G. (2002). Deliberate learning and the evolution of dynamic capabilities. *Organization science, 13*(3), 339–351.

THE VIRTUE OF IN-BETWEEN PRAGMATISM – A BALANCING ACT BETWEEN RESPONSIVENESS AND INTEGRATION IN A MULTINATIONAL COMPANY

Gabriel R. G. Benito, Randi Lunnan and Sverre Tomassen

ABSTRACT

In this paper, we offer insights that combine a network perspective of the multinational company (MNC) with an analysis of different types of interdependencies. We develop and illustrate our arguments with a company case (LIMO) and argue that types of interdependencies have consequences for the orchestration of MNC activities. The experience from LIMO suggests that extreme organizational designs, where orchestration is either purely local or mostly global, fail to capture the nuances necessary to ensure efficiency and profitability. The main theoretical contribution in this paper is to show that the search for orchestration through an organizational design must involve the combination of several perspectives of activity combinations and their interdependencies. Simply

Orchestration of the Global Network Organization
Advances in International Management, Volume 27, 75–97
ISSN: 1571-5027/doi:10.1108/S1571-502720140000027002

optimizing through a tight network or looking at the firm as a loose federation is too simple to understand the complex trade-off facing modern MNCs.

Keywords: Organizational design; organizational structure; integration; responsiveness; interdependence; linkages

INTRODUCTION

Any multinational company (MNC) faces important decisions concerning where to locate the activities it performs and how to coordinate them. Although these decisions have intrigued international business (IB) scholars for almost half a century (Ghoshal & Nohria, 1993; Hedlund, 1986; Stopford & Wells, 1972; see Egelhoff & Wolf, 2012, for an overview), organization design remains one of the least understood aspects of MNCs. In this paper, we offer insights into the organization of MNCs that combine an organizational network perspective (Astley & Zajac, 1990, 1991) with Thompson's (1967) seminal analysis of three distinct forms of interdependencies. We develop and illustrate our arguments with a company case (here called LIMO) and argue that types of interdependencies have consequences for the orchestration of MNC activities. Analyzing networks, Dhanaraj and Parkhe (2006) define orchestration as a "set of deliberate, purposeful actions undertaken by the hub firms as it seeks to create value and extract value from the network" (Dhanaraj & Parkhe, 2006, p. 659). Taking the notion of orchestration into an MNC context (Parkhe & Dhanaraj, 2003), we argue that it needs a somewhat different interpretation, as actions to create and extract value are not necessarily performed by one actor, but multiple, and these actors are not necessarily in the center (hub) of the MNC network. In this paper, we define orchestration as a set of deliberate, purposeful actions to create and extract value in the MNC. We particularly discuss actions of localization, coordination, and governance and argue that orchestration takes place within the overall design of the MNC.

According to Astley and Zajac (1991), two different, but also complementary theoretical models have been applied to understand the design of organizations. The coalitional model views organizations as market-like partnerships where units are bounded together in a rather loosely coupled network of other subunits. The tasks performed in these systems are not directly interdependent, which is in stark contrast to the rational model of organization where each subunit is part of a tightly coupled and machine-like network. While assuming bounded rationality, the rational model views value creation in the organization as "one system" to be optimized, and "precisely defined subunit activities interlock so that they complement each other as harmoniously as possible" (Astley & Zajac, 1991, p. 403). This "macro-logic" produces a hierarchy of dependence where organizational tasks are successively divided into "areas," "groups," "bundles," "modules," and "activities" into a sequentially dependent model (Astley & Zajac, 1990, 1991; Mackenzie, 1986).

Distinguishing between activities (*a*) and locations (*l*), a very basic view of the MNC implies that it occupies a two-dimensional space as illustrated in Fig. 1, which needs first to be demarcated and, subsequently, managed. Defining the boundaries of a company is a fundamental and crucial decision (Williamson, 1985) and one which has been at the very core of International Business as a discipline and central in internalization theory; one of its key theoretical perspectives (Buckley & Casson, 1976; Hennart, 1982; Rugman, 1986). While the sets of activities and locations chosen by a given MNC could be said to define it − at a certain level of abstraction, it is a description that provides limited understanding of how it actually operates, especially since internalization theory largely presupposes that organization issues are resolved through the use of hierarchy in combination with well-defined and accepted ownership rights (Tomassen, Benito, & Lunnan, 2012). Here, we argue that within the scope of internalization, organizational issues remain,

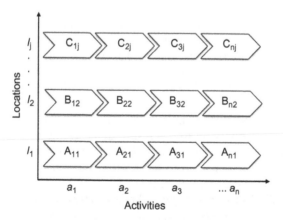

Fig. 1. The MNC as a Location-Activity Set.

which calls for bringing in perspectives that take a more nuanced view of the MNC.

ORGANIZING THE MNC: KEY ISSUES

The MNC can be portrayed as a global network, hence the two general theoretical perspectives that Astley and Zajac (1991) describe have been applied to a more specific setting, namely to understand the organization of the multinational corporation (Boehe, 2007). Both perspectives consider MNCs as networks that "possess internal linkages and coordination mechanisms that represent and respond to many different kinds and extents of dependency and interdependency in inter-unit exchange relationships" (Ghoshal & Bartlett, 1990, p. 604; see also Ghoshal & Nohria, 1989). First, the loosely coupled network model (Andersson, Forsgren, & Holm, 2002, 2007; Bartlett & Ghoshal, 1989) builds on a resource dependency logic where MNC subsidiaries are seen as rather autonomous. Each subsidiary has its own distinct network, "... it [the subsidiary] tends to strive either for autonomy in relation to the rest of the firm, or to influence other parts of the firm to move in a direction that supports the development of its own business" (Forsgren, 2008, p. 123). Thus, headquarters (HQ) are not necessarily the core orchestrating actor in the network, as subsidiaries may take on roles of coordination of interdependencies between units, and influence localization and governance.

On the other hand, Porter (1985, 1996) demonstrated with the value chain the efficiencies of localizing together similar processes in activities and showed that the way in which these activities are interlinked may have great effect on total cost and value as perceived by the customer. Scholars argue that value chains are increasingly sliced and activities specialized (Buckley & Ghauri, 2004). At the same time, activities become more global (Mudambi, 2008) with higher levels of intra-MNC transfers as a consequence (Beugelsdijk, Pedersen, & Petersen, 2009), resulting in a narrower and less strategic activity set for each subsidiary. In the MNC, central coordination offers a more homogenous delivery, as well as benefits of scale, scope, best practice sharing, and arbitrage (Birkinshaw & Pedersen, 2008; Ghemawat, 2007) facilitated by more sophisticated ICT systems (Yamin & Sinkovics, 2007). In this perspective, then, the HQs are undisputedly central in the network and will assume the role of orchestration based on logics of cost and value creation.

Thompson (1967) discusses three types of interdependencies; pooled, sequential, and reciprocal. We argue that a loosely coupled network for the most part represents pooled interdependency as subsidiaries A and B can perform their activities independently, but the total delivery depends on the jobs done in both A and B. Each subsidiary can be rather autonomous, and the sum of these interlinked subsidiaries constitutes the MNC. When the activity set is sliced according to scale and cost, B cannot perform its activity unless A has finished his part as an input, which leads to "sequential interdependency" (Thompson, 1967, pp. 54–55). In this paper, we will argue that the previous two approaches omit an important interdependency, namely Thompson's third type; reciprocity, which describes a situation where unit A's activities become input to B's and vice versa. Research, especially on service firms, offers insights into the interdependencies between production and consumption (Aharoni, 1996; Aung & Heeler, 2001). Moreover, activities from sales to delivery demands contact with the same professionals. Consequently, the development of globally sliced and specialized activity sets may conflict with the requirements of service deliveries. Hence, the traditional approaches, such as the integration – responsiveness framework (Ghoshal, 1987; Prahalad & Doz, 1987) as well as the research emphasis on issues "dismantled" from the overall design of the MNC, seem to be ripe for review and development.

All three types of interdependencies can coexist in MNCs, and, we argue, influence the efficiency and effectiveness of the MNCs' organizational design. When activities are linked reciprocally, we should expect to see more informal and cooperative strategies (Thompson, 1967). If outcomes of the interdependence are non-correspondent (competing), centralization becomes more important because the units to a lesser degree will be able to solve problems on their own (Victor & Blackburn, 1987). Ghoshal and Nohria (1989) argue that formalized routines may provide a structured context for reciprocal exchange, whereas centralization restrains interaction. Baliga and Jaeger (1984, p. 33) claim that "reciprocal interdependence generates the maximum need of control, coordination, and consistency in decision making." These studies suggest that several forms of coordination mechanisms handle reciprocal linkages, although we should expect to find more co-location and personal coordination to foster mutual adjustment when these types of linkages are present.

Recently, Puranam, Raveendran, and Knudsen (2012) have offered an expanded perspective on interdependencies, differentiating between task and agent interdependencies. Task interdependency occurs when the value of task A depends on the value of task B. As such, this logic is very close to

Thompson (1967). Agent interdependency is defined as the incentives of actor A depending on the incentives of actor B. Puranam et al. (2012) argue that designers of the organization can influence interdependencies due to variations in task allocations, scheduling and incentive breadth and as such use different designs of the organization to try to shape the need for coordination between organizational units. In our understanding, actions to influence interdependence are, in fact, actions of orchestration.

Most of the centralization/localization debate has taken place at the subsidiary level. If it is true that the integrated subsidiary is becoming less common (Birkinshaw & Pedersen, 2008), the activity level may become more interesting as a focus area, especially if "globalization occurs at the level of the function, not at the firm" (Malnight, 1995, p. 119); see also (Carpano & Chrisman, 1995; De Meyer, 1991; De Toni, Filippini, & Forza, 1992; Kim, Park, & Prescott, 2003; Mascarenhas, 1984; Nobel & Birkinshaw, 1998). Our approach in this paper is on activities, defined by Porter as "discrete, but related production functions" (Porter, 1985, p. 39) and our main concern is how these activities are related to each other in terms of interdependence (Victor & Blackburn, 1987). Interdependence has been defined as the state in which the activities and outcomes of one actor are influenced by the actions of another actor (Saavedra, Earley, & Van Dyne, 1993). International interdependence can be defined as the state in which the outcomes of a foreign subsidiary influence are influenced by the actions of another unit within the MNC operating in a different country (O'Donnell, 2000). As previously mentioned, Thompson (1967, pp. 54–55) describes three types of interdependence: Pooled, reciprocal, and sequential. Pooled interdependence takes place in a situation where units A and B can perform their activities independently, but the total delivery depends on the jobs done in both A and B. The second type of dependency is termed sequential dependency, and it occurs when part B cannot perform its activity unless A has finished his part. In this sense, A becomes a supplier to B. The third form of dependency is reciprocal dependency, describing a situation where unit A's activities become input to B's and opposite. The example used by Thompson is an airline that both operates and repairs airlines. Stabell and Fjeldstad (1998) have linked these interdependencies to the value creation logics in chains, shops, and networks, respectively.

Linkages or types of fit are interdependent relationships between the way one activity is performed and the cost or performance of another, and they are often subtle and go unrecognized (Porter, 1985, 1996). Linkages are examples of value and cost drivers, indicating that if these are discovered and managed, they may lead to competitive advantages, mainly through the two mechanisms of optimization and coordination. Optimization occurs when, for example, more stringent material inspection reduces service costs due to fewer breakdowns, while an example of coordination benefits occurs when the coordination of input and production reduces need for inventory. Linkages may be vertical reflecting interdependencies between a firm's activities and the value chains of suppliers and channels, or horizontal, coordinating activities with for instance alliance partners or competitors.

Global integration is defined as control and coordination of business operations across borders (Cray, 1984). Coordination concerns managing linkages between geographically dispersed units, whereas control may be seen as regulating business activities to align them with the expectations set in targets. The effectiveness of global integration has implications for business performance (Birkinshaw, Morrison, & Hulland, 1995), which means that a concern for business managers is to design an organization to achieve effective integration of global operations (Kim et al., 2003). Malnight (1995, p. 130) argues that coordination and control must be studied at the level of activities rather than the firm, because "without first enhancing the company's ability to perform individual functions globally, the potential for cross-functional integration would be limited." Kim et al. (2003) identify four forms of coordination mechanisms in multinational corporations: (1) people (or lateral relations) corresponding to personal, socialization, and cultural control (Edström & Galbraith, 1977); (2) information systems; (3) formalization, like rules, norms, and regulations; and (4) centralization or direct supervision.

We argue that when an activity can be linked to another in a sequential or pooled manner, the activity can to a higher degree be standardized and self contained since the interdependence is based on one activity being the input to another (sequential) or the activities happening in parallel (pooled). As such, coordination of the activities can be pre-planned, known and anticipated, and if something goes wrong, a centralized body may look at interfaces between the activities and resolve conflicts and new formalized rules for interaction may be developed. Therefore, when the activities are linked sequentially or pooled, there should be less need for personal interaction, and unless transportation costs or delivery times are high (as suggested by Porter (1985)), there should be little need for co-location of activities. When activities are linked reciprocally, however, we expect to see more informal, localized, and cooperative strategies (Thompson, 1967).

When outcomes of the interdependence are non-correspondent (competing), there may be a need for centralization because the units will to a lesser degree be able to solve problems on their own (Victor & Blackburn, 1987). Ghoshal and Nohria (1989) find that interdependence may increase formalization because it provides a structured context for reciprocity. Centrality, on the other hand, has the opposite effect on interdependency as HQ views are reflected and reciprocity is constrained by hierarchy. Although these studies suggest that there may be some formalization and centralization, we argue that reciprocal linkages create a need for increased coordination, and more personal interaction, implying that reciprocal linkages entail that the two activities are co-located.

THE CASE OF LIMO

Company Background

LIMO is a Norwegian service company with more than 500 employees at 22 units in 16 different countries in Europe, Asia, and North America. It provides global market access through services of testing, inspecting and certifying products, machinery, installations and systems worldwide. LIMO is recognized in its industry as a leading supplier of global market access and it is ranked among the top three providers of international CB-certificates (i.e., approval of electrical products). A global company today, LIMO was until the early 1990s a national monopoly protected by law. However, as a result of Norway adopting Pan-European (EU-EEA) directives for product safety at the expense of the former national approval schemes for electrical components, LIMO was transformed into an independent, self-owned private foundation in 1991 with a HQ in Oslo.

LIMO's Initial Internationalization: The MNC as a Loosely Coupled Network in a Period of International Growth

After 1991, LIMO grew rapidly through several international acquisitions and each acquired unit was left more or less autonomous to serve their local market. The reason was partly that each country unit had a unique technical strength, like luminaires in Italy and telecom in Canada, but also that the focus was on international expansion, not central coordination. An illustration of this growth period is the establishment in Taiwan. The CEO of LIMO had previously worked in a company with a subsidiary in

Taipei, and through his contacts LIMO rented space from this company. Two young engineers were sent out from HQ, one to USA, the other to Taipei. The young man in Taipei explained how they started to hire people for this new office mainly to tend to the growing IT industry. Growth in Taipei was organic, and interaction with other LIMO units scarce. After a period of 10 years, the unit was one of the most profitable in LIMO.

Analyzing this period, we argue in Fig. 2, in a somewhat exaggerated manner, that subsidiaries basically replicated the company's value system in each (major) market, without much interaction or coordination across them. Effectively, LIMO had become what can best be described as a "loose" network. Such an organizational model builds on a resource dependency logic (Pfeffer & Salancik, 1978) and has a rather federative character as "... issues of competency and power tend to be (more) contested within the MNC and interdependencies between units tend to be reciprocal as well as sequential" (Ghoshal & Bartlett, 1990, p. 607). Subsidiaries have autonomy, but also strategic influence, and the power base is their embeddedness in internal and external networks. The Taiwan subsidiary, for example, had a high status in LIMO due to their customer relationships and high performance. Headquarters have formal authority, but in reality they may have less power than a subsidiary with strong networks (Forsgren, 2008).

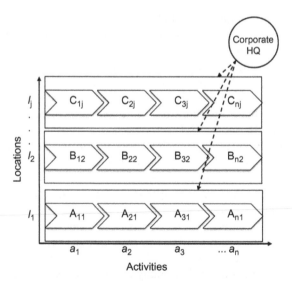

Fig. 2. The MNC as a Collection of Autonomous Units: the Loosely Coupled MNC.

Although this perspective opens up for different types of interdependence, we argue that this perspective has mostly focused on loosely coupled subsidiaries that are linked together in a federative network, where the dominating form of interdependence is pooled. Hence, close interaction takes place, from the initiative of a strong subsidiary or headquarters, but the main idea is based on subsidiaries operating autonomously within their local environment. In LIMO, established and stable units in Asia, North America, and Europe, that had strong subsidiary leadership, took more autonomy than emerging units in Asia and units close to HQ in Norway. Most of these units either had a strategically important customer, a specific product or market segment that they served. The units that were emerging were trying to expand their platform in a market that had become more mature, and the units close to HQs were partly serving units abroad, partly struggling with a declining market at home. A growing need to support emerging subsidiaries, particularly in China, and demands for more global coordination from units close to HQ, sparked discussions for a change in the organization structure of LIMO.

Tightly Controlling a Sliced-up MNC

At the turn of the millennium LIMO realized that the cost pressure had increased substantially in the industry, and hence, the company had to improve the efficiency of its daily operations. A growing part of worldwide production was being moved to low costs countries, especially to China. To increase and sustain their market share in a price sensitive industry, LIMO needed to improve efficiency and look for economies of scale and scope. More and more, these benefits were to be achieved through integration of their global subsidiaries.

The new structure initiated in 2004 focused on the three main activities that were crucial in the processes for achieving total service performance, sales, testing, and certification. (1) *Sales and marketing* was responsible for customer contact, sales, contract initiations, and customer support; (2) *testing* should facilitate testing and verification including technical labs and the engineers; and (3) *certification* should issue the final certificate. The main idea behind the reorganization was to standardize the service delivery and have sales and marketing done locally, but testing and certification globally. Most of the subsidiaries had many overlaps, for example several subsidiaries offered services within household and luminaries, and combining these services should yield benefits. Substantial investments were allocated to an advanced ICT system that should allocate resources efficiently regardless of location. When a new order was entered, for example, the ICT system should suggest where it would be most efficiently tested and verified. This would direct the service to the most efficient location, and the internal competitive effects were seen as favorable as they would encourage improvements in all parts of the process. Due to this reorganization, the formal structure of LIMO changed from a divisional geographical structure to a matrix, and the main formal profit and loss reporting lines were structured according to the above three sets of activities. The three reporting lines each had a vice president at HQ in Oslo.

This change corresponds to the "tight coupling" perspective (Astley & Zajac, 1991), which assumes behavior rationality and sees value creation in a MNC as "one system" to be optimized, and "precisely defined subunit activities interlock so that they complement each other as harmoniously as possible" (page 403). This is illustrated in Fig. 3.

According to Astley and Zajac (1991, p. 403), "this macro-logic produces a hierarchy of dependence where organization tasks are successively divided into areas, groups, bundles, modules, and activities." Astley and Zajac (1991) view this system as sequentially interdependent. The ICT system was designed to support the workflow and used incentive systems and key performance indicators to follow up the new organizational processes.

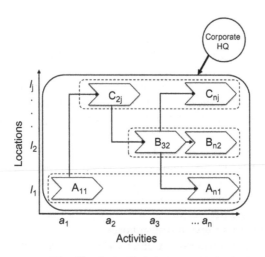

Fig. 3. The Sliced-Up Tightly Controlled MNC.

Formal procedures were designed to apply both within each activity as well as coordinate deliveries between activities.

However, the standardization efforts of LIMO were not trivial. Various local managers estimated that the amount of services that deviated from the planned procedure could amount to 50%, sometimes even more and gradually the company realized that they could not standardize the service delivery as much as they thought. Further, as explained by one engineer in Italy, distance made it hard to finish a project in time. He compared a local project to a project from China, where he in the local project could have new components within the next day, whereas from China, there were long delays. After a few years of operations, the conclusion was that the heavily integrated system proved overly complex to manage, and further, it resulted in unsatisfactory performance.

MNC Orchestration as a Balancing act

Observing two global meetings, one between all global sales managers in China and one between technical managers in Oslo, open confrontations between representatives from different subsidiaries were not rare. Most often, discussions took place between subsidiaries who complied with the integrated strategy, and tried to focus on global concerns, and those that were less interested in the global, more in their local business. A new CEO came to LIMO in 2008, and he quickly decided that to heavily insist on the global, integrated strategy to realize benefits of costs and scale would meet too much resistance. Therefore, in 2008, the new management at HQ changed the structure of LIMO (see Fig. 4) and initiated three major charter changes.

First, and arguably most important, was that the organization changed from a matrix to a line structure with three relatively independent regions — Europe, Asia, and North America as coordinating strategic bodies as illustrated in Fig. 4. All subsidiaries were given increased autonomy and profit and loss responsibilities. Many units saw this shift as procedurally fair as the matrix structure could be seen as mature locations "giving away" business to a more cost-efficient location. Why should they secure large contracts, for example in Norway, that were executed in China? With the new system, local sales were tested locally, and performance started to increase immediately in several subsidiaries.

Second, LIMO introduced a Center of Excellence system, where world mandate responsibilities were moved from HQ to designated subsidiaries in

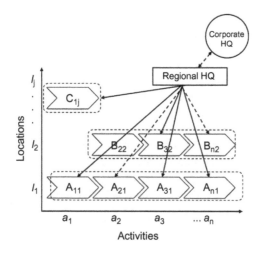

Fig. 4. MNC Orchestration as a Balancing Act.

North America, Europe, and Asia. Italy, for example, secured the lumi-naire Center of Excellence. This unit was expected to be "best in LIMO" within this field of competence, and to share best practices with the rest of the LIMO organization. Some hours a week to one individual at each CoE were dedicated to this function. Projects were established to explore mechanisms for knowledge sharing, for example using e-mail, company web pages, and a WIKI system where frequently asked questions were posted for everyone to consult if they had problems. Until formal struc-tures and responsibilities were established with these mandate shifts, the use and recognition from other subsidiaries concerning these technologies varied and the amount of knowledge transferred from these units to other units also initially followed established network structures. Particularly, people tended to ask those that they had met in person in global meetings. Expectations were high, however, that one-to-one knowledge transfer over time should be replaced with one-to-many.

Finally, at a regional level the charter for the China unit was also chan-ged, increasing its scope to a full-fledged set of activities. A new and up-to-date lab was constructed in Shanghai signaling increased importance to China. Most units saw the extreme growth in China and recognized the increased market opportunities. The extent that the China unit was grow-ing created some fear concerning a shift in global focus and loss of oppor-tunities elsewhere. On the other hand, the development of China relied on a wide range of knowledge inflow from other subsidiaries. Some subsidiaries sent experts on shorter and longer term assignments, and these experts greatly added to the learning curve of the newly hired Chinese employees, making the subsidiary able to perform gradually complex tasks. Still, there were also examples of experts who continued to serve their former subsidiary and to a lesser degree worked for the growth of the Shanghai unit. Since the reorganization in 2008, LIMO has had a steady growth in profit.

Whereas we in the first two periods could argue for clear structures – a loosely coupled network, or a tight integrated value activity system – the third period organization had no such clear structure, but rather was a mix between the local and the global, in an attempt to balance and get the best from both worlds. We call this a balancing act and explore this further in the next section.

IMPLICATIONS AND BOUNDARY CONDITIONS

The changes in organizational design over time in LIMO illustrate a balancing act between central and global orchestration. In the middle period, HQs created an efficient whole through advanced ICT systems, whereas the first period observed local and dispersed orchestration, where local subsidiaries orchestrated activities to form a customized and adapted service. We have argued, through our illustrative case, that both of these types of orchestrations have strengths as well as weaknesses. The loosely coupled, decentralized network structure failed to reap global synergies and learning was random. Further, costs surged as central authorities were reluctant to overrule local initiatives. Hence activities were duplicated and uncoordinated. The tight, centralized "activity slivering" structure, attempted in the second period, addressed costs and learning synergy optimization as projects were to be allocated to the lab with lowest costs and highest availability regardless of geographical location. Implications that were discussed but never realized was that this change over time could lead to some labs being more successful and to unsuccessful laboratories being closed. This design structure, however, failed to recognize the responses from local subsidiaries and, we argue, relatedly, interdependencies between activities. Although incentives between subsidiaries were intended to be broad, advanced structures were never fully implemented, and local employees distrusted broad incentives and followed the narrow, local performance indicators. In this sense, they were skeptical to giving away business to another subsidiary not recognizing the possibly higher global benefits.

Local subsidiary managers were dissatisfied with the tightly centralized model because the structure for them was unclear. Why should they send a product to be tested to another location far away when there was capacity in their local lab? And further, when their performance measures focused on local performance? Additionally, their customers often wanted to be closely linked to the testing, to learn and to make alterations quickly if the testing did not work out as planned. This, we argue, suggests there were reciprocal interdependencies between the two activities of sales/marketing and testing.

Interdependencies were mainly of two kinds: involvement and re-specifications. In some cases, the customer would like to be involved, to visit the lab, to learn how testing was done by observation and discussing with the lab engineers. It was not unusual to request a specific named lab engineer. In some situations, testing was not straightforward, but required the product to be redesigned, which entailed interactions between the company and the lab. Consequently, the activity set was not sequential, but in various situations, reciprocal. This meant that within a centralized structure, where testing was done far away, based on cost-efficiency, this type of interaction would not be allowed. These two factors, local resistance and reciprocal dependencies, led to customer complaints and ultimately the breakdown of the system – and highlighted the need to develop a new organization design.

Our analysis suggests that when product uncertainty and complexity are high, and the interaction between customers, front office, and labs is frequent, the cooperation resembles a team that comes together to solve a problem (Stabell & Fjeldstad, 1998). As the product becomes more complex, more units, standards, and types of equipment are involved, and the need for a co-location between the customer, marketing & sales, and lab increases. This co-location facilitates knowledge transfer of sticky and contextual knowledge (Szulanski, 1996; Szulanski & Cappetta, 2003) that is best transferred in close, personal relations. In addition, the co-location facilitates reversal of the workflow. In cases where the lab testing fails, instead of being sent to further testing, it goes back to the customer for further specifications creating reverse workflow patterns and loops between activities.

Without co-location, each time a complex or uncertain project is presented to the organization, the firm may design a project where members meet personally in addition to follow ups through electronic and virtual communication. For a relatively small, geographically dispersed organization where reciprocal linkages were fairly frequent, this type of "occasional fix" would not be feasible. These views were supported by several "war stories" in LIMO where they had failed to build on the efforts of other locations when the sequential logic broke down resulting in a failure of the total service delivery.

To summarize, for a company like LIMO, there are significant benefits of central orchestration to generate scale and scope effects, learning and low cost sourcing. We have also shown that there are disadvantages to this centralization related to poor problem-solving of projects with high complexity and uncertainty because of the reciprocal interdependencies between labs, front office, and customers. Finally, there is a need to align incentives. The final organization choices must therefore balance these two concerns in its orchestration, through its choices of localization, coordination, and governance. We therefore need to discuss conditions for which the choice of "in-between orchestration" is most efficient, and when.

We have argued that with orchestration we mean choice of localization of activities, how these are coordinated and governed within the overall design of the MNC. Our case illustrates that one company over time has tried different levels of coordination and governance (local subsidiaries, regional units, and global HQ), and different geographical locations of activities (local, regional, central). Our main argument is in line with Bartlett and Ghoshal (1989), who maintain that economies of scale and scope directs the choice of design toward a global, tightly connected choice, whereas the demand for local responsiveness directs the choice toward a local solution. Our contribution through the illustrative case of LIMO is to argue that we need to look beyond characteristics of each activity when designing the overall design, but take into account the linkages between activities. When these linkages are pooled, a loose network with local activities and local orchestration could be appropriate, whereas sequential linkages call for a more centralized localization with HQ governance and control. The more the linkages are reciprocal, necessitating reverse workflows between activities, the more co-location of these activities become efficient. In LIMO's case, the reciprocal loops between marketing & sales and labs involved the customer, which draws toward local activity localizations with local governance and control of these two activities.

However, the activities of re-testing and issuing of certificates were sequentially linked to the previous two activities and could therefore be localized and coordinated through different requirements such as scale and cost. In addition, to capture best practice identification and knowledge sharing across units, beneficial not only for an expanding unit like China, but also instrumental for improving daily operations in all locations, world mandates could be useful. The question then was: Should these be globally or regionally orchestrated? In the third period, LIMO chose a regional model, where three regional centers were given mandates to coordinate activities within their regions. The CEO of LIMO acknowledged to us that this could lead to three independent units with limited synergy focus between them. In LIMO's case, a regional unit, located within the region, would be closer to the need of each subsidiary and therefore better able to timely understand and meet the needs of local units while securing synergies on a regional level, for example by establishing regional re-testing, certification, and best practice centers of excellence. There is no doubt, however, that a regional level for these activities would miss out on the benefits of global knowledge transfer.

The insights from LIMO suggest that extreme organizational designs where orchestration is either purely local or mostly global fail to capture the nuances necessary to ensure efficiency and profitability. One managerial implication that emerges from our analysis points to the balancing act itself and suggests that managers should resist the understandable temptation to make simple and straightforward organizational design choices. Using an activity lens, we may analyze the lab activity and argue that there are great opportunities for scale and capacity utilization by centralizing this activity. Identifying the reciprocal interdependencies with the marketing & sales and customers, however, show that there are significant benefits of co-location between marketing & sales and labs. A balancing act could be to look into whether there are functions within the lab activity that require less reciprocal interaction, where scale and cost could be pursued. Further, in activities that are analyzed to be sequential (certification) or support day-to-day business (support or secondary activities) there is a balancing act between the regional (being close to subsidiaries) or the global (reaping synergies across regions). Another managerial implication that emerges from our analysis is that managers should exercise restraint in making organizational changes. Balancing acts take place within an overall organizational design but do not involve restructuring the company unnecessarily. In fact, our case company went through only three distinct phases over a period of 20 years.

The company that we have used as an illustrative case, LIMO, is a service firm operating in multiple locations around the world and where interdependencies of sequential, pooled, and reciprocal kinds are simultaneously present to a considerable extent. As such it is company that is particularly well suited to exemplify the need to perform a balancing act.

One could argue that service companies are more exposed to complex organizational design issues than manufacturing firms, and that our discussion therefore primarily deals with similar service firms. We think this is not the case. Although a sequential logic has historically been dominant in industrial firms, increasingly their activities are also characterized by pooled and reciprocal interdependencies. Factors such as rapid technological change, increased complexity, and increased demand for customization have their parts in this. In many industries, highly interactive and iterative processes have arguably been the norm for a long time already, for example in the oil and gas offshore industry. Also, the demarcation between goods and services is increasingly blurred, with many products being a combination of both, for example telecommunication, internet shopping, and restaurants – just to name a few. As such we believe that the organizational challenges we have looked at here are in fact of a general nature and affect manufacturing companies and service companies alike.

CONCLUSIONS

The main argument in this paper has been that effective and efficient orchestration in the MNC is a balancing act between different choices of localization of activities and how to coordinate and control them. Two different network perspectives (Astley & Zajac, 1991) claim that orchestration focus is either local, with each subsidiary pooled together in a network structure, or tightly coupled in a system orchestrated from global HQ. Using an illustrative case, we have shown that both of these choices have merits, but also weaknesses. A loose network system misses out on synergies, whereas a tight network orchestration overlooks the needs for local adaptation. Using the analysis of interdependencies introduced by Thompson (1967) we argue that an effective organizational design must acknowledge their different implications. For example, when interdependencies are reciprocal between two activities, these are best co-located and orchestrated locally. When interdependencies are pooled or sequential, activities can be located and governed by other considerations, such as scale and cost, with global orchestration. Further, designing broad but clear incentive structures, where incentives of one unit depend on incentives in another unit, stimulates global solutions (Puranam et al., 2012). While this seems trivial, there are some important implications.

First, these considerations always include trade-offs. In our case, there are important scale effects by centralizing the labs to get scale, capacity utilization and learning effects, effectuated by global or regional orchestration. An important choice is therefore to calibrate the importance of the reciprocal linkage with the benefits of centralization and trade-off these two concerns. It is probably not possible to find an optimal solution, hence the choice involves some trade-offs leading to a need for additional measures to make up for the concerns that are not met. In our case, if the lab is localized to optimize reciprocal linkages, an integrative project securing inter-lab efficiency could be needed, or if labs are centralized, virtual teams and visits could tend to customer interaction. The trade-off leading to a difficulty in finding an optimal solution would also lead to design temporality, as growing dissatisfaction often raises a need for a change in the design.

Second, we observe that the balancing act of orchestration will lead to the main responsibility being global, regional, or local. In the first period, the orchestration was done locally, in the second globally, and in the third period, the main responsibility was regional. Communicating an organizational design to the organization, we argue that one level of orchestration often takes the lead. This is necessary to make sure that important tasks are fulfilled and conflicts solved. It also implies, however, that it becomes more difficult for other levels to orchestrate. In our case, for example, a clear implication of giving the regional level the main orchestration prominence in the third period, was that the centers of excellence, a global set-up, were having difficulties. Going from a global to a regional structure, suddenly there was no infrastructure for global interaction, and therefore fewer initiatives to seek advice beyond the region. Combining global, regional, and local orchestration is therefore a challenge that must be carefully thought out, especially regarding the levels given lower prominence.

This means that MNC orchestration necessitates a balancing act, and the virtue of in-between pragmatism involves a comparative trade-off between a complex set of dynamic issues (Grøgaard, 2012). As such, there is no ONE best solution, but the search for a good design is a constant challenge in all complex MNCs; see Devinney, Midgley, and Venaik (2000) for a comprehensive discussion about organizational forms and performance of the global firm. Further, orchestration is not secured by one unit, but may be done by the central HQ, by regional HQ and/or by subsidiaries. In MNCs, therefore, orchestration takes place at different levels, and necessitates coordination between units that may have different interests.

The main managerial implication that emerges from our analysis is that making decisions about organizational design in MNCs will never be a quick fix with simple and static solutions. Organizations, as well as the environment they operate in, are highly dynamic. Hence, managers have to continuously evaluate the activity set with its linkages when they decide upon organizational structure. Whether activities can be globally centralized or dispersed will be a matter of what kind of linkages that are present in the activity set. If, for example, a majority of the deliveries have a low degree of reciprocal linkages, special attention to coordination may allow a high centralization of activities, whereas when deliveries have high customer interaction, high product complexity and uncertainty, the activities that are most involved in the reciprocal linkages should be identified and co-located. Our case shows nonetheless that even in such instances some activities (like certification) may still be centralized. Managers could use our framework to first identify activity linkages, then look at the totality of activities at a certain location, and may then identify the balancing act between globalization benefits and localization advantages due to co-localization of interdependent units.

A theoretical contribution in this paper is to show that orchestration in itself is performed at different levels by multiple actors, and not necessarily through one hub firm (Parkhe & Dhanaraj, 2003). Further, the search for optimal orchestration through an organizational design must involve the combination of several perspectives of activity combinations and their interdependencies, including actor interdependencies (Puranam et al., 2012). Optimizing through a tight network, or looking at the firm as a loose network, gives a too simple understanding of the complex trade-offs that modern MNCs face.

Finally, our analysis has focused on organizational design. Organizational challenges are obviously not resolved by design choices alone, even though we think they are important to the well-functioning of companies. Coordination mechanisms of various types still have to be designed and/or developed (Kim et al., 2003) and managers still play important roles in implementing organizational solutions.

ACKNOWLEDGMENTS

We thank Arnaldo Camuffo, Paul N. Gooderham and the Editors Timothy Devinney, Torben Pedersen, and Markus Venzin for many helpful comments and suggestions on an earlier version presented at the "Orchestration of the Global Network Organization" Workshop organized by Bocconi University, Milan, 22–23 November, 2013. The financial support of the Norwegian Research Council (NFR) is gratefully acknowledged.

REFERENCES

Aharoni, Y. (1996). The organization of global service MNEs. *International Studies of Management & Organization, 26*(2), 6–23.

Andersson, U., Forsgren, M., & Holm, U. (2002). The strategic impact of external networks: Subsidiary performance and competence development in the multinational corporation. *Strategic Management Journal, 23*(11), 979–996.

Andersson, U., Forsgren, M., & Holm, U. (2007). Balancing subsidiary influence in the federative MNC: A business network view. *Journal of International Business Studies, 38*(5), 802–818.

Astley, W. G., & Zajac, E. J. (1990). Beyond dyadic exchange: Functional interdependence & sub-unit power. *Organization Studies, 11*(4), 481–501.

Astley, W. G., & Zajac, E. J. (1991). Intraorganizational power and organizational design: Reconciling rational and coalitional models of organization. *Organization Science, 2*(4), 399–411.

Aung, M., & Heeler, R. (2001). Core competencies of service firms: A framework for strategic decisions in international markets. *Journal of Marketing Management, 17*(7/8), 619–643.

Baliga, B. R., & Jaeger, A. M. (1984). Multinational corporations: Control systems and delegation issues. *Journal of International Business Studies, 15*(2), 25–40.

Bartlett, C. A., & Ghoshal, S. (1989). *Managing across borders: The transnational solution.* Boston, MA: Harvard Business School Press.

Beugelsdijk, S., Pedersen, T., & Petersen, B. (2009). Is there a trend towards global value chain specialization? An examination of cross border sales of US foreign affiliates. *Journal of International Management, 15*(2), 126–141.

Birkinshaw, J., Morrison, A., & Hulland, J. (1995). Structural and competitive determinants of a global integration strategy. *Strategic Management Journal, 16*(8), 637–655.

Birkinshaw, J., & Pedersen, T. (2008). Strategy and management in MNE subsidiaries. In A. M. Rugman (Ed.), *The Oxford handbook of international business* (2nd ed., pp. 367–388). Oxford: Oxford University Press.

Boehe, D. M. (2007). Product development in MNC subsidiaries: Local linkages and global interdependencies. *Journal of International Management, 13*(4), 488–512.

Buckley, P. J., & Casson, M. C. (1976). *The future of the multinational enterprise.* London: Macmillan.

Buckley, P. J., & Ghauri, P. N. (2004). Globalisation, economic geography and the strategy of multinational enterprises. *Journal of International Business Studies, 35*(2), 81–98.

Carpano, C., & Chrisman, J. (1995). Performance implications of international product strategies and the integration of marketing activities. *Journal of International Marketing, 3*(1), 9–27.

Cray, D. (1984). Control and coordination in multinational corporations. *Journal of International Business Studies, 15*(2), 85–98.

De Meyer, A. (1991). Tech talk: How managers are stimulating global R&D Communication. *Sloan Management Review, 32*(3), 49–58.

De Toni, A., Filippini, R., & Forza, C. (1992). Manufacturing strategy in global markets: An operations management model. *International Journal of Operations and Production Management, 12*(4), 7–18.

Devinney, T. M., Midgley, D. F., & Venaik, S. (2000). The optimal performance of the global firm: Formalizing and extending the integration-responsiveness framework. *Organization Science, 11*(6), 674–695.

Dhanaraj, C., & Parkhe, A. (2006). Orchestrating innovation networks. *Academy of Management Review, 31*(3), 659–669.

Edström, A., & Galbraith, J. R. (1977). Transfer of managers as a coordination and control strategy in multinational organizations. *Administrative Science Quarterly, 22*(2), 248–263.

Egelhoff, W. G., & Wolf, J. (2012). New ideas about organizational design for modern MNEs. In A. Verbeke & H. Merchant (Eds.), *Handbook of research on international strategic management* (pp. 137–154). Chelterham: Edward Elgar.

Forsgren, M. (2008). *Theories of the multinational firm: A multidimensional creature in the global economy.* Cheltenham: Edward Elgar.

Ghemawat, P. (2007). Managing differences. *Harvard Business Review, 85*(3), 58–68.

Ghoshal, S. (1987). Global strategy: An organizing framework. *Strategic Management Journal, 8*(5), 425–440.

Ghoshal, S., & Bartlett, C. A. (1990). The multinational corporation as an interorganizational network. *Academy of Management Review, 15*(4), 603–625.

Ghoshal, S., & Nohria, N. (1989). Internal differentiation within multinational corporations. *Strategic Management Journal, 10*(4), 323–337.

Ghoshal, S., & Nohria, N. (1993). Horses for courses: Organizational forms for multinational corporations. *Sloan Management Review, 34*(2), 23–35.

Grøgaard, B. (2012). Alignment of strategy and structure in international firms: An empirical examination. *International Business Review, 21*(3), 397–407.

Hedlund, G. (1986). The hypermodern MNC – A heterarchy. *Human Resource Management, 25*(1), 9–35.

Hennart, J.-F. (1982). *A theory of multinational enterprise.* Ann Arbor, MI: University of Michigan Press.

Kim, K., Park, J. H., & Prescott, J. E. (2003). The global integration of business functions: A study of multinational businesses in integrated global industries. *Journal of International Business Studies, 34*(4), 327–344.

Mackenzie, K. D. (1986). *Organizational design: The organizational audit and analysis technology.* Norwood, NJ: Ablex Pub. Corp.

Malnight, T. W. (1995). Globalization of an ethnocentric firm: An evolutionary perspective. *Strategic Management Journal, 16*(2), 119–141.

Mascarenhas, B. (1984). The coordination of manufacturing interdependence in multinational companies. *Journal of International Business Studies, 15*(3), 91–106.

Mudambi, R. (2008). Location, control and innovation in knowledge-intensive industries. *Journal of Economic Geography, 8*(5), 699–725.

Nobel, R., & Birkinshaw, J. (1998). Innovation in multinational corporations. *Strategic Management Journal, 19*(5), 479–496.

O'Donnell, S. W. (2000). Managing foreign subsidiaries: Agents of headquarters, or an interdependent network? *Strategic Management Journal, 21*(5), 525–548.

Parkhe, A., & Dhanaraj, C. (2003). Orchestrating globally: Managing the multinational enterprise as a network. *Research in Global Strategic Management, 8*, 197–214.

Pfeffer, J., & Salancik, G. R. (1978). *The external control of organizations: A resource dependence perspective.* New York, NY: Harper and Row.

Porter, M. E. (1985). *Competitive advantage: Creating and sustaining superior performance.* New York, NY: Free Press.

Porter, M. E. (1996). What is strategy? *Harvard Business Review, 74*(6), 61–78.

Prahalad, C. K., & Doz, Y. (1987). *The multinational mission balancing local demands and global vision.* New York, NY: Free Press.

Puranam, P., Raveendran, M., & Knudsen, T. (2012). Organization design: The epistemic interdependence perspective. *Academy of Management Review, 37*(3), 419–440.

Rugman, A. M. (1986). New theories of the multinational enterprise: An assessment of internalization theory. *Bulletin of Economic Research, 38*(2), 101–118.

Saavedra, R., Earley, P. C., & Van Dyne, L. (1993). Complex interdependence in task-performing groups. *Journal of Applied Psychology, 78*(1), 61–72.

Stabell, C. B., & Fjeldstad, Ø. D. (1998). Configuring value for competitive advantage: On chains, shops, and networks. *Strategic Management Journal, 19*(5), 413–437.

Stopford, J. M., & Wells, L. T. (1972). *Managing the multinational enterprise: Organization of the firm and ownership of the subsidiaries.* New York, NY: Basic Books.

Szulanski, G. (1996). Exploring internal stickiness: Impediments to the transfer of best practice within the firm. *Strategic Management Journal, 17*(Winter), 27–43.

Szulanski, G., & Cappetta, R. (2003). Stickiness: Conceptualizing, measuring, and predicting difficulties in the transfer of knowledge within organizations. In M. Easterby-Smith & M. A. Lyles (Eds.), *Handbook of organizational learning and knowledge management* (pp. 513–534). Oxford: Blackwell Publishing.

Thompson, J. D. (1967). *Organizations in action: Social science bases of administrative theory.* New York, NY: McGraw-Hill.

Tomassen, S., Benito, G. R. G., & Lunnan, R. (2012). Governance costs in foreign direct investments: A MNC headquarters challenge. *Journal of International Management, 18*(3), 233–246.

Victor, B., & Blackburn, R. S. (1987). Interdependence: An alternative conceptualization. *Academy of Management Review, 12*(3), 486–498.

Williamson, O. E. (1985). *The economic institutions of capitalism: Firms, markets, relational contracting.* New York, NY: Free Press.

Yamin, M., & Sinkovics, R. R. (2007). ICT and MNE reorganisation: The paradox of control. *Critical Perspectives on International Business, 3*(4), 322–336.

FUNCTIONAL-LEVEL TRANSFORMATION IN MULTI-DOMESTIC MNCs: TRANSFORMING LOCAL PURCHASING INTO GLOBALLY INTEGRATED PURCHASING

Frank Elter, Paul N. Gooderham and Svein Ulset

ABSTRACT

This paper revisits Bartlett and Ghoshal's transnational theory of the MNC in relation to multi-domestic MNCs. We argue that the aggregate level of analysis adopted by Bartlett and Ghoshal is unhelpful for identifying significant changes in multi-domestic MNCs at the level of discrete functions. We argue that a more disaggregated level of analysis is required. Our analysis of two cases of multi-domestic MNCs that have undertaken the global integration of their locally distributed purchasing functions indicates that while significant change to the purchasing function has occurred, at the aggregate level both MNCs remain multi-domestic. In both cases the decision to integrate local purchasing was

Orchestration of the Global Network Organization
Advances in International Management, Volume 27, 99–120
Copyright © 2014 by Emerald Group Publishing Limited
All rights of reproduction in any form reserved
ISSN: 1571-5027/doi:10.1108/S1571-502720140000027007

regarded as having more obvious benefits than integrating other functions such as marketing. While both of our case multi-domestic MNCs may in future choose to integrate other functions and develop into full-fledged transnational companies we argue that there is no inevitability to this. Indeed global integration may cease with the purchasing function. A second theme in this paper is that we argue that Bartlett and Ghoshal's transnational theory has a biased view of what constitutes effective governance mechanisms for achieving global integration, local responsiveness and worldwide learning and that it would greatly benefit from a more balanced application of hierarchical and relational governance mechanisms.

Keywords: Transnational theory of the firm; functional-level analysis; procurement

INTRODUCTION

Employing a decentralized federation organization characterized by considerable local autonomy, multi-domestic multi-national companies (MNCs) compete by replicating their entire value chain in each of their foreign markets to produce locally customized products (Bartlett & Ghoshal, 1989; Roth, 1992; Yip, 1989). To the extent the global integration potential of the industry improves, multi-domestic MNCs will benefit from globally integrating their foreign operations. In general they will focus on those value-chain activities that offer the highest globalization potential first (Vahlne, Ivarsson, & Johanson, 2011). One obvious initial candidate for integration is the procurement of those inputs that are common to most foreign units (Yeniyurt, Henke, & Cavusgil, 2013). However, any such change is challenging for MNCs that have developed routines and structures dedicated to local adaptation to changing local conditions. They are confronted by a lack of MNC-wide networks to facilitate inter-business unit learning and an absence of appropriate hierarchical governance mechanisms to impose solutions that cut across the interests of individual business units (Gooderham, 2012).

In the late 1980s, Bartlett and Ghoshal (1987, 1989) introduced the concept of the transnational model of the multinational company, which they argued constituted a "new organizational model" in the sense that its structure was "significantly different to those employed by MNCs over the preceding five decades" (Bartlett & Ghoshal, 1993, p. 24). That is, whereas *international* companies seek to improve their performance by transferring technology and production closer to foreign markets, supported by a centralized federation organization (Dunning, 1980; Teece, 1986), and whereas *global* and *multi-domestic* companies may seek additional improvements either through cost-reducing global standardization (global companies) supported by a centralized hub organization or through value-increasing local customization (multi-domestic companies), supported by a decentralized federation organization (Bartlett & Ghoshal, 1989; Roth, 1992; Yip, 1989), *transnational* companies seek even further improvements by combining global integration with local responsiveness supported by an integrated network organization. The transnational strategy seeks to achieve both cost-efficient global integration and value-adding local responsiveness, in addition to the benefit of worldwide learning and regular transfer of local best practice.[1]

Although Bartlett and Ghoshal (2000, pp. 214−215) observed that the benefits of global integration vary across markets, businesses, companies, functions, and tasks they have consistently reiterated their assertion that "many worldwide industries were transformed in the 1980s and 1990s from the three established MNC forms, the multinational, international, and global forms into the transnational form" (Bartlett, Ghoshal, & Beamish, 2008, p. 339). However, Harzing (1999) failed to find any convincing empirical support for such a pervasive transformation. According to Harzing (1999), transnational companies were more likely to be born rather than to become transnational. While we agree with Bartlett and Ghoshal (2000, pp. 516−518) that conditions such as improved communications are more amenable to the transnational form, equally Harzing's (1999) findings imply that these have not been sufficient in themselves to drive any large-scale transformation of MNCs to the transnational form. Barriers to such transformation are clearly manifold, including subsidiary power (Bouquet & Birkinshaw, 2008; Dörrenbächer & Geppert, 2006; Vahlne et al., 2011), unresolved agency relations (Mudambi & Pedersen, 2007; Nohria & Ghoshal, 1994; O'Donnell, 2000), path dependency (Vahlne et al., 2011), the lack of inter-business unit social networks (Martin & Eisenhardt, 2010; Nahapiet & Ghoshal, 1998; Tsai, 2000), the lack of bonding social capital (Adler & Kwon, 2002; Burt, 1992; Edelman, Bresnen, Newell, Scarbrough, & Swan, 2004), the local embeddedness of business units (Forsgren, Holm, & Johanson, 2005), and the socially embedded nature of knowledge (Dimaggio & Powell, 1983; Hakkarainen, Palonen, Paavola, & Lehtinen, 2004; Lave & Wenger, 1991; Vygotsky, 1986). Thus we agree with Vahlne et al. (2011, p. 4) that global integration is often tortuous and proceeds through "incremental adjustments, with the most obvious and performance impacting changes handled early in the process." In all, we argue, that it should come as no great surprise that 25 years after Bartlett and Ghoshal launched their transnational transformation thesis evidence of any such large-scale transformation is lacking. However, we contend that to disregard the "incremental adjustments" that Vahlne et al. (2011) refer to is to ignore significant structural changes to specific functions.

The overall purpose of this paper is to argue for the importance of studying global integration on the functional level in multi-domestic MNCs. As such we develop a view that was initiated by Malnight (1995), who observed that global integration occurs at the level of particular functions rather than to the entire MNC. Rather than developing into full-fledged transnational MNCs, we argue that multi-domestic MNCs are significantly more likely to develop transnational capabilities in relation to specific high-potential value-chain activities. Further, we argue that the procurement function is a primary candidate for such integration and capability development. The outcome is an ambidextrous or hybrid solution resulting in a multi-domestic MNC with transnational capabilities limited to specific functions. The transnational thesis essentially ignored such a development. Its lack of attention to variations in global integration across functions may have caused it to "fall out of favour."

To support the development of transnational capabilities within functional areas, we argue not only for a focus on a more disaggregated activity level of analysis but also for a re-balancing of the use of hierarchical and relational governance mechanisms. Specifically, we argue that while relational governance mechanisms are significant their development is dependent on the corporate decision to employ hierarchical governance. Without the impetus of hierarchical governance the lateral mechanisms that are needed for inter-unit learning will not emerge. In line with Harzing (1999), we further argue that there is no inevitability that a multi-domestic MNC that has integrated across one function will necessarily chose to integrate other functions. Thus, we develop a significantly revised version of the transnational thesis that proposes that multi-domestic MNCs may achieve global efficiency, local responsiveness, and worldwide learning for high-potential value-chain activities at the functional rather than the aggregate level. Furthermore, they achieve this by applying hierarchical as well as relational governance mechanisms.

Our empirical setting is two Norwegian multi-domestic MNCs, Rieber & Son and Telenor. Both companies identified the integration of their globally dispersed purchasing activities as having particular potential.

In order to identify those governance mechanisms required to achieve higher-level globally integrated purchasing we compare their early, and less successful, initiatives to achieve purchasing integration with their more recent, and more successful, initiatives. Both cases illustrate that in the context of this single integrated function, cost-economizing was combined with value-increasing local responsiveness and worldwide learning.

PURCHASING INTEGRATION IN MULTI-DOMESTIC MNCS

MNCs in general, but multi-domestic MNCs in particular, are increasingly being challenged to compete by integrating their operating and functional activities that comprise dispersed value-chains activities while retaining their ability to respond to local market conditions (Kotabe & Mudambi, 2009; Yeniyurt et al., 2013). It is argued by Yeniyurt et al. (2013, p. 352) that, "in contrast to other mechanisms necessary for global integration (e.g., global product platforms, global talent pools, and global HR systems), global procurement has been enthusiastically adopted by multinationals, primarily because the benefits of uniform sourcing are more apparent."

Trent and Monczka (2003) describe the move from local purchasing to globally integrated and coordinated procurement as a series of evolving levels in a continuum. However, the implementation of the integration of purchasing units across a firm's worldwide locations poses severe organizational challenges (Trautmann, Bals, & Hartmann, 2009). Global procurement involves not just centralization but also the creation of lateral relations across geographically dispersed purchasing units. Not only do entirely new global sourcing capabilities have to be developed but there is the added challenge of deciding when globally integrated purchasing of components is advantageous and when elements of purchasing should remain the responsibility of the local purchasing unit (Trautmann et al., 2009). This calculation will not only involve an assessment of the profit impact and supply risk to individual components (Kraljic, 1983), but also of the extent to which common requirements and harmonized specifications are available across business units (Trent & Monczka, 2003). Thus, while the consideration of economies of scale for a particular purchasing category in order to improve the overall negotiation position is important, a lack of sensitivity to local needs may undermine local operations. Ensuring cross-unit learning in order to balance these considerations is therefore critical for sourcing responsiveness (Yeniyurt et al., 2013). Developing and maintaining concurrent sourcing knowledge and communication at the global and local levels involves creating social networks (Gooderham, 2012). For multi-domestic MNCs that have weak social networks their development constitutes a critical coordination cost (Tomassen & Benito, 2009)

Rather than considering the entire MNC, our approach is to focus our analysis on specific value-chain activities in terms of their contribution to competitive advantage (Porter, 2008). Additionally, we view normative social control as complementary, but still secondary, to the main governance mechanisms of administrative control, economic incentives and managerial dispute settlement, as outlined in transaction cost economics and its M-form thesis (Williamson, 1981, 1985).[2]

METHODOLOGY

Given the lack of a fully developed theory on how governance mechanisms are deployed by multi-domestic MNCs to deal with the challenge of developing an integrated purchasing function, our approach has been to engage in combined deductive/inductive theory building drawing on two case studies. To illustrate the relevance of developing a modified version of Bartlett and Ghoshal's (2000, 2008) transnational theory of the firm (TTF) on the functional level, we employ our cases to compare unsuccessful attempts at global integration of purchasing with successful attempts (Eisenhardt, 1989; Martin & Eisenhardt, 2010).

Our case studies are derived from two Norwegian multi-domestic MNCs, Rieber & Son and Telenor, which are dissimilar in terms of their size and industry but similar in their respective decisions to respond to competitive pressure by integrating purchasing. They share one other commonality and that is that both initially failed to achieve integrated purchasing prior to a successful transition. Each of these polar samples, an unsuccessful and a successful effort, makes it possible to observe emergent constructs and theoretical relationships (Martin & Eisenhardt, 2010). In so doing we distinguish between hierarchical and relational governance mechanisms. Discussion and implications conclude the paper.

Our primary source of data in Rieber & Son was a series of interviews with managers at corporate headquarters and its main subsidiaries in the period 2007–2013. In Telenor our primary source of data is a series of accessed interviews with mangers at corporate headquarters conducted in the Spring of 2013, internal management documents, internal news on the intranet portal, documents shared on capital market days, and a whole day workshop with the sourcing management team and a team of researchers. One of the authors is a Telenor employee.

THE CASE OF RIEBER & SON (R&S)

R&S is an MNC in the dry foods industry. In addition to its Norwegian subsidiary, Toro, it has a number of fully-owned foreign-based subsidiaries that it acquired during the 1990s. The most important of these were Delecta (Poland) and Vitana (Czech Republic). In addition it had smaller operations in five other European countries and sales and market offices in a further six countries. In 2007, R&S owned 28 brands in 12 countries. Its workforce comprised nearly 4,000 employees of whom 1,000 were located in Norway. While Toro (Norway) had for many years been highly profitable, its non-Scandinavian subsidiaries were markedly less so. Its approach to product development was summarized as that of being "a local taste champion." Marketing was also deemed purely local. In its search for sources of inter-subsidiary synergies it attempted to centralize production. However, these were largely abandoned because of the inability to reproduce the various "local taste preferences." In 2004, it was decided that the only contender for integration was purchasing which was largely uncoordinated with each subsidiary controlling its own purchasing function.

R&S made two attempts to integrate its purchasing. The first, the Harmonization Project, spanned 2004—2007, and was acknowledged by corporate and subsidiary managers and board members as having been largely unsuccessful. The second, the significantly more successful Future Purchasing, commenced September 2008 and was in the main completed by March 2010.

Under the Harmonization Project, a number of activities were implemented in order to take out purchasing synergies across subsidiaries. The approach was to harmonize raw material specification across subsidiaries and then for each category to allocate a central lead-buyer with responsibility for sourcing across subsidiaries. For the most part these individuals were Norwegians located at Toro. In addition the position of Group Purchasing Director was established whose task was to coordinate between the purchasing departments in the respective subsidiaries. This position was allocated to a senior Vitana manager. To support these initiatives a number of supporting measures were undertaken: SAP was introduced; inter-subsidiary networks for marketing and sales managers were formed; annual two-day strategy meetings for subsidiary heads were organized.

A feature of the Harmonization project was that no subsidiary was to be obliged to go against its business judgment and use the central lead-buyers. In other words each subsidiary had the latitude to decide the degree to which it was in their interest to employ the services of the central lead-buyers. At its launch at a gathering of subsidiary managers the project and its core idea of using central lead-buyers was generally greeted positively. However, despite this initial reaction, by the end of the project the subsidiaries had on the whole opted to continue to use local buyers. Because product development continued to be done locally, it was generally the case that business units considered it more efficient to use their respective local buyers rather than the central lead-buyer. Not only were the communication opportunities significantly greater, but mutual understanding was already established. At Vitana and Delecta an important aspect to this mutual understanding was that local purchasers were significantly more cost conscious than central lead-buyers based at Toro in affluent Norway.

This lack of confidence or trust on the part of Vitana managers in the central lead-buyers based at Toro was experienced in reverse by one of the few central lead-buyers located outside of Toro. Based at Vitana, his perception was that the view of managers at Toro was that "anything that originated from the Czech Republic was by definition sub-standard." As the Harmonization project concluded his experience was that rather than consulting with him "Toro managers would simply buy what they wanted behind my back." As a senior manager at R&S with long-term experience of purchasing for Toro emphasized, "the challenge for a purchaser is to get the precise quality needs of the subsidiary right. Otherwise the (local) brand suffers." Furthermore, getting the quality right depends not only on understanding the needs of the subsidiary but also on communicating these to suppliers. His experience was that getting the supplier relationship to work could take as much as two years of steady interaction (see, e.g., Johanson & Vahlne, 2009).

As the Harmonization project came to an end the view of managers at R&S was that the managing directors (MDs) of the various subsidiaries had failed to identify with its potential. One senior R&S manager ascribed this in part to their lack of involvement in the Harmonization project and in part to their remuneration being exclusively calculated on the basis of their local performance rather than on the basis of group-level performance. The view from the subsidiaries was that a unified group mentality across R&S remained underdeveloped.

The R&S board decided to engage in a second and, what it signaled, would be a final attempt at achieving group-wide purchasing integration. As a first step it initiated a purchasing and supply management (PSM) analysis conducted by external consultants from McKinsey. The PSM analysis benchmarked the group's overall PSM performance against other MNCs in the same industry. The McKinsey analysis concluded that purchasing represented an unexploited cost savings potential of NOK 300 million. On the basis of the McKinsey analysis the board took the decision to launch Future Purchasing starting early September 2008. The core aim of Future Purchasing was to integrate direct purchasing across the group. This would mean transforming the highly decentralized structure of the group. At the same time, the board reiterated the need for each subsidiary to be its respective country's "local taste champion."

Whereas the Harmonization project had been loosely structured the board was determined that Future Purchasing was to have a clear structure from the outset. Each purchasing category was assigned a management team by the Future Purchasing project organization which also had the responsibility for monitoring the progress of the category teams and reporting its findings to R&S corporate management. Each category team was to comprise about five category experts who would also have access to advice from an external purchasing consultancy. The category teams were charged with defining the group-wide needs within each category and signing new group-wide contracts with new suppliers.

In March 2010, our findings indicated that the initial scepticism to Future Purchasing that was prevalent across the various subsidiaries had largely evaporated. The Project Director viewed Future Purchasing as having delivered on its targets and as having been perceived as having done so by the subsidiary MDs. Not only had the category teams worked well together, but they had "created a lot of purchasing knowledge." One senior R&S manager observed that Future Purchasing had been so successful that McKinsey regarded it as an exemplar of "how things should be done."

THE DISTINCTIVE ELEMENTS OF FUTURE PURCHASING

Hierarchical Mechanisms

Governance Reconfiguration – The General Management Team (GMT)
When R&S's new CEO joined the company in late September 2008 his first action was to conduct one-to-one meetings with each of the MDs of

the main subsidiaries. He explicitly requested that they act on behalf of the whole business rather than their own subsidiaries. Late October 2008 he presented a two-page memo to subsidiary MDs, "From a food conglomerate to an integrated food company." However, a much more substantial action by the new CEO was his decision to form an entirely new GMT which, in addition to himself, the CFO, the head of human resources, the director of marketing and sales and the new supply chain director included the MDs of the main subsidiaries. For the first time in the history of R&S subsidiary managers were now integrated in the corporate center. From December 2008 the GMT held monthly meetings in different locations supplemented by telephone conferences half way through each month. At each and every GMT meeting the Project Director of Future Purchasing reported on the progress of the project including any personnel issues that had arisen in the wake of manning the category teams.

At its outset the new GMT was a brittle entity. One senior manager recalled "innumerable meetings" with the CEO "hammering home Future Purchasing." Unlike under the Harmonization project it was now no longer the case that subsidiaries could use their local needs as "an excuse for inaction." Such was the pressure from the CEO that those who opposed Future Purchasing thought "it wise to keep their scepticism to themselves." Overall what we observe at R&S is governance reconfiguration. The fiefdom mentality of the subsidiary MDs is not only challenged but the MDs are incorporated in a new group-wide governance mechanism. GMT meetings are an arena for exchanging views, for developing a common vision of the group and for reaching common binding decisions.

Realignment of Rewards

Coupled to the new GMT was a fresh approach to MD compensation. Whereas the former system had been primarily local in its orientation, rewarding subsidiary MDs on the basis of their unit's performance, the new CEO introduced a new rewards system that, to a significant extent, rewarded the subsidiary MDs on the basis of overall group performance.

Rolling Measures of Outcomes

Part of the design of Future Purchasing comprised the regular monitoring by a controller of each category team in order to objectively identify tangible savings. Thereafter these unambiguous outcomes were immediately communicated to the GMT by the Program Director. The communication of "early wins" (i.e., immediate substantial savings) to the GMT not only persuaded subsidiary MDs that Future Purchasing was working, but it even generated a conviction that further integration was both possible and desirable.

Mandated Category Teams

The overall task of the category teams was very similar to the task assigned to the central lead-buyers of the Harmonization project. It was to define the group-wide needs within each purchasing category and then to sign new contracts with suppliers on behalf of the group. However, in operational terms there were profound differences. The R&S approach to the operational integration of purchasing in the Harmonization Project was to appoint central lead-buyers for the various purchasing categories and to provide them with authorization to invite cooperation from the purchasing managers based in the various subsidiaries. The approach of Future Purchasing to developing category teams was not to devolve the responsibility for forming them but to centralize it. Category teams were formed at the outset of each phase of Future Purchasing with designated team members covering a variety of relevant competencies including production, product development, logistics and marketing. Furthermore, unlike the Harmonization project where central lead-buyers remained in their regular purchasing roles, category team leaders were designated on a full-time basis while the team members were to spend an average of 60 percent of their working week on category team-related activities.

Category team appointments were subject to GMT scrutiny and monitoring. The boundaries of the category teams had in effect been buffered by the GMT against disruptive, competing tasks thereby "enabling its members to work outside of their normal functions and to work across both functions and geographies."

Relational Mechanisms

Inter-Subsidiary Category Teams

The Harmonization project was spearheaded by central lead-buyers who for the most part were Norwegians located at Toro. The view of non-Toro colleagues was that they failed to understand their idiosyncratic local needs. Equally in relation to colleagues at Toro the central lead-buyer located at

Vitana fared no better. The approach to Future Purchasing was very different to that of the Harmonization project in that it aimed to form inter-subsidiary category teams. In so doing, Future Purchasing created arenas for the exchange and sharing of local purchasing knowledge.

Bridging Category Teams
The category teams of Future Purchasing were specifically instructed to interact not just with suppliers but with local stakeholders across the group. Furthermore, their success in doing this was monitored by the Project Director and the GMT. By contrast bridging ties were not an explicit priority of the Harmonization project.

On the whole, according to the supply chain manager, these arenas worked well and resulted in projected cost savings (NOK 300 mill) being realized, the half of which by means of effective contract renegotiation in the project phase (2008–2010), and the remaining half by means of volume concentration and supplier switching in the post-project phase (2010–2012).

THE CASE OF TELENOR

Telenor is one of the larger mobile operators in the world with more than 150 million mobile subscriptions. From being a legacy Norwegian state owned company, Telenor now has operations in 14 counties that can be grouped into three areas: Scandinavia, Central and Eastern-Europe and South-East Asia. It is headquartered in Norway. Telenor's corporate policy has been to treat each business unit as a stand-alone operation. Until 2008 integration initiatives were limited to knowledge transfer when establishing new operations and modest attempts at creating knowledge sharing arenas for on-going operations.

At this point corporate management responded to increasing competitive pressures and began to consider the global integration of selected functions. It recognized that the core of mobile telcos is to purchase, configure, and operate standardized technology to run the telecom engine and then to effectively sell and distribute services through multiple channels with appurtenant customer service. Whereas marketing, service composition and distribution need to remain locally adapted purchasing could be undertaken globally. However, it was not until 2010 that corporate management finally concluded that globally integrated purchasing had significant potential. In 2012, a new souring organization was established. The financial ambition of this move is to realize savings of 3 BNOK by the end of 2015.

PHASE 1 – GROUP PROCUREMENT AS A CORPORATE CENTER OF EXCELLENCE

Group Procurement was originally set up in 2001 as a center of excellence located at corporate headquarters to support and coordinate the purchasing functions located in each of the business units. The initial voluntary coordination of purchasing cases of telco equipment across BUs improved the negotiation power and significant benefits were achieved. During the mid-2000s, Group Procurement attempted to create a corporate policy for procurement. The autonomous BUs ignored this attempt and by 2008 it was recognized by corporate management that Group Procurement was failing to engage local purchasing managers in terms of gaining their trust and support for a centrally developed procurement strategy. Business unit informants reported that Group Procurement lacked a sufficient understanding of the local culture and business model. The result, as expressed by a Group Procurement informant, was: "There was nobody who wanted our purchasing strategy or support. The business units wanted us to sit here at headquarters and not interfere with their local business. We decided that we had to rethink our role and focus."

Responding both to failure but also to corporate management's strategy for global purchasing integration Group Procurement developed an entirely new approach that started with a thorough analysis of the needs of the local procurement functions. One major commonality that was identified was all of the business units needed to modernize their mobile networks in order to make the transition from voice to mobile data. Group Procurement decided to concentrate their efforts on meeting this one common need. However, the response from the business units was entirely negative. According to a Group Purchasing informant "they did not want anything to do with us." Attitudes only changed as Group Procurement demonstrated its capabilities in conjunction with Telenor's greenfield entry into India in 2009 when the entire "telecom machine" had to be swiftly purchased and rolled out in an extremely competitive market. For the India entry Group Procurement succeeded in achieving the lowest prices on infrastructure equipment ever witnessed at Telenor.

PHASE 2 – SERIES OF GROUP-WIDE GLOBAL SOURCING PROJECTS

Despite misgivings, on the back of the tangible achievements in India, Telenor's Norway business unit granted Group Procurement the opportunity to contribute to its network modernization. Bold moves were undertaken by Group Procurement that replaced two European vendors with a single Chinese vendor, Huawei. In this move Telenor was the first western telco to opt for Huawei. For the period 2010–2015, the estimated result was savings in relation to previous cost levels of the order of 10–12 BNOK for the whole Telenor group. Based on the successes of Global Procurement in India corporate management recognized that integrated purchasing was both feasible and necessary. Many of the business units shared this analysis and began to actively cooperate with Group Procurement.

New cases for global purchasing were identified such as modems, SIM cards, antennas, and microwave equipment that were purchased and used in all business units. For the individual business unit the savings on any one of these items were not significant, but taken together they amounted to considerable savings for Telenor as a whole. Deploying small category teams comprising relevant specialists the purchasing of equipment was bundled thereby fully utilizing Telenor's overall scale. One outcome was aggressive competition between vendor partners that led to the total number of vendor partners being significantly reduced. The upshot for Telenor was that unit prices dropped between 50 and 60 percent.

A feature of the globally led sourcing projects at this stage was that the participation of the business units remained voluntary. Group Procurement had to continuously demonstrate the benefits of global purchasing to the business units, a process that was costly, not least in terms of time. In the spring of 2012, corporate management felt sufficiently confident that Group Procurement had developed the necessary global purchasing capabilities and the trust of business units to move to a new stage. One of the members of Group Procurement recalled: "From GEM (corporate management) we were challenged: what could we achieve if we could build the sourcing organization from scratch? What would sourcing then look like?"

PHASE 3 – SOURCING 3.0

In response to this challenge a new purchasing function, Global Sourcing, was established in September 2012 that operated under the slogan "one integrated global organization." When launching it, Jon Fredrik Baksaas, Group President and CEO said: "Co-ordinated sourcing has delivered good results during the recent years and we see that there is still a large potential to tap into."

The centralized Group Souring function was set up to address three main areas. First, purchasing of strategic investments was centralized to ensure the adoption and execution of effective purchasing solutions. Second, purchasing of standardized goods was coordinated centrally to utilize Telenor's scale to achieve lower prices. To achieve scale, Global Sourcing had to engage in internal standardization processes of product specifications. Third, Group Sourcing was tasked with providing best practice purchasing solutions and support to local business unit sourcing functions who remained engaged in the purchasing of local services. As Bjørn Harald Brodersen, Head of Global Sourcing, stated: "We will continue to have strong and qualified sourcing teams in each Business Unit, but strengthen the coordination across the Group." Apart from the need to maintain local responsiveness in regard to purchasing in response to purely local needs, Telenor seeks to ensure that each business retains a significant proportion of its stand-alone capabilities in order to maintain the strategic option of divestment to any part of its portfolio.

THE DISTINCTIVE ELEMENTS OF SOURCING 3.0

Hierarchical Mechanisms

Governance Reconfiguration – Restructuring the Organization
When the Global Sourcing function was established in 2012, the governance and organization structure was changed to speed up decision processes, support transparency and facilitate collaboration, and better manage the resource base and working procedures. The change project prior to the establishment of Global Sourcing revealed multiple sourcing hierarchies and multiple sets of working procedures.

Prior to Global Sourcing, local purchasing departments reported to a local executive. Post Global Sourcing, sourcing personnel employed by local business units report directly to Global Souring with only a "dotted reporting line" to their local business unit top management. The new governance model provided Global Sourcing with the formal means to effectively coordinate all sourcing activities across the various business units.

Realignment of KPIs, Measures of Outcomes and Rewards
The change project identified a variety of goals, key performance indicators (KPIs) and plans across the business units. Sourcing and finance at corporate headquarters collaborated closely to define how savings were to be calculated and measured. The management initiated changes to KPIs, spend and saving definitions, sign-off sheets and reporting tools. The sign-off sheets were used as a means to commit stakeholders by having them sign a document that showed how much in savings were going to be achieved. These savings figures were then followed up in the reporting phase. The new souring planning process was integrated with the business planning processes. New KPIs were introduced as a motivation mechanism that balances corporate and local needs. Bonus agreements were aligned with the new KPIs to create incentives to act accordingly.

Relational Mechanisms

Global Category Teams
Teams that draw on employees located across business units were established in order to ensure relevant expertise for each product or service category. Local sourcing staff is allocated to one or more category teams each of which has a dedicated leader. Each category team operates as a virtual team. To overcome the significant geographical distances involved knowledge and procedures are codified and standardized. The category teams safeguard Telenor's ability to develop and maintain sufficient competences within each purchasing category.

Bridging Central and Local Category Teams
Global Sourcing makes extensive use of collaborative technology tools as a way to share updated documents and procedures as a means to coordinate across business units. It is common that members of category teams have never physically met, but they regularly have virtual meetings supported by real-time document sharing and phone-conferences. To mitigate cultural differences, selected local BU sourcing employees are inpatriated to work at global headquarters on 1−2 year contracts. These inpatriate assignments involve on-the-job training and experience from working with colleagues from various business units. Global Sourcing employs one person who is tasked with attending all of their management team meetings and

who is responsible for ensuring information sharing across all purchasing operations.

SUMMARY OF FINDINGS

Global integration benefits derive from enhanced scale and scope economies (cost savings) and by concentrating production of common inputs on significantly fewer vendors. As both cases show, resistance to global integration of purchasing only decreases under significant pressure from corporate forces. Such resistance to integration is to a large extent caused by local managers' perceptions of the relative costs and benefits associated with such integration. Such costs derive primarily from the need for more standardization which often, but not always, means less responsiveness to local conditions. While these costs are readily conceived by business unit managers, the benefits of purchasing integration for the MNC as a whole are less obvious to them.

Further, both cases suggest that purely voluntary approaches to integrated purchasing that rely on relational governance are ineffective. In moving to globally integrated purchasing both companies only achieved global integration of purchasing by employing hierarchical, corporate driven common purchasing initiatives that created a sufficient number of successes that objectively demonstrated significant cost savings for local business unit as well as the MNC as a whole. At that stage centralized purchasing organizations could be developed.

In both MNCs the model that was adopted for achieving centralized purchasing involved horizontal coordination in the form of globally dispersed category teams actively supported by hierarchical governance in the form of corporate category managers, supervised by Group Sourcing central management. This model shares many of the characteristics of the transnational model in that it combines local responsiveness with global efficiency and worldwide learning (see Table 1). However, the model is at the functional rather than the aggregate level and is predicated on the explicit use of hierarchical governance mechanisms.

As indicated in the Table common to both MNCs what emerged was a hybrid form of organization with a centralized hub structure for purchasing, interlinked with a decentralized federation structure for other functions. Responsiveness to local purchasing needs and conditions was taken

Table 1. Key Success Capabilities of Purchasing Integration.

MNC Organization	Key Success Capabilities			Preliminary Results
	Local Responsiveness	Global Integration		
		Global Efficiency	Worldwide Learning	
Hierarchically governed and horizontally coordinated purchasing within a decentralized federation structure (a hybrid form combining decentralized federation with centralized hub)	*BU Sourcing:* reports dotted line to BU management and solid line to Group Sourcing; makes routine call-off to global framework agreements; makes purchases for local BUs; represents Group Sourcing in local BUs	*Group Sourcing:* standardizes and aggregates common inputs (developed by Global Category Teams); negotiates global contracts with global suppliers offering large volume discounts	*Global Category Teams:* develop global sourcing categories; discovers, and transmits best purchasing practice	*Cost savings:* according to project plans

care of by BU Sourcing whereas the global efficiency was the main responsibility of Group Sourcing. In both MNCs valuable purchasing knowledge was developed by global category teams and diffused across business units.

DISCUSSION

Contrary to Bartlett and Ghoshal's transnationalization thesis, we have argued that multi-domestic MNCs will generally not engage in aggregate level transformation to the transnational form. In line with Vahlne et al. (2011), we expect integration in multi-domestic MNCs to be limited to those functions that have the most tangible impact on performance. Further, in line with Yeniyurt et al. (2013), we have argued that purchasing is the most obvious function for multi-domestic MNCs to engage with because in comparison with, for example, marketing or product development the benefits of uniform sourcing in terms of cost savings are significantly more apparent. While procurement is a natural first candidate for global integration, other value-chain activities such as technology development, marketing, and after-sales services may follow drawing on the organizational capabilities initially developed for procurement. However, there is no inevitability to this. In that, Harzing's (1999) research failed to identify any aggregate transformation of multi-domestic MNCs to transnationals this position is not novel. What is more novel is our argument that within the multi-domestic model profound changes can occur at the level of discrete functions. Although Malnight (1995, p. 121) argued along these lines nearly two decades ago, it remains the case that "there has been limited investigation of the process within firms as they move toward integrated network structures."

Our two cases indicate that at the functional-level multi-domestic MNCs can achieve the three key success capabilities — *local responsiveness, global integration and worldwide learning* — associated with the transnational model. However, our analysis indicates that this achievement is not just the product of the development of a "shared management understanding" in the sense of common values and "nonparochial personalities" as supposed by Bartlett and Ghoshal (1995, p. 483). Our findings correspond with Yeniyurt et al.'s (2013, pp. 351–362) observation in regard to purchasing integration: "As with any important endeavor, the success of an effective and efficient globally integrated organization begins with having the full and active support and leadership of top management." Thus we observed that "voluntarism" resulted in initial failure for both case MNCs. Instead

the transformation of purchasing was dependent on hierarchical initiatives
that generated objectively positive results that appealed to the self-interest
of local business unit managers.

NOTES

1. Bartlett and Ghoshal were by no means alone in arguing for the emergence of
a "new" MNC. Similar propositions are found in for example Hedlund and his
'heterarchy' concept (1986, 1994), and White and Poynter's (1990) notion of the
'horizontal organization'. It has also received broad support from Kogut and
Zander (1993), Birkinshaw and Morrison (1995) and O'Donnell (2000) to name but
a few.
2. Although alternative integration candidates exist such as product development, production and marketing, purchasing is often chosen due to its large cost
saving potentials and immediate cost saving effects.

REFERENCES

Adler, P. S., & Kwon, S. W. (2002). Social capital: Prospects for a new concept. *Academy of
    Management Review*, *27*(1), 17–40.
Bartlett, C., & Ghoshal, S. (1987). Managing across borders: New organizational responses.
    MIT Sloan Management Review, *29*(1), 43–53.
Bartlett, C. A., & Ghoshal, S. (1989). *Managing across borders: The transnational solution.*
    Boston, MA: Harvard Business School Press.
Bartlett, C. A., & Ghoshal, S. (1993). Beyond the M-form: Toward a managerial theory of the
    firm. *Strategic Management Journal*, *14*(Issue S2), 23–46.
Bartlett, C. A., & Ghoshal, S. (1995). *Transnational management. Text, cases and readings in
    cross-border management* (2nd ed.). Chicago, IL: Irwin.
Bartlett, C. A., & Ghoshal, S. (2000). *Transnational management. Text, cases and readings in
    cross-border management* (3rd ed.). Chicago, IL: Irwin.
Bartlett, C. A., Ghoshal, S., & Beamish, P. W. (2008). *Transnational management. Text, cases
    and readings in cross-border management* (5th ed.). Chicago, IL: MacGraw-Hill.
Birkinshaw, J., & Morrison, A. J. (1995). Configurations of strategy and structure in subsidi-
    aries of multinational corporations. *Journal of International Business Studies*, *26*(4),
    729–753.
Bouquet, C., & Birkinshaw, J. (2008). Managing power in the multinational corporation:
    How low-power actors gain influence. *Journal of Management*, *34*(3), 477–508.
Burt, R. S. (1992). *Structural holes: The social structure of competition*. Cambridge, MA:
    Harvard University Press.
Dimaggio, P. J., & Powell, W. W. (1983). The iron cage revisited – institutional isomorphism
    and collective rationality in organizational fields. *American Sociological Review*, *48*(2),
    147–160.

Dörrenbächer, C., & Geppert, M. (2006). Micro-politics and conflicts in multinational corporations: Current debates, re-framing, and contributions of this special issue. *Journal of International Management, 12*(3), 251–265.

Dunning, J. H. (1980). Towards an eclectic theory of international production: Some empirical tests. *Journal of International Business Studies, 11*(1), 9–31.

Edelman, L. F., Bresnen, M., Newell, S., Scarbrough, H., & Swan, J. (2004). The benefits and pitfalls of social capital: Empirical evidence from two organizations in the United Kingdom. *British Journal of Management, 15*(1), 59–69.

Eisenhardt, K. (1989). Building theories from case study research. *Academy of Management Review, 4*, 532–550.

Forsgren, M., Holm, U., & Johanson, J. (2005). *Managing the embedded multinational.* Cheltenham, UK: Edward Elgar.

Gooderham, P. N. (2012). The transition from a multi-domestic to globally integrated multinational enterprise — in an industry where local taste matters. *European Journal of International Management, 6*(2), 175–198.

Hakkarainen, K., Palonen, T., Paavola, S., & Lehtinen, E. (2004). *Communities of networked expertise: Professional and educational perspectives* (1st ed.). London: Elsevier.

Harzing, A.-W. (1999). *Managing the multinationals.* Cheltenham, UK: Edward Elgar.

Hedlund, G. (1986). The hypermodern MNC — A heterarchy? *Human Resource Management, 25*(1), 9–35.

Hedlund, G. (1994). A model of the knowledge management and the N-form corporation. *Strategic Management Journal, 15*(Summer, Special Issue), 73–90.

Johanson, J., & Vahlne, J.-E. (2009). The Uppsala internationalization process model revisited: From liability of foreignness to liability of outsidership. *Journal of International Business Studies, 40*(9), 1411–1431.

Kogut, B., & Zander, U. (1993). Knowledge of the firm and the evolutionary theory of the multinational corporation. *Journal of International Business Studies, 24*, 625–645.

Kotabe, M., & Mudambi, R. (2009). Global sourcing and value creation: Opportunities and challenges. *Journal of International Management, 15*, 121–125.

Kraljic, P. (1983). Purchasing must become supply management. *Harvard Business Review, 61*(5), 109–118.

Lave, J., & Wenger, E. (1991). *Situated learning: Legitimate peripheral participation.* New York, NY: Cambridge University Press.

Malnight, T. W. (1995). Globalization of an ethnocentric firm: An evolutionary perspective. *Strategic Management Journal, 16*(2), 119–141.

Martin, J. A., & Eisenhardt, K. M. (2010). Rewiring: Cross-subsidiary collaborations in multibusiness organizations. *Academy of Management Journal, 53*(2), 265–301.

Mudambi, R., & Pedersen, T. (2007). *Agency theory and resource dependency theory: Complementary explanations for subsidiary power in multinational corporations.* Copenhagen Business School. SMG Working Paper No. 5/2007.

Nahapiet, J., & Ghoshal, S. (1998). Social capital, intellectual capital, and the organizational advantage. *Academy of Management Review, 23*(2), 242–266.

Nohria, N., & Ghoshal, S. (1994). Differentiated fit and shared values: Alternatives for managing headquarters-subsidiary relations. *Strategic Management Journal, 15*(6), 491–502.

O'Donnell, S. (2000). Managing foreign subsidiaries: Agents of headquarters, or an independent network? *Strategic Management Journal, 2*(5), 525–548.

Porter, M. E. (2008). Competing across locations. In *On competition, updated and expanded edition* (pp. 305–344). Boston: Harvard Business School Publishing.

Roth, K. (1992). Implementing international strategy at the subsidiary level: The role of managerial decision-making characteristics. *Journal of Management, 18*(4), 769–789.

Teece, D. J. (1986). Transaction cost economics and the multinational enterprise: An assessment. *Journal of Economic Behavior and Organization, 7*(1), 21–45.

Tomassen, S., & Benito, G. (2009). The costs of governance in international companies. *International Business Review, 18*(3), 292–304.

Trautmann, G., Bals, L., & Hartmann, E. (2009). Integration in the global sourcing organization – An information processing perspective. *Journal of Supply Chain Management, 45*(2), 57–74.

Trent, R. J., & Monczka, R. M. (2003). International purchasing and global sourcing – What are the differences? *Journal of Supply Chain Management, 39*(4), 26–36.

Tsai, W. (2000). Social capital, strategic relatedness and the formation of intraorganizational linkages. *Strategic Management Journal, 21*, 925–939.

Vahlne, J.-E., Ivarsson, I., & Johanson, J. (2011). The tortuous road to globalization for Volvo's heavy truck business: Extending the scope of the Uppsala model. *International Business Review, 20*(1), 1–14.

Vygotsky, L. S. (1986). *Thought and language.* Cambridge, MA: MIT Press.

White, R. E., & Poynter, T. A. (1990). Organizing for worldwide advantage. In C. Bartlett, Y. Doz, & G. Hedlund (Eds.), *Managing the global firm* (pp. 95–113). New York, NY: Routledge.

Williamson, O. E. (1981). The modern corporation: Origins, evolution, attributes. *Journal of Economic Literature*, (December 1981), *19*(4), 1537–1568.

Williamson, O. E. (1985). *The economic institutions of capitalism.* New York, NY: Free Press.

Yeniyurt, S., Henke, J. W. Jr., & Cavusgil, E. (2013). Integrating global and local procurement for superior supplier working relations. *International Business Review, 22*(2), 351–362.

Yip, G. (1989). Global strategy – In a world of nations? *MIT Sloan Management Review, 31*(1), 29–41.

NETWORK ORCHESTRATION: VODAFONE'S JOURNEY TO GLOBALIZATION

Ayse Saka-Helmhout and Christopher J. Ibbott

ABSTRACT

This investigation provides an understanding of network orchestration as an impersonal, primordial driving force that challenges the view in organizational design that assigns human choice and deliberate intention a central role. The study highlights the importance of emerging strategy and the unintended consequence in bringing about a desirable outcome in MNCs' efforts to coordinate and integrate globally dispersed capabilities. It is based on a longitudinal action research that embraces a period of transformational change between Vodafone and Ericsson to achieve cash synergies in mobile network operations globally. The findings indicate that enabling knowledge mobility, appropriating knowledge, and fostering network stability contribute to a successful economic performance as interactive, self-governing processes of network orchestration. Accordingly, we conclude that the processes of network orchestration must be understood as driven by choice sets taken while creatively coping

Orchestration of the Global Network Organization
Advances in International Management, Volume 27, 121–147
ISSN: 1571-5027/doi:10.1108/S1571-502720140000027003

with change rather than as primarily choice sets deliberately taken in the sequential pursuit of goals.

Keywords: Network orchestration; Vodafone; inter-firm relationships; knowledge mobility

INTRODUCTION

There has been substantial research on various multinational corporation (MNC) configurations in their link to identifying and leveraging capabilities (e.g., Bartlett & Ghoshal, 1989; Gulati, Nohria, & Zaheer, 2000; Hedlund, 1994; Prahalad & Doz, 1981). Regardless of whether the MNC is conceptualized as a set of internalized cross-border transactions (Buckley & Casson, 1976), a differentiated network (Ghoshal & Nohria, 1989; Nohria & Ghoshal, 1997), or a social community that crosses national boundaries (Kogut & Zander, 1992), the ability to leverage dispersed capabilities effectively is seen by most international business (IB) scholars as a key source of competitive advantage for MNCs (Ernst & Kim, 2002; Zander, 1999). The significant idea here is that the structural pattern of a firm is unique, and has the potential to confer competitive advantage.

Although the work on organizational design carried out in IB between 1970 and 1990 has had a significant impact on the IB field and has largely faded since, it continues to have a strong influence on organization theory. Network forms of organization, typified by reciprocal patterns of communication and exchange (Powell, 1990; Powell, Douglas, Koput, & Owen-Smith, 2005), are seen as reshaping the global business architecture and marking the current period by their growing prevalence (e.g., Monge & Fulk, 1999; Parkhe, Wasserman, & Ralston, 2006). However, much of the theorizing on organizational design rests on the central role assigned to human choice and deliberate intention (e.g., Child, 1972; Pettigrew, 1987; Whittington, 1988). It is argued that deliberate actions of individuals determine the success and/or failure of organizations. Outcomes tend to be attributed to conscious choices, and purposeful actions of individuals (Chia & Holt, 2009). The same can be observed in accounts of network orchestration by MNCs (e.g., Dhanaraj & Parkhe, 2006). There is little room for theorizing the unexpected effects of unintended consequences of deliberate choices (MacKay & Chia, 2013). In this chapter, our objective is to show an interactive process of *network orchestration* that combines choice and change in an unexpected way to produce a desired organizational outcome. Network orchestration is defined by those who assign a heroic status to agency, that is, uphold the view that the deliberate actions of individuals determine the success or failure of an organization, as coordinating knowledge mobility, appropriating knowledge, and fostering network stability (Dhanaraj & Parkhe, 2006). Unlike arguments that celebrate the purposeful design processes led by hub firms in the formation and growth of a network (Dyer & Singh, 1998; Rowley, Behrens, & Krackhardt, 2000), we highlight the importance of emerging strategy and the unintended consequence in bringing about a desirable outcome in MNCs' efforts to coordinate and integrate globally dispersed capabilities.

We present a framework for network orchestration by drawing on organization theory in the following section. This is followed by an empirical illustration of key orchestration processes that Vodafone performed to create cash synergies in its key mobile network of infrastructure suppliers. The fourth section concludes the chapter by presenting the implications for IB of network orchestration.

NETWORK ORCHESTRATION

There is increasing attention given to networks in which hub firms (Jarillo, 1988) — prominent actors (Knoke, 1994), flagship firms (Rugman & D'Cruz, 2000), or network orchestrators (Hacki & Lighton, 2001) — lack the benefit of hierarchical authority (e.g., Fulk, 2001). With widespread disintegration of value chains in many high-tech industries (Lorenzoni & Baden-Fuller, 1995), the significance of network orchestration has become more prominent. The paradox here is how a hub firm or a network orchestrator coordinates and influences other network members over which it has no hierarchical control to achieve economic benefits.

Organization theory literature highlights both chance and prior history, that is, path dependence (Burton, Sørenson, & Beckman, 2002), and purposefully designed processes that are led by hub firms in the formation and growth of a network (Dyer & Singh, 1998; Rowley et al., 2000). In the intentional view, hub firms are seen to possess the attributes necessary to lead the process of pulling resources and capabilities of network members. As network orchestrators, they aim to create and extract value from the network by integrating and coordinating processes, resources, and assets (Hinterhuber, 2002). Intermediate levels of control and incentives in network organizations do not necessarily equate with overall inefficiency of such a structure (Demil & Lecocq, 2006). Mutual dependence, strong personal relationships and reputation preclude agents from pursuing their own interests exclusively (Jones, Hesterly, & Borgatti, 1997; Powell, 1990). However, in order to create value in such structures, it is commonly argued that there needs to be deliberate, purposeful action (e.g., Kogut, 2000). In the context of network orchestration, these are hypothesized as (i) coordinating knowledge mobility, (ii) appropriating knowledge, and (iii) fostering network stability (Dhanaraj & Parkhe, 2006).

Mobilizing Knowledge

Mobilizing knowledge is defined as the "ease with which knowledge is shared, acquired, and deployed within the network" (Dhanaraj & Parkhe, 2006, p. 660). This is necessary as significant value cannot be created where knowledge is retained by each network member. Hub firms are able to assess the value of relevant knowledge at different points in the network and to coordinate its transfer where it is needed (Gulati, 1999). They tend to follow three specific processes to mobilize knowledge: knowledge absorption, network identification, and inter-organizational socialization (Dhanaraj & Parkhe, 2006). Knowledge absorption involves combining existing capabilities in new ways (Kogut & Zander, 1996). By establishing a common identity, hence confidence, among network members, a hub firm encourages open sharing of valuable knowledge (Dyer & Nobeoka, 2000). This knowledge tends to be mobilized through socialization, that is, formal and informal linkages, among network participants (Brown & Duguid, 2001).

Appropriating Knowledge

Appropriating knowledge in network orchestration involves governing a network member's ability to capture value generated by mobilized knowledge (Teece, 1986, 2000). In its application to networks, appropriating knowledge implies evenly distributing the value created from knowledge mobility through an appropriability regime set up by the hub firm (Dhanaraj & Parkhe, 2006). This suggests a broad, consensual framework that averts any attempt to act opportunistically or leak information to external parties by the partners (Mowery, Oxley, & Silverman, 1996). Dhanaraj and Parkhe (2006) suggest trust, procedural justice, and joint asset ownership mitigate concerns in appropriation. Social interactions that foster trust and reciprocity among network members are crucial in minimizing the risk of opportunistic behavior (Gulati et al., 2000). A network orchestrator serves the role of a champion in building up this trust. Procedural justice or the fairness of the decision process encourages voluntary cooperation (Sheppard & Tuchinsky, 1996). This can be enacted by hub firms through network resource allocation, conflict resolution decisions, and consistency in decision making (Kim & Mauborgne, 1991). Dhanaraj and Parkhe (2006) also purport that joint asset ownership, which is commonly observed in networks, can reduce the risk of responsibility shirking, create room for joint problem solving, and provide incentives for sharing rewards.

Fostering Network Stability

The third task in network orchestration is fostering network stability that enables growth and flexibility for members to enter and exit the network (Dhanaraj & Parkhe, 2006). This rests on the assumption that loosely coupled networks may experience unstable linkages encouraging, for instance, defection of network partners to other networks (e.g., Uzzi, 1997). The type of coordination displayed in the network is acknowledged to be one of "subtle leadership" (Orton & Weick, 1990) rather than management. In other words, each network member is able to take initiatives. Change in the membership of a network through isolation, migration, cliques, and attrition poses a challenge to value creation (e.g., Lorenzoni & Lipparini, 1999), limiting opportunities for the creation of social capital (e.g., Inkpen & Tsang, 2005). The task of a hub firm as an orchestrator is to (i) enhance or sustain reputation so that network members see a benefit in maintaining their links (Stuart, 2000), (ii) encourage forward-looking expectations of gains, and (iii) promote multiplexity or interdependencies among network members through, for instance, multiple projects in order to reinforce ties (Kenis & Knoke, 2002).

In line with most previous research in organizational design, the three processes of network orchestration are perceived as planned, intentional actions. It is assumed that atomistic, rational calculation or a proactive ability to intentionally create, adapt, and control a specific network structure characterizes the process (e.g., Rowley et al., 2000). It is also contended that networks forms of organizations are driven initially by path-dependent processes, and subsequently adopt intentional management

(Hite & Hesterly, 2001). Although we see the role of human agency, choice, and deliberate intention in explaining the conduct of organizations as significant, we do not see decisive interventions as necessarily bringing about a desired state of affairs. Rather, we acknowledge the unintended effects of deliberate choices that contribute to shaping organizational circumstances (MacKay & Chia, 2013). The network orchestration processes that we highlight at Vodafone capture the very act of choosing a particular strategy in response to a specific objective that generated an unintended network form of organization.

RESEARCH METHODS

We draw on a longitudinal action research, embracing a period of transformational change (December 1998 to November 2000) between two MNCs, Vodafone Group Plc. ("Vodafone") and Telefonaktiebolaget LM Ericsson, that is, more specifically LM Ericsson AB ("Ericsson"). The transformational change was motivated, through a network infrastructure supply chain, by the Vodafone corporate objective to achieve cash synergies in its mobile network operations globally. Ericsson was a major supplier to Vodafone of said infrastructure and related services. The second author was the inaugural and co-leader of the initiative on behalf of Vodafone supported by an Ericsson counterparty. Though the primary stimulus was Vodafone, the two MNCs resolved to adopt a collective strategy to globalize their business relationship, recognizing and accepting that the financial benefits arising might be asymmetric.

It is noteworthy that the contextual background of the case company changed over the transition period. The initial Vodafone country quorum comprised the United Kingdom, Holland, Greece and Australia and the corresponding Ericson operations. Vodafone subsequently merged with AirTouch Communications, Inc. ("AirTouch") of California (1999), and this combination later acquired Mannesmann AG ("Mannesmann") of Germany (2000). The consequence of this acquisition was the expansion in the number of Vodafone operators, 10 in the longitudinal period of transition, that is, the phase terminating when the inter-organizational and inter-company relationships within each organization had evidenced transformed practices. Subsequently, two additional infrastructure suppliers became engaged with this synergy initiative. The Mannesmann AG acquisition resulted further in a range of synergy targets being committed to the financial markets.

In 1998, the second author as the IT and Project Management Director in Vodafone (United Kingdom), in advance of an impending merger with AirTouch, assumed responsibility for the achievement of the Vodafone financial targets. These could only be achieved through mobilizing the commitment of the operating companies that actually transacted business locally with Ericsson.

Data collection comprised a chronological sequence of all key meetings, with the venue and the purpose thereof, of the Vodafone and Ericsson members by organizational position, the Minutes of the meetings, and data sources and notations. Table 1 lists the chronology of all meetings in the case company.

Of note are the Global Supply Chain Management (GSCM) and eRelationship meetings supplemented by a series of country visits conducted by the second author. The purpose of the country and ad hoc meetings by the second author was to support the promotion of the infrastructure supply chain globalization initiative, and to establish transparency and trust to bring on board the local operating companies in the transformational activities. For data sources more generally, reference was made to memorandums, exchanges/interactions at meeting venues, forums, video recordings of presentations, and emails.

The second author was present at all listed meetings save for two, the Global Cost Synergies meeting in the United Kingdom in which he was a part-time attendee and that of April 2000. Throughout the longitudinal period of the transformation, the GSCM meeting remained the main coordination focal point to which the virtual works streams were subordinated, to which progress was reported and from which new initiatives were launched. The second author participated in all the eRelationship virtual work stream meetings and was in the latter stages appointed as its chairman. None of the meeting minutes were prepared by the second author. The meeting facts and observations were confirmed and/or supplemented by the observations and/or input noted by the actors present at the meetings.

Whilst this case study provides for the opportunity of deep insight given the leadership role and participation of the second author, it too has the potential disadvantage of introducing bias. In mitigation thereof and post the case analysis, the second author held a workshop for the purpose of validating outcomes. The workshop was attended by the Ericsson Global Contact (a Managing Director based in the United Kingdom), another senior Ericsson Contact (a Managing Director also based in the United Kingdom), an Ericsson Director from Sweden, a Vodafone Customer Executive based in the UK and two academic experts, who all confirmed

Table 1. Chronological Sequence of All Meetings.

Meeting Category	GSCM Meeting	eRelationship	Ad Hoc	Second Author Country Visits	Supplier	New GSCM Initiatives	Comments
Meeting Dates:							
February 25–26, 1999	X						Inaugural GSCM meeting in Newbury, UK
March 23, 1999				X			Libertel in Maastricht, Holland
April 14–15, 1999	X						Maastricht, Holland
May 26–27, 1999	X						Athens, Greece
July 26–27, 1999			X				Former AirTouch properties in Amsterdam
August 2, 1999				X			Ericsson in Holland
August 3–4, 1999				X			Panafon and Ericsson jointly in Athens, Greece
August 5–6, 1999				X			Misrfone and Ericsson jointly in Cairo, Egypt
August 13, 1999			X				Meeting that included eRelationship in Stockholm
September 2–3, 1999	X						Nynashamn, Near Stockholm, Sweden
September 10, 1999		X					Inaugural meeting in Amsterdam, Holland
September 14–15, 1999			X				Global Cost No. 1 Synergies in Newbury, UK
September 16, 1999				X			Libertel meeting in Maastricht, Holland
September 17, 1999				X			Düsseldorf, Germany
October 6, 1999				X			Airtel only in Madrid, Spain
October 11, 1999		X					Amsterdam, Holland
October 21, 1999						X	New infrastructure supplier presentation in Copenhagen, Denmark
November 2, 1999			X				Technical Operations Symposium in Newbury, UK

Date	Event / Location						
November 3, 1999	London, UK					X	
November 4, 1999	GSM Systems Program Managers in Stockholm		X				
November 22, 1999	Telecel and Ericsson separately in Lisbon, Portugal			X			
December 1, 1999	Panafon and Ericsson jointly in Athens, Greece		X	X			
December 7, 1999	TTS Global Workshop, Nr Stockholm						
December 9, 1999	D2 meeting in London, UK						
December 21, 1999	London, UK			X		X	
January 11–12, 2000	Cairo, Egypt						X
February 3–4, 2000	Vodafone and Ericsson jointly in Sydney, Australia			X			
February 4–5, 2000	Ericsson jointly with Vodafone, Fiji, then Vodafone, New Zealand both in Auckland			X			
February 18, 2000	Business Management Conference, Hong Kong		X				
March 14, 2000	London, UK					X	
March 21–22, 2000	Inaugural IT GSCM meeting in Sydney, Australia	X					
April 2–3, 2000	Global Cost Synergies in Bucharest, Romania				X		
May 5, 2000	London, UK					X	
May 10–12, 2000	Lisbon, Portugal						X
June 15, 2000	Financial Directors' Conference, UK				X		
June 21, 2000	D2 meeting in Münich, Germany; new supplier			X			
July 4–5, 2000	Ericsson meeting in Düsseldorf, Germany						X
October 2–5, 2000	Bucharest, Romania			X		X	

Source: Ibbott (2001).

the facts. For example, one of the Supplier Global Contacts stated "the Programme has, during the past two years, strengthened the relationship the Customer and Supplier in a way that never would have been possible in a purely commercial relationship."

ILLUSTRATION OF NETWORK ORCHESTRATION: VODAFONE'S INCEPTION OF A REQUISITE ORGANIZATION

By January 1998, the second author, as the IT and Project Management Director in Vodafone Limited (the UK mobile operating company) had initiated the functional transformation of procurement to a supply chain function, including for the provision of mobile network infrastructure sourced from Ericsson (Supplier). The infrastructure included mobile network equipment, software and a number of related supporting services. This activity was to transform and optimize supply, deploy processes and practices locally in addition to contributing to the achievement of the cost reductions sought by Vodafone.

An illustration of the point is the deployment of base station equipment in containers to field locations adjacent to masts on which the antennas are mounted. Hitherto, Vodafone procured to its warehouse the container and all equipment/parts to be installed therein. Then either field engineers assembled, installed and tested the equipment/parts locally in the warehouse, after which the completed container was transported to its assigned field location, or the container and the equipment/parts were all shipped unassembled to the field location and the installation and testing process was carried out there. This led to variability in the standards of quality and physical configuration of the installation owing to undefined assembly and test instructions, as well as costs in deploying field engineers in this mode. The transformed supply chain alternative was to contract Ericsson to source its own and all other required third party equipment/parts and to build, integrate and commission/test the configuration in a factory environment according to defined assembly, test and quality processes, after which they could organize the shipment of the completed container directly to its assigned field location. The impact was to relieve Vodafone of the cost of all component procurement, warehousing and the deployment of field engineers to system build and test, and to achieve higher quality and consistent factory output delivered directly to site.

Whilst perhaps not unique in practice, these and the ensuing other changes in the supply chain context marked the transformation and optimization of extant working processes and practices within and between operating divisions in Vodafone UK, namely supply chain, technology and operations. The inter-MNC processes and practices were enhanced too, not to mention that Ericsson was the benefactor of an increased services business. Although there was resistance to the variant propositions within Vodafone, business ambitions were realized by adopting an inclusive, progressive and incremental approach. In May 1998, the Board of Vodafone Limited approved the second author's proposals for a UK policy on the separation of roles and responsibilities of Supply Chain Management and the Technology.

In the latter part of 1998, and in advance of the impending merger of Vodafone with AirTouch Communications Inc. of California, the anticipated benefit of enhanced cost synergies between the extant Vodafone mobile operating company interests and those of AirTouch was promoted by the Vodafone M&A team. A financial benefit of the merger was anticipated to be the opportunity for enhanced synergies from lessons learned and shared due to the increase in number of mobile network operators in the merged businesses that may otherwise not have been realized. Initially, this prompted discussions internal to Vodafone between the extant operators led/hosted by the second author. However, all parties were constrained from commercial information exchanges due to each country operation being bounded by Non-Disclosure Agreement (NDA) obligations in the local contracts with Ericsson. This quorum of operators and the percentage equity ownership of Vodafone Group Plc. at that time were the United Kingdom (100%), Libertel of Holland (70%), Panafon of Greece (55%), and Vodafone Australasia (to include Fiji) (91%), each of which were existing Ericsson network infrastructure customers. The second author also established, with the Ericsson newly appointed global leader, a shared interest and a strategy in seeking to globalize inter-organizational commercial relationships by enhancing all aspects of the (end-to-end) network infrastructure supply chain management processes from the source of supply through to network deployment and the support thereof such as warranties, software updates, and reverse logistics.

There were no preordained agreed scope of work, organization structures, budget, levels of authority, or formal governance arising from the decision to implement a global supply chain. In other words, the intra- and inter-organizational processes and commercial outcomes were not envisaged, prescribed or planned. Rather, there was a polarizing Vodafone objective to attain cash synergies in the network infrastructure supply chain and with an acceptance that the benefits arising thereof may be asymmetric and not shared.

With the agreement of the Ericsson global leader, the second author invited the current Vodafone local operating company interests and their local Ericsson counterparts to the joint Vodafone-Ericsson inaugural GSCM meeting to be hosted by Vodafone Limited. In February 1999, to overcome the aforesaid issue of confidentiality, it was a requirement that each attending company sign a group NDA that enabled the open sharing between the parties of all hitherto confidential commercial information. This was the first globalizing step of an emerging and new inter-organizational relationship, each organization being treated as a homogenous whole and each country identified jointly as a single entity for the purposes of the new journey. This forum was to become the catalyst for transformational change within which social and intellectual capital could develop through sharing of knowledge and building of a common identity. These were hindered in the former silo-based disaggregated inter-organizational relationships.

To that end, it was agreed that the GSCM forum would be a Steering Group and that detailed (virtual) assignments should be assigned and delivered jointly by the Vodafone and Ericsson participating local companies. It was further agreed that the second author, through the UK Company, and with the Ericsson global leader would conclude the first commercial Global Agreement. This was an initiative that had already been underway in the UK and the outcome of which would now be of synergy benefit to the participating Vodafone operating companies, as the variant inter-organizational relationships would, through this unified collaboration, be treated as one by Ericsson.

A number of virtual work streams were initiated to include global terms and conditions for products procured from Ericsson (Global Price Book), to converge radio base station equipment configurations, to analyze and propose a network-converged switching requirement, and to establish common software, audit test and delivery methodologies (see Table 2).

A work stream, assigned by country, consisted of a combination of local resources of both MNCs and the support, as required and decided by those leading the work stream, of other interested countries. It was agreed that progress of these and any other/new work streams would be reported at the GSCM meetings. Virtual teams could be independently set up with invitees of a given country member's choice regardless of whether or not these members attended the GSCM meetings.

Table 2. The Key Virtual Work Streams Initiated.

Key Virtual Work Streams	Brief Description	Lead Country
Global agreement	The creation and agreement of a global "price book" that would cover all GSM products purchased from Ericsson	UK
Base station (BTS) configurations	An agreed convergence toward, and a set of, BTS configurations	UK
MSC and BSC switching configurations	Analysis and discovery of a set of MSC and BSC configurations that could be adopted by all countries	Greece, transferred later to Germany
Groupware	Analysis and creation of groupware (later known as eRelationship) for all inter-organizational Information Systems (IS) that allows information sharing and product ordering	Netherlands
Common software, audit, test, and delivery	The elimination of repeated software build and testing	Australia

Source: Ibbott & O'Keefe (2004).

Of significance here was the work stream that was to lead to the introduction, by the second author, of the concept of eRelationship (previously known as Groupware). The eRelationship environment was created and hosted by Ericsson on an IT platform in Stockholm in 1999. It was a bi-directional web portal or a virtual environment for both global and local inter-organizational information and knowledge sharing, all intended to epitomize the relationship within and between the two organizations. Key, however, was that the placement, the management thereof, of information and access rights were to be governed by the contributors utilizing a set of software tools. There was to be no centralized control. Save for commercially sensitive information, the ethos was that all information would be accessible by all employees of either MNC, whether or not they were involved in the Vodafone-Ericsson business relationship. This was achieved. A further objective through the virtual work streams was to promulgate new practice and learning to others in the end-to-end supply chain within and between the MNC organizations for the betterment of their MNC and/or country operations.

An impact of eRelationship was the increase in the unrestricted flow and/or exchange of unfiltered information within and between both MNCs. This was an open inter- and intra-organizational model, beyond the control of the HQ of both MNCs. It extended to all registered intranet users who were not engaged in this particular business relationship. The value creation of intellectual capital was under virtual control, but it was reinforced by the evolved social capital, the momentum of which could be extracted from the various global forums and meetings that also became a catalyst for engagement.

By May 2000, the eRelationship focus became formalized with clarity of strategic intent as is illustrated by the following highlights presented jointly by the Vodafone and Ericsson project leaders for the approval of the virtual working group.

> The Vodafone (Customer) − Ericsson (Supplier) Global Portal must reflect the entire global relationship, in all its aspects, between Vodafone and Ericsson. Further, it is the aim that this eRelationship virtual environment becomes that natural primary source of information and communication between the organizations, and as such is not constrained by time and/or location. It is anticipated that arising from this new paradigm will be the mutual requirements for changes in process, practices and organizations. In particular, this capability is crucial to the sustainable support of all global virtual workstreams and initiatives under the guidance of the GSCM virtual leadership. (Ibbott, 2001, pp. 262−263)

As a prime mover for the Vodafone Group, the second author became the catalyst within the network of its operating companies for the transformation of the network infrastructure supply chain, which was enabled through eRelationship to garner support from a critical mass of operating companies. None of the operating companies directly reported to the second author. Yet they were, in combination, the source of the realized cash synergies against which they were targeted in the Group business, because they were the ones to transact with Ericsson locally. The role required a non-hierarchical lead, transcending the vertical company hierarchies of the Vodafone operating companies and interceding in their collective local disaggregated business relationships with Ericsson.

In order to create the global inter-organizational community, following the inaugural meeting in the United Kingdom, the venue for the GSCM meetings was agreed to be variously convened in the countries of the participating joint MNC operating companies to engender an esprit de corps among the participants − to additionally include Holland, Greece, Sweden, Egypt, Australia, Portugal, and Romania. Although the forum comprised of actors of variant hierarchical position, it had no formal status. The local companies of the MNCs took decisions collectively in these meetings to which the second author offered guidance and/or ascent as appropriate. This was, in practice, a conformant accession, by the Vodafone operating companies, of local decision making authority to the globalizing leadership on matters of commerce and conditions related thereto, for example, the Global Price Book and its requirements for variant practices as a quid pro quo in return for supplier concessions. These GSCM meetings were observed to be highly inclusive regardless of country-of-origin, and company and/or job role. Of note too, was that the small global team of the second author comprised actors and/or secondees from Vodafone operating companies' supply chain or technical teams, recommended by the extant global team members and supported by the operating companies.

The case data shown in Table 3 provide clear evidence of the nature of the boundary crossing as observed in multi-level job roles of participating actors.

The vertical axis depicts the horizontal organization mix and hierarchical job roles within each MNC (Vodafone as Customer and Ericsson as Supplier). The horizontal axis documents the number of attendees at each of the GSCM meetings and of the eRelationship working group. In this context, the network organization was the plethora of the engaged and non-engaged operating companies of each of the MNC with Group/HQ engagement/support, whilst the eRelationship was an enabling means for the sharing of information and knowledge both globally and on projects locally.

Through the strength of the boundary-crossing actors in the horizontal inter-organizational structure, the local objections, resistance and/or reticence were overcome, for example, through the release of the Global Agreement. This Agreement provided for a consolidation of equipment and a limitation of configuration diversity in return for unified pricing and commercial terms. The following quote from the Listing of Particulars (page 9) offers a quantum to the magnitude of the synergy expectations in anticipation of the Vodafone AirTouch Plc. offer for Mannesmann AG:

> The Board expects the benefits of this transaction to generate synergies of approximately £500 million on a proportionate after tax cash flow basis in 2003 (with approximately 20 per cent of such synergies coming from increased revenues, 40 per cent from cost savings and 40 per cent from capital expenditure savings) and approximately £600 million on a proportionate after tax cash flow basis in 2004 (with approximately 25 per cent of such savings coming from increased revenues, 40 per cent from cost savings and 35 per cent from capital expenditure savings).

The network infrastructure synergies discussed here were substantially contributions made to the capital expenditure objectives, though operating

Table 3. Composition of Actors in the GSCM and eRelationship Meetings.

Actor positions	GSCM Meetings							eRelationship Working Group Meetings					
	No. 1	No. 2	No. 3	No. 4	No. 5	No. 6	No. 7	No. 1	No. 2	No. 3	No. 4	No. 5	No. 6
Customer organization													
Managing director	0	0	0	0	0	0	0	0	0	0	0	0	0
Director	3	2	1	2	2	2	2	1	1	1	2	1	1
Executive	1	2	2	3	7	6	6	1	1	1	1	2	1
Senior manager	2	3	3	8	8	8	13	0	0	0	1	1	0
Other actors	1	3	3	4	3	6	3	1	1	0	1	1	2
Total in attendance:	7	10	9	17	20	22	24	3	3	2	5	5	4
Supplier organization													
Managing director	2	2	2	3	2	2	2	1	1	1	1	1	1
Director	0	2	2	1	2	2	2	0	1	0	2	2	1
Executive	3	3	3	7	8	9	5	1	1	1	2	1	1
Senior manager	0	2	2	7	12	12	16	2	2	3	5	9	2
Other actors	1	1	4	2	1	1	1	0	0	1	0	0	2
Total in attendance	6	10	13	20	25	26	26	4	5	6	10	13	7

Source: Ibbott (2001).

Note: The GSCM meetings were the core forum, and the eRelationship Working Group meetings were a subordinated virtual work stream.

expense activities were also pursued. Vodafone reported, in its Interim Results Release for the Six Months to 30 September 2002, "Good progress has been made on the synergies arising from the Mannesmann transaction. It is expected that the £500m of forecast post-tax cash flow synergies for the year ending March 2003 will be exceeded." Further, in its 2004 Annual Report Vodafone stated "Mannesmann has been integrated into the Group and the expected synergies for the year ended 31 March 2004 announced at the time of the acquisition have been achieved, exceeding the target mainly as result of higher savings from capital expenditure, handset procurement and additional revenue opportunities." The Customer-Supplier GSCM forum enabled the transfer of experiential knowledge and the dispersion of lead responsibilities of internationalization to actors representing various customer operating company equity interests. For instance, as the Group Supply Chain Management (SCM) Director of Vodafone Procurement Company (VPC), Detlef Schultz, indicates, the supply chain management resulted in a paradigm shift by 2008. VPC became a strategic sourcing center. By 2011, the company was leveraging synergies beyond boundaries. The VPC was targeting new areas of spend (presentation by the GSCM Director). By the same token, the Customer senior lawyer from the US perceived the GSCM meetings as follows.

> For the first time, there was vigorous dialogue among the Customer's operating companies regarding the vendor's products, performance, price, and future plans ... [The second author] moderated the discussions, planned the ongoing meetings and work of the (global Customer-Supplier) team ... These small beginnings yielded large results. Through the improvement in communication and reductions in unnecessary product (configurations), the vendor was able to improve its efficiency ... the bulk of the improvements in pricing came from the supply chain process.

As a point of note, in 2001 Vodafone introduced formal governance in pursuit of a Mannesmann synergy commitment that formalized the relationship between the Vodafone Group functions and its local operating companies. Of developmental relevance to the period beyond the case study, was the formation of the SCM Council and the IT and Technology (ITTM) Council; the second author participated in both forums. These forums decided jointly on matters of technology, its sourcing and deployment, to which the Vodafone operating companies were obliged. The informal virtual organization remained intact and continued to function below the SCM Council, which comprised of representatives of large OpCos, representatives of smaller OpCos, Group CTO, and the Group Technology representatives. This body served to ratify what was informally agreed or to assert decisions taken outside the Council. The second author represented, on behalf of the informal virtual organization, proposals for adoption on Group matters relating to the mobile network infrastructure.

DISCUSSION

We began by asking what role network orchestration serves in MNCs' coordination and integration of capabilities that are globally dispersed. Our findings, as summarized in Table 4, progress a perspective on MNC configuration that takes into account the unexpected effects of unintended consequences of deliberate choices. This approach celebrates the importance of emerging strategy and unintended consequence in bringing about a desirable outcome in MNCs' efforts to coordinate and integrate globally dispersed capabilities.

Vodafone, in agreement with Ericsson, played a pivotal role in the formation, growth, and success of its network infrastructure. As the case suggests, knowledge absorption and inter-organizational socialization are significant in *enabling knowledge mobility*. GSCM meetings, work streams (which reflected boundary-crossing activity), and the eRelationship platform enabled the exchange of commercial knowledge and the development of a common understanding relevant for the case initiative. What is important to note here is that the hub firm or the orchestrator – Vodafone – neither aimed to control knowledge mobility, nor was it in a position to assess the value of relevant knowledge at different points in the network. Each local company was treated as an independent entity or node rather than as part of a hierarchical unity of command. Although the Vodafone objective was to attain cost synergies, this was pursued through mutually respected horizontal relationships. The role of Vodafone was one of a catalyst for learning at the organization's boundaries (Lyles & Salk, 1996). Each virtual work stream, led by a self-organized country and including local members from Vodafone and Ericsson, leveraged resources and interacted horizontally with other teams in their base companies, and in the broader joint MNC communities, as necessary. This reinforced a common identity among network partners (Dhanaraj & Parkhe, 2006). The GSCM forum also served as a socialization platform that encouraged the accrual of social capital (Ahuja, 2000).

Vodafone's effort in distributing value equitably in *appropriating knowledge* involved the signing of a group NDA. This was to facilitate the open

Table 4. Summary of Network Orchestration Process.

Governance Mechanism	Mobilizing Knowledge	Appropriating Knowledge	Fostering Network Stability
GSCM	Exchange of commercial knowledge and socialization for a common understanding (Pre-supplier and Vodafone meetings were held in advance of the GSCM meetings)	Trust formation through social interaction between the members of the second author's global team and operating companies, in particular, those having direct representation of the Global Supply Chain Council	Convincing members of a benefit in maintaining links: the early-day operating company engagement was based on an acceptance to act in the community's best interests; Drawing the core global team from the engaged operating companies for collaborative decision-making and execution; Creating the opportunity for participating operating companies to be the host location for the GSCM meetings
Work streams, in particular Groupware	Leveraging of resources and horizontal interaction with other teams in base companies and the broader joint MNC communities	Informally motivating the participation of trusted skilled resources from either organization that was perceived by the engaged work stream participants to add capability to work stream endeavors	Convincing local and global members of the economic benefits arising from the collaboration; The resource quantum of the quorums was flexible as to the dynamics of the leadership
eRelationship platform	Exchange of commercial, technical and operational knowledge and socialization for a common understanding;	Encouraging open and unfiltered communication and access to information by either organization, departments or resources therein	Providing for clusters locally to establish workspaces to manage businesses locally such as to establish a common set of country-specific documentation

Table 4. (Continued)

Governance Mechanism	Mobilizing Knowledge	Appropriating Knowledge	Fostering Network Stability
	The bi-directional portal was intended as the embodiment of the business relationship between Vodafone and Ericsson that was visible to all in either organization with corporate intranet access to encourage convergence of practice		
Group Non-Disclosure Agreement	Providing for the release of information otherwise considered to be confidential	"Grandfathering" of prior agreement locally in mitigating matters to be agreed globally	Achieving transparency through openness, cooperation, and collaboration on matters such as optimizing processes, configuration diversity, and acceptance procedures
Equity-based grouping	Actively publishing the Vodafone Group cost synergy ambitions	Engagement of management teams of each entity with operating companies for bilateral discussions and information sharing	Establishing interdependencies among network members through regular engagement to stimulate and guide toward Vodafone Group cost synergy ambitions

Source: Ibbott (2001).

sharing of confidential commercial information, and to dispel the fear that the openness of partners in the network would not be taken advantage of (Teece, 2000). Although there was a deliberate choice to attain cost synergies, it was well recognized by the partners that the benefits would be asymmetric. There was no conventional agreement around the provision of visibility or the sharing of the cost reductions achieved. It was simply acknowledged that any tangible and/or intangible benefits arising from joint endeavors would be retained solely by the party in question. For instance, Vodafone's equity-based grouping required the engagement of management teams of each entity who had to buy-in to ideas to support the organizational transformation. By contrast, Ericsson's fully owned subsidiaries had less scope to resist the propositions. Voluntary cooperation was also encouraged through social interactions with partner firms and the use of trust and joint problem-solving that was championed by Vodafone. High levels of trust prevailed, in particular, among key Vodafone and Ericsson individuals, whose relationship dated back to 1983.

What is striking in the case is that *fostering network stability* was not a critical task of the network orchestrator (cf. Kenis & Knoke, 2002). The interdependencies established among network members, or local operating companies of Vodafone and Ericsson, through GCSM meetings and virtual work stream activities convinced members of a benefit in maintaining their links. Reciprocity enabled continuity. Vodafone was tasked with delivering a reliable efficient network to its customers, and Ericsson had to provide its key customers such as Vodafone with reliable, cost-effective and technologically advanced products and support. However, the formalization of the network was never set as an objective. The emergent network, composed of the Vodafone global and virtual management team, Lead operating companies (supplier clusters) including Ericsson, Nortel, Nokia and Siemens, and remaining Vodafone operating companies, was an informal one (see Fig. 1).

The network was self-governing to assure relevant inputs and inclusion in execution. The network orchestrator upheld the view that the emergent informal structure should remain non-hierarchical in operation. This was seen as contributing to the successful economic performance of the network. Although a formal governance structure (Supply Chain Management (SCM) Council, and IT and Technology Management (ITTM) Council) was subsequently introduced, this did not intervene with the informal functioning of the virtual organization.

The case reported here demonstrates an interactive process of creative evolution, that is, choice and change interacting to produce consequences

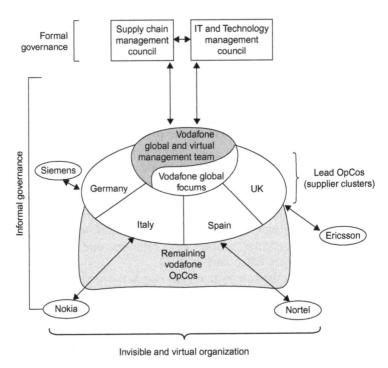

Fig. 1.   Governance Structure. *Source*: Ibbott (2007).

that influence organizational outcomes (the achievement of cost synergies) in an unexpected way (through the emergence of a network organization). It offers a process view that recognizes the importance of action, interaction, spontaneous change, and their unintended consequence. Although the intentional view offers insight into the reasons for Vodafone's search for an organizational means to achieve cost synergies, it is essentially limited in its ability to explain fully the emergence of a network organization to achieve such synergies. Throughout the transformation process, there was no predetermined underlying order that produced stable choice sets. Order emerged spontaneously as GSCM and work stream meetings were held. Therefore, we argue that the process of network orchestration must be understood as driven by choice sets taken while creatively coping with change rather than as primarily choice sets deliberately taken in the sequential pursuit of goals.

CONCLUSION

The IB literature is not foreign to the coordination tasks of managing a network of established foreign subsidiaries, and an analysis of the competitive advantages that arise from potential economies of scope (e.g., Ghoshal & Bartlett, 1990). An MNC's structure has been the most enduring idea of IB (Ghoshal & Nohria, 1993) up until the 1990s. Given the radical change in the way economic value is created, and empowered by the digital information technology, network organizations are taking a leading role in economic and social innovations (Birkinshaw & Hagström, 2000). Although the relevance of exploiting external resources (Teece, Pisano, & Shuen, 1997), and the ability to integrate efforts of different actors (Grant, 1996) have been acknowledged, the processes in orchestrating a network remain fairly unarticulated and projected as predetermined and intended. Drawing on organization theory, we shed light on the process of network orchestration consisting of mobilizing knowledge, appropriating knowledge, and fostering network stability. We emphasize action and process as opposed to position and structure. Structure alone does not create the benefit, but the entrepreneurial approach of a hub firm to turn the structure into a benefit is noteworthy. Unlike other studies that focus on the deliberate acts and intended consequences of central firms to exploit and manage the network (e.g., Ahuja, 2000), we consider the unintended consequence of an intentional action, thus recognizing the reality of in situ responses of network orchestrators themselves.

We suggest that cultivating an internalized agility involving on-going creative adaptation is crucial to dealing with the unintended consequences of action in a world of increased adversity. We emphasize that organizations encourage innovation from within a global virtual community, where appropriate, void of pre-emptive structure, and mandates save for alignment on the strategic ambition. Unintended but strategically consistent outcomes can be a bonus from wherever and whomever they emerge. A hierarchical position/role is not an exclusive domain within which effective outcomes may emerge. The case study also illustrates that endeavors into uncharted areas of the business do not necessarily require detailed planning, but instead allow leadership to orchestrate and guide the situational dynamics. It helps to consider acknowledging the doctrine of equivalence of the emergent participant contributions, being constrained only by a positive progression and momentum toward that espoused and agreed strategy.

The case reported here considers the interworking of two (Supplier–Customer) MNCs within a specific set of circumstances. This limits our ability to generalize some of our findings. However, our fundamental message applies across the board, that a dynamic analysis of networks, which recognizes the reality of change in inter-firm network relationships (e.g., Kenis & Knoke, 2002) and the role of emergent strategy and unintended consequences of strategic change (e.g., Balogun & Johnson, 2005; Boisot & McKelvey, 2010), is a more representative way of understanding the way in which today's MNCs coordinate and integrate globally dispersed capabilities. Future research can seek to explore network orchestration processes in differently sized organizations and sectors that are exposed to varying intensity of competition. This would help deepen understanding into the creative nature of network orchestration.

REFERENCES

Ahuja, G. (2000). Collaboration networks, structural holes and innovation: A longitudinal study. *Administrative Science Quarterly, 45*, 425–455.

Balogun, J., & Johnson, G. (2005). From intended strategies to unintended outcomes: The impact of change recipient sense-making. *Organization Studies, 26*, 1573–1601.

Bartlett, C., & Ghoshal, S. (1989). *Managing across borders: The transnational solution.* Boston, MA: Harvard Business School Press.

Birkinshaw, J., & Hagström, P. (2000). *The flexible firm: Capability management in network organizations.* Oxford: Oxford University Press.

Boisot, M., & McKelvey, B. (2010). Integrating modernist and postmodernist perspectives on organizations: A complexity science bridge. *Academy of Management Review, 35*, 415–433.

Brown, J. S., & Duguid, P. (2001). Knowledge and organization: A social-practice perspective. *Organization Science, 12*, 198–213.

Buckley, P. J., & Casson, M. (1976). *The future of the multinational enterprise.* London: The Macmillan Press.

Burton, M. D., Sørenson, J. B., & Beckman, C. M. (2002). Coming from good stock: Career histories and new venture formation. *Research in the Sociology of Organizations, 19*, 229–262.

Chia, R., & Holt, R. (2009). *Strategy without design: The efficacy of indirect action.* Cambridge, UK: Cambridge University Press.

Child, J. (1972). Organization structure, environment, and performance: The role of strategic choice. *Sociology, 6*, 1–22.

Demil, B., & Lecocq, X. (2006). Neither market nor hierarchy nor network: The emergence of bazaar governance. *Organization Studies, 27*, 1447–1466.

Dhanaraj, C., & Parkhe, A. (2006). Orchestrating innovation networks. *Academy of Management Review, 31*, 659–669.

Dyer, J. H., & Nobeoka, K. (2000). Creating and managing a high-performance knowledge sharing network: The Toyota case. *Strategic Management Journal, 21*, 345–368.

Dyer, J. H., & Singh, H. (1998). The relational view: Cooperative strategy and sources of inter-organizational competitive advantage. *Academy of Management Review, 23*, 660–679.

Ernst, D., & Kim, L. (2002). Global product networks, knowledge diffusion, and local capability formation. *Research Policy, 31*, 1417–1429.

Fulk, J. (2001). Global network organizations: Emergence and future prospects. *Human Relations, 54*, 91–99.

Ghoshal, S., & Bartlett, C. A. (1990). The multinational corporation as an interorganizational network. *Academy of Management Review, 15*, 603–625.

Ghoshal, S., & Nohria, N. (1989). Internal differentiation within multinational corporations. *Strategic Management Journal, 10*, 323–337.

Ghoshal, S., & Nohria, N. (1993). Horses for courses: Organizational forms for multinational corporations. *Sloan Management Review, 34*(Winter), 23–35.

Grant, R. M. (1996). Towards a knowledge-based theory of the firm. *Strategic Management Journal, 17*(Winter Special Issue), 109–122.

Gulati, R. (1999). Network location and learning: The influences of network resources and firm capabilities on alliance formation. *Strategic Management Journal, 20*, 397–420.

Gulati, R., Nohria, N., & Zaheer, A. (2000). Strategic networks. *Strategic Management Journal, 21*, 203–215.

Hacki, R., & Lighton, J. (2001). The future of the networked company. *McKinsey Quarterly, 3*, 26–39.

Hedlund, G. (1994). A model of knowledge management and the N-form corporation. *Strategic Management Journal, 15*, 73–90.

Hinterhuber, A. (2002). Value chain orchestration in action and the case of the global agrochemical industry. *Long Range Planning, 35*, 615–635.

Hite, J. M., & Hesterly, W. S. (2001). The evolution of firm networks: From emergence to early growth of the firm. *Strategic Management Journal, 22*, 275–286.

Ibbott, C. J. (2001). *An IS-enabled model for the transformation and globalization of interorganizational and inter-company relationships.* Unpublished DBA thesis, Brunel University.

Ibbott, C. J. (2007). *Global networks: The Vodafone–Ericsson journey to globalization and the inception of a requisite organization.* Hampshire: Palgrave MacMillan.

Ibbott, C. J., & O'Keefe, R. (2004). Transforming the Vodafone/Ericsson relationship. *Long Range Planning, 37*, 219–237.

Inkpen, A. C., & Tsang, E. W. K. (2005). Social capital, networks, and knowledge transfer. *Academy of Management Review, 30*, 146–165.

Jarillo, C. (1988). On strategic networks. *Strategic Management Journal, 9*, 31–41.

Jones, C., Hesterly, W. S., & Borgatti, S. P. (1997). A general theory of network governance: Exchange conditions and social mechanisms. *Academy of Management Review, 22*, 911–945.

Kenis, P., & Knoke, D. (2002). How organizational field networks shape interorganizational tie-formation rates. *Academy of Management Review, 27*, 275–293.

Kim, W. C., & Mauborgne, R. A. (1991). Implementing global strategies: The role of procedural justice. *Strategic Management Journal, 12*, 125–143.

Knoke, D. (1994). Networks of elite structure and decision making. In S. Wasserman & J. Galaskiewicz (Eds.), *Advances in social network analysis* (pp. 274–294). Thousand Oaks, CA: Sage.

Kogut, B. (2000). The network as knowledge: Generative rules and the emergence of structure. *Strategic Management Journal, 21*, 405–425.

Kogut, B., & Zander, U. (1992). Knowledge of the firm, combinative capabilities, and the replication of technology. *Organization Science, 3*, 383–397.

Kogut, B., & Zander, U. (1996). What do firms do? Coordination, identity, and learning. *Organization Science, 7*, 502–518.

Lorenzoni, G., & Baden-Fuller, C. (1995). Creating a strategic centre to manage a web of partners. *California Management Review, 37*, 146–163.

Lorenzoni, G., & Lipparini, A. (1999). The leveraging of inter firm relationships as a distinctive organizational capability: A longitudinal study. *Strategic Management Journal, 20*, 317–338.

Lyles, M. A., & Salk, J. E. (1996). Knowledge acquisition from foreign parents in international joint ventures: An empirical examination in the Hungarian context. *Journal of International Business Studies, 29*, 154–174.

MacKay, R. B., & Chia, R. (2013). Choice, chance, and unintended consequences in strategic change: A process understanding of the rise and fall of NorthCo Automative. *Academy of Management Review, 56*, 208–230.

Monge, P. R., & Fulk, J. (1999). Communication technology for global network organizations. In G. DeSanctis & J. Fulk (Eds.), *Shaping organizational form: Communication, connection, and community* (pp. 71–100). Newbury Park, CA: Sage.

Mowery, D. C., Oxley, J. E., & Silverman, B. S. (1996). Strategic alliances and interfirm knowledge transfer. *Strategic Management Journal, 17*(Winter Special Issue), 77–91.

Nohria, N., & Ghoshal, S. (1997). *The differentiated network: Organizing multinational corporations for value creation.* San Francisco, CA: Jossey-Bass Publishers.

Orton, J. D., & Weick, K. E. (1990). Loosely coupled systems: A reconceptualization. *Academy of Management Review, 15*, 203–223.

Parkhe, A., Wasserman, S., & Ralston, D. A. (2006). Introduction to special topic forum: New frontiers in network theory development. *Academy of Management Review, 31*, 560–568.

Pettigrew, A. (1987). Context and action in the transformation of the firm. *Journal of Management Studies, 24*, 649–670.

Powell, W. W. (1990). Neither market nor hierarchy: Network forms of organization. *Research in Organizational Behaviour, 12*, 295–336.

Powell, W. W., Douglas, R. W., Koput, K. W., & Owen-Smith, J. (2005). Network dynamics and field evolution: The growth of interorganizational collaboration in the life sciences. *American Journal of Sociology, 110*, 1132–1205.

Prahalad, C. K., & Doz, Y. L. (1981). An approach to strategic control in MNEs. *Sloan Management Review, 22*(Summer), 5–13.

Rowley, T., Behrens, D., & Krackhardt, D. (2000). Redundant governance structures: An analysis of structural and relational embeddedness in the steel and semiconductor industries. *Strategic Management Journal, 21*(Special Issue), 369–386.

Rugman, A. M., & D'Cruz, J. R. (2000). *Multinationals as flagship firms.* Oxford: Oxford University Press.

Sheppard, B. H., & Tuchinsky, M. (1996). Micro OB and the network organization. In R. M. Kramer & T. R. Tyler (Eds.), *Trust in organizations: Frontiers of theory and research* (pp. 166–195). Thousand Oaks, CA: Sage Publications.

Stuart, T. E. (2000). Interorganizational alliances and the performance of firms: A study of growth and innovation rates in a high-technology industry. *Strategic Management Journal, 21,* 791–811.

Teece, D. J. (1986). Profiting from technological innovation: Implications for integration, collaboration, licensing and public policy. *Research Policy, 15,* 285–305.

Teece, D. J. (2000). *Managing intellectual capital: Organizational, strategic, and policy dimensions.* Oxford: Oxford University Press.

Teece, D. J., Pisano, G., & Shuen, A. (1997). Dynamic capabilities and strategic management. *Strategic Management Journal, 18,* 509–533.

Uzzi, B. (1997). Social structure and competition in interfirm networks: The paradox of embeddedness. *Administrative Science Quarterly, 42,* 35–67.

Whittington, R. (1988). Environmental structure and theories of strategic choice. *Journal of Management Studies, 25,* 521–536.

Zander, I. (1999). How do you mean "global"? An empirical investigation of innovation networks in the MNC. *Research Policy, 28,* 195–213.

RE-THINKING A MNC: THE ROLE OF COGNITIVE INTERVENTIONS IN ORGANIZATIONAL DESIGN

Elizabeth Maitland and André Sammartino

ABSTRACT

Using a managerial cognition lens, we investigate the organizational design issues facing multinational corporation (MNC) managers. We apply concepts hitherto untested in the international management (IM) literature to a longitudinal study of reconfiguration efforts within a large, Asian MNC. We focus on how organizational design outcomes can be affected through mental interventions that provoke changes in senior executives' mental representations of what the MNC is and can be to achieve a strategic redirection and redesign. We draw on extensive interview and other qualitative data. Our study contributes to the literatures on MNC design and to our understanding of the important, but largely neglected, micro-foundational role of cognition in IM. This field research on executive judgment and decision-making in real time offers unique insights into the dynamics of MNC design.

Keywords: Managerial cognition; MNC design; strategic leadership

Orchestration of the Global Network Organization
Advances in International Management, Volume 27, 149–190
Copyright © 2014 by Emerald Group Publishing Limited
All rights of reproduction in any form reserved
ISSN: 1571-5027/doi:10.1108/S1571-502720140000027014

INTRODUCTION

The multinational corporation (MNC) is a nexus of decisions. Its architecture and strategy reflect repeated judgments and actions by senior managers, acting on what they believe are the opportunities, risks and best designs for its activities and assets. Yet, optimal MNC designs and superior strategic opportunities apparent with hindsight may be far from evident, if not totally obscured, to boundedly rational individuals assailed by complex and noisy information sets. Little is known about how managers engage in the critical cognitive tasks of strategic opportunity identification and MNC design, despite increasing calls for managerial cognition to be integrated into theoretical models and studies of the MNC (Devinney, 2011; Hutzschenreuter, Pedersen, & Volberda, 2007).

This neglect of explicit theorizing on cognition in international management (IM) contrasts the growing interest in managerial cognition and decision-making in the broader fields of organization science and strategy (Kaplan, 2011; Powell, Lovallo, & Fox, 2011).[1] The emerging school of behavioural strategy emphazises the importance of understanding the exercise of executive judgment and the psychological architecture of the firm to understanding heterogeneity in strategic decision choices and firm performance (Gavetti, 2011, 2012; Powell et al., 2011). A central tenet of this approach is that individuals engaged in *making sense* of an environment and determining a decision or set of decisions first develop a mental sketch of what they believe are the situation's salient characteristics (Gavetti, Levinthal, & Rivkin, 2005). These mental representations enable individuals to filter noisy and often ambiguous information to then determine strategic choices. Identifying a strategic opportunity and redesigning the MNC to pursue it is one such set of processes.

Recently, Gavetti (2011, 2012) proposed that the role of strategic leaders in complex organizations is to not only build their own representations of superior strategic opportunities but also to manage others to adopt these representations. To achieve this, he argues leaders need to engage in so-called *mental or cognitive interventions* that disrupt existing representations and provoke others to see — and commit to — these superior opportunities. However, Gavetti's (2011, 2012) theoretical work does not discuss the actual design, nature or possible deviations of these interventions, leading him to conclude: '[if] strategic leaders were to focus their limited attention on managing their own and others' mental processes, what are the nature and boundaries of the "mental interventions" that would most benefit their firms' performance?' (Gavetti, 2012, p. 268).

Building on Gavetti's (2012) theoretical propositions, we consider the potential design of mental interventions in a MNC looking to reconfigure its geographic and activity footprint. We argue designing effective interventions to prompt individuals to embrace a cognitively distant opportunity is a challenging task. It lies at the heart of MNC design and the multiple tensions involved in reaping the benefits of globalization, different locations and existing commitments to home markets, cultures and mindsets. Our overarching research question asks how can a MNC leader provoke changes in executives' mental representations of *what* the MNC *is* and *can be* to achieve its strategic redirection and redesign.

We report the findings of a longitudinal field study conducted within a large, Asian multinational bank, as it sought to become a regional financial leader by 2015. We draw on data from: two rounds of interviews, separated by a year (i.e. mid-2012 and mid-2013), with 20 of the bank's most senior decision-makers, including the entire executive management team; extensive discussions with the corporate strategy unit; internal planning documents; and external communications and media reporting. As the strategic change was motivated by the Chief Executive Officer (CEO) pursuing a new strategy, rather than a response to an external threat, our analysis of the type and impact of mental interventions on the executives' representations was free of confounding external drivers of change. The new strategic agenda was also cognitively distant from the bank's existing geographic and product configuration and rested on significant organizational redesign. Although the bank had a significant international network of operations, the scale of the home country businesses and the bank's strong home country identity dominated the thinking and attention of the senior executive ranks.

Our interviews allow us to track the impact of two distinct sets of mental interventions by the CEO, and the emerging redesign of the bank and its strategic agenda. We find a central role for cognition and for the nature of mental interventions used to initiate change in understanding the dynamics of MNC redesign. The case also enables us to explore MNC design and leadership in an industry − finance − undergoing very significant external shocks and changes to the competitive landscape. These changes encompass: ongoing, cross-border regulatory tightening and prudential supervision in the wake of the Global Financial Crisis (GFC) and the collapse or near collapse of established, large-scale multinational banks; shifts in the identification of strategic opportunities under the impact of ongoing technological change; and revisions to the notion and role of *leaders*, given widespread perceptions' of the industry's excessive risk-taking, bonus-driven culture.

We conclude with directions for future research. The MNC and IM decision-making are rich environments in which to explore the cognition of senior decision-makers, and IM has much to offer in this domain. Equally, work in behavioural strategy and managerial cognition provides valuable insights into the potential micro-foundations of IM and its impact on MNC design decisions and implementation.

MNC DESIGN

For many years, the foundation and scaffolding of MNC design have been to *think global, act local*; a mantra in which scale, learning and local sensitivity are cast as the bedrocks of the MNC. Managers have been exhorted to reap scale advantages by consolidating activities in low cost, high skill locations, and to integrate their networks of operations to promote knowledge accumulation and unique product development (Ghemawat, 2007; Ghoshal & Bartlett, 1990; Prahalad & Doz, 1987). Yet, while the MNC's overall design was once central to the IM oeuvre, over recent years there has been a tendency to theorize and investigate individual design elements, such as entry mode choice, outsourcing, subsidiary mandates and HRM, in isolation.[2] All too often, the broader strategic interplay between and around these elements has been obscured, diverting attention from the challenge of juggling the MNC into a suite of cohesive design elements pursuing a coherent corporate strategy.

Recently, we proposed a three-dimensional framework for examining the trade-offs of MNC faces when reconfiguring its geographic footprint of assets and activities (Maitland & Sammartino, 2012). Building on Ghemawat and del Sol's (1998) concepts of firm- and use-specificity, we added *location*, as a critical element of the strategic flexibility confronting the MNC. We argued reconfiguration choices are contingent on, and often constrained by, the specificity of assets to their current use, physical location and/or the extent to which they have been tailored to the needs of MNC itself. This is the classic *strategic commitment dilemma*, whereby firms must trade-off the benefits of constructing unique suites of resources and capabilities against the constraints of strategic rigidities, in the face of environmental and competitive dynamism (Leonard-Barton, 1992).

Applying the framework to illustrative MNC footprint reconfigurations, we highlighted these decisions as complex and involving levels of uncertainty that rely on the exercise of executive judgment (Maitland & Sammartino, 2012). To design a configuration for the MNC's activities and assets that best positions it to, for example, reap scale advantages, without neglecting localization concerns, managers must be able to first identify these constraints and opportunities, and then determine a design that *fits*. Such findings fit with the broader bodies of research in behavioural strategy and managerial cognition, which emphasize that interpretive tasks and strategic problem framing depend on the cognitive actions of senior decision-makers (Gavetti & Levinthal, 2000; Gavetti & Rivkin, 2007; Kaplan, 2011; Kiesler & Sproull, 1982; Porac & Thomas, 1990; Porac, Thomas, & Baden-Fuller, 1989).

Cognitive elements have implicitly informed IM theories, from the core assumption of bounded rationality through to assessments of psychic distance as a key differentiator of entry and mode choice dynamics (Hennart, 1991; Johanson & Vahlne, 1977; Kogut & Singh, 1988). However, the relationships between cognition and design decisions are poorly understood (Devinney, 2011; Hutzschenreuter et al., 2007). Similarly, early interest in how the MNC's *dominant logic*, or collective managerial mindset towards global-local pressures, informed the subsidiary network's design has faded (Murtha, Lenway, & Bagozzi, 1998; Prahalad & Bettis, 1986; Rhinesmith, 1992).

We argue that modelling the cognitive processes preceding the observable decisions typically studied in IM is vital to understanding why MNCs adopt different designs and identifying the resulting performance effects. In particular, how managers interpret the myriad environmental forces at play, and integrate these interpretations into design decisions, are central to descriptive and prescriptive research on MNCs. Drawing on the early understandings of the dominant logic literature, we argue that MNC design also involves: (1) the insights of more than one senior strategist, given the diversity of the business *landscapes* confronting a MNC (e.g. business models, customer requirements, scale and scope possibilities, government requirements, technological shifts); and (2) considerable internal convergence on the nature of the fit between the *internal* (what the MNC can do) and *external* (the possibilities landscape). In the following section, we set out the conceptual framework for investigating MNC design from a cognitive perspective.

COGNITION AND MNC DESIGN

MNCs are rich laboratories for studying strategic decision-making in context. Operating across multiple markets, cultures and institutional frameworks, MNC senior managers must make sense of a wide variety of forces, particularly compared to solely domestic firms. Each manager engages in separate and distinct cognitive processes, exercising judgment as to possible issues, options and solutions, yet also interacts with other decision-makers, their specific strategic responsibilities and the organizational routines of the MNC. The negotiated outcomes of their decisions then inform the MNC's collective design and behaviour.

Understanding how individual cognition scales to collective behaviour and how judgement is exercised in such complex organizations are key problems studied by the emerging behavioural strategy school (Powell et al., 2011, p. 1380). Since Simon, March and Cyert's seminal work on bounded rationality as a foundational concept for understanding firm behaviour (Cyert & March, 1963; March & Simon, 1958; Simon, 1947), individual cognition has shifted ever closer to the centre of strategic management theorizing and analysis (Daft & Weick, 1984; Felin, Foss, Heimeriks, & Madsen, 2012; Gavetti, 2012; Gavetti, Greve, Levinthal, & Ocasio, 2012; Kaplan, 2011; Powell et al., 2011; Winter, 2012). Behavioural strategy models of decision-making argue that as an individual attempts to make sense of an environment or problem space, they develop a sketch in their mind's eye of what they believe are a situation's salient characteristics (Gavetti et al., 2005). These mental representations then enable them to filter noise and navigate towards a strategic choice or problem solution by exercising judgment, based on their mental models of stored knowledge acquired through learning and experience (Eisenhardt & Sull, 2001; Gigerenzer, 2008).

Since superior strategic opportunities tend to be difficult to see — otherwise, others would readily imitate and adopt the same positions — Gavetti (2011, 2012) argues successful strategic leaders are those who can perceive such *cognitively distant* opportunities (based on their mental models) and, critically, *persuade* those within the organization and its stakeholders to commit to this mental leap. Gavetti contends that this commitment comes from leaders using mental interventions that disrupt existing representations of the organization and its opportunity landscape, and provoke others to build new representations that enable them to *see* these distant opportunities. He, thus, argues such interventions have the capacity to positively alter firm performance, through guiding more successful strategic decisions.

Gavetti (2012, p. 269) identifies three focal behavioural failures that must be overcome for strategists to seize upon cognitively distant opportunities. It is a term deliberately evocative of the recognized role of market failures, in that both types of failure allow firms to sustain competitive advantages over rivals. The three behavioural failures emanate from shortcomings or tendencies with regards to (1) rationality – 'the ability to identify opportunities', (2) plasticity – 'the ability to act on opportunities' and (3) shaping ability – 'the ability to legitimise opportunities and therefore "shape" or "construct" the opportunity space' (Gavetti, 2012, p. 269). The role of the leader (and/or leadership group) is to intervene and address these failures. Theoretically, interventions must thus attend to (1) short-sightedness – favouring the near, known and familiar; (2) 'cognitive or identity-based inertia' (Gavetti, 2012, p. 273) – current mental representations of what is possible and acceptable; and (3) preconceptions within the firm and external stakeholders about how the industry works. However, much of the work thus far on such interventions has been theoretical propositions or anecdotal illustrations, rather than in-depth investigation.

Building on Gavetti's (2011, 2012) theoretical, we investigate the mental interventions within a MNC looking to reconfigure its geographic and activity footprint. Our central premise is that a MNC leader faces a number of tasks in redesigning the organization to seize cognitively distant opportunities. First, they must disrupt existing frames to prompt discovery of distant opportunities (given the scope of possible changes and opportunities implicated in the redesign, a MNC cannot rely just on the strategic leader to see all possible opportunities). Second, they must coalesce the executive group around a coherent redesign that can be implemented, a process requiring ongoing management of politics, over-commitments to the existing footprint and vested interests. Third, they must also commence investments or simultaneously manage changes in key support platforms on which the ultimate design will be built. For a MNC, this includes investments in human capital (particularly with respect to mobility within the internal labour market across national and product boundaries), relations with existing and potential host governments (in the financial services sector this particularly includes central banks and monetary authorities) and technology.

In the following section, we set out our research design and method for capturing the dynamic process within a MNC of introducing mental interventions to disrupt existing executive representations and responses to these interventions.

RESEARCH METHOD AND DESIGN

Studies on managerial cognition employ a diverse range of research methods (see Devinney, 2013; Powell et al., 2011; Walsh, 1995). To investigate the role of cognition and strategic leadership in MNC reconfiguration design processes, we chose a case study method. It enabled us to study a dynamic process in context: a series of cognitive interventions by a strategic leader and their impact over time on key executives' mindsets and the MNC's design. While a simulation exercise with a senior leadership group would have enabled direct observations of responses to hypothesized interventions, such an approach relies on stylized abstractions, and cannot capture the rich interplay within high level executive groups, the context and their impact on mindsets and reconfiguration decisions over time (Detert, Treviño, & Sweitzer, 2008). The loss of vividness and rich detail is compounded by the difficulties of designing hypothetical events that are unambiguous and persuasive (March, Sproull, & Tamuz, 1991).

Case Selection

Our case selection was based on intentional sampling to address three key considerations (Eisenhardt & Graebner, 2007). First, the MNC was actively engaged in a strategic redesign, enabling us to study real-time processes in context. Second, the redesign was in response to the CEO seeking to pursue a new strategic objective, rather than an externally generated crisis forcing a redirection on the MNC. This implied the senior executives' mental representations of the MNC were not being heavily influenced by external considerations or drivers of change. Finally, the MNC had a sizeable international network of operations, for which there were numerous reconfiguration options and opportunities.

Our selected MNC is a large, Asian headquartered multinational bank, which we label with the pseudonym AsiBank.[3] The bank was seeking to pursue a regional financial leadership strategy that was a significant shift from its previous focus on home country objectives, supported by a strong, national identity. This very exposure to the home country had prompted AsiBank's Board of Directors to push the CEO to consider a new strategic orientation, as it was felt the home economy's long-term economic growth would eventually slow, at the same time as the bank potentially reaching saturation in its key markets. This strategic shift built on an existing 14 country footprint, encompassing sizable, but largely independent, subsidiaries throughout Southeast Asia and the Subcontinent, and offices in the world's leading financial centres in Europe, North America, Asia and the Middle East. The activity footprint covered the full range of financial services from classic retail banking, through commercial banking, asset and high net wealth management, investment banking, stock broking, insurance (general, life and commercial) and Islamic finance (retail, commercial and wholesale banking, and insurance), delivered outside the home country through over 300 wholly owned branches, as well as representative offices.

Data Collection

In late November 2011, we secured the organizational agreement of AsiBank's CEO and Board Chair to participate in the project. This agreement encompassed: interviews with all members of the Executive Committee (a formal grouping in the bank's corporate structure known as ExCo, comprising the divisional and Group function heads (HR, risk, legal, finance, IT and strategy)), the strategy heads of each division, and the Chief Marketing Officer (an *ex officio* ExCo member) and access to internal company documents. While the CEO's *sponsorship* was critical to securing the respondents' participation, the project was clearly delineated as independent research, with results made available to each participant outside the formal reports we prepared for the CEO and ExCo.

Over an 18-month period, we collected data from multiple primary and secondary sources. During a February 2012 headquarters site visit, we: met with the bank's corporate strategy and transformation group; were given access to confidential internal corporate planning and operational documents; and engaged in extensive background interviews and data collection. Individual interviews with the 20 senior executives were then conducted at two points in time: March–April 2012 and March–April 2013. The average interview was just over 110 minutes (the longest was over three hours). Each was digitally recorded and professionally transcribed.[4] The interviews explored the executives' views on AsiBank's regional redesign, including their: (1) conceptualization of the *region* in geographic and product market terms; (2) projection of the bank's 2015 and 2020 footprints; (3) explanations of the motivations for the regional ambitions; (4) assessment of existing and possible future sources of competitive advantage and (5) identification and evaluation of the scope to reconfigure key assets and activities. A representative sample of questions from both interview rounds is included in the Appendix.

Data Analysis

As self-reported information can be subject to problems, such as recollection biases (Bettman & Weitz, 1983; Huber & Power, 1985), we sought to confirm the internal and construct validity of the data through triangulation with additional data sources (Eisenhardt, 1989; Yin, 1994). For example, we compared timelines of key events identified by respondents with internal corporate documents to confirm the accuracy of both the timing of decisions and recollections of discussions. We developed cognitive maps for each individual, particularly checking for internal consistency within and between the two interview rounds (Axelrod, 1976; Eisenhardt & Graebner, 2007). The semi-structured interviews also used a mix of direct and indirect questions, as suggested by qualitative research methodologies to enhance theoretical insights and mitigate bias (Eisenhardt, 1989; Yin, 1994). To enhance the data collection's reliability, both authors were present at most interviews, each making concurrent notes, as well as extensive, independent notes at the end of each day (Kaplan, 2008).

From the first round interview data and internal corporate documents, we identified and classified the initial set of cognitive interventions, based on Gavetti (2012). Our interview data analysis then focused on the categorization of text, comparison of these categories and their organization within broader concepts. In the first analysis stage, we undertook a process of construct coding by reading through the data and coding text for issues and themes. To increase coding validity, we engaged in an ongoing discussion of concepts, definitions, and compared coding of common passages and documents (Van de Ven & Poole, 2002). This initial coding identified a series of coding concepts grouped into: the *perceived* corporate culture and mindset before the transformation project and before the external reorientation (e.g. 'complacent', 'resistance', 'politics', 'internally focused'); the cognitive interventions ('regional projects', 'financial target', 'centres of excellence', 'the Group'); the respondent's own mindset and emotions ('excited', 'concerned', 'frustrated'); definitions of the 'region' and 'leadership' ('Greater Asia', 'Southeast Asia', 'Greater China'); sources of competitive advantage *outside* the home country ('relationships with home country firms', 'client relationship management', 'knowledge of host country'); their assessment of reconfiguration options ('centralization', 'customer-touching', 'delivery platform', 'sequencing'); potential competitive responses ('nimble', 'premium segment'); ExCo dynamics ('operational', 'overwhelmed', 'tactical'); and responses to the interventions ('execution', 'where/what can we be', 'what can we do', 'loss of focus'). We repeated this process for the second set of interviews.

THE CASE

Having emerged as a closely government-linked national champion, AsiBank had pursued an aggressive strategy of domestic and foreign acquisitions throughout the 1990s and into the mid-2000s. A number of years of poor performance and perceived strategic mis-steps, however, led to a new (the incumbent) CEO being appointed to transform the bank and regain its dominant home market position. The early years of his tenure involved a large-scale, internally focused transformation project to address productivity problems and a deteriorating performance in the bank's core home country retail and commercial banking markets. Productivity shifts were pursued through: (1) an overhaul of the bank's IT platform; and (2) the introduction of performance-based individual to divisional-level incentives and metrics to disrupt an internal culture of life-time employment expectations. The metrics were explicitly referred to as the *dashboard*, an analogy to a car's on-road functioning thought to perfectly encapsulate their continuous performance management role.

By 2010, the transformation programme was generating visible successes, including a 375% increase in profit before tax (partially due to extraordinary write-downs in preceding years). Having restored stakeholder confidence in AsiBank, these achievements provided the platform for an external reorientation of the bank's strategic focus. Initially prompted by the Board of Directors, the strategic shift sought to redesign the bank's activities and assets in terms of their geographic, competitive and structural configuration to achieve a position of regional financial leadership by 2015.

However, it was contingent on several factors. The existing geographic and product footprint, while significant, was dominated by the scale of the home country operations and a strong, home country, national identity. The value chains for most products were highly independent, from a country and division perspective. The footprint's international scope was widely believed to have emerged from a haphazard, often poorly executed, series of international strategies.

Unsurprisingly, home country activities dominated not only AsiBank's balance sheet but also the senior executive group's attention (see Findings below). The transformation programme, while successful, also meant that for over four years the senior executive team's attention was not only home country focused, but was inward-looking, pursuing cost-cutting programs and productivity gains, rather than on developing new opportunities in the external business landscape.

We argue these four factors − (1) the existing design of AsiBank's value chain activities and assets, (2) its strong home country identity and scale, (3) its poor international growth history and (4) the overwhelming focus on the bank's inner functionings − collectively meant achieving the redesign and strategic redirection of AsiBank's activities required significant shifts in the mental representations of internal and external stakeholders. At the most senior executive ranks, we further argue that individuals' representations of what AsiBank *was* and *could be* were crucial to identifying the possible future configurations of activities and assets, and for binding the executives' political and reputational capital to achieving the regional financial leadership goal.

In addition to the four key legacy considerations and the standard MNC challenges of local responsiveness, integration and arbitrage (Ghemawat, 2007), AsiBank also needed to navigate longer-term structural issues. First, rapid product and process innovations based on information technology (IT) are rapidly changing distribution platforms (e.g. mobile banking) and threatening to dis-intermediate banking value chains, particularly through the threatened entry of powerful new players, such as Apple and Google, into the payments system. At the same time, established financial service providers are being subject to heightened levels of cross-border regulatory and prudential oversight that are raising the costs of providing capital to all but the most secure of borrowers (i.e. sovereign debt). This heightened scrutiny is a direct response to the GFC and the systemic risk problems from the collapse and near collapse of several very large and high-profile financial service providers. It has also been accompanied by broader calls for changes to the finance industry's perceived culture of excessive risk-taking and bonuses. For bank CEOs, this entails an added layer of complexity: profitability has to be achieved, while simultaneously juggling stakeholder demands for more ethical behaviour, longer-term rewards for employees, and tighter lending standards and trading practices that can be costly and distracting to implement.

Within its region, AsiBank also needed to determine how it would respond to: (1) the formalization of regional institutions to support trade and investment flows, particularly in Southeast Asia; and (2) China's growing dominance in East Asia and the world economy. With respect to the latter, China's rapid economic growth and sheer population size are counter-balanced by tight networks of government−bureaucracy−state−private business relations that represent significant barriers to entry and constraints on competition (Sheng, Zhou, & Li, 2011). By contrast, rapidly growing intra-regional trade and investment flows in Southeast Asia are increasingly supported by formal treaties and agreements, particularly centred around the formal grouping of ASEAN (Association of Southeast Asian Nations), and a large and increasingly highly educated population of over 600 million. ASEAN's attractiveness is tempered, however, by fears of systemic risk, given the commonality in economic structures across the region and the potential for a repeat of the 1997 Asian Financial crisis (World Bank, 2010).

These longer-term structural and legacy factors presented considerable challenges for the design of AsiaBank. Key considerations included: the scope of financial services offered to each market; the ability to centralize and/or standardize activities; the delivery mode (particularly physical vs. digital platforms); and market positioning relative to the global players (such as HSBC, Standard & Chartered and Citibank, who were potentially distracted by economic and regulatory issues in their core North American and European markets); local incumbents and potential new entrants. The following section sets out our findings with regard to the mental interventions implemented by the CEO and the responses of and within the executive group.

FINDINGS AND DISCUSSION

The CEO's Redesign Challenge

To address the pressures for strategic change from AsiBank's Board of Directors, the CEO required the input and support of the senior executives to map out the opportunity landscape – identifying avenues for growth within and across the bank's many lines of business and locations. He needed to draw the ExCo, and their strategy reports, together on a common vision that could be translated into a fully conceived and coherent strategy for AsiBank's regional footprint and competitive position. To do so, the CEO had to disrupt these decision-makers' existing representations of the bank, its markets and its competitive advantages. Two distinct objectives required balancing: (1) building the richest possible representations to identify cognitively distant opportunities; and (2) reaching sufficient convergence in individuals' representations to enable collective decision-making. Put differently, the CEO needed to manage the degree of dissension, such that there was healthy diversity and disagreement, without divisive politics, resource ring-fencing and business silo-isation.

The CEO outlined his challenge, and the inherent redesign aspects, as:

> you look at ASEAN and the promise of 650 million people. How we stitch together that, how we figure out what will be the regional platform for which set of customers, and then really executing on that − it's going to be a large challenge and probably one of our most profitable ones ... if we get it right.

He saw key strategic opportunities, which could be considered distant from the everyday, incremental expansion of the bank, in:

(1) online and mobile banking platforms
(2) digital payments
(3) Islamic finance, particularly in providing investment opportunities for the very large pools of capital in Southeast Asia and the Middle East seeking Islamic structured products and
(4) harnessing the spill-over from Asian regional economic growth to ensure the domestic retail franchise was secure.

To the CEO, it was evident that bank's home country activities could not be neglected in the pursuit of the regional strategy. These were the core, revenue generating markets that would support the regional redesign:

> I think in the first instance I realised that nobody can claim to be a real champion if you don't have a solid domestic base. So there was a time when our domestic leadership was challenged. And as a matter of priority we put in place a number of initiatives to strengthen our domestic leadership. So that's actually important, because, without domestic leadership, there's no way you will have the cash flow to invest overseas. And there's no way that you will have the human capability, the skills to be able to export this to the other countries as well. Now, we have set a clear target in the sense that as much as we want to be a regional bank we do believe that our domestic contributions must not be below 50%. So meaning that we still, you know, have our roots within [home country]. And that's why we have targeted in terms of our overseas contribution to around 40% come 2015. Now, we are also realistic enough to know that given the fact that banking is a very capital intensive business, so there's no way that we can have beyond regional exploration. But I guess it's a matter of knowing your limitations and your capabilities rather than setting very lofty targets that you're not going to be able to achieve.

We track the interplay between the CEO's mental interventions and the shifting representations of his ExCo and their direct strategy reports across two data collection points, 12 months apart. We identify two waves of interventions, one initiated in the months preceding our first data collection round and a second in the months following our delivery of an initial study report, approximately midway between the two data collection points.[5] We label these as *disruption phases*: bundles of formal and informal design actions that we argue constitute attempts to disrupt the mental representations AsiBank's senior executives held of the bank and its opportunity landscape.

Bringing ExCo on Board

With the launch of the new regional strategy, each ExCo member was expected to identify regional project opportunities, with an emphasis on identifying cross-unit projects. Each had their own mental representation of the opportunities that could and should be pursued, and of the challenges the bank faced. These representations reflected, in part, the legacy effects of where the bank had come from, its poor internationalization history, the existing geographic and product footprint, and the executives' existing ideas for strategic opportunities. Among the individual executives their initial representations differed with regard to: geography (particularly the extent of the region); and with respect to product mix and design, the platforms through which such products should be delivered, and the likely *reach* of these products into different markets. These initial representations informed each executive's attitude to which strategic opportunities should be prioritized.

Key to the evolving process was the two disruption phases. Each phase included redesign actions (summarized in Table 1), which should be viewed as mechanisms to shift thinking, rather than just ends in themselves. Among the reconfigurations and redesigns were a major acquisition of a financial services provider, and the grouping of all risk management, credit management and compliance into a central parent unit (which then initiated Group policies and processes for all these functions). The first disruption phase employed predominantly structural or formal mechanisms — efforts to shift reporting lines and responsibilities, and establish projects and objectives. These might be viewed as more *headline* actions (worthy of public announcement). The second phase saw greater emphasis on more normative disruptions — attempts to engender different behaviours among the decision-making group in terms of interactions and attitudes. These were less likely to be visible to external parties.

Disruption Phase One

As Table 1 indicates, the first set of interventions commenced with the high-profile, mid-2010 launch of a new corporate structure, creating a series

Table 1. Cognitive Interventions and Design Changes.

	Formal	Norms-Based	Actual Reconfigurations
Pre-round 1 (mid-2010–2011)	New corporate structure – *International* as a horizontal arm running across all divisions (but not a formal unit)	ExCo required to identify potential regional projects	Major acquisition of financial services provider in key ASEAN country
	Key strategic objectives defined: – Regional financial leadership by 2015 – Regional Group pre-tax profit target by 2015	Corporate *talent show* competitions held across bank network, with winners presenting at a showcase evening (continuing annual event) with Board and ExCo present and clear regional aspiration taglines	Group risk unit – All risk management, credit management and compliance centralized into one parent unit
	Targeted regional projects initiated: – Cards – High net wealth management – Auto finance – Virtual banking Brand refresh to incorporate regional vision tagline		Heads of all major foreign subsidiaries elevated to ExCo Ongoing investments in IT platform
Post-round 1 (May 2012–March 2013)	Centres of excellence – Cards – High net wealth management	*Non-work* dinners at CEO's home, one-on-one	Regional cash management system
	Regional talent initiative	*Non-work* dinners with several ExCo members and CEO	Regional trade finance platform
	All subsidiaries (country and product) co-branded with corporate identity Redefined home country as 'home markets' – the home country plus two ASEAN countries with the largest subsidiary networks	ExCo workshops on team culture ExCo members required to speak about the regional agenda to employees attending training session, at least once per month	Group treasury risk management rolled out to largest subsidiary All risk-management policies and processes made Group-level for regional roll-out

Post-round 2 (May 2013–)

Multi-country, large-scale advertising campaign across all forms of media focused on regional ambitions	ExCo required to identify staff for an international/non-domestic rotation	Ongoing investments in IT platform to support regional products and regional delivery
	Board meetings held in offshore locations to emphasize regional importance	Established Greenfield entries in two ASEAN countries, locally incorporated and expanded in a third, expanded China network
	More junior-level managers encourage to present to ExCo on regional initiatives	Re-launched India office to facilitate India–ASEAN trade and transactions business
		Spun-off over-lapping brokerage functions in a major subsidiary
		Head of International position created, at ExCo level
		Change in CEO

of core operating divisions, supported by enterprise systems, human capital and risk management. In visual representations, *International* was depicted running across the divisions, as a central responsibility and avenue for growth. This new structure was presented as the platform for a strategy of externally focused growth and constituted a highly visible disruption to the existing model of AsiBank as a nationally focused, market leader. Two new and clearly articulated strategic objectives were central: becoming a regional financial leader by 2015 and a clear expression of the 2015 revenue percentage to be derived from international operations. A significant redesign initiative was the formation of special project teams to build four banner *regional* products. Over the following 18 months, the operational focus continued to be on business unit driven productivity and performance improvements.

Responses to Disruption Phase One

Identification of Cognitively Distant Opportunities
As noted, the CEO had expressed concerns about the home country's slowing growth, and the countervailing appeal of the much larger regional market with the scope to build and leverage substantial economies of scales. Yet, only five of the other twenty respondents cited this as a key motivation for pursuing a regional agenda. These five respondents were aware that the pace of innovation in the payments space meant AsiBank's pool of cheap funds from its large, low cost domestic retail savings franchise was vulnerable to alternative savings vehicles (including growth of superannuation products, a shift to higher consumption lifestyles in line with the country's economic development and share-trading) and to new, non-financial services players, such as Google and Apple (see previous section) taking advantage of innovations in *electronic* wallets. For AsiBank to remain competitive in the pricing and design of its retail products, these challenges needed to be met with an ability to innovate product offerings quickly, while operating at a low cost of capital through achieving scale and scope advantages in the core IT architecture, costs of digital processing and warehousing, templates for product design and so forth.

These scale advantages were apparent to many of the executives, but only 6 (including the CEO) of the 21 respondents explicitly touched on their importance in maintaining a cost of capital position. These six respondents also showed the clearest appreciation of the nuances in distinguishing centralization from standardization of processes, policies and products, and the ability to flexibly design product *pipelines* and supporting activities thereby achieving significant scale and scope economies along up to 80–90% of the value chain. The final 10–20% could then be customized to local requirements and sensitivities, as shown in the second column of Table 2.

In this sense, the true use, firm and location flexibility of existing assets and the need for innovation in the physical footprint to ensure ongoing performance (see Maitland & Sammartino, 2012) were not widely appreciated. Each of the five respondents (other than the CEO), who did demonstrate such an awareness, was in a role working (and thinking) across divisional boundaries. This suggests that exposure to cross-functional and cross-divisional views on banking was potentially contributing to their ability to construct rich mental representations that overlaid product value chains with geographic footprint considerations. As one of these six respondents illustrated:

> Why we want to have [subsidiary country A] for deposits is because of Brunei money. Brunei, they have a lot of Islamic funds ... they can't put the money in [our subsidiary in] Brunei, because we don't have a licence for Islamic, it's conventional ... so the first thing we were thinking about is – let's have a quick win, let's have our Treasury out of [subsidiary country A], we put it [there], and I think we've got some traction and we've got close to achieve about 400 million dollars out, so that's a start for example. There's no risk, because for the two countries, it's backed against [country A's currency]. So, this allows our global markets team to talk that sort of conversation, to open up that door. So, this is where the regional dividend is – we need to look at this connectivity, we need to unleash this. (CEO, Islamic Banking)

Differences in Representations of what AsiBank should be

While most believed in adopting a regional strategy, there was considerable divergence in this early period on (1) what constituted the region, (2) the regionalization value proposition and (3) the extent of regional standardization that should be pursued.

One of the most compelling footprint issues was determining what constituted the *region* of AsiBank's leadership objectives. As Table 3 indicates, while the centrality of ASEAN was universally agreed, there were disparate views on whether additional countries, such as China and India, should be targeted. Most interviewees explicitly raised China as a hard to ignore market that they had very mixed feelings about. Engagement was seen as necessary, but the investment required, the regulatory hurdles, and the nature of competition were intimidating. The Middle East was also identified, specifically regarding Islamic banking.

This heterogeneity of geographic representations appears to stem from each executive focussing primarily on country-level issues and opportunities,

Table 2. Examples of Flexible-Specificity Frames.

	Flexible Thinking	Specificity Thinking
First round	'We cannot apply the same standard of credit that we do, say in Singapore, given for example if you lend to corporates, you get good financials, you know the auditors, you know the information access would be a lot more than say a corporate in Cambodia or something like that. So, we really have to customise or modularise how we do it in different markets'.	'There is no way that [Asibank] can compete effectively domestically in China'
	'Now this is where I talk about "regionally" on the retail front: the alchemy is there for us to standardise the regional technology platform so that we can have a standardised approach. It doesn't need to mean that customers have to be able to do a deposit in Indonesia, but we build a platform that we can roll out a standard functionality and a higher level functionality across the countries'.	'We can't possibly be crazy enough to want to compete in the retail banking sector in China'
	'I think the challenge for us will be to figure out how do you give perceived flexibility. So, the basic building blocks for product are not that different, I mean, a mortgage is a mortgage. Our challenge is to identify what these building blocks of any product are, even in the business, within the business, so we can standardise those components and then have other components which give the flexibility for them to market or make it look and feel and touch a bit different'.	'Profitability is tough: the rules of the game favour locals' 'China is the one. China is the elephant in the corner ... China is hard, hard, hard' 'If you take a look at China, even Hong Kong, you question whether you can ever build a retail franchise that is meaningful, because of the very high cost and extremely competitive nature of the business there' 'We're far from being at a critical mass, the right size to be a serious retail banker [in China] ... and I don't think this Bank has the appetite to put in billions and billions of dollars'
Second round	'we are still a country based/centric transformation programme, so why don't we have a transformation that looks across the Group and make sure that the levers that we want to put in place across a region are being monitored across the Group'.	'I think as far as the unified approach from a corporate level, it's there, but from a business level, as far as the products are concerned, and the services are concerned, it's still not there yet'
	'the market is moving very fast, so it's about the relative speed of change, of internal resources versus external speed of the change and how nimble and how agile. So if you ask me it's a case of versatility, adaptability'.	'On the flipside is instinctively when we think of new ideas regional is not our first thought. So when we ... a new customer service idea or anything, it's still not ingrained in the psyche, so we've still got ... we opportunistically do it, but we're not doing it across the board yet'

'I think one area we probably have done well on is IT. We have an IT transformation that cuts across the group. So to me, we should also have business area transformation that cuts across the Group ... sometimes it can be quite painful ... But if there is that periodic monitoring and review of key things that we need to do throughout the Group that is being anchored by ExCo, I think that can go far'.

'[what] AsiBank group need to do is to start building the pool of people who can be – who already have the regional experience and who already are geared up to take regional roles so that at the end of the day whenever we say we need somebody to come in here and help us, they have people to deploy'.

'But, of course, it is not going to be 100% the same for one country. You'll be like 80-20, like a car: 80% the same, but in Europe you drive left hand drive, but here right hand drive; and in a car there, you need a heater, here you need aircon. So the same thing applies'.

'when it comes to implementation, I think there is probably a danger of trying to standardise implementation throughout the Group and, hence, we may fall into the trap of moving too slowly, when we need to move faster. So, for that matter, how can we then expedite the development of that infrastructure in [host country] first? So, I think, on the one hand, yes, we want to standardise and we can have the best practices, etc., but I suppose there is a need to recognize that certain units have to move faster to capture the market, to improve infrastructure. And I think that is one area where a big improvement is required'.

Table 3.   Imagining AsiBank's Footprint in 2015 and 2020.

Footprint	By 2015 (%)	By 2020 (%)
ASEAN	100	100
… with key home markets	28	7
+ Greater China	39	20
+ Greater China and India	6	53
+ Middle East	33	47
+ Wider world	17	27

Notes: The table reports the frequency with which particular footprints were identified in our Round 1 interviews (i.e. the percentage of interviewees). As all mentioned ASEAN, the subsequent responses (in italics) indicate further specific detail. Those with '+' indicate mention of these locations. '+Greater China and India' is a distinct response from just '+Greater China'.

rather than building representations of region-wide strategic niches or gaps. This may reflect the legacy of the bank's poor internationalization history. The existing footprint was seen as the outcome of a disjointed series of decisions to expand into particular markets, without a coherent plan for how to grow within and across these markets:

> The success [at home] has become, I guess, a stumbling block, although maybe that is a mindset right, when it comes to looking at the region. With [the home country], the Group, the growth was great, leadership is positioned and all that kind of stuff, we want to go to [large ASEAN country], or maybe we tiptoe around it, we want to go to another market, tiptoe around. For example, we have had branches in Cambodia for such a long time, we've had a branch in China for such a long time, but almost at the same time when [major competitor] had a branch in China, you know, today [major competitor] has about 18 branches in China. We still have one. (Deputy CEO & Head of Global Wholesale).

> We have been such a dominant bank [at home] for such a long time, that we became very complacent outside of [the home country]. We had footprints that we did not leverage on. (Head of Strategy, Retail)

This historical indecision fuelled many of the respondents' concerns that there was no clear strategy or even parameters for the regional agenda, more than 18 months after the initial introduction of the broad leadership and revenue objectives. The regional aspiration was frustratingly viewed as a geographic footprint issue, detached from key questions of the strategy to create and capture value well into the future:

> We have strategic targets, but what is the strategy to get there? (Head of Strategy, Islamic)

we talk about it, but do not have a clear roadmap and we're not executing that road-map. So, you know, we don't have a plan of a plan. (Deputy Head, Group Strategy)

I have seen a lot of regional projects, I've seen lengthy presentations on the regional cards, on the regional wealth management ... I mean, all these projects I have seen. Regional strategy discussion? I cannot remember that I have seen that. (CEO, Insurance)

With differences amongst the decision-making group in terms of this basic geographic representation, and also different levels of awareness that such heterogeneity of representations even existed, it would remain difficult to conduct commonly understood conversations around more substantial strategic issues.

While the value proposition from regionalization painted a series of aspirational goals, there were not clear statements outlining why these goals and not others. For some, the *regional dividend* was obvious (and carried connotations of greater prestige). Others raised concerns about a lack of clarity causing difficulties in articulating the goals to those outside ExCo and their immediate direct reports and in initiating and guiding the necessary resource allocation choices.

For nearly all the respondents, the clearest divergence was between the domestic retail and the wholesale banking divisions in terms of their business models and willingness to embrace change. Relatively few recognized that this, in part, reflected the physical delivery modes of the different divisions. Retail was genuinely multi-locational, operating a large domestic network of branches, as well as providing input to the subsidiary network's retail operations. Wholesale had the luxury of already thinking about many of its products competing in regional and global markets, whereas retail was necessarily focused on less mobile customers (individuals, households, small–medium size businesses) requiring higher degrees of localization of product, communication, delivery mode and risk assessment. In a number of subsidiary countries, a reluctance to embrace mobile and virtual banking and ongoing tight supervision by local monetary authorities (including extended vetting processes for key staff, and in-country requirements on the physical location of data warehousing) also presented significant location constraints.

While the Head of Retail was fully supportive of the regional agenda and had a highly developed mental representation of the footprint possibilities, the other executives frequently ascribed his division's home country focus to an inward looking bias on his behalf.[6] This ascription overlooked that the Head of Retail's performance metrics mandated by the CEO explicitly required him to *prioritize* the home country and ensure all operational efficiencies were being pursued, including a major overhaul of the branch banking network's physical and IT design. As noted earlier, the domestic retail division's low cost of capital (from its large, low-interest bearing deposit base) position was essential to funding AsiBank's regional aspirations. In effect, the retail Head's personal enthusiasm for the regional strategy and desire to include his division in its realization was being held back by significant legacy factors from both the existing MNC design and his colleagues' mental representations.

Commonly Recognized Constraints
The executives often expressed awareness of the constraints on AsiBank's capacity to reach for regional opportunities emanating from its current design and its legacy of underwhelming internationalization. Intriguingly, one major concern reflected a delay in pushing disruptions further down in the organization. There was universal concern expressed about the ability of employees below the bank's top two to three layers to adjust their mental representations to accept an identity defined by the region, rather than the home country. At a practical level, this presented challenges in convincing staff to pursue offshore appointments or to prioritize non-local initiatives and demands. Reticence about expatriate assignments was linked to fears about losing close relationships within the bank's hierarchy, and concerns that a secondment or international appointment was a demotion, since all the overseas subsidiaries were smaller in scale than the home country operations and perceived as less advanced and technologically sophisticated. Maintaining a home country focus also meant that overseas subsidiaries struggled to gain attention from parent employees or have a voice in the design of regional projects, processes and policies:

> So, to me, the business is there, the footprint is there, but how do we link them together and how do we get our people to drive the business regardless of geography, regardless of products? (CEO, country subsidiary)

It was also clear that the notion of a corporate group (a key element of the new regional structure) was only slowly gaining traction outside AsiBank's most senior ranks, with performance metrics again raising a complicating element:

> When we saw this opportunity we felt, hang on, let's book here, because the withholding tax is the same, the client is a [home country] corporate, he'll feel more comfortable if it is here. But, we had this challenge, surprise surprise − our guys in [subsidiary country]

are saying 'no, no, no, hang on — book here'. Because they want the income. I said 'hang on guys, you have got to look at it as a totality: your cost of funding per dollar is 50 to 80 basis points much more expensive. I can get cheaper and for the Group this income is tax free, and I'm not even passing this to the customer.' So that is where the challenge is. We've got to look at it as a Group. (CEO, Islamic Banking)

The perceived lack of a Group-level regional strategy was the source of greatest frustration and concern during the interviews. For many, this was a direct outcome of a disjuncture between espoused objectives and the operational mechanics of ExCo meetings. These were seen as overwhelmed by reporting and operational detail, thus lacking in rigorous debate, with the more powerful members using off-line discussions and political plays to grab regional mandates and resolve strategic differences:

We have ExCo meetings, we have [the home country and key subsidiaries] and then we talk about regional things. Honestly, we have not been to any ExCo meetings in the last two years, when really there was discussion of regional issues. It's really [the home country]. The only regional matters we talk about is the financial performance ... this is what [wholesale and the investment bank] is doing, this is what [subsidiary country A] is doing, this is what [subsidiary country B] is doing, the performance. That takes one hour when we can actually read it ourselves. So yes, it's a committee that finishes at 10pm, which can be done in three hours. (CEO, Investment Bank)

These commonly recognized constraints, and our reporting of them to the CEO and ExCo, formed part of the motivation for Disruption Phase Two.

In Summary

At the time of our first data collection, in the midst of the first disruption phase, the mental interventions used to initiate strategic change (particularly the articulation of very broad regional leadership statements, a projected regional revenue target, and the implementation of a limited number of high profile, but tightly proscribed regional projects) had created frustration and divergence in mindsets and actual initiatives (see Table 1). The challenge for AsiBank's psychological architecture was that the rich diversity of opportunities identified by executives risked being hijacked by the development of entrenched positions on the outcome of the redesign. Divisional-level regional projects were increasingly non-complementary and supported by investments in human capital, and product and technology changes that needed to be defended from or justified to fellow executives in an increasingly political battle.

Disruption Two — A New Redesign Challenge

The disquiet expressed in the first interviews about the lack of a clearly articulated strategy and disharmony in the operation of ExCo surprised the CEO. It explicitly prompted him to use more *normative* mechanisms within ExCo and with other parts of the bank to communicate the strategy, its logic and its objectives (see Table 2):

> I must say that some of the comments did come as a surprise to me ... I guess that means that we haven't done enough. So over the past six months, for example, we've been increasing our various levels of communication. So, for example, I've been engaging with many smaller groups and including spending two mornings in a month at our [AsiBank] academy ... basically I will pop into two classrooms for those mornings. Each classroom on average would have about 20 people. So they are going through the normal training programmes. So we just ask them to just allocate that one hour for a session with me or with any of the ExCo members to articulate three things: one is our progress, secondly our regional aspirations and third, reinforce the core values that we must have within the organisation.

The CEO switched to using much more informal processes to manage the cognitive dissonance his direct reports were experiencing from the perceived disconnect between *espousing* regional ambitions and the lack of an immediate, concrete regional strategy. By providing forums away from the bank's formal processes for ExCo members to interact (see Table 1), the CEO argued that he was seeking to build a team identity that tied each ExCo member explicitly to a Group corporate identity, rather than their division/functional roles. This redesign of the senior management environment was, in many ways, two steps removed from the formal regional strategy formation process. It was most directly a response to the ExCo's response to the initial redesign.

For the CEO, the shift to normative mechanisms from more formal targets was also undertaken in the context of increasing external validation and visible success for the regional initiatives:

> I think what made the big difference is the fact that when you started to see the real hard evidence of your hard work being reflected in both the profit and loss account and the balance sheet, and those were carefully reported by the analysts. So now it's incredible that if you get the analysts' reports of four years ago and then the evolution in terms of how positive the analysts have been on our results, it has been quite incredible.

This is testament to the success of the first disruption phase in shifting external stakeholder representations of AsiBank's strategic agenda. It is consistent with Gavetti's (2012) argument that reaching for distant opportunities requires building legitimacy with external stakeholders. The strategic leader's shaping ability – in this instance, the CEO's communication of intent through the publicly visible elements of disruption phase one – was crucial to this process.

Normative mechanisms were required to insure against complacency and constantly communicate a representation of opportunities (and threats) that emphasized the need to be ahead of technological changes:

> the view for us now is that we must not let our people be complacent: we need to actually keep on running. This means we are not perfect still, there are too many areas where we are under a lot of threat, especially when it comes to electronic payments and internet banking … we do need to realise that things will change and be at the forefront of those changes … it's worth it to leverage on that belief, that trust in financial institutions to handle all their financial transactions, but making sure that we are able to operate in that electronic space. Again there are so many views on that. There are some banks that have gone ahead and tried to create a completely separate internet bank. But that hasn't worked so far. But that doesn't mean that things will not work in the future. So I always argue, provide the example of the iPad. The iPad is basically a tablet computer. So a tablet computer was first invented by Microsoft. (CEO)

Alongside the new normative interventions, the pace of reconfiguration accelerated. This included changes to the physical footprint, the introduction of a number of key platforms and systems for a regional architecture, and a continuing harmonization of a coherent, but less home country focused, corporate identity (see Table 2). Surprisingly, these very significant actual reconfigurations attracted very little attention in the thinking of the executives. In particular, that core IT platforms and risk systems had been flexibly implemented to support any number of footprint configurations attracted very little consideration. They were much more focussed on the shift in the decision-making culture, the convergence of thinking within the group, and the remaining (and new) shortcomings and constraints of the bank's design.

Responses to Disruption Phase Two

Identification of Cognitively Distant Opportunities
There had been a clear convergence in the individuals' representations of opportunities over the 12 months between our first and second data collection rounds, with the more cognitively distant prospects coming to the fore. In this second round, a larger proportion of interviewees identified the virtual banking and mobile payments systems as key strategic opportunities, and, in particular, the need to monitor the efforts of global technology giants rather than banking rivals in this space. So too, more executives expressed concern that Islamic finance was not being properly incorporated

into the regional agenda, and that opportunities to promote and distribute such products within Asia and the Middle East were being neglected. The CEO appeared to have been successful in bringing the majority of the ExCo towards his more cognitively distant representations of opportunity.

Definition of the region was also no longer a source of particular dissension, with the importance of focusing on ASEAN plus Greater China (China, Hong Kong and Taiwan), the predominant and accepted geographic frame. However, the scale and nature of AsiBank's engagement with Greater China remained contentious. The decision to open a number of new offices in very different parts of China (see Table 2) was directly ascribed to a poorly developed and discussed initiative from Group Strategy and the Head of Wholesale Banking, that five other respondents explicitly identified as an unnecessary distraction and allocation of time and capital away from developing a coherent regional strategy that would genuinely deliver a sustainable regional dividend.

The twin aims of (1) shifting to and converging upon richer representations while also (2) allowing for disagreement had been achieved. This was typically attributed to the normative interventions. With very few exceptions, the respondents believed that ExCo meetings had improved in terms of their openness and cohesiveness. All espoused the importance of devoting time to discussions and decisions relating to strategic, rather than operational, issues. All respondents (ExCo and non-ExCo members) also recognized that the scale of redesign needed to achieve AsiBank's ambitions meant pushing responsibility for operational issues down the organization and breaking a culture of deferring to hierarchy to ensure ideas were being pushed forward and constructively challenged. These process and innovation challenges were acknowledged to be partially issues of mindset, with leadership needing to be taken from ExCo to achieve these shifts:

> we are actually in some ways taking away opportunities for our direct reports ... I believe that in terms of empowering people one layer down from the ExCo members. We probably need to be much, much more strategic, in terms of the mobilising process, for example, in terms of validation. (CFO)

> So, that conversation [about the regional dividend] is much more frequent now than it was a year ago and there's some members who are quite good at catalysing and provoking, because, whether you like it or nor, you get caught in your tactical deliveries. (Head of Group IT)

The changes in ExCo and the CEO's very deliberate attempts to provide supporting mechanisms appeared to prompt greater ownership of the regional agenda and identification with the Group, rather than individual role responsibilities. Numerous respondents spoke to the need for Group processes to be formally restructured and normatively practiced to ensure ExCo was not the 'final stop' for reporting on projects, outcomes and operational tasks. Across all the respondents, there were numerous mentions of how ExCo seemed to be less driven by internal politics, operating at much higher levels of trust, and resolving issues within formal decision bodies, rather than off-line, one-on-one accommodations. This had two clear outcomes.

First, there was a common desire to *increase* the pace of regionalization by developing a clear strategy articulating exactly what the bank would look like by 2015 and 2018 (a new, unofficial time horizon). The redesign efforts designed to disrupt representations had had their desired effect, rendering a more ambitious ExCo group.

Second, there was recognition that the sequencing of design changes was paramount, but had received very little attention thus far. The redesign efforts had thus fuelled an appetite for more design, but with a clearer link between these design elements and the strategic outcomes. For example, there were universal calls for ExCo to change its meeting structures and objectives to devote its time to explicit deliberation of strategic trade-offs and alternative configurations for achieving the bank's goals. Developing metrics and decision tools that emphasized Group regional outcomes, shared value chains and subsumed individual geographic/product thinking were also seen as critical. This partially reflected how strongly embedded the quantitative measurement method was in ExCo, as a result of the previous transformation programme. Among the suggestions for changes were: comparative rates of return on assets and equity across the Group; calculating and privileging long-term returns on high, up-front investments; identifying Group-level returns for business-level expenditures; recognizing how different divisions/business units contribute to shared value streams and creating a genuine regional compensation formula (effectively internal transfer pricing); and the opportunity costs of allocating resources to alternative uses:

> I would like operational matters to be left to the sector heads to manage and we [ExCo] focus a lot more on strategies and articulating, rather than direct operation reporting – articulating the strategic road map. Measuring the strategy, using more strategic method. (Head of country subsidiary)

While the representations of opportunities had approached consensus, there were differences in opinion about how the bank should progress towards these various strategic prospects. In essence, these reflected differences in terms of how individuals saw redesign playing out.

Differences in Design Preferences

The use of projects to foster cross-divisional collaboration and pursue regionalization was a continuing source of difference. A clear preference for projects and initiatives generated by a select number of centres of excellence was apparent for executives with career backgrounds in consulting and investment banking. This may reflect the nature of their skill set and mental models: both consultants and investment bankers tend to engage in project-based work, typically with clear objectives and timelines. In contrast, executives with career backgrounds primarily in corporate and retail banking, with a greater focus on task and functional expertise, were frustrated by what they felt was a *chunky* approach to evolution, that failed to achieve regional platforms pooling best practices from across the bank. The project approach was viewed as strangling agility and innovation, forcing business units into templates that were neither sensitive to local requirements nor flexible enough to be adapted to purpose:

> are we going to have 40, or 50, or 60 individual projects that deliver on their own vertical? … if they don't tie in and get an aggregate versus an additive response, we're wasting a lot of time and energy. (Head of Group IT)

So too, the centres of excellence model that had evolved from the initial regional projects was seen by some executives as a brake on the speed of regionalization: the need to establish clear mandates, assign staff, reporting protocols, budgets and cost responsibilities was time consuming and seen to reinforce divisional silos, rather than encouraging Group collaboration.

As noted above, the two disruption phases had fuelled an appetite for strategic decision-making. There was a considerable majority of the interviewees who felt constrained by two key design elements that were seen to emanate from the Group Strategy unit. They ascribed the continued use of projects and centres of excellence directly to a desire within Group Strategy to control the regional agenda, rather than act as a source of knowledge and integration. Three quarters of the respondents were critical of Group Strategy, describing it as operating opaquely and failing to provide leadership on strategy issues. The Corporate Counsel, who was the only respondent other than the CEO who sat on both ExCo and the Board of Directors, believed that the unit was not fulfilling its potential to provide consideration of the external environmental dynamics, nor of developing the very financial and decision-metrics that AsiBank's senior executives had identified they needed to design and manage AsiBank to be a regional financial services leader. The Deputy Head of Group Strategy recognized the problem, yet appeared to have very little voice to temper the Chief Strategy Officer's (CSO) apparent preference for projects:

> if we are eventually grow to be a big regional player, we do need to grow beyond what we have today, which is to leave the countries to themselves and try to add value through centres of excellence and regional projects ... as long as we have this country-by-country priorities and reporting line, and overall targets, it's hard to have a conversation − a serious conversation − about regional priorities and regional numbers, when at the end of the day, we're all individuals in our own geographies. I think something's got to change. And it can't be changed on a line-by-line business or this is the model for cards, but mortgages and private banking, and wealth management will do something else − it will just confuse everyone.

By contrast, the CSO made numerous references to the need for greater strategic thinking amongst the executive and a freeing up of ExCo meeting time from *business as usual* issues to achieve this. Yet, he made no reference to the clearly emerging tensions between the project and centres of excellence approach he directly oversaw, and a second design element − the cost management programme he designed and championed. Implemented during 2012, the Group-wide programme was explicitly designed to 'nurture a cost-conscious culture' and instil 'a return-on-investment mindset' (to lower the immediate, short-term cost-to-income ratio in line with Board determined annual metrics). Others saw the programme as hampering AsiBank's ability to build an organization with potential to seize the real value of regional leadership − through the scale and scope economies from integrated product designs, management and delivery. Such innovations relied on heavy, up-front investments − the very things that a cost management programme sought to discourage. As such, the CSO's mental representation seemed less attuned to the cognitively distant opportunities identified by the CEO and a handful of senior executives more than 12 months earlier − and to the challenges of design that these opportunities presented.

Commonly Recognized Constraints
There was also growing recognition of the constraints imposed by the cost and productivity agendas on innovation and initiative. The *dashboard* system of performance management had become (see Section 'The Case') so deeply embedded in the very fabric of how processes were structured right through to the Board level, that it was exerting a countervailing pressure to the regional redesign. From being a strength of the transformation programme, it was becoming apparent that its lack of use-flexibility was constraining the shift from productivity-based to geographic and product-based growth. The Group-wide cost management programme only exacerbated

the problem. Faced with additional pressures to perform on cost-to-income metrics, individuals, subsidiaries and business units turned inwards and fought to avoid expenses linked to regional projects and platforms, while grabbing any potential revenue such initiatives might produce.

Finally, a continuing lack of skilled human capital that could operate across geographies and product lines was identified by all respondents as a constraint on the pace of redesign, although only the Head of Group Human Capital, the CEO of Islamic Banking and the CEO of a large country subsidiary recognized that the bank's cost management programme was exacerbating the problem.

Some also queried whether a senior team that had been built to tackle internally generated problems could build an externally focused, leading edge organization. There was also a voice of caution regarding how far the executives' representations had converged on the importance of committing to a single coherent strategy, over-riding individual political games. The corporate counsel, with his unique insights into strategy at the Board and ExCo levels was again insightful, stated that the key sensitive strategy issues that he knew were being presented to the Board, were still not being fully and openly shared in ExCo.

In Summary

Both disruption phases saw tensions and dissension. Variance in executives' mental representations was a significant contributor to this discord. Some executives were quicker to identify cognitively distant opportunities, including in the virtual banking and mobile payments space, in Islamic finance, and with regard to more finely sliced value chain configurations. Tensions arose from these individuals' perceptions that others did not see these prospects or lacked the will to pursue them. These tensions correspond with Gavetti's (2012) *rationality* and *plasticity* behavioural failures. The variation in representations often aligned with differences in individuals' roles and backgrounds, and whether their position cut across the bank's business lines. Some of the narrower representations reflected long entrenched views and interests in maintaining the *status quo* within a business unit. Such differences speak to both the justification for interventions and the outcomes thereof, as the cross-divisional roles were in several instances the direct outcome of the structural redesign of disruption phase one.

Over the 12 months of our observations, the executives' representations of the strategic opportunities converged to a considerable extent, with previously marginalized distant opportunities shifting centre stage. For example, calls to innovate in the mobile payments arena had spread, and building centres of excellence located away from the home country to support regionally standard products had moved from being a contentious opportunity to an accepted initiative. Likewise, more executives spoke of the need to distinguish a different set of geographic opportunities for Islamic products. Again, it can be argued that these outcomes in terms of wider recognition of cognitively distant opportunities reflect some success in addressing behavioural failures, including *shaping ability*.

IMPLICATIONS

Our field research on executive judgment in real time is a unique insight into the dynamics of a MNC's (re)design. It demonstrates the extent to which shifting an organization is as much about modifying mindsets, as it is an architectural challenge. In particular, reaching for cognitively distant opportunities − those strategic options beyond most rivals' line of sight, and thus with huge potential upside − is a mental stretch requiring explicit management interventions. Our case offers invaluable insight into what Gavetti (2011, p. 125) has dubbed *strategic leadership:* 'the mental capacity to spot opportunities that are invisible to rivals and to manage other relevant parties' perceptions to get them on board'. As Gavetti (2011, 2012) warns, behavioural failures mean *near* opportunities are much more likely to appear on the radar. For AsiBank to stretch beyond the near option of domestic dominance and a peripheral international presence, these senior decision-makers' mental representations needed to be altered considerably. Indeed, for MNC redesign to occur, the mental representations of the executives charged with such design also needed to be *redesigned*.

In the behavioural strategy school, cognition is seen as central to heterogeneity in firm performance (Daft & Weick, 1984; Felin et al., 2012; Gavetti, 2012; Gavetti et al., 2012; Kaplan, 2011; Powell et al., 2011; Winter, 2012). A firm with well-developed routines for framing strategic opportunities − the requisite cognitive architecture − may outperform less adept rivals. The two cognitive intervention phases we identified in AsiBank had many of the desired effects on such architecture: senior decision-makers were identifying new regional strategic opportunities and, as a group, had coalesced around a logic of distance compression advantages for competing across the region, but not beyond. They agreed technology, and technological innovations, would serve as a key driver of advantage across these markets and as a tool for further organizational redesign. They were now delineating the differences in the opportunities between product lines, while also looking for commonalities across products.

This micro-foundational perspective on advantage is equally relevant to MNC performance. IM scholars have made numerous efforts to determine a multinationality—performance relationship (Contractor, Kundu, & Hsu, 2002; Hennart, 2007; Lu & Beamish, 2004) and to investigate links between adoption of various architectural elements (e.g. entry mode choice) and performance. Simply looking for such choice—outcome relationships is likely to miss the more fundamental explanatory impact of cognition and executive judgment.

Our findings also demonstrate the interconnectedness of MNC redesign. A mix of design mechanisms were utilized across the spectrum, from the more formal and structural to the normative and behaviourally oriented. Incentive and monitoring systems, reporting lines and accounting practices added to the complexity of the more visible organizational structures, while also forming part of the mental intervention arsenal. The CEO used them to disrupt and shape the cognition of decision-makers and implementers throughout the MNC. An immediate implication for IM scholars is that examinations of any one type of design element in isolation may be mis-guided, as much of the explanations for and impacts of such redesigns may rest on a multitude of different motivations and understandings among the executive group. Furthermore, these executives may be viewing the design element as part of a suite of elements. Design elements may themselves be introduced as mental interventions, rather than purely as a desired out-come. Put differently, MNC architecture should be treated as neither just a means nor just an ends. Instead, IM would benefit from conceptualizing the MNC's organizational architecture as part of the firm's *mindset*, recog-nizing it is initially the individual executives' mindsets warranting closest examination.

Our study also provides specific insights into how senior MNC bankers are grappling with the broader structural factors impacting the finance industry. Since 2007, the industry has undergone radical changes in the availability of funds, regulatory oversight, technological innovation and the threat of powerful new entrants. While it is an industry built on notions of stability and continuity, IT advances and globalization continue to bring demands for greater flexibility and nimbleness in MNC design and strategy. Yet, the typical divisional structures of full-service, multinational banks, demarcated into wholesale, retail and geographic groupings, are arguably inimical to such flexibility. At AsiBank, breaking down the strong internal silos between wholesale and retail, domestic and international activities and enabling greater flexibility in how the bank responded to the risks and opportunities in the external landscape was as much about cognition as it was formal structure of responsibilities and reporting. Initially, only AsiBank's CEO and a handful of the senior executives were attuned to the possibilities of inter-weaving product value chains to achieve significant economies of scale and scope, without necessarily sacrificing local sensitivity. They were also aware of the pace of change in IT, its impact on traditional banking products (particularly retail) and the attendant threat to secure, long-term low cost funding. Compared with the initial round of targeted cognitive interventions, the second phase of normative mechanisms appears to have been much more effective in achieving significant cognitive shifts among those executives, who had initially continued to think within their immediate silo contexts and opportunity landscapes. This highlights the clear imperative for bank CEOs to show Gavetti-style leadership in pushing their executives outside their cognitive comfort zones and reach for previously unseen distant opportunities.

Our findings on the effectiveness of normative mechanisms also speak to the challenges faced by bank CEOs of achieving significant changes in internal cultures and approaches to risk-taking in financial service providers. Such changes arguably rest on disrupting existing representations of *what is* and *can (or should) be*; disruptions by Gavetti (2011, 2012) and our preliminary findings suggest require carefully designed cognitive interventions, rather than short-term changes to performance bonuses and vision statements. As the Deputy CEO and Head of Wholesale Banking observed:

> I guess everybody is in the stage of trying to find meaning in what they do and are tired with what is going on especially in the US. When investment bankers get paid $1,200 Million, and you know, screw the Government tax payers at the same time. They want to find something that is more, I don't know, what is the word, I guess have a meaning to what they do in the Bank. At the same time, we also realised that in the marketplace, more and more banks are behaving on a transaction basis, dealing with clients, and what they do with the clients, all they see is the dollar sign, most of the time, and we know for a fact that most clients don't like it.

FUTURE RESEARCH DIRECTIONS

MNCs are frequently the innovators within and across industries, redefining what is viable in terms of product designs, business models, value chain structures and organizational forms. Such decisions typically rest on CEOs and their senior executive teams identifying, reaching out for and attaining cognitively distant opportunities unseen by rival firms. IM has a real opportunity to contribute to research on managerial and organizational cognition, by investigating the cognitive efforts and interactions among MNC senior decision-makers.

The AsiBank setting provides insight into the reconfiguration of a MNC with pre-existing subsidiaries across a region. Future research should explore cognition within: (1) more globally distributed MNCs and (2) firms just starting out on internationalization. The opportunity framing and mental representations of executives in these two settings are likely to differ substantially.

Alternative causes of such differences in cognition are also promising avenues for research. IM has long argued for the value of experience in shaping MNC performance. Executives themselves may well be the foundation for such experience. The AsiBank executives' mental representations did not shift at a uniform pace. Some were faster to see new, more distant opportunities; others were laggards. There were ongoing differences in what they viewed as constraints on strategic progress. As noted, some perspective differences appear to reflect variations in experience and expertise among the group. Exploring the link between individuals' prior work experiences (e.g. in multiple countries, engaged in international strategy decisions), and their cognition may shed new light on this performance relationship.

Our study also demonstrated the use of assorted disruptive mechanisms to shape and shift the executives' cognition. We distinguished between formal structural and norms-based behavioural interventions, drawing on existing notions of formal and behavioural forms of control and coordination in subsidiary networks. We found the two types served different, but complementary, roles in *nudging* mindsets. Future work could more carefully delineate different types of interventions and explore the impact of different cultures and industry effects on the use and effectiveness of the different types of interventions. For example, Barkema and Shvyrkov (2007) argued high levels of diversity can create *faultlines* within top management teams (TMTs). These faultlines can hamper foreign expansion decisions, undermining the required consensus for crucial strategic innovations. Only after sustained interaction over three to four years were the faultline effects overcome. Studies on the impact of executives' home country background have also suggested TMTs from different countries and cultures may have different overall levels of uncertainty and ambiguity tolerance (Barkema & Vermeulen, 1997; Carpenter & Fredrickson, 2001). It may also be that individual executives' prior experiences of certain interventions shape their cognition and also their responsiveness and implementation of such interventions.

Within AsiBank, the CEO played an especially dominant and interventionist role in driving the executive team towards more cognitively distant opportunities. Future studies should deliberately sample for scenarios where the interventions are driven by other stakeholders, such as other executive team members, active investor blocks, management buyout consortia or strategy consultants. Likewise, the push for new *ways of thinking* was not triggered by a major external shock. Investigations of cognition and redesign during crises may reveal a different dynamic and need for alternative types of cognitive interventions. Given the complexity and interconnectedness of such events in the global business arena (e.g. the GFC), this is a rich opportunity for IM scholars.

CONCLUSION

For senior leaders attempting to change a MNC's strategic direction and design, attending to the cognitive architecture of the organization is critical. Designing successful mental interventions that prompt individuals to abandon outdated understandings of what the MNC is and can be to embrace cognitively distant strategic opportunities is a challenging task, but one that may lie at the heart of achieving superior outcomes for the organization.

NOTES

1. For brevity, we use IM to refer to work by IM and international business (IB) scholars.
2. For an overview of IM's treatment of a number of these design elements see Westney and Zaheer (2001) and Whitley (2009).
3. The country has been disguised to maintain participant anonymity, in line with the authors' universities' research ethics requirements.
4. The first round interviews were conducted in each respondent's office/meeting room (including for offshore subsidiaries); the second, by individual teleconferences. Recordings were made with each participant's explicit written permission and we guaranteed de-identification of quotes.
5. Based on the first round interviews, we prepared a report for the ExCo that included a variety of de-identified quotes and extensive analysis. As discussed

below, the more normative aspects of the second disruption phases were partially a response by the CEO to our findings of discontent among the ExCo about the decision-making culture and lack of clear articulated vision.

6. During our interview with the Head of Retail, he presented a document setting-out his views on the two possible regional models for AsiBank (multi-local and integrated), moving through four phases of implementation from independent franchises in different countries (no regional reporting, high autonomy, limited *ad hoc* collaboration), through collaboration (regional taskforces for select initiatives, *ad hoc* staff movement), standardization (introduction of common business models and practices, beginnings of regional reporting structure, extensive guidelines for standardization, shared infrastructure where possible, formal secondment programme) and full integration. Against this transition map, four key businesses within retail were plotted, with only one achieving full integration by 2015.

REFERENCES

Axelrod, R. M. (1976). *Structure of decisions: The cognitive maps of political elites*. Princeton, NJ: Princeton University Press.

Barkema, H. G., & Shvyrkov, O. (2007). Does top management team diversity promote or hamper foreign expansion? *Strategic Management Journal, 28*(7), 663–680.

Barkema, H. G., & Vermeulen, F. (1997). What differences in the cultural backgrounds of partners are detrimental for international joint ventures? *Journal of International Business Studies, 28*(4), 845–864.

Bettman, J. R., & Weitz, B. A. (1983). Attributions in the board room: Causal reasoning in corporate annual reports. *Administrative Science Quarterly, 28*(2), 165–183.

Carpenter, M. A., & Fredrickson, J. W. (2001). Top management teams, global strategic posture, and the moderating role of uncertainty. *Academy of Management Journal, 44*(3), 533–545.

Contractor, F. J., Kundu, S., & Hsu, C. C. (2002). A three-stage theory of international expansion: The link between multinationality and performance in the service sector. *Journal of International Business Studies, 34*(1), 5–18.

Cyert, R. M., & March, J. G. (1963). *A behavioral theory of the firm*. Englewood Cliffs, NJ: Prentice-Hall.

Daft, R. L., & Weick, K. E. (1984). Toward a model of organizations as interpretation systems. *Academy of Management Review, 9*(2), 284–295.

Detert, J. R., Treviño, L. K., & Sweitzer, V. L. (2008). Moral disengagement in ethical decision making: A study of antecedents and outcomes. *Journal of Applied Psychology, 93*(2), 374–391.

Devinney, T. M. (2011). Bringing managers' decision models into foreign direct investment research. In R. Rammamurti & N. Hashai (Eds.), *The future of foreign direct investment and the multinational enterprise* (pp. 1069–1094). Bingley, UK: Emerald Group Publishing.

Devinney, T. M. (2013). Is microfoundational thinking critical to management thought and practice? *The Academy of Management Perspectives, 27*(2), 81–84.

Eisenhardt, K. M. (1989). Building theories from case study research. *Academy of Management Review, 14*(4), 532–550.

Eisenhardt, K. M., & Graebner, M. E. (2007). Theory building from cases: Opportunities and challenges. *Academy of Management Journal, 50*(1), 25−32.

Eisenhardt, K. M., & Sull, D. N. (2001). Strategy as simple rules. *Harvard Business Review, 79*(1), 106−119.

Felin, T., Foss, N. J., Heimeriks, K. H., & Madsen, T. L. (2012). Microfoundations of routines and capabilities: Individuals, processes, and structure. *Journal of Management Studies, 49*(8), 1351−1374.

Gavetti, G. (2011). The new psychology of strategic leadership. *Harvard Business Review, 89*(7−8), 118−125.

Gavetti, G. (2012). Toward a behavioral theory of strategy. *Organization Science, 23*(1), 267−285.

Gavetti, G., Greve, H. R., Levinthal, D. A., & Ocasio, W. (2012). The behavioral theory of the firm: Assessment and prospects. *Academy of Management Annals, 6*(1), 1−40.

Gavetti, G., & Levinthal, D. (2000). Looking forward and looking backward: Cognitive and experiential search. *Administrative Science Quarterly, 45*(1), 113−137.

Gavetti, G., Levinthal, D., & Rivkin, J. W. (2005). Strategy making in novel and complex worlds: The power of analogy. *Strategic Management Journal, 26*(8), 691−712.

Gavetti, G., & Rivkin, J. W. (2007). On the origin of strategy: Action and cognition over time. *Organization Science, 18*(3), 420−439.

Ghemawat, P. (2007). *Redefining global strategy: Crossing borders in a world where differences still matter.* Boston, MA: Harvard Business Press.

Ghemawat, P., & del Sol, P. (1998). Commitment vs. flexibility. *California Management Review, 40*(4), 26−42.

Ghoshal, S., & Bartlett, C. A. (1990). The multinational corporation as an interorganizational network. *Academy of Management Review, 15*(4), 603−626.

Gigerenzer, G. (2008). Why heuristics work. *Perspectives on Psychological Science, 3*(1), 20−29.

Hennart, J.-F. (1991). The transaction costs theory of joint ventures: An empirical study of Japanese subsidiaries in the United States. *Management Science, 37*(4), 483−497.

Hennart, J.-F. (2007). The theoretical rationale for a multinationality-performance relationship. *Management International Review, 47*(3), 423−452.

Huber, G. P., & Power, D. J. (1985). Retrospective reports of strategic-level managers: Guidelines for increasing their accuracy. *Strategic Management Journal, 6*(2), 171−180.

Hutzschenreuter, T., Pedersen, T., & Volberda, H. W. (2007). The role of path dependency and managerial intentionality: A perspective on international business research. *Journal of International Business Studies, 38*(7), 1055−1068.

Johanson, J., & Vahlne, J. E. (1977). The internationalization process of the firm-a model of knowledge development and increasing foreign market commitments. *Journal of International Business Studies, 8*(1), 23−32.

Kaplan, S. (2008). Framing contests: Strategy making under uncertainty. *Organization Science, 19*(5), 729−752.

Kaplan, S. (2011). Research in cognition and strategy: Reflections on two decades of progress and a look to the future. *Journal of Management Studies, 48*(3), 665−695.

Kiesler, S., & Sproull, L. (1982). Managerial response to changing environments: Perspectives on problem sensing from social cognition. *Administrative Science Quarterly, 27*(4), 548−570.

Kogut, B., & Singh, H. (1988). The effect of national culture on the choice of entry mode. *Journal of International Business Studies, 19*(3), 411−432.

Leonard-Barton, D. (1992). Core capabilities and core rigidities: A paradox in managing new product development. *Strategic Management Journal, 13*(1), 111–125.

Lu, J. W., & Beamish, P. W. (2004). International diversification and firm performance: The S-curve hypothesis. *Academy of Management Journal, 47*(4), 598–609.

Maitland, E., & Sammartino, A. (2012). Flexible footprints: Reconfiguring MNCs for new value opportunities. *California Management Review, 54*(2), 92–117.

March, J. G., & Simon, H. A. (1958). *Organizations.* New York, NY: Wiley.

March, J. G., Sproull, L. S., & Tamuz, M. (1991). Learning from samples of one or fewer. *Organization Science, 2*(1), 1–13.

Murtha, T. P., Lenway, S. A., & Bagozzi, R. P. (1998). Global mind-sets and cognitive shifts in a complex multinational corporation. *Strategic Management Journal, 19*(1), 97–114.

Porac, J. F., & Thomas, H. (1990). Taxonomic mental models in competitor definition. *Academy of Management Review, 15*(2), 224–240.

Porac, J. F., Thomas, H., & Baden-Fuller, C. (1989). Competitive groups as cognitive communities: The case of Scottish knitwear manufacturers. *Journal of Management Studies, 26*(4), 397–416.

Powell, T. C., Lovallo, D., & Fox, C. R. (2011). Behavioral strategy. *Strategic Management Journal, 32*(13), 1369–1386.

Prahalad, C. K., & Bettis, R. A. (1986). The dominant logic: A new linkage between diversity and performance. *Strategic Management Journal, 7*(6), 485–501.

Prahalad, C. K., & Doz, Y. (1987). *The multinational mission.* New York, NY: Free Press.

Rhinesmith, S. H. (1992). Global mindsets for global managers. *Training and Development, 46*(10), 63–69.

Sheng, S., Zhou, K. Z., & Li, J. J. (2011). The effects of business and political ties on firm performance: Evidence from China. *Journal of Marketing, 75*(1), 1–15.

Simon, H. A. (1947). *Administrative behavior.* New York, NY: Macmillan.

Van de Ven, A. H., & Poole, M. S. (2002). Field research methods. In J. A. C. Baum (Ed.), *The Blackwell companion to organizations* (pp. 867–888). Oxford, UK: Blackwell Publishers.

Walsh, J. P. (1995). Managerial and organizational cognition: Notes from a trip down memory lane. *Organization Science, 6*(3), 280–321.

Westney, D. E., & Zaheer, S. (2001). The multinational enterprise as an organization. In A. M. Rugman & T. L. Brewer. (Eds.), *Oxford handbook of international business* (pp. 349–379). Oxford, UK: Oxford University Press.

Whitley, R. (2009). The multinational company as a distinct organisational form. In S. Collinson & G. Morgan (Eds.), *Images of the multinational firm* (pp. 145–166). Oxford, UK: Blackwell Publishing.

Winter, S. G. (2012). Purpose and progress in the theory of strategy: Comments on Gavetti. *Organization Science, 23*(1), 288–297.

World Bank. (2010). *East Asia and Pacific economic update: Emerging stronger from the crisis* (Vol. 1). Washington DC: The World Bank.

Yin, R. K. (1994). *Case study research: Design and methods* (2nd ed.). Newbury Park, CA: Sage.

APPENDIX: SAMPLE INTERVIEW QUESTIONS

How would you describe AsiBank's regional position right now?

What are the key drivers for greater pursuit of a regional presence?

   a. How do the drivers vary across the different lines of business of the Bank?

   b. Is this regional leadership strategy a response to your competitors' regional strategies?

   c. How will AsiBank's regional strategy change the competitive dynamics?

Does the AsiBank group brand have value in other countries?

   a. How do you believe the brand is perceived outside the domestic market?

   b. Would you develop different brands for different countries and product classes/groups?

   c. In instances of inorganic growth (i.e. acquisition), would rebranding be your default approach?

How do you identify which assets or activities can be leveraged into new markets/locations?

   a. Do you have a specific programme to do so? (*or approach for doing this?*)

   b. Does any one person or team have direct responsibility for assessing and identifying roles, activities and staff capable of performing at a regional level?

   c. What channels/means are there for such assessments to 'flow up' from below in your division?

Is there broad support for the regional strategy at the Exec level?

   a. (And at the next level down?)

   b. Are some people more or less enthusiastic about the strategy?

   c. Why do you think that is?

   d. How does this shape the priorities and decision-making around the roll-out of the strategy?

   e. Do you feel there has been sufficient debate and scrutiny of the arguments for the regional approach?

   f. Is there scope for dissent?

What is your absolute priority in terms of achieving the regional strategy?

    a. Why?
    b. What does this mean in terms of activities?
    c. How does this differ from your colleagues' priorities?
    d. Is this likely to cause any tension?

"THE MOST PUBLIC SECRET": CONCEALING AND SILENCING ETHNOCENTRISM IN THE MNC

Marianne Storgaard, Janne Tienari and Rebecca Piekkari

ABSTRACT

In this paper, we focus on ethnocentrism as a practice that persists among top managers at MNC headquarters and steers their efforts in orchestrating the global network of subsidiaries. While the extant literature has viewed ethnocentrism as a detrimental attitude that top management seek to remedy, we offer a different reading. On the basis of our fieldwork in Danish MNCs, we argue that top management may deliberately cling to ethnocentrism. At the same time, however, they silence ethnocentrism and conceal it from view. In turn, people in subsidiaries engage in self-silencing. We argue that this sustained yet concealed and silenced ethnocentrism has important implications for orchestration of the global MNC network.

Keywords: Ethnocentrism; MNC; management; headquarters; subsidiaries; global networks

Orchestration of the Global Network Organization
Advances in International Management, Volume 27, 191–212
ISSN: 1571-5027/doi:10.1108/S1571-502720140000027027

INTRODUCTION

In multinational corporations (MNCs), a wide array of actors — managers at headquarters (Hedlund & Kogut, 1993), expatriates (Thomas, 1996; Zeira, 1976), local subsidiary managers (Florkowski & Fogel, 1999; Templer, 2010), and customers (Riefler, Diamantopoulos, & Siguaw, 2012; Sharma, 2011) — are said to possess ethnocentric attitudes. However, following Howard Perlmutter's (1969) seminal article "The Tortuous Evolution of the Multinational Corporation," most research attention has been devoted to studying management ethnocentrism at MNC headquarters (HQ).

According to Perlmutter (1969), top managers at HQ have a tendency to portray a sense of superiority towards foreign subsidiaries. In ethnocentric MNCs decision-making is centralized, communication typically flows from headquarters to foreign subsidiaries, and "home-made" standards are applied in managing subsidiaries regardless of local conditions. What is crucial about ethnocentrism is that home country nationals "are recruited and trained for key positions everywhere in the world" and foreigners are seen as "second-class citizens" (Perlmutter, 1969, p. 12). Ethnocentrism in the MNC is embedded in the culture of the HQ's country of origin and reproduced in and through its practices. This is argued to have dire consequences for the organization and its functioning.

Perlmutter (1969) described MNC development as a move away from ethnocentrism towards geocentrism, which he regarded as the most advanced model of organizing. His ethnocentric-polycentric-geocentric model offered the foundation for a number of contributions on organizational design in MNCs such as the transnational corporation (Bartlett & Ghoshal, 1989), the heterarchy (Hedlund, 1986), and the differentiated network (Nohria & Ghoshal, 1997), all of which aimed to tackle the various challenges posed by ethnocentrism in the international business context. Inspired by Perlmutter's work, researchers have turned their attention from the design of formal structures to the mindsets and "mentality of those who constitute the structure" (Bartlett & Ghoshal, 1987, p. 53; see also Bartlett & Ghoshal, 1990, 1992; Gupta & Govindarajan, 2002; Hedlund, 1986; Maljers, 1992).

It has been argued that formal structure can no longer capture the increasing internal and external complexity required to orchestrate an MNC. Bartlett and Ghoshal (1990), who were in the forefront of the popularization of these notions, encourage top managers to build the "physiology" and "psychology" of their organizations, and introduce the model of the geographically dispersed network as a way to accomplish this (Bartlett & Ghoshal, 1989; Nohria & Ghoshal, 1997). As the argument goes, the role of subtle, indirect, and informal mechanisms such as shared values, practices, and personal relationships is paramount in managing this network. They "glue" the geographically dispersed organization together and provide managers and employees with a shared sense of purpose and direction (see also Martinez & Jarillo, 1989).

The onus of having common values and shared practices to support orchestration of the MNC turned the attention of researchers to its particular management challenges. The demands placed upon individual top managers were considerable: they "must have a broad, nonparochial view of the company and its operations yet a deep understanding of their own business, country, or functional tasks" (Bartlett & Ghoshal, 1992, p. 132). A suitable mindset for internalizing this understanding was associated with characteristics such as curiosity about the world, self-consciousness, openness to diversity and novelty, and the discipline required to develop an integrated perspective that would weave together diverse strands of knowledge about cultures and markets (Gupta & Govindarajan, 2002). Moreover, it was the task of top management to identify and further develop junior talent with a "global mindset" who would be free from allegiances to any particular culture and nation (Gupta & Govindarajan, 2002).

However, all this has proved to be a quixotic task. Perlmutter (1969, pp. 16–17) himself described the evolution from ethnocentrism towards geocentrism as "long and tortuous" because "[t]he human demands of ethnocentrism are great." Since Perlmutter's ground-breaking contribution, several studies have shown that ethnocentrism persists in MNCs (Adler & Bartholomew, 1992; Kristensen & Zeitlin, 2005; Levy, Beechler, Taylor, & Boyacigiller, 2007). Researchers have also provided various explanations for this, including the advantages of ethnocentrism such as the cost-effectiveness of recruiting home country nationals (Mayrhofer & Brewster, 1996) as well as their familiarity with HQ policies and practices and loyalty to them (Banai, 1992). At the same time, as Westney (1993) has shown, top managers are often unaware of their lingering ethnocentric attitudes and the impact they have on organizational practices and outcomes.

In this paper, we complement these findings on why ethnocentrism persists in orchestration of the MNC. We take departure in the stance that HQ managers are often aware of their own ethnocentrism, but opt to hold onto it. With reference to empirical examples from Danish MNCs, we show how HQ management deliberately cling to this outlook in orchestrating the MNC. For some, it constitutes a dilemma of political incorrectness.

In order to cope with it, they may forcefully downplay ethnocentrism and then exclude it from discussion. For others, ethnocentrism is a question of practical coping and as natural as "common sense." In the subsidiaries, HQ ethnocentrism looks very different. It may be perceived as a lack of respect and as a sign of marginalization and exclusion of the subsidiaries' knowledge and competence.

Against this backdrop, we suggest that HQ ethnocentrism in the modern MNC can be depicted as "the most public secret," as a manager in one of our case companies put it. It is widely known in the organization, but concealed and silenced. To make sense of this state of affairs, and to consider its implications for research on orchestrating the global network organization, we outline some of the ways in which ethnocentrism is concealed and silenced in the MNC. In doing so, our attention shifts from top management attitudes to practices of ethnocentrism.

The remainder of the paper unfolds as follows. We first review how ethnocentrism has been treated in the literature and identify the most common reasons provided for its persistence. We proceed to offer empirical illustrations, relate these observations to the relevant literature, and pose the following question: what can be done about ethnocentrism in the MNC? We conclude by specifying our contribution to international management research and by outlining ideas for future research.

THE MANY FACES OF ETHNOCENTRISM

HQ ethnocentrism has been presented as parochialism and (a false portrayal of) "common sense" that draws on locally anchored mindsets and taken-for-granted assumptions as well as locally preferred practices (Thomas, 1996; Westney, 1993). Our reading of international management research suggests that three main assumptions govern discussion about ethnocentrism (Storgaard, Michailova, Piekkari, & Tienari, 2014). Firstly, ethnocentrism is detrimental to the MNC because it has negative consequences for business performance (Caligiuri & Tarique, 2012; Thomas & Hill, 1999). It hampers the mobility of subsidiary managers, reduces their motivation, and prevents them from participating in decision-making of the MNC (Banai, 1992; Perlmutter, 1969; Zeira, 1976).

Secondly, ethnocentrism is associated with the early stages of internationalization (Hedlund, 1993; Hedlund & Kogut, 1993; Muratbekova-Touron, 2008; Perlmutter, 1969). As the MNC matures, key actors are increasingly expected to embrace polycentric and later geocentric attitudes. Consequently, the degree of ethnocentrism in the organization will diminish. Perlmutter (1969), for example, was of the opinion that ethnocentric attitudes evolved as the MNC progressed towards more advanced stages of development. Thirdly, the literature assumes that ethnocentrism is an attitude that can and should be overcome (Caligiuri & Tarique, 2012; Leiba-O'Sullivan, 1999; Zeira, Harari, & Nundi, 1975) through training offered to various groups of managers in the MNC (Gupta & Govindarajan, 2002).

Despite these widespread assumptions about the undesirability of ethnocentrism, it persists in practice although it is rarely voiced (Storgaard et al., 2014). Ethnocentrism is a multidimensional phenomenon; it has many "faces." Researchers have identified "ingrained ethnocentrism and transcending nationally-entrenched perceptions" (Levy et al., 2007, p. 233) as well as the endurance of a single country perspective (Adler & Bartholomew, 1992). The findings of Kristensen and Zeitlin (2005, p. 173) suggest that the MNC headquarters is characterized by a "local outlook" visible only to those in the periphery, that is, the subsidiaries. In a similar vein, Barner-Rasmussen, Piekkari, Scott-Kennel, and Welch (2010, p. 9) argue that headquarters is often "too far removed from the operational realities that dominate daily experiences at the subsidiary level."

Following this line of thinking, a stream of studies suggests that HQ takes its departure from its own local knowledge − locally preferred values and practices − when designing the global "best" practices to be transferred to foreign subsidiaries. Frenkel (2008) questions whether top managers at HQ are in the position to define what is "best" for the rest of the organization. Edwards, Colling, and Ferner (2007) concur by problematizing the task of identifying "best" practices in the first place. They argue that organizational practices are not "governed solely by rational choices made by one group of calculating economic actors" but also by self-interest and aggrandizement (Edwards et al., 2007, p. 202). In a similar vein, Vaara, Tienari, and Björkman (2003) argue that choosing what practices are "best" is always a political process in the MNC and that transferring practices involves a complex process of recontextualization. Morgan and Kristensen (2006, p. 1471) summarize the HQ ethnocentric tendency as follows: "When they go global, they will take these practices, national templates and routines of control and coordination with them and create subsidiaries that reflect the organizational forms of their home country." In this context, the term "miniature replica" (Poynter & White, 1985) is sometimes used to refer to the foreign subsidiary as the mirror image of the corporate HQ.

Using "culture" – typically defined in terms of the basic assumptions, values, and practices that an organization carries (Schein, 1984) – as an informal control and coordination mechanism in the organization is a case in point. Rather than reflecting ways of doing things that are unique and specific to the company in question, so-called corporate values often reflect deeply ingrained national preferences, for example in terms of decision-making or lines of authority and command. As a management mechanism, corporate culture provides the opportunity to universalize a belief system that stems from the home country of the MNC across its network. In this regard, domestically oriented attitudes are masked in a supposedly legitimate and acceptable form of shared values and practices that are then disseminated within the MNC (Westney, 1993). HQ offers these values and practices as neutral – or based on "common sense" – and promotes them among subsidiary managers in order to ensure their cooperation (Nobel & Birkinshaw, 1998).

Nevertheless, foreign subsidiary managers often perceive such imposition as a sign of HQ ethnocentrism. As Westney (1993, p. 68) puts it, "[w]hat appears to the home country manager as 'the way things are done' (indicating a lack of awareness of genuine alternatives) or 'the way we do things' (indicating a belief that the patterns are company-specific rather than country-specific) often appears to locals as the product of the parent's home country." In other words, what is taken as legitimate assimilation by top managers at HQ can be perceived in the subsidiaries as HQ domination and marginalization and exclusion of subsidiary knowledge and competence. In this regard, views on ethnocentrism straddle company- or HQ-specific and subsidiary-specific practices, global and local outlooks, and the various perceptions expressed by HQ and subsidiary representatives that give ethnocentrism its many "faces."

WHY DOES ETHNOCENTRISM PERSIST?

The literature in international management offers several reasons for the persistence of ethnocentric attitudes. Explanations range from the advantages associated with ethnocentrism, crude attributions of success, unquestioned privilege, narrow-mindedness, and groupthink. In their study entitled "In praise of ethnocentricity," Mayrhofer and Brewster (1996, p. 772) argue that "there are good reasons for retaining ethnocentric policies" as an efficient management approach. They explain that "with regard to HRM, most organizations remain solidly ethnocentric [...] not because they are backward, but because it is a cost-effective way of handling the crucial problem of integration" (Mayrhofer & Brewster, 1996, p. 750).

Mayrhofer and Brewster (1996) detail the main advantages and disadvantages of an ethnocentric approach to international staffing in a European context and argue that the advantages exceed the disadvantages. They include in the advantages expatriates, who spread the values and practices of the parent company, contribute to high levels of communication between the HQ and subsidiaries, and possess extensive expertise on HQ operations that benefits the local subsidiary. Overall, Mayrhofer and Brewster (1996, p. 772) are convinced that "the assumptions of a progression towards a truly global approach to international staffing need to be challenged."

Banai (1992) agrees with Mayrhofer and Brewster (1996) that there are many advantages to ethnocentrism. Since parent country nationals share their origin with HQ, they tend to be more familiar with and loyal to the organization's mission, policies, and practices than host country nationals. Banai (1992, p. 464) finds that MNCs may be stuck in the self-fulfilling prophecy of ethnocentrism because "[t]heir success may suppress any incentive to change the policy." Nadler and Shaw (1995) echo this thinking. They maintain that success often sets the stage for failure as top managers in successful organizations tend to cling to patterns of existing thinking and behavior that were perceived to be the cause and source of success. They become "learning disabled," as Nadler and Shaw (1995, p. 11) put it. Over time, top managers become incapable of accepting new ideas and insights. Like all human beings, they have a tendency to attribute success to their own actions and regard failure as something that is not of their own making.

Another perspective to the persistence of ethnocentrism is provided by Thomas (1996, p. 218) who suggests that it may in part be "a result of privilege" that is granted to an individual without him or her investing effort in earning it. Thomas argues that "those who are privileged in their home cultures, simply due to race or ethnicity, are so ingrained in their culture that they are incapable of perceiving those privileges that are afforded to them by virtue of their group membership. Likewise, they are likely to use their own cultural context as a standard against which others should be judged and to which others should aspire" (Thomas, 1996, p. 218). Top managers at corporate headquarters may be unaware of having adopted their position by means other than individual competence such as the "right" nationality or ethnic background. Instead, they are likely to believe that they have risen to the top in what is essentially a meritocracy. Such unawareness of privilege makes it more difficult to detect and remove ethnocentric attitudes.

Finally, Hamel and Breen (2007, p. 158) posit that lack of diversity in the top management team can lead to a narrow-mindedness that often reinforces ethnocentrism: "Managers tend to marry their cousins. Not literally of course, but they often surround themselves with people whose life experience mirrors their own." The authors argue that the greater the degree of diversity − of thought, skills, attitudes, and capabilities − the greater the range of adaptive capabilities in the organization. In reverse situations, lack of diversity may lead to "groupthink" − a joint desire for conformity − that paralyzes decision-making (Aldrich & Kasuku, 2012).

In sum, in spite of the questionable aspects of ethnocentrism detailed in the previous section, there are sound business reasons as well as cognitive, emotional, and behavioral rationales for maintaining an ethnocentric outlook in the MNC. However, it is apparently an ambiguous and contested theoretical concept and a complex empirical phenomenon. In the following, we provide empirical insights into how ethnocentrism is sustained in the global network of the MNC while at the same time concealed and silenced. Our focus is on ethnocentric behaviors and practices rather than on ethnocentric "attitudes."

CONCEALING AND SILENCING
ETHNOCENTRISM IN THE MNC

The following insights are based on our analysis of two Danish-owned MNCs. For purposes of anonymity, we refer to the case companies as Alpha (operating in the business-to-business environment) and Beta (operating in the consumer goods market). Our empirical evidence from these companies has given rise to theorizing about ethnocentrism in terms of concealing and silencing. Firstly, in what we call "concealing ethnocentrism with culture," top managers at HQ attempt to convince themselves and each other that they do not orchestrate the MNC in an unjustly ethnocentric way. They create and sustain a common culture at the top, which is then spread throughout the organization. Secondly, in "concealing ethnocentrism with discipline" HQ management convinces the rest of the organization, including the foreign subsidiaries, that their approach to management is not ethnocentric. Any criticism voiced about HQ's potential ethnocentrism is effectively dismissed and subsidiaries are disciplined to take part in concealing ethnocentrism, in other words, to silence themselves.

Concealing Ethnocentrism with Culture

In the first form of concealing and silencing ethnocentrism, elements of "national culture" and "corporate culture" are intertwined and mixed with each other. Cultural traits and virtues that are represented as essentially Danish are depicted as superior to those of other local cultures in the MNC. However, this ethnocentric outlook of HQ is converted into corporate culture talk, which is then used as a pretext for concealing ethnocentrism. Individually and as a group, managers at HQ in Alpha and Beta are convinced that this conversion is possible and that it can be used to align the global network of foreign subsidiaries.

Top management at Alpha has purposefully made an effort to "spread the Danish way" of operating throughout the global organization, which consists of some 80 foreign subsidiaries around the world. The following quotation shows that HQ is fully aware of its own ethnocentrism, which takes the form of corporate culture and which everybody outside the HQ has to adopt and learn:

> [We] are already today rather good at making our overseas employees [...] feel like a part of the company. [...] There are some cultural differences that may conflict, but only because we have chosen a set of rules that originate from our part of the world. And we do not intend to change that! [...] They are willing to put their own preferences aside, because they are in a company that has a certain culture, which we call our company culture but which, to be honest [...] is a version of Danish culture. (Top manager, HQ, Alpha)

The top manager admits in the research interview that Alpha's corporate culture consists of "a set of rules" that originate from his "part of the world" and that it is "a version of Danish culture." He emphasizes that despite some cultural differences between Denmark and the host countries, subsidiary staff buy into Alpha's corporate values. This justifies keeping the culture intact. The above comment also shows that the top manager is fully aware of Alpha's ethnocentrism but does not find it odd or inappropriate in any way. In contrast, it is natural to disseminate "best" practices across Alpha's foreign subsidiaries. At the same time, however, Alpha's mission statement conveys a very different message:

> Our company is an international and a globally thinking corporation with production and sales in all parts of the world. We believe that it is not possible to run a global corporation from one central office. We rely on regional production and local establishment because we want to show respect for local values, cultures, and ways of doing things. We do not do this by forcing the Danish culture upon international subsidiaries,

but by creating optimal space for their own cultures. (Mission, vision and core values pamphlet, Alpha)

The discrepancy related to the notion of culture is noteworthy. A shared corporate culture is emphasized as a management mechanism in Alpha because it prevents cultural disintegration of the geographically dispersed network of foreign subsidiaries. At the same time, its Danishness is concealed in the official communications. The following extract from an internal HR document further illustrates this point:

> The cultural uniqueness which we have built into our company and which we try to transplant to our many subsidiaries, is part of what we see to be the most important to preserve. Based on our values, our company culture has evolved over many years. This is the backbone of our company and our major asset. In order to be able to meet future challenges, we must ensure that despite fast growth and globalization, we live our values throughout the company at all times and continuously strengthen its distinct identity. (Internal HR document, Alpha)

There is a conscious and deliberate strategy at HQ to spread "best" practices that serve orchestration of the MNC network. However, representatives of foreign subsidiaries are well aware of the dangers associated with this kind of ethnocentrism. As long as people at HQ do not want to learn about other cultures, nothing is going to change. A Danish expatriate in one of Alpha's subsidiaries in Asia commented as follows:

> The problem is that the people at HQ, who grant the resources and define the strategies, do not have their finger on the pulse.[...] In Denmark they have a world map that they bring along when they travel around the world. And they think that everything is the same as in Denmark. They are so naïve, thinking that everybody is like the Danes. Yet people are not the same all over. (Danish expatriate, Asian subsidiary unit, Alpha)

Imposition of the corporate culture in the subsidiaries is a powerful means for concealing and silencing ethnocentrism. Similar conversions of the ethnocentric outlook of HQ into corporate culture talk can be found at Beta, which has operations in over 40 countries around the world. The following comment by a top manager at Beta's HQ suggests that much could be learned from other ways of doing things. This is, however, difficult when things are proceeding well enough from the top management's perspective:

> We are 500 people in this house and close to 100 come from other countries. We have at least 20 different nationalities here. But I don't think that having all these nationalities here benefits the headquarters. The headquarters don't really learn from all these foreign people. It could be much better. We could listen more to other people's experiences and be much more humble. There are several issues to be learned. But the main thing would be to understand the different mindsets. We could do it in a much more

organized way if we wanted to. Why don't we? Well, nobody has asked this question. (Top manager, HQ, Beta)

The above quotation suggests that the top management in Beta's HQ precludes itself from the possibility of receiving inputs from outside. International assignments tend to be mind-stretching experiences that offer opportunities for professional and personal development and thus, learning: "We need international experience because you become more humble when you open your eyes to what the different cultures are. [...]. So you have to have that international experience [...]. It's a must."

In this top manager's view, the majority of the managers at Beta's HQ lack the beneficial international experience that teaches humility and the ability to listen to other viewpoints based on different assumptions. Such experience would also provide a common ground for mutual understanding between the core team of Danish top managers at the HQ and the "inpatriates" who are brought in from Beta's network of foreign subsidiaries for shorter and longer visits. These inpatriates feel that their contribution to creating a more global mindset at Beta is marginalized. An inpatriate top manager explains this as follows:

I don't think that we as "inpats" are seen as part of the globalization process in the organization. I rather think that we make a difference when we go back home and bring the Danish — sorry (smiles) — the organizational ways of thinking with us. (Top manager, HQ, Beta)

The slip of the tongue — deliberate, perhaps — in the above quotation suggests that the top manager equates Beta's corporate culture with Danish culture. Several of our respondents suggest that top management at Beta act as if they think that if they start hiring foreigners for key positions in Denmark the strategy of assimilation (expecting that everyone adapts to what in effect is the Danish way of doing things) may be compromised. Another inpatriate top manager at HQ put it this way:

It is convenient to hire your own mirror image because you know how this person works, thinks, and handles things. And most people normally think that "my way is the right way." And if you work together with "another you", you get confirmation all the time that your way is the right way. It is much more uncomfortable to work with a diverse team because people say things and propose things that you don't expect. (Top manager, HQ, Beta)

Beyond this top management homosociality — the preference for people who are considered similar in some significant way — there is also evidence to suggest that at Beta's HQ in Denmark there is increasing awareness about how the current practices of recruiting top managers are limiting.

They aim at selecting individuals who resemble the decision-makers themselves:

> "Our recruitment processes and policies state that everyone has equal opportunities and that we do not discriminate. But when you start analyzing the whole process and the steps you go through, you realize that in every single step of the process there are discriminating factors. They are just so embedded in our taken-for-granted practices that they are invisible to those who work with it on a daily basis. (Human resources manager, HQ, Beta)

By limiting the diversity in the executive management team, HQ silences itself — or rather, it silences any potential participant in the team who might challenge the ethnocentric Danish outlook of the HQ. Hence HQ creates a corporate club whose members persist in convincing each other that they are right. They blind themselves from their own biases and reject any opportunities to learn. In this way, Beta maintains a core group of top managers who agree on how to run the company.

In sum, there seems to be a tendency among HQ top managers at Alpha and Beta to convince each other that they have developed a particular corporate culture. Being in the HQ, in the nexus of power and in the place where all nationalities of the company meet, it is easy to ignore — and even forget about — your own ethnocentrism, and use corporate culture as a pretext to silence claims to the contrary. However, in an ethnocentric HQ there is a danger that this will become a cliché which blinds the top team from seeing its own lack of a global mindset. This concealed and silenced ethnocentrism has repercussions for relationships between HQ and the subsidiaries in the global network.

Concealing Ethnocentrism with Discipline

At Alpha, top managers not only silence critical or deviating voices within their own group, but also reject critical views originating from the rest of the organization such as the foreign subsidiaries. Since HQ top managers appear unable to admit or openly defend their own ethnocentrism, the only alternative is to forcefully silence any organizational talk about it. A Danish expatriate in one of Alpha's subsidiaries in Asia comments on this very issue:

> The problem is that the HQ people have a narrow Danish background and a narrow-minded view on things. [...] They deliberately choose to focus on the positive things to suppress any critique or negative attitudes. They simply do not acknowledge the problems. (Danish expatriate, Asian subsidiary unit, Alpha)

In the following, the local general manager of another Alpha subsidiary explains how unwelcome it is to ask what he calls "nasty questions" about ethnocentrism at HQ. Top managers at HQ demonstrate their power in a way that renders it risky to challenge them:

> I'm asking these nasty questions [...] I believe that within the top management we have to have [an] opportunity to discuss our internal problems. But they say: "blah, blah, blah – why do you ask just now? We are so satisfied with the results." There are colleagues who would like to help me, but for some reason they do not like to ask these questions. It's not easy. Sometimes it's risky. (General manager, subsidiary, Alpha)

Moreover, there is no international forum within Alpha that would provide an institutional channel for asking these "nasty questions" and feed them back to the executive management team, as one Danish middle manager who had recently been on an expatriate assignment pointed out:

> I think that we need a forum where we can discuss strategic issues with our colleagues from outside HQ. I am talking about more than three quarters of the employees in the company and some of the most skilled people that we have. We need them to participate, discuss, and give feedback to our top management here in Denmark. But we do not have an international forum where we can have such strategic discussions. That kind of relationship between top management and the international employees is completely lacking today. (Middle manager, HQ, Alpha)

Another manager based in a subsidiary in Asia explains that it would be only fair to resist HQ ethnocentrism, but people do not dare to do so as it is associated with the risk of losing your job:

> There is a social safety net for most of Europe, which means that people in Europe can survive without having a job for a relatively long period. That is not the case in Asia. We have to pay for our children's education and health care. On top of that, with the high degree of power distance in most Asian countries, employees are afraid to speak out and have a direct confrontation with their manager [sic]. (Human resources manager, Asian subsidiary unit, Alpha)

Another subsidiary general manager describes how it would be "tremendously beneficial" to challenge the ethnocentric HQ, but that this is not done because subsidiary managers engage in self-silencing behavior:

> Danes come here and they see the way we do it [...] It would be beneficial though [to challenge HQ], tremendously beneficial. But again, my opinion is the reason why people don't is because it is the mother ship, it is the heart and soul of the company, it is where everything started and the respect that you have. Your role is to learn about the way they do it, not to challenge or question or suggest the way they do it. [...] Denmark has all the money, so they just close in and say I won't give you any help. So you have to collaborate, you have to work with them. (General manager, North American subsidiary, Alpha)

However, in our interview with the Chairman of the Board of Alpha he invites a particular kind of resistance, what he calls "qualified." His meaning remains obscure, as his comment confirms the message that if subsidiary managers are not aligned with Alpha's corporate culture they need to be disciplined or "corrected" as he put it:

> I have always wished for qualified resistance. I have never demanded that people should agree with me. But I have always demanded that if they wish to be right, they need to work hard and argue firmly for what they want. There have not been many easy compromises. [...] It is a given that now and then there are challenges that need to be discussed, for instance when we observe that managers abroad have not always been aligned with our culture and our standards. These are normal things and they need to be corrected. (Chairman of the Board, HQ, Alpha)

Turning to Beta, concealing and silencing is achieved through personal control by physically co-locating individuals and teams at HQ in Denmark who think and talk in a similar way. A Danish middle manager who had been on a foreign assignment in Beta commented as follows:

> To some managers it means a lot that they physically sit almost in the same office, that they are able to just walk into each other's offices and talk about things. I just think that we cannot hold on to that way of thinking – we need to put an end to it. Otherwise we will never be global... It is not going to be possible to attract all kinds of talented and competent people to Denmark. [As if] the people who either live or want to live in Denmark would be the world's most competent individuals. I have a vague suspicion that this is not the case – without in any way offending Danes. (Middle manager, HQ, Beta)

In a similar vein, an inpatriate middle manager based at the Beta HQ in Denmark commented that "inbreeding" reduces the diversity of views and impoverishes the HQ:

> At headquarters they need to have a much more global outlook and mindset. Often it is only teams of Danes located in close physical proximity that are steering the global operations without [a] particular awareness of the diversity in the company. I find it hard to see that good intensions are enough. There is simply a lack of the skills and knowledge at headquarters needed to be able to effectively embrace all the managerial challenges you encounter in a global company. (Middle manager, HQ, Beta)

In sum, HQ at Alpha and Beta disguise ethnocentrism in statements about corporate culture that builds on the Danish national culture. They draw on various practices such as selective recruitment and foreign assignments to further conceal and silence ethnocentrism in their respective organizations. This has also led to self-silencing among subsidiary managers who are disciplined not to reveal the most public secret that is kept in Alpha and Beta.

DISCUSSION

Our vantage point in this paper was to offer a new take on ethnocentrism and approach it both from HQ and subsidiary perspectives in order to advance understanding of the orchestration of global networks in MNCs. Starting from the HQ's perspective, it has been argued that criticism and alternative solutions seldom reach the HQ because of the "corporate immune system" (Birkinshaw & Ridderstråle, 1999) or because subsidiaries themselves avoid raising delicate issues with the HQ that is known to be strongly ethnocentric in its outlook (Storgaard, 2010). Consequently, foreign subsidiaries often remain silent about locally experienced injustice and conflicts (Blazejewski, 2006). Either subsidiaries "passively resist and simply ignore" (Blazejewski, 2006, p. 89) HQ or they react to conflict with "unofficial, below-the-line venting of frustration" (Blazejewski, 2006, p. 87). Morrison and Milliken (2000) concur that employees tend to feel compelled to remain silent in the face of concerns related to the HQ mode of operation. The most common reason for not raising important issues is fear of negative repercussions, which was also a dominant theme in our case studies of Alpha and Beta. Alternatively, people in subsidiaries may feel that speaking up would make no difference. Morrison and Milliken (2000, p. 707), however, argue that "silence is a potentially dangerous impediment to organizational change and development and is likely to pose a significant obstacle to the development of truly pluralistic organizations."

In our case studies top managers at HQ concealed and silenced their own ethnocentrism through practices that reinforced a strong corporate culture and discipline. These top managers did not consider their own behavior detrimentally ethnocentric and rejected any criticism that suggested so. Furthermore, they disciplined subsidiaries into self-silence. Consequently, the ethnocentric status quo at HQ in Alpha and Beta was difficult to challenge − despite the rhetoric on global mindsets and integration fostered in the international management literature (Bartlett & Ghoshal, 1990, 1992; Gupta & Govindarajan, 2002).

Turning to the subsidiary perspective, Morgan and Kristensen (2006, p. 1479) distinguish between "boy scout subsidiaries" and "subversive strategists" who arguably differ in the extent to which they are prepared to react openly and critically towards the ethnocentric behavior of HQ management. The boy scouts "follow the demands of the head office and do not seek to develop or go beyond their existing mandate … [their] main concern is to implement … practices that head office recommends"

(Morgan & Kristensen, 2006, p. 1479). In contrast, the subversive subsidiary strategists are characterized by "a continuous search for mandate extension," irrespective of the rules the HQ tries to impose on them (Morgan & Kristensen, 2006, p. 1480). Either way, it is argued that subsidiaries must learn to "play the HQ game" if they want to retain influence in the MNC (Kristensen & Zeitlin, 2005, p. 196).

Our case studies indicate that a clear-cut distinction between two kinds of subsidiary strategists is a crude caricature of the complexity of the MNCs as an organization. Also, the HQ is not a monolithic entity. Those managers who had been on assignments abroad at Alpha and Beta voiced their readiness to adjust their views in order to accommodate to changing circumstances within the firm. Many insisted in our research interviews on voicing their doubts and concerns about how to run the geographically dispersed multinational. Yet, practices of ethnocentrism seem to be pervasive in the two organizations. Our field notes from Alpha suggest that these practices remain a highly sensitive issue at HQ. When contacting subsidiary respondents and expatriates for factual verification, they commented that "statements like this are almost enough to get you sacked," "you are touching upon a topic that is taboo in our organization," and that "this issue is about the most public secret in [Alpha]."

The question remains: What can be done about ethnocentrism in the MNC? At least four different answers suggest themselves. First, if the genuine objective is to achieve a form of geocentrism (Perlmutter, 1969), the challenge in orchestrating the global network of the MNC may lie in how those vested with power (more often than not top managers at the HQ) are able to engage in self-reflection and change their own ways of operating. The top management team must be able to reflect on the assumptions underlying the policies and practices that they seek to implement, and build feedback mechanisms and forums across organizational units. Also, because the composition of the top team carries symbolic meaning they could become an example in encouraging plurality and inclusion in the organization. Drawing on this signaling effect, a strong message could be sent to the organization by composing a top management team that reflects diversity.

The other answers are more unorthodox, at least viewed in the light of extant literature in international management. Second, top managers at the HQ could openly admit their ethnocentrism and argue for its benefits. A transparent management system could be built where this ethnocentrism could be capitalized through openly strict standards set by HQ. This would also entail a particular kind of brand-building, drawing from specific national and cultural symbols, icons, stories, and other discursive resources, rather than from a global image of the MNC (Vaara & Tienari, 2011). Perlmutter (1969) notes that MNCs pay particular attention to how their aspirations toward multinationality are conveyed externally in the eyes of the general public. If a particular form of ethnocentrism works in practice, why not pragmatically take advantage of it (Mayrhofer & Brewster, 1996)? Third, ethnocentrism could be turned into a management model where the subsidiaries would each be given clear targets, on the one hand, and substantial leeway in finding their own solutions to achieve these targets, on the other. The task of HQ (consisting of home country nationals) would be to make sure that a sufficient return on investment for the MNC is generated in the "portfolio" of different subsidiaries, taking advantage of the variety of localized solutions. Fourth, and finally, there is always the possibility to keep calm and carry on. One can seek to continue hiding ethnocentrism and pretending that it does not exist. Such a paradox of political correctness can be handled if HQ's belief in its own superiority is strong enough and if top managers have the courage to persevere in the pursuit of its chosen strategy while maintaining a facade of global integration.

CONCLUSION

As an organizational form, the global network of interdependent yet differentiated foreign subsidiaries is often depicted as the most advanced stage in the development of the MNC (Bartlett & Ghoshal, 1989; Gupta & Govindarajan, 2002; Nohria & Ghoshal, 1997). According to Perlmutter's (1969) seminal model, top managers should possess, at least in theory, a geocentric outlook and state of mind to orchestrate such a network. Perlmutter (1969, p. 11) yet warns us that a deeper analysis of the orientation of top managers towards "foreign people, ideas, and resources" may reveal a gulf between "public pronouncements about the firm's multinationality" and the living reality of the MNC. This is because many MNCs remain for considerable periods of time in a transitional stage from ethnocentrism toward polycentric and geocentric management models. They experience serious obstacles to geocentrism, which are in part associated with top management's cognitive, emotional, and behavioral limits. This renders the journey away from ethnocentrism "long and tortuous" (Perlmutter, 1969, p. 16).

Perlmutter's (1969) contribution to international management research lies in emphasizing the role of key decision-makers' attitudes towards foreignness and difference in contrast to more external and quantitative parameters of multinationality such as percentage of investments overseas, number of foreign nationals who have reached top positions, and foreign ownership. While his ethnocentric-polycentric-geocentric model has been highly influential in the field, Perlmutter's skepticism towards the evolutionary movement of MNCs from ethnocentrism to polycentrism and geocentrism has received less attention. Our reading of Perlmutter's work suggests that not only did he pinpoint the perils of ethnocentrism as a top management attitude, but also detailed some its fundamental causes and consequences, which are related to the social fabric and the behavioral aspects of managing and orchestrating the MNC. Our case studies of Danish MNCs confirm that persistent ethnocentrism is first and foremost contained in the *practices* that the HQ sustains and imposes on the subsidiaries, rather than in the "attitudes" of top managers per se. We offer cultural and disciplinary practices as examples of this. Further, we argue that practices related to *concealing* and *silencing* ethnocentrism are particularly important here. They not only sustain ethnocentrism, but render it an ambiguous and paradoxical condition in the functioning of the MNC.

In this paper, we have detailed practices of concealing and silencing ethnocentrism for further theory development. We have thus joined Perlmutter (1969) in his quest to understand why ethnocentrism persists in the MNC. The different forms of silencing complement his findings, and those of Westney (1993), and enable us to better understand why certain MNCs may not experience a need for evolutionary movement from ethnocentrism towards supposedly more "advanced" stages in the first place. Top management's recurring efforts to conceal and silence ethnocentrism are widely known and recognized in our case companies; "the most public secret" in the MNC. Our findings thus open interesting avenues for further research. We envisage that future studies could focus on silencing as a powerful mechanism to exercise culture control and engineer mindsets in the MNC (Welch & Welch, 1997). It would also be important to shed light on the lack of self-reflection and learning on the part of HQ managers who actively maintain ethnocentric practices. As Perlmutter (1969, p. 17) writes, the question is about a pervasive change "not only in attitude but in dress and speech" to alter the course in the development of the MNC. Finally, how the HQ works on the MNC's "global" reputation and brand in inter-organizational relationships and the media while operating in an ethnocentric way is a topic that calls for attention. Anecdotal evidence from our case companies suggests that this form of "silencing through branding" – through various communication channels to convince both external and internal audiences that ethnocentrism does not exist – would be a relevant subject of further inquiry. In fact, Perlmutter (1969) identified for more than 40 years ago that the "public eye" may reinforce or challenge MNC top managers' aspirations towards multinationality. This perspective on the MNC from "outside-in" could offer uncharted opportunities for international management researchers, potentially in collaboration with colleagues from other disciplines such as marketing and organizational communications.

ACKNOWLEDGMENT

We would like to acknowledge D. Eleanor Westney's and the guest editors' insightful suggestions and comments on an earlier draft of this paper.

REFERENCES

Adler, N., & Bartholomew, S. (1992). Globalization and human resource management. In A. M. Rugman & A. Verbeke (Eds.), *Research in global strategic management: Corporate response to global change* (Vol. 3, pp. 179–201). Greenwich, CT: JAI Press.

Aldrich, R. J., & Kasuku, J. (2012). Escaping from American intelligence: Culture, ethnocentrism and the Anglosphere. *International Affairs, 88*, 1009–1028.

Banai, M. (1992). The ethnocentric staffing policy in multinational corporations: A self-fulfilling prophecy. *International Journal of Human Resource Management, 3*, 451–472.

Barner-Rasmussen, W., Piekkari, R., Scott-Kennel, J., & Welch, C. (2010). Commander-in-chief or absentee landlord? Key perspectives on headquarters in multinational corporations. In U. Andersson & U. Holm (Eds.), *Managing the contemporary multinational: The role of headquarters* (pp. 85–105). Cheltenham: Edward Elgar.

Bartlett, C. A., & Ghoshal, S. (1987). Managing across borders: New organizational responses. *Sloan Management Journal, 29*, 43–54.

Bartlett, C. A., & Ghoshal, S. (1989). *Managing across borders: The transnational solution.* Boston, MA: Harvard Business School.

Bartlett, C. A., & Ghoshal, S. (1990). Matrix management: Not a structure, a frame of mind. *Harvard Business Review, 68*, 138–145.

Bartlett, C. A., & Ghoshal, S. (1992). What is a global manager? *Harvard Business Review, 70*, 124–132.

Birkinshaw, J., & Ridderstråle, J. (1999). Fighting the corporate immune system: A process study of subsidiary initiatives in multinational corporations. *International Business Review, 8*, 149–180.

Blazejewski, S. (2006). Transferring value-infused organizational practices in multinational companies: A conflict perspective. In M. Geppert & M. Mayer (Eds.), *Global, national and local practices in multinational companies* (pp. 63−104). Houndmills: Palgrave Macmillan.

Caligiuri, P., & Tarique, I. (2012). Dynamic cross-cultural competencies and global leadership effectiveness. *Journal of World Business, 47*, 612−622.

Edwards, T., Colling, T., & Ferner. A. (2007). Conceptual approaches to the transfer of employment practices in multinational companies: An integrated approach. *Human Resource Management Journal, 17*, 201−217.

Florkowski, G. W., & Fogel, D. S. (1999). Expatriate adjustment and commitment: The role of host-unit treatment. *The International Journal of Human Resource Management, 10*, 783−807.

Frenkel, M. (2008). The multinational corporation as a third space: Rethinking international management discourse on knowledge transfer through Homi Bhabha. *Academy of Management Review, 33*, 924−942.

Gupta, A. K., & Govindarajan, V. (2002). Cultivating a global mindset. *Academy of Management Perspectives, 16*, 116−126.

Hamel, G., & Breen, B. (2007). *The future of management*. Boston, MA: Harvard Business School Press.

Hedlund, G. (1986). The hypermodern MNC: A heterarchy? *Human Resource Management, 25*, 9−35.

Hedlund, G. (1993). Introduction: Organization and management of transnational corporations in practice and research. In G. Hedlund (Ed.), *Organization of transnational corporations*, The United Nations Library on Transnational Corporations (Vol. 6, pp. 1−21). London: Routledge.

Hedlund, G., & Kogut, B. (1993). Managing the MNC: The end of the missionary era. In G. Hedlund (Ed.), *Organization of transnational corporations*, The United Nations Library on Transnational Corporations (Vol. 6, pp. 343−358). New York, NY: Routledge.

Kristensen, P. H., & Zeitlin, J. (2005). *Local players in global games: The strategic constitution of a multinational corporation*. Oxford: Oxford University Press.

Leiba-O'Sullivan, S. (1999). The distinction between stable and dynamic cross-cultural competencies: Implications for expatriate trainability. *Journal of International Business Studies, 30*, 709−725.

Levy, O., Beechler, S., Taylor, S., & Boyacigiller, N. A. (2007). What we talk about when we talk about "global mindset": Managerial cognition in multinational corporations. *Journal of International Business Studies, 38*, 231−258.

Maljers, F. A. (1992). Inside Unilever: The evolving transnational corporation. *Harvard Business Review, 70*, 46−52.

Martinez, J. I., & Jarillo, J. C. (1989). The evolution of research on coordination mechanisms in multinational corporations. *Journal of International Business Studies, 20*, 489−514.

Mayrhofer, W., & Brewster, C. (1996). In praise of ethnocentricity: Expatriate policies in European multinationals. *The International Executive, 38*, 749−778.

Morgan, G., & Kristensen, P. H. (2006). The contested space of multinationals: Varieties of institutionalism, varieties of capitalism. *Human Relations, 59*, 1467−1490.

Morrison, E. W., & Milliken, F. J. (2000). Organizational silence: A barrier to change and development in a pluralistic world. *Academy of Management Review, 25*, 706−725.

Muratbekova-Touron, M. (2008). From an ethnocentric to a geocentric approach to IHRM: The case of a French multinational company. *Cross Cultural Management: An International Journal, 15*, 335–352.

Nadler, D. A., & Shaw, R. B. (1995). Change leadership: Core competency for the twenty-first century. In D. A. Nadler, R. B. Shaw & A. E. Walton (Eds.), *Discontinuous change: Leading organizational transformation.* San Francisco, CA: Jossey-Bass.

Nobel, R., & Birkinshaw, J. (1998). Innovation in multinational corporations: Control and communication patterns in international R&D. *Strategic Management Journal, 19*, 479–496.

Nohria, N., & Ghoshal, S. (1997). *The differentiated network: Organizing multinational corporations for value creation.* San Francisco, CA: Jossey-Bass.

Perlmutter, H. V. (1969). The tortuous evolution of the multinational corporation. *Columbia Journal of World Business, 4*, 9–18.

Poynter, T. A., & White, R. E. (1985). The strategies of foreign subsidiaries: Responses to organizational slack. *International Studies of Management and Organization, 14*, 91–106.

Riefler, P., Diamantopoulos, A., & Siguaw, J. A. (2012). Cosmopolitan consumers as a target group for segmentation. *Journal of International Business Studies, 43*, 285–305.

Schein, E. (1984). Coming to a new awareness of organizational culture. *Sloan Management Review, 25*, 3–16.

Sharma, P. (2011). Country of origin effects in developed and emerging markets: Exploring the contrasting roles of materialism and value consciousness. *Journal of International Business Studies, 42*, 285–306.

Storgaard, M. (2010). *Lokale syn på globale horisonter: Et kritisk perspektiv på HQ's rolle i den globaliserende MNC (Local views on global horizons: A critical perspective on HQ's role in the globalizing MNC).* Ph.D. thesis, Aarhus University Press, Aarhus School of Business.

Storgaard, M., Michailova, S., Piekkari, P., & Tienari, J. (2014). *Rethinking ethnocentrism in the evolution and management of the multinational corporation.* Unpublished manuscript.

Templer, K. J. (2010). Personal attributes of expatriate managers, subordinate ethnocentrism, and expatriate success: A host-country perspective. *International Journal of Human Resource Management, 21*, 1754–1768.

Thomas, K. M. (1996). Psychological privilege and ethnocentrism as barriers to cross-cultural adjustment and effective intercultural interactions. *The Leadership Quarterly, 7*, 215–228.

Thomas, M., & Hill, H. (1999). The impact of ethnocentrism on devising and implementing a corporate identity strategy for new international markets. *International Marketing Review, 16*, 376–390.

Vaara, E., & Tienari, J. (2011). On the narrative construction of MNCs: An antenarrative analysis of legitimation and resistance in a cross-border merger. *Organization Science, 22*, 370–390.

Vaara, E., Tienari, J., & Björkman, I. (2003). Best practice is west practice? A sensemaking perspective on knowledge transfer in a merging organization. *Nordiske Organisasjonsstudier (Nordic Organization Studies), 5*, 37–57.

Welch, D. E., & Welch, L. S. (1997). Being flexible and accommodating diversity: The challenge for multinational management. *European Management Journal, 15*, 677–685.

Westney, E. (1993). Institutionalization theory and the multinational corporation. In S. Ghoshal & E. Westney (Eds.), *Organization theory and the multinational corporation* (pp. 53–76). Houndmills: Macmillan.

Zeira, Y. (1976). Management development in ethnocentric multinational corporations. *California Management Review, 18*, 34–42.

Zeira, Y., Harari, E., & Nundi, D. I. (1975). Some structural and cultural factors in ethnocentric multinational corporations and employee morale. *Journal of Management Studies, 12*, 66–82.

THE OMNIPOTENT MNC –
A REVIEW AND DISCUSSION

Håkan Pihl and Alexander Paulsson

ABSTRACT

Until the late 1990s researcher described a new strategy and organiza-tion for MNCs. The new MNC was omnipotent in character, striving for many new competitive advantages. This paper reviews the literature and synthesizes the ideas behind this Omnipotent MNC. General themes and key organizational characteristics are identified. A survey among large Swedish companies illustrate that many of the identified changes has occurred during recent years. Finally, we discuss why this kind of research more or less vanished.

Keywords: The Omnipotent MNC; new MNC organization/strategy; Transnational; Integrated network

INTRODUCTION

The idea of a new strategy/organization for multinational corporations emerged as a theme in international business research during the late 1980s

Orchestration of the Global Network Organization
Advances in International Management, Volume 27, 213–233
ISSN: 1571-5027/doi:10.1108/S1571-502720140000027028

and 1990s. Traditional choices between different alternative strategies and organizational trade-offs were replaced by all-enhancing ambitions, which were to be realized by a new and more complex organizational model. Units belonging to MNCs were expected to be globally specialized as well as locally adapted, to exploit existing knowledge as well as contribute with new innovations, to be decentralized, entrepreneurial and a node in an informal network without losing its predictability as part of a formal hierarchical system. The new model was omnipotent.

Different researchers described the characteristics of this new phenomenon by developing new concepts and models. Below we list names given to this new strategy/organization, to illustrate the rich flora of contributions:

Geocentric (Perlmutter, 1969), Dynamic network (Miles & Snow, 1984), Heterarchy (Hedlund, 1986), Transnational (Bartlett, 1986), Multinational Mission (Prahalad & Doz, 1987), Integrated Network (Bartlett, 1986; Bartlett & Ghoshal, 1992), Horizontal (White & Poynter, 1990), Multicenter (Forsgren, 1990), Integrated player (Gupta & Govindarajan, 1991), Wired (Hagström, 1991), Holographic (Ridderstråle, 1992), Transcontinental (Humes, 1993), Multidimensional (Jansson, 1994), N-form (Hedlund, 1994), Integrated global (Malnight, 1995), Dynamic MNE (Sölvell & Zander, 1995), Network-based (Malnight, 1996), Less Hierarchical (Marschan, 1994), Metanational (Doz, Asakawa, Santos, & Williamson, 1996), Differentiated network (Nohria & Ghoshal, 1997), Individualized enterprise (Ghoshal & Bartlett, 1997), W-form (Pihl, 2000), The Network Firm (Forsgren, 2002), The modern firm (Roberts, 2004).

At the time, a widespread belief among researchers was that they witnessed a new and path-breaking organizational innovation, as important as − for example − the innovation of the divisionalized organization in the early 1900s (Bartlett & Ghoshal, 1993; Egelhoff, 1998; Hedlund, 1994; Miles & Snow, 1984). But then, within only a few years, researchers turned their back to the discussion. In the early 2000s, the stream of research on the new strategy and organization for MNCs almost had vanished. The idea of the Omnipotent MNC, however, has later become part of the established popular view of MNCs, for example as expressed in today's textbooks in International Business and Organization theory (i.e., Child, 2005; Daft, Murphy, & Willmott, 2010; Hill, 2011). Hence, the idea of an Omnipotent MNC might have died as a research field, but it is still a living part of the general perception of MNCs, shared by thousands of business students and, by extension, managers globally.

What was the idea of a new strategy/organization all about? Did it resemble real changes in strategic orientation and organization? Why did the research so suddenly vanish? This paper will focus on the first question. We look back on the literature of the early years and synthesize the contributions. Common themes among researchers are identified and the various suggested organizational changes are summarized. Then we discuss if changes have been realized and why research vanished. A survey is presented on managers' perceptions of organizational change in large Swedish firms.

EARLY CONTRIBUTIONS

A pioneering contribution to the idea of a new organization was presented by Perlmutter in the late 1960s. Perlmutter (1969) described the new orientation of MNCs as "geocentric" rather than "ethnocentric" or "polycentric." Perlmutter's contribution is today mostly known for his view on staffing policies; geocentric organizations used the best managerial competence regardless of the nationality of managers whereas ethnocentric organizations used managers from the home country and polycentric organizations used nationals from host countries. But Perlmutter also described the emergence of a more general change in organizations, which was perceived to be very promising.

> the senior executives engaged in building the geocentric enterprise could well be the most important social architects of the last third of the twentieth century. For the institution they are trying to erect promises a great universal sharing of wealth and a consequent control of the explosive centrifugal tendencies of our evolving world community.
>
> Perlmutter (1969, p. 18)

Characteristic for the new organization was that headquarters and subsidiaries all shared a worldwide approach. Subsidiaries were described as "neither satellites nor independent city states, but parts of a whole whose focus is on worldwide objectives as well as local objectives, each part making its unique contribution with its unique competence" (Perlmutter, 1969, p. 13).

The headquarter approach toward subsidiaries was to be more complex and interdependent, more collaborative and with more communication from headquarters to subsidiaries, from subsidiaries to headquarters, as well as between subsidiaries. The subsidiaries were to be both local and universal oriented and standards and rewards were to be both universal and local. Local subsidiary managers should ask themselves where in the world they could get help to serve their local customers and to where in the world they could export their local products, which should meet global standards.

Another early contribution along similar lines was presented by Edström and Galbraith in the late 1970s. Edström and Galbraith (1977) observed an increase in complexity in MNCs, with more need for novel decision-making in the subsidiaries. To coordinate this complexity Edström and Galbraith suggested an increase in coordination by socialization (today also named normative or cultural control), in addition to the centralization and bureaucratic methods used in earlier stages of development. The latter methods were to be modified to fit the new structure. Edström and Galbraith also identified frequent transfers of managers as a method for changing the organization. By transferring managers between units they would become more socialized into corporate views and values and they would also develop a network of personal relations to people in many units and locations, with whom they could continuously communicate. Hereby a "verbal information network" would evolve; a more informal and flexible system for decision-making, parallel to the formal structure. Subsidiary managers that were socialized into corporate values and that actively participated in the corporate verbal information network would gain power and influence. Over time a more interdependent network of more decentralized and autonomous subsidiaries would evolve which, according to Edström and Galbraith (1977), was an efficient way to coordinate increasingly complex operations.

A NEW ORGANIZATIONAL FORM

The idea of a new organization developed further in the 1980s. Hedlund (1986) named the new organization "Heterarchical," an organization characterized by many different centers. Subsidiaries should be more independent and given strategic roles for the MNC as a whole. An important mechanism for coordination was, again, the normative, cultural control. Concerning the organizational structure, Hedlund suggested that different models could be used simultaneously with flexibility. The organization should be multidimensional and more subtle measures than organizational structure needed to be developed, that is, new management processes, developed HRM and communication networks. Some years later, Hedlund (1994) elaborated the ideas further and emphasized the use of knowledge and dynamic capabilities and identified a new "N-form" (N as in Novelty, a form that comes after the M-form). The N-form was characterized by combining different parts by temporary constellations and horizontal communication. The critical organizational level was middle management, who should facilitate horizontal relations. Top managers should be catalysers and architects rather than controllers and allocators. Other researchers continued along similar lines. White and Poynter (1990), for example, described a new organization in MNCs as a "horizontal organization," a network with lateral decision-making processes as a way to balance global and local dimensions.

Was there empirical evidence supporting the idea of a new organization? Most contributions used case studies to generate ideas about the characteristics of a new form, but few attempts were made to analyze how general the phenomenon was. Martinez and Jarillo (1989) synthesized 85 empirical studies between 1952 and 1988 and concluded that there was support for a more general emerging phenomenon. They summarized the development in three phases. In the 1920–1950s, MNCs were loosely coupled with subsidiary managers from the home country reporting to headquarters. In the period of 1950–1980, headquarters centralized control over production and development and introduced more formalized divisional structures. After the 1980s, a more integrated structure emerged with responsibilities for production becoming more decentralized to specialized plants, and with strong interdependencies and inter-organizational transfers of technology and ideas within the network. Coordination developed from simpler to more complex mechanisms covering more multidimensional perspectives. The corporate structure for this new era was, according to Martinez and Jarillo (1989), a global matrix built on the former divisionalized structure. They also observed that coordination increased with the use of more mechanisms. Decision-making was more centralized but subsidiary mandates were also more upgraded. There was still a high degree of formalization but output control was also tight and complex. And, beyond these mechanisms, there was an increase in informal coordination mechanisms with the use of temporary teams, task forces and integrators. The new form was characterized by a more elaborated use of informal channels of communication, personal relationships between managers, and a strong organizational culture. The study by Martinez and Jarillo (1989) confirms that, at the turn of 1980–1990s, the idea of a new organization in MNCs was widely shared among researchers.

The probably most influential and popular contributions describing this new phenomenon was presented by Bartlett and Ghoshal in the late 1980s and early 1990s. Bartlett (1986) presented a framework of different strategies and structural configurations in MNCs and identified a new future development as a "Transnational" strategy using the coordinating configuration "Integrated network" (Bartlett, 1986). Earlier strategies/ organizations had been either focused on local adaption ("Multinational strategy/Decentralized federation") or global scale ("Global strategy/ Centralized hub"). The Transnational strategy aimed at both. In the new form subsidiaries had globally specialized roles and integrated with each other to support different local customer demands. The integrated network was characterized by large flows of resources, products, people and information in all directions. At the time, MNCs striving for being global and local was also elaborated by other researchers, that is, Prahalad and Doz (1987) argued for sensitivity for local demand and a global vision.

Bartlett and Ghoshal (1988) also observed the possibilities for subsidiaries to contribute with new knowledge and innovation, and found that socialization and dense intra- and inter-unit communication had a positive impact on a subsidiary's ability to contribute. Later, Bartlett and Ghoshal (1992) added the dimension of innovation and knowledge diffusion to the analysis of alternative strategies/configurations and identified the transfer of firm-specific knowledge from headquarters to subsidiaries as an "International strategy/Coordinated federation." They also added knowledge transfers into the "Transnational/Integrated Network," but in this context knowledge and ideas were expected to be transferred in all directions, also between subsidiaries and from subsidiaries to headquarters. Innovations and learning in MNCs have since then been a popular theme in research. (For some early contributions, see Cantwell, 1989; Kogut & Zander, 1993; Liebeskind, 1996).

On the question of formal structure, Bartlett and Ghoshal (1992) differed from Martinez and Jarillo (1989) and argued against the use of a matrix. Instead they emphasized other dimensions than structure, especially managerial roles and the development of a multidimensional "mind matrix" where managers managed with flexibility, and different managerial groups had different roles for different activities, balancing each other. Managers with global, functional, and local responsibilities should all have a say in this complex organization. Coordination should be sophisticated and altering between different mechanisms. Informal communication and temporary integrating projects and committees should be added to the formal structure.

In a later contribution (Bartlett & Ghoshal, 1993), the new strategy and organization was compared to the traditional divisional form (M-form) and, again, the authors argued for a developed managerial perspective for coordinating the Integrated Network. Inspired by a new organization in ABB (Taylor, 1991) they also, argued for radical decentralization and that stronger entrepreneurial responsibilities should be given to front line managers. In later contributions, they continued to argue for the idea that highly decentralized units for profits and development should collaborate and interact with each other with flexibility, as a response to disadvantages in earlier divisionalized structures where units were locked into divisions and divisional management limited management responsibility at lower levels. The divisional borders of the M-form should be opened up and units at sub-divisional levels should be given more responsibilities for operation efficiency as well as strategic development. For coordination, Bartlett & Ghoshal (1997), again, emphasized on management skills rather than structure and control mechanisms, and called the new organization an "Indivualized corporation" (Bartlett & Ghoshal, 1997). Units should be free to interact with others, over divisional borders in the whole MNC. Middle-managers were expected to facilitate such collaborations, and act as horizontal information brokers and integrators of capabilities. Top management should create and communicate purpose and challenge the status quo by selective interventions.

Other strands of research elaborated on similar ideas during these years. Here follows some examples from the Scandinavian horizon: Forsgren (1990) identified "Mulit-center firms" as an internalization process of second degree. Hagström (1991) identified the "Wired MNC" as an organization that uses new information technology and therefore manages to be more differentiated and specialized. The new technology makes it possible to report and evaluate more dimensions; hence a more complex coordination is possible. Ridderstråle (1992, 1996) argued for a "Holographic Organization" where the different parts resembled the whole enterprise. Also Ridderstråle (1992, 1996) argued for a radical decentralization, geographical diffusion of strategic assets and global coordination of these assets. Jansson (1994) identified a new, more boundary free "multidimensional organization" with several strategic dimensions, organized as a more informal, differentiated and decentralized form with both internal hierarchal and market mechanisms. Sölvell and Zander (1995) discussed the organization of the Dynamic MNE and argued that heterarchy is a structure that selectively taps into different home bases.

The writing on a new organization in MNCs continued during the late 1990s. Malnight (1995, 1996) used case studies to learn about the process when firms transform to a transnational strategy. Nohria and Ghoshal (1997) argued for a flexible use of coordination mechanisms, different for different kind of subsidiaries, and labeled such an organization a "Differentiated Network." Doz et al. (1996) named the new organization "Metanational" and emphasized the function to orchestrate multiple capabilities from different external environments. Buckley and Casson (1998) explained the need for more flexible structures in MNCs with the increase of environmental volatility and suggested more flat, federative organizations with more networking among managers and an increased use of internal market relations. Forsgren (2002) reflected on the socio-economic implications of the "Network MNC" and concluded that it was the most preferable structure compared to the earlier "Multi-domestic" and "Global MNC," especially because "the Network MNC" is well suited for knowledge transfers across borders.

ADJACENT FIELDS OF RESEARCH

The writings on the Omnipotent MNC emphasized the strategic importance of subsidiaries and a special branch of research developed with a focus on subsidiaries. Some examples: Gupta and Govindarajan (1991) described innovative roles among subsidiaries, as implementers, local innovators, global innovators and integrated players. Andersson and Forsgren (1994) analysed how subsidiaries are affected by their local business networks, as well as their corporate belonging. Birkinshaw (1996) and Birkinshaw and Hood (1998) discussed subsidiary mandates and entrepreneurial initiatives and Taggart (1998) studied strategy shifts in subsidiaries.

The emerging perception of a new organization in MNCs was also coherent with a more general discussion of a new and more networked organizational form for firms in general, and the use of networks as a coordinating mechanism between markets and hierarchies, early observed by, for example, Powell (1991). One such example is Miles and Snow (1993) who analyzed a development where large corporations dissolved into dynamic networks of firms coordinated by "broker firms" using market mechanisms rather than chains of control. (For an analysis of these brand name firms, responsible for design and orchestration, see Dhanaraj & Parkhe, 2006; Pihl, 2013.)

The internal organization of large organizations could also develop more networked structures. Fulk and DeSanctis (1995) summarized the literature on firm-internal networked forms and suggested that they would be flatter with more cross-functional collaborations and process-orientation.

The new information technology would make these structures more coordination-intensive and make it possible to combine increased decentralization with elements of centralization. Coordination by shared culture and internal market mechanisms would increase. Ostroff (1999) described a similar development but emphasized that the traditional functional structure of large organizations would change to more cross-functional and process-oriented structures with more decentralized decision-making.

Disadvantages with these new organizational structures were seldomly discussed. One exemption was Marschan (1994) who concluded that frequent personal transfers might harm informal, personal relations between subsidiaries and that decentralized units might develop a myopic perspective. The contributions also rather seldomly provided a more elaborate theoretical analysis of the development, comparable to i.e. the analysis of the divisionalized form presented by Williamson (1975, 1985). Kogut and Zander (1993) used evolutionary theory and analyzed MNCs as an institution for transferring knowledge. Attempts were also made to analyze the development by transaction cost analysis. Rugman and Verbeke (1992) related the transnational strategy to the ability to develop both location-bound and not location-bound firm-specific advantages. Pihl (2000) identified the new organization as a new W-form, following on the earlier M-form and U-form. Dunning (2000) integrated writing on the new organization into the Eclectic Paradigm by identifying the specific competence of managers as a kind of ownership advantage. Roberts (2004) presented a "modern firm", with similarities to the Omnipotent MNC, and related it to later developments in economics, that is, theory on complementarities. (For a more extensive overview of different theoretical perspectives on MNCs, see Forsgren, 2008.)

THE CHARACTERISTICS OF THE OMNIPOTENT MNC

As has been illustrated, multiple contributions researched the emergence of a new strategy and organization of MNCs, especially during the 1980s and 1990s. What did the Omnipotent MNCs aim for? Some interlinked set of ideas can be identified.

A first idea concerned the solution to the contradiction of global specialization and local adaption. The Omnipotent MNC developed a new kind of global specialization and a new kind of local adaption. Earlier globally specialized MNCs had one center that was globally specialized, responsible for the main part of the value creating process. In the Omnipotent MNC, value creation was divided among several dispersed globally specialized units, each with unique advantages due to their different skills and locations. This was a more widespread and sophisticated strategy of global specialization.

On the other hand, earlier locally adapted MNCs had their units supporting different local markets by developing their own different value creation processes. Here, the Omnipotent MNC expected local units to adapt to local variations, not by developing the necessary skills and components themselves, but by collaborating with other specialized units in a network. This was a more widespread and sophisticated strategy for local adaption.

The above global specialization and local adaption involved more specialization among disperse units and collaborations between units in a new and more intensive way. Therefore it is perhaps not surprising that, as a second set of ideas, knowledge development and knowledge transfers came into focus. In earlier structures knowledge and skills were developed at the center and exploited by satellites, or – with local adaption – developed at satellites for the various local demands. In the Omnipotent MNC, new knowledge was developed at many locations by dispersed units, isolated or in collaborations, and shared wherever it was needed around the network. This was a more widespread and sophisticated strategy for developing and exploiting knowledge.

With these more integrated processes for production, marketing and development, it is perhaps also natural that research focused also on entrepreneurial and networking capabilities, a third set of ideas related to the Omnipotent MNC. The new strategic ambitions required managers to act and interact with flexibility and speed over the borders of functions, units and levels. In earlier structures such entrepreneurial and cross-boundary activities were reserved for managers at top positions. The Omnipotent MNC encouraged such entrepreneurial activities in a more widespread and sophisticated way.

Hence, the perception of the aim of a new organization changed over time, and new organizational characteristics were added accordingly. With the strategic purpose to be both more global and more local, the organization allocated specialized roles to different parts of the organization, making use of different localization advantages. At the same time, it should be more flexible and adaptive to local customer needs. With the purpose to increase organizational learning, knowledge development in different parts was encouraged, with collaborations and transfers of knowledge in multiple directions. More decentralized responsibilities were needed to vitalize entrepreneurial initiatives in different parts of the organization, as well increased flexibility. The divisions were opened up and responsibilities for profits and development were decentralized to units at lower levels.

To sum up the organizational characteristics of the Omnipotent MNC: The literature suggests that the MNC should allocate specialized roles to dispersed "global centres" and, at the same time, decentralize responsibilities for local customer adaption to local units. The units should be involved in extensive interactions and cross-functional collaborations over organizational borders. In this decentralized structure, there is still some selective centralization – managers at corporate and divisional/functional levels control sub-units when it is perceived necessary. Formalization is modified with an increase of standardized measures and communication tools. More performance evaluations and exchanges between units increase control by internal market measures. The Omnipotent MNCs also emphasize socialization (normative, cultural control) and an extensive use of informal communication, at all levels. Informal, horizontal communication, cross-border collaborations and new initiatives are encouraged throughout the organization. In this context managers develop new roles – local unit managers become more entrepreneurial, divisional, and functional managers become more focused on cross-unit integration and top management more focused on visions, values and overall direction. The characteristics of the Omnipotent MNC are summarized in Table 1.

Table 1. Characteristics of the Omnipotent MNC.

Ten Organizational Characteristics

1. Responsibilities decentralized to front level units, with selective centralization.
2. Adaption to customers by the flexible use of the whole network of the MNC.
3. Dispersed units with specialized roles, that is, for production and research.
4. Informal communication between people in different parts of the corporation.
5. Evaluations and comparisons of output and performance.
6. Middle-managers facilitate collaborations and coordination among local units.
7. Knowledge shared between different units in the corporation.
8. Functions are integrated (i.e., R&D and production).
9. Multiple sources for new ideas and development initiatives.
10. Members of the corporation share common visions and values.

SURVEY OF ORGANIZATIONAL CHANGES

Research on the new model was highly conceptual. Many of the contributions above were inspired by observations from case studies of successful MNCs. More general surveys of the change toward Omnipotent MNCs were rare. The inventory of 85 empirical studies made by Martinez and Jarillo (1989) covered about 60 large-sample studies describing the use of coordination mechanisms in MNCs. To identify a development in the use of mechanisms, Martinez and Jarillo compared the studies, concluding that the focus changed over time and that more informal mechanisms were observed in later studies. This was interpreted as an actual general change in MNCs. A later survey by Harzing (1999) studied the use of control mechanisms in more than one hundred MNCs in different nations. Harzing mapped an extensive use of different mechanisms and concluded that the use varied in various contexts.

Few, if any, surveys have been made to study if MNCs actually have been changing their organization in the direction discussed in literature. And there are few, if any, studies on how general the change is. Is the new organization a model for all or is it an organizational model for corporations in specific contingencies, that is, complex and dynamic environments? The contingency tradition was strong at the time of the contributions, but the literature on a new organization is remarkably generalistic.

Longitudinal studies of organizational changes on large populations of MNCs are complex to conduct. A more feasible approach is to ask managers in MNCs about their experiences during a range of years. Have they experienced the predicted changes? One such study was presented by Pihl (2008) who surveyed 56 large international corporations with substantial activities in Sweden. Managers from each corporation were interviewed about their perception of organizational changes. The result strongly supported an increase in knowledge sharing, in integration of functions, in more informal communication and in the allocation of specialized roles to units for production and research. It also found support for more decentralization and adaption to local demands. However, the study did not provide support for more supportive roles of middle-managers and more comparisons and competition among units. The study was conducted in the early 2000s and a question is if the predicted changes are still going on today? Below we present a study of large corporations in Sweden, investigating changes toward the predicted characteristics of a new organization.

PROCEDURE, SAMPLE, AND MEASURES

Telephone interviews were made by a group of 147 business students, each interviewing one manager at one of the 200 largest companies in Sweden, as measured by turnover. (The largest company had 102,082 employees, the company on place 199 had 827 employees.) The respondents had a management position and had been working in the company for at least 5 years. In all, 123 managers representing 122 large corporations were interviewed; the response rate was about 80 percent. In general, the students believed that the managers understood the questions well. After the students had done their interviews, they were asked to write a few sentences where they reflected on the process and its outcomes. The respondents were asked to answer "Yes," "No" or "Don't know" to 10 statements describing organizational change, corresponding to the characteristics identified in the literature review. Each statement started with "Compared to some years ago, today there is ...," followed by the statement (see Table 2).

ANALYSIS AND RESULTS

Had the managers experienced the organizational changes? The "yes"-answers dominated over the "no"-answers, and there were also "don't know"-answers. To compensate for a possible yes-bias (more discussed later) "don't know" answers were coded as "no" answers. The answers were compared and, again, a descriptive analysis showed that "yes"-answers were more frequent than "no" answers. A binomial test was used to analyze the outcome, using a two-tailed test with a 95% confidence interval. The test was analyzed by using SPSS and the result is summarized in Table 2.

Statements with more than 50% on the lower tail of the interval, as shown in the right column of Table 2, have a statistically significant Yes-majority. Seven of the ten statements are supported by this analysis. The strongest support was shown for statement 2 (flexible and adapting to different customer demands), 7 (sharing of knowledge and experiences between different units), and 10 (emphasis on visions and values). Support was also given to statement 8 (integration between different functions) and 9 (people from a wider range of units and management levels contribute with ideas for development). Some support was finally also found for statement 1 (more decentralization but also more centralization in some areas) and 5 (increase of comparisons between units and more evaluation on

Table 2. Binominal Analysis of Managers' Perception of Organizational Change.

Variables/Statements	Category	N	Observed Proportion	Test Proportion	Lower Tail 95% Confidence Interval
1. There is more decentralization of responsibilities but also more centralization in some areas.	Yes No	81 42	0.74 0.36	0.50	0.57
2. There is more emphasis on being flexible and adapting to different customer demands.	Yes No	109 14	0.90 0.10	0.50	0.83
3. Units for production and research have more specialized roles.	Yes No	63 60	0.68 0.32	0.50	0.42
4. There is more informal communication between people in different parts of the corporation.	Yes No	69 54	0.64 0.36	0.50	0.47
5. There are more comparisons between units in the corporation, and more evaluations of performance.	Yes No	83 40	0.76 0.24	0.50	0.59
6. Middle-managers are more supportive, less controlling.	Yes No	69 54	0.65 0.35	0.50	0.47
7. There is more sharing of knowledge and experiences between different units in the corporation.	Yes No	101 22	0.84 0.16	0.50	0.75
8. There is more integration between different functions (i.e., R&D and production work more close together).	Yes No	92 31	0.76 0.34	0.50	0.67
9. More people from a wider range of organizational units and management levels contribute with ideas for development.	Yes No	92 31	0.80 0.20	0.50	0.67
10. There is more emphasis on visions and values in the corporation.	Yes No	98 25	0.82 0.18	0.50	0.72

performance). Three statements did not reach significant support in the binominal analysis: statement 3 (specialized roles of production and research), statement 4 (informal communication), and statement 6 (middle-managers are more supportive and less controlling).

The results must, of course, be interpreted with caution. There is probably a "yes-bias" in this kind of surveys. Managers want to make a good impression and might believe that "yes" is a better answer for a modern, effective organization. Some respondents answered "yes" very fast, without time for reflection, which can indicate such a bias. On the other hand, the questions asked about changes "compared to some years ago". Perhaps the identified changes had occurred earlier, or will be implemented soon, which would support that the change in the organizations has happened or will happen. Some respondents said that they answered "no" due to such reasons, which, together with treating "don't know" as "no-answers", might compensate for the yes-bias.

AND THEN … WHAT HAPPENED TO THE OMNIPOTENT MNC?

The view in the late 1990s was that MNCs were in a state of transition, as illustrated by Egeloff:

> it is difficult to describe with any certainty what we are changing to. International stra-
> tegies and organizational designs are still in a period of high transition. The dominant
> designs of the recent past are gone, and new dominant designs have not yet emerged.
> /…/ No one knows when this period of transition will come to an end or what the
> dominant organizational forms will look like when this occurs.
>
> Egelhoff (1998, p. xiii)

Why did the changes in MNC strategy/organization occur at this specific time? From a perspective of institutional economics the development could be explained by lower transaction costs for integrated global network struc-tures, with new and organizational innovations that over time became insti-tutionalized. For a recent contribution following these lines of thoughts, see Teece (2014). The world went through an era of liberalization in the 1990s, costs for transports were reduced and new information technology and telecommunications made it possible to communicate and interact in novel ways. There were opportunities for increased expansion and speciali-zation and for new ways of integration.

An alternative explanation sees new organizational phenomena such as this as the result of institutional isomorphism (Meyer & Rowan, 1977). Firms not only search efficiency, managers mimic each other to legitimize their activities. In this process, the writings on the Omnipotent MNC may be an influencing factor in itself. Bartlett and Ghoshal, and others have been part of the management literature which has influenced management thinking, directly and indirectly. (For a critical discussion on this perspective, see Kostova, Roth, & Dacin, 2008.)

But, with new dominant designs emerging, why did the research on this new phenomenon so suddenly vanish? One answer could be that the different contributions were inconsistent with each other and too difficult to synthesize. This paper has shown that this was not the case.

Another answer could be that there was a general loss of interest for holistic models of organizations. In the past there are many examples of contributions in organization studies describing dominant designs, with names such as Weber, Chandler, Williamson, and Mintzberg. But few, if any, researchers have continued this theoretical tradition in the past decades. Organization scholars have become more specialized which is perhaps part of an even more general development in social sciences – maybe under influence of post-modern philosophy and its criticism of grand narratives.

This can also be related to a change in the view on research versus more popular writings. Today, the descriptions of ideal models are often written by management consultants and journalists – the kind of literature we find in airport bookstores. In the 1980s and 1990s, these idealized approaches might more often have found their way into research conferences and academic journals, especially if they were written by well-known "management-gurus." Some of the writers on the Omnipotent MNC fit the description of successful management gurus, i.e., Bartlett and Ghoshal. And some, for example Ridderstråhle, continued along that track and wrote popular books such as "Funky Business," "Karaoke Capitalism," and "Re-energizing the Corporation." From this point of view, it might be understandable that the general, ideal, and popular holistic perspectives of the Omnipotent MNC transformed to more specialized lines of research.

Another explanation can be found in difficulties to operationalize the new model, of which the lack of empirical testing can be an indication. The contributions described organizational changes that were complex; existing structures were modified with new elements added in the more elusive dimensions of coordination – informal personal networks and cultural control. Such changes are difficult to measure. (Compare with the formal, structural transformation to a divisionalized form, as described by Chandler, 1986; Williamson, 1985.)

Besides, the literature did not discuss in any detail how these changes would come about. Would it be a top-down process, a clear managerial decision of a shift to a new organization, a radical change concentrated to a specific point of time and implemented by support of change agents such as management consultants? Or would the new organization emerge gradually at different lengths and paces for different organizations, as an ongoing incremental process with many participating internal decision makers learning somewhat coincidentally about new opportunities to organize?

The change was probably more of the latter kind, a changes that is more difficult to measure. That would imply that the contributors describing a new organization in the late 1980s and 1990s summarized various organizational modifications and synthesized them, but these changes were probably seldom one large transformation in the organizations at a certain point of time. Over time, large corporations gradually changed their organization in a direction that is coherent, but not always as extreme, with the ideas of the Omnipotent MNC.

One can perhaps compare the development in this field to the writings of the new Information Society (or Knowledge Economy, etc.) that was popular during the same era, with contributions from authors such as Drucker, Toffler, Naisbitt, and others. Few would argue that societies have not changed in the prescribed direction but there are not so many attempts made to measure the change. Researchers today seem to have lost interest in the issue and turned to more specific questions.

It might seem strange that research on the Omnipotent MNC disappeared. But research normally starts with hypothetical, visionary conceptualizations and then, later, transform into more specialized, well-defined sub-fields. This process might have been accelerated at the turn of the century when the "grand narratives" and holistic perspectives fell out of fashion, a trend that also affected studies of the Omnipotent MNC.

REFERENCES

Andersson, U., & Forsgren, M. (1994). *Degree of integration in some Swedish MNCs.* Working paper 1994/4. Företagsekonomiska Institutionen, Uppsala Universitet.

Bartlett, C. A. (1986). Building and managing the transnational: The new organizational challenge. In M. E. Porter (Ed.), *Competition in global industries.* Cambridge: Harvard Business School Press.

Bartlett, C. A., & Ghoshal, S. (1988). Organizing for worldwide effectiveness: The transnational solution. *California Management Review, 31*(1), 54–74.

Bartlett, C. A., & Ghoshal, S. (1992). *Transnational Management.* Text, Cases, and Readings in Cross-Border Management, Irwin.

Bartlett, C. A., & Ghoshal, S. (1993). Beyond the M-form: Toward a managerial theory of the firm. *Strategic Management Journal, 14*(S2), 23–46.

Bartlett, C. A., & Ghoshal, S. (1997). *The individualized corporation. A fundamentally new approach to management. Great companies are defined by purpose, process, and people.* Random House Business Books.

Birkinshaw, J. (1996). How multinational subsidiary mandates are gained and lost. *Journal of International Business Studies, 27*(3), 467–496.

Birkinshaw, J., & Hood, N. (1998). Multinational subsidiary evolution: Capability and charter change in foreign-owned subsidiary companies. *Academy of Management Review, 23*(4), 773–795.

Buckley, P. J., & Casson, M. (1998). Models of the multinational enterprise. *Journal of International Business Studies, 29*(1), 21–44.

Cantwell, J. A. (1989). *Technological innovation and multinational corporations.* Oxford: Basil Blackwell.

Chandler, A. D. (1986). The evolution of modern global competition. In M. E. Porter (Ed.), *Competition in global industries.* Harvard University Press.

Child, J. (2005). *Organization. Contemporary principles and practice.* Cambridge: Blackwell Publishing.

Daft, R. L., Murphy, J., & Willmott, H. (2010). *Organization. Theory and design.* Hampshire: South-Western Cengage Learning.

Dhanaraj, C., & Parkhe, A. (2006). Orchestrating innovation networks. *Academy of Management Review, 31*(3), 659–669.

Doz, Y. L., Asakawa, K., Santos, F. P., & Williamson, P. (1996). The Metanational Corporation. Paper prepared for the Academy of International Business Annual Meeting in Banff, Canada, September 26–29.

Dunning, J. H. (2000). The eclectic paradigm as an envelope for economic and business theories of MNE activity. *International Business Review, 9*(2), 163–190.

Edström, A., & Galbraith, J. R. (1977). Transfer of managers as a coordination and control strategy in multinational organizations. *Administrative Science Quarterly, 22,* 248–263.

Egelhoff, W. G. (Ed.). (1998). *Transforming international organizations.* Cheltenham: Edward Elgar. (Elgar Reference Collection).

Forsgren, M. (1990). Managing the international multi-centre firm: Case studies from Sweden. *European Management Journal, 8*(2), 261–267.

Forsgren, M. (2002). Are multinational firms good or bad? In V. Hvila, M. Forsgren, & H. Håkansson (Eds.), *Critical perspectives on internationalisation.* London: Pergamon.

Forsgren, M. (2008). *Theories of the multinational firm. A multidimensional creature in the global economy.* Cheltenham: Edward Elgar Publishing.

Fulk, J., & DeSanctis, G. (1995). Electronic communication and changing organizational forms. *Organization Science, 6*(4), 337–349.

Ghoshal, S., & Bartlett, C. A. (1997). *The individualized corporation.* London: Harper Collins Publishers.

Gupta, A. K., & Govindarajan, V. (1991). Knowledge flows and the structure of control within multinational corporations. *Academy of Management Review, 4*(16), 768–792.

Hagström, P. (1991). *The "Wired" MNC. The role of information systems for structural change in complex organizations.* Institute of International Business. Stockholm School of Economics.

Harzing, A.-W. K. (1999). *Managing the multinationals: An international study of control.* Cheltenham: Edward Elgar.

Hedlund, G. (1986). The hypermodern MNC – A heterarchy? *Human Resource Management,* *25*(1), 9–35.

Hedlund, G. (1994). A model of knowledge management and the n-form corporation. *Strategic Management Journal, 15*(S2), 73–90.

Hill, C. W. L. (2011). *International business. Competing in the global marketplace.* New York, NY: McGraw-hill.

Humes, S. (1993). *Managing the multinational. Confronting the global–local dilemma.* New York, NY: Prentice Hall.

Jansson, H. (1994). *Transnational industrial corporations in South East Asia, an institutional approach to industrial organization.* Aldershot: Edward Elgar.

Kogut, B., & Zander, U. (1993). Knowledge of the firm and the evolutionary theory of the multinational corporation. *Journal of International Business Studies, 24*(4), 625–645.

Kostova, T., Roth, K., & Dacin, M. T. (2008). Institutional theory in the study of multinational corporations: A critique and new directions. *Academy of Management Review, 33*(4), 994–1006.

Liebeskind, J. P. (1996). Knowledge, strategy, and the theory of the firm. *Strategic Management Journal, 17*(Winter Special Issue), 93–107.

Malnight, T. W. (1995). Globalization of an ethnocentric firm: An evolutionary perspective. *Strategic Management Journal, 16*(2), 119–141.

Malnight, T. W. (1996). The transition from decentralized to network-based MNC structures: An evolutionary perspective. *Journal of International Business Studies, 27*(1), 43–65.

Marschan, R. (1994). *New structural forms and inter-unit communication in multinationals.* Helsinki: HSE Press.

Martinez, J. I., & Jarillo, J. C. (1989). The evolution of research on coordination mechanisms in multinational corporations. *Journal of International Business Studies, 20*(3), 489–513.

Meyer, J. W., & Rowan, B. (1977). Institutionalized organizations: Formal structures as myth and ceremony. *American Journal of Sociology, 83*(2), 340–363.

Miles, R. E., & Snow, C. C. (1984). Fit, failure and the hall of fame. *California Management Review, 26*(3), 10–28.

Miles, R. E., & Snow, C. C. (1993). Internal markets and network organizations. In W. E. Halal (Ed.), *Internal markets. bringing the power of free enterprise INSIDE your organization.* New York, NY: Wiley.

Nohria, N., & Ghoshal, S. (1997). *The differentiated network. Organizing multinational corporations for value creation.* San Francisco: Jossey-Bass Inc.

Ostroff, F. (1999). *The horizontal organization.* Oxford: Oxford University Press.

Perlmutter, H. V. (1969). The tortuous evolution of the multinational corporation. *Columbia Journal of World Business, 4*(1), 9–18.

Pihl, H. (2000). *Multinationella företags organisation. Ett nyinstitutionellt perspektiv på samordning.* Dissertation. Lund University. School of Economics and Management. Department of Business Administration. Lund.

Pihl, H. (2008). Transnational tendencies in multinational enterprises. *Baltic Journal of Management, 3*(3), 328–345.

Pihl, H. (2013). The firm as an institution for product design and value web orchestration. *Business and Economics Journal, 4* (BEJ-85), 1–14.

Powell, W. W. (1991). Neither market nor hierarchy: Network forms of organization. In G. Thompson, J. Frances, R. Levacic, & J. Mitchell (Eds.), *Markets, hierarchies & networks.* London: Sage Publications.

Prahalad, C. K., & Doz, Y. (1987). *The multinational mission: Balancing local demands and global vision*. New York, NY: The Free Press.

Ridderstråle, J. (1992). Developing product development. Holographic design for successful creation in the MNC. (Paper) *EIBA Annual Meeting*, Reading, December.

Ridderstråle, J. (1996). *Global innovation — Managing international innovation projects at ABB and Electrolux*. Dissertation. Institute of International Business, Stockholm School of Economics.

Roberts, J. (2004). *The modern firm, organizational design for performance and growth*. Oxford: Oxford University Press.

Rugman, A. M., & Verbeke, A. (1992). A note on the transactional solution and the transaction cost theory of multinational strategic management. *Journal of International Business Studies*, *23*(4), 761–771.

Sölvell, Ö., & Zander, I. (1995). Organization of the dynamic multinational enterprise. The home-based and heterarchical MNE. *International Studies of Management and Organization*, *25*(1–2), 17–38.

Taggart, J. H. (1998). Strategy shifts in MNC subsidiaries. *Strategic Management Journal*, *19*(7), 663–681.

Taylor, W. (1991). The logic of global business. An interview with ABB's Percy Barnevik. *Harvard Business Review*, *69*(2), 91–105.

Teece, D. J. (2014). A dynamic capabilities-based entrepreneurial theory of the multinational enterprise. *Journal of International Business Studies*, *45*, 8–37.

White, R., & Poynter, T. A. (1990). Organizing for world-wide advantages. In C. Bartlett, Y. Doz, & G. Hedlund (Eds.), *Managing the global firm* (pp. 95–113). London: Routledge.

Williamson, O. E. (1975). *Markets and hierarchies: Analysis and antitrust implications*. New York, NY: Free Pres.

Williamson, O. E. (1985). *The economic institutions of capitalism*. New York, NY: Free Press.

APPENDIX A: DESCRIPTIVE STATISTICS

Category	$N_{divided}$	N_{total}	Mean	Standard Deviation	Standard Error Mean
S1 Yes	81	110	0.74	0.443	0.042
S1 No	42				
S2 Yes	109	121	0.90	0.300	0.027
S2 No	14				
S3 Yes	63	92	0.68	0.467	0.049
S3 No	60				
S4 Yes	69	107	0.64	0.481	0.046
S4 No	54				
S5 Yes	83	109	0.76	0.428	0.041
S5 No	40				
S6 Yes	69	106	0.65	0.479	0.047
S6 No	54				
S7 Yes	101	120	0.84	0.367	0.033
S7 No	22				
S8 Yes	92	121	0.76	0.429	0.039
S8 No	31				
S9 Yes	92	115	0.80	0.402	0.037
S9 No	31				
S10 Yes	98	119	0.82	0.383	0.035
S10 No	25				

APPENDIX B: BINOMINAL ANALYSIS

			Test Value $= 0$			
	T	df	Significance (two-tailed)	Mean difference	95% Confidence interval of the difference	
					Lower	Upper
S1	15.339	122	0.000	0.659	0.57	0.74
S2	30.820	122	0.000	0.886	0.83	0.94
S3	11.318	122	0.000	0.512	0.42	0.60
S4	12.486	122	0.000	0.561	0.47	0.65
S5	15.911	122	0.000	0.675	0.59	0.76
S6	12.486	122	0.000	0.561	0.47	0.65
S7	23.666	122	0.000	0.821	0.75	0.89
S8	19.028	122	0.000	0.748	0.67	0.83
S9	19.028	122	0.000	0.748	0.67	0.83
S10	21.869	122	0.000	0.797	0.72	0.87

COMPLEMENTARITY VERSUS SUBSTITUTION AMONG POLITICAL STRATEGIES

Stefan Heidenreich, Jonas F. Puck
and Igor Filatotchev

ABSTRACT

Prior research on political strategies has predominantly analyzed singular political activities or drivers for firms to become politically active and, overall, only scarcely obtained insights on performance consequences of political strategizing. To further develop the realm of political strategy, this study analyzes the effects of two "generic" political strategies on firms' (1) stakeholder network development and (2) performance. Specifically, we provide theoretical and empirical evidence whether the two political strategies add to or substitute each other in their effect on the corresponding outcome variable. We find that an information strategy significantly affects the stakeholder network development, whereas no influence of a financial incentive strategy could be detected. Moreover, we find that the stakeholder network drives firm performance and, more importantly, that the two political strategies substitute each other in their effect on firm performance. Thus, we provide initial insights on the efficiency of political strategies when firms

Orchestration of the Global Network Organization
Advances in International Management, Volume 27, 235–262
Copyright © 2014 by Emerald Group Publishing Limited
ISSN: 1571-5027/doi:10.1108/S1571-502720140000027032

opt to execute an information strategy and financial incentive strategy simultaneously. The results of our study have important implications for research as they put a new light on the efficiency of political strategies.

Keywords: Political strategies; subsidiary performance; stakeholder networks

INTRODUCTION

Foreign firms are in many kinds underprivileged compared to their domestic counterparts (Zaheer, 1995). Therefore, scholars (e.g., Batjargal, 2007; Li, Poppo, & Zhou, 2008; Peng & Heath, 1996; Peng & Luo, 2000; Xin & Pearce, 1996) emphasize the importance for firms to establish informal ties with decision makers and to set up a stakeholder network in order to enhance firm performance. To develop high quality informal ties, firms do not solely rely on market strategies, but more and more on political strategies (Baysinger, 1984; Epstein, 1969; Hillman & Hitt, 1999; Hillman & Wan, 2005). Companies thus frequently apply "action[s] intended to influence governmental policy or process" (Getz, 1997, pp. 32–33) and employ strategies and tactics that are supposed to affect non-market decision makers in a way favorable for the firm (Baysinger, 1984; Deng, Tian, & Abrar, 2010; Keim & Baysinger, 1988). Political strategies thus constitute a means to develop and maintain ties with relevant market and non-market stakeholders. Nevertheless, political strategies do not just aim toward the development of stakeholder networks but are also implemented to directly contribute to performance. Baron (1995, p. 47), for example, characterizes political strategies as "a concerted pattern of actions taken in the nonmarket environment to create value by improving overall performance" (see also Deng et al., 2010; Hillman, Withers, & Collins, 2009; Peng & Luo, 2000; Salamon & Siegfried, 1977). In this study, we specifically focus on the two "generic" political strategies that target political decision makers directly: information strategy and financial incentive strategy (Hillman & Hitt, 1999). We acknowledge that with constituency-building a third political strategy is suggested, however, this strategy is aimed at individuals and toward the support of the public, who then in turn are supposed to affect political decision makers. Thus, the constituency-building strategy targets political decision makers indirectly, what is why we do not include it into this study. Both the information strategy and financial incentives strategy are characterized by a set of tactics: Firms using an information strategy provide their targets with information about firm-specific objectives, problems, desires, etc., whereas a financial incentive strategy furnishes political decision makers with financial inducements (Cho, Patten, & Roberts, 2006; Hillman & Wan, 2005; Schuler, Rehbein, & Cramer, 2002; Wan & Hillman, 2006).

Although a significant amount of international business research has dealt with political strategies so far (e.g., Elg, Ghauri, & Tarnovskaya, 2008; Holtbrügge, Berg, & Puck, 2007; Mattingly, 2007; Taminiau & Wilts, 2006), existing studies do not capture whether different types of political strategies add to or substitute each other in their effect on the outcomes of political activity. On the one hand, Hillman and Hitt (1999, p. 835) argue that "the use of one political strategy (or tactic within) does not preclude the use of another. Rather, a configuration of strategies may be used." They thus explicitly assume additive effects of the distinct strategies on the outcome of political action. On the other hand, one could argue that the joint execution of two political strategy types leads to substituting effects for resource reasons. Both strategies require substantial but mostly unconnected resource endowments (Keim & Baysinger, 1988) with relatively high fixed costs. That is, deploying an information strategy requires resources, for instance, extensive activities by lobbyists, whereas financial inducements are rather managed by consultants. The intense execution of a single strategy may thus require fewer resources than the joint execution of both, subsequently affecting the performance outcome of such activities. Overall, it thus remains unclear if firms benefit from the simultaneous execution of two "generic" political strategies.

In this study, we consequently aim at unraveling the question whether an information-based and a financial incentive-based political strategy have additive or substituting effects on firms' stakeholder network development and performance when they are deployed jointly. We thus intend to contribute to political strategy theory by answering the question: Does a simultaneous implementation of the two specific political strategies lead to an enhanced stakeholder network as well as to an improved firm performance, thus implying additive effects, or do the political strategies substitute each other when they are employed concurrently?

To test substitution or additivity of those political strategies, we use a sample of foreign subsidiaries in Russia. Russia ranks 143th among 183 countries worldwide in the Corruption Perceptions Index (Transparency International, 2011) and 144th among 180 countries in the Economic Freedom Index (Heritage Foundation, 2012). Previous empirical contributions show that firms in such contexts frequently apply political strategies (e.g., Deng et al., 2010; Elg et al., 2008; Holtbrügge & Berg, 2004; Holtbrügge et al., 2007; Spencer & Gomez, 2011). We conduct our analysis on the subsidiary level as we expect political strategies to be heavily context-specific. Multinational corporations (MNCs) are exposed to a variety of stakeholders who are likely to differ in their structure and importance depending on the specific national conditions. Blumentritt and Nigh (2002, p. 58) stress in this regard that "the 'international' aspect of political activities has been considered largely from the perspective of 'what MNCs do outside of their home countries', implicitly assuming that MNC subsidiaries undertake similar political activities." However, the strategies deployed in MNC subsidiaries might differ considerably since subsidiary strategy is affected by the local environment and subsidiary capabilities (Bartlett & Ghoshal, 1986; Birkinshaw & Morrison, 1995; Blumentritt & Nigh, 2002). We address this issue by taking the context-specificity of strategies into account and therefore focus on MNC subsidiaries in one specific national environment.

The remainder of this article is organized as follows: In the next paragraph, we outline the theoretical background of the study and derive our hypotheses. In a next step, we describe the methodological approach followed by the analysis and presentation of our results. We conclude with limitations and implications and highlight potential alleys for further research.

LITERATURE REVIEW AND HYPOTHESES DEVELOPMENT

Motives and Strategies of Political Activities

Owing to their foreignness, foreign firms usually face several detriments when competing with local firms (Zaheer, 1995). These disadvantages also apply to the access and embeddedness into local networks (Uhlenbruck, Rodriguez, Doh, & Eden, 2006). Therefore, firms are challenged to deploy strategies enabling them to obtain access to important stakeholders. The relationships to, for example, government authorities are supposed to ensure firms' existence in the host country and to enhance firm success. For example, in the United States, informal ties between corporate leaders play a significant role to manage uncertainty stemming from resource dependency (Westphal, Boivie, & Ming Chng, 2006). In the Russian context, scholars stress the notion of *svyazi*, referring to social networks, and *blat*, highlighting the essential role of relationships, similar to *guanxi* in China (Batjargal, 2007; Ledeneva, 1998; Li et al., 2008; Peng & Luo, 2000; Peng, Sunny Li, Pinkham, & Hao, 2009; Puffer & McCarthy, 2007; Yakubovich, 2005). However, such examples can be found in probably every market around the world. This implies that firms, no matter where, attempt to "exercise some degree of control or influence over the resource environment or the organization's exchange partners for purposes of achieving stability" (Oliver, 1991, p. 149).

Pfeffer and Salancik (1978, p. 189) propose that "the organization, through political mechanisms, attempts to create for itself an environment that is supporting for its interest." Firms thus employ political strategies to shape their non-market surroundings and to complement their market strategies (Baron, 1995, 1997; Blumentritt, 2003; Frynas, Mellahi, & Pigman, 2006). In doing so, firms attempt "to influence political decision making in order to manage and control their business environments" (Skippari, 2005, p. 83). To analyze "how" to develop such a network, we look at the concept of the "political market" (Hillman & Keim, 1995). The actors operating on this market can be considered as suppliers (e.g., politicians, judicial and regulatory bodies, etc.) and demanders (e.g., firms, unions, consumers, etc.) in the political process (see Bonardi, Hillman, & Keim, 2005; Bonardi, Holburn, & Vanden Bergh, 2006; Hillman & Keim, 1995). Therefore, Buchanan's (1987, p. 246) assertion that "markets are institutions of *exchange*; persons enter markets to exchange one thing for another" is applicable to the political market as well. On the political marketplace, actors behave self-interested, are seeking for their own benefit, and are susceptible for incentives (Bonardi et al., 2005). That is, demanders request specific policy outcomes (or access to policy makers), whereas suppliers are seeking for exchange resources that are beneficial for themselves. As a result, there are incentives for political decision makers, which are (1) information and (2) direct incentives, such as financial inducements (Hillman & Hitt, 1999), to provide a desired outcome (from the demander's perspective). Consequently, firms can use different options to address political stakeholder needs. As Hillman & Hitt (1999) argue, firms can apply two distinct generic strategies to influence their non-market stakeholders: an information strategy or a financial incentives strategy (see also Hillman & Wan, 2005).

Applying an information strategy, firms incorporate a relationship management in their operations and interact with their stakeholders by means of, for instance, press releases, reports, and discussions (Roloff, 2008, p. 245).

Neville and Menguc (2006) as well as Holtbrügge and Puck (2009) outline similar approaches suggesting that firms engage in, for example, lobbying activities as well as information exchange in order to develop their stakeholder network. More precisely, Elg and colleagues (2008, p. 686) show in their study that the "network was strengthened and extended step by step through personal contacts (...) [and developed by] all kinds of activities such as business conferences, personal formal and informal meetings." Firms, thus, engage in a relationship management and apply certain tactics comprised in an information strategy, to develop a network that is considered to be decisive for firms' operations.

The financial incentive strategy suggests that access can also be gained by providing financial stimuli. In this respect, the supplier of those incentives tries to "buy" the stakeholders' "friendship" or at least the access to them. Generally, providing financial support to politicians and parties has become a legal means (McWilliams, Van Fleet, & Cory, 2002), particularly pervading the United States (Lord, 2003; Mitchell, Hansen, & Jepsen, 1997), but is also evident in many other regions of the world, entailing access to political stakeholders. In doing so, firms "decide to buy political access through political campaign contributions" (Dahan, 2005, p. 15) in order to develop their stakeholder networks. To align the incentives of policy makers and the firm, firms might also invite host-country governors to their headquarters (Holtbrügge & Puck, 2009), or provide travel and speaking fees (Hillman & Hitt, 1999; Mullins, 2005). Furthermore, firm members might serve at the political level as elected politicians or consultants, which enables them to establish networks with policy makers at the top level (Getz, 1993; Hillman, Zardkoohi, & Bierman, 1999). In sum, we thus argue in line with existing research that firms implement financial incentives strategically and target political stakeholders to enlarge their network.

Outcomes of Political Strategizing

Existing research has conceptualized the two strategies as independent from each other in their effects on outcomes of political activity. Specifically, scholars assumed either explicitly or implicitly that the two strategies are additive in their effects on outcomes. For example, Hillman and Hitt (1999) refer in their study to Grant (1993, p. 129), who proposes that organizations engaging in political activity "are not so naive as to rely solely on one channel of access." Hence, firms should implement a combination of different political strategies (suggested by Hillman & Hitt, 1999) to develop an extensive stakeholder network. However, this assumption has not been tested explicitly. We argue that the combined effect of the two strategies depends on the respective output variable. As shown above, firms on the one hand intend to develop their stakeholder network, that is, the quality and quantity of accessible supportive stakeholders (Gulati, 1999; Peng & Luo, 2000) when applying political strategies. On the other hand and subsequently, performance is definitely the ultimate output variable of every activity in the host market.

Applying the "political market" view outlined above, we argue that providing stakeholders with both resources (information and financial incentives) simultaneously has additive effects on firms' stakeholder network development. We believe that this is the case for the following two reasons:

First, a concurrent use of the two political strategies increases the likelihood that multiple stakeholder demands are addressed and, thus, different access possibilities are exploited. Holburn and Vanden Bergh (2008, p. 526) emphasize this assumption stating that generally "politicians value the resources that the firm can provide (financial or informational)." Thus, the various relationships in a network "differ in terms of transactional content, such as information or money" (Mahon, Heugens, & Lamertz, 2004). As different stakeholders most probably have different preferences in terms of rather informational or financial resources, the likelihood to satisfy those preferences when deploying both strategies simultaneously is higher than by opting for only one strategy, thus entailing a larger network. Consequently, owing to the different levels that are addressed by the two incentives, we propose that a simultaneous implementation of an information and financial incentive strategy enlarges the network in terms of size.

Furthermore and second, we propose that a simultaneous implementation of both strategies increases the "stickiness" of the established contacts. Thus, if a stakeholder is more susceptible to informational resources but additionally endowed with financial incentives, one can assume that this relation is unlikely to deteriorate as a result of providing financial incentives but rather strengthens. Given this situation and considering the firm as the agent and the political stakeholder as the principal, we argue that in this case the agent initially does not expect a specific *quid pro quo* when providing financial inducements since the principal is amenable to information. However, providing both resources entails a situation where the agent ingratiates herself with the principal, and thus possibly improves the principals' goodwill because of an additional favor provided. Consequently, this might lead to both an increase of the relationship's quality as well as an increased likelihood to access the stakeholder more easily.

Based on our arguments, it thus seems reasonable that a joint use of an information and financial incentive strategy additively and positively influences stakeholder network development. We thus hypothesize:

Hypothesis 1. Information strategy and financial incentive strategy have additive effects on stakeholder network development.

As outlined above, firms engage in political strategies to "achieve strategic objectives" (Boddewyn & Brewer, 1994, p. 121), such as the development of a stakeholder network. However, they also do so to directly "create value for the firm" (Schuler et al., 2002, p. 661). As firms implement political strategies to influence the policy process in a way entailing outputs favorable for the own success (Keim & Baysinger, 1988), they also constitute an important direct determinant of firm performance (Tian, Hafsi, & Wu, 2009).

Despite the urging of scholars (e.g., Bonardi et al., 2006; Epstein, 1980), however, insights on the effectiveness of political strategies on firm performance are scarce compared to market strategies (see Hillman et al., 1999; Marsh, 1998; Shaffer, Quasney, & Grimm, 2000 for exceptions). For the information strategy, Shaffer et al. (2000) show that the implementation of an information strategy leads to significant above-average firm performance. For the financial incentive strategy, Hillman et al. (1999) show that firms benefit from linkages to the government through personal service (e.g., a CEO is appointed as elected politician), and demonstrate that, as a result, increased performance accrue to the former employer. Similarly, Wu (2006) finds a significantly positive effect of a financial incentive strategy on firms' market and financial performance. As Lord (2000, p. 81) states in this regard: "Although any explicit quid pro quo would be illegal, PAC [political action committee] contributions are considered to be means by which corporations may 'purchase' favorable public policy." Furthermore, Lord (2003, p. 118) outlines that "former legislators and other policy makers are more than willing to help provide advice, counsel, and whatever influence they might have, for a price." What is more, firms use political strategies at decisive moments: "Just before the Nigerian Council of Ministers discussed negotiations with Shell-BP regarding oil licenses (...), the company donated funds for the expansion of technical education in Nigeria to obtain more favorable treatment" (Frynas et al., 2006, p. 329). Consequently, political strategies are individually deployed to achieve firm objectives and to result in improved performance.

But what are the effects on performance when both political strategies are deployed simultaneously? Mahon (1993) suggests that a combination of different political tactics and approaches might lead to policy outcomes favorable for the firm. Similarly, Schuler et al. (2002) make an initial contribution providing insights that firms apply certain political tactics concurrently (lobbying and campaign contributions). Generally, "many scholars assume that because we witness firms engaging in political strategies, these firms must believe the benefits outweigh the costs of such activities" (Hillman et al., 1999, p. 68). However, research falls short of answering explicitly "how" political strategies interact when deploying them simultaneously in terms of their effect on firm performance, and some recent research actually questions a positive performance contribution (Hadani & Schuler, 2013).

We again refer to the "political market" view outlined above and consider the political market as an arena of demanders and suppliers engaged in the political process, who interact self-interestedly to exchange one thing for another (Bonardi et al., 2005; Buchanan, 1987; Hillman & Keim, 1995). In this process, suppliers provide resources in terms of specific policy outcomes, whereas demanders provide resources such as information or direct incentives (e.g., financial inducements) in exchange. From a policy supplier's perspective, "politicians exchange policy favors for resources from organized interest groups to maximize their electoral prospects" (Bonardi et al., 2006, p. 1210). From a firm (demander's) perspective, "the favorable application or a change in a current public policy is (…) the final goal to be achieved through the implementation of a political strategy that requires specific resources, which some have called "political resources" (Dahan, 2005, p. 11).

In line with the assumptions on stakeholder networks, we argue that from a firm's perspective the simultaneous application of an information strategy and a financial incentive strategy has additive effects on performance – when not considering the resource commitment necessary to "produce" the strategy. However, and contrary to the establishment of stakeholder networks, when analyzing the effect of information and financial incentive strategy on firm performance, the committed resources need to be considered. In other words, the whole input–output relationship needs to be taken into account. We argue that deploying both political strategies (information and financial incentive) concurrently, has substituting effects on firm performance. We do so because of economies of scale and learning curve effects associated with the implementation of the strategies.

Applying both an information and financial incentive strategy not only addresses the political stakeholders on different preference levels (thus contributing additively to outputs), but also necessitates significant set-up costs for realizing these strategies. When "implementing political strategies, the key questions are whether the organization has the proper financial, human, and material resources to influence legislators' decision making. These organizational requirements will differ across the menu of potentially valuable political strategies available to firms" (Keim & Baysinger, 1988, p. 175). Arguably, an information strategy and financial incentive strategy are rooted in and applied by different resource bases entailing different set-up costs. That is because "political strategies vary in the skills they require and the organizational resources needed to implement them" (Keim & Baysinger, 1988, p. 175). More precisely, for instance, an information strategy is conducted by the use of lobbyists whereas a financial incentives strategy entails hiring consultants, which act on behalf of the firm. Both strategies, however, inherently involve financial expenditures, for example, to pay lobbyists and to make political action committee contributions (Fainsod, 1940).

We base this line of reasoning on insights regarding the generic business strategies developed by Porter (1980, 1985) (cost leadership and differentiation). In this regard, scholars stress that firms should not apply those strategies simultaneously, but opt exclusively for one strategy type (Miller, 1986; Porter, 1980). More precisely, Porter (1980, p. 40) outlines that "sustained commitment to one of the strategies as the primary target is usually necessary to achieve success" since both strategies relate to a different set of resources (Hitt, Ireland, & Hoskisson, 2001), as we assume political strategies do as well.

As the resources needed to execute the single strategies seem to be unrelated, economies of scales as well as learning curve theory suggest cost advantages when applying a singular strategy more intensely (e.g., intensity 4) compared to applying two strategies with the same overall intensity (e.g., intensity 2 each). Looking at the firm as a set of resources (Barney, 1991; Penrose, 1959) and applying economies of scale reasoning, the allocation of firm resources to only one strategy leads to cost degression effects. This is the case since increasing the intensity of one political strategy involves that the share of costs to set up this strategy is distributed to a larger amount of political strategizing, thus entailing cost reduction. In addition, "repeated practice is an important learning mechanism" helping us "to understand processes more fully and so [to] develop more effective routines" (Eisenhardt & Martin, 2000, p. 1114), thus emphasizing the notion of a learning curve. Consequently, the intense application of a single strategy leads to comparative cost advantages. Referring to Lieberman (1987, p. 441), this effect can be clearly depicted in the functional form

$$c(x) = ax^{-b} \tag{1}$$

where $c(x)$ is marginal cost, a constitutes the cost of the first unit (such as set-up costs for the corresponding political resources base), x is the cumulative output (such as the outcome of political strategizing), and b represents learning elasticity. Coming back to our assumption, thus, costs would double when executing both political strategies. When opting for one strategy (information in this case), however, the "firm's operating costs increase at a lower rate than its output" (Katrishen & Scordis, 1998, p. 305) owing to learning effects.

Overall, we thus argue that the simultaneous execution of two strategies has additive effects on the outcomes of political activity (without considering inputs). However, both the literature on economies of scale and the literature on the learning curve suggest that deploying both strategies simultaneously with a given intensity entails higher costs than executing one of them with the same overall intensity. Costs thus exceed stronger than benefits of the strategies. Consequently, we hypothesize:

Hypothesis 2. Information strategy and financial incentive strategy have substituting effects on firm performance.

METHODS

Data

In order to test our hypotheses, we collected firm-level data from foreign firms located in Russia through a questionnaire survey. Contact addresses were compiled through the database "Polpred – Foreign Investors in Russia." The questionnaire, accompanied by a cover letter explaining the aim of the study, was distributed via e-mail to 714 German, Austrian, Swiss, and U.S. companies located in Russia. After having excluded questionnaires that were sent back incompletely, we had received 85 usable questionnaires (response rate of 11.9 percent). This rate is fairly satisfying, particularly if we take into account that obtaining a double-digit response rate in surveys has been becoming an increasingly challenging target for researchers (Harzing, Reiche, & Pudelko, 2013). We tested for non-response bias by using the approach of Armstrong and Overton (1977) and compared early and late arriving responses. Non-response bias exists, if the "persons who respond differ significantly from those who do not"

(Armstrong & Overton, 1977, p. 396). *T*-test statistics revealed no significant differences for any independent variable. Therefore, non-response bias
was not considered to be a problem. To reduce common method bias, we
employed the strategies suggested by Podsakoff, MacKenzie, Lee, and
Podsakoff (2003). In particular, we separated items measuring the same
construct in the questionnaire, protected and assured respondent anonymity, and reduced the danger of evaluation apprehension by explaining in
the cover letter that there are neither "right" nor "wrong" answers. In addition, we subjected the data collected through the questionnaire survey to
Harman's (1967) one-factor test, which showed negative for common
method bias.

Statistical Approach

We argue that the execution of political strategies affect subsidiary
stakeholder network and subsidiary performance differently. However, in
line with existing research, we also expect that subsidiary performance is
partially determined by the subsidiary's stakeholder network (both are thus
not independent from each other) (e.g., Harrison, Bosse, & Phillips, 2010;
Hillman et al., 1999; Johanson & Vahlne, 2009). More specifically,
Donaldson and Preston (1995, p. 67) state that "corporations practicing
stakeholder management will, other things being equal, be relatively
successful in conventional performance terms" thus explicitly highlighting
that a firm's actively managed stakeholder network positively affects performance. Owing to the direct effects of political strategies on both variables
(stakeholder network and firm performance), and the effect of stakeholder
network on performance, thus, performance is endogenously determined by
the stakeholder network. To encounter the endogeneity issue, we therefore
need to apply an econometric technique that corrects for endogeneity. By
not implementing such techniques, we would run into danger to compute
biased coefficient estimates and to draw "faulty conclusions about theoretical propositions" (Hamilton & Nickerson, 2003, p. 52).

Consequently, to test our hypotheses, we thus model these associations
as a system of simultaneous equations using a three-stage least square
(3SLS) method in STATA. The 3SLS method represents a proper technique because it allows considering endogenously determined variables.
Moreover, in a 3SLS method the estimation for the model's parameters is
performed concurrently thus obtaining the target with simultaneous equations more effectively compared to a separated estimation of the equations

(Jiménez & Delgado-García, 2012). Hence, we construct two equations with one dependent variable per equation and control for several other effects based on both theoretical and methodological deliberations. In Eq. (1), *Stakeholder Network Development* represents our dependent variable. *Information Strategy*, *Financial Incentive Strategy*, and the interaction term *Information Strategy × Financial Incentive Strategy* enter the equation as independent variables. Furthermore, we controlled for *Share of Expatriates*, and *Share of B2C*. In Eq. (2), *Performance* builds our dependent variable. We include the same independent variables as in Eq. (1) but additionally include *Stakeholder Network Development* as an explanatory variable as well as control for *Risk*. We also added instrumental variables, namely an industry dummy, establishment mode, value activities performed in the subsidiary, and relative turnover.

Measures

Dependent Variable
Market-based Performance is measured following the suggestions of Dunning (1993). We developed three market-related items, which capture the subsidiaries' market-related goal achievement in Russia (e.g., "To what extent do you have achieved the following goals during your activity in Russia?"; "developing a new market"; "securing an existing market"; "following important customers"). Respondents were asked to assess these items on a 7-point Likert scale. We ran a factor analysis and extracted one factor, which we subsequently used in our analysis (explaining 60.51 percent of the variance). As Grice (2001) notes that averages can be considered a specific type of factor score (using unit weights instead of a weight matrix derived mathematically) and they typically yield highly similar and robust results, we also calculated scales by averaging item scores. We test Grice's assumption and found that factor scores were highly correlated with simple averages (i.e., $0.99 > r < 1.00$).

Independent Variables
Based on various suggestions in the literature (e.g., Gulati, 1999; Peng & Luo, 2000), we measure a subsidiary's *Stakeholder Network Development* on three dimensions: size, quality, and accessibility. Respondents were requested to assess their stakeholder network in Russia based on these categories on a 7-point Likert scale. These items, again, were clearly captured

by one factor, which we used in our analysis (explaining 90.31 percent of the variance).

Information Strategy and Financial Incentive Strategy. In order to measure the subsidiaries' execution of political strategies, respondents were requested to assess how frequently several tactics were applied within the past year on a 5-point Likert scale. In line with previous research (Hillman & Hitt, 1999; Hillman & Wan, 2005), we used well-established items to measure the political activity. However, three items (1 financial incentive item, 2 information items) showed contradicting factor loadings and were thus excluded. The remaining seven items could be explicitly classified into information strategy and financial incentive strategy (explaining 67.77 percent of the variance) and were clearly captured by one factor each.

Substitution Effect

We include an interaction term of information strategy and financial incentive strategy in order to analyze a possible substitution of those political strategies in their effect on stakeholder network development and performance (see Abdi & Aulakh, 2012; Bresnahan, Brynjolfsson, & Hitt, 2002; Filatotchev & Piesse, 2009 for a similar approach).

Controls

Share of Expatriates. We requested the share of expatriates who were delegated from both headquarters and third countries and were employed on the first or second hierarchical level of the subsidiary. The percentages are summed up resulting in a composite variable of the total share of expatriates on the management level of the subsidiary. Owing to the fact that people on a subsidiary's managerial level are often expatriates from the head office, managers on both the subsidiary and headquarter level maintain strong personal interrelations (Birkinshaw & Hood, 1998). Therefore, we expect those subsidiaries as having a significant role within the MNC, thus inevitably influencing the subsidiary's network development.

Share of B2C. We asked for the subsidiary's B2C turnover in Russia. This information enables to draw inferences about the intensity the subsidiary usually interacts with the public. In line with Holtbrügge et al. (2007), we assume that firms with intensive end-customer contact are exposed to the attention of political stakeholders to a larger extent and more visible in general, thus affecting a subsidiary's network development.

Risk. Following Kobrin's (1979) suggestions, we measured the subsidiary's risk exposure. Respondents evaluated on a 7-point Likert scale the level of legal, political, economic, and cultural risks, the subsidiary was exposed to. In order to prevent misunderstandings, we explained each of the categories more in detail in the questionnaire. As all items loaded on one risk factor, we again used this factor for our analysis (explaining 64.71 percent of the variance).

We implemented additional exogenous variables, which were not used in any of our equations but as instruments (Reeb, Sakakibara, & Mahmood, 2012). *Industry.* Following the distinction between service and manufacturing firms, which has been applied in a variety of IB studies (e.g., Brouthers & Brouthers, 2003; Filatotchev & Piesse, 2009; Habib & Victor, 1991), we implemented a dichotomous industry variable in our study, indicating whether a subsidiary operates in the service (0) or manufacturing (1) sector. *Establishment mode.* Respondents had to answer whether the subsidiary emerged as a brownfield or greenfield investment in Russia. *Value activities performed.* Following similar approaches in the literature (e.g., Cuypers & Martin, 2010), we asked respondents to state whether or not the subsidiary was active in R&D, procurement, production, and sales & marketing to subsequently measure the scope of value-added activities within the subsidiary in percentages. *Relative turnover.* Respondents were requested to provide information on the turnover of the corresponding subsidiary and the MNC. We divided the subsidiary's turnover by the turnover of the parent firm.

RESULTS

In this study we argue that two political strategies, information strategy and financial incentive strategy, affect subsidiary stakeholder network and subsidiary performance differently. Furthermore, we posit that subsidiary performance is, at least partially, determined by the subsidiary's stakeholder network, thus leading to an endogeneity problem. Consequently, we run 3SLS and construct two equations with one dependent variable per equation. The bivariate Pearson correlations, means and standard deviations are depicted in Table 1. Table 2 shows the results of the 3SLS model.

In hypothesis 1 we proposed that executing both political strategies simultaneously entails additive effects on stakeholder network development. As can be seen in the first equation (Table 2), the coefficient of the information

Table 1. Means, Standard Deviations, and Bivariate Pearson Correlations.

	Variable	Mean	SD	1	2	3	4	5	6	7	8	9	10	11
1.	Performance	-0.079	0.968	1.000										
2.	Stakeholder network development	-0.022	1.040	0.519**	1.000									
3.	Information strategy	0.001	0.989	0.292**	0.548**	1.000								
4.	Financial incentive strategy	0.027	1.001	0.278*	0.389**	0.546**	1.000							
5.	Risk	0.031	1.023	0.020	-0.039	0.098	0.300**	1.000						
6.	Share of expatriates	46.217	34.007	0.116	0.175	0.004	0.085	0.030	1.000					
7.	Share of B2C	37.754	31.625	-0.170	0.093	0.113	-0.073	-0.114	-0.136	1.000				
8.	Relative turnover	20.120	70.859	-0.067	-0.205	0.038	-0.044	0.032	-0.138	0.070	1.000			
9.	Value activities performed	0.345	0.210	0.190	0.126	0.290**	0.161	0.091	-0.188	-0.089	-0.087	1.000		
10.	Establishment mode	0.93	0.258	-0.050	-0.136	0.177	0.204	0.041	0.067	-0.055	0.041	0.103	1.000	
11.	Industry	0.41	0.495	0.021	-0.121	-0.116	-0.189	0.005	0.101	-0.248*	0.121	0.091	0.044	1.000

$N = 85$; ** $p < 0.01$; * $p < 0.05$.

Notes: Results of *P*, *SND*, *IS*, *FIS*, and *R* are calculated with corresponding factors *P* = Performance, *SND* = stakeholder network development, *IS* = information strategy, *FIS* = financial incentive strategy, *R* = Risk.

Table 2. 3SLS Model Predicting Subsidiary Performance.

	Stakeholder Network Development	Performance
Stakeholder network development	–	0.4204**
	–	(0.2123)
Information strategy	0.4717***	−0.0640
	(0.1055)	(0.1378)
Financial incentive strategy	0.1483	0.0248
	(0.1092)	(0.1104)
Information × financial	−0.0408	−0.1712***
	(0.0557)	(0.0629)
Share of expatriates	0.1454**	
	(0.0740)	
Share of B2C	0.0837	
	(0.0943)	
Risk		−0.1271
		(0.1107)
Constant	−0.0057	0.0106
	(0.0936)	(0.0898)
R^2	0.3594	0.3401
χ^2	47.71***	31.43***
$n = 85$		

Notes: Coefficients are standardized. Standard errors in parentheses.
Significance at 0.1% and 1% is denoted by *** and ** respectively.

strategy on stakeholder network is positive and statistically significant (0.4717; $p < 0.001$). However, our findings show no significant effect of the financial incentive strategy on stakeholder network development, thus, hypothesis 1 is only partially supported. We also test for an interaction effect of the political strategies on stakeholder network development; however, the interaction term is insignificant implying that the political strategies do neither complement nor substitute each other. Besides, the share of expatriates in the subsidiary positively and statistically significantly affects stakeholder network development (0.1454; $p < 0.01$). The share of B2C conducted in Russia, however, shows no significant effect. Overall, the equation for stakeholder network development shows an R^2 value of 35.94 percent and a Chi-square value of 47.71 at a highly significant $p < 0.001$ level. In a next step, we hypothesized that the joint execution of the two political strategies has substituting effects on firm performance. As can be seen in the second equation, both political strategies have no significant direct effect on

Fig. 1. Interaction Plot of Information Strategy and Financial Incentive Strategy
on Firm Performance.

performance. Our findings show, however, a negative and strongly significant (-0.1712; $p < 0.001$) negative interaction effect of information strategy
and financial incentive on performance. This finding provides evidence for a
substituting effect of the two political strategies on firm performance when
executing them simultaneously, thus supporting hypothesis 2. The substituting effect is visualized in Fig. 1, showing nearly perfect substitution of the
two strategies. Furthermore, as theoretically outlined above, we find a positive and statistically significant effect (0.4204; $p < 0.01$) of stakeholder network on firm performance. Risk, which entered our equation as a control
variable, is found to be insignificant. The analysis shows an R^2 value of
34.01 percent and a Chi-square value of 31.43, on a highly significant
$p < 0.001$ level.

DISCUSSION AND IMPLICATIONS

Our study provides a number of implications and contributes to political
strategy research by looking at so far unanswered questions. We demonstrate how an information strategy and financial incentive strategy affect
the stakeholder network development as well as firm performance when

both political strategies are executed simultaneously. In doing so, we provide evidence on whether the political strategies add to or substitute each other in their effect on stakeholder network development and firm performance. More precisely, first, we show that the assumed additive effect of the political strategies on stakeholder network development is only partially supported, and second, our results lend support for our assumption that the joint execution of political strategies has substituting effects on firm performance. Our findings thus emphasize that the commonly assumed positive effect (e.g., Hillman et al., 1999; Keim & Baysinger, 1988; Schuler et al., 2002; Shaffer et al., 2000; Tian et al., 2009) of combining political strategies on firm outcomes has to be queried. First, contrary to our assumption that both political strategies show additive effects on stakeholder network development, our results only partially support this hypothesis as no significant effects could be detected for the financial incentive strategy. Obviously, an information strategy is more apt to develop a well-functioning relationship on a long-term basis between demander and supplier in the political arena, than a financial incentive strategy.

At this point we refer to Hillman and Hitt (1999) who distinguish between a relational and transactional approach to political strategy. In their line of reasoning, a transactional approach to political strategy implies that firms engage in political strategizing when the necessity to do so arises, indicating a rather short-termed and issue-based approach. On the contrary, a relational approach constitutes an attempt to establish relationships with long-termed perspective, suggesting an ongoing political strategizing activity. When looking at the firm's objective to establish a stakeholder network and to obtain access to political stakeholders, one can argue that the network develops based on the exchange of demanded resources, recurring interactions, and mutual trust.

Given this situation, providing political stakeholders with information involves the supplying actor (the firm) and its position and commitment more intensely, whereas the provision of financial inducements takes place rather anonymously and more issue-based. What is more, the boundary of financial inducements within the legal frame and illegal corruption activities is sometimes difficult to draw (Dieleman & Boddewyn, 2012). Considering the fact that usually "any journalist has a strong incentive to investigate and uncover stories on wrongdoing" (Brunetti & Weder, 2003, p. 1801), political stakeholders might be increasingly cautious with regard to accepting financial inducements of firms. This might be the case because of the possible consequences involved: If illegal activities come to the surface, for example, politicians accepting bribes or enjoying complimentary favors paid by firms, a boomerang effect might occur diminishing their chances of re-election. On the other hand, if a firm is recognized as corrupt, "it is difficult for it to survive and grow" (Luo, 2006, p. 754). This uncertainty associated with financial incentives seems to be depicted in our data entailing an insignificant effect of a financial incentive strategy on stakeholder network development.

In sum, a relational approach to political strategy and the deployment of an information strategy seems to be more effective when attempting to establish a stakeholder network. This might be the case owing to the long-term perspective, higher involvement, and trust-building effect when providing information. Financial inducements, on the contrary, although deployed by the firms in our sample, show no significance in their effect on stakeholder network development. We conjecture that this is the case because of the rather short-termed nature of financial incentives, the lacking trust-building effects compared to the informational counterpart, and an associated uncertainty due to blurry boundaries in terms of legality of this activities.

Second, we hypothesized that an information strategy and financial incentive strategy substitute each other in their effect on firm performance when they are executed simultaneously. In doing so, we plunged into a so far untapped field in political strategy research and challenge the common thought that political strategizing generally entails outcome effects favorable for the firm (e.g., Keim & Baysinger, 1988; Lord, 2000). Moreover, we thus address a call made by Hillman and Hitt (1999) who suggest that firms might combine different political strategies. Schuler et al. (2002) accordingly show that firms combine several political tactics rooted in different strategy types, however, do not provide inferences about the effectiveness of their joint application. In our study, we find support for the hypothesized substituting effect of political strategies on performance when they are executed concurrently and, thus, contribute to strategy research and theory building.

As depicted in Fig. 1, the interaction of the political strategies shows a substitution effect. We argue that this might be the case because of resources needed and hence costs associated to execute those strategies. Since both strategies root in different resource bases and, thus, require different skills for their implementation (Keim & Baysinger, 1988), efficiency cutbacks occur when they are deployed simultaneously, given the firm does not hold infinite resources. We argue that the insights on the "generic" strategies developed by Porter (1980, 1985) might be transferrable to the political market as well. Ever since their establishment, scholars contend that firms must decide for one strategy in order to avoid a "stuck in the middle" position. In the meantime, however, scholars point to "hybrids" and "combinations" of those strategies too, or treat the generic strategies as dimensions instead of considering them as "mutually exclusive" (Spanos, Zaralis, & Lioukas, 2004, p. 142). Looking at this evolvement, the suggestion made by Hillman and Hitt (1999) that firms might deploy political strategies simultaneously, seems reasonable. However, the simultaneous application is shown to be inefficient in our data. One can argue that the potential to generate economies of scale and learning curve effects remains unexploited when opting for a simultaneous execution of both political strategies. As a result, efficiency losses occur that, in turn, could be gained if a firm devotes a given set of resources to the execution of a single political strategy instead of executing both strategies.

In sum, we find a substituting interaction effect of information strategy and financial incentive strategy on firm performance in our data. This insight further develops theory on political strategies since it sheds initial light on the so far unrevealed question whether certain political strategies add to or substitute each other in their effect on firm performance. We assume that the substituting effect takes place for cost reasons.

LIMITATIONS

Despite the theoretical implications of our study, it is not without limitations. First, we analyzed foreign subsidiaries located in a single country, Russia. We used this approach since we believe that political strategies are heavily context-specific and, as outlined by many scholars (Bartlett & Ghoshal, 1986; Birkinshaw & Morrison, 1995; Blumentritt & Nigh, 2002), are affected by the local environment and subsidiary capabilities. Therefore, our results are context-specific and might yield different results in other regions. Thus, generalizability should be undertaken with caution. Future research should comparatively test the substitution effect of political strategies in different contexts to broaden our knowledge and to assess whether the findings at hand can be validated across contexts.

Second, our measures are vulnerable to common method variance, which is one of the core problems in IB research other scholars already pointed toward (e.g., Puck, Holtbrügge, & Mohr, 2009; Sireci, Yang, Harter, & Ehrlich, 2006). However, we applied several remedies to minimize common method bias (Armstrong & Overton, 1977; Podsakoff et al., 2003), as outlined above. Furthermore, we used a complex statistical approach, which is seen as an ex post procedural remedy to reduce the likelihood of common method variance (Chang, Van Witteloostuijn, & Eden, 2010). We cannot completely preclude any common method variance in our data; however, our findings do suggest that it is of no great concern.

The study at hand serves as a starting point for future research to more precisely investigate the interacting effect of political strategies and their performance consequences. What is more, studies should develop research frameworks to test whether the substituting effect of political strategies de facto depends on the costs associated with different resources bases, as argued in this study.

CONCLUSION

Building on political strategy reasoning, we analyze whether two political strategies add to or substitute each other in their effect on firm performance, when they are executed simultaneously. First, we show that an information strategy significantly affects firms' stakeholder network development, whereas no significant effect of a financial incentive strategy could be detected in our data. More importantly, the political strategies substitute each other in their effect on firm performance. We argue that this might be the case for resource and cost reasons, impairing the efficiency. Overall, we indicate that general inferences on the positive effect of political strategizing have to be questioned. Our study thus provides important implications for political strategy research and builds a helpful starting point for future research.

REFERENCES

Abdi, M., & Aulakh, P. S. (2012). Do country-level institutional frameworks and interfirm governance arrangements substitute or complement in international business relationships? *Journal of International Business Studies, 43*(5), 477–497.

Armstrong, J. S., & Overton, T. S. (1977). Estimating nonresponse bias in mail surveys. *Journal of Marketing Research, 14*(3), 396–402.

Barney, J. (1991). Firm resources and sustained competitive advantage. *Journal of Management, 17*(1), 99–120.

Baron, D. P. (1995). Integrated strategy: Market and non-market components. *California Management Review, 37*(2), 47–65.

Baron, D. P. (1997). Integrated strategy, trade policy, and global competition. *California Management Review, 39*(2), 145–169.

Bartlett, C. A., & Ghoshal, S. (1986). Tap your subsidiaries for global reach. *Harvard Business Review, 64*(6), 87–94.

Batjargal, B. (2007). Network triads: Transitivity, referral and venture capital decisions in China and Russia. *Journal of International Business Studies, 38*(6), 998–1012.

Baysinger, B. D. (1984). Domain maintenance as an objective of business political activity: An expanded typology. *Academy of Management Review, 9*(2), 248–258.

Birkinshaw, J., & Hood, N. (1998). Multinational subsidiary evolution: Capability and charter change in foreign-owned subsidiary companies. *Academy of Management Review, 23*(4), 773–795.

Birkinshaw, J. M., & Morrison, A. J. (1995). Configurations of strategy and structure in subsidiaries of multinational corporations. *Journal of International Business Studies, 26*(4), 729–753.

Blumentritt, T. P. (2003). Foreign subsidiaries' government affairs activities: The influence of managers and resources. *Business & Society, 42*(2), 202–233.

Blumentritt, T. P., & Nigh, D. (2002). The integration of subsidiary political activities in multinational corporations. *Journal of International Business Studies, 33*(1), 57–77.

Boddewyn, J. J., & Brewer, T. L. (1994). International-business political behavior: New theoretical directions. *Academy of Management Review, 19*(1), 119–143.

Bonardi, J.-P., Hillman, A. J., & Keim, G. D. (2005). The attractiveness of political markets: Implications for firm strategy. *Academy of Management Review, 30*(2), 397–413.

Bonardi, J.-P., Holburn, G. L. F., & Vanden Bergh, R. G. (2006). Nonmarket strategy performance: Evidence from U.S. electric utilities. *Academy of Management Journal, 49*(6), 1209–1228.

Bresnahan, T. F., Brynjolfsson, E., & Hitt, L. M. (2002). Information technology, workplace organization, and the demand for skilled labor: Firm-level evidence. *Quarterly Journal of Economics, 117*(1), 339–376.

Brouthers, K. D., & Brouthers, L. E. (2003). Why service and manufacturing entry mode choices differ: The influence of transaction cost factors, risk and trust. *Journal of Management Studies, 40*(5), 1179–1204.

Brunetti, A., & Weder, B. (2003). A free press is bad news for corruption. *Journal of Public Economics, 87*(7–8), 1801–1824.

Buchanan, J. M. (1987). The constitution of economic policy. *American Economic Review, 77*(3), 243–250.

Chang, S.-J., Van Witteloostuijn, A., & Eden, L. (2010). From the editors: Common method variance in international business research. *Journal of International Business Studies, 41*(2), 178–184.

Cho, C. H., Patten, D. M., & Roberts, R. W. (2006). Corporate political strategy: An examination of the relation between political expenditures, environmental performance, and environmental disclosure. *Journal of Business Ethics, 67*(2), 139–154.

Cuypers, I. R., & Martin, X. (2010). What makes and what does not make a real option? A study of equity shares in international joint ventures. *Journal of International Business Studies, 41*(1), 47–69.

Dahan, N. (2005). Can there be a resource-based view of politics? *International Studies of Management & Organization, 35*(2), 8–27.

Deng, X., Tian, Z., & Abrar, M. (2010). The corporate political strategy and its integration with market strategy in transitional China. *Journal of Public Affairs, 10*(4), 372–382.

Dieleman, M., & Boddewyn, J. J. (2012). Using organization structure to buffer political ties in emerging markets: A case study. *Organization Studies, 33*(1), 71−95.

Donaldson, T., & Preston, L. E. (1995). The stakeholder theory of the corporation: Concepts, evidence and implications. *Academy of Management Review, 20*(1), 65−91.

Dunning, J. H. (1993). *Multinational enterprise and the global economy*. Wokingham, UK: Addison-Wesley.

Eisenhardt, K. M., & Martin, J. A. (2000). Dynamic capabilities: What are they? *Strategic Management Journal, 21*(10−11), 1105−1121.

Elg, U., Ghauri, P., & Tarnovskaya, V. (2008). The role of networks and matching in market entry to emerging retail markets. *International Marketing Review, 25*(6), 674−699.

Epstein, E. (1969). *The corporation in American politics*. Englewood Cliffs, NJ: Prentice-Hall.

Epstein, E. (1980). Business political activity: Research approaches and analytical issues. In L. E. Preston (Ed.), *Research in corporate social responsibility and policy* (pp. 1−55). Greenwich: JAI Press.

Fainsod, M. (1940). Some reflections on the nature of the regulatory process. In C. J. Friedrich & E. S. Mason (Eds.), *Public policy* (pp. 297−323). Cambridge, MA: Harvard University Press.

Filatotchev, I., & Piesse, J. (2009). R&D, internationalization and growth of newly listed firms: European evidence. *Journal of International Business Studies, 40*(8), 1260−1276.

Frynas, J. G., Mellahi, K., & Pigman, G. A. (2006). First mover advantages in international business and firm-specific political resources. *Strategic Management Journal, 27*(4), 321−345.

Getz, K. A. (1993). Selecting corporate political tactics. In B. Mitnick (Ed.), *Corporate political agency* (pp. 242−273). Newbury Park, CA: Sage Publications.

Getz, K. A. (1997). Research in corporate political action: Integration and assessment. *Business & Society, 36*(1), 32−72.

Grant, W. (1993). Pressure groups and the European community: An overview. In S. Mazey & J. Richardson (Eds.), *Lobbying the European community* (pp. 123−142). New York, NY: Oxford University Press.

Grice, J. W. (2001). Computing and evaluating factor scores. *Psychological Methods, 6*(4), 430−450.

Gulati, R. (1999). Network location and learning: The influence of network resources and firm capabilities on alliance formation. *Strategic Management Journal, 20*(5), 397−420.

Habib, M. M., & Victor, B. (1991). Strategy, structure, and performance of U.S. manufacturing and service MNCs: A comparative analysis. *Strategic Management Journal, 12*(8), 589−606.

Hadani, M., & Schuler, D. A. (2013). In search of El Dorado: The elusive financial returns on corporate political investments. *Strategic Management Journal, 34*(2), 165−181.

Hamilton, B. H., & Nickerson, J. A. (2003). Correcting for endogeneity in strategic management research. *Strategic Organization, 1*(1), 51−78.

Harman, H. H. (1967). *Modern factor analysis*. Chicago, IL: University of Chicago Press.

Harrison, J. S., Bosse, D. A., & Phillips, R. A. (2010). Managing for stakeholders, stakeholder utility functions, and competitive advantage. *Strategic Management Journal, 31*(1), 58−74.

Harzing, A.-W., Reiche, S., & Pudelko, M. (2013). Challenges in international survey research: A review with illustrations and suggested solutions for best practice. *European Journal of International Management, 7*(1), 112−134.

Heritage Foundation. (2012). *Index of economic freedom.* Washington, DC: The Heritage Foundation.

Hillman, A., & Keim, G. (1995). International variation in the business–government interface: Institutional and organizational considerations. *Academy of Management Review, 20*(1), 193–214.

Hillman, A. J., & Hitt, M. A. (1999). Corporate political strategy formulation: A model of approach, participation and strategy decisions. *Academy of Management Review, 24*(4), 825–842.

Hillman, A. J., & Wan, W. P. (2005). The determinants of MNE subsidiaries' political strategies: Evidence of institutional duality. *Journal of International Business Studies, 36*(3), 322–340.

Hillman, A. J., Withers, M. C., & Collins, B. J. (2009). Resource dependence theory: A review. *Journal of Management, 35*(6), 1404–1427.

Hillman, A. J., Zardkoohi, A., & Bierman, L. (1999). Corporate political strategies and firm performance: Indications of firm-specific benefits from. *Strategic Management Journal, 20*(1), 67–81.

Hitt, M. A., Ireland, R. D., & Hoskisson, R. E. (2001). *Strategic management: Competitiveness and globalization.* Cincinatti, OH: Southwestern College Pub.

Holburn, G. L. F., & Vanden Bergh, R. G. (2008). Making friends in hostile environments: Political strategy in regulated industries. *Academy of Management Review, 33*(2), 521–540.

Holtbrügge, D., & Berg, N. (2004). How multinational corporations deal with their socio-political stakeholders: An empirical study in Asia, Europe and the U.S. *Asian Business & Management, 3*(3), 299–313.

Holtbrügge, D., Berg, N., & Puck, J. F. (2007). To bribe or to convince? Political stakeholders and political activities in German multinational corporations. *International Business Review, 16*(1), 47–67.

Holtbrügge, D., & Puck, J. F. (2009). Stakeholder networks of foreign investors in Russia: An empirical study among German firms. *Journal for East European Management Studies, 14*(4), 369–394.

Jiménez, A., & Delgado-García, J. B. (2012). Proactive management of political risk and corporate performance: The case of Spanish multinational enterprises. *International Business Review, 21*(6), 1029–1040.

Johanson, J., & Vahlne, J.-E. (2009). The Uppsala internationalization process model revisited: From liability of foreignness to liability of outsidership. *Journal of International Business Studies, 40*(9), 1411–1431.

Katrishen, F. A., & Scordis, N. A. (1998). Economies of scale in services: A study of multinational insurers. *Journal of International Business Studies, 29*(2), 305–323.

Keim, G., & Baysinger, B. (1988). The efficacy of business political activity: Competitive considerations in a principal–agent context. *Journal of Management, 14*(2), 163–180.

Kobrin, S. J. (1979). Political risk: A review and reconsideration. *Journal of International Business Studies, 10*(1), 67–80.

Ledeneva, A. V. (1998). *Russia's economy of favors: Blat, networking and informal exchange.* Cambridge, UK: Cambridge University Press.

Li, J. J., Poppo, L., & Zhou, K. Z. (2008). Do managerial ties in China always produce value? Competition, uncertainty, and domestic vs. foreign firms. *Strategic Management Journal, 29*(4), 383–400.

Lieberman, M. B. (1987). The learning curve, diffusion, and competitive strategy. *Strategic Management Journal, 8*(5), 441–452.

Lord, M. (2000). Corporate political strategy and legislative decision making. *Business & Society, 39*(1), 76–93.

Lord, M. D. (2003). Constituency building as the foundation for corporate political strategy. *Academy of Management Executive, 17*(1), 112–124.

Luo, Y. (2006). Political behavior, social responsibility and perceived corruption: A structuration perspective. *Journal of International Business Studies, 37*(6), 747–766.

Mahon, J. F., Heugens, P. P. M. A. R., & Lamertz, K. (2004). Social networks and non-market strategy. *Journal of Public Affairs, 4*(2), 170–189.

Mahon, J. F. (1993). Shaping issues/manufacturing agents: Corporate political sculpting. In B. Mitnick (Ed.), *Corporate political agency* (pp. 22–39). Newbury Park, CA: Sage Publications.

Marsh, S. J. (1998). Creating barriers for foreign competitors: A study of the impact of anti-dumping actions on the performance of U.S. firms. *Strategic Management Journal, 19*(1), 25–37.

Mattingly, J. E. (2007). How to become your own worst adversary: Examining the connection between managerial attributions and organizational relationships with public interest stakeholders. *Journal of Public Affairs, 7*(1), 7–21.

McWilliams, A., Van Fleet, D. D., & Cory, K. D. (2002). Raising rivals' costs through political strategy: An extension of resource-based theory. *Journal of Management Studies, 39*(5), 707–723.

Miller, D. (1986). Configurations of strategy and structure: Towards a synthesis. *Strategic Management Journal, 7*(3), 233–249.

Mitchell, N. J., Hansen, W. L., & Jepsen, E. M. (1997). The determinants of domestic and foreign corporate political activity. *Journal of Politics, 59*(4), 1096–1113.

Mullins, B. (2005). More lawmakers take trips funded by corporations. *The Wall Street Journal.* Dow Jones & Company.

Neville, B. A., & Menguc, B. (2006). Stakeholder multiplicity: Toward an understanding of the interactions between stakeholders. *Journal of Business Ethics, 66*(4), 377–391.

Oliver, C. (1991). Strategic responses to institutional processes. *Academy of Management Review, 16*(1), 145–179.

Peng, M. W., & Heath, P. S. (1996). The growth of the firm in planned economies in transition: Institutions, organizations and strategic choice. *Academy of Management Review, 21*(2), 492–528.

Peng, M. W., & Luo, Y. (2000). Managerial ties and firm performance in a transition economy: The nature of a micro-macro link. *Academy of Management Journal, 43*(3), 486–501.

Peng, M. W., Sunny Li, S., Pinkham, B., & Hao, C. (2009). The institution-based view as a third leg for a strategy tripod. *Academy of Management Perspectives, 23*(3), 63–81.

Penrose, E. T. (1959). *The theory of the growth of the firm.* New York, NY: Wiley.

Pfeffer, J., & Salancik, G. R. (1978). *The external control of organizations: A resource dependence perspective.* New York, NY: Harper & Row.

Podsakoff, P. M., MacKenzie, S. B., Lee, J.-Y., & Podsakoff, N. P. (2003). Common method biases in behavioral research: A critical review of the literature and recommended remedies. *Journal of Applied Psychology, 88*(5), 879–903.

Porter, M. (1980). *Competitive strategy*. New York, NY: Free Press.

Porter, M. (1985). *Competitive advantage: Creating and sustaining competitive advantage*. New York, NY: Free Press.

Puck, J. F., Holtbrügge, D., & Mohr, A. T. (2009). Beyond entry mode choice: Explaining the conversion of joint ventures into wholly owned subsidiaries in the People's Republic of China. *Journal of International Business Studies, 40*(3), 388–404.

Puffer, S. M., & McCarthy, D. J. (2007). Can Russia's state-managed, network capitalism be competitive? Institutional pull versus institutional push. *Journal of World Business, 42*(1), 1–13.

Reeb, D., Sakakibara, M., & Mahmood, I. P. (2012). From the editors: Endogeneity in international business research. *Journal of International Business Studies, 43*(3), 211–218.

Roloff, J. (2008). Learning from multi-stakeholder networks: Issue-focussed stakeholder management. *Journal of Business Ethics, 82*(1), 233–250.

Salamon, L. M., & Siegfried, J. J. (1977). Economic power and political influence: The impact of industry structure on public policy. *The American Political Science Review, 71*(3), 1026–1043.

Schuler, D. A., Rehbein, K., & Cramer, R. D. (2002). Pursuing strategic advantage through political means: A multivariate approach. *Academy of Management Journal, 45*(4), 659–672.

Shaffer, B., Quasney, T. J., & Grimm, C. M. (2000). Firm level performance implications of nonmarket actions. *Business & Society, 39*(2), 126–143.

Sireci, S. G., Yang, Y., Harter, J., & Ehrlich, E. J. (2006). Evaluating guidelines for test adaptations. *Journal of Cross-Cultural Psychology, 37*(5), 557–567.

Skippari, M. (2005). Intrafirm variation and change in the political strategies of a multidivisional firm. *International Studies of Management & Organization, 35*(3), 82–110.

Spanos, Y. E., Zaralis, G., & Lioukas, S. (2004). Strategy and industry effects on profitability: Evidence from Greece. *Strategic Management Journal, 25*(2), 139–165.

Spencer, J., & Gomez, C. (2011). MNEs and corruption: The impact of national institutions and subsidiary strategy. *Strategic Management Journal, 32*(3), 280–300.

Taminiau, Y., & Wilts, A. (2006). Corporate lobbying in Europe, managing knowledge and information strategies. *Journal of Public Affairs, 6*(2), 122–130.

Tian, Z., Hafsi, T., & Wu, W. (2009). Institutional determinism and political strategies. *Business & Society, 48*(3), 284–325.

Transparency International. (2011). *Corruption perceptions index 2011*. Berlin: Transparency International Secretariat.

Uhlenbruck, K., Rodriguez, P., Doh, J., & Eden, L. (2006). The impact of corruption on entry strategy: Evidence from telecommunication projects in emerging economies. *Organization Science, 17*(3), 402–414.

Wan, W., & Hillman, A. (2006). One of these things is not like the others: What contributes to dissimilarity among MNE subsidiaries' political strategy? *Management International Review, 46*(1), 85–107.

Westphal, J. D., Boivie, S., & Ming Chng, D. H. (2006). The strategic impetus for social network ties: Reconstituting broken CEO friendship ties. *Strategic Management Journal, 27*(5), 425–445.

Wu, W. (2006). The relationship among corporate political resources, political strategies and political benefits of firms in China: Based on resource dependency theory. *Singapore Management Review*, *28*(2), 85–98.

Xin, K. R., & Pearce, J. L. (1996). Guanxi: Connections as substitutes for formal institutional support. *Academy of Management Journal*, *39*(6), 1641–1658.

Yakubovich, V. (2005). Weak ties, information, and influence: How workers find jobs in a local Russian labor market. *American Sociological Review*, *70*(3), 408–421.

Zaheer, S. (1995). Overcoming the liability of foreignness. *Academy of Management Journal*, *38*(2), 341–363.

THE DARK SIDE OF MULTI-UNIT FRANCHISING: THE DRAWBACKS OF LOCAL RESPONSIVENESS

Andrey Kretinin, Todd Morgan and Sergey Anokhin

ABSTRACT

In attempting to solve agency issues associated with single-unit franchising and international adaptation issues with company-owned outlets, franchisors engage in multi-unit franchising. Extant research has examined the antecedents and positive outcomes of multi-unit franchising, but the dark side has largely been neglected. In a sample of 16 corporations that operate 25 brands from the period of 2005–2012, we examine how the density of multi-unit franchising impacts overall franchise system growth and internationalization growth. The results of our study show that multi-unit franchising negatively impacts franchise system growth and a franchise system's internationalization efforts. While benefits of multi-unit franchising have been explicated by previous research, our results show that companies should be concerned about the long-term impact of multi-unit franchising and that there is indeed a dark side.

Keywords: Multi-unit franchising; franchise internationalization; integration-responsiveness

Orchestration of the Global Network Organization
Advances in International Management, Volume 27, 263–281
ISSN: 1571-5027/doi:10.1108/S1571-502720140000027029

INTRODUCTION

As economies become more globally competitive, the need to withstand pressure from increasing competition and market specificities rises tremendously. Companies compete with international rivals not only abroad, but also in their home markets, and service industries are no exception to this phenomenon (Doherty, 2007; Jindal, 2011). However, the nature of the service industries creates a multitude of obstacles and dilemmas for companies. First, services are consumed almost simultaneously with their production and thus cannot be exported (Vargo & Lusch, 2004). Second, market specifications such as culture, government, and other administrative regulations, and the level of economic development demand that companies alternate and adapt their offerings to satisfy the given international market (Elango, 2007; Ghemawat, 2007a; Prahalad & Doz, 1987). As a result, the classical tradeoff between integration and responsiveness becomes crucial for service providers. In attempting to solve this tradeoff and survive greater competitive intensity, companies in service industries utilize franchising. By varying different ownership types in franchising, they create a flexible system allowing fast expansion and desired degrees of adaption and standardization (Barthelemy, 2008). Extant research has argued that a particular ownership type, multi-unit franchising (MUF) is the most beneficial one, as it solves agency problems associated with single-unit franchising (SUF) and low adaptation of company-owned locations (Perryman & Combs, 2012). While theoretical arguments that examine the antecedents and benefits of MUF have been covered by extant research (e.g., Dant & Gundlach, 1999; Kaufmann & Dant, 1999), adverse consequences of MUF have largely been neglected. In this paper, we argue that MUF may adversely impact the franchise system and its internationalization growth rates.

Franchisors, the owners of the company or brand, may choose to expand either through opening company-owned outlets or franchised ones. Extant research suggests that company-owned outlets are best suited for integration/standardization (Bradach, 1997) due to managers of the outlets being hired to operate with directives from the corporation. Alternatively, there is evidence to suggest that they tend to shirk and fail to adapt to the given market conditions (Sorenson & Sørensen, 2001). These two issues are solved by franchised outlets, which are run by franchisees, licensees of the brand, who are interested in self-profit maximization (Combs & Ketchen, 2003). Unfortunately, by trying to solve issues associated with corporate owned outlets, franchising leads to an alternative set of opportunistic behavior problems because of the misalignment of interests between the franchisee and the corporation. Since franchisees are self-profit motivated, they may behave opportunistically and damage the company's brand image (Perryman & Combs, 2012). In an attempt to reduce agency issues in franchising, existing research and industry practice has shown that franchisors should assign new outlets to existing franchisees, instead of attracting new ones (Perryman & Combs, 2012; Sanchez Gomez, Suarez Gonzalez, & Vazquez, 2010). When a franchisee owns multiple outlets they are considered a MUF (Combs, Ketchen, & Short, 2011). Existing research argues that MUFs should be more motivated to grow the corporate brand in the long run and avoid opportunistic behavior because they would damage their own investments across multiple locations (Dant & Gundlach, 1999). Extant research has only explicated antecedents and positive outcomes of MUF, with the exception of Kalnins and Lafontaine (2004) who never empirically tested negative outcomes.

Adopting the integration-responsiveness framework for international expansion and applying agency theory, we argue that franchisors should solve agency issues with SUF. First, MUFs are assigned to specific homogeneous areas (i.e., state, country, or region) to develop outlets. While initial development of the area may be fast and efficient, further saturation may be questionable: if a MUF opens too many locations, it may cannibalize its profits (e.g., encroachment will occur; Kalnins, 2004). As a result, MUFs may not be willing to fully develop the area in order to maximize their profit margins. Second, due to the increased bargaining power of MUFs, franchisors may experience declining growth rates and lack of control to remedy the situation (Dant, Weaven, Baker, & Jeon, 2013). We claim that the positive effect of MUF diminishes as MUFs grow. In particular, we argue that an increase in MUF density will eventually slow down the company's overall growth rate.

When a company operates internationally, its growth rate results from growth in both the home market and international markets. According to the integration-responsiveness framework, international companies become vulnerable and lose their competitiveness when their home market is penetrated (Prahalad & Doz, 1987). Therefore, franchisors continually develop their home markets by either opening company-owned outlets or attracting new franchisees. However, according to existing research and agency theory, international markets are best penetrated by MUFs (Jindal, 2011; Perryman & Combs, 2012). As a result, the home market is constantly developed, while development of international markets may lag behind due to the slow MUF growth rates. Thus, we argue that the positive effects of MUF on a company's internationalization may decrease as MUF increases.

We test and provide support for our hypotheses using a unique dataset that contains quarterly data on 25 US brands with international franchising operations over the 8-year period. Our multi-step estimation helps us conclude that MUF indeed has nonlinear negative effects on franchising growth and internationalization. MUF initially helps the growth rate of corporations but after a certain point it becomes detrimental for the corporation.

The paper proceeds as follows. The following section provides a literature review of existing franchising research and development of our specific hypotheses. We apply the integration-responsiveness framework to show how franchising companies handle international expansion and competition. Next, we detail our methodology and results of our analysis. Last, we provide a discussion of our findings, including managerial and theoretical implications along with the limitations of our study.

LITERATURE REVIEW

I-R Framework

A substantial body of academic research has recognized the issues of international expansion — the need for standardization and adaption along with tradeoffs between them (e.g., Prahalad & Doz, 1987). However, the majority of research has focused on hard, manufactured goods, while services have been neglected. Due to substantial differences between hard and soft goods, it is necessary that services be examined. Existing research claimed that companies' integration plays a key role in the global marketplace. Centralized management helps companies to coordinate geographically dispersed units and achieve efficiency. However, the flow of hard manufactured goods is limited to supplies in service industries. As a result, economies of scale may not provide a substantial benefit to companies' performance (Johnson, Arya, & Mirchandani, 2013). One of the reasons for such issues is that unlike hard manufactured goods, manufacturing and consumption of services occur almost simultaneously (Vargo & Lusch, 2004). As such, the production and exporting of services from the parent facility is not possible for these industries. Second, service industries closely interact with customers. Services provided at different locations should be of high value and consistent in order to create and maintain customer loyalty (Doherty, 2007; Moorman & Rust, 1999). Therefore, customers' experiences at different service outlets should be consistently positive in terms of service, taste, or quality. For example, fast food chains try to provide the same taste of its products in the United States and Europe to maintain their brand identity. Interaction with customers creates certain customer expectations, which can be fulfilled by ensuring a high quality of supplies and extensive employee training, (e.g., standardization of service practices; Moorman & Rust, 1999). On the other hand, close interactions with customers are influenced not only by expectations, but also by customers' culture and market specifications. Cultural differences may prevent companies from standardizing its practices by imposing constraints based on religious and traditional specifications of the host country (Elango, 2007; Ghemawat, 2007a). For example, McDonald's chains should not offer beef products in the Indian market due to the religious specificity of the country. Deviations in a company's offerings impacts change in supply and may also include different positioning strategies (e.g., midscale vs. luxury hotels in different countries) (Taggart, 1997). Service companies struggle between standardization across different markets in order to provide consistent offerings and adaptation to host market conditions in order to successfully operate in a given country.

Considering the nature of the service industries, service providers cannot export their offerings, but instead they have to establish their presence in the given geographic market. The most common and efficient way for entering international markets for service providers is licensing, in particular, franchising (Doherty, 2007; Elango, 2007). The franchise business model represents a contract that grants a franchisee the right to operate under a given brand in exchange for an initial fee and ongoing royalty fees paid to the brand's owner, the franchisor (Combs & Ketchen, 2003). Expansion in franchising may come from two possible sources: opening company-owned outlets or franchised outlets. The company's choice between these two options represents the tradeoff between integration and responsiveness.

The franchisor may decide to keep complete control over its brand by opening company-owned outlets. This way of expansion allows a franchisor to operate directly in the given area and expose itself to extensive learning of the focal market (Bradach, 1997). Company-owned locations are shown to adhere to the brand's corporate strategy and behave less opportunistically than franchised units (Oxenfeldt & Kelly, 1969). In other words, company-owned locations provide ample opportunity to expand in a given market with a high degree of standardization (Sorenson & Sørensen, 2001). With a higher degree of standardization, the franchisor's learning and control come at the cost of market risk, capital expenditures on new outlets, and monitoring of existing outlets (Perryman & Combs, 2012).

However, once brands expand geographically, the need for local responsiveness starts to become more important than standardization; responsiveness across geographic markets for service industries becomes resource intensive (Elango, 2007). It involves conformity to administrative procedures, level of economic development, political conditions, competition, and customer preferences (Ghemawat, 2007a; Prahalad & Doz, 1987). Failure to account for any of the aforementioned specifications will most likely lead to retreat from the given geographic market, leading to sunk costs for the franchisor. In order to adapt to the host market conditions, companies mandatorily have to deviate from existing practices. Previous research has demonstrated that franchised locations may be best suited to operate in foreign markets for the franchisor due to their understanding of the market (Perryman & Combs, 2012; Shane, 1998) and the lack of resource commitment by the franchisor (Sorenson & Sørensen, 2001).

Multi-Unit Franchising

Although franchising provides a very convenient and efficient way of international expansion, it has certain drawbacks. Since franchisees invest a large amount of capital in opening new locations, they seek to maximize their profitability, sometimes at the expense of the franchisor (Combs & Ketchen, 2003), resulting in goal conflict. Opportunistic behavior, which may be reflected in shirking on employee training or the quality of supplies, damages the corporate brand image but may help maximize short-term profitability for the franchisee (Barthelemy, 2008; El Akremi, Mignonac, & Perrigot, 2011). Although a franchisor may attempt to align goals and mitigate opportunistic behavior by the franchisee, given geographical distance and information asymmetry, it is not always efficient.

Existing research suggests that the potential solution to agency problems in franchising is to adopt a MUF strategy by assigning new outlets to existing franchisees instead of new franchisees. Dant and Gundlach (1999) argue that MUFs are more discouraged from opportunistic behavior compared to SUFs because they own several outlets and have more to lose if the overall brand image is tarnished. As such, they may adopt behaviors that strengthen the overall brand instead of their individual outlets and become more interested in the long-term performance instead of short-term maximization. Second, MUF creates greater efficiency when new outlets are opened due to the lack of information withholding from new franchisees (Kaufmann & Dant, 1999). Existing franchisees learn existing business practices and find ways to adapt to the market conditions by trial-and-error method, which may be fairly costly. Since franchisees have invested time and effort in their own market learning, they have no incentive to share their knowledge and adaptation practices with the franchisor or other franchisees. However, by assigning new outlets to the existing franchisees that have demonstrated acceptable performance, the franchisor ensures no information withholding between existing and newly opened location.

It may be that MUF solves some of the agency problems between a franchisee and franchisor and helps more efficient operations of the franchise system. However, none of the consequences or potential negative impacts of MUF on the franchise system have been empirically tested although they have been theoretically discussed (see Kalnins & Lafontaine, 2004).

Total Franchise System Growth

One of the major benefits of franchising is the ability to quickly increase the number of outlets with minimal capital expenditure by the franchisor. The majority of costs of opening a new location are borne by the franchisee; thus, from the franchisor's perspective, franchising provides a very inexpensive and fast expansion strategy using the franchisees' funds instead of its own. However, if franchisors decide to engage only in MUF, the benefits of fast expansion may not be continually increasing.

First, MUFs may not possess sufficient funds to quickly open several new locations. In the case of SUF, every additional franchisee brings a sufficient amount of resources to open a new location. However, one MU franchisee requires more aggregate resources to open multiple locations. In other words, the amount of resources needed by MUF is directly proportional to the number of new locations − more new locations require more resources from a single MU franchisee. However, MUF is still an agent on behalf of the franchisor and, according to agency theory, is motivated by self-interest (e.g., profit maximization). Therefore, the development of the MUF system will be dictated by the amount of resources available to MU franchisees and their willingness to open new locations. Once an MUF invests funds to open a certain number of outlets, it may postpone additional outlet growth and reap the rewards of its existing outlets to pay off initial investments. If the franchisee is granted the right to operate in a given region (i.e., area development agreement), the growth rate in that region may be low until the franchisee acquires sufficient funds to open several locations or pay off its original investments.

Second, MUFs may be hesitant to open new locations. Since franchisees may open several locations in a given geographic area, the probability of encroachment will increase with every subsequent new outlet (Kalnins, 2004; Nair, Tikoo, & Liu, 2009). Encroachment occurs when the outlets of a single brand are located too close to each other and compete for the same customers. If encroachment occurs among SUFs, they compete with each other, and may potentially increase the service level to achieve a higher level of satisfaction for the customer. In this case, encroachment diminishes profits at the brand level, instead of franchisees' level. However, if encroachment affects an MUF, it simply decreases its profits margin per store. Naturally, since MUFs are granted the rights to develop a certain region, they may avoid encroachment by not saturating that region with opening new outlets that compete with its existing outlets.

Third, MUFs may not be forced to open new locations. When MUFs grow, they possess more bargaining power and tend to behave as franchisors (i.e., act as principals instead of agents) (El Akremi et al., 2011; Kalnins & Lafontaine, 2004). MUFs' bargaining power is directly proportional to the number of outlets they possess – more outlets means more bargaining power with the franchisor. In this case, franchisees may simply refuse to open new locations, and may successfully bargain against the franchisor. Such refusals may occur if the MUF believes that the market is saturated and tries to avoid encroachment or simply wants to pay off its investments.

Existing research and our argumentation suggest that there is a non-linear impact of MUF on the overall system growth. Summarily, existing literature argues that MU franchisees tend to lose their motivation, but there is no claim or evidence that MUFs' motivation should increase after some decline. Therefore, we argue that:

H1. There is negative curvilinear relationship between the franchise system growth and the density of MUF.

Internationalization of the Franchise System

In franchising industries, companies follow patterns that are well described in the literature: the franchisor first develops its domestic market with company-owned outlets, SUF and MUF, while MUF prevails when expanding internationally (Jindal, 2011; Perryman & Combs, 2012). According to the I-R framework, companies should protect their home market in order to generate stable cash flows to then compete internationally (Prahalad & Doz, 1987). As such, a franchisor may saturate its domestic market while trying to expand initially. It may use all possible resources to achieve maximal expansion – company resources through opening company-owned locations and licensees' capital through attracting more franchisees. As a result, the domestic market is consistently being developed regardless of a company's international operations. The degree of a company's internationalization is defined as the ratio between its international operations to its total operations (Wright, Madura, & Wiant, 2002). Following our previous arguments, we purport that a company's internationalization may be subject to inconsistent patterns because of MUF activity. While the domestic market continuously develops through multiple sources, the international market development led by MUF may demonstrate diminishing growth rates. As a result, the degree of internationalization will diminish due to the continual development of the domestic market. Therefore, we argue that the growth of the company's internationalization will show patterns similar to the overall system growth:

H2. There is negative curvilinear relationship between the density of MUF and the company's internationalization growth.

METHODOLOGY

Data

We utilize a unique dataset to test our theory described above. We developed our sampling frame from multiple databases. We accessed financial data from COMPUSTAT and additional franchising data from companies' annual reports and from the International Franchise Association database. We focused on public companies with headquarters in the United States that meet the following criteria: (1) the company utilizes or has utilized franchising practices during the period of observation and (2) the company had presence in at least one non-US country during the period of observation. As a result, our panel dataset contains information about 16 corporations that operate 25 brands representing fast food, rental, and hotel industries from the period of 2005–2012. We utilize quarterly periods to enhance our panel and reduce the impact of a yearly aggregated panel dataset. In effect, the dataset includes 800 unique quarterly observations for the 25 brands explicated. According to the Rosenberg International Franchise

Center (Peter T. Paul College of Business and Economics, University of New Hampshire, 2013), public companies in these industries account for the vast majority of market share in the global franchise industry. Therefore, we may consider our sample to be representative of the franchise business model.

Variables

Dependent Variables
Franchise System Growth (Total Growth) represents the percentage change in the total number of units of the given brand. This variable is calculated as a ratio of the total number of outlets at time $(t+1)$ divided by the total number of outlets at time t. Our operationalization of franchise system growth is widely used within franchising research (e.g., Combs & Ketchen, 2003; Szulanski & Jensen, 2008).

   Internationalization Growth (Internationalization Growth) represents the degree of internationalization, calculated as the ratio of the number of international outlets divided by the number of total outlets. This variable helps capture the internationalization rate as a function of MUF. This operationalization of international growth has been used in previous research (e.g., Wright et al., 2002).

Independent Variables
Density of MUF represents the average number of outlets owned by franchisees. It is calculated as the ratio of the number of franchised outlets divided by the number of franchisees. The greater the ratio is, the more outlets belong to the single franchisee (Gómez, González, & Vázquez, 2010).

Control Variables
In order to rule out extraneous factors that could have an impact on our dependent variables of interest, we needed to control for a number of variables. The *Number of Countries of a Company's Operations* controls not only for the size of the company, but also serves as a proxy for company's internationalization (Baena & Cervino, 2012). *CAGE* distance controls for the environmental heterogeneity. Following Ghemawat (2007b), we utilize a composite CAGE distance for every country in which the company operates. Our dataset consists of US corporations, therefore we obtained the distance from the US to every country included in the dataset.

We then summed the distances for every international market per company as follows[1]:

$$CAGE = \sum_{1}^{n} CAGEi$$

Introduction of this control variable enabled us to account for cultural, administrative, and economic differences between countries along with the geographical distance between them (in km). *Parent Brand* controls for the heterogeneity between the corporations and the homogeneity of the brands operating under the parent corporation. Our sample includes the companies that possess more than one brand and the variable controls for unique factors that are associated with the parent company (Combs & Ketchen, 2003). The *Royalty Rate* indicates the percentage of revenues that franchisees have to pay the franchisor for the right of using the brand name (Combs & Ketchen, 2003). *Franchising Experience* needs to be controlled for because more experience in operating as a franchisor will serve as a proxy for dealing with opportunistic franchisee efficiency. Moreover, the franchising literature has not reached a consensus regarding the overall trend of franchising companies – some authors argue that companies should become fully franchised with time, other argue oppositely (Oxenfeldt & Kelly, 1969; Perryman & Combs, 2012). Therefore, we control for that experience factor that may affect a franchisor's strategy (Combs & Ketchen, 2003; Sorenson & Sørensen, 2001). Finally, we control for the *Total Number of Company-Owned Locations (LnCO)*. This variable controls for a company's growth and accounts for the expansion through company-owned locations. It is calculated as a natural log transformation from the number of company-owned outlets. We transformed it in order to avoid multicollinearity between the number of company-owned locations, franchisor's experience, and MUF (Combs & Ketchen, 2003).

Models and Estimation

Our arguments claim that the relationship among the variables of interest is curvilinear. First, we established a baseline model to examine the control variables in the study. Second, we tested the linear effect of MUF on our dependent variable in the main effect models to examine whether the relationship among the variables exists. Our third set of models includes the squared MUF variable that tests the nonmonotonic effect of MUF.

While inclusion of the squared term is the most common way to test for inverted U-shaped patterns, our theoretical argument claims that the relationship is characterized by diminishing returns. Therefore, a parabola may not fit the data because there is no claim the function should rise as MUF increases (Sorenson & Sørensen, 2001). Therefore, we set up the fourth model that includes MUF^{-1}, the multiplicative inverse term. We argue that the mathematical properties of this variable should most accurately fit the diminishing effect function. Therefore, we expect to find the following estimation results: a negative linear effect, a positive squared term (U-shape), and a positive multiplicative inverse term. Moreover, we expect that the multiplicative inverse term will better fit the data and be more significant than squared term.

Results

Since our dataset consists of several quarters and years of observation, we utilized panel data estimation procedures to obtain unbiased estimators and correct for autocorrelation and heteroskedasticity (Greene, 2000). We conducted GEE Population-averaged linear model (Crouchley & Davies, 1999). Descriptive statistics of our variables is presented in Table 1. As can be seen from Table 1, the correlations show reasonable patterns and multicollinearity should not be a concern.

As indicated above, we performed four models to test each of our hypotheses. First, we established the base model according to the existing research. Next, we tested the linear effect of the MUF density on overall franchise system growth. Our estimation shows an insignificant linear effect of MUF ($\beta = -0.72$, $p = 0.18$). Such insignificance may be caused by more complex and nonlinear relationship between MUF and system growth. Second, we tested the quadratic relationship of MUF density on franchise system growth. Again, the obtained result is insignificant ($\beta = -0.41$, $p = 0.2$). Finally, we test the multiplicative inverse of MUF density. As expected, the multiplicative inverse term is positive and significant ($\beta = 3.62$, $p < 0.01$). Therefore, we obtained support for Hypothesis 1. The summary of the models used to test Hypothesis 1 is presented in Table 2.

We used a similar procedure to test Hypothesis 2. We began with the estimation of the linear effect of MUF density of the company's internationalization and obtained insignificant estimator ($\beta = -0.72$, $p < 0.16$). We proceeded further by estimating the quadratic relationship, and observed a significant U-shape pattern ($\beta = 1.92$, $p < 0.05$). We finally tested the

Table 1. Descriptive Statistics and Correlations.

	Mean	SD	1	2	3	4	5	6	7
1 Franchise system growth	0.01	0.06	1						
2 Internationalization growth	0.11	0.15	-0.06†	1					
3 Countries	17.92	28.02	-0.06	0.68**	1				
4 Royalty	0.05	0.01	0.00	0.09**	0.32**	1			
5 Experience	32.28	15.29	-0.15**	0.23**	0.45**	-0.00	1		
6 LN(CO)	3.62	3.06	-0.03	-0.09**	0.41**	0.55**	0.27**	1	
7 CAGE	2412.56	2654.54	-0.11**	0.34**	0.40**	-0.14**	0.23**	-0.06†	1
8 MUF	14.58	24.26	0.00	-0.22**	-0.12**	-0.20**	0.08*	-0.19**	0.05

†$p < 0.10$, *$p < 0.05$, **$p < 0.01$.

Table 2. Estimation Results for Hypothesis 1.

| | Franchise system growth | | | | | | | |
| Model | Control | | Linear | | Squared | | M. Reverse | |
Variable	β	Standard error	β	Standard error	β	Standard error	β	Standard error
Countries	-1.60	1.33	-2.06	1.38	-1.57	1.44	-6.05**	1.48
Royalty	-2.10**	0.62	-2.17**	0.63	-2.04**	0.63	-3.66**	0.63
Experience	-0.12	0.32	-0.01	0.34	-0.05	0.34	-0.01	0.32
Ln(CO)	-0.33	1.19	-0.03	1.22	-0.20	1.23	1.04	1.17
CAGE	-0.31	0.42	-0.28	0.43	-0.39	0.44	-0.39	0.41
MUF			-0.24	0.18	0.24	0.43	1.02*	0.42
MUF^2					-0.41	0.34	-0.82*	0.33
MUF^{-1}							3.62**	0.47
Constant	0.37	0.49	0.28	0.50	0.40	0.51	-0.51	0.50
Parent brand	Included		Included		Included		Included	
χ^2	32.64		33.59		35.15		100.10	
n	650							

$*p < 0.05$, $**p < 0.01$.

Table 3. Estimation Results for Hypothesis 2.

	Control		Internationalization					
			Linear		Squared		M. Reverse	
Model								
Variable	β	Standard error	β	Standard error	β	Standard error	β	Standard error
Countries	4.41	5.28	7.52	5.13	10.95*	4.86	10.33*	4.68
Royalty	−3.56	2.69	−1.57	2.64	0.38	2.45	0.87	2.23
Experience	0.68	1.73	0.54	1.62	0.22	1.46	−0.26	1.27
Ln(CO)	−2.12	3.70	−2.29	3.67	−2.35	3.59	−1.13	3.48
CAGE	3.60*	1.57	3.03*	1.54	2.56†	1.47	1.94	1.38
MUF			−0.72	0.52	−3.20*	1.19	−2.69*	1.17
MUF²					1.93*	0.89	1.71†	0.89
MUF⁻¹							5.34**	1.28
Constant	9.68**	2.54	10.92**	2.37	12.30**	2.12	12.95**	1.86
Parent Brand	Included		Included		Included		Included	
χ^2	71.00		81.49		104.27		159.35	
n	748							

†$p < 0.10$, *$p < 0.05$, **$p < 0.01$.

multiplicative inverse term, which supported our hypothesis ($\beta = 5.33$, $p < 0.01$). Therefore, we found support for Hypothesis 2, the summary of which is presented in Table 3.

As a robustness check, we examined alternative models that account for potential autocorrelation and heteroscedasticity in our data; we conducted a Prais–Winsten regression with panel corrected standard errors and AR1 disturbance. The results of our analysis hold and provide support for our hypotheses. The estimation procedure and results are available from the authors upon request.

DISCUSSION AND CONCLUSION

Our statistical analysis provides support to both of our hypotheses, which indicate that the density of MUF decreases the growth of the overall franchise system and reduces companies' internationalization efforts. Existing theory on MUF indicates multiple benefits of MUF and, according to agency theory, claims that MUF has an overall positive effect on franchisors. Our findings support the argument that MUFs have a negative impact on the growth of the franchise system, but do not create a decline of franchise system or internationalization. However, we contribute to the MUF dialogue by showing the nature of the positive effect of MUF density – its effect on overall franchising system is positive, but has a form of diminishing returns, because of its negative association with system growth. The support of Hypothesis 1 suggests that the growth of MU franchisees slows down the growth of the overall franchise system. Slow system growth rates may create problems for franchisors in the long run. Based on agency theory, we expect that MUFs may be too concerned with paying off their own investments instead of furthering system development. As a result, MUFs will not saturate the market with outlets in order to avoid any sort of encroachment and further investments. As observed from our empirical study, as the density of MUF increases, the growth rates become close to zero. Our second hypothesis provides further support for our arguments. Due to a franchisor's home market being developed by company-owned outlets and both types of franchisees, SUF and MUF, it continually grows. However, international markets are developed by MU franchisees. The difference between growth rates causes a company's internationalization to decrease. Our paper provides a valuable contribution to the literature on franchising by highlighting a negative effect of MUF.

Our study also provides some valuable suggestions for practitioners. We claim that franchisors have to account for potential slowdowns in franchising by modifying the franchise contract and stating additional requirements for MUF. Franchisors have to provide further alignment between its own goals the ones of MUFs to ensure acceptable grow rates. For example, franchisors may specify the minimum number of outlets that should be opened in a given period of time. Our conclusion also suggests that the area development contracts should be reviewed more carefully, since they grant MUF with an indisputable right and responsibility for the particular region. Given the findings above, we believe that franchisors should keep the system diversified, keeping all three outlet ownership types, CO, SUF, and MUF. Such diversification will enable company to stay flexible by mixing different growth, adaptation, and standardization rates.

Limitations and Suggestions for Further Research

While we have found support for our hypotheses in this study, the paper does have its limitations. Due to the examination of public franchisors with US headquarters, we may have limited the overall generalizability of our findings. Private franchising systems may operate differently due to the differences in ownership (Combs, 2008). Future research should address the impact of MUF density on system growth in privately held corporations, since there might be significant differences due to the ownership type. Second, even though our sample consists of international corporations, it may not fully represent MUF's impact on a global scale. Additional research should be conducted in order to investigate franchising companies that originate in other countries. There might be substantial distinctions due to the differences in legal, economic, and cultural systems among nations. Third, our estimation techniques defined the general relationship between MUF and growth rates. However, we did not obtain any optimum points. Further research may attempt to find the MUF density, which creates the highest growth rates. In addition, it may be helpful for research to examine more franchises collectively and extending the panel characteristics of the data to see the longer-term impact on the variables examined in this study.

NOTE

1. n is the number of international markets in which the company operates and i is the distance from the US headquarters to a given international market.

REFERENCES

Baena, V., & Cervino, J. (2012). International franchise expansion of service chains: Insights from the Spanish market. *The Service Industries Journal, 32*(7), 1121–1136.

Barthelemy, J. (2008). Opportunism, knowledge, and the performance of franchise chains. *Strategic Management Journal, 29*(13), 1451–1463. doi:10.1002/smj.719

Bradach, J. L. (1997). Using the plural form in the management of restaurant chains. *Administrative Science Quarterly, 42*(2), 276–303.

Combs, J. G. (2008). Commentary: The servant, the parasite, and the enigma: A tale of three ownership structures and their affiliate directors. *Entrepreneurship Theory and Practice, 32*(6), 1027–1033.

Combs, J. G., & Ketchen, D. J. (2003). Why do firms use franchising as an entrepreneurial strategy? A Meta-Analysis. *Journal of Management, 29*(3), 443–465.

Combs, J. G., Ketchen, D. J., & Short, J. C. (2011). Franchising research: Major milestones, new directions, and its future within entrepreneurship. *Entrepreneurship Theory and Practice,* 35(3), 413–425.

Crouchley, R., & Davies, R. B. (1999). A comparison of population average and random-effect models for the analysis of longitudinal count data with base-line information. *Journal of the Royal Statistical Society: Series A (Statistics in Society), 162*(3), 331–347.

Dant, R. P., & Gundlach, G. T. (1999). The challenge of autonomy and dependence in franchised channels of distribution. *Journal of Business Venturing, 14*(1), 35–67. doi:10.1016/S0883-9026(97)00096-7

Dant, R. P., Weaven, S. K., Baker, B. L., & Jeon, H. J. (2013). An introspective examination of single-unit versus multi-unit franchisees. *Journal of the Academy of Marketing Science, 41*(4), 473–496. doi:10.1007/s11747-011-0265-2

Doherty, A. M. (2007). The internationalization of retailing: Factors influencing the choice of franchising as a market entry strategy. *International Journal of Service Industry Management, 18*(2), 184–205.

El Akremi, A., Mignonac, K., & Perrigot, R. (2011). Opportunistic behaviors in franchise chains: The role of cohesion among franchisees. *Strategic Management Journal, 32*(9), 930–948.

Elango. (2007). Are franchisors with international operations different from those who are domestic market oriented? *Journal of Small Business Management, 45*(2), 179–193.

Ghemawat, P. (2007a). Redefining Global Strategy: Crossing borders in a world where differences still matter. Boston, MA: Harvard Business School Press.

Ghemawat, P. (2007b). CAGE comparator™ – custom analysis and mapping of cross-country distances and differences. Retrieved from http://www.ghemawat.com/cage/. Accessed on December 30, 2012.

Gómez, R. S., González, I. S., & Vázquez, L. (2010). Multi-unit versus single-unit franchising: assessing why franchisors use different ownership strategies. *The Service Industries Journal, 30*(3), 463–476.

Greene, W. H. (2000). *Econometric analysis* (4th ed.). Upper Saddle River, NJ: Prentice-Hall, Inc.

Jindal, R. (2011). Reducing the size of internal hierarchy: The case of multi-unit franchising. *Journal of Retailing, 87*(4), 549–562. doi:10.1016/j.jretai.2011.07.003

Johnson, J. H., Arya, B., & Mirchandani, D. A. (2013). Global integration strategies of small and medium multinationals: Evidence from Taiwan. *Journal of World Business, 1*(48), 47–57.

Kalnins, A. (2004). An empirical analysis of territorial encroachment within franchised and company-owned branded chains. *Marketing Science, 23*(4), 476–489.

Kalnins, A., & Lafontaine, F. (2004). Multi-unit ownership in franchising: Evidence from the fast-food industry in Texas. *Rand Journal of Economics 35*(4), 747–761. doi:10.2307/1593771

Kaufmann, P. J., & Dant, R. P. (1999). Franchising and the domain of entrepreneurship research. *Journal of Business Venturing, 14*(1), 5–16. doi:10.1016/S0883-9026(97)00095-5

Moorman, C., & Rust, R. (1999). The role of marketing. *Journal of Marketing, 63*, 180–197.

Nair, S. K., Tikoo, S., & Liu, S. (2009). Valuing exclusivity from encroachment in franchising. *Journal of Retailing, 85*(2), 206–210.

Oxenfeldt, A. R., & Kelly, A. O. (1969). Will successful franchise systems ultimately become wholly-owned chains. *Journal of Retailing, 44*(4), 69–83.

Perryman, A. A., & Combs, J. G. (2012). Who should own it? An agency-based explanation for multi-outlet ownership and co-location in plural form franchising. *Strategic Management Journal, 33*(4), 368–386. doi:10.1002/smj.1947

Peter T. Paul College of Business and Economics, University of New Hampshire. (2013). Rosenberg International Franchise Center – Research. University of New Hampshire: Retrieved from https://paulcollege.unh.edu/research/rosenberg-international-franchise-center/rosenberg-international-franchise-center-research. Accessed on December 8, 2012.

Prahalad, C. K., & Doz, Y. L. (1987). *The multinational mission: Balancing local demands and global vision.* New York, NY: The Free Press.

Sanchez Gomez, R., Suarez Gonzalez, I., & Vazquez, L. (2010). Multi-unit versus single-unit franchising: Assessing why franchisors use different ownership strategies. *Service Industries Journal, 30*(3), 463–476. doi:10.1080/02642060802252027

Shane, S. A. (1998). Making new franchise systems work. *Strategic Management Journal, 19*(7), 697–707.

Sorenson, O., & Sørensen, J. B. (2001). Finding the right mix: Franchising, organizational learning, and chain performance. *Strategic Management Journal, 22*(6–7), 713–724.

Szulanski, G., & Jensen, R. J. (2008). Growing through copying: The negative consequences of innovation on franchise network growth. *Research Policy, 37*(10), 1732–1741.

Taggart, J. H. (1997). An evaluation of the integration-responsiveness framework: MNC manufacturing subsidiaries in the UK. *Management International Review, 37*(4), 295–318.

Vargo, S., & Lusch, R. (2004). Evolving to a new dominant logic for marketing. *Journal of Marketing, 68*(1), 1–17.

Wright, F. W., Madura, J., & Wiant, K. J. (2002). The differential effects of agency costs on multinational corporations. *Applied Financial Economics, 12*(5), 347–359.

ORGANIZING EXPORT STRATEGIES

Gabriella Lojacono and Markus Venzin

ABSTRACT

This article supports managers in their attempts to organize effective export strategies. Exporting is not just an initial low-commitment internationalization strategy that leads naturally into higher commitment entry modes such as FDI or acquisitions. For many firms, location advantages do not justify foreign direct investments and they therefore decide to service foreign markets from their domestic markets. But despite the relevance of this internationalization mode, there does not seem to be much consolidated knowledge about the organization of successful export strategies. As a result, firms are not just confronted with the choice between export or FDI but with numerous distinct strategic exporting alternatives. The article unfolds as follows: after a brief introduction on the relevance of international trade and the characteristics of export strategies, we describe four distinct export archetypes: (1) export manager, (2) centralistic export developer, (3) export skimmer, (4) integrated export developer. This article concludes with a discussion on the impact different export models have on firm performance.

Keywords: Export strategies; foreign market commitment; international expansion; Italian furniture industry

Orchestration of the Global Network Organization
Advances in International Management, Volume 27, 283–298
Copyright © 2014 by Emerald Group Publishing Limited
All rights of reproduction in any form reserved
ISSN: 1571-5027/doi:10.1108/S1571-502720140000027011

THE RELEVANCE OF EXPORT STRATEGIES

The volume of export has continuously increased in recent years and exceeds 20% of total world output. Exporting is for many small as well as large companies the main market-servicing mode. Total world export accounted for 11.8 trillion dollars in 2006. If we compare exporting to the total world output of 58.6 trillion dollars (The World Bank, 2008), we see how important cross-border trade has become. In fact, the total volume of the world merchandise trade grew by 8% in the period from 2000 to 2006 compared to an average GNP increase of less than half (3.5%) in the same period. However, exporting is not equally important for all product classes: manufactures were the fastest growing category with 10% in constant prices in 2006 and thereby outpaced its average annual growth rate since 1950 by 2.5%. Most other product categories show an annual growth rate in constant prices that is only half as big. CAGE (cultural, administrative, geographical, and economic) differences still matter. Only 23% of total exports can be accounted to inter-regional merchandise trade flows between North America, Europe, and Asia. There are also strong regional differences in terms of export composition: 84% of total trade is manufactured from Asia but just 20% in Africa and 22% in the Middle East.[1]

This snapshot on international trade statistics illustrates the relevance of exporting for most economies and firms. The importance of this topic for business is reflected in a rich stream of literature on market entry modes and the organization of international strategies (Agarwal & Ramswami, 1992; Anderson & Gatignon, 1986; Brown, Dev, & Zhou, 2003; Buckley & Casson, 1998; Buckley & Ghauri, 2006; Pan & Tse, 2000; Root, 1987). Many of these articles, however, are more concerned with large companies choosing between FDI, strategic alliances, and exporting. Few authors give pragmatic advice on how companies that do not have the resources, ambitions, or market conditions to directly invest equity abroad may find an effective export mode (Cavusgil, 1984; Cavusgil & Zou, 1994; Cunningham & Spigel, 1971; Pavord & Bogart, 1985; Piercy, 2001; Piercy, Kaleka, & Katsikeas, 1998). The goal of this article is therefore to provide a rich description of export behavior of the Italian furniture industry, which will serve as a basis to develop a framework for the organization of export strategies.

EMPIRICAL SETTING: THE ITALIAN FURNITURE INDUSTRY

We chose this industry because it heavily depends on exporting and initial interviews with entrepreneurs has shown that many different approaches to exporting co-exist. The following paragraphs describe the research method, the industry structure and competitive dynamics as well as international challenges of the global furniture industry and their implications for the Italian firms.

Research Method

Data on the export behavior and performance implications were collected in three consecutive stages. First, we conducted 30 in-depth cases studies on the international growth patterns of firms within the Italian furniture industry. This qualitative analysis indicated that various export behaviors exist and that higher commitment to export activities may translate into a higher degree of success for the exporting company. This first investigation helped identify the elements that constitute export behavior. In the second stage, we consolidated our preliminary findings by reviewing the relevant literature on market entry modes and export performance (Cadogan, Diamantopoulos, & De Mortanges, 2002; Cavusgil & Zou, 1994; Katsikeas, Leonidou, & Morgan, 2000; Katsikeas, Piercy, & Ioannidis, 1996; Lu & Beamish, 2004; Pan, Li, & Tse, 1999; Samiee & Roth, 1992; Zou & Stan, 1998). However, only a small stream of the literature studied exporters' profiles, and previous studies of internationalization strategies and resulting performance generated only ambiguous findings. The third phase was dedicated to the development and subsequent analysis of the questionnaire. We tested the survey with four respondents and improved its clarity and effectiveness. The final version was translated into Italian and administered to the sample of 263 firms. The Italian questionnaire was translated back into English to check its consistency with the original English version of the survey. After the clusters were built, we organized a workshop to which we invited the 97 responding firms to share and interpret the results, of which 37 accepted the invitation. Not surprisingly, 34 of these belong to the two most successful archetypes in terms of export performance. To improve our understanding of the four archetypes, we conducted five follow-up interviews with a selected group of entrepreneurs.

Industry Structure and Competitive Dynamics

The Italian furniture industry is mainly composed of small and medium sized firms with an average of six employees.[2] Those firms are mostly family controlled and located in only a few of Italy's regional industrial areas: Lombardy, Veneto, Tuscany, Friuli-Venezia Giulia, and the Marches.

The high level of industry fragmentation[3] and small size together with the ownership structure enable furniture firms to react with flexibility and quick decision making to industry changes. But at the same time, these small family owned and family run companies were limited by scarce availability of resources (financial and human) as well as conservative mindsets of the owners. Most companies are more risk adverse than their international peers. In Germany, for example, the furniture industry is less fragmented: although the top 10 firms have a similar turnover (see Table 1), the 36,000 Italian firms are on average much smaller than the approximately 1,700 German firms. A major difference, however, is that the top German firms are run by external managers. They also tend to be less risk adverse since their ownership structure is more diversified. In Italy, only two Italian furniture companies are listed: Natuzzi (NYSE) and Poltrona Frau Group (Milan Stock Exchange).

The most widespread way to segment the Italian furniture industry is to distinguish the level of vertical integration and the product scope. By combining these two factors, we get the following four sub-segments:

- *Integrated and specialized companies*: This category includes enterprises where the majority of production takes place inside the company or group of companies. These enterprises normally invest substantial resource in innovation. Natuzzi is part of this cluster: This company is focused on the production and commercialization of a narrow offer

Table 1. Top 10 Companies in Italy Compared to Top 10 in Germany.

	Italy		Germany	
	Company name	Turnover 2007 (0.000 euro)	Company name	Turnover 2007 (0.000 euro)
1	Natuzzi	629.805	Nobilia-Werke J. Stickling Gmbh & Co. Kg	650.800
2	Poltrona Frau[a]	269.841	Alno Ag	608.395
3	Snaidero	247.905	Hülsta-Werke Hüls Gmbh & Co. Kg	284.000
4	Scavolini	223.953	Nolte Küchen Gmbh & Co. Kg	280.000
5	Chateau d'Ax	214.763	Häcker Küchen Gmbh & Co. Kg	258.000
6	B&B Italia	176.447	Rauch Möbelwerke Gmbh	205.000
7	Calligaris[a]	247.717	Himolla Polstermöbel Gmbh	179.294
8	Veneta Cucine	149.929	Schüller Möbelwerk Kg	165.351
9	Cucine Lube	137.967	Pino Küchen Gmbh	125.000
10	Santarossa	111.891	Bulthaup Gmbh & Co Kg[a]	106.666

[a]2006.

(i.e., armchairs and sofas) but decided to control the entire value system – from the production of leather covers, metal and wooden frames to the trucks that deliver the goods to the sales outlets. Higher levels of integration allowed Natuzzi to improve reliability and times of delivery as well as reduce its costs by economies of scale in production.

- *Integrated and diversified companies:* In this category, direct control of production activities is combined with an offer covering various products, from kitchen units to fully equipped wall modules and bedroom furniture. Production is often diversified by means of external growth (acquisitions). As a result, companies belonging to this cluster often have a multi-brand strategy. Diversification in many firms has been triggered by the need to obtain greater negotiating power with the distribution channels as well as economies of scope in production. For example, it often happens that wardrobe and "equipped wall module" companies decide to apply their carpentry expertise in kitchen unit production. What appears to be fundamental here is that the acquisitions always concern homogeneous brands with a high intrinsic value. Some of the best-known cases of external growth strategy are the acquisitions of Varenna by Poliform, Ernesto Meda by Scavolini, Cassina and Cappellini by Poltrona Frau. Decisions to diversify are usually linked to basic technology. One particular example of this category is the Meritalia Group, which is specialized in large turnkey contract business for private and institutional customers that led to the acquisition of specialized companies (in wood, metal and marble and stone-cutting) and the launch of a lighting unit production. Companies, such as Molteni, that carry out all stages of woodworking also fall within this group.
- *Specialized "assembler" companies*: These companies outsource heavily and purchase even complex components from suppliers with whom they typically have consolidated relationships based on personal ties of entrepreneurs, their reputation in the local area and their brand recognition in the market. The offer mainly comprises mattresses, upholstery, or kitchens. Accessories (for example, bedside tables and carpets) are purchased from external companies and marketed under their own brand. Companies operating with this business model are Flou (mattresses and beds), Chateau d'Ax (upholstered furniture and mattresses), and Calia (upholstered furniture).
- *Diversified "assembler" companies*: This category includes both large companies focused on a volume strategy and small concerns of an artisan nature whose unique skills are gradually being lost (for instance, gilding and polishing). The latter have no standardized product offering but

make to order based on specific customer requirements. As a result, they have to be highly flexible in terms of production. For example, Kartell offers many items (from lighting to chairs to trolley to bookcase) linked to the firm's original specialization in plastics technology; the company coordinates the design and marketing process but all the components are manufactured by external suppliers.

This description could be complemented using other two segmentation criteria: branding strategy and design intensity. For the purpose of this article, it is essential to understand whether furniture producers market their products using their own brands − the most frequent case − or whether they sell unbranded products (e.g., the private label agreement between the Italian kitchen producer Snaidero and Ikea). Producers distinguish themselves also by different approaches towards design. *Design-driven companies* (e.g., B&B Italia, Kartell, Zanotta) substantially invest in innovation capabilities. Their products are created through a close collaboration with external designers. As a result, these companies position themselves in the high end of the market. *Market-driven companies* (e.g., Scavolini, Snaidero, Natuzzi) use their internal technical office to create new product prototypes based on detailed market research.

Meeting the Challenges of International Markets

Italian furniture producers have started to successfully export in the late Seventies. As a result, Italy was leading the global furniture export ranking from 1979 until 2003 when it was overtaken by China. Since then, the global furniture industry underwent a dramatic change: producers from low-cost countries (e.g., China, Malaysia, Vietnam, and Mexico) have established a deep-rooted presence in primary markets for European firms (e.g., USA). Once considered as least relevant, the low-cost competition is now becoming a significant concern for most producers. In addition to a low-cost advantage, critical sources for building the primary position of Chinese manufacturers have been their ability to develop new models quickly according to dealers' requests and in big volumes. Today, competitors in the low-end market can easily go out of business if they do not have a reactive and flexible product development.

Consider the following example: In 2006, the buyer of one of the leading furniture retailing chains in the United Kingdom (including 35 stores) was thinking about the modification of its purchasing policy to be price-aggressive and to create a more differentiated product assortment. The firm started from upholstered furniture (i.e., armchairs and sofas – the most sold product category) to restructure its offer. Furthermore, its collection of upholstered was originally bought from five Italian manufacturers. According to the buyer: "Italian producers are the luxury side of the low end." The traditional approach of these companies towards retailers has been to ignore them and to neglect requests for product and service adaptation. They prefer to promote their standard product portfolio (ideated by their technical office) under their brands; while in countries like UK clients are more loyal to retailers than manufacturers." To revise its product scope, the buyer with his staff organized meetings with potential Chinese suppliers on the basis of a collection of catalogues of Italian full with personal sketches reflecting customers' input. Surprisingly, one of them was able to create a prototype of one the sketches in 10 hours; this company delivered a dozen containers of that model in 20 days from the order. This was the beginning of a lasting cooperation and the closing of commercial relationships with all Italian suppliers. Today, appealing and cheap Chinese upholstered is widely sold in their UK stores under two Italian-style private labels.

This example documents that many Italian exporting companies are not positioned to implement effective low-cost strategies and this market could be considered as lost. One of the major challenges while addressing international markets is therefore to find ways to reinforce competitive advantage in the high end market. This requires capabilities to transfer branding and high-value design to foreign markets. As a result, export strategies of many firms have evolved in the past years and have increased in their complexity as described in the following paragraphs.

EXPORT STRATEGY ARCHETYPES

Our data from the Italian furniture industry suggests that there are two main variables that shape the organization of export strategies: (1) the orientation (strategic vs. opportunistic) and (2) the locus (home market vs. dispersed) of decision making. The following paragraphs describe both design variables.

Organization Variable 1: The Orientation of Decision Making

Firms can approach international markets in an opportunistic or a strategic way. Many entrepreneurs choose not to choose. They decline to make strategic decisions that commit a substantial amount of resources to foreign markets in a way that it hard to reverse. This situation is symptomatic of a "hit and run" approach to the company's international presence. They engage in cross-border business if opportunities arise without a profound knowledge about foreign markets. An opportunistic market approach is characterized by the absence of a clear competitive positioning and an idea of how to get there in the long term. To service the market in an opportunistic approach often works well in emerging markets with little international competition. But as soon as other international players enter the market with a higher commitment and a strategic approach, the opportunists often quickly lose market share and instead of increasing their commitment they look for the next emerging market to address. Exporters with an opportunistic approach often service a large number of markets but with small market shares.

In turn, exporters with a strategic approach aim at creating a "second home market," i.e., a foreign market where they are nearly as strong as they are in their home market. These exporters have explicit mechanisms for investment decisions. The marketing budgets, for example, may vary substantially from one market to another because they investment priorities are based on an assessment of the attractiveness as well as penetrability of those markets. Strategic exporters base their decisions on detailed market research that allow them to cluster their markets according to their level of attractiveness and penetrability. This profound foreign market knowledge allows those firms to make differentiated decisions about the right local marketing mix including pricing, promotion and distribution. To have a strategic approach to exporting does not necessarily mean to adapt to local conditions but to make an informed decision about the level of local adaptation.

Organization Variable 2: The Locus of Decision Making

The locus of decision making refers to the issue of who is deciding and how the strategic decisions are integrated. When a firm decides to service international markets through exporting, it naturally expands the list of stakeholders that eventually influence the decision-making process. Most exporters make all decisions at their headquarters located in the domestic market. The local partners or subsidiaries serve as pure sales units and execute strategic directions coming from the center. However, over the years, successful subsidiaries increasingly gain importance as sources of competitive advantage in. As a result, various subsidiary types emerge as they grow

(Birkinshaw & Hood, 1998) and most exporters today do not rely solely on sources of competitive advantage created in the home-country, but facilitate the peripheral development of knowledge, competences, or other sources of competitive advantage. But to unleash this potential, headquarters have to learn how to involve subsidiaries in strategic decision-making processes. They have to find the right balance between subsidiary initiatives and central control.

The potential impact of locus of decision making and orientation of decision making on a firm's export behavior is represented in Fig. 1.

Export Manager

Most of the analyzed firms of our sample started their internationalization process as "export managers." These firms typically regard their home markets as the most important reference points for strategic decisions. They look at international markets as a way to increase volume without much effort. Foreign business partners have few possibilities to adapt their offerings to local needs. These firms tend to replicate their success recipes

	Strategic	**Centralistic Export Developer**	**Integrated Export Developer**
Orientation of Decision Making			
	Opportunistic	**Export Manager**	**Export Skimmer**
		Home Market	Dispersed

Locus of Decision Making

Fig. 1. Export Strategies Clusters Classified on Locus and Orientation of Decision Making.

abroad using a naïve approach – they have a single market entry mode for all markets and do not adapt their products at all. Most of these firms choose a low-commitment entry mode using multi-branded agents or importers that have no preferred relationship with any of their suppliers. Export managers seek little feedback from their foreign business partners on the general local market conditions or their end-customers. As a consequence they do not develop local market knowledge and therefore invest little in adapting their products or marketing mix to the needs of their foreign customers. All export managers in our sample have no brand recognition outside their home market. We could not identify a clear pattern regarding vertical integration and product specialization.

To illustrate the export behaviors of firms within the "export manager" cluster, this paragraph describes a typical firm ("Company A") from this cluster. The focal firm is a famous traditional brand in the Italian luxury industry of upholstered furniture. Company A has experienced very low international growth serving a few clients in European countries mainly. It also made some attempts to break into new overseas markets to replace declining local sales. It was hoped that geographic diversification would lower the firm's dependence on the declining domestic market and increase market share in other parts of the world. However this strategy failed. We identified a number of structural and organizational constraints that at least partly account for its incomplete internationalization: (1) high investments in differentiation that in order to be perceived need an adequate level of communication and service that doesn't match with the standard international retailing structure. The more suitable distribution strategy should be the opening of direct operating stores that require investments this SME couldn't afford; (2) internal organizational practices that are focused on product development and on extreme centralization of decision making. Local units are not real subsidiaries but offices that intermediate between representatives and the headquarters in Italy; (3) the belief that the primary market is Italy; orders coming from foreign dealers are just a good opportunity to increase turnover and saturate production capacity.

Centralistic Export Developer
Compared to the previous export archetype, this cluster is characterized by higher levels of market knowledge, which allows firms to approach exporting in a more strategic way. Explicit mechanisms exist for resource allocation, and investment priorities are set and revised regularly. Products, brands, and distribution channels are, however, mostly replicated in a

naïve way (i.e., without changes from the home-market model) in carefully selected foreign markets. Centralistic Export Developers work like mainframe computers; they are receptive for information that is collected and stored centrally. But action is steered by the 'main frame' of the top management. The main decisions are still made by the founder at the headquarters level and the distant outposts are used to gather information and to execute the commands that come from the center. In such a model, the foreign subsidiaries or partners work like terminals without computing power. They gather data and maybe deliver strategic options but the center is deciding how to approach the single foreign markets. Typically, centralistic export developers have not a very strong brand name in foreign countries. Most of them are specialized assemblers.

"Company B," a typical representative of this cluster, is not only one of the biggest industrial group in the Italian kitchen industry, but also a leading firm in the global contract business (i.e., turnkey projects). It started its international expansion in the early sixties targeting distant markets like Canada and USA since the origins. The geographical and cultural proximity never represented a pre-requisite for market entry. However, like the major part of its competitors, the internationalization of Company B has been provoked by the occasional request of Made in Italy products coming from international dealers. Although there is a strong level of coordination amongst the headquarters (including logistics) in Friuli and locals subsidiaries, the product development (without any adaptation to local markets) and the commercial and marketing plan are defined in Italy. Subsidiaries are in charge of order management and post-sale assistance. Local intermediaries have to periodically analyze local distribution in order to submit a proposal of potential clients. The organizational structure for international operations is composed of a commercial director, three area manager, two training manager, a service team (members are specialized by language/Country) for order management, one Middle East sales director and one sales director dedicated to business development in emerging markets.

Export Skimmer
This export archetype shows a high degree of foreign market autonomy and decentralization. Firms in this cluster tend to be relatively small and are positioned in the low-end market. Their approach to foreign markets is opportunity driven – once they have identified a valid foreign business partner, they delegate substantial elements of the marketing mix to them. This can be done because all firms in this cluster do not have strong brand

names that need to be protected or exploited. Consequently, export skimmers make all potential adaptation to the product if this is economically feasible. In this archetype, subsidiaries cannot be compared to dummy terminals that gather data for a central mainframe computer. Instead, the organizational model of this international network is more similar to an internet based model where computing power can come from anywhere in the web. Foreign market partners are fairly autonomous and as long as they produce the desired economic outcomes, headquarters will not interfere. The network of foreign subsidiaries is linked to each other by arms lengths market agreements. Little formal integration of foreign subsidiaries or cross-border arbitrage (i.e., knowledge specialization and sharing) is made. Export skimmers typically appoint home-market managers with their office at the headquarters to lead the sales areas. Most of them are unbranded and specialize in a narrow product range. They are typically not highly vertically integrated.

In 1970, Company C, a family business firm specialized in leather sofas, was born for sales in European markets. Till now, France is the main market (60% of total export). With exception of sporadic orders, C doesn't serve Italian dealers. Since the origins, the product portfolio was suited to European dealers and basic models were adapted to the specific requirements of local clients. Country managers at headquarter accumulated experience in the marketplace and knowledge in running relationships with buyers and purchasing offices of large retailing chains. Effective sales force in main countries (the vertical channel is differently organized around the world) has been selected to understand and help clients abroad. The path that C experienced in its internationalization showed different cornerstones towards the other models. Notably, the entrepreneur and his management team attached scarce importance to brand awareness and related investments. Brand was considered somewhat unnecessary to boost sales while participation to local fairs, update knowledge of domestic regulations, constant information flows with clients, "no-frills" product models and product adaptation, monitoring of competitors' strategies were essential for an effective local action.

Integrated Export Developer
Due to the higher local market adherence in terms of a firm's marketing mix activities and the autonomy of competitive strategies, we labeled this cluster as "integrated export developer." Firms in this cluster delegate more decision power to local markets but do not adapt their marketing mix to local partners. This can be explained by the increased international

orientation in product design, development and distribution policies. In other words, products are not mainly conceived of for home-market clients, but as a viable compromise for global clients. As a result, the company manages to achieve economies of international integration and allows local adaptation in areas where it is not too costly. As opposed to export skimmers, integrated export developers typically appoint foreign market managers as head of their respective areas. This way, they have a direct impact on the strategic decisions that are made for their markets. The home-market sales area is integrated in a larger region and has no particular position in relation to the other areas. Most firms in this category pursue an articulated branding strategy and show an elevated level of up- and down-stream integration.

Company D is a significant player among this group including many firms with a well-known brand (domestically or worldwide). It was founded in the Fifties and has its headquarter in North Italy (in the Brianza District, the area in between Como and Milan). Its main product lines are chairs, tables, sofas, and wardrobes. The high proportion of managerial activity that takes place overseas makes it a host-oriented firm and places it alongside the majority of home-region dependent firms in terms of influence that local players may have on strategic decisions. Like the others companies of this cluster, with very few exceptions, Company D approached European markets (e.g., Belgium, Netherlands) at a first stage (Sixties and Seventies). In that initial period, Italian design is diffusing in nearest countries following the well-recognized primacy of both Italian designers and product quality. However, Company D has been also stimulated to go abroad by the intuition and vision of its founder: "I always thought that the company I started up had no geographical boundaries and it could face the international challenges successfully. Travelling abroad and participating to industry fairs supported my beliefs and the search of ideas and innovation worldwide." The three main subsidiaries (in USA, UK, and Japan) are like autonomous firms responsible for the following activities: (1) management of the showroom; (2) management of sales force; (3) scouting of contract projects (i.e., turnkey projects); (4) implementation of contract projects in strict coordination with the contract division in Italy. To ensure the best quality standard service, a logistic platform has been created in New York. No product adaptation is provided for two reasons. First, the product is designed by external international designers who have an international feeling in their ideas and sketches. Second, a unique product collection is considered as leverage for promoting a coherent brand image worldwide. In Italy, the organizational structure includes one commercial director and three area managers (East Europe, Western Europe, Far East-Australia) who coordinate the efforts of local mono-brand representatives.

EXPORT PERFORMANCE

After identifying and describing the four export archetypes, we were naturally interested in whether some export archetypes are more successful than others. We created a composite index to measure export performance based on six qualitative questions with equal weight. The results were rather surprising: The export skimmer had the best export performance of the archetypes in our sample, closely followed by the integrated export developer. This indicates that a high commitment to foreign markets, paired with a high dispersion of marketing value chain activities, a high level of independence of competitive actions and a high level of adaptation of marketing mix elements results in better export performance. The firms in our sample that are highly committed to foreign markets and delegate substantial decision power to local entrepreneurs are able to exploit ownership advantages in the home and host markets through higher levels of coordination and control. On the other hand, our results indicate that very low levels of commitment, together with superficial knowledge of target markets and an opportunistic, passive approach to internationalization, lead to poor export performance. This confirms the general assumption that internationalizing firms need to develop profound market knowledge and deploy dedicated resources if they aim for a successful international market presence.

CONCLUSION

The value of this article lies in bringing a more differentiated approach to the organizing of export strategies. We stress the importance of exporting as an internationalization mode. For many firms, exporting is not an initial experimental market entry strategy that is naturally substituted by a higher commitment entry mode. We argued that exporting is the dominant cross-border market-servicing mode in the Italian furniture industry and it is most likely to remain this way. Based on our data, we were able to show that fundamentally different exporting modes exist. We distinguished four exporting modes based on the locus (central versus dispersed) and orientation (opportunistic versus strategic) of decision making and linked them to subjective performance assessments.

Firms that integrated foreign operations in the decision-making processes (i.e., export skimmers and integrated export developers) had significantly superior performance as opposed to firms that centralized decision-making power at the home-country level. However, our interview data reveal that most industry experts do not think that export skimmers will be successful in the long run, especially since competition from low-cost suppliers of furniture from Asian countries is steadily increasing. Export skimmers usually do not have their own identity and foreign market knowledge. This makes them easily replaceable with suppliers that are more flexible, speedy and less costly. We therefore conclude that integrated export developers have a marginally lower export performance today but they are investing in a stronger foreign market position that will secure future success.

Our findings also suggest that a common exporting strategy represented by the "export manager" archetype is the least successful. Even small firms seem to be able to achieve superior returns from international activities by responding more proactively to foreign market conditions — either strategically as integrated export developers or opportunistically as export skimmers that adopt their offerings to the requests of rather autonomous foreign sales agents. The more integrated and mature international markets get, the lower will be the number of firms operating as export managers.

NOTES

1. If not indicated otherwise, international trade data in this section was taken from International Trade Statistics (2007).

2. For more details, see the annual statistics provided by the Italian Furniture Trade Association (www.federlegno.it).

3. In total, over 36,000 firms are classified as furniture producers in Italy.

REFERENCES

Agarwal, S., & Ramswami, S. N. (1992). Choice of foreign market entry mode: Impact of ownership, location and internalization factors. *Journal of International Business Studies*, 23(1), 1–27.

Anderson, E. M., & Gatignon, H. (1986). Modes of foreign entry: A transaction cost analysis and propositions. *Journal of International Business Studies*, 17(3), 1–26.

Birkinshaw, J., & Hood, N. (1998). Multinational subsidiary evolution: Capability and charter
    change in foreign-owned subsidiary companies. *Academy of Management Review, 23*(4),
    773–795.
Brown, J. R., Dev, C., & Zhou, Z. (2003). Broadening the foreign market entry mode decision:
    Separating ownership and control. *Journal of International Business Studies, 34,*
    473–488.
Buckley, P. J., & Casson, M. C. (1998). Analyzing foreign market entry strategies: Extending
    the internalization approach. *Journal of International Business Studies, 29*(3), 539–561.
Buckley, P. J., & Ghauri, P. N. (2006). *The internationalization of the firm* (2nd ed.). London:
    Thomson.
Cadogan, J. W., Diamantopoulos, A., & De Mortanges, C. P. (2002). Export market-oriented
    activities: Their antecedents and performance consequences. *Journal of International
    Business Studies, 33*(3), 615–626.
Cavusgil, S. T. (1984). Differences among exporting firms based on their degree of internatio-
    nalization. *Journal of Business Research, 12*(2), 195–208. Elsevier.
Cavusgil, S. T., & Zou, S. (1994). Marketing strategy–performance relationship: An investigation
    of the empirical link in export market ventures. *Journal of Marketing, 58*(January), 1–21.
Cunningham, M. T., & Spigel, R. I. (1971). A study in successful exporting. *British Journal of
    Marketing, 5*(Spring), 2–12.
International Trade Statistics. (2007). World Trade Organization. Retrieved from http://www.
    wto.org/english/res_e/statis_e/statis_e.htm
Katsikeas, C. S., Leonidou, L. C., & Morgan, N. A. (2000). Firm-level export performance
    assessment: Review, evaluation, and development. *Journal of the Academy of Marketing
    Science, 28*(4), 493–511.
Katsikeas, C. S., Piercy, N. F., & Ioannidis, C. (1996). Determinants of export performance in
    a European context. *European Journal of Marketing, 30*(6), 6–35.
Lu, J. W., & Beamish, P. W. (2004). International diversification and firm performance: The
    s-curve hypothesis. *Academy of Management Journal, 47*(4), 598–609.
Pan, Y., Li, S., & Tse, D. K. (1999). The impact of order and mode of market entry on profit-
    ability and market share. *Journal of International Business Studies, 30*(1), 81–104.
Pan, Y., & Tse, D. (2000). The hierarchical model of market entry modes. *Journal of
    International Business Studies, 31,* 535–554.
Pavord, W. C., & Bogart, R. G. (1975). The dynamics of the decision to export. *Akron
    Business and Economics Review, 6*(Spring), 6–11.
Piercy, N. (2001). Company internationalisation: Active and reactive exporting. *European
    Journal of Marketing, 15*(3), 26–40.
Piercy, N. F., Kaleka, A., & Katsikeas, C. S. (1998). Sources of competitive advantage in high
    performing exporting companies. *Journal of World Business, 33*(4), 378–393.
Root, F. R. (1987). *Entry strategies for international markets.* New York, NY: Lexington
    Books.
Roth, K. (1992). International configuration and coordination archetypes for medium-sized
    firms in global industries. *Journal of International Business Studies, 23*(3), 533–549.
Samiee, S., & Roth, K. (1992). The influence of global marketing standardization on perfor-
    mance. *Journal of Marketing, 56*(2), 1–17.
The World Bank. (2008). World development indicators, p. 193. Retrieved from http://web.
    worldbank.org
Zou, S., & Stan, S. (1998). The determinants of export performance: A review of the empirical
    literature between 1987 and 1997. *International Marketing Review, 15*(5), 333–356.

MNC HEADQUARTERS AS GLOBAL NETWORK ORCHESTRATORS: INSIGHTS FROM HEADQUARTERS RELOCATION PATTERNS IN EUROPE

Alfredo Valentino, Phillip C. Nell and Jasper J. Hotho

ABSTRACT

Despite increased interest in headquarters (HQ) and their activities, we still lack a comprehensive understanding of the drivers of HQ relocations and their consequences. We seek to address this gap by examining whether HQ relocations are primarily driven by cost-reduction or value-creation motives, whether these motivations vary by HQ type and how these relocation patterns vary over time. We explore these questions on the basis of a unique hand-collected database of 227 HQ relocations in Europe between 2000 and 2012. Our findings illustrate that different types of HQ units play their orchestrating role in different ways and that their relocations are driven by different motives. Furthermore, our data

Orchestration of the Global Network Organization
Advances in International Management, Volume 27, 299–323
ISSN: 1571-5027/doi:10.1108/S1571-502720140000027015

suggest that although all types of HQ units are increasingly mobile, the implications of relocations for the MNC may differ considerably by HQ type. These findings contribute to a more fine-grained understanding of the drivers of HQ relocations and open up various new avenues for future research on HQ relocation and the role of HQ units in the orchestration of MNCs' internal networks.

Keywords: Headquarters; HQ relocation; parenting advantage; HQ role; value creation; cost reduction

INTRODUCTION

Within global network organizations, much of the "orchestrating" of the organizational architecture takes place in corporate and divisional headquarters (HQs) who take on the role of network orchestrators (Foss & Pedersen, 2002; Ghoshal, Moran, & Almeida-Costa, 1995). The geographical locations of these HQs have historically tended to be relatively stable. Recently, however, it was reported that multinational corporations (MNCs) increasingly relocate individual HQs activities (Birkinshaw, Braunerhjelm, Holm, & Terjesen, 2006) or even their entire HQs across borders (Baaij, Mom, Van den Bosch, & Volberda, 2012; Benito, Lunnan, & Tomassen, 2011; Laamanen, Simula, & Torstila, 2011). For example, in 2008, Nissan, the Japanese car producer, moved the divisional HQs of its truck division from France to Switzerland. Other recent examples include relocations by corporations such as Philips, IKEA, and Maersk.

While scholarly attention to the relocation of value chain activities has increased considerably, explicit attention to the cross-border relocation of HQs functions has not followed suit. Laudable exceptions aside (e.g., Baaij et al., 2012; Birkinshaw et al., 2006; Laamanen et al., 2011), there have been few attempts to understand the antecedents and consequences of such relocation decisions. For example, little attention has been paid to the question whether HQ relocations are associated with cost-reduction or value-creation motives. Similarly, we still lack insight into how the drivers of relocation decisions and their consequences may differ between different HQ types, such as corporate, regional, and divisional headquarter units. Laamanen et al. (2011) find that regional HQs are more mobile than corporate HQs, and Birkinshaw et al. (2006) argue that the relocation of corporate and divisional HQs activities are driven by different contextual factors. Nevertheless, we still lack a more comprehensive understanding of how relocation patterns differ between all three types of HQ units.

A related concern is we still have little insight into how HQ relocation patterns have developed over the past years. Although it is often claimed that HQ relocations occur even more frequently, evidence of this is often anecdotal and empirical studies on HQ relocations tend to draw on datasets that are relatively small (e.g., Benito et al., 2011; Laamanen et al., 2011), or cross-sectional (e.g., Birkinshaw et al., 2006). As a result, while global network organizations increasingly see the relocation of HQ activities as the next step in the optimization of their global networks (Forsgren, Holm, & Johanson, 1995; Laamanen et al., 2011), our understanding of these relocation patterns is still relatively limited (Baaij et al., 2012; Birkinshaw et al., 2006).

This lack of attention to HQ relocations is surprising, both because of the economic impact of such relocations and because of the theoretical and practical interest in the central role of HQs in the overall orchestration of global network organizations. A shift in HQ location reorganizes critical parenting activities, changes the interaction between HQs and subunits, and moves key decision makers of the firm (Barner-Rasmussen, Piekkari, & Bjorkman, 2007; Birkinshaw et al., 2006). As a result, such relocations are likely to have a considerable impact on the way in which global network organizations are orchestrated. Drawing on parenting theory (e.g., Nell & Ambos, 2013) and the literature on the role of HQ in the MNC (Foss & Pedersen, 2002; Ghoshal et al., 1995) we focus on how HQs increase the net value that they create for the MNC. This can be done either by increasing the value that they create for the subunits or by reducing the costs that the HQ activities incur.

Thus, we aim to contribute to the emergent research agenda on HQ relocations by unraveling the key motivations for these relocation decisions, as well as how these motivations differ between different types of HQ and have developed over time. Specifically, given the central role of HQs for global network organization, we aim to shed light on three questions:

1. Are HQ relocations related to cost-reduction or value-creation motives?
2. Are there differences in these relocation patterns between different types of HQs?
3. Have these relocation patterns changed over time?

For our exploratory analysis, we work with a hand-collected dataset that is unique with regard to its comprehensiveness and scope, covering 227 relocation incidences of corporate, regional, and divisional HQs in Europe over a 13-year period between 2000 and 2012. To our knowledge, this is the largest dataset with cross-border HQ relocations. The findings contribute to the development of a research agenda in which the link between relocations and the role of HQs as orchestrators of the global network takes center stage.

HQ ROLES AND RELOCATIONS

The Role of HQs in Global Network Organizations

Much like orchestra conductors, who face the challenge of bringing together a diverse set of specialized musicians, MNC HQs are considered to be the orchestrators of the various operations of the global network organization. Previous work has highlighted various ways in which effective HQs create value for the MNCs through their orchestrator role.

First, HQs have been found to positively influence knowledge transfers between their dispersed units; both by providing appropriate incentives and through the allocation of resources to places where knowledge transfers would otherwise be difficult to achieve. For example, work by Dellestrand, Kappen, and Ciabuschi (Ciabuschi, Dellestrand, & Holm, 2012; Ciabuschi, Dellestrand, & Kappen, 2012; Dellestrand, 2010; Dellestrand & Kappen, 2012) illustrates that HQs may selectively allocate attention and managerial resources in order to encourage innovation transfer projects; or projects in which an innovation is to be transferred from one MNC location to another. They find that the allocation of resources to enhance knowledge transfer is related to several variables, such as the distance that is to be bridged between the two different units as well as characteristics of the innovation.

Second, HQs have been found to positively contribute to the resources and capabilities of their subunits and to influence the way in which dispersed value chain activities fit together. For example, Parmigiani and Holloway (2011) show that HQs can transfer their operational capabilities to subunits which enables them to perform better. Similarly, Nell and Ambos (2013) highlight that MNC HQs can improve the performance of their subunits even when these subunits operate in distant and contextually different environments. Furthermore, when outsourcing and offshoring decisions are taken, the HQs involvement orchestrating the process has implications for the success of outsourcing and offshoring. For example, Larsen, Manning, and Pedersen (2012) show how the orchestrating role of

HQs can reduce hidden costs related to offshoring operations especially when the complexity of offshoring increases.

Third, classic MNC literature has highlighted the HQs' importance in building a "differentiated" control system. Control and coordination mechanisms such as central control (centralization), formal control (formalization), and behavioral control (socialization) are supposed to be used in a differentiated manner across the whole subunit portfolio (Bartlett & Ghoshal, 1989; Ghoshal & Bartlett, 1988; Nohria & Ghoshal, 1994). The reasoning is based on the idea that subsidiaries in established MNCs differ strongly from each other in terms of local capabilities and environmental context. The only exception is found with socialization (also called normative integration or integration mechanisms). The establishment of strong normative integration that enables to restrict and channel the behavior of subsidiary managers is considered to be one of the most important mechanisms that is valuable across all kinds of subsidiaries (O'Donnell, 2000). Problems with building up an effective differentiated control system are one of the drivers toward setting up regional HQs (Nell, Ambos, & Schlegelmilch, 2011).

Fourth, HQs units may also add value through their effect on subsidiary evolution (e.g., Birkinshaw & Hood, 1998). In contemporary MNCs, subsidiaries frequently develop their own subsidiary-level strategies. In fact, subsidiaries are striving for an enlargement of their activity scope or in continuous upgrading of their capabilities. In turn, such charter change does not only increase the status of the subsidiary in the MNC, it also makes the subsidiary a more important contributor to the performance of the whole MNC. Although not all subsidiary initiatives are warranted by the MNC, in the context of subsidiary initiatives and entrepreneurship, the HQs orchestrating role takes on two different functions (Birkinshaw, 1997; Birkinshaw & Fry, 1998; Bouquet & Birkinshaw, 2008). On the one hand, HQs may drive charter change processes by developing an overall idea of how their portfolio of subsidiaries should develop and by trying to implement this logic (Hoenen, Nell, & Ambos, forthcoming; Rugman & Verbeke, 2003). On the other hand, HQs function as a fundamental part of the firm's immune system. That is, subsidiary initiatives that are too alien to the rest of the MNC's activities are not further supported with MNC resources or sanctioned (Ambos, Andersson, & Birkinshaw, 2010; Schotter & Beamish, 2011).

In sum, there are different ways in which HQs' orchestrating function adds value to the firm. While many of these value-creating activities are highlighted in the literature, less emphasis has been paid on the net value that HQs create. In fact, the strategy literature highlights that the net value added by HQs is composed of the created value minus the costs that the HQs activities, initiatives, and staff cost (Nell & Ambos, 2013). In fact, some authors claim that in increasingly complex, geographically dispersed, and interdependent MNC structures, the HQs value-creation activities are hampered. For example, Andersson, Forsgren, and Pedersen (2001) claim that in the "federative MNC" (i.e., in strongly network-oriented MNC structures), HQs might not have an important role anymore as its powerbase is diluted vis-à-vis the power of established and locally embedded subsidiaries. Foss, Foss, and Nell (2012) argue that today's complex organizations might increasingly lead to net value destruction by HQs. This is because HQs might intervene in an ineffective or inefficient manner leading to costs in terms of opportunity costs, motivation loss, or errors. Firms that perceive limited or even negative net value added by their HQs can engage in three types of initiatives. First, they attempt at making their HQ more efficient, for example, by streamlining processes or cutting costs such as reducing HQ staff (Fischer & Rush, 2011; Ghosh, Rodriguez, & Sirmans, 1995; Heenan, 1989). Second, they attempt at making their HQ activities better by upgrading the HQ staff's capabilities or by reorganizing the way how the HQ interacts with the subsidiaries (Holcomb, Holmes, & Connelly, 2009; Nell & Ambos, 2013). Third, some firms attempt a combination of the first two factors.

HQ Relocations and Their Link to HQs' Value Creation

HQ relocations may assume different forms and patterns. While some firms engage in full relocations, in which all HQ functions are moved to a different location (see, for example, Barner-Rasmussen et al., 2007; Birkinshaw et al., 2006), firms may also engage in partial relocations, meaning that only some parenting activities are relocated (Benito et al., 2011; Birkinshaw et al., 2006; Forsgren et al., 1995).

Most of the cross-border relocation literature (see Table 1 for an overview) has focused on relocations in Europe, in particular the attempts by Scandinavian enterprises to relocate their HQs to countries that are larger and more central (Barner-Rasmussen et al., 2007; Benito et al., 2011; Birkinshaw et al., 2006; Forsgren et al., 1995). Since the Nordic countries are small, peripheral, and highly dependent on foreign trade and investments (Benito & Narula, 2007), when a Scandinavian firm with important cross-border activities decides to relocate its HQs there is a high probability that they will relocate outside national borders (Benito et al., 2011). These studies tend to focus especially on the effects of different firm-specific

Table 1. Previous Studies on HQs Relocations.

References	Focus	Findings
Forsgren et al. (1995)	Reasons that push MNCs to relocate division HQs abroad	• The degree of internationalization of company's divisions has a positive effect on divisional HQs relocation. • The degree of MNCs internationalization has a negative effect on divisional HQs relocation.
Birkinshaw et al. (2006)	Business unit HQs and corporate HQs relocation abroad	Business unit HQs relocation is influenced positively by: • the degree of MNCs internationalization; • the attractiveness of host country. Corporate HQs relocation is related positively to: • foreign ownership; • the listing of company on a foreign stock exchange.
Barner-Rasmussen et al. (2007)	Corporate HQs relocation overseas	Corporate HQs relocation is full, partial, and virtual and it is driven by symbolic and pragmatic motivations.
Benito et al. (2011)	Division HQs relocation abroad	Divisional HQs relocation is affected positively by: • the number of divisions. Divisional HQs relocation is affected negatively by: • degree of diversification; • MNCs' size; • concentration of ownership.

Table 1. (*Continued*)

References	Focus	Findings
Laamanen et al. (2011)	Relocations of both corporate and regional HQs in a multi-country setting	The likelihood of HQs relocation is positively influenced by: • corporate taxes at home country; • employment rate at home country; • the amount of foreign revenues of the firm (a proxy for the degree of internationalization); • the type of HQs unit. HQs units are attracted by locations characterized by: • low corporate taxes.
Voget (2011)	The cross-borders mobility of HQs units through a multi-country dataset	The relocation of HQs serves to avoid the controlled foreign corporation legislation. Taxation plays an important role in this decision.
Baaij et al. (2012)	The relocations of parenting activities, that is, some parts of corporate HQs, to alternative host countries	EMT is driven by: • internationalization of stakeholders and assets. Legal domicile and corporate functions are driven by: • target country attractiveness.

characteristics, such as the degree of internationalization or the type and the nationality of ownership structure, to explain relocations (Benito et al., 2011; Birkinshaw et al., 2006; Forsgren et al., 1995). Such studies highlight that, after the internationalization of sales, marketing and R&D functions (the first degree of internationalization), and the creation of centers of excellence, where subsidiaries are responsible for specific tasks and product groups (the second degree), the relocation of HQs units is the "third stage" to foster the MNCs' international involvement (Forsgren et al., 1995).

In contrast, Laamanen et al. (2011) consider a broader set of country specific characteristics of both the home country and the destination country. They propose a first attempt to distinguish between push (cost minimization) and pull (value creation) motives of HQs relocations. Using their multi-country dataset, they show that companies are attracted by low tax countries and by locations close to big cities or capitals for their HQs. Moreover, they show that regional HQs are characterized by more dynamism in terms of relocation than corporate HQs. Voget (2011) underlines the role of taxation in the relocation decision, offering more empirical evidences. In this direction, Baaij et al. (2012) examine the relocations of individual parenting activities, or the relocation of individual activities of corporate HQs, to alternative host countries. They find that legal domicile and corporate functions are driven by target country attractiveness, while executive management team (EMT) is driven especially by the internationalization degree of stakeholders and assets.

Based on this literature, HQ relocations can be conceptualized as either a strategic move to cut the costs of the HQ's activities, to increase the value that the HQs create, or both. Cost reductions, for example, might occur when HQs are transferred in their entirety to locations where lower tax rates are applied or when the HQ reduces its size. On the other hand, some HQs are transferred because the increasing internationalization of the firm has created new, important markets and customers that are more distant from the HQs than previous markets and customers. Thus, relocating toward these markets might enable the HQs to better understand and comprehend these markets, and the subsidiaries located in them, which, in turn, enables them to increase the value of their parenting activities.

Although previous studies have contributed substantially to our understanding of the HQ relocation phenomenon, we contend that some questions still remain unanswered. Three questions are particularly pertinent: first, we still lack insight into whether HQ relocations are predominantly driven by cost-reduction or value-creation motives. Apart from Laamanen et al. (2011), there is limited empirical work which addresses this question.

As a result, we still lack a clear understanding of how HQ relocations are linked to the orchestrating role of HQ units as well as how relocations add value to the MNC. Second, are there differences in relocation patterns between different types of HQ units? Laamanen et al. (2011) show differences in mobility between global and regional HQ units, and Birkinshaw et al. (2006) highlight that corporate and divisional HQ relocations are affected differently by contextual drivers. Nevertheless, there have been few systematic attempts to assess differences in relocation patterns among all three HQ types, that is, corporate, divisional, and regional HQ units. And third, how do these patterns change over time? Despite an alleged trend toward more frequent relocations (e.g., Baaij et al., 2012; Wanner, Leclef, & Shimizu, 2004), studies on HQ relocations are often cross-sectional (e.g., Birkinshaw et al., 2006) and those studies that use panel data (e.g., Benito et al., 2011; Laamanen et al., 2011) pay relatively little attention to changes over time.

METHODS

In order to explore these questions, we constructed a unique dataset of HQ relocations in Europe. Specifically, we focus on HQs relocations that occurred in 27 European countries (EU-25 plus Norway and Switzerland) during 2000–2012. To shed light on our research questions, we take into account corporate, divisional, as well as regional HQs. That is, along the lines of the parenting literature (e.g., Nell & Ambos, 2013), we assume that the orchestrating role of HQs (e.g., knowledge transfer, synergy-creation, maintaining the corporate immune system) is important for all types of HQs, including regional and divisional ones.[1]

We interpret a relocation of a HQ as a strategic initiative to change the orchestrating role of this HQ. That is, we capture if and in what way a relocation is linked to either value-creation logic, a cost-reduction logic (efficiency logic), or both simultaneously.

We define a HQ as a unit composed by two essential characteristics: a management group with a specific location where they meet to take strategic decisions, and several parenting activities that give the possibility to fulfill the HQs roles discussed above in the literature review (Birkinshaw et al., 2006).

We define relocations as processes in which a firm moves a HQ from one country to another and where the relocated HQs unit maintains "a degree of continuity in identity" (Laamanen et al., 2011, p. 9).

Relocations were identified on the basis of two different databases: LexisNexis and Factiva, two different news databases that collect articles from magazines and journals. We paid particular attention on the issue of potential false positives and on the opposite case of potential false negatives in sampling. To reduce these two sampling errors, we tried to complement our data with several other sources of information in addition to LexisNexis and Factiva. We gathered information from stock market notifications, local business press, financial press, Google news and annual reports, and by cross-checking news articles in other languages.

Moreover, we obtained information about the reasons of HQs relocations from annual reports and announcements in the international and local press. Considering the possible impact of relocation on firm performance, we summarized these explanations in two main groups: cost reduction and value creation. In the first group, the improvement of firm performance is due to the reduction of costs. So, relocation is explained as a way to reorganize the internal organizational structure to cut costs. Similarly, locating HQs in a country with low corporate taxation helps reducing costs. In the second group, we counted all possible explanations that relate HQs relocation to create more value. Here, HQs relocation is a way to implement a new growth strategy or to be closer to main markets, clients and stakeholders to reduce "outsidership" and to improve external relations.

Before conducting the analysis, we give a brief introduction into our sample. We identified 227 HQs relocations in our time frame (2000–2012). Going into details, we found 72 corporate relocations, 42 divisional, and 113 regional ones. On average, in our sample each HQ operates with roughly 180 employees.

Looking at parent firms, they operate with about 33,000 employees on average. This is in line with previous literature that has emphasized how especially larger firms are prone to moving HQs units (Laamanen et al., 2011; Strauss-Kahn & Vives, 2009). However, it could be a consequence of sampling process. Since we identified relocations based on press data, it is likely that we have a bias toward more important firms and more important relocation events. Most of them come from Europe. Only a small percentage stems from Asia-pacific.

A breakdown by industry indicates that 50% of all parent firms are operating in service activities such as transportation, finance, retail, and wholesaling. 45% is of the firms belong to manufacturing industries. The rest (5%) operates in other sectors, like mining and construction.

Measures

Here we describe the main variables used in the analysis and how we operationalize them on the basis of previous literature. The degree of internationalization of the relocating MNC is measured as the ratio between the amount of foreign revenues on the total amount of firm revenues one year before relocation. Following Laamanen et al. (2011), data on this variable comes from several sources: we used data from the Orbis database; collected data directly from annual reports; and combined data from these different sources.

The frequency of managerial explanations of the relocation "is measured as the number of occurrences when a reason falling into that category was used as a justification for the relocation" (Laamanen et al., 2011, p. 13). Some firms give more than one justification, while for some few firms we do not have any reason for the movement of HQs. We identified managerial explanations from the announcement of relocation decision in newspapers or annual reports.

To further investigate some details regarding cost-related relocations, we also capture the change in corporate tax exposure before and after the relocation as well as the change in total HQ staff. We collected data on corporate taxes from the OECD database. The staff savings were compiled using information from the Orbis database and from annual reports.

To further investigate details of value-creation relocations, we capture the change in institutional quality of the HQ location measured with the Kauffman index. We used the six dimensions of the Kauffman index, namely the HQ location's political stability and absence of violence; voice and accountability; government effectiveness; regulatory quality; the rule of law; and control of corruption (Kaufmann & Kraay, 2003; Kaufmann, Kraay, & Mastruzzi, 2009). High values of the Kauffman index indicate that a country has high institutional quality for these dimensions. The institutional quality is usually related to the quality of business services to HQs and thus it represents one way of how HQs can improve its value-creating role within the MNC.

ANALYSIS

In line with our aim to describe the HQ relocation phenomenon and advance the research agenda on this topic, we conduct a descriptive and explorative analysis. To check the statistical significance of our results, we perform some statistical tests. Especially, we run *t*-tests when our variables are normally distributed, and non-parametric tests (Chi-squared and Wilcoxon−Mann−Whitney tests) when the previous assumption is not satisfied.

In the next sections, we describe our main results answering to the three research questions. Then, we conduct a more fine-grained analysis regarding the cost versus value motives per type of HQs and over time.

Cost-Reduction or Value-Creation Motives Related to the HQ Relocations?

Counting the frequencies of managerial explanations, Fig. 1 shows the five most frequent reasons across the three types of HQs (divisional, regional, and corporate HQs). HQs relocation seems predominantly a strategic decision to increase the value added of the HQs since the two most important reasons for relocations are closeness to main markets, clients, or growth. This explanation is used especially for regional and divisional HQs relocations. Cost minimization seems to play a less prominent role and it is used predominantly to justify CHQs relocations. This result contrasts somewhat with previous studies on the phenomenon that consider cost cutting and efficiency motives as the main drivers of HQs relocation. Presumably, this is due to the fact that some cost-aspects (such as tax rates or sizes of HQs) can be captured more easily as compared to strategic, value-creating reasons.

Grouping the managerial explanations in cost minimization and value creation, Table 2 relates them to the full sample and to the type of HQs.

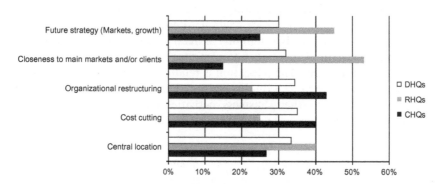

Fig. 1. The Five Most Frequent Managerial Explanations of HQ Relocation Across the Three Types of HQs.

Table 2. Total Number and Percentage of Relocations per Managerial
Explanation and Type of HQs.

	Cost Minimization Explanations Whole Period	Value Creation Explanations Whole Period	Both Explanations (Cost and Value) Whole Period
Full sample	83 (37%)	96 (42%)	46 (20%)
CHQs	31 (43%)	24 (33%)	17 (24%)
RHQs	34 (30%)	56 (50%)	23 (20%)
DHQs	17 (40%)	19 (45%)	6 (14%)

Table 2 shows that 42% of all relocations in our sample are driven by value creation reasons while 37% by cost minimization. The remaining 20% are relocations for which both value and cost reasons are given. Thus, overall, cost and value creation reasons are pretty balanced with some higher relevance of value-creation reasons. This corresponds to the frequencies of Fig. 1.

Are There Differences in These Relocation Patterns between Different Types of HQs?

However, the results change when differentiating between the types of HQs (see Table 2). They underline the different roles played by corporate, divisional, and regional HQs, and in particular on their ability to create parenting value for MNCs: first, corporate HQs relocations are more strongly justified with cost reasons (43% of the total number of CHQs relocations). To reduce their problems in creating more additional value, they are looking for new locations where, for example, lower tax rates apply. Second, divisional and regional HQs mobility is related rather to the creation of additional value, implementing future strategies or being closer to main customers and markets. The relocation is related to their intermediate position within MNC organizational structure. They are operative units that need to be closer to their business activities (Birkinshaw et al., 2006; Forsgren et al., 1995).

Have Relocation Patterns Changed Over Time?

Global competition is pushing firms to be more dynamic and to change quickly their center of gravity. Table 3 shows the mobility of HQs over

Table 3. Number of Relocations in Total, Across Different HQ Types, and Across Time.

	Total Number of Relocations Whole Period	Average No. of Relocations 2000–2005	Average No. of Relocations 2006–2012	*t*-Test Statistic, Significance
Full sample	227	15.0	19.6	1.36*
CHQs	72	5.3	6.7	0.21
RHQs	113	7.0	10.1	1.66**
DHQs	42	2.7	3.7	1.37*

Notes: *, **, and *** denote significance at the 10%, 5%, and 1% levels, respectively.

Table 4. Total Number and Percentage of Relocations Per Managerial Explanations and Type of HQs Over Time.

	Managerial Explanations 2000–2005			Managerial Explanations 2006–2012		
	Cost	Value	Both	Cost	Value	Both
Full sample	29 (33%)	35 (40%)	24 (27%)	54 (39%)	61 (45%)	22 (16%)
CHQs	10 (31%)	10 (31%)	12 (38%)	21 (53%)	14 (35%)	5 (13%)
RHQs	16 (38%)	16 (38%)	10 (24%)	18 (25%)	40 (56%)	13 (18%)
DHQs	4 (25%)	10 (63%)	2 (13%)	13 (50%)	9 (35%)	4 (15%)

time. Our results are in line with Wanner et al. (2004) and Laamanen et al. (2011) who report a growing number of HQs relocations in Europe. Splitting up our time frame in two periods (2000–2005 and 2006–2012), there is growth in the number of relocations per year and this growth is statistically significant. Thus, HQ units seem increasingly mobile and they are searching for new locations where they can improve parenting value through cost reduction or more value creation. These movements are characterized by cost/benefit ratios that seem to indicate higher parenting value. This trend holds also if we differentiate the analysis for the type of HQs. There is an increasing number of relocations/year for all types of HQs.

Looking at the evolution of managerial explanations over time for the full sample and for the type of HQs, Table 4 seems to show that in the more recent period, the reasons for relocations become more clearly separated – either cost or value creation whereas in the beginning of the 2000s, there are substantially more relocations justified with both cost and value-creation motives.

This observation particularly holds for corporate HQs, where the number of relocations with both justifications simultaneously drops from 38% to 13%. For these HQs, the cost justification becomes much more important. It increases by 22% points. Thus, it seems that firms have substantial problems with the parenting value of their corporate HQs, especially the costs, associated with it.

For divisional and regional HQs, we observe an opposite behavior between the two time periods. For DHQs, cost justifications become much more important from the first to the second period, while RHQs relocations are characterized by a stronger focus on value-creation justifications over costs.

More Detailed Analysis on the Cost versus Value Motives of HQs Relocation

In order to investigate some more details regarding the cost versus value motives, we focus on some additional data. With regard to cost reasons, we particularly focus on corporate tax levels and the size of the HQs. Reducing the size of the HQs while relocating it indicates that the relocation went hand in hand with an overall restructuring of the orchestrating role of the HQs.

Table 5 shows the mean savings in terms of corporate tax rates achieved by the relocation. A negative result means a reduction in tax rates for the firm. The overall tax rate savings are on average 5% and the tax rate decrease becomes more prevalent during the last years. This decrease is statistically significant at 1% confidence level. This trend is consistent

Table 5. Average Corporate Tax Savings in Percentage Points per Type of HQs and Over Time.

	Average Tax Savings Whole Period (%)	Average Tax Savings 2000–2005	Average Tax Savings 2006–2012	Z (Mann–Whitney test), Significance
Full sample	−5	−3	−6	−2.02***
CHQs	−6	−4	−7	−1.61**
RHQs	−6	−3	−8	−1.20*
DHQs	−3	−1	−5	−1.56**

Notes: *, **, and *** denote significance at the 10%, 5%, and 1% levels, respectively.

across all HQs types. Thus, relocations achieved on average at maximum three times higher corporate tax savings in the last years since 2006 than in the first half of the decade.

Firms can relocate HQs also to restructure their internal configuration. So, the cost savings derive from the change in the HQs staff after the movement. Table 6 shows the average of staff savings in percent achieved by moving HQs in a new location. We take particular attention to reduce the effects of missing values and outliers. A negative result means a reduction in staff costs for firm. The results show that the overall staff savings are on average 22% after relocation. It means that firms use relocation as a way to reduce the number of HQs employees minimizing internal HQs costs. This reduction is stronger in divisional HQs than in corporate and regional ones. Over time this reduction appears to become more important for every type of HQs, and *t*-test is statistically significant at 5% confidence level for the full sample and for regional HQs.

Similarly to the more fine-grained analysis for the cost-side, we are also considering some more details regarding the value creation side. We are investigating the institutional quality of the location the HQs is moving to. HQs can move to locations with high institutional quality (in terms of low corruption, bureaucracy, and so on), where they can foster relations with stakeholders and operate closer to main markets and customers.

Table 7 shows the number and the percentage of HQs relocations to high institutional quality locations over time. To be a good orchestrator, it is important to be in a good location.

The results show how 55% of the relocated HQs in our sample relocate to high institutional quality locations. These locations improve the value HQs are able to create for firms. Corporate HQs are more sensitive to such

Table 6. Average Staff Savings in Percentage Per Type of HQs and Over Time.

	Average Staff Savings Whole Period (%)	Average Staff Savings 2000–2005 (%)	Average Staff Savings 2006–2012 (%)	Chi-Squared Test, Significance
Full sample	−22	−16	−26	−1.85**
CHQs	−20	−19	−21	−0.08
RHQs	−19	−10	−27	−1.98**
DHQs	−27	−22	−31	−0.76

Notes: *, **, and *** denote significance at the 10%, 5%, and 1% levels, respectively.

Table 7.   Number and Percentage of HQs Relocations to High
Institutional Quality Locations per Type of HQs and Over Time.

	Relocation to High Institutional Quality Locations Whole Sample	Relocation to High Institutional Quality Locations 2000–2005	Relocation to High Institutional Quality Locations 2006–2012	Chi-Squared Test, Significance
Full sample	124 (55%)	46 (37%)	78 (63%)	0.10
CHQs	46 (64%)	20 (43%)	26 (57%)	2.75*
RHQs	54 (48%)	19 (32%)	35 (68%)	0.50
DHQs	24 (57%)	9 (35%)	15 (65%)	0.01

Notes: *, **, and *** denote significance at the 10%, 5%, and 1% levels, respectively.

quality (64% of the total CHQs relocations). They need to foster relations with external stakeholder (such as investors) and high institutional locations can offer these opportunities. For divisional and regional HQs, the percentage of high-quality institutional contexts is still high but, respectively, 7% and 16% points lower than for corporate HQs. This is not surprising given that especially regional HQs often have to relocate to emerging regions (e.g., Central and Eastern Europe) because of the value-creation motives (closeness to customers and growing markets) and they accept somewhat lower institutional quality in such places. The chi-squared test is significant at 10% confident level only for CHQs relocations.

Value creation could be achieved also by moving to locations closer to main markets and clients. Being closer to their center of gravity, HQs can better orchestrate their internal network creating additional value. We define centrality as the proximity to main markets. Since we focus on European relocations, we consider the centrality relative to the most important European markets. According to Wanner et al. (2004), the main markets are located in the central part of Europe. Our results show that 60% of our sample HQs relocate to central locations. Especially, divisional and regional HQs are moving to these locations (51% of the total RHQs relocations and 50% of the total DHQs ones), because they need to be closer to the demands of their products/services. To create value they have to know their main markets, customers, and competitors and make relations with them (Birkinshaw et al., 2006). Moreover, the trend is positive at each level of analysis. The Chi-squared test is statistically significant at 10% confidence level for CHQs relocations and the full sample and at 5% confidence level for DHQs relocations (Table 8).

Table 8. Number and Percentage of HQs Relocations to Central
Locations Per Type of HQs and Over Time.

	Relocation to Central Locations Whole Sample	Relocation to Central Locations 2000–2005	Relocation to Central Locations 2006–2012	Chi-Squared Test, Significance
Full sample	113 (60%)	54 (40%)	82 (60%)	2.72*
CHQs	32 (44%)	14 (44%)	18 (56%)	2.70*
RHQs	58 (51%)	16 (27%)	42 (73%)	3.89**
DHQs	21 (50%)	9 (43%)	12 (57%)	0.48

Notes: *, **, and *** denote significance at the 10%, 5%, and 1% levels, respectively.

DISCUSSION AND CONCLUSION

Recent work in International Business demonstrates a renewed interest in the movement of HQ units or parenting activities overseas (Baaij et al., 2012; Barner-Rasmussen et al., 2007; Benito et al., 2011; Birkinshaw et al., 2006; Forsgren et al., 1995; Laamanen et al., 2011; Strauss-Kahn & Vives, 2009). This work has focused especially on the antecedents of HQ relocations, which are seen as a strategic decision to minimize internal and external costs, and to create growth opportunities for the firm. While increased attention to these relocation decisions is clearly important and needed given the apparent growing trend of this phenomenon (Laamanen et al., 2011; Wanner et al., 2004), little emphasis has thus far been paid to how relocations impact on the role of HQs as the "orchestrators" of the global network organization.

In this paper, we have sought to address this gap and some of the limitations of previous studies. To this end, we conducted an explorative and descriptive analysis of HQ relocations in Europe to illustrate how these relocations relate to HQs orchestrating role. Previous work on the orchestrator role of HQs has underlined these units' ability to create additional value for the internal MNCs network. There are two ways to play this role: cutting internal and external costs or increasing the value that HQs create. In this paper, we show that these two value creation roles are related to HQ relocations, and that the motivations for HQ relocations vary between different types of HQ units and over time.

Our results contribute to the emergent research agenda on HQ relocations in a number of ways. First, the insights of this paper are relevant for our understanding of the parenting roles, activities and responsibilities of

HQ units (e.g., Chandler, 1991; Goold, Pettifer, & Young, 2001). Our findings illustrate that HQ relocations are indeed driven by both types of motives. A central challenge for MNCs is to find the optimal configuration and geographical distribution of their HQ units. Choosing the right location allows HQs to better exploit their parenting role, cut taxes or internal costs, or create additional value by being closer to main markets or customers. Nevertheless, the results illustrate the different types of HQs play their orchestrating role in different ways and they are, thus, pulled and pushed differently to alternative locations abroad.

Specifically, our results suggest that relocations of corporate HQ units tend to do little to enhance the value-creating role of these units. Instead, these units tend to move to locations where they can maximize tax and staff savings, or foster relations with important external influencers, such as stakeholders, good institutions, and shareholders. In contrast, divisional and regional HQs appear to be especially sensitive to the demands of their products and services. They tend to relocate closer to main markets and customers in order to maximize added value and foster their parenting role. Thus, while corporate HQs predominantly tend to move for reasons associated with cost minimization, divisional and regional HQs tend to relocate for reasons associated with the creation of parenting value. These results suggest the need for a more differentiated understanding of the drivers of HQ relocations that accounts for the different parenting role played by the different types of HQ units within MNCs.

Second, our results confirm that the relocation of HQ units is a growing trend. This might be symptomatic of the challenges for the "orchestrator" units within the MNC network to create additional value for their firms. These challenges may push HQ units, which have historically tended to be relatively bound to their geographic locations, to become more mobile in order to better play their parenting role. This finding is in line with the view by Wanner et al. (2004, p. 65) that "the new holy grail of management is that any function, also parenting activities, has to add to the bottom line." However, our findings go beyond previous work by demonstrating differences in the degree of mobility between different types of HQ units. Specifically, we find that corporate HQs are geographically less mobile than divisional and regional headquarter units. This may support the claim by Lamaanen et al. that "the relocation of the corporate headquarters [...] is likely to be treated with more emotional attachment than the relocation of regional headquarters" (Lamaanen et al., 2011, pp. 8–9). It might also signal that corporate HQ faces greater incentives or constraints from national governments. Another explanation is that regional and divisional HQ relocations are less costly than corporate HQ relocations, since these

Table 9. Degree of Internationalization: Average Values in Total and Over Time.

	Average Degree of Int. Whole Period (%)	Average Degree of Int. 2000–2005 (%)	Average Degree of Int. 2006–2012 (%)	Z (Mann–Whitney Test), Significance
Full sample	45	50	40	−2.53***
CHQs	42	48	38	−1.57*
RHQs	40	46	37	−1.88**
DHQs	58	65	53	−1.37*

Notes: *, **, and *** denote significance at the 10%, 5%, and 1% levels, respectively.

units usually manage a more limited number of parenting activities (Lamaanen et al., 2011).

Thus, our findings also speak to the internationalization process perspective on which previous HQ relocation papers have built on (Benito et al., 2011; Birkinshaw et al., 2006; Forsgren et al., 1995; Laamanen et al., 2011). In this view, HQ relocations are seen as the final step in the internationalization process of firms. Accordingly, especially large enterprises with a high internationalization degree are expected to engage in the decision to move HQs overseas. Given that we find an overall trend toward more mobile HQs, we were wondering if this is linked to fact that the requirement of the very high degree of internationalization is still valid.

Table 9 shows the average degree of internationalization of the firms for which we have collected relocation data.

In total, as well as across different types of HQs, we find that firms engage in HQ relocations earlier in their internationalization process. Specifically, we find a statistically significant decline in the degree of internationalization of 10 percentage points across the whole sample and with very similar results for the individual HQ types. This signals that, increasingly, less-international firms are moving their HQs to new locations where they can better orchestrate internal units and add more value. Thus, even among less internationalized firms, relocations are increasingly considered an important level to improve the parenting role of HQ units.

FUTURE RESEARCH

Our objective for this contribution was to develop a more comprehensive understanding of HQ relocations and their implications for the pivotal role of HQ units within MNCs. Our exploratory analysis highlights several recent trends and developments which support a more differentiated view on the drivers of relocation decisions. Nevertheless, this descriptive and explorative effort should be combined with empirical research along several lines. One interesting avenue would be to measure empirically the net value added of HQ relocations. This would require a strict comparison of the full operational costs related to the relocation with the benefits by the relocation of the HQ units (rather than focusing only on efficiency drivers). Longitudinal studies are needed to investigate this aspect and to understand how HQ relocations can add or destroy value. This also opens up lines of inquiry into the consequences of HQ relocations for MNCs' performance, as well as the relocation decision process itself.

A second line of inquiry lies in the determinants of HQ relocation decisions. For example, our exploratory study paid little attention to the fact that institutions may differ considerably in their effects on internationalization decisions (Hotho & Pedersen, 2012). It would therefore be worthwhile to complement assessments of the effects of institutional quality on HQ relocations with the effects of other types of societal institutions, such as those highlighted in organizational institutionalism (DiMaggio & Powell, 1991) or the national business systems approach (Hotho, 2014; Whitley, 1999). Considering other types of institutions may allow for a more detailed assessment of how the relocation of HQ units is hampered and facilitated by issues related to legitimacy and power.

Finally, we also encourage a shift in research focus from the drivers of relocation decisions to the consequences of HQ relocations for the organization of the global network. For example, more work is needed to analyze, both theoretically and empirically, how the relocation of HQ units affects the relations between HQ units and subsidiaries as well as among HQ units. Similarly, more work is needed to understand how relocations influence internal knowledge transfers and the allocation of resources and capabilities. As our findings suggest, such studies would benefit from adopting a differentiated view of HQ units and the motivations for relocation.

NOTE

1. We consider only relocations of HQs themselves, that is, any movements of subsidiaries or individual corporate functions such as R&D or purchasing are not included.

REFERENCES

Ambos, T. C., Andersson, U., & Birkinshaw, J. (2010). What are the consequences of initiative-taking in multinational subsidiaries. *Journal of International Business Studies*, *41*(7), 1099–1118.

Andersson, U., Forsgren, M., & Pedersen, T. (2001). Subsidiary performance in multinational corporations: The importance of technology embeddedness. *International Business Review*, *10*(1), 3–23.

Baaij, M. G., Mom, T. J., Van den Bosch, F. A., & Volberda, H. W. (2012). Why do multinational corporations relocate core parts of their corporate headquarters abroad? *Long Range Planning*. doi:http://dx.doi.org/10.1016/j.lrp.2012.07.001

Barner-Rasmussen, W., Piekkari, R., & Björkman, I. (2007). Mobility of headquarters in multinational corporations. *European Journal of International Management*, *1*(3), 260–274.

Bartlett, C. A., & Ghoshal, S. (1989). *Managing across borders: The transnational solution.* Cambridge, MA: Harvard Business School Press.

Benito, G., Lunnan, R., & Tomassen, S. (2011). Distant encounters of the third kind: Multinational companies locating divisional headquarters abroad. *Journal of Management Studies*, *48*(2), 373–394.

Benito, G. R., & Narula, R. (Eds.). (2007). *Multinationals on the periphery*. London: Palgrave Macmillan.

Birkinshaw, J. (1997). Entrepreneurship in multinational corporations: The characteristics of subsidiary initiatives. *Strategic Management Journal*, *18*(3), 207–229.

Birkinshaw, J., Braunerhjelm, P., Holm, U., & Terjesen, S. (2006). Why do some multinational corporations relocate their headquarters overseas? *Strategic Management Journal*, *27*(7), 681–700.

Birkinshaw, J., & Fry, N. (1998). Subsidiary initiatives to develop new markets. *Sloan Management Review*, *39*(3), 51–61.

Birkinshaw, J., & Hood, N. (1998). Multinational subsidiary evolution: Capability and charter change in foreign-owned subsidiary companies. *Academy of Management Review*, *23*(4), 773–795.

Bouquet, C., & Birkinshaw, J. (2008). Weight versus voice: How foreign subsidiaries gain attention from corporate headquarters. *Academy of Management Journal*, *51*(3), 577–601.

Chandler, A. D. (1991). The functions of the HQ unit in the multibusiness firm. *Strategic Management Journal*, *12*(S2), 31.

Ciabuschi, F., Dellestrand, H., & Holm, U. (2012). The role of headquarters in the contemporary MNC. *Journal of International Management*, *18*(3), 213–223.

Ciabuschi, F., Dellestrand, H., & Kappen, P. (2012). The good, the bad, and the ugly: Technology transfer competence, rent-seeking, and bargaining power. *Journal of World Business*, *47*(4), 664–674.

Dellestrand, H. (2010). *Orchestrating innovation in the multinational enterprise: Headquarters involvement in innovation transfer projects.* Doctoral dissertation, Uppsala University.

Dellestrand, H., & Kappen, P. (2012). The effects of spatial and contextual factors on headquarters resource allocation to MNE subsidiaries. *Journal of International Business Studies*, *43*(3), 219–243.

DiMaggio, P. J., & Powell, W. W. (Eds.). (1991). *The new institutionalism in organizational analysis* (Vol. 17). Chicago, IL: University of Chicago Press.

Fischer, A. K., & Rush, T. (2011). Staffing after mergers and acquisitions: A human resource management case study. *Journal of Business Case Studies (JBCS)*, *4*(12), 29–36.

Forsgren, M., Holm, U., & Johanson, J. (1995). Division headquarters go abroad: A step in the internationalization of the multinational corporation. *Journal of Management Studies*, *32*(4), 475–491.

Foss, K., Foss, N. J., & Nell, P. C. (2012). MNC organizational form and subsidiary motivation problems: Controlling intervention hazards in the network MNC. *Journal of International Management*, *18*(3), 247–259.

Foss, N. J., & Pedersen, T. (2002). Transferring knowledge in MNCs: The role of sources of subsidiary knowledge and organizational context. *Journal of International Management*, *8*(1), 49–67.

Ghosh, C., Rodriguez, M., & Sirmans, C. F. (1995). Gains from corporate headquarters relocations: Evidence from the stock market. *Journal of Urban Economics*, *38*(3), 291–311.

Ghoshal, S., & Bartlett, C. A. (1988). Creation, adoption, and diffusion of innovations by subsidiaries of multinational corporations. *Journal of International Business Studies*, *19*(3), 365–388.

Ghoshal, S., Moran, P., & Almeida-Costa, L. (1995). The essence of the megacorporation: Shared context, not structural hierarchy. *Zeitschrift für die gesamte Staatswissenschaft [Journal of Institutional and Theoretical Economics (JITE)]*, *151*(4), 748–759.

Goold, M., & Campbell, A. (2002). Parenting in complex structures. *Long Range Planning*, *35*(3), 219–243.

Goold, M., Pettifer, D. & Young, D. (2001). Redesigning the corporate centre. *European Management Journal*, *19*(1), 83–91.

Heenan, D. A. (1989). The downside of downsizing. *Journal of Business Strategy*, *10*(6), 18–23.

Hoenen, A., Nell, P. C., & Ambos, B. (forthcoming). Entrepreneurial capabilities at the regional level — The role of intra-regional similarity and regional embeddedness. *Long Range Planning*.

Holcomb, T. R., Holmes, R. M., & Connelly, B. L. (2009). Making the most of what you have: Managerial ability as a source of value creation. *Strategic Management Journal*, *30*(5), 457–485.

Hotho, J. J. (2014). From typology to taxonomy: A configurational analysis of national business systems and their explanatory power. *Organization Studies*. doi:http://10.1177/0170840613502767

Hotho, J. J., & Pedersen, T. (2012). Beyond the 'rules of the game': Three institutional approaches and how they matter for international business. In G. Wood & M. Demirbag (Eds.), *Handbook of institutional approaches to international business* (pp. 236–273). Cheltenham: Edward Elgar.

Kaufmann, D., & Kraay, A. (2003). Governance and growth: Causality which way? — Evidence for the world, in brief. Washington, DC: World Bank Publication.

Kaufmann, D., Kraay, A., & Mastruzzi, M. (2009). *Governance matters VIII: Aggregate and individual governance indicators, 1996–2008*. Washington, DC: World Bank Policy Research Working Paper 4978.

Laamanen, T., Simula, T., & Torstila, S. (2011). Cross-border relocations of headquarters in Europe. *Journal of International Business Studies*, *43*(2), 187–210.

Larsen, M. M., Manning, S., & Pedersen, T. (2012). Uncovering the hidden costs of offshoring: The interplay of complexity, organizational design, and experience. *Strategic Management Journal, 34*(5), 533–552.

Nell, P. C., & Ambos, B. (2013). Parenting advantage in the MNC: An embeddedness perspective on the value added by headquarters. *Strategic Management Journal, 34*(9), 1086–1103.

Nell, P. C., Ambos, B., & Schlegelmilch, B. B. (2011). The benefits of hierarchy? – Exploring the effects of regional headquarters in multinational corporations. In C. G. Asmussen, T. Pedersen, T. M. Devinney, & L. Tihanyi (Eds.), *Dynamics of globalization: Location-specific advantages or liabilities of foreignness?* (Vol. 24, pp. 85–106). Advances in International Management. Bingley, UK: Emerald Group Publishing Limited.

Nohria, N., & Ghoshal, S. (1994). Differentiated fit and shared values: Alternatives for managing headquarters-subsidiary relations. *Strategic Management Journal, 15*(6), 491–502.

O'Donnell, S. W. (2000). Managing foreign subsidiaries: Agents of headquarters, or an interdependent network? *Strategic Management Journal, 21*(5), 525–548.

Parmigiani, A., & Holloway, S. S. (2011). Actions speak louder than modes: Antecedents and implications of parent implementation capabilities on business unit performance. *Strategic Management Journal, 32*(5), 457–485.

Rugman, A. M., & Verbeke, A. (2003). Extending the theory of the multinational enterprise: Internalization and strategic management perspectives. *Journal of International Business Studies, 34*(2), 125–137.

Schotter, A., & Beamish, P. W. (2011). Performance effects of MNC headquarters–subsidiary conflict and the role of boundary spanners: The case of headquarter initiative rejection. *Journal of International Management, 17*(3), 243–259.

Strauss-Kahn, V., & Vives, X. (2009). Why and where do headquarters move? *Regional Science and Urban Economics, 39*(2), 168–186.

Voget, J. (2011). Relocation of headquarters and international taxation. *Journal of Public Economics, 95*(9), 1067–1081.

Wanner, H., Leclef, X., & Shimizu, H. (2004). Global headquarters on the move: From administrators to facilitators. Arthur D. Little Corporation Report.

Whitley, R. (1999). *Divergent capitalisms: The social structuring and change of business systems.* Oxford: Oxford University Press.

STRATEGIC ARCHETYPES OF EMERGING MARKET MULTINATIONALS: ANALYSIS OF OUTWARD FDI OF INDIAN FIRMS

Amit Karna, Rajesh Upadhyayula and Vikas Kumar

ABSTRACT

Emerging Market Multinationals (EMNCs) are often seen as firms with singular identity. While they may share certain characteristics, EMNCs are seldom orchestrated and managed in the same manner. Through a cluster analysis of outward foreign direct investment data of EMNCs from India, we propose taxonomy of EMNCs based on their mode of operation, industry in which they operate, region where they invest and the amount invested. We use a dataset spread over 2007–2013, constituting investment data of 4,824 Indian firms into 7,238 foreign entities. Based on a two-step clustering approach, we propose three strategic archetypes of EMNCs: Global Service Providers, Integrated Manufacturers, *and* Established Internationalizers. *The Global Service Providers mainly consists of firms operating in developed markets with an intention to serve their client needs through wholly owned subsidiaries. Integrated Manufacturers are firms that are primarily operating in other developing*

Orchestration of the Global Network Organization
Advances in International Management, Volume 27, 325–347
ISSN: 1571-5027/doi:10.1108/S1571-502720140000027030

markets to sell their products through joint ventures and also present in developed markets through wholly owned subsidiaries — to acquire technology and other resources. The Established Internationalizers are large EMNCs with highest levels of investments, and relatively similar to the Western multinationals. We analyze the characteristics of these three groups of EMNCs based on their strategy and investment behavior, to derive insights into the heterogeneity across EMNCs. We discuss our findings and lay out future directions for research in the area.

Keywords: Emerging Market Multinationals; outward FDI; cluster analysis; India

INTRODUCTION

Emerging Market Multinationals (EMNCs) — a term used to describe internationalizing firms from emerging economies — are fast gaining significance in the academic literature (Cuervo-Cazurra, 2012; Gammeltoft, 2008; Gammeltoft, Barnard, & Madhok, 2010; Kumar, Mudambi, & Gray, 2013; Luo & Tung, 2007; Ramamurti & Singh, 2009a). Although it is well accepted that these EMNCs differ from traditional multinationals (MNCs) from the developed markets (Guillén & García-Canal, 2009) in terms of their internationalization paths and processes, there is need to further investigate how they operate in international markets. EMNCs have several characteristics in common, however, they are rife with inherent heterogeneity (Ramamurti, 2013) arising out of the varied institutional and cultural landscape of emerging economies (Hoskisson, Wright, Filatotchev, & Peng, 2013). Although classifications of EMNCs exist (Luo & Tung, 2007; Ramamurti & Singh, 2009b), given their continuous transformation as a result of rapid internationalization, there is need to empirically segregate them into distinct categories based on the outcomes of their strategic choices. We do so through a cluster analysis of outward foreign direct investment (OFDI) of Indian EMNCs.

Many EMNCs invest overseas in order to augment their resource base rather than to exploit a proprietary asset (Luo & Tung, 2007), in contrast to the vast majority of MNCs from the developed markets. However, the internationalization of EMNCs is often motivated by multiple factors such as overcoming scale disadvantage in the home market (i.e., acquiring globally competitive scale), to accessing raw materials or knowledge, or to overcome export barriers (Deng, 2007; Gaur & Kumar, 2010). While the motivations can be several, they often manifest in the way the investments eventually occur – in form of joint ventures (JV) or wholly owned subsidiaries (WOS). Based on the industry and region the EMNC chooses to invest over a period of time, the mode of operation and the amount of investment, one can classify these EMNCs into different categories.

EMNCs are a heterogeneous group exhibiting a variety of internationalization strategies (Ramamurti, 2012), primarily being shaped by home country characteristics (Luo & Wang, 2012). They are distinct in terms of their internationalization speed (accelerated instead of incremental) and motive (asset-augmentation instead of asset-exploitation) when compared to traditional MNCs from the West (Luo & Tung, 2007; Makino, Lau, & Yeh, 2002). Many of them have internationalized from positions of weakness rather than on the basis of strong ownership advantages, and have done so through consistently leveraging their global linkages (Gaur & Kumar, 2009; Mathews, 2006). While there is ongoing debate on EMNCs not following the traditional internationalization theories, there is clearly a growing acceptance of potential to enrich these theories (Cuervo-Cazurra, 2012). However, in order to theorize appropriately around the EMNC internationalization, there is also a need to differentiate within the group of EMNCs.

In this paper, we propose strategic archetypes of EMNCs based on a cluster analysis of 4,824 Indian EMNCs OFDI behavior. Our archetypes further build on the classification by Ramamurti and Singh (2009b) in three ways. First, while the earlier classifications have been based on the choices that the EMNCs can make, our taxonomy is based on archival data and therefore takes into account the outcome of the strategic and organizational choices these EMNCs have made. Second, we use the most recent data on OFDI of EMNCs, that is, for the period 2007–2013, which takes into account the most recent developments within the emerging economies and EMNCs. In a way, our analysis is a natural sequel and to the earlier proposed typologies. Third, our description of strategic archetypes builds on the generic international strategies of EMNCs proposed by Ramamurti and Singh (2009b) on two specific dimensions of target markets and mode of operation. Finally, by looking at a large number of firms using a rigorous analysis, we believe our classification is robust enough to make theoretical inferences that can be extended to a larger set of EMNCs.

EMNC CLASSIFICATION

Based on an extensive review of EMNC literature, Gaur and Kumar (2010), call for investigating the differences within EMNCs from different emerging economies, and during different time periods. The main argument for such a difference has been attributed to the motivations, paths and processes adopted by these EMNCs during their history of existence. The ownership advantages possessed by the EMNCs to overcome the liability of foreignness can be firm-specific or, in some cases, also country-specific (Gaur, Kumar, & Sarathy, 2011). Based on this argument, they also call for newer theoretical approaches to study this EMNC phenomenon in greater detail. Our review did not find any study that classifies EMNCs into distinct categories that present an empirical taxonomy of EMNCs. While the literature is replete with theoretically derived typologies, we could not find a classification of EMNCs, which is based on empirical observations of EMNCs from real life.

EMNCs have mostly been looked at in the literature from the resource-based (possessing little or no distinctive resources) as well as institutional perspectives. However, we find a lack of literature that classifies EMNCs into categories based on their investment behavior. Ramamurti and Singh (2009b) suggest, in their classification of EMNC international strategies, five clusters in which emerging multinationals can be grouped: local optimizers, low-cost partners, global consolidators, natural resource vertical integrators, and global first movers. They discuss the theoretical foundation of these generic internationalization strategies to describe how EMNCs can achieve competitive advantage using each of these. In his classification, Ramamurti and Singh (2009b) also compare the likely mode of entry, target markets and industry conditions under which these EMNCs operate.

Another classification of EMNCs was proposed by Luo and Tung (2007), based on a springboard perspective to divide firms based on their ownership structure (state-owned and non-state-owned) and their international expansion strategy (broad and narrow). Their typology focuses primarily on the motivations and strategies to overcome risk while expanding internationally to acquire strategic resources.

While both Ramamurti and Singh's (2009b) and Luo and Tung's (2007) classifications present overarching frameworks to analyze uniqueness of EMNCs and their path to international expansion, they do not explicitly group firms based on the internationalization behavior across the multiple dimensions. The focus in the literature so far, has largely been on the dimensions of industry conditions, target markets, ownership (and therefore risk-taking) structure of the firms. Much of this literature not only posits common country-specific advantages (CSA) these EMNCs have access to, but also similar firm-specific advantages that helps them leverage the CSAs. While these classifications have shed light on differences within EMNCs, we see a need to introduce more strategic and organizational dimensions into dividing the group of firms.

Originating from weaker institutional environments, investigating EMNCs' internationalization steps and mode of operation are likely to add to our understanding of international business theories. In a recent review, Xu and Meyer (2013) find that much of the literature has focused on institutional distance where EMNCs have to overcome the differences they face in host-countries. However, the review concludes there is limited literature (e.g., Gubbi, Aulakh, Ray, Sarkar, & Chittoor, 2010; Lu, Zhou, Bruton, & Li, 2010) focusing on firm-level decisions and in particular from a resource-based perspective to explain the internationalization of EMNCs and their motives. Ramamurti and Singh (2009b) argue that some EMNCs do possess unique resources which can be exploited in foreign markets, however, these resources do not fall in the typical categories of R&D, marketing or advertising. EMNCs resources are more closely linked with their institutional context and hence hard to identify (Dunning & Lundan, 2010). For example, the ability of the firm to negotiate uncertainty and work in sub-optimal conditions is strongly present in many EMNCs (Cuervo-Cazurra & Genc, 2008), which they do exploit while operating in other similar emerging or developing market. In this paper, we introduce mode of operation and investment size as additional dimensions to industry and target markets to analyze the investment behavior of a set of EMNCs.

CLUSTER ANALYSIS OF INDIAN EMNCS

Through a cluster analysis of the OFDI transactions of Indian firms over the period 2007—2013, we attempt to classify the Indian EMNCs to suggest that there are distinct categories among these EMNCs. The comprehensive dataset, of the OFDI investments by Indian firms, is compiled of the actual data filed with the regulator by every Indian EMNCs that carries out an overseas transaction. We seek to contribute to the literature on EMNCs by proposing a classification of EMNCs based on multiple dimensions. Broadly speaking, we find three categories of EMNCs that are characterized by the type of industry in which they operate, the region in which they invest, the mode with which they operate, and the amount they have invested within their foreign operations.

Through our empirical investigation of the OFDI of Indian EMNCs, we derive several insights. First, we find that there is an overwhelming tendency of Indian firms to invest in form of WOS route rather than JVs. We also find that the three sectors that make up for more than three-fourth of the overseas investments are (a) manufacturing, (b) wholesale and consumer services, and (c) finance, insurance and business services. Secondly, we find three categories of Indian EMNCs, based on their overseas investment behavior and classify them as: *Global Service Providers, Integrated Manufacturers*, and *Established Internationalizers*. These three categories serve as archetypes of EMNCs and the strategies they follow. They also correspond directly to the three (out of the four) generic strategies provided by Ramamurti and Singh (2009b), and to two EMNC typologies prescribed by Luo and Tung (2007).

The Global Service Providers or service multinationals consists of firms primarily operating in developed markets with an intention to serve their client needs through WOS. Most of these service multinationals markets have the necessary skills, process and project management techniques. They do serve as the low-cost partner for their clients in developed markets. An interesting aspect is that these global service providers do not operate simultaneously across emerging and developed markets. Integrated Manufacturers or manufacturing multinationals are firms that are primarily operating in emerging markets as well as developed markets. Although a majority of these firms are operating on a WOS basis, the mode of operation also favors JVs in comparison to service multinationals. Further, the integrated manufacturers also do not operate simultaneously across emerging and developed markets. Established Internationalizers are firms that have high levels of investment into both developed and emerging markets. On an average, they undertake significantly higher investments and their mode of operation can be either JV or WOS. These firms are the most similar among the EMNCs to the Western multinationals.

Research Methodology

In order to distinguish between strategies adopted by EMNCs, it is appropriate to use a classification system (Enright & Subramanian, 2007). Studies have suggested that a numerical technique such as cluster analysis would either aid in corroborating the internationalization strategy typology defined ex-ante or help in classifying the internationalization strategies on the basis of data (Enright & Subramanian, 2007). Bailey (1994) has argued that the classification system should be derived from the theoretical constructs (ex-ante). Apart from Ramamurti and Singh (2009b), there is hardly any study which develops a theoretically developed typology on internationalization strategies of EMNCs. Ramamurti and Singh (2009b) have highlighted that national roots of competitive advantage (CSA), international competitive advantage (FSA), industry conditions, target markets, mode of international expansion as factors affecting strategies of emerging market multinationals. However, a taxonomy of EMNC firms has so far not been empirically derived using a rigorous mechanism or analysis of a large dataset of EMNCs. Empirically derived classification schemes are suggested for disciplines that require classification (Lorr, 1983; Mezzich & Solomon, 1980; Smith, 2002). Accordingly, this study adopts an empirically derived classification. This sort of classification system would help in the development of the basis for a theoretically developed classification system, like Bailey, Carron, Teece, and Wehner (1970) or aid in refining the theoretically defined classification system.

Outward FDI Data

Much of the EMNC literature either looks at export data at the firm level (e.g., Chittoor, Ray, Aulakh, & Sarkar, 2008; Gubbi et al., 2010) or at case-studies of individuals or a group of firms (e.g., Cuervo-Cazurra, 2008; Sim & Pandian, 2003) for explaining the internationalization strategies of EMNCs. There has been sparse but increasing literature on overseas investments in general (e.g., Witt & Lewin, 2007) and overseas investments by EMNCs in particular (e.g., Gammeltoft, 2008; Gammeltoft, Pradhan, & Goldstein, 2010). However, much of the literature focuses on the country-level determinants and outcomes of outward FDI to draw reasoning for evaluating the behavior of population of firms. Much of the literature has also been devoid of any firm-specific insights due to lack of data on variables that have relevance at the firm level. With respect to EMNC internationalization, a firm-level analysis of FDI has also been missing for a similar set of reasons. However, as EMNCs expand, and data becomes more widely available, there will be more insights to draw from FDI by EMNCs. In this paper, we use the data recently published by the Reserve Bank of India (India's central bank) on every FDI move made at a firm level, in order to draw inferences on how EMNCs choose their mode of operation in foreign markets, and learn from the differences across different sectors, geographies and firms.

Our dataset includes all the OFDI investments made by Indian firms over the period July 2007 to August 2013. The data is sourced from the Reserve Bank of India who in turn has compiled it on the basis of OFDI by Indian companies as reported by Authorized dealers in Form OFDI. The dataset captures an overall overseas investment of approximately USD 164 billion made by 4,824 Indian firms from July 2007 to August 2013. The dataset has investments made by Indian firms into 7,238 foreign entities.

Variables

To examine the EMNC internationalization strategy, the data was further transformed. The dataset compiled by RBI captures the name of the firm, name of the JV or WOS, the country in which the investment is made, the industry to which the firm belongs, financial commitment in USD million, whether debt, equity or guarantee issued, year and month of investment. Although the data is provided on a monthly basis by RBI, we aggregate the data at a firm level for examining the internationalization strategy choices of EMNCs.

a. *Country*: Every firm in our dataset was classified as making investments into emerging markets, developed markets or both. Countries in which the investment was made by the firm were classified as emerging or developed as per the IMF Classification.[1]

b. *Industry activity*: RBI has classified the major activities into Agriculture, Fishing, Forestry, and Mining; Community, Social, and Personal Services; Construction; Electricity, Gas, and Water; Finance, Insurance, and Business Services; Manufacturing; Transport, Storage, and Communication Services; Wholesale, Retail Trade, Restaurants and Hotels; Miscellaneous. We have classified these major activities into five distinct categories (Agriculture, Mining, and Forestry; Financial, Insurance, and Business Services; Manufacturing; Utilities and Transportation; Wholesale and Consumer Services) and the remaining firms are classified as Miscellaneous.

c. *Number of JV*: From the dataset, every firm can make more than one investment into a foreign subsidiary. Each of these subsidiaries can be operated either as a WOS or a JV. We computed the number of JVs that each firm has invested into.

d. *Number of WOS*: As in the previous measure, we computed the number of WOS that each firm has invested into.
e. *Amount invested*: We have computed the *amount invested* by every firm in US Dollars.

Analytical Approach

Using an exploratory cluster analysis, we classified the Indian EMNCs on the *Country, Industrial activity, Number of JV, Number of WOS,* and *Amount Invested* between 2007 and 2013. While the first two variables were categorical, the latter three were continuous variables. Since there are both categorical and continuous variables in our dataset, we carry out a two-step clustering approach. Among the three clustering procedures: two-step, k-means, and hierarchical, this is the only approach that enables the mixing of both categorical and continuous variables while adopting a numerical based classification technique (Noruésis, 2011). One can allow the two-step algorithm to determine the number of clusters or you can specify the number of clusters. In order to not impose a criteria, we allowed the algorithm to determine the number of clusters that emerge naturally from the data. In this approach, during the first step, cases are assigned into pre-clusters and these pre-clusters are treated as single cases in the second step. During the second step, the hierarchical algorithm is used to further cluster the pre-clusters. In the approach where the algorithm determines the number of clusters, they are determined on the basis of the lowest information criterion measure and the highest ratio of distance measures.

OFDI Analysis of Indian EMNCs

Out of a total of 7,238 foreign entity level investments, 30% (2,156) of the investments were made through the JV route whereas 70% (5,082) of the investments were made through the WOS route. The data shows that a single firm made a maximum investment of USD 19.5 billion (BhartiAirtel) with a standard deviation of USD 380 million. The investments by Indian firms during 2007–2013 were made across 145 countries across different regions, namely Africa, Americas, Asia, Oceania, and Europe. Moreover, a single firm has made investments into a single foreign entity (and country) to as many as 31 different foreign entities; however, the median is one foreign entity. The highest number of transactions goes up to 31 foreign

Table 1.   Distribution of Firms across Three Distinct Clusters of EMNCs.

Clusters	No. of Firms	% of Total	No. of Subsidiaries	% of Subsidiaries
Global Service Providers	2,370	49	2,801	39
Integrated Manufacturers	1,847	38	2,215	31
Established Internationalizers	607	13	2,222	31
Total	4,824	100	7,238	100

entities in as many countries (by the state-owned oil firm ONGC). Furthermore, we also find two firms (On Mobile Global and Videocon Industries) to have invested regularly every year up to USD 1.5 billion in 47 transactions outside India every year, and eight firms (Cox and Kings, GMR Energy, Godrej Consumer Products, Infosys Technologies, Intelenet Global Services, Metro Wireless Engineering, Shapoorji & Pallonji, and Tata Consultancy Services) to have invested six out of the seven years under study. Their total investment of USD 4 billion was done through 80 transactions.

From our analysis, we found the ratio of distance measures to be the highest for three clusters (see Appendix). Therefore, we explain the strategies of the three distinct groups. Table 1 provides a distribution of firm membership across the three distinct clusters. We summarize the factors affecting the three distinct clusters of EMNCs below.

STRATEGIC ARCHETYPES OF EMNCS

Based on the cluster analysis of Indian EMNC firms over the last seven years, we empirically derive three archetypes of EMNCs based on multiple dimensions. So far, the literature (e.g., Luo & Tung, 2007; Ramamurti & Singh, 2009b) has provided generic strategies based on target markets, activity, and strategic intent of the firm. While these generic strategies provide clarity on the ways EMNC firms could achieve competitive advantage, it leaves open the question of whether there are differences across the EMNC group in terms of which strategies they have selected in the recent years. In other words, while the literature has outlined a theoretical classification of what EMNCs can do, we contribute to this literature by proposing three archetypes that empirically differentiate EMNCs from each other.

Global Service Providers

Our first type of EMNC we find is a global service provider – either in consumer, wholesale, or financial services. Table 2 provides the distribution of firms across defined industrial activities.

Among the three groups, this group has the highest number of firms, that is, 2,370 firms (nearly 50% of our sample). However, the average amount of investment made by these firms is only USD 9 million with a standard deviation of USD 59 million (Table 3). An interesting attribute of this group of firms is that they are primarily in the service business (87.5% of firms from Financial, Insurance, and Business services as well as 90% of firms from wholesale and consumer services). Fig. 1 shows the distribution of firms across emerging and developed markets. 66% of firms are in developed markets in comparison to 34% in emerging markets. Interestingly, none of the firms operates in both developing and developed economies.

While 69% of firms operate 2,017 subsidiaries through WOS mode alone, 27% of firms operate 756 JVs and 4% seek to operate their foreign entities using both the modes of operation. The strategy of these global service providers has been similar to Ramamurti and Singh's (2009b) typological framework of low-cost partner. Most of these firms have national roots competitive advantage, such as factor cost advantage, process excellence and project management skills. They have abundant skills and factor costs are low. The primary markets for such firms are developed countries and the reasons for their internationalization are primarily based on serving their clients from other low-cost locations or moving into high cost locations to build their own capabilities. Most of these firms have invested abroad to seek markets or acquire a global foot print to provide services to their clients globally. Accordingly, the mode of operations is primarily through WOS (Figs. 2 and 3).

Integrated Manufacturers

We propose a second type of EMNC that is an integrated manufacturer. 38.3% of Indian EMNCs (or 1,847 firms) fall under this category. The average amount of investment made by these firms is USD 14.87 million (much higher than that for the global service provider) with a standard deviation of USD 71.5 million. An interesting attribute of this group of firms is that they are primarily in manufacturing or utilities as an industry (85.2% of all manufacturing firms and 86.7% of all utilities that are in

Table 2. Distribution of Firms across Industries.

Clusters	Agriculture, Mining, and Forestry	Financial, Insurance, and Business Services	Manufacturing	Miscellaneous	Utilities and Transportation	Wholesale and Consumer Services	Total
Global Service Providers	0	1,339	0	0	0	1,031	2,370
	0%	87%	0%	0%	0%	91%	49%
Integrated Manufacturers	249	0	1,084	51	463	0	1,847
	87%	0%	85%	81%	87%	0%	38%
Established Internationalizers	36	192	189	12	71	107	607
	13%	13%	15%	19%	13%	9%	13%
Total	285	1,531	1,273	63	534	1,138	4,824

Table 3. Average Investment and Average Number of Subsidiaries.

Clusters	Investment (in USD Million)		No. of WOS		No. of JV	
	Mean	σ	Mean	σ	Mean	σ
Global Service Providers	9.54	59.54	0.85	0.667	0.33	0.528
Integrated Manufacturers	14	71.50	0.77	0.663	0.43	0.587
Established Internationalizers	187.5	1032.61	2.72	2.237	0.94	1.27
Total	34.03	375.59	1.05	1.19	0.45	0.714

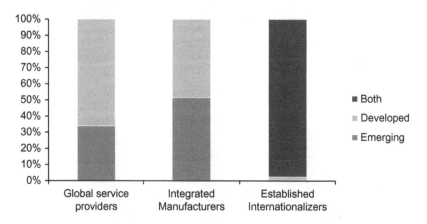

Fig. 1. Distribution of Firms across Target Markets.

our sample). Moreover, 52% of firms operate in emerging economy whereas 48% operate in developed economies. Interestingly, as with global service providers, none of these firms too operate in both developing and developed economies. 60% of firms operate on a WOS basis, whereas 34% of firms on a JV mode in this category. The number of firms operating on a JV mode is higher in comparison to the first strategic group. Out of a total 2,215 subsidiaries, 36% of subsidiaries are operated on a JV mode, whereas 64% of them are operated on a WOS mode. This EMNC usually masters the art of producing a successful product in its home country, with which it can then expand into other emerging economies to sell their product. With its ability to cater to low-end customers and

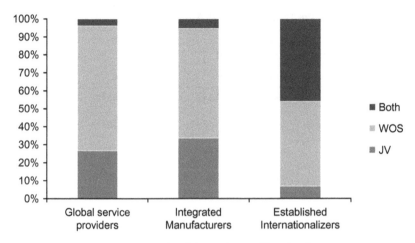

Fig. 2. Mode of Operation at Firm level.

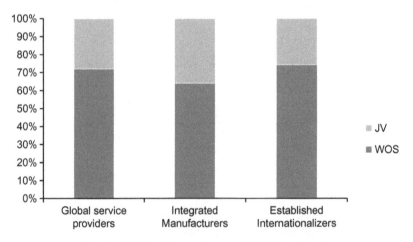

Fig. 3. Mode of Operation at a Subsidiary Level.

operate in underdeveloped soft and hard infrastructures, it usually relies on low-cost production to achieve competitive advantage. This type of EMNC often follows the generic strategy of local optimizer (Ramamurti & Singh, 2009b). These EMNCs opt for either JV or WOS as the mode of operation depending on the institutional environment of the host country (target market). While 38% of these EMNCs from emerging markets opt for JVs, only 29% of the firms in developed markets opt for JV mode.

Established Internationalizers

The third type of EMNC we propose contains established internationalizers. A small but significant proportion of firms in our sample were found to be established multinationals much like their Western counterparts. 12.6% of the Indian EMNCs (607 firms) follow this strategy. They can be represented as the most mature of the EMNCs because of the size of their investments. The average investment is USD 187 million (significantly higher than that for the earlier two strategic groups) with a standard deviation of USD 1,032 million. Around 10% of firms from across various industries form a part of this segment. They are spread across a number of emerging and developed economies worldwide. This type of EMNC did not have a dominant industry or target market and were typically large and established firms. This type of EMNCs also contained oil and gas explorer including the state-owned ones. While 46% of firms choose both JV and WOS as mode of operation, 47% choose only WOS and 7% of firms chose only JV as a mode of operation. 74% of the total subsidiaries (2,222 subsidiaries) are operated on a WOS mode, whereas 26% are operated on a JV mode. This archetype of EMNC follows, what Ramamurti and Singh (2009b) calls generic strategies of Global consolidator and Natural resource vertical integrator. Established Internationalizers are often found in mature industries, and are present in developed as well as other emerging economies, based on where they find natural resources and the best place to process them. This corroborates with broad diversification strategy proposed in the literature (Luo & Tung, 2007).

Internationalization Behavior of Indian EMNCs

Apart from the three clusters, our analysis also outlines a few more interesting insights into how EMNCs operate internationally. First, we find that the Indian EMNCs, at least a good majority, are choosing WOS as the mode of operation in their international operations. This trend also supports the argument that the majority of EMNCs invest in developed economies to acquire resources and therefore prefer larger control over their foreign operations. In contrast, the Indian EMNCs investing in developing countries also prefer WOS. This can be attributed to the relatively similar institutional environment and ease of acquiring targets in lesser-developed countries.

Second, we find a clear distinction between service providers and integrated manufacturers on one hand, and established EMNCs on the other.

The established EMNCs have a significantly larger size of investments in foreign operations and they cut across different industries in which they operate. The established EMNCs have been actively investing in foreign operations as we find them to be exhibiting repeated investment behaviors of large magnitude. These firms are also similar to the developed country MNCs and follow similar internationalization approaches. This suggests that EMNCs over time may converge with the internationalization patterns of the Western multinationals, and that the differences that are currently debated (Narula, 2012; Ramamurti, 2012) are temporary and an artifact of the different time periods and stages of internationalization.

DISCUSSION

Our categorization of EMNCs, we believe, is a significant step in advancing the field investigating EMNCs in general. Based on their larger scale and scope of operations, we argue that established EMNCs pose a larger competitive threat in sectors that have historically been dominated by traditional MNCs (namely manufacturing, utilities and transportation). The EMNCs, particularly from India, were thought to be coming from the services domain – earlier due to availability of low-cost and abundant human resources, and later due to a rise in expertise of the software development and project management capabilities (see Luo, Wang, Zheng, & Jayaraman, 2012; Peng, Wang, & Jiang, 2008). However, as our classification as well as those in the past proved, there are different types of firms that internationalize into different markets. By proposing strategic archetypes of EMNCs, we not only provide a more fine-grained understanding of EMNCs, but also a more qualitative view of strategies that the service and manufacturing EMNCs follow in order to establish themselves in the later stages of their lifecycle.

Our archetypes of EMNCs build on the categorization of generic internationalization strategies of EMNCs by Ramamurti and Singh (2009b). As shown in Table 4, our three archetypes correspond one-to-one with the various dimensions proposed by Ramamurti and Singh (2009b) viz. FSA, CSA, industry conditions, and value-chain scope. However, our analysis adds to the target markets and industries in which these firms following specific generic strategies are, and the mode of operation they adopt. We find additional insights that help us theorize about the internationalization behaviors of EMNCs. First, that global service providers (that mostly

Table 4. Classification of EMNCs.

Dimension	Cluster		
	Global Service Providers	Integrated Manufacturers	Established Internationalizers
Generic International Strategy (Ramamurti and Singh, 2009b)	Low-cost partner	Local optimizer	Global consolidator
International competitive advantage (FSA)	• Factor cost arbitrage • Process excellence • Project management	• Products and processes optimized for emerging markets	• Operational excellence • Restructuring/turnaround capabilities
National roots of competitive advantage (CSAs)	• Technological absorptive capacity, developed in prior decades (during import-substituting industrialization) • Cheap brainpower • Entrepreneurial tradition • Low wages • Skill supply	• Low-income consumers • Underdeveloped hard and soft infrastructures • Low-cost production	• Large, high-growth home market in "mature industry" • Access to capital • Barriers to acquisition of local firms by foreign
Value-chain scope	• Narrow and specialized	• Functionally integrated	• Functionally integrated • International horizontal and vertical integration
Industry conditions	• Mostly mature industries, but possible also in emerging industries	• Mature industries • Products not standardized across income, culture, etc.	• Mature industries • Relatively standard products and processes across income, cultures, etc.

Table 4. (*Continued*)

Dimension	Cluster		
	Global Service Providers	Integrated Manufacturers	Established Internationalizers
Industries	• Financial and Business Services (56%) • Wholesale and Consumer Services (44%)	• Manufacturing (59%) • Utilities and Transportation (25%) • Agriculture, Mining, and Forestry (13%)	• Financial and Business Services (32%) • Manufacturing (31%) • Wholesale and Consumer Services (18%) • Utilities and Transportation (12%) • Agriculture, Mining, and Forestry (6%)
Target foreign markets	• Developed Countries for markets (66%) • Emerging Markets for sourcing resources (34%)	• Emerging Markets for market access (52%) • Developed Countries for resource/technology acquisition (48%)	• Both Developed and Emerging countries (98%)
Modes of international expansion	• WOS (69%)	• JV in Emerging Markets • WOS in Developed countries	• WOS in Emerging Markets (47%) • JV in Both Developed and Emerging countries (46%)

Note: Adapted based on generic internationalization strategies dimensions by Ramamurti and Singh (2009b). The shaded cells are based on our analysis.

follow low-cost partner internationalization strategy) have internationalized to developed markets, rather than emerging markets. This leads us to believe that the low wage benefit as a CSA supports the firm's internationalization in other markets regardless of the ability of the firm to source low-cost resources from other emerging markets. Second, integrated manufacturers (that mostly follow local optimization strategy) have internationalized to emerging as well as developed economies. However, their mode of operations is different in the two markets. While the dominant mode of operation in emerging markets is JV, they expand to developed countries using WOS route. This finding regarding emerging market expansion corroborates with Ramamurti and Singh (2009b) who posit that EMNC's optimized products and processes will find markets in other similar markets; whereas the finding regarding developed countries confirms the argument that EMNCs often go to developed countries to acquire resources and technology. However, it is worth noting here that most firms that go to either type of the target country do not target the other type.

The third archetype of established internationalizers throws up the most interesting finding of our study. This cluster contains firms that are very similar to Western multinationals in size as well as conduct of their international operations. This cluster of firms not only spans different industries, but also tends to internationalize to a wide variety of markets. Almost all the firms (98%) within this cluster have internationalized to developed as well as emerging markets. We believe these firms are truly global consolidators that take advantage of all country advantages that they possess. This archetype is also in contrast with Ramamurti and Singh (2009b) because it contains firms such as Mahindra and Infosys to be following local optimizer and low-cost partner, respectively, in their illustration of generic strategies. In our analysis, these two firms – and other similar ones – fall under the archetype of established internationalizers (global consolidators), because since 2007 these firms have been internationalizing to achieve global scale and therefore have grown out of being just a low-cost partner or a local optimizer.

Based on these findings, we believe that the lifecycle development stages of EMNCs enable them to start off with either of the two fundamental generic strategies – low-cost partner or local optimizer – eventually making them all global consolidators. What remains to be seen is whether the development of the firm from either of the two fundamental generic strategies into global consolidator is due to firm's internal activities, or if it is caused by external factors.

CONCLUSION

Our categorization of EMNCs hints on reducing the broad theoretical focus on EMNCs and make it more focused to differentiate between those EMNCs. The conceptual literature and empirical evidence indicate that EMNCs are continuing to pursue different strategies to internationalize depending on their individual competitive advantages and combination of the country advantages they can leverage. Our analysis is based on a large dataset comprising of comprehensive actions by EMNCs as compared to existing literature, which looks at a small section of firms and their internationalization motives. With a descriptive and aggregate analysis of the trends of OFDI by Indian firms, we empirically categorize the Indian EMNCs.

Our study is limited by way of context as it only contains transactions by EMNCs from one country and for a fixed period of time. It remains to be seen how these firms performed in this period and beyond. Moreover, there is a need to employ more qualitative research on the actions of EMNCs to theoretically advance the phenomenon, the investment data indicating the actions by the firms presents an opportunity to differentiate between the different types of EMNCs, and analyze the trends from several different perspectives.

Future research in the area will benefit from more in-depth studies on the internationalization of EMNCs, as also on how firms chose a particular mode of operation and the method in which organizational learning accumulates in such a firm. The transition from being a low-cost partner or a local optimizer into being a global consolidator also represents an interesting research theme. Evaluating the performance of the archetypes of EMNCs and how it is affected by the strategy for internationalization also represents a useful theme for future research.

NOTE

1. International Monetary Fund (2012), "World Economic Outlook: Growth Resuming, Dangers Remain."

REFERENCES

Bailey, D. A., Carron, A. V., Teece, R. G., & Wehner, H. J. (1970). Vitamin C supplementation related to physiological response to exercise in smoking and nonsmoking subjects. *The American Journal of Clinical Nutrition, 23*(7), 905–912.

Bailey, K. D. (1994). *Typologies and taxonomies: An introduction to classification techniques* (Vol. 102). Thousand Oaks, CA: Sage.

Chittoor, R., Ray, S., Aulakh, P. S., & Sarkar, M. B. (2008). Strategic responses to institutional changes: "Indigenous growth" model of the Indian pharmaceutical industry. *Journal of International Management, 14*(3), 252−269. doi:10.1016/j.intman.2008.05.001

Cuervo-Cazurra, A. (2008). The multinationalization of developing country MNEs: The case of multilatinas. *Journal of International Management, 14*(2), 138−154.

Cuervo-Cazurra, A. (2012). Extending theory by analyzing developing country multinational companies: Solving the Goldilocks debate. *Global Strategy Journal, 2*(3), 153−167. doi:10.1111/j.2042-5805.2012.01039.x

Cuervo-Cazurra, A., & Genc, M. (2008). Transforming disadvantages into advantages: Developing-country MNEs in the least developed countries. *Journal of International Business Studies, 39*(6), 957−979.

Deng, P. (2007). Investing for strategic resources and its rationale: The case of outward FDI from Chinese companies. *Business Horizons, 50*(1), 71−81.

Dunning, J. H., & Lundan, S. M. (2010). The institutional origins of dynamic capabilities in multinational enterprises. *Industrial and Corporate Change, 19*(4), 1225−1246.

Enright, M. J., & Subramanian, V. (2007). An organizing framework for MNC subsidiary typologies. *Management International Review, 47*(6), 895−924.

Gammeltoft, P. (2008). Emerging multinationals: Outward FDI from the BRICS countries. *International Journal of Technology and Globalisation, 4*(1), 5−22.

Gammeltoft, P., Barnard, H., & Madhok, A. (2010). Emerging multinationals, emerging theory: Macro-and micro-level perspectives. *Journal of International Management, 16*(2), 95−101.

Gammeltoft, P., Pradhan, J. P., & Goldstein, A. (2010). Emerging multinationals: Home and host country determinants and outcomes. *International Journal of Emerging Markets, 5*(3/4), 254−265.

Gaur, A. S., & Kumar, V. (2009). International diversification, business group affiliation and firm performance: Empirical evidence from India. *British Journal of Management, 20*(2), 172−186.

Gaur, A. S., & Kumar, V. (2010). Internationalization of emerging market firms: A case for theoretical extension. In T. Devinney, T. Pedersen, & L. Tihanyi (Eds.), *The past, present and future of international business & management* (Vol. 23, pp. 603−627). Advances in International Management. Bingley, UK: Emerald Group Publishing Limited.

Gaur, A. S., Kumar, V., & Sarathy, R. (2011). Liability of foreignness and internationalisation of emerging market firms. In C. G. Asmussen, T. Pedersen, T. M. Devinney, & L. Tihanyi (Eds.), *Dynamics of globalization: Location-specific advantages or liabilities of foreignness?* (Vol. 24, pp. 211−233). Advances in International Management. Bingley, UK: Emerald Group Publishing Limited.

Gubbi, S. R., Aulakh, P. S., Ray, S., Sarkar, M. B., & Chittoor, R. (2010). Do international acquisitions by emerging-economy firms create shareholder value? The case of Indian firms. *Journal of International Business Studies, 41*(3), 397−418. doi:10.1057/jibs.2009.47

Guillén, M. F., & García-Canal, E. (2009). The American model of the multinational firm and the "new" multinationals from emerging economies. *The Academy of Management Perspectives, 23*(2), 23−35.

Hoskisson, R. E., Wright, M., Filatotchev, I., & Peng, M. W. (2013). Emerging multinationals from mid-range economies: The influence of institutions and factor markets. *Journal of Management Studies, 50*(7), 1295−1321. doi:10.1111/j.1467-6486.2012.01085.x

International Monetary Fund. (2012). *World economic outlook: A survey by the staff of the International Monetary Fund.* Washington, DC: International Monetary Fund.

Kumar, V., Mudambi, R., & Gray, S. (2013). Internationalization, innovation and institutions: The 3 I's Underpinning the competitiveness of emerging market firms. *Journal of International Management, 19*(3), 203–206.

Lorr, M. (1983). *Cluster analysis for social scientists.* San Francisco, CA: Jossey-Bass.

Lu, Y., Zhou, L., Bruton, G., & Li, W. (2010). Capabilities as a mediator linking resources and the international performance of entrepreneurial firms in an emerging economy. *Journal of International Business Studies, 41*(3), 419–436.

Luo, Y., & Tung, R. L. (2007). International expansion of emerging market enterprises: A springboard perspective. *Journal of International Business Studies, 38*(4), 481–498.

Luo, Y., & Wang, S. L. (2012). Foreign direct investment strategies by developing country multinationals: A diagnostic model for home country effects. *Global Strategy Journal, 2*(3), 244–261.

Luo, Y., Wang, S. L., Zheng, Q., & Jayaraman, V. (2012). Task attributes and process integration in business process offshoring: A perspective of service providers from India and China. *Journal of International Business Studies, 43*, 498–524.

Makino, S., Lau, C.-M., & Yeh, R.-S. (2002). Asset-exploitation versus asset-seeking: Implications for location choice of foreign direct investment from newly industrialized economies. *Journal of International Business Studies, 33*(3), 403–421.

Mathews, J. A. (2006). Dragon multinationals: New players in 21st century globalization. *Asia Pacific Journal of Management, 23*(1), 5–27.

Mezzich, J. E., & Solomon, H. (1980). *Taxonomy and behavioral science.* New York, NY: Academic Press, Inc.

Narula, R. (2012). Do we need different frameworks to explain infant MNEs from developing countries? *Global Strategy Journal, 2*(3), 188–204.

Noruésis, M. J. (2011). *IBM SPSS Statistics 19 guide to data analysis.* Boston, MA: Pearson Education.

Peng, M. W., Wang, D. Y. L., & Jiang, Y. (2008). An institution-based view of international business strategy: A focus on emerging economies. *Journal of International Business Studies, 39*(5), 920–936.

Ramamurti, R. (2012). What is really different about emerging market multinationals? *Global Strategy Journal, 2*(1), 41–47.

Ramamurti, R. (2013). The role of international M&A in building the competitive advantage of Indian firms. In P. W. Williamson, R. Ramamurti, A. C. C. Fleury, & M. T. L. Fleury (Eds.), *The competitive advantage of emerging market multinationals.* Cambridge, UK: Cambridge University Press.

Ramamurti, R., & Singh, J. V. (2009a). *Emerging multinationals in emerging markets.* Newyork, NY: Cambridge University Press.

Ramamurti, R., & Singh, J. V. (2009b). Indian multinationals: Generic internationalization strategies. In *Emerging multinationals in emerging markets* (pp. 110–165). Newyork, NY: Cambridge University Press.

Sim, A., & Pandian, J. R. (2003). Emerging Asian MNEs and their internationalization strategies—Case study evidence on Taiwanese and Singaporean firms. *Asia Pacific Journal of Management, 20*(1), 27–50.

Smith, K. B. (2002). Typologies, taxonomies, and the benefits of policy classification. *Policy Studies Journal, 30*(3), 379–395.

Witt, M. A., & Lewin, A. Y. (2007). Outward foreign direct investment as escape response to home country institutional constraints. *Journal of International Business Studies, 38*(4), 579–594.

Xu, D., & Meyer, K. E. (2013). Linking theory and context: "Strategy Research in Emerging Economies" after Wright et al. (2005). *Journal of Management Studies, 50*(7), 1322–1346. doi:10.1111/j.1467-6486.2012.01051.x

APPENDIX: CRITERION FOR SELECTING CLUSTERS

	Auto-Clustering Algorithm Results			
Number of Clusters	Schwarz's Bayesian Criterion (BIC)	BIC Change[a]	Ratio of BIC Changes[b]	Ratio of Distance Measures[c]
1	34180.831			
2	27252.159	−6928.672	1.000	1.187
3	21431.631	−5820.528	0.840	1.899
4	18418.274	−3013.357	0.435	1.240
5	16008.525	−2409.749	0.348	1.211
6	14037.686	−1970.839	0.284	1.389
7	12650.156	−1387.530	0.200	1.105
8	11405.269	−1244.887	0.180	1.220
9	10404.520	−1000.750	0.144	1.094
10	9498.815	−905.704	0.131	1.364
11	8864.030	−634.785	0.092	1.155
12	8329.187	−534.843	0.077	1.265
13	7929.675	−399.512	0.058	1.125
14	7586.862	−342.813	0.049	1.294
15	7346.944	−239.918	0.035	1.172

[a]The changes are from the previous number of clusters in the table.
[b]The ratios of changes are relative to the change for the two cluster solution.
[c]The ratios of distance measures are based on the current number of clusters against the previous number of clusters.

ORGANIZING MNC INTERNAL NETWORKS TO MANAGE GLOBAL CUSTOMERS: STRATEGIES OF POLITICAL COMPROMISING

Elina Pernu, Tuija Mainela and Vesa Puhakka

ABSTRACT

The present study approaches multinational corporations as internal networks that are constantly newly organized on the basis of relationships, operations, activities, and tasks at hand. It combines MNCs-as-networks view with the research on supplier−customer relationship development to conceptualize the relational dynamics in the MNCs. The dynamics are seen created as the interplay of organizing within internal networks and managing of the global customer relationships. Through an empirical study on a project business MNC and analysis of the events in its global customer relationship the study defines strategies of political compromising in MNC internal networks.

Keywords: Multinational corporation; internal network; global customer; politics; strategy

Orchestration of the Global Network Organization
Advances in International Management, Volume 27, 349−376
Copyright © 2014 by Emerald Group Publishing Limited
All rights of reproduction in any form reserved
ISSN: 1571-5027/doi:10.1108/S1571-502720140000027010

INTRODUCTION

MNC Alpha has been operating two years in India through its Subunit I that has Project I with a locally headquartered MNC Beta's Unit India. Based on the Project I, Project II is initiated between Alpha's Subunit II and Beta's Unit Zambia. Alpha's Subunit I has a local office in Zambia and therefore Subunits I and II cooperate in the Zambian operations. Subunit II can use the local office of Subunit I and, because Subunit I does not have direct contacts to Beta's Unit Zambia, Subunit II acts as Alpha's representative in all local matters. Initial contacts between Alpha's Subunit II and Beta's Unit Zambia lead to negotiations on Project II with many meetings and debates, about price, in particular. After half a year communications Alpha's KAM and project manager of Beta's Unit India are invited to the negotiations because of their previous good relationship developed in Project I. These two individuals agree on the Project II terms. Subsequently, the CEO of Beta's Unit Zambia states that he would have never agreed on the project with that price. A significant supplementary agreement is added to Project II after half a year of implementation.

As illustrated above, multinational corporations (MNCs) are organizationally complex multi-dimensional entities (Galbraith, 2012; Ghoshal & Bartlett, 1990; Gupta & Govindarajan, 2000) that consist of the headquarters and often numerous of local units and multiple inter-unit relationships (Holm & Sharma, 2006). Hence, MNCs are typical network organizations that are in practice much less hierarchical than the organizational charts imply (Hedlund, 1986; Noorderhaven & Harzing, 2009). Some units belong to multiple functional groups and any given unit may be a member of several technological systems. As a result, an MNC is not a single network but consists of multiple internal networks that are constantly newly organized in relation to relationships, operations, activities and tasks at hand. As the above case example also illustrates, the MNC internal networks are formed at several levels. The use of teams and project groups, in particular, leads to formation of both planned and emerging intra-organizational networks based on the relationships and expertise of individuals without regard to the unit borders (Möller & Rajala, 1999).

Furthermore, the case example presents the process of managing global customer relationships as a major change catalyst in the organization's internal network (Campbell, 2003). Internal networks in MNCs differ between customers and over time. The handling of these intra-organizational and inter-personal relationships between different units in two MNCs is a prerequisite for successful management of inter-organizational customer relationships (see Möller & Rajala, 1999). We focus on this dynamism of the MNC internal networks in relation to its global customers. The research question of the study is: how are the MNC internal networks organized in relation to managing of the global customer relationships.

We approach an MNC as a loosely coupled organization that is embedded in external networks of relationships to variety of different actors (Piekkari & Welch, 2010). The research on MNCs has for long discussed the MNC structures and also the managing of different levels within the heterogeneous organizations. However, the interfaces of the internal and external structures are covered primarily as a question of standardization versus local adaptation in the process of internal decision making (Bartlett & Ghoshal, 2002; Meyer, Mudambi, & Narula, 2011; Nohria & Ghoshal, 1997). What we emphasize is that there is a need to create connections between internal and external structures that exist both at organizational and individual levels. Moreover, we claim that the collective and intentional orchestration behaviors in relation to the global customers are crucial boundary work in MNCs (cf. Santos & Eisenhardt, 2009). We delve into the details of this boundary work by analysing changes in the internal networks of a project business MNC in specific events over development of its global customer relationship. In MNCs boundary work is by necessity circumscribed by politics and constant negotiations (Mintzberg, 1985; Williams & Lee, 2009). This makes political compromising a key to orchestration of MNC internal networks.

In the following we will discuss the MNCs-as-networks view and research on supplier–customer relationship development. MNCs-as-networks view has focused on, for example, subunits' external networks (e.g., Forsgren, 2008) and headquarter–subunit relationships (e.g., Birkinshaw, Holm, Thilenius, & Arvidsson, 2000; Holm, Johanson, & Thilenius, 1995). This study extends the discussion by emphasizing that there are multiple internal networks in MNCs built around specific customer relationships and that these networks are the dynamic platforms and driving forces of the operations of the organization. The customer occupies a key role in defining the internal network and the internal networks activated in specific events influence the customer relationship.

The empirical research follows process research strategy to examine how things evolve and why they evolve in a particular way based on data on a selected global customer of an MNC. As a result, the study shows how the changes of the internal network in connection to various relationship events are related to the variety of strategic ways of behaving to create common views. We explicate strategies for political compromising as the finding of the study.

ORGANIZING MNC INTERNAL NETWORKS IN RELATION TO CUSTOMERS

Business network perspective on MNCs focuses on the network of relationships in which the operations of the firm are embedded (Forsgren, 2008; Piekkari & Welch, 2010). A fundamental characteristic of this network is the headquarters being an outsider in the subunit's network and considered to be one player among others (Forsgren, 2008, pp. 121–122). Furthermore, we rely on the notion that an organization's ability to develop and manage successfully its relationships with other actors is a core competence and source of competitive advantage (Möller & Halinen, 1999; Ritter, Wilkinson, & Johnston, 2004; Wilson, 1995). For the purposes of examining the change of internal networks in relation to evolvement of global customer relationships we'll discuss prior research on organizing in MNCs and on customer relationship development.

Organizing in MNC Internal Networks

The answer to the question "what is an MNC?" is not straightforward. Concepts such as multinational corporation (e.g., Birkinshaw & Morrison, 1995; Dörrenbächer & Gammelgaard, 2010), multinational enterprise (e.g., Giroud & Scott-Kennel, 2009; Manev, 2003; Yamin & Forsgren, 2006), transnational corporation (Bartlett & Ghoshal, 2002) and global firm (Vahlne, Schweizer, & Johanson, 2012) are often used interchangeably (see also Aggarwal, Berrill, Hutson, & Kearney, 2011). The roots of the MNC research are already in Hymer's studies in 1960s when it was primarily a question of foreign direct investment. In later study of the role and functions of different MNC units the research has focused on MNCs as structures that consist of headquarters and subsidiaries and their relationships. Whether named as "heterarchies" (Hedlund, 1986), "interorganizational networks" (Ghoshal & Bartlett, 1990), "differentiated networks" (Andersson, Forsgren, & Holm, 2002; Nell, Ambos, & Schlegelmilch, 2011;

Nohria & Ghoshal, 1997) or "internal networks" (Dörrenbächer & Gammelgaard, 2010), MNCs are network organizations. There is always a question of behaviors by multiple actors and of interactions in various kinds of relationships between them.

The traditional, hierarchical definition of MNCs draws a picture of single country mandated subunits each focusing on their own supplier and customer relationships. Todays diversified MNCs cover multiple geographical markets with multiple product lines (Doz & Prahalad, 2005, p. 21). Although the subunits may be internally differentiated in their products, business conditions, structures, and coordination processes (Forsgren, 2008, p. 86; Ghoshal, Korine, & Szulanski, 1994), the subunits are required to cooperate in terms of various country operations and projects. Therefore, MNCs actually consist of multiple internal networks embedding the units differently over time in the home and host country networks (Dörrenbächer & Gammelgaard, 2010) as well as in the technological, functional, and project-based networks. The MNC internal network, hence, is a dynamic structure that needs to be understood in its particular context.

In the MNC internal networks, the actors are quite independent in relation to many issues (see Ritter & Gemünden, 2003). Multiple perspectives always exist on choices and decisions and there are multiple internal and external stakeholders (Doz & Prahalad, 2005, p. 21). Different units develop in different and inconsistent directions (Holm et al., 1995). Still, the subunits may act in the same country markets or serve the same global customers in different markets. The strength of MNCs is fundamentally in their nature as social communities (Kogut & Zander, 1993; Piekkari & Welch, 2010) that develop competitive advantage through accumulation of knowledge and competencies from different parts of the world (Adenfelt & Lagerström, 2006; Andersson et al., 2002; Gupta & Govindarajan, 2000; Holm & Sharma, 2006). However, quite often headquarters do not have sufficient knowledge of the networks and actions of the subunits (Vahlne et al., 2012). Coherent worldwide operations require extensive inter-unit coordination and integration (Ghoshal et al., 1994) and, therefore, there is a need for structuring the interfaces between functions and units. This structuring we see as the process of organizing.

Organizing is an internal process to which belong activities, such as, creating organizational structures, staffing and implementation of the ways of communication in relation to particular operations (e.g., Ritter, 1999). Furthermore, organizing denotes processes that take place in constantly changing relationship networks (Håkansson & Snehota, 1995, p. 10). Thus, organizing is a behavioral process, in which the internal networks become re-formulated when new relationships are built, old decay or existing relationships change their character (cf. Möller, 2010). Organizing affects the organizational level operations but also includes the enactment of individuals in internal networks (cf. Weick, 1979). Critical events in internal networks or in customer relationships are always an occasion for organizing (Weick, 1979, pp. 3–4). Organizing can thus be seen as the production of collective understanding in organizational networks developing over time.

The dilemma confronting MNCs is how to reconcile the global role of the operating subunits with the need for cross-divisional communication and coordination at corporate, continent and country levels. As networks with some hierarchical, but varying, powers, MNCs feature struggles between headquarters and subsidiaries as well as between different subsidiaries (Forsgren, 2008, p. 123). This means that politics are significant part of organizing MNC internal networks.

Managing Global Customer Relationships

All companies need to be engaged in exchange relations, and some of those relationships develop into close, long-term relationships (Håkansson, Ford, Gadde, Snehota, & Waluszewski, 2009; Wilson, 1995). Customer relationships, in particular, are described as the most important resources that companies have (e.g., Dwyer, Schurr, & Oh, 1987; Ritter et al., 2004). Therefore, an organization's ability to successfully develop and manage its relationships with other actors is a core competence and important source of competitive advantage (Möller & Halinen, 1999; Ritter et al., 2004; Wilson, 1995). Management of customer relationships is a question of understanding and serving customer needs and often also co-developing new products and services (Ritter et al., 2004).

As organizations become more global, their need to deeply understand customers and carry on a meaningful dialog with them even increases (Young & Javalgi, 2007). Multinational customers demand global-based contracts, prices, and products instead of just country-based services (Harvey, Myers, & Novicevic, 2003; Montgomery & Yip, 2000). This means that if a supplier is unable to serve a customer globally, it is unlikely to continue to serve the customer at a national level (Campbell, 2003; Wilson & Weilbaker, 2004).

The management of customer relationships in MNCs requires the reconciliation of the need for global coordination and control with the local needs of customers in the context of increased levels of organizational complexity and cultural diversity (Luo, 2001, 2002; Millman, 1996; Wilson & Weilbaker, 2004). Thus, MNCs are striving to meet both the global and local needs of their customers (Wilson & Weilbaker, 2004) for which cooperation between different units, locations, and projects in MNCs is needed (Evaristo & van Fenema, 1999). This is often a question of political compromising between different interests.

The relationships between suppliers and customers are dynamic and affected by the individual episodes, which take place within them (Håkansson, 1982). Interactions in the episodes affect the technical, knowledge, social, administrative, and legal aspects of the relationships although they may be beyond the control of individuals acting in organizations (Håkansson & Snehota, 1995). Still, it is important to know what precedes the current situation and frames the evolution (see Ford & Håkansson, 2006; Tidström & Hagberg-Andersson, 2012). This comes about as understanding of relationship events, that is, changes caused by nature or outcomes of human acts (Hedaa & Törnroos, 2008), and how they are connected with each other in the past, present, and the future of the relationship development (Hedaa & Törnroos, 2008; Tidström & Hagberg-Andersson, 2012). The events can be regional, local, or global in scope but they act as engines for relationship and network change as mediated by the actors (Hedaa & Törnroos, 2008; Kamp, 2005; Schurr, 2007).

Human actors give meanings based on their previous experiences (Arthur, 2001); therefore, also events are actually socially constructed (Halinen, Medlin, & Törnroos, 2012; Tidström & Hagberg-Andersson, 2012). In differentiated MNCs, events and their causes in the global customer relationships are often perceived and interpreted by the actors in different manner. This opens up relationship management challenges whose solving is a process of politics, in particular.

Politics at the Structural and Behavioral Interfaces

Developing spaces connecting structures and action that cut across the established boundaries within the MNC are critical for its competitiveness (Lee & Williams, 2007). These spaces are the arenas for boundary work (Santos & Eisenhardt, 2009) at both structural and behavioral interfaces of the MNCs, in which MNC politics take place. The political arenas are organizational situations of influence in conflict between individuals (Mintzberg, 1985; Williams & Lee, 2009), organizational units (Williams & Lee, 2011) or between the existing structures and behaviors of organizing and managing (cf. Foss, Foss, & Nell, 2012).

Individuals within MNCs often interpret events in a different manner and give multiple meanings to the cause of the events (cf. Hedaa & Törnroos, 2008). Especially when experiences differ, the understandings tend to clash with each organizational group representing its opinions to the other in the form of an argument that stands for its unique model of what makes sense (Drazin, Glynn, & Kazanjian, 1999). In these situations conflict and political influence appear and affect the organizational action (Drazin et al., 1999). When significant enough an event to be called a crisis occurs, negotiated order between opposing groups is needed (Drazin et al., 1999). This negotiated order within the MNC internal network we name as the act of political compromising at the interface of organizing behaviors and internal network structures.

Furthermore, political tensions also arise in managing the customer relationships, in particular, when the customer's situation and networks change (cf. Forsgren, Holm, & Johanson, 2005). Due to the local market embeddedness the MNC customer relationship management involves significant amount of decentralized bargaining and negotiations (cf. Dörrenbächer & Geppert, 2006). We see this as the act of political compromising at the interface of the managing behaviors by the MNC and the customer relationship.

Crossing boundaries is, in particular, needed to organize MNC internal networks in relation to the inter-organizational level customer relationships, which in practice develop through projects and personal relationships. Views of the customer by necessity differ at different organizational levels and in units as well as the actions of individuals in relation to the customer inside the MNC. Still, creating a collective understanding of the customer is needed to successfully manage inter-organizational level customer relationships. Organizations are thus required to make political compromises between opposing groups and units (Drazin et al., 1999) and through that ensure the overall development of the customer relationship. Understandings may not be completely shared, but will nonetheless guide the behavior in the organization. How conflicts are solved between different views determines how MNC internal network is organized and how customer relationships are managed and thus guides the development of an MNC as a whole. Thus, we see that the last act of political compromising exists at the interface of organizing internal networks and managing customer relationships.

In this research the concept of internal network is used to describe the operations of an MNC in relation to specific customers. Networks are not seen as permanent structures, instead, it is seen that each network in relation to specific customer is unique and dynamic. Internal networks consist both of formal structures between headquarters, different technological and geographical units as well as of informal relationships in projects and between individuals involved with specific customers. Fig. 1 connects internal MNC networks and global customer relationships and shows the interfaces where political compromises are made.

MNCs organize their internal networks including both organizing informal relationships between actors and, in the long term, adjusting their organizational structures to become more customer-centric. As different understandings of the customer relationships exists based on the different experiences, actions and actors involved, political compromises in organizing MNC internal networks are made. MNCs manage their customer relationships at multiple levels, including continuous inter-organizational level relationships and discontinuous project-level relationships. Developing inter-organizational level relationships may require different understanding and actions than managing single, discontinuous projects (Alajoutsijärvi, Mainela, Salminen, & Ulkuniemi, 2012). MNCs strive to organize both formal structures and informal relationships in their internal networks as well as to manage customer relationships at inter-organizational and project level. Combining different levels is bound to include disagreements as the objectives differ, thus, creating the need for political compromises.

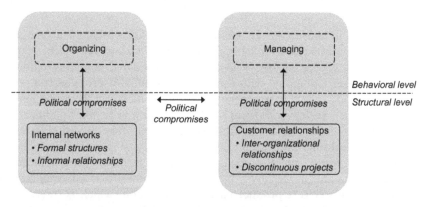

Fig. 1. Conceptual Framework of the Study.

RESEARCH DESIGN

The research paradigm adopted is moderate constructionism (see, e.g., Guba & Lincoln, 1994, p. 109; Järvensivu & Törnroos, 2010). Constructionism is interested in how people, as individuals or as groups, interpret and understand social events and settings (Crotty, 1998, p. 43; Eriksson & Kovalainen, 2008, p. 19). In the moderate form of constructionism utilized in this research, it is seen that the truth exists as dialogue, critique and consensus in different communities and new, usable knowledge can be created through these multiple viewpoints of the truth (Järvensivu & Törnroos, 2010). In line with relativism, the underlying assumption here is that there are multiple, sometimes conflicting, social realities based on human experience and therefore the form and content of reality is dependent on individual persons or groups holding the constructions (Guba & Lincoln, 1994, pp. 110–111). Knowledge is seen as personal and dependent on the individual (Guba & Lincoln, 1994, p. 111).

Research Strategy and the Selection of the Case

Following process research strategy (see Feldman & Orlikowski, 2011) the study strives to understand how and why things evolve and uses process data consisting of stories about what happened and who did what when — events, activities, and choices over time (Langley, 1999). Historical data collected through retrospective interviews and documents are combined with data collected in real time to examine relationship development over time.

Case study is chosen as the method to gain knowledge in a complicated, cross-cultural research setting (Marschan-Piekkari & Welch, 2004, pp. 7–8). The case company is a global, consolidated company (subsequently, Supplier Company) with three business units. It provides technology to entire value chain in processing minerals to metals in the mining and metals industries. It deliveries from single equipment to turnkey plants and comprehensive services having multiple simultaneous projects with different subunits and customer units around the globe.

Subunit I offers mostly smaller projects through geographically mandated units and is seen by other subunits primarily as an equipment supplier. Subunit II is a product based business unit, which is internally divided based on the used technologies. Subunit III offers most comprehensive services, which means that the projects are bigger and last longer.

Subunit III was acquired in 2001 and its main unit is in Germany and therefore it operates quite independently. Each of the subunits has multiple geographical units, which are typically located near the main customers.

This research focuses on a selected customer relationship (subsequently, Customer A) of the Supplier Company. Customer A was defined as important to the Supplier Company by its top management. It is a senior mining house that has multiple production units mainly operating in India, Zambia and Australia and it can have projects with all Supplier Company's subunits. A more intensive relationship with Customer A started in 2003 but not all supplier subunit have equal relationships with the customer. Still, multiple units both on customer's and supplier's side are involved in the relationship.

Data Collection and Analysis

The empirical study builds on altogether 48 interviews. The first set of primary data consists of 16 interviews, which were done with the managers of the Supplier Company in multiple organizational units and at various levels in relation to Customer A. The interviews lasted from one hour to two and a half hours and were all tape-recorded. The interviews produced 18 hours and 16 minutes of recording. The interviews concentrated on the specific customer relationship and the internal events and actions of the Supplier Company in it. The themes discussed were the history and development of customer relationship, features of the relationship, features of the projects with the customer, cooperation between the companies and roles of different internal units. According to the multilevel approach, the interviewees tell about their own personal relationships (individual level) inside their own unit (unit level) and these relationships form an overall relationship with the customer (organizational level). Another set of primary data consists of 32 interviews that are made within the case company by other researchers of the larger research project on relationships in MNCs. These interviews are not directly linked with Customer A but offer data at the overall company level. These interviews were utilized before the first set's interviews to create understanding of the company, its operation logics and its customer relationships.

This research also utilized a multitude of complementary data. Various written sources, such as the web-pages of the firm and its customer, annual reports, offering circular and brochures, were reviewed. A number of project memos and other workshop and seminar materials provided case-specific data. The complementary data was extensively used during the research process and especially before the interviews to create comprehensive understanding of the industry's context and the operations of the case firm.

Data analysis has been done in several phases intertwined with several phases of literature review, data collection, and the process of casing. The iterative nature of data collection and analysis (Dubois & Gadde, 2002; Zalan & Lewis, 2004) allows theory to develop simultaneously with the formulation and reformulation of the research problem (see Ghauri, 2004). QSR Nivo program was used to store the data and to assist systematic coding of it.

As the first analytical step, a story of the customer relationship was written based on the experiences of the interviewed individuals. Then, the network-like customer relationships at multiple organizational levels were depicted. After this, the focus was shifted into the events and from each interview the actions in events and the meanings that individuals give to them were mapped. In the following, the narrative of the customer relationship development is presented through the internal networks in relation to the events in the customer relationship development. In the end, events are analyzed in terms of strategies employed for political compromising as they present conflict and influence within the internal networks.

EMPIRICAL ANALYSIS

Customer A is an Indian metal producing company that has grown by acquisitions as a significant global player. It owns mines in India, Zambia, and Australia. It has experienced rapid growth, which offers substantial opportunities to the Supplier Company. Customer A does not invest in research and development; rather, it focuses on producing metals at a low cost and attempts to find ways to conduct projects as inexpensively as possible. Although Customer A is listed on the stock market, it can be defined as family-owned; the top management of the company is two brothers. The internal cooperation is strong, and top management is well informed about business and project details. Table 1 summarizes the development of the relationship in terms of six major events.

Table 1. Relationship Development with Customer A.

Events in Relationship	Importance	Timing	Organizational Units Involved
1. Equipment sales	Start of the relationship, using agents	Beginning in the 1970s	All
2. Activating the relationship	Defining the current stage and possibilities of the relationship, creating contacts	Early 2003	HQ (CustA KAM)
Project I	Growing market share, closer relationship, contact with top management, role of CustA KAM is strengthened	2003	Sub I Finland HQ (CustA KAM)
3. Internal marketing	Creating unified ways of actions and one point of contact to the customer	2004 onwards	HQ (CustA KAM) Sub I Finland Sub II Finland, Sub III Germany
Project II	Having a wider relationship to the customer	2006	Sub II Finland (unit 2) Sub I Southern Africa HQ (CustA KAM)
4. New unit to India	Creating a local presence	2007	HQ Local office in India
Toward strategic relationship	Customer's desire to have a closer relationship	Fall 2008	HQ (CustA KAM) Sub III Germany
5. Problems in Project II	Customer plant suffered downtime, which affected production numbers	December 2008	Sub II Finland Sub I Southern Africa HQ
Loss of sale	Sub III loses a sale because of problems in Project II with Sub II	Spring 2009	Sub III Germany HQ (CustA KAM)
6. Improving relations	Working together and building the trust that was lost	Summer 2009	Sub II Finland Sub III Germany HQ (CustA KAM)

The Development Process of the MNC's Global Customer Relationship

The relationship between Supplier Company and Customer A started with a few equipment sales in 1980s and 1990s. During this time, the Supplier Company was using agents, and each of the subunits had its own agents. The Supplier Company did not regard the Indian market and Customer A as very important. Personal contacts were scarce and the relationship distant. The coordination of agent relationships was perceived as a challenge and handling cultural differences difficult.

The relationship experienced a second start in 2003 when the President of Market Area India was appointed (subsequently, CustA KAM). His role was to enhance the company's involvement in the Indian market and to act as a global account manager in the relationship with Customer A. CustA KAM went to India to explore the possibilities for different subunits of the Supplier Company and to activate the relationship at the personal level. The good reputation of the Supplier Company helped to create relationships and open doors, and CustA KAM first created contacts at the lower organizational levels in the customer organization.

In May 2003, the first negotiations of a large project between Customer A (Unit India) and Subunit I commenced (subsequently, Project I). The Supplier Company heard about the project through an agent, and CustA KAM was able to present the Supplier Company to the customer. Subsequently, the Supplier Company was asked to place an offer. In the project negotiations, CustA KAM acted as a chair of a separate committee and did not belong to the project organization. Four companies were initially involved in project negotiations, which lasted from May to December, and the longest individual negotiation lasted six weeks. At the end of 2003, there were two companies remaining, but price was an issue. The Supplier Company first refused the project at the suggested price, but the contract was created the following night. The relationship with Customer A (Unit India), and the contacts with the top management were created solely through this project. The Supplier Company was the main contracting party, but it also had an Indian engineering office as a partner and supervised the partner's actions. Customer A would have wanted the project to be turnkey project, but the Supplier Company saw the risk too big in an unknown country. The duration of the project bidding and launching phase was a year and a half.

The relationship with unit India was created through Project I, but the relationship with other parts of customer organization did not yet develop. Since 2004, the Supplier Company strived to create new relationships to

Customer A and to obtain knowledge of its decision makers and ways of action. Customer A experienced rapid growth and made big investments in the 2003–2006 period. The Supplier Company was able to participate in the bidding, but Customer A aggressively strived to find the least expensive solution and emphasized completion with different suppliers. During this period, the contacts at different levels and between different units multiplied. CustA KAM acted as the global account manager and marketed the Customer A project openings internally to different subunits and geographical units and participated in the sales negotiations.

The two year activity in India led to major Project II between Subunit II and Customer A (Unit Zambia). Project II was located in Zambia, where the local office of Supplier Company was Subunit I's office. Subunit II used the local office of Subunit I and, because Subunit I did not have direct contacts to Customer A, Subunit II acted as Supplier Company's representative in the market. In spring 2005, a project manager from Customer A (Unit Zambia) contacted Subunit II with interest in their technology. The requested information package with references was provided with a rough cost estimate. Negotiations lasted until the end of 2005 and included many meetings, debates and misunderstandings. In December 2005, CustA KAM became involved as the technology used by the Supplier Company was better than that of its competitors, but price was an issue. The representative from Customer A (Unit India) was invited to the negotiations because of his previous connection with CustA KAM in Project I. These two individuals made the final negotiations, and the representative from Customer A (Unit India) ultimately asked CustA KAM to make the final decision because he perceived CustA KAM as fair. Subsequently, the CEO of Customer A Unit Zambia stated that he would have never agreed on that price. The contract was signed on January 3, 2006. In fall, a significant supplementary agreement containing technical support was added.

Simultaneously to Project II with Subunit II, Subunit III had multiple projects with Customer A and the cooperation as a whole grew and diversified. In 2007, the technological management of the Supplier Company made the decision to establish a local unit in India and a local managing director was hired in fall 2008. The Indian unit was designed to be a local full-service unit with sales, engineering, manufacturing, and service because local operations were deemed necessary in India. In fall 2008, Subunit III and CustA KAM met with Customer A's top management. Customer A's managers expressed their desire to develop the relationship as closer and more long-term to strive for a strategic partnership. The request was generally viewed as positive development. However, for Subunit III, the revenue logic in the arrangement remained a question, as the customer would still want to invite many companies to bid. Therefore, the Supplier Company decided to contemplate the answer to this question. Local personnel were recruited to the Indian unit in 2009 and the remaining agent relationships were terminated.

Meanwhile, Project II ran into trouble. Project II was technically demanding because the raw material used was not typical for the chosen technology. The project consisted of the sale of a technology package involving a certain process, instructions on how the process works and the guarantee for the end result. The Supplier Company provided specifications on the equipment, but customer was able to decide how strictly it wanted to follow the instructions. The execution had begun in spring 2007 and the customer hoped that the plant would be operational in February 2008. The Supplier Company foresaw that the plant would be operational in the summer of 2008 at the earliest. Launch included several problems and after many changes, the plant commenced operations in October. On Christmas Eve 2008, a serious technical problem emerged in the plant. It disrupted the operations, and there was also a risk of a great accident, which was fortunately avoided. The local office in Zambia, Subunit II in Finland and CustA KAM were informed about the problems. After the first incident, two more technical problems emerged in February and April 2009 and also affected the operating of the plant. The problems were reported in news all over the globe, and the customer was not satisfied with how the problems were addressed.

The challenges with Project II strained the relationship in the following six months, and because of the problems in Project II between Subunit II and Customer A (Unit Zambia), Subunit III lost a sale with Customer A (Unit India). In a technological sense, the Supplier Company would have had strong know-how and references. The negotiations with Customer A progressed normally, but Customer A had an order from top management not to buy anything from the Supplier Company, which was subsequently told to CustA KAM. The operations of Customer A are highly centralized. If there are problems in one field or with one delivery, it will affect the overall relationship. The negotiations for a more strategic relationship ended, and all discussions at different organizational levels centered on the problems of Project II.

Despite the loss of the bigger project, there were smaller deliveries. As CustA KAM states, "we were not on a corporate-wide black list." There have also been improvements in the relationship after the problems were solved. All of the subunits have had sales during the development of the customer relationship. Subunit I has had a few sales. Subunit II has had the most actions with the customer. Monetarily, Subunit III has had the largest sales. Today, the greatest potential in the relationship with Customer A exists with Subunits II and III. The importance of the customer also varies inside of the subunits; Customer A is notably more important to Subunit II, unit 1 than to unit 2. Subunit III has the closest and longest relationship with the greatest potential with Customer A. Fig. 2 illustrates the change of the internal network of the Supplier Company in relation to the Customer A over time.

Political Compromising Strategies Over the Relationship Development

As the relationship in question consists of multiple unit and individual level relationships, conflicts are bound to exist. Units and individuals are required to make compromises to ensure the overall development of the customer relationship. Political compromising is a key for creating collective understandings of the customer relationship and having these shared understandings gives MNCs the possibility to organize internal networks in relation to the customers. Fig. 2 in the previous chapter depicted the changes in the Supplier Company's internal network in relation to Customer A. As the customer relationship develops, also the internal network evolves and the individuals and units involved change. From the development of customer relationship, we identified five transitions involving a *conflict-compromise* situation.

In the beginning, the customer relationship consisted of equipment sales conducted by agents of each subunit, which meant that each subunit had substantial autonomy to act with the customer. In the first transition, the relationship shifted from equipment sales through agents to a relationship coordinated through key account manager. The conflict aroused as each subunits' agent relationships were eventually terminated and the relationships coordinated through a headquarter level key account manager. The decision came from the corporate level and affected all subunits. We name this as the strategy of *mandating customer interface*.

In the second transition, the single unit and single project relationship changed to a multiple unit relationship and simultaneously from one customer production unit to another. As multiple units become involved the conflict arises from different ways of operations.

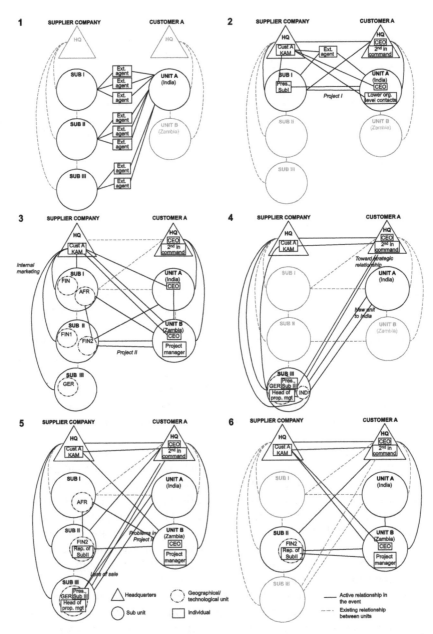

Fig. 2.   Change of Supplier Company's Internal Network in Relation to Customer A.

I was able to get in to our [subunits] negotiation teams. Some were willing to take me in, others managed it so cunningly that I was not involved; we are not in matrix organization or so disciplined. So I had to sell myself internally which is understandable. Why would for example Canadian or German team want me to come with? What do I bring into that? (CustA KAM)

For example, after Project I with Subunit I, another project negotiation between Customer A and Subunit III failed. CustA KAM explained that the sale was brought to them and that the failure had a negative effect on the relationship. According to him, the failure was not caused by the price; rather, it stemmed from the lack of understanding on the Supplier Company's side. This way of behaving is focused on the *selling of oneself as internal trustee*.

Another conflict arouse when negotiating Project II. When Subunit II negotiated with Customer A's business Unit Zambia with respect to Project II, the negotiations did not progress beyond a certain point, and the customer called the Indian manager from Project I to negotiate with CustA KAM because of their previous connection in Project I. The incident both showed the existing gaps in the internal networks as well as the need for stabilizing the relationship and creating common practices through *personally mediated problem solving*. The same Project II illustrates the strategy of *project-based resource combining* as the Subunits I and II worked closely together hiring the resources needed from each other to avoid conflict in the internal network in relation to representation towards the customer.

The negotiations for Project I and II were difficult and individuals and units involved described the Customer A as challenging. With both projects the negotiations, execution, payment and lack of clarity created the third transition when the Supplier Company shifted from challenging project negotiations into the era of more continuous projects. For example, the relationship between Customer A and Subunit I was built through Project I, and the challenges in that project lead Subunit I to conclude that the relationship with Customer A is less important to them.

In [Sub I], many key individuals felt that they had burned their wings. It was like poorly aimed shots in hunting season; the poor bird didn't die but got hurt badly – this is the metaphor that comes to mind. Still the same persons have done business or tried to do business with [Customer A], but that project strained the relationships on a personal level; many decent engineers felt that they got criticized without reason and too few compliments. (CustA KAM)

Subunit I supports other units in their relationship with Customer A, even though Subunit I feels that the relationship is not beneficial for them. The compromising strategy has originated from the need to stabilize and maintain the relationship. Actions of Subunit I were thus directed towards the customer relationship and as a strategy showed *collective responsibility taking*. The challenges in project negotiations and resistance towards the customer have led also to another outcome. The Supplier Company has learned how customer operates and the correct ways to operate with the customer. In addition, units are more responsive towards organizationally coordinated relationship.

The fourth transition occurred when Customer A wanted to develop the relationship into a strategic partnership with Subunit III. This development was interrupted when Project II run into problems. The relationship between Customer A and the Supplier Company grew tense after these problems, which also affected the actions of Subunit III. According to Subunit III, the customer was not satisfied with the technical support that the Supplier Company was giving, but Subunit II was viewing the situation differently − there were differences in opinions, which, according to the head of proposal management at Subunit III, "*left a bit of a bad taste.*" Subunit III feels that it was blamed for something that was not their fault.

> I was in a meeting, and [the top manager] was shouting at me for things for which we were not responsible. He told me, "you're in the [Supplier Company's] management group. You have to tell that your people." So they were not happy about that. (Vice President, Sub III)

According to CustA KAM, the project loss occurred because the top management of Customer A momentarily lost trust in the Supplier Company. Customer A had difficulties understanding why the attitude of the Supplier Company was so distant with respect to their massive problems. Eventually, the customer relationship shifted from the stage of emerging strategic cooperation through loss of sales toward recovering the relationship. This was seen as an important turning point in the relationship.

Behind the shift we see intense *sharing of experiences for corporate level narrative* in relation to the customer. The problems in Project II harmed the relationship from both sides. The important transition occurred when the attitude towards the customer inside the Supplier Company shifted from disaffection towards collective understanding of the importance of the customer. From the Supplier Company's side, different views on why the Project II ran into problems meant that the situation was not dealt with sufficiently, including both technical problem solving and relationship management. CustA KAM in charge of the overall customer relationship felt that the Supplier Company did not react to customer needs sufficiently quickly. CustA KAM feels that Subunit II acted correctly in terms of engineering, but the management of the overall customer relationship did not succeed. The representative of Subunit II describes Project II as highly technical and feels that the customer lacked sufficient expertise in plant operations. The delayed launch of the project was caused, among other reasons, by the late deliveries of equipment that the customer had ordered. Because of these delays there was an insufficient number of personnel to supervise and educate the customer. The subunit representatives also felt that the customer did not listen to them on how things should be done and that advices were accepted only when problems already existed. The need for creating shared understanding arouse when it was seen how closely connected different customer's units are and how one problem also affects the operations of others. The transition included a lot of resistance but eventually led to a shared feeling of customer's importance.

> I think I used the metaphor of sitting on the same bench and looking in the same direction. After April, both organizations finally realized that, hey, this is a shared problem, and only by working together can we make this right. (CustA KAM)

To conclude, the MNC internal network evolves as the customer relationship is developed. Formal structures may stay stable in the short run, but informal relationships related to the customer relationship change as well as the role of these relationships as the importance of the customer to different supplier units varies in time and vice versa. Eventually, this will also lead to changes in organizational structures, e.g. establishing a local unit to India to create local presence that reflects the strategy of *mandating customer interface*. The actors involved in compromising differ and can be individuals, units or corporate actors. Also the level of compromise differs, as it can be done within the MNC internal network or on the customer relationship. In any case, these compromises in MNC internal network are needed to develop and manage customer relationships. Table 2 summarizes the strategies for political compromising in organizing the MNC internal networks to manage its global customers.

CONCLUDING REFLECTIONS

Our aim was to examine the relational dynamics in the MNCs as the interplay of organizing within internal networks and managing of the global customer relationships. We argued that the MNCs-as-networks view,

Table 2.   Behavioral Strategies for Political Compromising.

Behavioral Strategy	Actor	Level of Compromising
Personally mediated problem solving	Individual	Relationship
Collective responsibility taking	Unit	Relationship
Mandating customer interface	Corporate	Relationship
Selling oneself as internal trustee	Individual	Internal network
Project-based resource combining	Unit	Internal network
Sharing experiences for corporate narrative	Corporate	Internal network

combined with the research on supplier—customer relationship research, is appropriate for studying the orchestration processes in MNCs; the core activity is the creation of shared views. We suggest political compromising as the crucial boundary work and social practice at the structural and behavioral interfaces of the MNCs through which the challenges in customer relationship management can be solved. Political compromising manifests as concrete ways of behaving, named as behavioral strategies, activated in particular in the transition periods of the internal networks. Fundamentally, political compromising is a productive force of orchestration creating places for new thinking, convincing others of possible solutions, narrating the value of contradictions for the further development and telling stories of the common past to strengthen the shared social spaces. Rather than showing that there are certain beneficial outcomes of the political compromising, the emphasis was placed on the transforming and moving of the complex situations as orchestrated settings. Inspired by our observations, we propose three directions into which research on orchestration of network MNCs might develop.

Many theories on MNCs are based on the descriptions of activities of an efficient bureaucracy (cf. Meyer et al., 2011). We have a strong theoretical and practical legacy to see and apply the image of a bureaucratic organization with clear responsibilities, structures and positions of power (cf. Hodgson, 2004). However, we stand for the usefulness of flexible organizational and organizing forms in realization of MNC activities in relation to their global customers. MNCs, are, and should nowadays be, rather loosely coupled mycorrhizaes (Engeström, 2007), in which the objects of the organizational work are easily redefined, constantly escaping, and loosely associated webs of tasks. The key activities of orchestration in MNCs might best be directed towards the so called non-places (Augé & Howe, 2008), that is, spaces of transition and movement that are part of the organizational work but do not happen under the official organizational structure.

These might be the most typical of the spaces for political compromising in MNCs.

There is also a growing body of research that sees organizations to be constructed in everyday work by people (e.g., Lee & Williams, 2007; Santos & Eisenhardt, 2009). MNCs could be conceptualized as behavioral objects of organizational work that develops the MNC level operations. By analyzing the everyday practices within MNCs we would be able to capture the dynamism and processuality inherent in the activities of MNCs (cf. Feldman & Orlikowski, 2011). Actualization of organizational work can be investigated only if research takes place close to the practice itself. We should search for possibilities to observe and record the practice and allow for discussing and reflecting on it. Acknowledgment and understanding of the everyday practice at the individual and unit levels is a key to orchestrating MNCs at corporate level.

Finally, network MNCs are about knowledge. But they should not be primarily about superior knowledge as an outcome of MNC activity but about knowledge as learning to renew itself (cf. Williams & Lee, 2009). Knowledge as learning is a process in which experimentation, experience, reflection and interpretation are in interaction. Global customer relationships of MNCs provide a particularly interesting setting for the organizational and individual behaviors that relate to learning for renewal. We further encourage the future research to recognize the historical embeddedness of knowledge. Knowledge does not exist but it has a history, is produced and edited, and it "fights against and bites back" (cf. Autio, Sapienza, & Almeida, 2000). It is in the use of symbolic language, like speech, expressions of emotions and conceptual reasoning when people share and develop their opinions and worldviews. All these create corporate experiences and common understanding, which we argue to be the key activities in orchestrating network MNCs in relation to their global customers.

REFERENCES

Adenfelt, M., & Lagerström, K. (2006). Knowledge development and sharing in multinational corporations: The case of a centre of excellence and a transnational team. *International Business Review*, *15*(4), 381−400. doi:10.1016/j.ibusrev.2006.05.002

Aggarwal, R., Berrill, J., Hutson, E., & Kearney, C. (2011). What is a multinational corporation? classifying the degree of firm-level multinationality. *International Business Review*, *20*(5), 557−577. doi:10.1016/j.ibusrev.2010.11.004

Alajoutsijärvi, K., Mainela, T., Salminen, R., & Ulkuniemi, P. (2012). Perceived customer involvement and organizational design in project business. *Scandinavian Journal of Management, 28*(1), 77–89. doi:10.1016/j.scaman.2011.07.001

Andersson, U., Forsgren, M., & Holm, U. (2002). The strategic impact of external networks: Subsidiary performance and competence development in the multinational corporation. *Strategic Management Journal, 23*(11), 979–996. doi:10.1002/smj.267

Arthur, N. (2001). Using critical incidents to investigate cross-cultural transitions. *International Journal of Intercultural Relations, 25*(1), 41–53. doi:10.1016/S0147-1767(00)00041-9

Augé, M., & Howe, J. (2008). *Non-places*. London: Verso.

Autio, E., Sapienza, H., & Almeida, J. (2000). Effects of age at entry, knowledge intensity, and imitability on international growth. *Academy of Management Journal, 43*(5), 909–924. doi:10.2307/1556419

Bartlett, C. A., & Ghoshal, S. (2002). *Managing across borders: The transnational solution* (2nd ed.). Boston, MA: Harvard Business School Press.

Birkinshaw, J., Holm, U., Thilenius, P., & Arvidsson, N. (2000). Consequences of perception gaps in the headquarters–subsidiary relationship. *International Business Review, 9*(3), 321–344. doi:10.1016/S0969-5931(00)00004-4

Birkinshaw, J. M., & Morrison, A. J. (1995). Configurations of strategy and structure in subsidiaries of multinational corporations. *Journal of International Business Studies, 26*(4), 729–753.

Campbell, A. J. (2003). Creating customer knowledge competence: Managing customer relationship management programs strategically. *Industrial Marketing Management, 32*(5), 375–383. doi:10.1016/S0019-8501(03)00011-7

Crotty, M. (1998). *The foundations of social research: Meaning and perspective in the research process*. London: Sage.

Dörrenbächer, C., & Gammelgaard, J. (2010). Multinational corporations, inter-organizational networks and subsidiary charter removals. *Journal of World Business, 45*(3), 206–216. doi:10.1016/j.jwb.2009.12.001

Dörrenbächer, C., & Geppert, M. (2006). Micro-politics and conflicts in multinational corporations: Current debates, re-framing, and contributions of this special issue. *Journal of International Management, 12*(3), 251–265. doi:http://dx.doi.org/10.1016/j.intman.2006.07.001

Doz, Y. L., & Prahalad, C. K. (2005). Managing MNCs: A search for new paradigm. In S. Ghoshal & D. E. Westney (Eds.), *Organization theory and the multinational corporation* (2nd ed., pp. 20–44). New York, NY: Palgrave Macmillan.

Drazin, R., Glynn, M. A., & Kazanjian, R. K. (1999). Multilevel theorizing about creativity in organizations: A sensemaking perspective. *The Academy of Management Review, 24*(2), 286–307.

Dubois, A., & Gadde, L. (2002). Systematic combining: An abductive approach to case research. *Journal of Business Research, 55*(7), 553–560. doi:10.1016/S0148-2963(00)00195-8

Dwyer, F. R., Schurr, P. H., & Oh, S. (1987). Developing buyer–seller relationships. *Journal of Marketing, 51*(2), 11–27.

Engeström, Y. (2007). From communities of practice to mycorrhizae. In J. Hughes, N. Jewson, & L. Unwin (Eds.), *Communities of practice: Critical perspectives*. London: Routledge.

Eriksson, P., & Kovalainen, P. (2008). *Qualitative methods in business research.* London: Sage.

Evaristo, R., & van Fenema, P. C. (1999). A typology of project management: Emergence and evolution of new forms. *International Journal of Project Management, 17*(5), 275–281. doi:10.1016/S0263-7863(98)00041-6

Feldman, M. S., & Orlikowski, W. J. (2011). Theorizing practice and practicing theory. *Organization Science, 22*(5), 1240–1253. doi:10.1287/orsc.1100.0612

Ford, D., & Håkansson, H. (2006). The idea of business interaction. *The IMP Journal, 1*(1), 4–20. Retrieved from http://www.impjournal.org/

Forsgren, M. (2008). *Theories of the multinational firm: A multidimensional creature in the global economy.* Cheltenham, UK: Edward Elgar.

Forsgren, M., Holm, U., & Johanson, J. (2005). *Managing the embedded multinational: A business network view.* Cheltenham, UK: Edward Elgar.

Foss, K., Foss, N. J., & Nell, P. C. (2012). MNC organizational form and subsidiary motivation problems: Controlling intervention hazards in the network MNC. *Journal of International Management, 18*(3), 247–259. doi:http://dx.doi.org/10.1016/j.intman.2012.03.001

Galbraith, J. (2012). The evolution of enterprise organization designs. *Journal of Organization Design, 1*(2), 1–13.

Ghauri, P. (2004). Designing and conducting case studies in international business research. In R. Marschan-Piekkari & C. Welch (Eds.), *Handbook of qualitative research methods for international business* (pp. 109–124). Cheltenham, UK: Edward Elgar.

Ghoshal, S., & Bartlett, C. A. (1990). The multinational corporation as an interorganizational network. *Academy of Management Review, 15*(4), 603–625.

Ghoshal, S., Korine, H., & Szulanski, G. (1994). Interunit communication in multinational corporations. *Management Science, 40*(1), 96–110.

Giroud, A., & Scott-Kennel, J. (2009). MNE linkages in international business: A framework for analysis. *International Business Review, 18*(6), 555–566. doi:10.1016/j.ibusrev.2009.07.004

Guba, E. G., & Lincoln, Y. S. (1994). Competing paradigms in qualitative research. In N. K. Denzin & Y. S. Lincoln (Eds.), *Handbook of qualitative research* (pp. 105–117). Thousand Oaks, CA: Sage.

Gupta, A. K., & Govindarajan, V. (2000). Knowledge flows within multinational corporations. *Strategic Management Journal, 21*(4), 473–496.

Håkansson, H. (1982). *International marketing and purchasing of industrial goods.* Ringwood: Wiley.

Håkansson, H., Ford, D., Gadde, L., Snehota, I., & Waluszewski, A. (2009). *Business in networks.* Chichester: Wiley.

Håkansson, H., & Snehota, I. (1995). *Developing relationships in business networks.* London: Routledge.

Halinen, A., Medlin, C. J., & Törnroos, J. (2012). Time and process in business network research. *Industrial Marketing Management, 41*(2), 215–223. doi:10.1016/j.indmarman.2012.01.006

Harvey, M., Myers, M. B., & Novicevic, M. M. (2003). The managerial issues associated with global account management: A relational contract perspective. *The Journal of Management Development, 22*(1/2), 103–129.

Hedaa, L., & Törnroos, J. (2008). Understanding event-based business networks. *Time & Society, 17*(2–3), 319–348. doi:10.1177/0961463X08093427

Hedlund, G. (1986). The hypermodern MNC – A heterarchy? *Human Resource Management*, *25*(1), 9–35. doi:10.1002/hrm.3930250103

Hodgson, D. E. (2004). Project work: The legacy of bureaucratic control in the post-bureaucratic organisation. *Organization*, *11*(1), 81–100.

Holm, U., Johanson, J., & Thilenius, P. (1995). Headquarters' knowledge of subsidiary network contexts in the multinational corporation. *International Studies of Management & Organization*, *25*(1–2), 97–119.

Holm, U., & Sharma, D. D. (2006). Subsidiary marketing knowledge and strategic development of the multinational corporation. *Journal of International Management*, *12*(1), 47–66. doi:10.1016/j.intman.2005.11.001

Järvensivu, T., & Törnroos, J. (2010). Case study research with moderate constructionism: Conceptualization and practical illustration. *Industrial Marketing Management*, *39*(1), 100–108. doi:10.1016/j.indmarman.2008.05.005

Kamp, B. (2005). Formation and evolution of buyer–supplier relationships: Conceiving dynamism in actor composition of business networks. *Industrial Marketing Management*, *34*(7), 658–668. doi:10.1016/j.indmarman.2005.04.006

Kogut, B., & Zander, U. (1993). Knowledge of the firm and the evolutionary theory of the multinational corporation. *Journal of International Business Studies*, *24*(4), 625–645.

Langley, A. (1999). Strategies for theorizing from process data. *Academy of Management Review*, *24*(4), 691–710. doi:10.5465/AMR.1999.2553248

Lee, S. H., & Williams, C. (2007). Dispersed entrepreneurship within multinational corporations: A community perspective. *Journal of World Business*, *42*(4), 505–519. doi:10.1016/j.jwb.2007.08.001

Luo, Y. (2001). Determinants of local responsiveness: Perspectives from foreign subsidiaries in an emerging market. *Journal of Management*, *27*(4), 451–477. doi:10.1016/S0149-2063(01)00103-9

Luo, Y. (2002). Organizational dynamics and global integration: A perspective from subsidiary managers. *Journal of International Management*, *8*(2), 189–215. doi:10.1016/S1075-4253(02)00053-4

Manev, I. M. (2003). The managerial network in a multinational enterprise and the resource profiles of subsidiaries. *Journal of International Management*, *9*(2), 133–151. doi:10.1016/S1075-4253(03)00009-7

Marschan-Piekkari, R., & Welch, C. (2004). Qualitative research methods in international business: The state of the art. In R. Marschan-Piekkari & C. Welch (Eds.), *Handbook of qualitative research methods for international business* (pp. 5–24). Cheltenham, UK: Edward Elgar.

Meyer, K. E., Mudambi, R., & Narula, R. (2011). Multinational enterprises and local contexts: The opportunities and challenges of multiple embeddedness. *Journal of Management Studies*, *48*(2), 235–252. doi:10.1111/j.1467-6486.2010.00968.x

Millman, T. F. (1996). Global key account management and systems selling. *International Business Review*, *5*(6), 631–645. doi:10.1016/S0969-5931(96)00031-5

Mintzberg, H. (1985). The organization as political arena. *Journal of Management Studies*, *22*(2), 133–154. doi:10.1111/j.1467-6486.1985.tb00069.x

Möller, K. (2010). Sense-making and agenda construction in emerging business networks – How to direct radical innovation. *Industrial Marketing Management*, *39*(3), 361–371. doi:10.1016/j.indmarman.2009.03.014

Möller, K., & Halinen, A. (1999). Business relationships and networks: Managerial challenge of network era. *Industrial Marketing Management, 28*(5), 413–427. doi:10.1016/S0019-8501(99)00086-3

Möller, K., & Rajala, A. (1999). Organizing marketing in industrial high-tech firms: The role of internal marketing relationships. *Industrial Marketing Management, 28*(5), 521–535. doi:10.1016/S0019-8501(99)00059-0

Montgomery, D. B., & Yip, G. S. (2000). The challenge of global customer management. *Marketing Management, 9*(4), 22–29.

Nell, P. C., Ambos, B., & Schlegelmilch, B. B. (2011). The MNC as an externally embedded organization: An investigation of embeddedness overlap in local subsidiary networks. *Journal of World Business, 46*(4), 497–505. doi:10.1016/j.jwb.2010.10.010

Nohria, N., & Ghoshal, S. (1997). *The differentiated network: Organizing multinational corporations for value creation.* San Francisco, CA: Jossey-Bass.

Noorderhaven, N., & Harzing, A. (2009). Knowledge-sharing and social interaction within MNEs. *Journal of International Business Studies, 40*(5), 719–741. doi:10.1057/jibs.2008.106

Piekkari, R., & Welch, C. (2010). The human dimension in multinational management: A way forward. *Scandinavian Journal of Management, 26*(4), 467–476. doi:10.1016/j.scaman.2010.09.008

Ritter, T. (1999). The networking company: Antecedents for coping with relationships and networks effectively. *Industrial Marketing Management, 28*(5), 467–479. doi:10.1016/S0019-8501(99)00075-9

Ritter, T., & Gemünden, H. G. (2003). Interorganizational relationships and networks: An overview. *Journal of Business Research, 56*(9), 691–697. doi:10.1016/S0148-2963(01)00254-5

Ritter, T., Wilkinson, I. F., & Johnston, W. J. (2004). Managing in complex business networks. *Industrial Marketing Management, 33*(3), 175–183. doi:10.1016/j.indmarman.2003.10.016

Santos, F. M., & Eisenhardt, K. M. (2009). Constructing markets and shaping boundaries: Entrepreneurial power in nascent fields. *Academy of Management Journal, 52*(4), 643–671. doi:10.5465/AMJ.2009.43669892

Schurr, P. H. (2007). Buyer–seller relationship development episodes: Theories and methods. *Journal of Business & Industrial Marketing, 22*(3), 161–170.

Tidström, A., & Hagberg-Andersson, Å. (2012). Critical events in time and space when cooperation turns into competition in business relationships. *Industrial Marketing Management, 41*(2), 333–343. doi:10.1016/j.indmarman.2012.01.005

Vahlne, J., Schweizer, R., & Johanson, J. (2012). Overcoming the liability of outsidership – The challenge of HQ of the global firm. *Journal of International Management, 18*(3), 224–232. doi:10.1016/j.intman.2012.04.002

Weick, K. E. (1979). *The social psychology of organizing* (2nd ed.). New York, NY: Random House.

Williams, C., & Lee, S. H. (2009). International management, political arena and dispersed entrepreneurship in the MNC. *Journal of World Business, 44*(3), 287–299. doi:10.1016/j.jwb.2008.11.008

Williams, C., & Lee, S. H. (2011). Political heterarchy and dispersed entrepreneurship in the MNC. *Journal of Management Studies, 48*(6), 1243–1268. doi:10.1111/j.1467-6486.2010.00996.x

Wilson, D. (1995). An integrated model of buyer–seller relationships. *Journal of the Academy of Marketing Science, 23*(4), 335–345. Retrieved from http://www.springerlink.com/content/k281456kgnj13452/

Wilson, K., & Weilbaker, D. (2004). Global account management: A literature based conceptual model. *Mid-American Journal of Business, 19*(1), 13–21.

Yamin, M., & Forsgren, M. (2006). Hymer's analysis of the multinational organization: Power retention and the demise of the federative MNE. *International Business Review, 15*(2), 166–179. doi:10.1016/j.ibusrev.2005.07.006

Young, R. B., & Javalgi, R. G. (2007). International marketing research: A global project management perspective. *Business Horizons, 50*(2), 113–122.

Zalan, T., & Lewis, G. (2004). Writing about methods in qualitatitve research: Towards a more transparent approach. In R. Marschan-Piekkari & C. Welch (Eds.), *Handbook of qualitative research methods for international business* (pp. 507–528). Cheltenham: Edward Elgar.

TO ORCHESTRATE MNC INTRA-FIRM RELATIONSHIPS, ONE NEEDS TO UNDERSTAND THEM

Snejina Michailova and Smita Paul

ABSTRACT

For over four decades, IB scholars have been conceptualizing and empirically examining the organizational structure of the multinational corporation (MNC) without really placing relationships at the center of attention. It therefore remains unclear what characterizes those relationships beyond subunits' roles, motivation, or control mechanisms. Relationship as a term has often been used but rarely defined in the IB literature on intra-firm networks. We develop arguments that position such relationships as the focal unit of analysis. We extend current IB literature to examine in detail the nature and dynamics of relationships in MNCs by borrowing insights from Industrial Marketing and Purchasing research, which focuses on the relational nature and dynamics of interactions between actors. We offer a theoretical framework and develop a conceptual model that brings to the fore the multiplexity and temporality of relationships in MNCs. We also argue that intra-MNC network relationships can be seen as an evolving process and advocate for shifting away from variance-based and typological views toward a process view

Orchestration of the Global Network Organization
Advances in International Management, Volume 27, 377–402
ISSN: 1571-5027/doi:10.1108/S1571-502720140000027006

*for examining relationships. Theoretically, understanding what charac-
terizes the nature of MNC intra-firm relationships and what processes
contribute to structuring them provides important insights into the global
configuration of the MNC and the required organizational design
mechanisms needed for MNC existence and resilience. The study is
timely and practically relevant in the sense that considering intra-firm
relationships deserves even more attention in the current global economic
environment when accessing external resources becomes costly and/or
inefficient.*

Keywords: MNC; intra-firm relationships; multiplexity; temporality;
process view

INTRODUCTION

Our study is positioned within the scholarly conversation on multinational
corporation (MNC) design. We argue for the need to examine relationships
between subunits in the MNC not as secondary to other issues, but as
the focal unit of analysis and suggest ways of how this can be done. True
to the context of our study, the MNC, in the center of our attention are
relationships between headquarters (HQ) and subsidiaries as well as those
between peer subsidiaries. Along the lines suggested by Alvesson and
Sandberg (2011, 2013), we problematize the fact that the past focus of prevailing International Business (IB) literature has not interrogated relationships as the primary focus of interest. We also will argue that relationships
cannot be orchestrated well as their essence and dynamics are not well
understood (see also Forsgren, Holm, & Johanson, 2005; Håkansson &
Snehota, 1995).

For over four decades, IB scholars have been conceptualizing and
empirically examining the organizational structure of the MNC without
really placing relationships at the center of attention. It therefore remains
unclear what characterizes those relationships beyond subunits' roles, motivation or control mechanisms. Also, while relationships between MNC
units have been viewed as master/servant, principle/agent, and contractual
relationships, there could be other forms awaiting discovery. Neither do we
have a thorough understanding of how relationships are dynamic, specifically how their structure changes over time. We are missing a process view

on intra-firm MNC relationships. This hampers the understanding of the complexity of the phenomenon and grasping what makes it distinctive from other related IB phenomena (see Devinney, Pedersen, & Tihanyi, 2010).

This state of affairs is puzzling given two circumstances: (1) that relationships between MNC subunits are of vital importance regardless of the difference between earlier (more hierarchical) and recent (more heterarchical) conceptualizations of the MNC and (2) that relationships can be seen as the core of the organizational design of the MNC and a key mechanism for adding value to the MNC. It is unjustified that research on relationships remains fragmented and findings are difficult to compare or aggregate for a more nuanced understanding.

We offer two theoretical contributions. First, we propose a conceptual model that advances current thinking about MNC intra-firm relationships by bringing the key concepts of multiplexity and temporality to the fore. In order to do so, we combine the theoretical lenses of IB and Industrial Marketing and Purchasing (IMP). We choose IMP as it focuses on the relational nature of interactions between actors and authentically integrates the notion of temporality into conceptual and empirical examinations. Second, we shift from variance-based and typological views to a process perspective on relationships. Understanding what processes contribute to structuring MNC intra-firm relationships can provide theoretical insights into the global configuration of the MNC and the required organizational design mechanisms needed for MNC existence and resilience. Our study is timely and practically relevant in the sense that considering intra-firm relationships deserves even more attention in the current global economic environment when accessing external resources becomes costly and/or inefficient.

Our arguments unfold in the following way. In the next section, we provide a brief overview of existing research on MNC organizational design. We use the review as a base to conceptually model our key notions and how they are linked. We then define and elaborate on the three notions — intra-firm relationships, multiplexity, and temporality — that are positioned centrally in our contribution. This is followed by explaining the rationale behind combining insights from IB and IMP to examine intra-firm relationships. In particular, we elaborate on the proximity and the compatibility of the two streams of literature. The subsequent section argues for the appropriateness and the advantages of utilizing a process view on relationships. We finish by summarizing our key arguments and contributions and suggesting directions for future research.

BACKGROUND OF THE STUDY: BRIEF OVERVIEW OF RESEARCH ON MNC ORGANIZATIONAL DESIGN

In order to ascertain the current conceptualizations of the relationship as such in IB and IMP literature, we conducted a systematic literature review to establish the basis for combining relevant concepts and the development of the conceptual model. Our literature search took place in three stages. First we conducted a wider systematic search using the targeted search string of "relationship*" AND "time" AND "intra" within five IB journals (*International Business Review, Journal of International Business Studies, Journal of International Management, Journal of World Business*, and *Management International Review*). As the result was humble, we extended the search to include management journals (*Academy of Management Journal, Academy of Management Review, Administrative Science Quarterly, California Management Review, Harvard Business Review, Journal of Management, Journal of Management Studies, Journal of Organizational Behavior, Long Range Planning, Management Science, MIT Sloan Management Review, Organizational Science, Strategic Management Journal*, and *Organizational Dynamics*). This resulted in 82 articles that focus on relationships and their dynamic nature. We studied carefully these articles to derive our key concepts. Second, we conducted a more focused search of IMP and IMP-related journals (*Industrial Marketing and Management, Journal of Business and Industrial Marketing, Journal of Marketing Management, Journal of Marketing Research*, and *Journal of Supply Chain Management*) and captured over 300 articles which we analyzed further to determine the extent to which they engage with these concepts.

Relationships as a term has often been used but rarely defined in IB literature (Hohenthal, Johanson, & Johanson, 2014), especially in the case of intra-firm networks. From our systematic review of IB network literature, we find that this is likely to be due to two reasons. First, most IB scholars equate relationships to the particular resource being studied (e.g., knowledge in knowledge transfer between parties). Second, relationships between actors are often studied secondary to other issues, such as the actors themselves or outcomes of relationships (e.g., firm performance).

The organizational structure of MNC has been traditionally conceptualized as a hierarchy with formal lines of control and communication (Ambos & Mahnke, 2010; O'Donnell, 2000). Inherent in this conceptualization is that HQs hold the necessary resources to coordinate and command subordinate business units in order to achieve desired overall organizational outcomes. However, MNC structure has evolved over time as internal and external operating environments increased in size, complexity, and ambiguity (Forsgren, 2013; Ghoshal & Bartlett, 1990).

Hedlund's (1986, 1994, 1999) heterarchical model of the MNC and Zander and Mathews' (2010) elaboration on it offer a more egalitarian view in light of the problems MNCs were having to control locally embedded foreign subsidiaries with centralization strategies. Some MNCs were moving toward a geocentric model where there is collaborative decision-making between HQ and subsidiaries (Harzing & Van Ruysseveldt, 2003; Perlmutter, 1969) and where relationships between peer subsidiaries are as important as the HQ/subsidiary relationships. As a result, the MNC was viewed as a transnational firm (Bartlett & Ghoshal, 1989), inter-organizational network (Ghoshal & Bartlett, 1990), and differentiated network (Nohria & Ghoshal, 1997). The transnational and inter-organizational model characterizes the MNC as an interdependent network with diffused expertise and subsidiaries as strategic units (Harzing, 2000). Within IB literature, an established stream of research that utilizes these conceptualizations of networked MNCs predominantly examines the strategic roles of subsidiaries as they hold specialized knowledge and capabilities. Others concentrate on the role of subsidiaries as a relevant unit of analysis (Andersson & Forsgren, 2000; Birkinshaw & Morrison, 1995), as sources of knowledge (Michailova & Mustaffa, 2012), or centers of excellence (Holm & Pedersen, 2000; Paterson & Brock, 2002).

Egelhoff (2010) argues for a more fine-grained understanding of the contemporary heterarchical MNC, pointing out that there are two views on the heterarchical MNC that researchers seldom explicate. One follows Hedlund's (1986), Bartlett and Ghoshal's (1989), and Nohria and Ghoshal's (1997) perspective of the heterarchy as a superior organizational structure and another follows Andersson, Forsgren, and Holm's (2002) conceptualization of the MNC as a business network. Following Egelhoff's (2010) line of reasoning, the business network perspective is inclusive of both hierarchical and heterarchical design and so, further research needs to explicate when and where the heterarchical MNC structure is relevant and more useful than other structures.

There are two notions that appear randomly and are mentioned, although only in passing, in the IB literature on intra-firm relationships — multiplexity and relationships changing over time. We examine them next, but already here we emphasize that because relationships are rarely the focal unit of analysis, researchers do not analyze them in-depth and neither do they integrate the two notions within MNC relationship research. In fact, more often than not, they are only mentioned as potential future research avenues. A notable exception is the work by Ferriani, Fonti, and Corrado (2013) who, on the basis of their longitudinal research, conclude that relationships in multiplex networks evolve over time, an insight that combines multiplexity and temporality in relationships. This is an issue we examine next.

INTRA-FIRM RELATIONSHIPS, MULTIPLEXITY, AND TEMPORALITY

We define intra-firm relationships as a series of complex interactions that evolve over time between MNC subunits, which have the primary aim of pursuing an activity and/or exchanging or transforming a resource. There are two central elements in this definition. First, relationships are *multiplex* in that they comprise of multiple co-existing sub-relationships that may differ in content and type. Sub-relationships can be economic or social, formal or informal, old or new, and last longer or shorter time. Relationships that enjoy high multiplexity may be more resilient. Research that only examines one type of sub-relationship does not take into account the existence or influence of other, sometimes hidden, existing sub-relationships. Doing so would bring us closer to understanding the true complex nature of MNC subunit relationships. Second, relationships are dynamic in the sense that sub-relationships can differ in *temporality* — they may be new or established, raise or decline. Sub-relationships are in a constant state of flux: growing, lapsing into latency, or terminating. Relationships may change over time due to critical events that subunits experience at their level, such as the acquisition and integration of a new subsidiary (Tran, Mahnke, & Ambos, 2010) and at the MNC level, such as de-internationalization processes (Turcan, 2013). Understanding how relationships change over time is important, as each phase may be more complex than initially thought. Assessing the value of a relationship may not be based on continuous growth. For example, termination itself may be planned (e.g., the end of a contractual agreement), an acceptance of an error (e.g., a contractual agreement gone sour) or a consequence of sudden external changes (war or natural disaster in the host country). We therefore suggest that the relationship is a process that changes over time and is affected by critical events.

In order to illustrate our conceptualizations, we integrate examples from Bouteiller, Evans, and Assen's (2004) case of La Compagnie Générale des

Eaux. Formed in 1853, it is the precursor to a number of successful MNCs, including Veolia Environnement and VINCI. Although originally not an MNC, its expansion story serves to illuminate the issues around the increasing complexity of a large networked company. A large expansion into diverse business activities between 1980 and 1996 serves as the background to the illustrative examples we use. This serves as a focus on the issues inherent to the increasing complexity of intra-firm network relationships and highlights our key notions of multiplexity and temporality.

Multiplexity

The majority of IB articles see relationships as differing in content. This is because the key outcome of such relationships is value-addition — to the subunits and the MNC as a whole. Tran et al. (2010) simply argue that the quality and quantity of resources from global HQ affect the performance of the receiving subsidiary. This argument is also offered in research that looks at inter-organizational network linkages (Giroud & Scott-Kennel, 2009). However, Ciabuschi, Martín Martín, and Ståhl (2010) point out that HQ/subsidiary relationships are multifaceted — there are a number of interactions that differ in content and are therefore *multiplex*. In essence, relationships between organizations (and actors) encapsulate multiple types of sub-relationships or ties (Shipilov & Li, 2012). HQs are able to allocate decision-making rights and resources to subsidiaries for successful knowledge and innovation transfer to occur (Ciabuschi et al., 2010).

Subsidiary/HQ relationships can also differ in content in regard to whether the interactions are formal or informal (Chiao & Ying, 2013). In addition, relationships can encompass social and economic ties (Ferriani et al., 2013) and be a mix of new and old ties (Ahuja, Soda, & Zaheer, 2012). Provan, Fish, and Sydow (2007) go further by highlighting that multiplexity is a better predictor of relationship strength and durability as a dissolution of a tie (as a sub-relationship) does not necessarily amount to the dissolution of a relationship. However, IB literature does not explicitly consider the specific factors that influence the formation, persistence, dissolution, and differing content of subunit relationships within MNC networks (Ahuja et al., 2012). We argue that it is important to do so, specifically in the MNC context, because of the variety of units comprising the MNC and hence, the richness of relationships between them. In more practical terms, appreciating the multiplex content of MNC intra-firm relationships can assist MNCs to structure and orchestrate these relationships in an optimal manner.

Pre WWI, La Compagnie Générale des Eaux's expansion policy was based on the horizontal integration of a number of local competing firms. Originally in potable water treatment and distribution, the company invested in a number of related spin-off acquisitions, such as hydraulic heating and factory construction. Into the early 1980s, La Compagnie Générale des Eaux followed an aggressive diversification expansion policy, such as entering the health market. However, this increasing complexity of business activities within a networked company led to "sources of contradiction and conflict among redundant business units in certain professions or territories" (Bouteiller et al., 2004, p. 9).

As the intra-firm network expanded, the role of the HQ moved away from operational responsibility toward administrative tasks. The relationship between the HQ and subsidiaries became multiplex and included activities such as managing information systems, cash-flow management, and communication. Interdependencies existed within these streams of activities, adding to our argument that these are sub-relationships that cannot be simply aggregated. An obvious emergent property of the overall relationship would be that a well-managed information system would impact on the quality of the communication and in-deed cash-flow management issues.

A clear example is Bouteiller et al.'s (2004) explanation of a specific case related to corporate restructuring. In the SAS case, La Compagnie Générale des Eaux recognized the problems of internal competition within its local subsidiaries. They grouped subsidiaries and created a "multi activity" agency to achieve network coherence and address key business activities – transport and cleanliness. Although the restructuring was ultimately a failure as the agency had to defer important decisions to the regional management centers, it can be seen that the company attempted to address the issues of the differing nature of intra-firm relationships and how it affected the overall nature of the company network structure.

Temporality

One way in which the IB literature addresses the dynamic nature of relationships between subunits is to highlight the dyadic nature of relationships. HQ/subsidiary relationships are understood mainly as a "mixed motive" pairing of two actors (i.e., MNC subunits), whereby any transfer of resource is affected by the willingness and ability of the partner to share and absorb that resource (Yamin, Tsai, & Holm, 2011; Yang, Mudambi, & Meyer, 2008). In this case, the dyad is conceptualized as the basic component within a business network. A second theme is the consideration of prior interactions on current relationships (Hohenthal et al., 2014). Subsidiaries develop "firm-specific competencies [that] originate from ongoing interactions in embedded relationships" (Andersson & Forsgren, 2000, p. 346). Therefore prior interactions influence the quality of the current relationship (Björkman, Barner-Rasmussen, & Li, 2004) and the probability of forming future relationships (Andersson & Forsgren, 2000; Foss & Pedersen, 2002). At the organizational level, prior interactions build cumulative relational content that can be conceptualized as network memory (Ahuja et al., 2012). In other words, current networks contain memories of past interactions. This line of thinking adds to the argument that subunit relationships are a process that evolves over time.

The two ways in which IB research addresses relationship processes between subunits that we just described lend credence to the significance of time. Not directly discussed in the literature however is the issue of how sub-relationships at different stages of development (e.g., formation, growth or decline) exist within a relationship process as a whole. Some IB literature does consider the issue of time and how relationships are not static. For instance, timing of resources transfer affects the outcome of the relationship and whether future relationships would be likely (Tran et al., 2010). The age of the subunits and their relationship also are found to affect the quality and ease of resource transfer. For example, older subsidiaries are likely to create more value for the MNC as they have developed cumulative relational capital than newer subsidiaries (Rabbiosi & Santangelo, 2013) but also experience relational capital decay (Alnuaimi, Singh, & George, 2012). Nevertheless, these are only initial attempts to look more closely into the temporality issue. We agree with Tsai (2000) that further research on the dynamic and evolving nature of intra-organizational relationships is needed.

More relevant to the issue of time is the discussion on time-bound dynamics of organizational structure (Phelps, Adams, & Bessant, 2007; Volberda & Lewin, 2003). The life cycle concept offers some categorizations of the different trajectories of network relationships but falters in integrating temporality and a process view of relationships. The life cycle concept offers a form of comparative statics (Pettigrew, Woodman, & Cameron, 2001) and views time as a form of linear progression. In reality, interactions are "loaded with the past and linked to the future"

(Chou & Zolkiewski, 2012, p. 248), influenced by critical events and can experience reactivation, such as a return from declining to a growth state (Zerbini & Castaldo, 2007).

To return to our illustrative case, the temporal aspect of intra-firm relationships is evident in Bouteiller et al.'s (2004) further explanation of particular projects undertaken by subsidiaries. They describe the issues surrounding a particular project – whereby a contract was offered to design and run a modern water treatment plant. Three subsidiaries worked together to coordinate a joint project that won the contract and further sub-contractor work was filled by sister subsidiaries. The selection of such subsidiaries, although still subordinate to price competitiveness, was based on previous "good understanding" between individuals. The specific relationship established was influenced by prior interactions and knowledge of interactions with other subsidiaries.

It becomes clear from the above analysis that researchers only indirectly offer an understanding of the different trajectories that relationships may take. As explained earlier, a key theme has been the emphasis on prior interactions and how they specifically influence the formation of relationships. We take this observation further and contend that if prior interactions can build relational capital before a new formal relationship between MNC subunits starts, the age of the relationships becomes highly relevant. For example, the death of a relationship between subunits may take longer as there is a cumulative "buffer" of good will developed during prior interactions that needs to be negated.

A cautionary note is warranted here. A number of IB researchers use social capital and social network theory concepts to examine relationships in MNCs (Inkpen & Tsang, 2005; Nahapiet & Ghoshal, 1998). We take Kostova and Roth's (2003) argument that MNCs lack the ability to establish (socially based) network closure through creating a strong shared set of values because spatial, cultural, and language barriers give limited opportunities for all MNC employees to interact and develop social capital as a public good. The relationship structure of subunits can be considered more transactional in nature (Hawkins, Wittmann, & Beyerlein, 2008). As a result, integrating concepts of trust and shared values is omitted from our discussion. Furthermore, IB scholars who use social network theory concepts rely on the problematic notion of interaction frequency to measure relationship strength, which does not take into account issues such as relationship reactivation (Levin, Walter, & Murnighan, 2008, 2011). Using "density" for measuring the "tightness" of relationships is problematic as it does not explicate its attributes and any data on the number of actors and relationships is estimated by the parties involved (Forsgren et al., 2005).

The drawback of IB studies that apply concepts as the ones we discussed so far is that they often "source" rather than genuinely "borrow" them from other fields and disciplines. To "borrow" concepts from one discipline and use in another relates to authentically examining whether both fields have theoretical fit − that is they have underlying assumptions that are similar enough for borrowing to occur but dissimilar enough for theoretical extensions and deeper understanding to arise (Okhuysen & Bonardi, 2011). We try to overcome the superficial and dangerous path of just sourcing and using concepts developed outside of IB research and borrow in a disciplined and systematic manner. In the next section, we look to the related research field of IMP, as this field focuses on network relationships as the unit of analysis. In doing so, we extend concepts related to the dynamic nature of intra-firm MNC subunit relationships. We start by establishing the appropriateness of combining IB and IMP.

COMBINING IB AND IMP: DIMENSIONS OF PROXIMITY AND COMPATIBILITY

Given that we conceptualize the MNC as a network of subunit relationships and the lack of focus and sophistication in extant IB research on such relationships, we borrow from IMP literature to understand in more detail the nature of these relationships. IMP scholars authentically integrate a business network perspective to examine relationships (Möller, 2013). Different from IB scholars, they offer a far more fine-grained understanding of the nature of relationships in a network (multiplexity) and utilize a process view to understand relationships over time (temporality).

It is possible to combine theoretical lenses from IB and IMP because they both share and differ in dimensions for opportunities for extension and further theorizing to be employed (Okhuysen & Bonardi, 2011). Proximity refers to "the conceptual distance that exists between the phenomena that the lenses address in their original conception" (Okhuysen & Bonardi, 2011, p. 7). This can be extended to empirical examinations that describe the "domain, goals and content of the theory or school" (Möller, 2013, p. 3). The degree of compatibility refers to how theories "rely on similar or dissimilar [...] properties in the development of their explanations" (Okhuysen & Bonardi, 2011, p. 7). This is extended to the idea of congruence or the "permeability of paradigmatic boundaries" and describes "the theory's underlying meta-theoretical assumptions" (Möller, 2013, p. 7). Meta-theoretical assumptions can be examined by considering the disciplinary background, ontological views of relevant concepts, context of the focal phenomena, epistemological views, and utilized methodologies.

In Table 1, we outline the differences in the business network perspective in IB and IMP literature categorized by dimensions for proximity and

Table 1.   Business Network Perspective in IB and IMP Literature.

Dimensions of proximity and compatibility	IB	IMP
Primary goals and empirical domain	– Internationalization and internalization advantages and processes. Relationships are intra- and inter-organizational. – *Empirical domains*: FDI, MNC subsidiaries, and HQ.	– Relationship marketing and business network perspective on markets, intra- and inter-organizational relationships. – *Empirical domains*: interactive and service marketing and channel systems research.
Disciplinary background	– Classical economics, neo-classical economics, sociology.	– Political science, neo-classical economics, sociology.
Epistemological view and common methodologies	– *Multidisciplinary*: large range of research epistemologies and methodologies (from post-positivist to interpretivist). – Quantitative (e.g., statistical modeling) and qualitative methods (e.g., interviews) are common.	– *Relationship management*: reductionist, uses techniques such as structural equation modeling, casual modeling frameworks. – *Business network perspective*: qualitative case analysis.
Ontological assumptions of key concepts: – Relationships – Multiplexity – Temporality	– *Relationships*: multiple contexts, conduit for resource transfer, predominantly individual level of analysis. – *Multiplexity*: relationships differ in content. – *Temporality*: control variable, time is chronological, prior interactions of partners influence future interactions.	– *Relationships*: Refined conceptualizations from the business network perspective. Relationships are reciprocal, value-adding, dyadic/triadic and embedded, organizational and individual level of analysis. – *Multiplexity*: Relationship differences in content, substance, and temporality. – *Temporality*: Linked to networks as a process, time can be chronological or kairological; prior interactions influence future interactions.

compatibility. On this basis, we demonstrate how it is appropriate for IB to borrow insights from IMP to develop a more nuanced viewpoint on inter-firm network relationships.

As shown in Table 1, two key organizational processes that are examined in IB using the business network perspective are internationalization and internalization (Vahlne & Johanson, 2013). IB is primarily a phenomenon-driven research area (Doz, 2011) and so, processes are studied in a variety of contexts. For example, FDI research uses country-level and industry-level data (Werner, 2002), internationalization research looks at "born-globals" (Madsen & Servais, 1997) and network focused MNC research examines the embeddedness of subsidiaries in local markets (Andersson, Forsgren, & Holm, 2007; Gammelgaard, McDonald, Stephan, Tüselmann, & Dörrenbächer, 2012; O'Donnell, 2000; Santangelo, 2012). The disciplinary background draws primarily from neo-classical economics and sociology and uses theories such as transaction cost economics (Ghoshal & Moran, 1996) and social capital and social network theory.

In IMP, scholars also examine relationships at different levels of analysis but are more network theory focused (Möller, 2013). Business networks are primarily examined in relation to buyer–seller interaction and industrial networks (Choi & Wu, 2009; Johnsen & Ford, 2008; Kamp, 2005; Kim, Choi, Yan, & Dooley, 2011; Roseira, Brito, & Ford, 2013). Möller (2013) highlights two areas in IMP – the dominant view of relationship marketing (RM) and the business network perspective (BN). The theoretical goals of RM are determining the antecedents, elements, and outcomes of dyadic relationships. While the BN literature utilizes the network perspective on inter- and intra-organizational relationships and markets to understand how they evolve. The managerial goals of RM are to enhance marketing efficiency and to optimize the value of customer portfolios. In contrast, the BN literature aims at understanding actor relationships within a network for more effective management processes. Similar to IB, IMP shares an eclectic disciplinary background. RM is often phenomena-driven and behavioral RM utilizes social exchange theory with some use of transaction cost economics. BN similarly is influenced by social exchange theory, transaction cost economics, and resource dependence theory.

The multidisciplinarity of IB as a field and the multiplicity of contexts it examines is reflected in the variety of research epistemologies and methodologies applied in the field. At the organizational and country-level post-positivist and quantitative methodologies are commonly used, with regression models performed on FDI data and surveys being a prominent example. At the individual and group level, such as employees and projects, subjective perceptions are often examined and so epistemologies tend to be interpretivist and methodologies are primarily qualitative. In IMP, Möller (2013) argues that RM and channels research tend to be reductionist and reliant on methods such as structural equation modeling and casual modeling frameworks. However, research that focuses on networks, such as markets-as-networks and focal network research, use qualitative case analysis, as they are more interested in developing in-depth understanding of the network phenomena they examine.

More important yet are the ontological assumptions behind multiplexity and temporality in the two fields (see Table 1). In IB literature, there is a varied understanding of relationships from a number of different contexts (Chiao & Ying, 2013). There is no similar research stream that echoes the focus of IMP's research areas of RM and BN. Relationships are often conceptualized as a conduit for resources transfer or sharing, such as knowledge (Brass, Galaskiewicz, Greve, & Tsai, 2004) and examined at the individual level, such as between employees (Barner-Rasmussen & Björkman, 2007; Chow & Chan, 2008). As a result, the role of trust and shared perspective in the willingness for common use of resources is often examined (Li, 2005; Phelps, Heidl, & Wadhwa, 2012). Relationships are typically seen in terms of dyads, embedded in networks and measured in terms of levels of interaction (Huggins, Johnston, & Thompson, 2012; Maurer, Bartsch, & Ebers, 2011). Relationships are path-dependent and although not explicitly stated, they are mere aggregates of sub-relationships that differ in content/substance, such as between formal and informal relationships (Chiao & Ying, 2013). In IB, the majority of studies on relationships do not explicitly consider multiplexity beyond the simple observation that relationships may differ in content or substance. In contrast to IB, the concept of multiplexity is better developed and explored explicitly in IMP. Understanding multiplex relationships is part of the focus on "understanding and predicting patterns of interactions and relationships among network members" (Ansari, Koenigsberg, & Stahl, 2011, p. 713).

In IMP, the BN research stream is more refined than in IB. Relationships are treated as reciprocal and multiplex since a variety of resources are exchanged through different actors, such as individuals, firms, and government. Although traditionally BN research was primarily on inter-organizational networks within industries, more recent research focuses on the organizational level. Furthermore, following Ghoshal and Bartlett's (1990) argument that MNCs can be structured similarly to inter-organizational networks, we find that recent BN research on relationships and networks offers insights at the organizational level. Relationship multiplexity is a more adequate measure of total relationship strength as the former "increases the number of ways one can reciprocate favors" (Ansari et al., 2011, p. 714). Relationships are value-adding through accessing, controlling or transforming resources. They can be dyadic or triadic (Iacobucci & Hopkins, 1992; Pilbeam, Alvarez, & Wilson, 2012; Roseira, Brito, & Henneberg, 2010), are embedded in networks, and are influenced by past interactions (Corsaro & Snehota, 2012; Wilkinson & Young, 2013). Originally, relationships were perceived as dyads (Håkansson & Snehota, 1995; Iacobucci & Hopkins, 1992), but research on supply chain networks argues that triads more accurately reflect network phenomena (Choi & Wu, 2009; Havila, Johanson, & Thilenius, 2004). These refined conceptualizations have unfortunately so far not risen to a similar level of appreciation in IB literature although it has been used in inter-organizational network studies (Bergenholtz & Waldstrøm, 2011; Ferriani et al., 2013; Phelps et al., 2012). Of note in IB is Forsgren et al.'s (2005) diagramming of the basic component of a networked MNC as one type of triad — with the HQs situated on top and controlling/influencing two subsidiaries below, with all three experiencing dependencies. We firmly believe that the role of HQ is as such, but put forward that not all triads within a networked MNC may involve the HQ. Some triads, especially given that subsidiaries may be "centers of excellence," may just consist of subsidiaries.

As we pointed out in Table 1, time is often demoted to a control variable within IB literature on relationships (Reeb, Sakakibara, & Mahmood, 2012). Although not explicated prominently, time does influence the process of relationships (Alnuaimi et al., 2012; Gammelgaard et al., 2012). Some scholars borrow from the life cycle concept but their studies suffer from problems of bracketing time in the sense that the process of relationships is often reduced to comparative statics (Langley, Smallman, Tsoukas, & Van de Ven, 2013). Furthermore, time is often seen as chronological. This, we argue, is problematic as purely chronological time does not emphasize critical events within a specific process (Medlin, 2004; Tidström & Åhman, 2006). For example, Levin et al. (2011) sustain that dormant strong relationships can be reactivated quickly for a critical event, such as gathering resources for a current organizational project. Forsgren et al. (2005) similarly argue that subunit relationships within a networked MNC are based on historical events. They add that such relationships are in a constant state of stability and change. Whilst the overall MNC network structure has continuity, relationships are constantly changing through processes of termination, establishment, and business activities. Temporality is taken more seriously in IMP research than in IB as time is seen as kairological (i.e., segmented by critical events) and relationships are seen as a process. This has resulted in a research stream that aims to develop theories to inform their understanding of time in business networks as business network change (Edvardsson & Strandvik, 2009; Halinen, Medlin, & Törnroos, 2012; Halinen, Salmi, & Havila, 1999; Peters, Vanharanta, Pressey, & Johnston, 2012).

The IMP literature concludes that relationships success is not reliant on constant growth – the end of a relationship is inevitable in some cases and therefore should be a managed process (Havila & Medlin, 2012; Havila & Salmi, 2000; Havila & Wilkinson, 2002) as it can among other things influence network status (Milanov & Shepherd, 2013). In addition, business networks are in constant flux between stability and change (Araujo & Easton, 2012; Tidström & Åhman, 2006). Business network relationships in aggregate can be seen as continual but the sub-relationships within are constantly developing and decaying (Håkansson & Snehota, 1995). Lastly, a kairological view that stresses critical events and timing in business relationships is emphasized (Degbey & Pelto, 2013; Edvardsson & Strandvik, 2009; Medlin, 2004; Tidström & Hagberg-Andersson, 2012). These refined conceptualizations are, perhaps, an answer to the call by Håkansson and Snehota (1995) to develop a range of models, descriptive and explanatory, that delve into the elements and formation processes of business relationships.

Based on our observations and analysis so far, we now outline the points of departure that arise from integrating IMP conceptualizations into IB on the key concepts of time, relationship structure and the process view. This is summarized in Table 2 and is followed by introducing a conceptual model on MNC intra-firm relationships.

A CONCEPTUAL MODEL ON MNC INTRA-FIRM RELATIONSHIPS

We take the points of departure outlined in the previous sections to develop a conceptual model grounded in theories and concepts in IB and IMP. Our model is depicted in Fig. 1. While relationship structure is primarily understood as dyads, monoplex in composition and resource-based, we emphasize that relationships are in triads, multiplex and not wholly resource-based. Furthermore, in our model, relationships are not seen as simple sum of lower level sub-relationships but enjoy emergent properties

Table 2. Points of Departure From Established IB Conceptualizations of Key Concepts.

Concepts	At First Glance (IB)	Points of Departure (IMP)
Relationship structure	– Dyads – Monoplex in composition and interactions are a measurement of strength	– Dyads and triads – Multiplexity as a measurement of strength and complexity
Multiplexity	– Resource-based – Aggregate of lower levels – for example, individuals properties aggregate to group level – Borrows primarily from social capital theory and focuses on social aspects of relationships	– Structurally based (resources is only one part of the reason for the relationship) – Emergent properties at subunit level that is not strictly based off aggregates of individual level – Borrows from but also develops social network theory concepts – Relationships can be transactional at the organizational level
Temporality	– Path-dependency and prior interactions – Static – life cycle concept – Age-less or controlled for empirically	– Latency and reactivation – Dynamic – temporality – Age is an issue as relationships change over time
Process view	– Comparison of "snapshots" of a process and variance-based models – Network structures measured at certain points of time	– Process view of relationships and networks – Networking not just networks; networks as flows of activity, resources and interactions in a continual state of transformation

when taken in aggregate. Finally, we follow the process view of networks and relationships in line with current thinking in IMP.

The basic building block of an MNC network is the processes within a triad. The triad consists of three subunits, which may be HQ, subsidiaries, and regional HQ. We assume that there are strong/highly complex, weak/less complex or null relationships between the three subunits (see left part of the model). We also emphasize that multiplexity of relationships is a better predictor of relationships strength and complexity (middle part in Fig. 1). The model overcomes the idea (grounded in IB) that time and temporality are path-dependent. Instead, it emphasizes that age of relationships is not merely a variable to be controlled for, but a factor to be taken seriously into account on its own right, an idea we take from IMP research (right part of model). Relationships are seen to experience latency (and reactivation), they are dynamic (and a process) and the age of the relationship should be taken into consideration as they can change over time. Temporality is depicted in the model in two ways. First, relationships can change over time in terms of strength and complexity (and as measured by multiplexity). Second, the configuration of the triad can change over time in response to critical events.

The model offers answers to important questions like: What are the content and substance of the sub-relationships that make up the multiplexity of subunit relationships? What types of critical events trigger changes in multiplexity and triad configurations over time? Analyzing these questions will allow the elucidation of how MNC managers may chart and

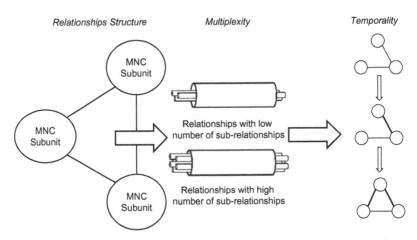

Fig. 1.   MNC Subunit Triad, Multiplexity and Temporality of Relationships.

orchestrate the value-adding relationships at the subunit level. Managing such relationships can lead to more efficient use of connections between subunits and in that way improve the orchestration of overall MNC design and operation.

Based on the arguments so far, a legitimate question is what type of research would be able to comprehensively integrate the issues around the temporality of relationships. Process research examines phenomena that evolve over time (Langley, 2009; Mohr, 1982; Van de Ven, 1992) by explicitly incorporating "temporal progressions of activities as elements of explanation and examination" (Langley et al., 2013, p. 1). In our model, this is illustrated through the various permutations of the triad, which is in response to business activities evolving over time (please refer to the right part of Fig. 1). Process research differs from variance research in that it looks at patterns of occurrence as opposed to the variation between independent and dependent variables (Bizzi & Langley, 2012; Van de Ven, 1992). Nonetheless, Langley (2009) stresses that both types are not mutually exclusive: process data can be gathered to develop variance-based theoretical interpretations. However, process research does not reduce research to an exercise in comparative statics such as the case with life cycle analysis (Pettigrew et al., 2001). A key guideline is that process research should seek to understand "recurrent patterns in the process, for structure and underlying logics" (Pettigrew, 1997, p. 341). The epistemological and methodological choices inherent in process research fit well with the logic of the model we propose.

A key issue to be conscious about is retrospective bias, which refers to the disparity between operational (true behavior) and presentational data (Cox & Hassard, 2007) and which needs to be mitigated. Furthermore, etic (general, outside perspective) explanations of research subjects often include their emic (contextual, internal perspective) meanings. However, this may not be a significant issue as presentational data offers a more nuanced view of previous events that includes awareness of the actual outcomes. In addition, this bias can be mitigated through careful multi-method procedures and making sure to not introduce further systematic errors (Golden, 1992; Pettigrew, 1997).

CONCLUSION AND FUTURE RESEARCH DIRECTIONS

We argue for positioning intra-firm relationships within MNCs as a focal unit of analysis in IB research when examining MNC organizational design. We are particularly interested in the dynamic nature of such relationships. Based on our systematic review of IB, Management, and IMP studies, we highlight the concepts of multiplexity and temporality of intra-firm relationships. We offer relevant extensions to IB by borrowing and integrating ideas and insights from IMP research. We chose IMP as it offers a more fine-grained understanding of network relationships. We can do so as both research fields are proximate and compatible with regards to borrowing and extending the key concepts of relationships, multiplexity, and temporality. Specifically, relationships can be embedded within a triadic structure and are multiplex. More importantly, they are not simply conduits for resource transfer but a process that evolves over time in reaction to critical events within the MNC. We propose a conceptual model for studying intra-firm MNC relationships that takes seriously such relationships as the focal unit of analysis when studying the orchestration of resources, activities, and actors within the networked MNC. In line with this thinking, we advocate for a process view to focus on patterns of occurrence rather than the traditional variance-based and typological views.

Given the nascent nature of the business network perspective in IB with regard to intra-firm relationships, we offer some focused future research considerations on the key concepts of relationships, multiplexity and temporality. We conceptualize intra-firm relationships using network concepts. We suggest future research on the predictive power of triads over the traditional dyadic perspective in the MNC context. The former is a closer approximation of the complexity of relationships between subunits in the MNC. We see considerable value in scholars continuing to focus on intra-firm relationships explicitly as we have done and examine how they influence network memory, dynamics, and development. A complementary route of future theoretical and empirical work could be delineating the boundary between intra- and inter-firm relationships and the usefulness of this conceptualization in understanding MNC network-based phenomena. In regard to multiplexity, we suggest that future research not only gathers empirical data on content and substance of relationships, but also attempts to understand how sub-relationships may influence each other and what are the emergent properties that occur at the subunit relationship level.

We argued that the boundarying of network phenomena within a MNC can be temporal. For instance, a critical event may be temporary but have lasting effects on organizational processes and future expectations of interactions and outcomes. Triadic and dyadic relationship structures may only be useful in specific stages within a particular situation, for example, a triadic relationship structure with a regional headquarter and peer subsidiary may enable better integration of a newly acquired subsidiary. The same could be said for multiplex relationships — rather than measuring interaction frequency, would the age or density of sub-relationships be a better indicator? Regarding temporality, do relationships experience latency and/or reactivation and does that affect future interactions with peer subunits? In essence, we suggest future research that explores the fertile ground of temporality-focused research and how it may modify underlying assumptions of current conceptualizations of the networked MNC. Lastly, we acknowledge that traditional longitudinal research design may be impractical and suggest scholars look toward process studies in order to investigate temporality in MNC network research, such as utilizing retrospective case study research design.

Examining the processes that structure intra-firm relationships in MNCs can allow scholars to grasp better the conceptual complexities inherent in MNC network research. Understanding such processes can elucidate the required organizational design network mechanisms for effective and efficient orchestration of MNC resources and actors. Furthermore, by starting to chart how relationships as such change over time, scholars can understand in what situations resilient relationships are a boon and when they should be terminated as a managed process. This is essential given that intra-firm relationships are at the very core of adding value to an MNC.

REFERENCES

Ahuja, G., Soda, G., & Zaheer, A. (2012). The genesis and dynamics of organizational networks. *Organization Science, 23*(2), 434–448.

Alnuaimi, T., Singh, J., & George, G. (2012). Not with my own: Long-term effects of cross-country collaboration on subsidiary innovation in emerging economies versus advanced economies. *Journal of Economic Geography, 12*(5), 943–968.

Alvesson, M., & Sandberg, J. (2011). Generating research questions through problematization. *Academy of Management Review, 36*(2), 247–271.

Alvesson, M., & Sandberg, J. (2013). *Constructing research questions: Doing interesting research.* Thousand Oaks, CA: Sage.

Ambos, B., & Mahnke, V. (2010). How do MNCs headquarters add value? *Management International Review, 50*(4), 403–412.

Andersson, U., & Forsgren, M. (2000). In search of centres of excellence: Network embeddedness and subsidiary roles in multinational corporations. *Management International Review, 40*(4), 329–350.

Andersson, U., Forsgren, M., & Holm, U. (2002). The strategic impact of external networks: Subsidiary performance and competence development in the multinational corporation. *Strategic Management Journal, 23*(11), 979–996.

Andersson, U., Forsgren, M., & Holm, U. (2007). Balancing subsidiary influence in the federative MNC: A business network view. *Journal of International Business Studies, 38*(5), 802–818.

Ansari, A., Koenigsberg, O., & Stahl, F. (2011). Modeling multiple relationships in social networks. *Journal of Marketing Research, 48*(4), 713−728.

Araujo, L., & Easton, G. (2012). Temporality in business networks: The role of narratives and management technologies. *Industrial Marketing Management, 41*(2), 312−318.

Barner-Rasmussen, W., & Björkman, I. (2007). Language fluency, socialization and inter-unit relationships in Chinese and Finnish subsidiaries. *Management and Organization Review, 3*(1), 105−128.

Bartlett, C. A., & Ghoshal, S. (1989). Managing across borders: The transnational solution. Boston, MA: Harvard Business Press.

Bergenholtz, C., & Waldstrøm, C. (2011). Inter-organizational network studies − A literature review. *Industry & Innovation, 18*(6), 539−562.

Birkinshaw, J. M., & Morrison, A. J. (1995). Configurations of strategy and structure in subsidiaries of multinational corporations. *Journal of International Business Studies, 26*(4), 729−753.

Bizzi, L., & Langley, A. (2012). Studying processes in and around networks. *Industrial Marketing Management, 41*(2), 224−234.

Björkman, I., Barner-Rasmussen, W., & Li, L. (2004). Managing knowledge transfer in MNCs: The impact of headquarters control mechanisms. *Journal of International Business Studies, 35*(5), 443−455.

Bouteiller, C., Evans, D., & Assens, C. (2004). *La compagnie générale des eaux: The dynamic of corporate networking [case study].* Cranfield, UK: The European Case Clearing House.

Brass, D. J., Galaskiewicz, J., Greve, H. R., & Tsai, W. (2004). Taking stock of networks and organizations: A multilevel perspective. *Academy of Management Journal, 47*(6), 795−817.

Chiao, Y.-C., & Ying, K.-P. (2013). Network effect and subsidiary autonomy in multinational corporations: An investigation of Taiwanese subsidiaries. *International Business Review, 22*(4), 652−662.

Choi, T. Y., & Wu, Z. (2009). Triads in supply networks: Theorizing buyer-supplier-supplier relationships. *Journal of Supply Chain Management, 45*(1), 8−25.

Chou, H.-H., & Zolkiewski, J. (2012). Decoding network dynamics. *Industrial Marketing Management, 41*(2), 247−258.

Chow, W. S., & Chan, L. S. (2008). Social network, social trust and shared goals in organizational knowledge sharing. *Information & Management, 45*(7), 458−465.

Ciabuschi, F., Martín Martín, O., & Ståhl, B. (2010). Headquarters influence on knowledge transfer performance. *Management International Review, 50*(4), 471−491.

Corsaro, D., & Snehota, I. (2012). Perceptions of change in business relationships and networks. *Industrial Marketing Management, 41*(2), 270−286.

Cox, J. W., & Hassard, J. (2007). Ties to the past in organization research: A comparative analysis of retrospective methods. *Organization, 14*(4), 475−497.

Degbey, W., & Pelto, E. (2013). Cross-border M&A as a trigger for network change in the Russian bakery industry. *Journal of Business and Industrial Marketing, 28*(3), 178−189.

Devinney, T. M., Pedersen, T., & Tihanyi, L. (2010). The past, present and future of international business & management. In T. Devinney, T. Pedersen, & L. Tihanyi (Eds.), *The past, present and future of international business & management* (Vol. 23, pp. 33−41). Advances in International Management. Bingley, UK: Emerald Group Publishing Limited.

Doz, Y. (2011). Qualitative research for international business. *Journal of International Business Studies, 42*(5), 582–590.

Edvardsson, B., & Strandvik, T. (2009). Critical times in business relationships. *European Business Review, 21*(4), 326–343.

Egelhoff, W. G. (2010). How the parent headquarters adds value to an MNC. *Management International Review, 50*(4), 413–431.

Ferriani, S., Fonti, F., & Corrado, R. (2013). The social and economic bases of network multiplexity: Exploring the emergence of multiplex ties. *Strategic Organization, 11*(1), 7–34.

Forsgren, M. (2013). *Theories of the multinational firm.* Massachusetts, MA: Edward Elgar.

Forsgren, M., Holm, U., & Johanson, J. (2005). *Managing the embedded multinational: A business network view.* Massachusetts, MA: Edward Elgar.

Foss, N. J., & Pedersen, T. (2002). Transferring knowledge in MNCs: The role of sources of subsidiary knowledge and organizational context. *Journal of International Management, 8*(1), 49–67.

Gammelgaard, J., McDonald, F., Stephan, A., Tüselmann, H., & Dörrenbächer, C. (2012). The impact of increases in subsidiary autonomy and network relationships on performance. *International Business Review, 21*(6), 1158–1172.

Ghoshal, S., & Bartlett, C. A. (1990). The multinational corporation as an interorganizational network. *Academy of Management Review, 15*(4), 603–625.

Ghoshal, S., & Moran, P. (1996). Bad for practice: A critique of the transaction cost theory. *Academy of Management Review, 21*(1), 13–47.

Giroud, A., & Scott-Kennel, J. (2009). MNC linkages in international business: A framework for analysis. *International Business Review, 18*(6), 555–566.

Golden, B. R. (1992). The past is the past – or is it? The use of retrospective accounts as indicators of past strategy. *Academy of Management Journal, 35*(4), 848–860.

Håkansson, H., & Snehota, I. (Eds.). (1995). *Developing relationships in business networks.* London: Routledge.

Halinen, A., Medlin, C. J., & Törnroos, J.-Å. (2012). Time and process in business network research. *Industrial Marketing Management, 41*(2), 215–223.

Halinen, A., Salmi, A., & Havila, V. (1999). From dyadic change to changing business networks: An analytical framework. *Journal of Management Studies, 36*(6), 779–794.

Harzing, A.-W. (2000). An empirical analysis and extension of the Bartlett and Ghoshal typology of multinational companies. *Journal of International Business Studies, 31*(1), 101–120.

Harzing, A.-W., & Van Ruysseveldt, J. (2003). *International human resource management.* London: Sage.

Havila, V., Johanson, J., & Thilenius, P. (2004). International business-relationship triads. *International Marketing Review, 21*(2), 172–186.

Havila, V., & Medlin, C. J. (2012). Ending-competence in business closure. *Industrial Marketing Management, 41*(3), 413–420.

Havila, V., & Salmi, A. (2000). Network perspective on international mergers and acquisitions: What more do we see? In V. Havila, M. Forsgren, & H. Håkansson (Eds.), *Critical perspectives on internationalisation* (pp. 457–472). Oxford: Pergamon.

Havila, V., & Wilkinson, I. A. N. (2002). The principle of the conservation of business relationship energy: Or many kinds of new beginnings. *Industrial Marketing Management, 31*(3), 191–203.

Hawkins, T. G., Wittmann, C. M., & Beyerlein, M. M. (2008). Antecedents and consequences of opportunism in buyer−supplier relations: Research synthesis and new frontiers. *Industrial Marketing Management, 37*(8), 895−909.

Hedlund, G. (1986). The hypermodern MNC − A heterarchy? *Human Resource Management, 25*(1), 9−35.

Hedlund, G. (1994). A model of KM and the N-form corporation. *Strategic Management Journal, 15*(2), 73−90.

Hedlund, G. (1999). The intensity and extensity of knowledge and the multinational corporation as a nearly recomposable system (NRS). *Management International Review, 39*(1), 5−44.

Hohenthal, J., Johanson, J., & Johanson, M. (2014). Network knowledge and business-relationship value in the foreign market. *International Business Review, 23*(1), 4−19.

Holm, U., & Pedersen, T. (2000). *The emergence and impact of MNC centres of excellence.* London: Macmillian Press.

Huggins, R., Johnston, A., & Thompson, P. (2012). Network capital, social capital and knowledge flow: How the nature of inter-organizational networks impacts on innovation. *Industry & Innovation, 19*(3), 203−232.

Iacobucci, D., & Hopkins, N. (1992). Modeling dyadic interactions and networks in Marketing. *Journal of Marketing Research, 29*(1), 5−17.

Inkpen, A. C., & Tsang, E. W. K. (2005). Social capital, networks, and knowledge transfer. *Academy of Management Review, 30*(1), 146−165.

Johnsen, R. E., & Ford, D. (2008). Exploring the concept of asymmetry: A typology for analysing customer−supplier relationships. *Industrial Marketing Management, 37*(4), 471−483.

Kamp, B. (2005). Formation and evolution of buyer−supplier relationships: Conceiving dynamism in actor composition of business networks. *Industrial Marketing Management, 34*(7), 658−668.

Kim, Y., Choi, T. Y., Yan, T., & Dooley, K. (2011). Structural investigation of supply networks: A social network analysis approach. *Journal of Operations Management, 29*(3), 194−211.

Kostova, T., & Roth, K. (2003). Social capital in multinational corporations and a micro-macro model of its formation. *Academy of Management Review, 28*(2), 297−317.

Langley, A. (2009). Studying processes in and around organizations. In D. A. Buchanan, & A. Bryman (Eds.), *The sage handbook on organizational research methods* (pp. 409−429). London: Sage.

Langley, A., Smallman, C., Tsoukas, H., & Van de Ven, A. H. (2013). Process studies of change in organization and management: Unveiling temporality, activity, and flow. *Academy of Management Journal, 56*(1), 1−13.

Levin, D. Z., Walter, J., & Murnighan, J. K. (2008). Dormant ties: The value of reconnecting. *Academy Of Management Annual Meeting Proceedings* (pp. 1−6). doi:10.5465/AMBPP.2008.33641687

Levin, D. Z., Walter, J., & Murnighan, J. K. (2011). Dormant ties: The value of reconnecting. *Organization Science, 22*(4), 923−939.

Li, L. (2005). The effects of trust and shared vision on inward knowledge transfer in subsidiaries' intra- and inter-organizational relationships. *International Business Review, 14*(1), 77−95.

Madsen, T. K., & Servais, P. (1997). The internationalization of born globals: An evolutionary process? *International Business Review, 6*(6), 561−583.

Maurer, I., Bartsch, V., & Ebers, M. (2011). The value of intra-organizational social capital: How it fosters knowledge transfer, innovation performance, and growth. *Organization Studies, 32*(2), 157–185.

Medlin, C. J. (2004). Interaction in business relationships: A time perspective. *Industrial Marketing Management, 33*(3), 185–193.

Michailova, S., & Mustaffa, Z. (2012). Subsidiary knowledge flows in multinational corporations: Research accomplishments, gaps, and opportunities. *Journal of World Business, 47*(3), 383–396.

Milanov, H., & Shepherd, D. A. (2013). The importance of the first relationship: The ongoing influence of initial network on future status. *Strategic Management Journal, 34*(6), 727–750.

Mohr, L. B. (1982). *Explaining organizational behaviour.* San Francisco, CA: Jossey-Bass.

Möller, K. K. (2013). Theory map of business marketing: Relationships and networks perspectives. *Industrial Marketing Management, 42*(3), 324–335.

Nahapiet, J., & Ghoshal, S. (1998). Social capital, intellectual capital, and the organizational advantage. *Academy of Management Review, 23*(2), 242–266.

Nohria, N., & Ghoshal, S. (1997). *The differentiated network: Organizing multinational corporations for value creation.* San Francisco, CA: Jossey-Bass.

O'Donnell, S. W. (2000). Managing foreign subsidiaries: Agents of headquarters, or an interdependent network? *Strategic Management Journal, 21*(5), 525–548.

Okhuysen, G., & Bonardi, J. P. (2011). The challenges of building theory by combining lenses. *Academy of Management Review, 36*(1), 6–11.

Paterson, S. L., & Brock, D. M. (2002). The development of subsidiary-management research: Review and theoretical analysis. *International Business Review, 11*(2), 139–163.

Perlmutter, H. V. (1969). The tortuous evolution of the multinational corporation. *Columbia Journal of World Business, 4*, 9–18.

Peters, L. D., Vanharanta, M., Pressey, A. D., & Johnston, W. J. (2012). Taking time to understand theory. *Industrial Marketing Management, 41*(5), 730–738.

Pettigrew, A. M. (1997). What is processual analysis. *Scandinavian Journal of Management, 13*(4), 337–348.

Pettigrew, A. M., Woodman, R. W., & Cameron, K. S. (2001). Studying organizational change and development: Challenges for future research. *Academy of Management Journal, 44*(4), 697–713.

Phelps, C., Heidl, R., & Wadhwa, A. (2012). Knowledge, networks, and knowledge networks: A review and research agenda. *Journal of Management, 38*(4), 1115–1166.

Phelps, R., Adams, R., & Bessant, J. (2007). Life cycles of growing organizations: A review with implications for knowledge and learning. *International Journal of Management Reviews, 9*(1), 1–30.

Pilbeam, C., Alvarez, G., & Wilson, H. (2012). The governance of supply networks: A systematic literature review. *Supply Chain Management: An International Journal, 17*(4), 358–376.

Provan, K. G., Fish, A., & Sydow, J. (2007). Interorganizational networks at the network level: A review of the empirical literature on whole networks. *Journal of Management, 33*(3), 479–516.

Rabbiosi, L., & Santangelo, G. D. (2013). Parent company benefits from reverse knowledge transfer: The role of the liability of newness in MNCs. *Journal of World Business, 48*(1), 160–170.

Reeb, D., Sakakibara, M., & Mahmood, I. P. (2012). From the editors: Endogeneity in international business research. *Journal of International Business Studies*, *43*(3), 211–218.

Roseira, C., Brito, C., & Ford, D. (2013). Network pictures and supplier management: An empirical study. *Industrial Marketing Management*, *42*(2), 234–247.

Roseira, C., Brito, C., & Henneberg, S. C. (2010). Managing interdependencies in supplier networks. *Industrial Marketing Management*, *39*(6), 925–935.

Santangelo, G. D. (2012). The tension of information sharing: Effects on subsidiary embeddedness. *International Business Review*, *21*(2), 180–195.

Shipilov, A., & Li, S. X. (2012). The missing link: The effect of customers on the formation of relationships among producers in the multiplex triads. *Organization Science*, *23*(2), 472–491.

Tidström, A., & Åhman, S. (2006). The process of ending inter-organizational cooperation. *Journal of Business & Industrial Marketing*, *21*(5), 281–290.

Tidström, A., & Hagberg-Andersson, Å. (2012). Critical events in time and space when cooperation turns into competition in business relationships. *Industrial Marketing Management*, *41*(2), 333–343.

Tran, Y., Mahnke, V., & Ambos, B. (2010). The effect of quantity, quality and timing of headquarters-initiated knowledge flows on subsidiary performance. *Management International Review*, *50*(4), 493–511.

Tsai, W. P. (2000). Social capital, strategic relatedness and the formation of intraorganizational linkages. *Strategic Management Journal*, *21*(9), 925–939.

Turcan, R. V. (2013). The philosophy of turning points: A case of de-internationalization. In T. M. Devinney, T. Pedersen, & L. Tihanyi (Eds.), *Philosophy of science and metaknowledge in international business and management*. (*Vol. 26*, pp. 219–235). Advances in International Management. Bingley, UK: Emerald Group Publishing Limited.

Vahlne, J.-E., & Johanson, J. (2013). The Uppsala model on evolution of the multinational business enterprise – From internalization to coordination of networks. *International Marketing Review*, *30*(3), 189–210.

Van de Ven, A. H. (1992). Suggestions for studying strategy process: A research note. *Strategic Management Journal*, *13*(S1), 169–188.

Volberda, H. W., & Lewin, A. Y. (2003). Co-evolutionary dynamics within and between firms: From evolution to co-evolution. *Journal of Management Studies*, *40*(8), 2111–2136.

Werner, S. (2002). Recent developments in international management research: A review of 20 top management journals. *Journal of Management*, *28*(3), 277–305.

Wilkinson, I. F., & Young, L. C. (2013). The past and the future of business marketing theory. *Industrial Marketing Management*, *42*(3), 394–404.

Yamin, M., Tsai, H.-J., & Holm, U. (2011). The performance effects of headquarters involvement in lateral innovation transfers in multinational corporations. *Management International Review*, *51*(2), 157–177.

Yang, Q., Mudambi, R., & Meyer, K. E. (2008). Conventional and reverse knowledge flows in multinational corporations. *Journal of Management*, *34*(5), 882–902.

Zander, I., & Mathews, J. A. (2010). Beyond heterarchy: Emerging futures for the hypermodern MNC. In U. Andersson & U. Holm (Eds.), *Managing the contemporary multinational: The role of headquarters* (pp. 33–59). Cheltenham, UK: Edward Elgar.

Zerbini, F., & Castaldo, S. (2007). Stay in or get out of Janus? The maintenance of multiplex relationships between buyers and sellers. *Industrial Marketing Management*, *36*(7), 941–954.

ORGANIZATIONAL RECONFIGURATION AND STRATEGIC RESPONSE: THE CASE OF OFFSHORING

Marcus M. Larsen and Torben Pedersen

ABSTRACT

The purpose of this paper is to investigate the effect of the organizational reconfiguration of offshoring on firms' strategies. A consequence of offshoring is the need to reintegrate the geographically relocated organizational activities into a coherent organizational architecture. In order to do this, firms need a high degree of architectural knowledge, which is typically gained through learning by doing. We therefore argue that firms with more offshoring experience are more likely to include organizational objectives in their offshoring strategies. We develop and find support for this hypothesis using a mixed-method approach based on a qualitative case study and comprehensive data from the Offshoring Research Network. These findings contribute to research on the

Orchestration of the Global Network Organization
Advances in International Management, Volume 27, 403–432
ISSN: 1571-5027/doi:10.1108/S1571-502720140000027000

organizational design and architecture of offshoring and the dynamics of organizational architectures.

Keywords: Offshoring; strategic response; architectural knowledge; mixed-method approach

INTRODUCTION

How does the organizational reconfiguration of offshoring influence firms' strategies? In recent years, the practice of offshoring administrative and technical services to foreign locations has gained vast popularity. Firms are not only offshoring standardized IT and business processes but also more complex and knowledge-intensive activities such as product design and development (Kenney, Massini, & Murtha, 2009; Lewin, Massini, & Peeters, 2009). However, while much research has provided rich insights into questions such as which functions firms decide to offshore, which governance modes they choose, where they offshore to, and what outcomes they achieve (e.g., Doh, Bunyaratavej, & Hahn, 2009; Lewin et al., 2009; Mol, van Tulder, & Beije, 2005), less research has been devoted to understanding the dynamics of offshoring (Contractor, Kumar, Kundu, & Pedersen, 2010; Kedia & Mukherjee, 2009; Maskell, Pedersen, Petersen, & Dick-Nielsen, 2007). In particular, little research has questioned how firms realize strategies of offshoring. Our paper contributes to filling this gap by studying firms' strategies following the offshoring implementation.

When firms implement offshoring activities abroad, they initiate an organizational reconfiguration where they relocate disaggregated organizational activities abroad to either independent suppliers, to wholly owned subsidiaries or in joint ventures (Jensen, Larsen, & Pedersen, 2013). Although the offshoring decision may provide firms with an array of advantages, such as lower costs, access to new resources, and markets (Dossani & Kenney, 2003; Hutzschenreuter, Lewin, & Dresel, 2011; Lewin et al., 2009), it also presents firms with substantial challenges (Larsen, Manning, & Pedersen, 2013). For example, Dell Inc., the US based multinational IT corporation, decided in 2003 after much problems and challenges regarding cultural differences, language difficulties, and time delays to eventually close and source back its Indian service centers that it had offshored and outsourced some years earlier (Graf & Mudambi, 2005). Aron and Singh (2005, p. 135) argue that many firms are caught up by the "harsh realities of offshoring" as they fail to pick up the right processes, calculate the operational and structural risks, and match organizational forms to live up to the initial expectations of the offshoring activities.

Since the organizational reconfiguration of offshoring encapsulates new architectural challenges and complexities (Larsen et al., 2013), firms subsequently need to reintegrate the geographically dispersed organizational elements so that they can be supportive of the organizational objectives (Mudambi & Venzin, 2010). In particular, firms need to identify and uncover the new international interdependencies spanning across geographies, cultures, and institutions. In this respect, the role of architectural knowledge – knowledge on how different activities are integrated and linked together in a coherent organizational system (Brusoni & Prencipe, 2001, 2006; Henderson & Clark, 1990) – is important. As firms gain experience with the offshoring implementation and thereby accumulate architectural knowledge, decision makers increasingly understand the true nature of the organizational activities and the interdependencies between these and will therefore acknowledge this in their strategies. Hence, we propose that as firms' experience with particular offshoring implementations increases they will growingly consider organizational objectives in their strategies.

We develop this idea by employing a mixed-method approach (Edmondson & McManus, 2007). First, we report the findings of an in-depth case study of offshoring in a product development project in Nokia, the worlds' largest mobile phone manufacturer. The case shows how the decision to offshore was initially driven by locational objectives such as lower costs and access to strategic resources but that this changed over time toward organizational objectives that could increase organizational performance. We then test and find support for a hypothesis that offshoring experience is positively associated with firms' organizational strategy orientation on comprehensive data from the Offshoring Research Network (ORN).

A contribution of this paper is the emphasis on the role of knowledge accumulation in the offshoring process, where architectural evolution should be understood as an iterative process between decision makers' accumulation of architectural knowledge and the deployment of this in their strategic behavior. This means that strategy follows structure (Chandler, 1962; Hall & Saias, 1980), but only to the extent that the decision maker successfully accumulates architectural knowledge. Thus, rather than assuming that the effective architecture of firms' offshoring activities can a priori be planned and implemented, we suggest that this is more a subject of learning. The locus of understanding the antecedents of different organizational architectures and their performance contingencies should therefore acknowledge the process in which decisions makers derive architectural knowledge on which decisions are taken.

The paper proceeds as follows: First, we briefly introduce the literature on organizational architectures and the role of architectural knowledge, before we discuss how offshoring may be regarded as an organizational reconfiguration. Second, we present the research methodology, before we introduce the qualitative analysis (based on Nokia) and the quantitative analysis (based on large-scale ORN data). Finally, we conclude the paper by discussing its implications for theory on offshoring and architectural knowledge.

THEORETICAL BACKGROUND

Organizational Architecture and Architectural Knowledge

An organizational architecture can be defined as decision makers' more or less intentional choices to ensure that organizational components and activities coexist and are linked to each other in the most effective way (Nadler & Tushman, 1997; Sah & Stiglitz, 1986). According to Sah and Stiglitz (1986, p. 716), "The [organizational] architecture describes how the constituent decision-making units are arranged together in a system, how the decision-making authority and ability is distributed within a system, who gathers what information, and who communicates to whom." As such, the organizational architecture depicts the architectural decisions on how activities interact, how they are interdependent on one another, and where tasks and organizational boundaries are drawn (Ethiraj & Levinthal, 2004).

Several different organizational architectures have been identified in the literature. For example, Sah and Stiglitz (1986) distinguish between the polyarchy architecture as a system in which there are several and possibly competing decision makers who can undertake projects or ideas independently of one another, and the hierarchy architectures where only a few individuals undertake projects while others provide support in decision making. Another example is the modular organizational architecture which can be characterized as a loosely coupled organizational form (Orton & Weick, 1990; Weick, 1976) with few and standardized interfaces between different organizational activities (Baldwin & Clark, 2000; Sanchez & Mahoney, 1996). This can be seen in contrast to an integral organizational architecture consisting of a low degree of standardization of interfaces between the different organizational elements (Schilling, 2000).

Central to the organizational architecture is the underlying interdependency structure. Organizations can be viewed as systems of tasks and individuals that to various extents are interdependent on each other (Lawrence & Lorsch, 1967; Perrow, 1967; Thompson, 1967). Interdependencies link together individual parts of an organization in such a way that the joint outcome of the activities depends on the contributions of these individual parts (van de Ven, 1976). Thus, a purpose of the organizational architecture is to meet the coordination requirements generated by individuals and groups undertaking interdependent activities. An essential role of interdependencies between tasks and individuals is therefore the "gathering, interpreting and synthesis of information in the context of organizational decision making" (Tushman & Nadler, 1978, p. 614) so that coordinated action can be exercised.

In terms of making effective architectural decisions, decision makers thus need to understand the underlying interdependency structure of firms' organizational architectures. For example, it is well established that the performance of the organizational architectures is highly correlated with the architectural fit (Drazin & Ven, 1985; Khandwalla, 1973; Siggelkow, 2002), that is, "an organizational system with no inconsistent core elements and a number of reinforcing core elements" (Siggelkow, 2002, p. 128). Architectural fit describes the degree to which the different architectural elements in the organization are consistent with one another and supportive of the organizational objectives. Modular architectural forms can be argued to be superior to integral forms in contexts of high organizational complexity due to standardization and minimization of interdependencies between different activities (Baldwin & Clark, 2000; Sanchez & Mahoney, 1996), whereas it may be less beneficial in contexts with little complexity due to the costs of modularizing a system (Brusoni, Marengo, Prencipe, & Valente, 2007). However, in order to make effective decisions toward achieving fit in modular systems (e.g., standardize interdependencies), decision makers need to know how changes within the parameters of an existing architecture as well as how broader changes in the architecture itself are geared toward improving organizational performance (Ethiraj & Levinthal, 2004). For example, decision makers need to know where the organizational boundaries, and hence also interdependencies, are drawn, how change in one activity will influence another activity, and how change in the overarching architecture will impact organizational performance.

Much research has emphasized firms' architectural knowledge — that is, the understanding of how components in an organizational system are related to each other (e.g., Baldwin & Clark, 2000; Brusoni & Prencipe, 2001, 2006; Henderson & Clark, 1990) — as a crucial factor in taking effective architectural decisions. For example, Brusoni and Prencipe (2006) show how radical organizational evolution in the tire manufacturing industry is strongly mediated by the evolution of firms' engineering knowledge. Indeed, deviations in the performance of organizational architectures have often been associated with the level of architectural knowledge of decision makers (Baldwin & Clark, 2000; Henderson & Clark, 1990). Henderson and Clark (1990) refer to architectural knowledge in relation to product technologies as consisting of two parts: knowledge about the different components underlying a distinct system and knowledge about how the components are integrated into an orchestrated systemic whole. The same applies to architectural knowledge in an organizational context: To make effective architectural decisions, decision makers need knowledge about the individual activities and about the ways that the different activities are integrated and linked together in a coherent organizational system. Without knowledge on how the organization with its activities and interdependencies function — that is, the underlying interdependency structure — there is a higher risk that incorrect and even deteriorating architectural decisions are taken. Indeed, assuming that decision makers suffer from bounded rationality (Simon, 1955; Simon & March, 1958), the likelihood of making incorrect architectural decision increases with the lack of knowledge.

By contrast, the more knowledge and experience the decision maker have, the more likely it is that effective architectural decisions are taken (Argyres, 2007; Gulati & Puranam, 2009; Jacobides & Winter, 2005; Tsoukas, 2001). Through cumulative learning-by-doing over time, firms gain experience with different organizational architectures in different contexts, and more knowledge is gained on what is effective and what is not (Nelson & Winter, 1982). This view is supported by Ethiraj and Levinthal (2004, p. 411): "While bounded rationality suggests that they [decision makers] are unlikely to discover the appropriate structure in the first attempt, it is certainly possible that repeated, small adaptive attempts will generate progress toward the appropriate structure." Thus, seeing the effective organizational architectural as the result of a joint discovery process of collective trial-and-error learning (Lounamaa & March, 1987) or as the outcome of firms' successfully managed search for new architectural options and the exploitation of these options once found (Siggelkow, 2002), it is evident that architectural knowledge plays a pivotal role in this process.

The Organizational Reconfiguration of Offshoring

From an architectural perspective, offshoring describes an organizational reconfiguration in which originally colocated activities become relocated abroad in different governance modes (Jensen et al., 2013). The organizational architecture is reconfigured on issues such as the contractual ownership and relationship of the offshoring setup (Hutzschenreuter et al., 2011), the geography of the host location (Graf & Mudambi, 2005), the interdependencies and coordination mechanisms between the spatially differentiated organizational tasks and activities (Kumar, Van Fenema, & von Glinow, 2009; Srikanth & Puranam, 2011), and the overall coherency of the globally dispersed organizational system (Ernst & Kim, 2002).

In the reconfiguration process, the organizational architecture incurs new complexities by adding distances (e.g., geographical, institutional, and cultural) to the interdependencies between the organizational activities. When activities are colocated, firms may not see the rationale of formalizing coordination mechanisms as day-to-day challenges can be solved in an informal face-to-face manner (Storper & Venables, 2004). However, as activities become dispersed, opportunities for informal coordination are reduced (Allen, 1977) and project teams find it more difficult to build collegial social environments and common ground due to less communication and shared context (Bartell & Ghoshal, 1989; Clark & Brennan, 1991; Kraut, Egido, & Galegher, 1990; Martinez & Jarillo, 1989). Moreover, research suggests that firms have a tendency of disaggregating or "fine-slicing" their value chain activities as they engage in offshoring processes (Contractor et al., 2010; Mudambi & Venzin, 2010; Tanriverdi, Konana, & Ge, 2007). Consequently, with increased offshoring firms are often presented with a higher number of organizational activities and interdependencies that must be coordinated across distance. In other words, decision makers need to take decisions that can restore fit among the geographically dispersed organizational elements so that they can be supportive of the organizational objectives.

Obviously, the governance mode of the offshoring implementation (captive vs. outsourced) has important implications for the extent to which the decision maker in the offshoring firm are able to implement architectural decisions. For example, it is less likely that a decision maker is able to exercise decision-making authority in outsourced arrangement where the activity is conducted by an external provider. However, we argue that firms' organizational architecture encapsulates both captive and outsourced implementations by stressing that a central task in offshoring relates to reintegrating offshored organizational activities (irrespective of governance mode) into a value-adding system (Mudambi & Venzin, 2010). The decision-maker possesses control in terms of facilitating the reintegration process and can make important architectural decisions on issues such as how the offshored activities should interact, to what extent they should be interdependent on one another, and where tasks and organizational boundaries should be drawn. In this respect, the offshoring companies presume the role of systems integrators in which they "lead and coordinate from a technological and organizational viewpoint the work of suppliers involved in the network" (Brusoni, Prencipe, & Pavitt, 2001, p. 613).

Thus far, little research has questioned and investigated how the organizational reconfiguration of offshoring impacts firms' strategies. Indeed, much research has successfully pointed out that firms are driven by offshoring for a number of reasons, such as achieving lower costs, gaining market proximity, and securing strategic resources (Kedia & Lahiri, 2007; Manning, Massini, & Lewin, 2008). Moreover, research suggests that firms with predefined corporate-wide offshoring strategies that articulate deliberate plans and guidelines for the adoption and implementation of offshoring activities are more likely to generate higher offshoring performance compared to firms that engage in offshoring more opportunistically (e.g., Heijmen Lewin, Manning, Perm-Ajchariyawong, & Russell, 2009; Lewin & Couto, 2007; Massini, Pern-Ajchariyawong, & Lewin, 2010). However, we know little about the consequences on firms' strategies as they reconfigure their organizations on a global scale. For example, how do firms accommodate for the new complexities in the organizational architecture after relocating activities abroad? Is the successful offshoring implementation only attainable by firms with overarching and supportive corporate strategies? Or, is it also possible that firms approach offshoring more as a learning-by-doing process? Accordingly, the research question we pose in this paper is: How does the organizational reconfiguration of offshoring influence firms' strategies?

In order to operationalize this research question, we discriminate between two types of offshoring strategies to illustrate how firms' strategies may change as a response to the organizational reconfiguration of offshoring. On the one hand, firms' offshoring strategies can be oriented toward objectives such as new markets, lower production costs, and talented labor. Indeed, the main objective for most firms engaging in offshoring is to access labor and other costs in low-cost locations (Lewin & Peeters, 2006). Whether firms offshore knowledge-intensive services or more standardized IT activities, a main offshoring objective relates to cutting costs by accessing labor and resources at a comparatively lower cost than in the home country. We thus label the strategies directed toward achieving benefits derived from the environment as *locational strategy orientation.* This strategy thus captures firms' desire to achieve objectives derived from being present in the host location.

On the other hand, research has also pointed out that firms' offshoring drivers can be devoted toward more organizational objectives. For example, firms may focus on objectives such as reducing systems redundancy, increasing operational and organizational flexibility, and improving business process redesign (Lewin & Peeters, 2006). As such, firms view offshoring as a facilitator for organizational change (e.g., Jensen, 2009). We label these strategies as *organizational strategy orientation.*

RESEARCH METHODOLOGY

We employ a mixed-method approach that combines qualitative and quantitative methodologies (Edmondson & McManus, 2007) to investigate how the organizational reconfiguration of offshoring influences firms' strategies. More specifically, first we employ an inductive analysis of a qualitative case study of the organizational reconfiguration of an offshoring event to accurately examine the phenomenon and eventually derive a testable hypothesis (Eisenhardt, 1989; Siggelkow, 2007; Yin, 2003). This enables us to capture the evolution of the offshoring process; from the offshoring decision to the organizational reconfiguration and further to the strategic response. However, in order to better discuss the generalizability of our finding, we subsequently use quantitative methods on comprehensive survey data to test the hypothesis induced from the qualitative results. Accordingly, we use the two methodological approaches as compliments to explore and explain how the organizational reconfiguration of offshoring influences firms' strategies.

The unit of analysis for both methodological approaches is firms' specific offshoring implementations, defined as relocations of particular tasks or processes to locations outside the home country. Thus, rather than investigating firms' general experience with offshoring, the aim of this study is to study the strategic implications of offshoring a specified firm activity. Hence, we investigate how the added complexities and distances (e.g., geography, institutions, and cultures) to the interdependencies in the organizational architecture affect firms' strategies.

Qualitative Data

The qualitative part of this study consists of a case study of an offshoring decision in Nokia Denmark in which certain product development activities were offshored to China. Nokia Denmark was founded in 1996 as a subsidiary of the Nokia Corporation, one the largest mobile phone manufacturers in the world, and contains the largest Nokia R&D unit outside Finland concentrating on the development of mobile phones. The Danish site houses approximately 1200 employees, in which 60% are engineers, equally distributed between software and hardware engineers. In 2007, Nokia Denmark received instructions from corporate headquarters to drastically increase the number of mobile phones developed. Motivated by the need to release pressure on its in-house capacity, Nokia Denmark decided to offshore certain product development projects to the Taiwanese company Foxconn in a joint R&D (JRD) setup. Foxconn, one of the world's largest electronic component manufacturers, who was also developing products for many of Nokia's competitors, was given the responsibility of developing and testing selected standardized and less complex mobile phones, while more complex and sophisticated technology projects were retained in Denmark.

The case of Nokia Denmark was theoretically selected for this research (Eisenhardt & Graebner, 2007; Pettigrew, 1990) as it highlights a process whereby a firm decides to offshore certain organizational tasks to a foreign location in order to release capacity and reduce costs. It can be argued that this case rather deals with international joint ventures rather than offshoring (e.g., Geringer & Hebert, 1989; Inkpen & Beamish, 1997; Lou, 2002) in which two companies establish a joint architecture for product development. However, since the theoretical motivation of using this case relates to the transfer of product development tasks from Denmark to China, rather than the choice of contractual governance mode, we argue that the case is well positioned to discuss the organizational reconfiguration of offshoring. Moreover, the case concerns offshoring of a technologically complex process (product development of mobile phones) rather than more standardized activities such as volume production. Accordingly, as the case pinpoints a number of central challenges and complexities of offshoring (Contractor et al., 2010; Srikanth & Puranam, 2011), it is well positioned to investigate how an organizational reconfiguration influences firm strategy.

We use both archival and interview data to gather longitudinal information of the case, to generate interference, and for triangulation (Silverman,

2006). The archival data consist of published academic cases, academic papers, company reports, industry reports, and news articles related to the Nokia Corporation, Nokia Denmark, and Foxconn. The interview data consist of six semi-structured interviews with central JRD stakeholders at Nokia Denmark (head of program management, product development manager, product program manager). Each interview ranged from one to two hours and was conducted in-person by either both authors or one of the authors of this paper. The interviews were used to gain an in-depth picture of offshoring in Nokia and particularly the evolution of the JRD with Foxconn. Moreover, a number of informal discussions with informants during site visits also served as an important source of data. Since the offshoring process started prior to our involvement in the case, some events relevant to the study had to be captured in retrospect.

Quantitative Data

For the quantitative part of this study, we use comprehensive survey data from the ORN. Accordingly, our study connects to a stream of research utilizing ORN data (Lewin et al., 2009; Manning et al., 2008; Massini et al., 2010). Since its foundation in 2004, the ORN research team has primarily conducted two major annual surveys based on which offshoring-related data has been collected: the corporate client survey and the service provider survey. Both surveys are utilized for this particular study. The corporate client survey collects data from U.S. firms and European firms on their offshore implementations, including information on tasks offshored, launch year, location choice, choice of delivery model (both captive and outsourced) and performance data. The dataset used for this study consists of data from 129 firms, out of which 73 are U.S. based and 56 are European. These firms reported a total of 353 offshoring implementations. Tasks may include IT infrastructure, administrative services (e.g., HR, legal, finance and accounting), call centers, software and product development, marketing and sales, and procurement. The statistical analysis is conducted on the level of these 353 offshore implementations.

In addition, we also use data from the ORN service provider survey. The service provider survey annually collects a range of firm- and service-specific data from service providers in the United States, Western and Eastern Europe, India, China, Latin America, and other regions. The survey informs about features of services provided (e.g., degree of commoditization), locations from which services are provided, and performance of service delivery. Particularly important for us are control variables measuring the degree of standardization and commoditization of particular services, from the perspective of service providers. Moreover, using data from two independent and unrelated surveys helps us address the common method variance problem (Chang, van Witteloostuijn, & Eden, 2010).

QUALITATIVE ANALYSIS

Product Development in Nokia Denmark

The primary activity of Nokia Denmark is the development of new mobile phone models, including every aspect from R&D to sourcing and logistics to marketing and market segmentation. The development of the mobile phone can be divided into the following sub-categories: mechanics, electro-mechanics, electronics, and software. In support of these are operations, product validation, quality, display, sourcing, and customer care. Together, these groups form the organization of the project development unit in Nokia Denmark in which each team is responsible for optimizing the different technologies and supply chain of the mobile phone. Each year, about six to ten new mobile phones are developed in Denmark. The Danish site is renowned in the global Nokia organization for the many bestselling and path-breaking products and technologies it has developed. For example, the Nokia 3310 − one of the most successful Nokia mobile phones with almost 200 million units sold around the world − was developed in Denmark. Moreover, the Series 40 software platform and application user interface software used on Nokia's broad range of mid-tier mobile phones was also developed in Denmark.

The organizational architecture of Nokia's product development process describes how different activities located in Denmark follow a generic process with the purpose of developing new products and related process capabilities based on orders from the product and portfolio management (see Fig. 1). The different activities are organized according to five distinct milestones (PD0 to PD4) that can only be reached if an assigned steering committee approved the development. PD0 marks the initiation of the product program; PD1 the product development release (full functionality of the product); PD2 the manufacturing release (full performance of the product); PD3 the delivery release (ready for the market); and PD4 the determination of product development (handover to product maintenance).

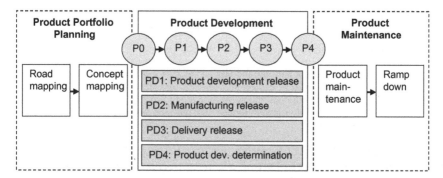

Fig. 1. Nokia Product Development. *Source*: Larsen and Pedersen (2012).

The intention of this setup is to funnel and convert "good ideas" into marketable products. One product development manager explained it as follows:

> Concept mapping is creating a lot of different ideas and finding the ones with most promise; product development is basically maturing what we now have – a concept; and product maintenance is to keep the product alive and integrate different components. We have divided the process into these three parts as each phase requires different competences and mindsets.

Offshoring to China

In 2007, the management of the Nokia product development unit located in Denmark decided to offshore parts of selected product development projects to the Chinese facilities of Foxconn – a major multinational electronics components manufacturer – in a joint R&D (JRD) setup. Faced with internal capacity constraints, the Danish Nokia management approached Foxconn with the purpose of cutting costs, reducing time to market, and tapping into Foxconn's rich pool of technological knowledge. In the JRD setup, Nokia would be responsible for development of the advanced parts of new mobile phones, while Foxconn would be responsible for the development of more standardized parts, such as the molding and fitting of plastic components.

This JRD presented a new situation for the Danish Nokia management. The product development of the mobile phones had traditionally been regarded a core competence at Nokia Denmark and had previously been carried out in-house. The Nokia management therefore had little experience or knowledge on how to best design and manage a JRD project across vast geographical and cultural distances. According to one Nokia JRD manager:

> It wasn't a top-down, but a bottom-up decision. The individual development sites were told that they should make X number of products, and then it was up to the local management to find out what we should do. We didn't have the capacity to make all these products, and our guys couldn't deliver it. We then found out that we should make some joint R&D.

Specifically, in the JRD Foxconn presumed responsibility of the product development phase (PD0-PD4) of selected projects (carried out in China) while the product portfolio management and the product maintenance was still done in Denmark (see Fig. 1). This meant that the entire product development function was reconfigured from being exclusively colocated in Denmark to become dispersed between Denmark and China. An effective organizational architecture would consequently depend on the extent to which the remaining in-house product development activities in Denmark and the activities outsourced to Foxconn were fully consistent and reinforcing of each other. While the architecture may have been effective while the activities were still colocated in Denmark, the decision to relocate certain activities to China incurred new complexities for the Nokia management in the coordination of the development projects. For example, while the crucial interdependencies between concept mapping and product development release and between product development determination and product maintenance could originally be coordinated through more informal mechanisms such as face-to-face coordination in Denmark, the introduction of the JRD signified that new and alternative mechanisms that could account for the distances.

From a Locational to an Organizational Strategy Orientation

Nokia's initial expectations for the JRD had been that they would simply hand the product specification over to Foxconn after the Concept Mapping phase and receive it back for Product Maintenance some months later. The Danish management saw the JRD as a case of simple outsourcing with limited communication with the Foxconn between the ordering and final delivery of the tasks. The attention and strategy was more concerned with the benefits of offshoring to China and Foxconn. Besides the obvious cost-saving motivation of relocating product development capacity to China, Foxconn – as one of the largest companies in the field of electronic component manufacturing – had much relevant knowledge and expertise that Nokia Denmark saw the potential of tapping into. For instance, it had a long history of developing technological products for major contractors around the world and possessed much experience of optimizing product development processes. In addition, Foxconn had supplied electronics components to Nokia for a number of years prior to the full-scale offshoring decision. Their already established relationship would therefore ease the process of relocating entire product development projects to China.

During the process of implementing the JRD, however, the Nokia management began to face challenges of aligning and reintegrating the two geographically dispersed organizational units. For example, while the Nokia management had hoped that the outsourced activities would be largely self-manageable and requiring minimum intervention from their side, they soon realized that safeguarding against misinterpretations and misbehavior required substantially more resources than initially expected. Moreover, the increased engagement with Foxconn created internal resistance among Nokia engineers toward relocating PD projects to a supplier and toward teaching a partner how to make Nokia phones. One JRD manager elaborated:

> People in Nokia see it as if we are selling our core competences. On a design level, people have been very nervous and cautious towards the JRD. In the old days, it was rocket science to make good mobile phones. That's not the case today, however. Everybody can easily buy all the necessary phone components on the market. But if you have made these components internally for the last 20 years, you will think that it is still a core competence for the company.

Consequently, the Danish management began to experiment with different architectural solutions, such as disaggregating the value chain differently, standardizing the interdependencies, and implementing new coordination mechanisms. For example, the Nokia management learned that frequent meetings and monitoring of the tasks were highly necessary to ensure that the products were developed according to Nokia standards. Among other things, they experienced that they needed to diligently control and coordinate the JRD to ensure the projects' adherence to Nokia's quality standards. They also realized that it was necessary to transfer substantially more knowledge to Foxconn on how the products should be developed. It was only after Nokia Denmark had faced the challenges of aligning technological and organizational specifications between the

Danish site and the Chinese site that it began to use weekly video conference meetings.

The realized challenges of offshoring product development to China therefore prompted the Nokia management to align the coordinative task with the requirements of geographically dispersed work. This was particularly increasing the monitoring of the JRD. For example, eight full-time Nokia employees were assigned to follow the JRD from Denmark while the product was being developed by 30–50 engineers in China. In order to supervise the life cycle of the PD projects, Nokia Denmark and Foxconn arranged weekly video conference meetings to discuss the status of each project as well as specific technological and organizational challenges or alterations that might have occurred. Moreover, the two partners also met either in Denmark or in China every six to eight weeks. Nokia also began to experiment with different ways of transferring the required knowledge, such as extensive process codification and frequent coordination. Eventually, the collaboration turned into becoming a Joint R&D rather than just outsourcing of R&D, in which the Nokia management presumed more responsibility regarding integrating the Chinese activities with the remaining Danish activities. Over time, the Nokia management gained knowledge on how the different organizational activities in China and Denmark functioned both individually in the two locations and together in an organizational system, and started to form its strategies on improving the collaboration. Based on this knowledge, the Nokia management learned how to most appropriately take decisions for the inter-organizational architecture in which better fit between the two dispersed units could be achieved. According to a Nokia JRD manager:

> It's really learning-by-doing. Nokia is kind of a cowboy company. We plunge into things, muddle our way through and eventually become wiser. It is not that much design in the things we do. We go out and try, and then we adjust.

Theoretical Implications from Qualitative Study

The findings of this case are to a large extent supportive of much offshoring research that views the offshoring process as a learning-by-doing process (e.g., Jensen, 2009; Manning et al., 2008; Maskell, Pedersen, Petersen, & Dick-Nielsen, 2007). For instance, Maskell et al. (2007) suggest how offshoring to low-cost countries is best described as a learning-by-doing process in which "over a period of time the outsourcing experience lessens the cognitive limitations of decision makers as to the advantages that can be achieved through outsourcing in low-cost countries: the in-sourcer/vendor may not only offer cost advantages, but also quality improvement and innovation" (Maskell et al., 2007, p. 239). Equally, based on evolving organizational learning in both home and host country firms, Jensen (2009) proposes how offshoring of advanced services should be understood as an antecedent for strategic business development and organizational change.

The uniqueness of the Nokia case relates to how experience is an important antecedent of architectural knowledge. It was only after the Nokia management had gained experience on the collaboration with Foxconn (in China) that they were able to understand the nature of the challenges and thus to take architectural decisions that could improve the effectiveness of the newly derived organizational architecture. Nokia's experience with the JRD was therefore central in the accumulation of architectural knowledge on the dispersed activities and how they could be integrated and linked into one value-adding system. Thus, as Nokia accumulates architectural knowledge over time, its decision makers increasingly understood the nature of the organizational activities and how these are interdependent on each other.

We therefore induce that firms with low offshoring experience are less likely to have acquired architectural knowledge, and do therefore not have the propensity to include architectural considerations in their offshoring strategies. The firms only have little experience with the implementation and have therefore not yet been faced with the challenges of reintegrating the international organizational architecture. Without architectural knowledge, the decision maker has no aspiration to consider the organizational architecture, and will therefore devote less attention to (cf. Ocasio, 1997).

With higher offshoring implementation maturity, however, firms are more likely to have been exposed to architectural challenges and thereby gained architectural knowledge. Accordingly, firms are more likely to include organizational objectives in their offshoring strategies with the purpose of increasing organizational performance. Massini et al. (2010) find that more experienced firms are more likely to adopt a corporate-wide offshoring strategy with a more nuanced view of offshoring that looks beyond short-term costs advantages, but also includes a broader set of drivers and risks. Similarly, both Maskell et al. (2007) and Jensen (2009) show how offshoring experience mediates a sophistication of firms' offshoring operations. Thus, we argue that the more experience a firm has with an offshoring implementation, the more likely it is to have accumulated architectural knowledge, and, as a result, the more likely they are to include organizational objectives in their offshoring strategies. With architectural knowledge, the decision maker has therefore aspiration to consider the organizational architecture, and will therefore devote more attention on. Based on the Nokia case and the previous reasoning, we formulate the following research hypothesis to be tested on a large-N sample:

> **Research hypothesis.** Offshoring experience has a positive effect on firms' organizational strategy orientation.

QUANTITATIVE ANALYSIS

Methods and Variable Construction

Building on the insights of the qualitative analysis, we go a step further by testing the effect of experience on firms' offshoring strategies using data from the ORN. The variables include a dependent variable – *organizational strategy orientation* – one independent variable – *offshoring experience* – and a number of control variables. For this analysis, we run ordinary least square (OLS) regression analysis. The OLS models are most suitable for this analysis as both our dependent and independent variables are measured on a continuous scale. The operationalization of these variables is outlined in the following.

Organizational strategy orientation is measured by asking respondents to indicate on a 5-point-Likert scale about the importance of different strategic drivers (1 = not important at all and 5 = very important). The three strategic drivers that constitute the organizational strategy orientation variable are: "Enhancing efficiency through business process redesign," "Enhancing system redundancy," and "Improving service levels." The three items have a Cronbach Alpha value of 0.64 indicating that they are manifest items of an underlying variable that we label and interpret as "Organizational strategy orientation." The three items are averaged in order to form the composite measure of organizational strategy orientation. The mean value of the organizational strategy orientation variable is 3.29 with a standard deviation 0.96 (see Table 1), which indicate that we have substantial variation in our dependent variable. This variable should thus be seen in contrast to *locational strategy orientation,* which captures the strategy orientation toward more external factors like customers, suppliers, etc. The locational strategy orientation is measured by asking respondents to indicate on a 5-point-Likert scale about the importance of different strategic

Table 1. Correlation Matrix Including All Variables (*N* = 353).[a]

	1	2	3	4	5	6	7	8	9	10	11	12	13	14
1. Offshoring experience	1.00													
2. Functional experience	0.29	1.00												
3. Country experience	0.37	0.76	1.00											
4. Employees offshored	0.08	−0.03	−0.06	1.00										
5. Standardization of task	0.04	−0.09	−0.09	−0.02	1.00									
6. Commoditization of task	−0.11	−0.15	−0.16	−0.01	0.26	1.00								
7. Collaborative technologies	−0.03	−0.05	−0.04	−0.03	0.33	0.02	1.00							
8. Locational strategy orientation	−0.05	0.13	0.01	0.13	0.05	0.08	−0.03	1.00						
9. BPO	0.11	0.15	0.22	−0.03	0.35	−0.32	0.09	−0.04	1.00					
10. KPO	−0.06	−0.03	−0.11	0.07	−0.52	−0.43	−0.42	−0.03	−0.55	1.00				
11. Organizational strategy orientation	0.13	0.21	0.15	−0.02	−0.20	−0.27	−0.02	0.35	−0.02	0.17	1.00			
12. Geographical distance	−0.01	−0.08	0.04	0.03	−0.02	0.07	0.08	−0.08	0.07	−0.14	0.06	1.00		
13. Cultural distance	−0.05	−0.04	−0.01	−0.03	0.03	0.04	−0.03	0.01	0.05	−0.06	−0.04	0.18	1.00	
14. Language distance	−0.11	−0.16	−0.10	0.10	−0.07	0.01	0.07	−0.05	−0.03	0.01	−0.02	0.43	−0.39	1.00
Mean	8.88	6.06	3.03	110	3.15	3.01	3.32	3.04	0.13	0.23	3.29	8,521	8.89	0.44
Standard deviation	4.70	5.01	2.53	259	0.28	0.30	0.13	0.93	0	0.42	0.96	4,186	5.49	0.49
Minimum value	0	1	1	1	2.72	2.38	2.97	1	0	0	1	0	0	0
Maximum value	44	21	10	2,000	3.54	3.45	3.75	5	1	1	5	16,244	31.5	1

[a] All coefficients above 0.10 are significant at 5% level.

drivers (1 = not important at all and 5 = very important). The three strategic drivers that form the organizational strategy orientation variable are: "Access to new markets for products and services," "Increasing speed to market," and "Growth strategy." The three items that are averaged in order to form the composite measure of locational strategy orientation have a Cronbach Alpha value of 0.65. This variable is included as a control variable to investigate the effect of firms' general strategy orientation.

Offshoring experience is a measure of time (in years) since the focal off-shoring implementation was launched. The assumption is that the longer the firm has been engaged in this particular offshoring project the more experience is accumulated related to this offshoring implementation. This approach is akin to other papers investigating the role of offshoring experience (e.g., Lewin et al., 2009; Maskell et al., 2007). While the firm may have offshoring experience from other offshoring activities, the gist of this measure is that it measure the experience specific to the particular offshoring implementation. However, we will control for other types of offshoring experience. The mean value of offshoring experience with the focal implementation is 8.88 years and it varies from 0 (two very recent implementations) to 44 years of offshoring experience (see Table 1).

Firms will gain more general offshoring experience through other off-shoring projects than the focal one and this general offshoring experience might in a similar way speed up the accumulation of architectural knowledge. Therefore, we control for this more general offshoring experience by taking into account number of employees, functions and locations that the firm previously has offshored to. More specifically, we construct a variable measuring the *number of service functions* (e.g., IT, HR, legal, finance, and accounting) that the firm has previously offshored and a variable measuring the *number of locations* that the firm has offshoring projects in. The third variable capturing the general offshoring experience is a measure of the *number of employees* that has previously been offshored.

In addition, we control for the nature of the offshored tasks as firms response to the organizational reconfiguration of offshoring may vary with the nature of the activities; for example, one would expect that more standardized and self-manageable tasks provide less need for strategic response than less standardized activities (e.g., Sanchez & Mahoney, 1996). For this reason, we first control for the degree of *standardization of tasks* in each function. Another variable, taken from the ORN Provider Survey, include *commoditization of tasks* since offshoring projects in functions with high level of commoditization might be less prone to architectural challenges (see, e.g., Manning, Lewin, & Schuerch, 2011). Commoditization refers to a process by which services and processes become more standardized, and knowledge less specific to firm or product characteristics, lowering transaction and coordination costs for firms offshoring these processes (see Davenport, 2005 for a similar definition). The use of *collaborative technologies* in the function is added to control for the use of information- and communication technology in the firm (Manning et al., 2008). The above mentioned three control variables are measured as 5-point-Likert scale variables based on the perception of service providers. Assuming that international interdependencies are more challenging to coordinate than colocated interdependencies (Srikanth & Puranam, 2011), we have added control variables for interaction distance that are based on secondary data on the distance between the home location and the foreign location of the offshore implementation. The interaction distance includes three dimensions: *geographical distance* measured as air miles between the home location and the offshore location, *cultural distance* between two locations based on the Kogut & Singh-index (Kogut & Singh, 1988), and *language distance* as a dummy variable indicating whether the same language is spoken both in the home location and in the offshore location. Finally, two dummies were added to control for whether the offshoring implementation was a business process offshoring (*BPO*) or a knowledge process offshoring (*KPO*). The third possible type, information technology outsourcing (ITO), was omitted and therefore serves as the baseline when interpreting the coefficients for BPO and KPO.

RESULTS

The descriptive statistics (mean, standard deviation, minimum and maximum values) and correlation matrix for all variables are provided in Table 1. Since the data included some high correlation coefficients, in particular between functional and country experience and between the BPO- and KPO-dummies, we tested for the variance inflation factor (VIF) in all models as well as tested the models with and without the highly correlated variables. However, since the high correlations were only among our control variables the results for our key variables remained qualitatively the same irrespective of the specification of the model. The VIF values for all models were below six, which is considered to be the threshold for detection of problems of multicolinearity (expect for KPO which has a VIF value slightly above the threshold, however, this is expected as KPO, BPO and ITO is negatively correlated by design). See Table 2 where all VIF value are included.

The results of the OLS regressions are presented in Table 2. The model includes our independent variable, offshoring experience, and all the control variables. Our independent variable comes out significant and positive ($\beta = 0.02$ and $p < 0.05$) indicating that offshoring experience related to the focal implementation is explaining the organizational strategy orientation.

Table 2. OLS-Regression Models with Standard Error in Parentheses and VIF Values in Italics.

	Organizational Strategy Orientation
Intercept	5.21*
	(2.24)
Offshoring experience	0.02*
	(0.01) *1.25*
Function experience	0.02
	(0.01) *2.64*
Country experience	−0.01
	(0.03) *2.80*
Employees offshored	−0.01
	(0.01) *1.07*
Standardization of task	−0.46*
	(0.20) *1.66*
Commoditization of task	−0.95**
	(0.32) *4.09*
Collaborative technologies	0.26
	(0.47) *1.97*
Locational strategy orientation	0.40***
	(0.05) *1.09*
BPO	−0.20
	(0.20) *4.98*
KPO	−0.06
	(0.26) *6.41*
Geographical distance	0.01*
	(0.01) *1.53*
Cultural distance	−0.01
	(0.01) *1.83*
Language distance	−0.19
	(0.14) *2.34*
F-value	10.50
R-square	0.287
Adjusted R-square	0.260

***, **, and * indicate significance on 0.1%, 1%, and 5% level, respectively.

Stronger organizational strategy orientation is following with more experience on the focal offshore implementation. It is further notable that the other more general experience variables are all insignificant (functional experience, country experience, and number of employees offshored) signifying that it is specific experience related to the focal offshoring implementation that matters rather than more general offshoring experience. As expected the more standardized and commoditized the offshored tasks the less scope for organizational strategy orientation, therefore both of these variables are significant negative. Locational strategy orientation, on the other hand, is significant positive reflecting that locational and organizational strategy orientation is not at the expense of each other, but rather that they reinforce each other. Among the distance variables it is only the geographical distance that turns significant.

In order to test for potential multilevel problems, a random coefficient model was conducted with Region (i.e., the region that hosts the implementation) as the group variable. However, only 5% of the variation in our dependent variable could be related to the region (i.e., an intra-class correlation of 0.05 in the empty models) and the random effects of the intercept at the between-level was insignificant ($p = 0.04$). This indicates that a random coefficient model is inferior to the applied OLS models.

DISCUSSION

This paper investigates how the organizational reconfiguration of offshoring impacts firms' strategies. Offshoring describes the disintegration and relocation abroad of business services that support domestic or global operations (Contractor et al., 2010; Manning et al., 2008). A major challenge in this respect is thus reintegration of the offshored activities into the organizational architecture (Mudambi & Venzin, 2010). In respect to offshoring, the organizational architecture can be defined as decision makers' more or less intentional choices to ensure that geographically dispersed organizational components and activities coexist and are linked to one another in an effective way (cf. Ethiraj & Levinthal, 2004; Nadler & Tushman, 1997; Sah & Stiglitz, 1986).

Using a mixed methods approach, we have first presented the case of Nokia Denmark and its decision to offshore certain product development activities to Taiwanese Foxconn in a joint R&D model. The case shows how the decision to offshore was initially driven by external objectives such as lower costs and access to strategic resources, but that this changed over time toward internal objectives. Based on this analysis, we induced a testable research hypothesis that argues that firms with offshoring experience are more likely to acknowledge and consider the organizational architecture in their strategies than firms with little experience. The assumption is therefore that firms with experience are more likely to have been exposed to architectural challenges, and are as a result more likely to have accumulated architectural knowledge. We found empirical support for this hypothesis using a dataset with 353 offshoring implementations reported by 129 U.S. and European firms. This suggests that the more experience the firm has with a specific offshoring project, the more likely it is to encapsulate the organizational architecture in its strategies. Interestingly, while we found experience measured in years since the implementation to be significant in explaining organizational strategy orientation, other experience measures such the number of countries and activities on a firm level turned out insignificant. This may suggest that architectural knowledge within the single implementation is residual and sticky (von Hippel, 1994) and, as such, is difficult to transfer across implementations and organizations.

This paper contributes to research on the organizational design and architecture of offshoring as well as on the dynamics of organizational architectures (Jensen et al., 2013). First of all, previous research on offshoring has been biased toward understanding either the antecedents or the outcomes of offshoring implementations (Doh et al., 2009; Kedia & Mukherjee, 2009; Lewin et al., 2009; Mol et al., 2005) and has ignored how firms actually approach offshoring. In contrast, this paper seeks to investigate the organizational architecture of offshoring implementations and how this impacts offshoring strategies. By showing that firms only seem to acknowledge the organizational architecture of offshoring with experience, we add a perspective on firm behavior that is in support of research that finds that most offshoring decisions are taken opportunistically, without corporate-wide strategies that delineate specific plans and guidelines for the adoption and implementation of offshoring activities (Lewin & Peeters, 2006; Massini et al., 2010). However, rather than assuming that the successful architecture of firms' offshoring activities can a priori be planned and implemented, we suggest that this is more a subject of continuous learning and improvement through accumulation of architectural knowledge within the given implementation. An interesting topic for future research thus relates to understanding firms' specific offshoring knowledge strategies and how this impacts performance. Moreover, while this research has focused on strategic orientation to illuminate this strategic response, future research could investigate how firms actually interact with the organizational design – that is, which changes they implement – as they gain offshoring experience and architectural knowledge.

More broadly, this research has implications for literature that seeks to understand how different architectural forms and practices correlate to organizational performance (e.g., Datta, 1991; Foss, Laursen, & Pedersen, 2011; Sah & Stiglitz, 1986; Zott & Amit, 2008). In particular, our argument is that firms adopt their strategies to accommodate for architectural inefficiencies. As such, we pose that strategy follows structure (Hall & Saias, 1980), but that this causality is contingent upon the accumulation of architectural knowledge. Thus, while certain organizational architectures may prove superior to others, this research suggest that superior organizational performance is more a result of a process where decision makers accumulate architectural knowledge than it is a result of a conscious strategy. Decision makers need to identify and uncover underlying interdependency structures in the organizational architecture by systematizing and accumulating knowledge and learning processes within the firm. This is in line with research that notes that architectural effectiveness is an outcome of the organization's ability to balance the search for organizational decisions and the exploitation of these once found (Rivkin & Siggelkow, 2003; Siggelkow, 2002). However, we extend this research by suggesting that it is the bounded rational decision maker who incrementally gains and accumulates knowledge on how to design the organizational architecture with the purpose of optimizing performance.

LIMITATIONS

This study does not go without limitations. For example, we argue that firms' organizationally oriented strategies can be explained by firms' experience. As firms face organizational challenges deriving from an international architecture, they will begin to search and accumulate architectural knowledge that can be deployed in offshoring strategies. However, our quantitative research design does not allow us to consider the actual challenges that firms face following the implementation (although the qualitative part provides some indications). Similarly, we have not empirically been able to say anything about different types of experience within the single implementation. For example, Madsen and Desai (2010) find that experience with failure leads to higher organizational performance than experience with success. Thus, future research could investigate what type of experience contributes more to the successful organizational adaptation following the offshoring implementation.

CONCLUDING REMARKS

A key issue in this paper is how organizational architectures evolve to become more effective. By studying how offshoring experience prompts firms to formulate more organizationally oriented strategies, we have emphasized the role of knowledge accumulation following an organizational reconfiguration (i.e., the offshoring implementation). This conceptualization builds on previous research on architectural evolution that observes that the successful organizational architecture is the result of a process in which the organization is able to search for new and good organizational decisions and to exploit these decisions once found (Rivkin & Siggelkow, 2003; Siggelkow, 2002). Yet, we go beyond this by aligning the theoretical development with the bounded rational decision maker who incrementally gains and accumulates knowledge on how to most appropriately design the organizational architecture with the purpose of optimizing performance. The Nokia management's decision to relocate product development activities to China disrupted the effectiveness of the organizational architecture, which consequently prompted them to search for alternative architectural arrangements so that the fit could be restored. Thus, we propose an evolutionary view on the organizational architecture that can be depicted as an iterative process between decision makers' search for architectural opportunities and the accumulation of architectural knowledge, which increases the likelihood of taking decisions that will lead to more effective organizational architectures. Accordingly, strategy follows structure (Hall & Saias, 1980), but only to the extent that the decision maker successfully accumulates architectural knowledge.

REFERENCES

Allen, T. J. (1977). *Managing the flow of technology*. Cambridge, MA: MIT Press.

Argyres, N. (2007). Contract design as a firm capability: An integration of learning and transaction cost perspectives. *Academy of Management Review, 32*(4), 1060–1077.

Aron, R., & Singh, J. V. (2005). Getting offshoring right. *Harvard Business Review, 83*(12), 135–143.

Baldwin, C. Y., & Clark, K. B. (2000). *Design rules. Vol. 1 — The power of modularity.* Cambridge, MA: The MIT Press.

Bartell, C. A., & Ghoshal, S. (1989). *Managing across borders: The transnational solution.* Boston, MA: Harvard Business School Press.

Brusoni, S., Marengo, L., Prencipe, A., & Valente, M. (2007). The value and costs of modularity: A problem-solving perspective. *European Management Review*, *4*(2), 121−132.

Brusoni, S., & Prencipe, A. (2001). Unpacking the black box of modularity: Technologies, products and organizations. *Industrial & Corporate Change*, *10*(1), 179−205.

Brusoni, S., & Prencipe, A. (2006). Making design rules: A multidomain perspective. *Organization Science*, *17*(2), 179−189.

Brusoni, S., Prencipe, A., & Pavitt, K. (2001). Knowledge specialization, organizational coupling, and the boundaries of the firm: Why do firms know more than they make? *Administrative Science Quarterly*, *46*(4), 597−621.

Chandler, A. D. (1962). *Strategy and structure.* Cambridge, MA: MIT Press.

Chang, S. J., van Witteloostuijn, A., & Eden, L. (2010). From the editors: Common method variance in international business research. *Journal of International Business Studies*, *41*(2), 178−184.

Clark, H., & Brennan, S. (1991). Grounding in communication. In L. B. Resnick, J. M. Levine, & S. D. Teasley (Eds.), *Perspectives on socially shared cognition* (pp. 127−149). Washington, DC: APA Books.

Contractor, F. J., Kumar, V., Kundu, S. K., & Pedersen, T. (2010). Reconceptualizing the firm in a world of outsourcing and offshoring: The organizational and geographical relocation of high-value company functions. *Journal of Management Studies*, *47*(8), 1417−1433.

Datta, D. K. (1991). Organizational fit and acquisition performance: Effects of post-acquisition integration. *Strategic Management Journal*, *12*(4), 281−297.

Davenport, T. H. (2005). The coming commoditization of processes. *Harvard Business Review*, *83*(6), 100−108.

Doh, J. P., Bunyaratavej, K., & Hahn, E. D. (2009). Separable but not equal: The location determinants of discrete services offshoring activities. *Journal of International Business Studies*, *40*(6), 926−943.

Dossani, R., & Kenney, M. (2003). "Lift and shift": Moving the back office to India. *Information Technologies & International Development*, *1*(2), 21−37.

Drazin, R., & Ven, A. H. Vd. (1985). Alternative forms of fit in contingency theory. *Administrative Science Quarterly*, *30*(4), 514−539.

Edmondson, A. C., & McManus, S. E. (2007). Methodological fit in management field research. *Academy of Management Review*, *32*(4), 1155−1179.

Eisenhardt, K. M. (1989). Building theories from case study research. *Academy of Management Review*, *14*(4), 532−550.

Eisenhardt, K. M., & Graebner, M. E. (2007). Theory building from cases: Opportunities and challenges. *Academy of Management Journal*, *50*(1), 25−32.

Ernst, D., & Kim, L. (2002). Global production networks, knowledge diffusion, and local capability formation. *Research Policy*, *31*(8), 1417−1429.

Ethiraj, S. K., & Levinthal, D. (2004). Bounded rationality and the search for organizational architecture: An evolutionary perspective on the design of organizations and their evolvability. *Administrative Science Quarterly*, *49*(3), 404−437.

Foss, N. J., Laursen, K., & Pedersen, T. (2011). Linking customer interaction and innovation: The mediating role of new organizational practices. *Organization Science, 22*(4), 980–999.

Geringer, J. M., & Hebert, L. (1989). Control and performance of international joint venture. *Journal of International Business Studies, 20*(2), 235–254.

Graf, M., & Mudambi, S. M. (2005). The outsourcing of IT-enabled business processes: A conceptual model of the location decision. *Journal of International Management, 11*(2), 253–268.

Gulati, R., & Puranam, P. (2009). Renewal through reorganization: The value of inconsistencies between formal and informal organization. *Organization science, 20*(2), 422–440.

Hall, D. J., & Saias, M. A. (1980). Strategy follows structure! *Strategic Management Journal, 1*(2), 149–163.

Heijmen, T., Lewin, A. Y., Manning, S., Perm-Ajchariyawong, N., & Russell, J. W. (2009). *Offshoring reaches the c-suite. 2007/8 ORN survey report.* Duke University & The Conference Board, Durham, NC.

Henderson, R., & Clark, K. B. (1990). Architectural innovation: The reconfiguration of existing product technologies and the failure of established firms. *Administrative Science Quarterly, 35*(1), 9–30.

Hutzschenreuter, T., Lewin, A. Y., & Dresel, S. (2011). Governance modes for offshoring activities: A comparison of US and German firms. *International Business Review, 20*(3), 291–313.

Inkpen, A., & Beamish, P. W. (1997). Knowledge, bargaining power, and the instability of international joint ventures. *Academy of Management Review, 22*(1), 177–202.

Jacobides, M. G., & Winter, S. (2005). The co-evolution of capabilities and transaction costs: Explaining the institutional structure of production. *Strategic Management Journal, 26*(5), 395–413.

Jensen, P. D. Ø. (2009). A learning perspective on the offshoring of advanced services. *Journal of International Management, 15*(2), 181–193.

Jensen, P. D. Ø., Larsen, M. M., & Pedersen, T. (2013). The organizational design of offshoring: Taking stock and looking forward. *Journal of International Management, 19*, 315–323.

Kedia, B. L., & Lahiri, S. (2007). International outsourcing of services: A partnership model. *Journal of International Management, 13*(1), 22–37.

Kedia, B. L., & Mukherjee, D. (2009). Understanding offshoring: A research framework based on disintegration, location and externalization advantages. *Journal of World Business, 44*(3), 250–261.

Kenney, M., Massini, S., & Murtha, T. P. (2009). Offshoring administrative and technical work: New fields for understanding the global enterprise. *International Journal of Business Studies, 40*(6), 887–900.

Khandwalla, P. N. (1973). Viable and effective organizational designs of firms. *Academy of Management Journal, 16*(3), 481–495.

Kogut, B., & Singh, H. (1988). The effect of national culture on the choice of entry mode. *Journal of International Business Studies, 19*, 411–432.

Kraut, R. E., Egido, C., & Galegher, J. (1990). Patterns of contact and communication in scientific research collaboration. In J. Galegher, R. E. Kraut, & C. Egido (Eds.), *Intellectual teamwork: Social and technological foundations of cooperative work* (pp. 149–171). Hillsdale, NJ: Erlbaum Associates.

Kumar, K., Van Fenema, P. C., & von Glinow, M. A. (2009). Offshoring and the global distribution of work: Implications for task interdependence theory and practice. *Journal of International Business Studies, 40*(4), 642–667.

Larsen, M. M., Manning, S., & Pedersen, T. (2013). Uncovering the hidden costs of offshoring: The interplay of complexity, organizational design and experience. *Strategic Management Journal, 34*(5), 533–552.

Larsen, M. M., & Pedersen, T. (2012). Nokia: From in-house to joint R&D. Case: 9B11M114. Ivey Management Services. London, Canada, October 10, pp. 1–15.

Lawrence, P. R., & Lorsch, J. W. (1967). *Organization and environment. managing differentiation and integration.* Boston, MA: Harvard University Press.

Lewin, A. Y., & Couto, V. (2007). *Next generation offshoring: The globalization of innovation.* CIBER/Booz Allen Hamilton report, Duke University, Durham, NC.

Lewin, A. Y., Massini, S., & Peeters, C. (2009). Why are companies offshoring innovation? The emerging global race for talent. *Journal of International Business Studies, 40*(8), 901–925.

Lewin, A. Y., & Peeters, C. (2006). Offshoring work: Business hype or the onset of fundamental transformation? *Long Range Planning, 39*(3), 221–239.

Lou, Y. (2002). Contract, cooperation, and performance in international joint ventures. *Strategic Management Journal, 23*(10), 903–919.

Lounamaa, P. H., & March, J. G. (1987). Adaptive coordination of a learning team. *Management Science, 33*(1), 107–123.

Madsen, P. M., & Desai, V. (2010). Failing to learn? The effects of failure and success on organizational learning in the global orbital launch vehicle industry. *Academy of Management Journal, 53*(3), 451–476.

Manning, S., Lewin, A. Y., & Schuerch, M. (2011). The stability of offshore outsourcing relationships: The role of relation specificity and client control. *Management International Review, 51*(3), 381–406.

Manning, S., Massini, S., & Lewin, A. Y. (2008). A dynamic perspective on next-generation offshoring: The global sourcing of science and engineering talent. *Academy of Management Perspectives, 22*(3), 35–54.

Martinez, J. I., & Jarillo, J. C. (1989). The evolution of research on coordination mechanisms in multinational corporations. *Journal of International Business Studies, 29*, 489–514.

Maskell, P., Pedersen, T., Petersen, B., & Dick-Nielsen, J. (2007). Learning paths to offshore outsourcing: From cost reduction to knowledge seeking. *Industry & Innovation, 14*(3), 239–257.

Massini, S., Pern-Ajchariyawong, N., & Lewin, A. Y. (2010). Role of corporate-wide offshoring strategy on offshoring drivers, risks and performance. *Industry and Innovation, 17*(4), 337–371.

Mol, M. J., van Tulder, R. J. M., & Beije, P. R. (2005). Antecedents and performance consequences of international outsourcing. *International Business Review, 14*(5), 599–617.

Mudambi, R., & Venzin, M. (2010). The strategic nexus of offshoring and outsourcing decisions. *Journal of Management Studies, 47*(8), 1510–1533.

Nadler, D. A., & Tushman, M. (1997). *Competing by design: The power of organizational architecture.* New York, NY: Oxford University Press.

Nelson, R. R., & Winter, S. G. (1982). *An evolutionary theory of economic change.* Cambridge, MA: Belknap Press of Harvard University Press.

Ocasio, W. (1997). Towards an attention-based view of the firm. *Strategic Management Journal, Summer Special Issue, 18*, 187–206.

Orton, J. D., & Weick, K. E. (1990). Loosely coupled systems: A reconceptualization. *Academy of Management Review, 15*(2), 203–223.

Perrow, C. (1967). A framework for the comparative analysis of organizations. *American Sociological Review, 32*(2), 194–208.

Pettigrew, A. (1990). Longitudinal field research on change: Theory and practice. *Organization Science, 1*(3), 267–292.

Rivkin, J. W., & Siggelkow, N. (2003). Balancing search and stability: Interdependencies among elements organizational design. *Management Science, 49*(3), 290–311.

Sah, R. K., & Stiglitz, J. E. (1986). The architecture of economic systems: Hierarchies and polyarchies. *The American Economic Review, 76*(4), 716–727.

Sanchez, R., & Mahoney, J. T. (1996). Modularity, flexibility, and knowledge management in product and organization design. *Strategic Management Journal, 17*, 63–76.

Schilling, M. A. (2000). Toward a general modular systems theory and its application to interfirm product modularity. *Academy of Management Review, 25*(2), 312–334.

Siggelkow, N. (2002). Evolution toward fit. *Administrative Science Quarterly, 47*(1), 125–159.

Siggelkow, N. (2007). Persuasion with case studies. *Academy of Management Journal, 50*(1), 20–24.

Silverman, D. (2006). *Interpreting qualitative data*. London: Sage.

Simon, H. A. (1955). A behavioral model of rational choice. *The Quarterly Journal of Economics, 69*(1), 99–118.

Simon, H. A., & March, J. G. (1958). *Organizations*. Oxford, England: Wiley.

Srikanth, K., & Puranam, P. (2011). Integrating distributed work: Comparing task design, communication, and tacit coordination mechanisms. *Strategic Management Journal, 32*(8), 849–875.

Storper, M., & Venables, A. J. (2004). Buzz: Face-to-face contact and the urban economy. *Journal of Economic Geography, 4*(4), 351–370.

Tanriverdi, H., Konana, P., & Ge, L. (2007). The choice of sourcing mechanisms for business processes. *Information System Research, 18*(3), 280–299.

Thompson, J. D. (1967). *Organizations in action: Social science bases of administrative theory*. New York, NY: McGraw-Hill.

Tsoukas, H. (2001). What is organizational knowledge? *Journal of Management Studies, 38*(7), 973–993.

Tushman, M. L., & Nadler, D. A. (1978). Information processing as an integrating concept in organizational design. *Academy of Management Review, 3*(3), 613–624.

van de Ven, A. H. (1976). On the nature, formation, and maintenance of relations among organizations. *Academy of Management Review, 1*(4), 24–36.

von Hippel, E. (1994). "Sticky information" and the locus of problem solving: Implications for Innovation. *Management Science, 4*(40), 429–439.

Weick, K. E. (1976). Educational organizations as loosely coupled systems. *Administrative Science Quarterly, 21*(1), 1–19.

Yin, R. K. (2003). *Case study research*. London: Sage.

Zott, C., & Amit, R. (2008). The fit between product market strategy and business model: Implications for firm performance. *Strategic Management Journal, 29*(1), 1–26.

EXPERIENTIAL LEARNING AND INNOVATION IN OFFSHORE OUTSOURCING TRANSITIONS

Christopher Williams and Maya Kumar

ABSTRACT

We use experiential learning theory to develop new conceptual insights into offshore outsourcing of innovation. In particular, we show how off-shore vendor firms are able to overcome liability of outsidership and eventually learn how to innovate on behalf of their onshore clients as a result of their embedment with clients across multiple teams. We theorize that the cross-border relocation of innovative activities from a client firm to an offshore vendor is only possible when teams within the vendor team have assumed a double-loop learning capability from the client allowing them to determine governing variables relating to the client's organizational environment. Through direct on-the-job experience working with each other, international teams comprised in part from the vendor and in part from the client can undergo different learning transitions, which we classify as either relationship-oriented or task-oriented. These transitions determine the extent to which double-loop learning can be developed in offshore locations and are influenced by intra-team dynamics and the way the joint teams organize and manage themselves. Our perspective

Orchestration of the Global Network Organization
Advances in International Management, Volume 27, 433–461
ISSN: 1571-5027/doi:10.1108/S1571-502720140000027005

has implications for our understanding of organizational designs asso-
ciated with both client and vendor multinational enterprises seeking to
benefit from innovation in offshore outsourcing.

Keywords: Organizational learning; experiential knowledge; offshore
outsourcing; innovation; communication; social linkages

INTRODUCTION

Early internationalization theories stress how foreign direct investment
(FDI) is driven by the firms' need to internalize transactions across national
boundaries (Buckley & Casson, 1976) and to gain access to new knowledge
(Dunning, 1981; Kuemmerle, 1999). A more recent approach emphasizes
the role of a firm's networks and the firm's position relative to those networks in determining internationalization strategy (Johanson & Vahlne,
2009). This approach posits that, following entry, relationships develop
with local customers, suppliers, competitors, and different types of institutions, allowing the firm to overcome costs associated with being an "outsider" (Johanson & Vahlne, 2009). Such market-specific networks build trust
and help the internationalizing firm to reduce the effects of "liability of
outsidership" in the foreign market (Johanson & Vahlne, 2009, p. 1411).

The central theme of this chapter is how firms overcome this "liability of
outsidership" when they are engaged in the offshore outsourcing of innovative activities. Driven by a shortage of innovative talent in home countries
of firms, potential of cost advantages of sourcing innovative talent abroad,
and access to knowledge and other nonhuman capital resources (Levy,
2005; Lewin, Massini, & Peeters, 2009), firms have intensified their international search for human capital and innovative capabilities in product
design, engineering and research and development (R&D) (Lewin & Couto,
2006). Over the past 15 years, global sourcing of innovative capabilities
has been achieved increasingly through offshore outsourcing (Lewin, Lin,
Aird, & Sappenfield, 2011) − contracting a firm in another country (henceforth a "vendor") to innovate on behalf of the focal firm (a "client"). Client
firms such as U.S.-based Otis Elevator, the world's largest designer and
builder of vertical transportation systems (Govindarajan & Bagla, 2013),
have given the responsibility of several of their innovation activities to an
offshore vendor in India.

Many vendors have also developed a global presence themselves.
The top 50 outsourcing service vendors include the Indian information

technology (IT) firms Wipro and Infosys, Brazilian firms like TIVIT, Chinese firms such as Neusoft, and Western-based firms such as Accenture and ISS (IAOP, 2013). Such vendor firms continue to grow and reap the benefits of offering higher value-added services, including innovating for their clients.

Client and vendor firms must collaborate when offshoring business activity from one location to another, transferring knowledge and technology. Knowledge transfer in this context relates not only to the sending of knowledge from a source (a client) to a recipient (a vendor), but also its integration, understanding, and application in innovative ways (Cohen & Levinthal, 1990; Inkpen & Tsang, 2005). However, issues arise from a lack of proximity, and in many cases an initial unfamiliarity associated with distance between client and vendor (Armstrong & Cole, 2002; Grote & Täube, 2007; Jarvenpaa & Leidner, 1999). It can take time for the transfer of innovative capabilities to occur (Bardhan, 2006), and distance can further hinder the building of relational norms and opportunities for socialization, resulting in poor communication and a lack of trust (Jarvenpaa & Leidner, 1999; Maznevski & Chudoba, 2000; Nardi & Whittaker, 2002).

We argue that the way in which clients and vendors learn from each other has a vital role to play in determining the extent to which both types of firms can overcome issues of outsidership in order to benefit from globalization of innovation. Recent studies on this topic have looked at the construct of learning over time. Benito, Dovgan, Petersen, and Welch (2013) suggest that the process of offshore outsourcing parallels conventional internationalization theory (Johanson & Vahlne, 1977), with incremental organizational learning occurring during the internationalization process and subsequent gradual intensification of outsourcing activities in foreign markets. Client firms internationalize gradually through offshore outsourcing as they learn and gain experience (Maskell, Pedersen, Petersen, & Dick-Nielsen, 2007). Concurrently, vendors grow and coevolve during the offshore outsourcing process (Lahiri & Kedia, 2011). Through the partnership with clients, vendors enhance their skills and expertise, enabling them to incorporate some of their clients' practices into their own businesses. This has resulted in vendors being able to offer an increasingly advanced level of service to their clients as experience is accumulated (IAOP, 2013; Lahiri & Kedia, 2011).

Given these recent trends and insights, we ask: what are the organizational design implications for offshore outsourcing of innovation and how do these learning relationships develop over time? Some guidance is provided by the international management literature. Particular literature focuses on governance modes (Hutzschenreuter, Lewin, & Dresel, 2011), while others focus on the competence of team members in overcoming cultural distance (Hallén & Wiedersheim-Paul, 1984; Johnson, Lenartowicz, & Apud, 2006; Kogut & Singh, 1988). Other IB literature delves into the practices firms can implement to improve coordination of global offshoring teams (Sidhu & Volberda, 2011) and knowledge transfer mechanisms that could help overcome distances between clients and vendors (Williams, 2011) and improve the building of shàred mental models (Chen, McQueen, & Sun, 2013). The team-working literature also sheds light on the question, suggesting that overcoming issues arising from distance between clients and vendors can be achieved by effective communications, building trust, and maintaining a heterogeneous and flexible team composition (Ancona & Caldwell, 1992; Eby & Dobbins, 1997; Jarvenpaa & Leidner, 1999; Majchrzak, Rice, Malhotra, King, & Ba, 2000).

Our approach is to extend this stream of research by utilizing experiential learning theory. This allows us to propose a new model of the process by which client and vendor firms engage in offshore outsourcing for innovation. Learning is defined here as "a process whereby knowledge is created through the transformation of experience" (Kolb, 1980, p. 38). Our model suggests that both onshore clients and offshore vendors establish teams to be involved in the offshore outsourcing transition of innovation and that these teams undergo different types of experiential learning. The transition period is the passage of time in which knowledge-intensive work is relocated from a client to a vendor (Beulen, Tiwari, & van Heck, 2011). We focus on how learning is influenced by the way clients and vendors organize and manage relationships and tasks within these cross-border teams that are often newly formed. Onshore clients learn how to relinquish knowledge and control over innovative activities while offshore vendors gradually learn how to innovate from direct on-the-job experience with clients. Our approach is to understand this process by referring to Argyris' model of single and double-loop learning.[1] We theorize that vendor-led innovation in a given team is only possible when the vendor part of the team has assumed a double-loop learning capability from the client and is willing and able to establish governing variables relating to its client's industry within a learning process (Argyris, 1976). Using this assumption, we propose there are two paths to vendor-led innovation in offshore outsourcing: a *task-oriented learning transition*, characterized by the transfer of explicit knowledge that is relatively easy to codify and articulate, and *relationship-oriented learning transition*, characterized by the transfer of tacit, difficult to articulate knowledge and trust. Finally, we discuss the organizational implications of various constellations of learning transitions *across multiple teams* involved in global offshore outsourcing between a client and vendor firms.

Our approach has implications for theory development on knowledge transfer and the learning microprocesses in global offshore outsourcing of innovation. Furthermore, we contribute to the global innovation literature in our examination of learning modes adopted by clients and vendors at different times during the transfer of innovation capabilities. Practical implications for managers of client firms involved in the geographic dispersion and offshore outsourcing of innovation and vendor firms aspiring to innovate for their clients are also discussed.

ORGANIZATIONAL FEATURES OF OFFSHORE OUTSOURCING FOR INNOVATION

The literature on inter-firm learning, the knowledge-based view, and dynamic environments suggests there are particular organizational features of offshore outsourcing that impact how we theorize around offshore outsourcing for innovation. Our approach is to analyze these at a team level and consider: (1) the formation and evolution of the actual client—vendor teams involved in the offshore outsourcing process; (2) how these client—vendor teams each have a common locus for exploring and exploiting; and (3) how the transferring of tacit knowledge is necessary for innovative activities between client and vendor teams.

The Formation and Evolution of Client—Vendor Teams

Transitioning knowledge-intensive work from a client firm to an offshore vendor is a process whereby knowledge and expertise within multiple teams in the client firm are bundled and relocated over a period of time to teams within the vendor (Beulen et al., 2011). The client and vendor are able to learn from each other through the exchange of knowledge between these teams. The team involved in this knowledge transfer process needs to be assembled with members from each of the client and vendor firms. Newly formed client—vendor teams will evolve and change over time. Before the transition period begins, locations of expertise for the client are organized according to the client's previous strategic and operational decisions; that is, they are under the hierarchical control of the client. At this point, vendor resources are only potential sources of expertise and value for the client.

During and after the transition, a newly formed team consists of an onshore client part and an offshore vendor part (referred hereafter as "client sub-team" and "vendor sub-team"). Knowledge residing in the client sub-team is shared with the vendor sub-team. Often in the offshore outsourcing of knowledge-intensive work, some vendor human resources are relocated "onshore" to work physically alongside the client team (Fig. 1). At a later time, vendor sub-team members may be transferred back offshore.

Over time, this will lead to a scenario in which the client and vendor firms are embedded with each other, stressing cooperation and interdependency between them (Barkema, Shenkar, Vermeulen, & Bell, 1997; Dyer & Singh, 1998; Hamel, 1991; Jarillo, 1988; Simonin, 1997). Such organizational embedment can be seen in long-standing offshore outsourcing relationships between Tata Consultancy Services Ltd., India and Asia's largest IT consultancy, and firms such as Scandinavian Airlines Systems and Citigroup. Through this integration process, both the client and vendor firms have developed close relationships, trust and shared knowledge that allows TCS as a vendor to provide unique IT services relevant to the changing business needs of their clients (Mehrotra & Agrawal, 2013).

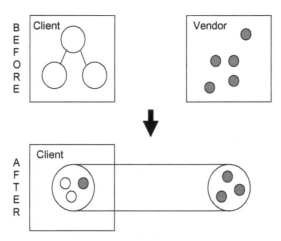

Fig. 1. Schematic of Client–Vendor Team Formation During Offshore Outsourcing.

Team Locus — Revolving Around a Common Focal Point

Despite many offshore outsourcing activities taking place across geographic and cultural distances, to be effective, the client−vendor teams that are formed in offshore outsourcing must adopt certain properties similar to a colocated team. In particular, they must share a common goal, contribute to a collective work-product, and be accountable on a mutual, rather than individual basis (Katzenbach & Smith, 1998). Often firms will put the goals and time frame for an offshore outsourcing project into service level agreements. This can be relatively easy for noncreative and non-innovative tasks, but more challenging in innovation projects where the product or service being developed is not yet fully conceptualized and requires a high degree of inventiveness.

A compounding factor is that vendor employees are not captive employees of the client, and many will not be colocated with client employees. The client must therefore take a deliberate stance to allow the transfer of knowledge to employees within the vendor. If this knowledge is not willingly shared via the client or cannot be explicitly stated, inter-firm barriers could make it even more challenging to share knowledge effectively. Therefore, the building of an effective offshore outsourcing team that is able to perform this knowledge transfer across both firm and national boundaries becomes critical to the success of the offshore outsourcing project (Oshri, Kotlarsky, & Willcocks, 2007).

The Transfer of Tacit Knowledge for Innovation

The transfer of knowledge and expertise to an offshore vendor, such that the vendor can innovate for the client, is not a trivial process. First, tacit knowledge is notably difficult to express and articulate. Its ambiguous nature can make it challenging to share between client and vendor sub-team. Nevertheless, tacit knowledge may act as an important source of competitive advantage (Baumard, 1999; Polanyi, 1966). Key personnel in the client firm can build up tacit knowledge over the years that allow them to undertake innovation in the client firm.

Second, the transfer of tacit knowledge can also be complicated in offshore outsourcing by a parallel reduction in key personnel within client firms. This results in additional issues in transferring knowledge to vendor sub-teams. Vendor sub-team members receiving knowledge during the transition not only lack a history of experience within the client's business context but also lack access to personnel with key knowledge that have left the client firm. Over time, this leads to a shift in relative absorptive capacity between client and vendor firms (Lane & Lubatkin, 1998), where client sub-teams, due to their "brain drain," will be less able to assimilate and apply new knowledge, let alone transfer new knowledge to a vendor sub-team.

Third, motivation significantly impacts the level of individuals' sharing of discretionary information. Remaining members of the client sub-team may lack motivation to articulate and communicate knowledge that would enable offshore vendor sub-teams to innovate. Kalman, Monge, Fulk, and Heino (2002) define motivation as a multiplicative function comprising organizational commitment, organizational instrumentality, connective efficacy, and information self-efficacy. Various researchers have highlighted the role of individuals' motivation and willingness to share and receive knowledge, particularly when their personal interests are impacted (Gooderham, Minbaeva, & Pedersen, 2011; Minbaeva & Pedersen, 2010). For instance, motivation and willingness to share knowledge can be affected by communication styles within the firm, performance beliefs, and job satisfaction (De Vries, Van den Hooff, & De Ridder, 2006). Furthermore, whether the motivation is extrinsic or intrinsic can differently impact the knowledge generation and transfer of explicit and tacit forms of knowledge (Osterloh & Frey, 2000). Client employees that remain after downsizing may develop a "Not-Invented-Here" (NIH) syndrome (Katz & Allen, 1982), blocking any behavior that would encourage innovative ideas to originate from an offshore vendor sub-team for fear of undermining their own power base and threatening their employment status.

EXPERIENTIAL LEARNING – SINGLE- VERSUS DOUBLE-LOOP

The three aforementioned features of offshore outsourcing (the team formation and evolution period, the team locus, and the challenges and motivations behind tacit knowledge transfer at a team level) challenge how we theorize around offshore outsourcing for innovation and support the need for an experiential learning approach to understand the process of offshore outsourcing to source innovation. The learning process occurs as knowledge-intensive work is increasingly relocated over time between client and vendor sub-teams (Maskell et al., 2007).

Experiential learning is described as an "integrated perspective on learning that combines experience, perception, cognition, and behavior" (Kolb, 1980, p. 21). Kolb (1980) reviews three models of experiential learning (those from Lewin, 1942; Dewey, 1938; Piaget, 1964) and identifies common characteristics of these models that: (1) learning is a process in which ideas are continuously formed and re-formed through experience, (2) learning happens as a consequence of conflicts between different ways of dealing with the world, (3) learning is an interaction of objective and internal conditions, between an individual and their environment, and (4) learning is a process of creating knowledge through the transaction of objective and subjective experiences.

Building on the experiential learning concept, Argyris and Schön (1978) and Argyris (1976) develop the idea that there may be important differences between individuals' espoused theories (those that they publically support) and their theories-in-use (actual behaviors). People are often unaware of the difference between their espoused theories and their theories-in-use, and hence, true beliefs are generally best understood by observing individuals' actions. The model proposes that governing variables affect actions, which affect consequences. Governing variables are underlying assumptions and beliefs that influence actions and may be displayed through the purpose and goals, design, and activities within organizations (Argyris, 1976). When expected consequences result, there is a match. Learning occurs when there is a "detection and correction of errors" (Argyris, 1976, p. 365), that is, when there is a mismatch, prompting the cycle of one of two types of learning, single-loop or double-loop, and subsequent corrective action.

In single-loop learning, organizational members are able to learn only within the constraints of governing variables imposed on them by others. As a result, in a single-loop learning mode, an actor's theory-in-use does not attempt to challenge or modify governing variables, and any correction of error is made within the rationality defined by others. If a mismatch occurs, a cycle of corrective actions leading to consequences continues to occur until the mismatch is corrected.

In double-loop learning, errors may be detected and corrected in a way that alters the governing variables. According to Argyris (1976), the double-loop model of learning invites actors to confront assumptions used to establish governing variables to gain sufficient valid information that ensures internal commitment to change. Therefore, in double-loop learning, if a mismatch occurs, a cycle of modifying governing variables leading to corrective actions will continue to occur until the mismatch is corrected.

This mode of learning encourages "the widest possible exploration of views" and requires the meaning and inference processes behind new concepts to be scrutinized by those expected to use them (Argyris, 1976, p. 369). This exploration process is particularly important in rapidly changing environments, where existing governing variables may not suit the evolving situation. Double-loop learning may be inhibited, however, in more established firms by entrenched defensive routines (Argyris, 2000).

OFFSHORE OUTSOURCING AND LEARNING TRANSITIONS

This experiential learning perspective is very relevant to the offshore outsourcing of knowledge-intensive work because different parts of a combined client–vendor team will experience and learn from their respective work environments in different ways throughout the transition period. The knowledge-creating process during the transition period is likely to be grounded in the detection of errors and in the communication of information concerning errors to those members of a vendor sub-team responsible for applying a correction. Innovation will require a capability in double-loop learning, in particular a willingness to confront past assumptions and an acceptance that governing variables may need to change as the transition proceeds.

At the beginning of the offshore outsourcing transition, we propose vendors partake in single-loop learning and may not question how and what they need to learn. Instead, they are informed by what information the client chooses to share. However, with two increasingly embedded sub-teams involved (the client part and the vendor part), the espoused theories and theories-in-use of team members within the team environment will change over time.

Both the client sub-team and the vendor sub-team will be capable of double-loop or single-loop learning and can adopt different learning modes at different stages of an offshore outsourcing transition. We propose that the transition of knowledge and expertise from a client sub-team to a vendor sub-team can be assessed by the positioning of each sub-team's learning mode on orthogonal learning dimensions (Fig. 2).

At the outset of an offshore outsourcing transition, the combined team will generally operate within the *Offshore Entry Mode* (Cell 1). Here, the client sub-team continues to learn on a double-loop basis and the vendor

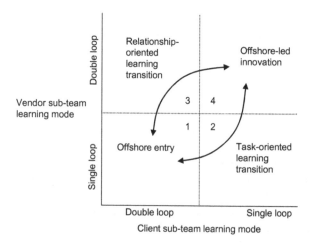

Fig. 2. Typology of Learning Transitions During an Offshore Outsourcing Transition.

sub-team on a single-loop basis. The client sub-team will set the parameters for delivery and performance and will be primarily responsible for new innovative ideas at this stage. Similarly, the choice of technology and the projects initiated will initially be defined by the client sub-team. For example, when Nokia Denmark, a subsidiary of the world's largest telephone manufacturer, the Nokia Corporation, decided to outsource some of their R&D activities for mobile phones to Taiwanese-based Foxconn, Nokia Denmark carefully defined how products should be developed and their expectations for the technology and expectations for the products' development (Larsen & Pedersen, 2011). Governing variables that set conditions for action and learning are typically defined and altered only by the client at this stage.

Over time however, we expect these governing parameters will change as experiential learning takes place and the vendor increasingly performs innovation. *Offshore-led Innovation* will commence (Cell 4) when the client sub-team has relinquished its ability to modify governing variables (performing single-loop learning), and the vendor sub-team has adopted this governing role where it is able to alter team goals, technology, priorities, and operating mechanisms. Vendor double-loop learning is demonstrated through willingness to question and confront governing variables. The offshore vendor increasingly grows to understand the client business context and the issues that the client faces, is able to question, detect errors, and alter priorities, contribute new innovative ideas for product enhancements and process improvements, and adopt a more proactive role in the team environment.

Task-Oriented versus Relationship-Oriented Learning Transitions

We propose two types of learning transitions — *task-oriented* and *relationship-oriented* — that determine the evolution of the client–vendor team from onshore client-led innovation to offshore vendor-led innovation. In task-oriented learning (a path via Cell 2), the client sub-team relinquishes double-loop learning capability before the vendor sub-team adopts double-loop learning and assumes control over governing variables. A period of time then transpires in which both teams are in single-loop learning and neither part of the team takes a leading role in confronting past assumptions about organization, process, or technology choices. Instead, they continue to rely on previously set governing variables. Any learning the teams undertake is on the basis of actions and consequences only.

The vendor continues to execute tasks that were previously assigned to them, and any errors that are identified are corrected and rechecked within a governing framework that has not fundamentally altered. This "hands-off" establishment of governing variables in task-oriented learning limits the type of knowledge transfer to explicit knowledge — knowledge that is relatively easy to codify and articulate. Such knowledge is also likely modularized, in which activities are decomposed into standard operating procedures and rules. This creates relative stability, based on high volumes of well-defined, transactional tasks to be performed by the vendor, and minimizes the need for regular coordination between the client and vendor (Srikanth & Puranam, 2011).

By contrast, in relationship-oriented learning (a path via Cell 3), client–vendor teams are able to develop relationships through regular interactions that help build common ground between the client and the vendor (Srikanth & Puranam, 2011). While the client sub-team retains double-loop learning capabilities, the vendor sub-team increasingly assumes the same. This means that both client and vendor sub-teams learn by adjusting governing variables, as well as by undertaking actions and reviewing their consequences. Attempts to change and redefine the purpose and priorities of the team, the technology used by the team, or the way in which the team operates, can be made by team members situated in either sub-team. This can potentially lead to confrontation associated with control and organization because knowledge sharing and creation related to the locus of the team is taking place in both onshore and offshore locations and at both the client and the vendor side. Differences in espoused theories may emerge between the two sub-teams. Moreover, client sub-team members may exhibit entrenched defensive routines that act to prevent learning (Argyris, 2000). Energy will be expended reconciling and agreeing on changes to governing variables that emerge as a result of the whole composite team attempting to "re-program" the project system, including its organization and control, making this learning transition potentially quite turbulent.

An increase in tacit knowledge sharing during the innovation process will lead to intensive two-way communication in client−vendor teams in a relationship-oriented learning transition. This can potentially lead to interdependence and a need for coordinating activities between teams (Srikanth & Puranam, 2011), as well as the ability to influence, question, and challenge the governing variables set by others. Therefore relationship-oriented learning also has the potential to lead to cocreation and collaboration on innovation.

It is possible that once offshore-led innovation is attained, client−vendor teams will return to an offshore entry mode again − where the client sub-team is able to learn on a double-loop basis and the vendor sub-team on a single-loop basis. The double-headed arrows of the learning transitions in Fig. 2 depict this potential forward and backward movement between learning transitions at the team level.

There may be several reasons for a transition back to an offshore entry mode, including a lack of success in offshore vendor innovation or a disagreement in establishing governing variables. Furthermore, changes in employees at either the client or vendor location that modify relationships or a change in strategic direction of the client firm may require more internally led innovation due to factors such as protection of proprietary technology and lack of knowledge and experience on the vendor side. In other words, our argument does not suggest that clients "unlearn" how to perform double-loop learning, but rather that they relinquish the need to set and control governing variables for projects that require innovation to be performed by an offshore vendor. It may be challenging to fully relinquish control however. In the case of Nokia Denmark and Foxconn, Nokia found that despite their long-standing relationship with Foxconn and early handover of control, their outsourcing projects were not self-manageable and required ongoing monitoring and meetings to discuss updates (Larsen & Pedersen, 2011).

ORGANIZATIONAL FACTORS INFLUENCING TEAM LEARNING TRANSITIONS

The type of learning transition used in offshore outsourcing of innovation is affected by the organizational contexts of the client and vendor sub-teams. We propose that the type of learning transition that is undertaken is influenced by the organizational properties that underpin the relationship between the client and vendor. We propose two sets of factors that have been shown to influence knowledge sharing and that will be relevant in determining the learning transition used in an offshore outsourcing transition. These are: (1) frequency and strength of interactions during team communication (Kumar, van Fenema, & von Glinow, 2009) and (2) social linkages and trustworthy norms (Larson, 1992; Ring & Van de Ven, 1994). We consider these factors because scholars have shown how building inter-personal trust can promote effective knowledge sharing (Penley & Hawkins, 1985; Tsai & Ghoshal, 1998; Zand, 1972), and bilateral informa-tion sharing and other relational norms are thought to facilitate the build-ing of trust (Aulakh, Kotabe, & Sahay, 1996).

Intensity of Team Communication

Team output is dependent on its ability to communicate internally, coordi-nate work, enable feedback to be provided to members, and share informa-tion about technical and market aspects of the environment (Ancona & Caldwell, 1992). Here, we define intensity of team communication as the frequency and openness of the interaction between sub-teams. The coher-ence of internal team discussions is related to its ability to engage in com-munication, and thus to influence outcomes (Pavitt & Johnson, 1999).

Matching the communication channel between client and vendor sub-teams to the task at hand is a predictor of international team effectiveness (Jarvenpaa & Leidner, 1999; Maznevski & Chudoba, 2000). When global offshore outsourcing teams are formed, the majority of communication is computer-mediated, similar to what takes place in virtual teams. Remote team members may never actually meet each other. This level of communi-cation works well for explicit knowledge: knowledge that is codified and articulated. However, tacit knowledge is more difficult to articulate and transfer virtually. It generally requires additional time and effort, as well as frequent and strong interactions, to transfer between client and vendor teams (Kumar et al., 2009).

In a task-oriented learning transition, rapid client downsizing or a lack of client sub-team motivation to share knowledge may initially lead to poor quality information flows between client and vendor sub-teams. Activities that are carried out during task-oriented learning are more likely to be explicit tasks that can be quantitatively measured, requiring less intense communications between team members. In this scenario, the combined team's ability to communicate will be impacted by the reduction of learning capability within the client sub-team from a double-loop to a single-loop one. Moreover, the client sub-team will no longer provide suggestions for changes to governing variables. At this stage, when errors are detected, attempts are made to correct them without questioning the underlying values of the surrounding system of governance. This results in the vendor sub-team being less able to learn through experience of the client sub-team's innovative ideas and initiatives.

In a relationship-oriented learning transition, both client and vendor sub-teams have the potential to communicate ideas and suggestions for changes to governing variables at the same time. Given the tacit nature of the communications, more qualitative measurements are likely to be used to assess knowledge sharing and learning. The client sub-team has not lost its ability to take a leading role in project innovation and the vendor sub-team is confident enough to also make an innovative contribution. This is likely to lead to an intense bi-directional flow of communications between the two parts of the team. Contained within these communications will be an articulation of knowledge about the client's environmental constraints, particularly as feedback flows between client and vendor sub-teams on the viability and appropriateness of vendor sub-team suggestions. This feedback amounts to a consequence of an action in Argyris' terms, and therefore enables the vendor sub-team to learn through its experience of communication exchange relating to ideas for changing governing variables.

Social Linkages and Face-to-Face Socialization

Research suggests that socialization can build shared experiences (Chen et al., 2013) and the social capital needed to access resources embedded in social relations can facilitate effective knowledge exchange and knowledge flows (Maurer, Bartsch, & Ebers, 2011). This has also been confirmed in research on distributed work, which stresses that social linkages are vital for information exchange (Noorderhaven & Harzing, 2009). Team socialization is a determinant of trust within teams, which, in an offshore outsourcing transition, may act to enhance the transfer of knowledge from client to vendor sub-team, as well as enable a growing dependence on the vendor sub-team as a reliable source of innovation.

Trust, however, requires time to develop and increases with the number and quality of positive interactions in the relationship (Ramchurn, Huynh, & Jennings, 2004). Moreover, in relationships where interactions are equitable and efficient, there is a chance of follow-up, repeated interactions where the team members are more likely to be willing to take on increasingly substantial and risky investments. Each subsequent positive interaction increases trust between the vendor and the client and strengthens the relationship (Kumar & Becerra-Fernandez, 2007).

Furthermore, social linkages can be built and enhanced through face-to-face communication (Nardi & Whittaker, 2002). In the task-oriented learning transition, face-to-face socialization will not be completely absent but is likely to be relatively low. As both client and vendor sub-teams adopt single-loop learning, social interactions based on face-to-face meetings will be considered less important than when either (or both) of the sub-teams engage in double-loop learning. One reason for this is that the governing variables are less challenged. Therefore, over time, clients may be reluctant to fund staff travel to remote locations for the purpose of meeting and socializing with vendor staff face-to-face, especially when a rapid downsizing of the client team has taken place. This in itself is an indication that clients who follow a task-oriented learning transition are typically focused on cost-savings through offshore outsourcing. Although it may be more cost effective to fund onshore placement of vendor staff for short spells to enable socialization and trust-building, the client may not see the value in this if the socialization does not result in the vendor sub-team being able to initially contribute to innovation through double-loop learning. As a result, rather than implementing socialization activities to build trust, control is maintained through contractual agreements in task-oriented learning transitions.

In contrast, in the relationship-oriented learning transition, the client will be very aware of the potential contribution of the vendor sub-team to learn and contribute during double-loop learning. Here, the vendor sub-team has the confidence and ability to make suggestions on changes to the governing variables for the project or system in question. It is the face-to-face interactions between client and vendor that reinforce these relationships and build trust and social linkages between client and vendor sub-teams engaged in an offshore outsourcing transition. Furthermore, socialization through face-to-face meetings may be essential to discuss the viability of innovative suggestions made by the vendor sub-team, as well as to reconcile new ideas and initiatives that the client may have with those of the vendor. These interactions reinforce the relationship, further strengthening trust between parties, and facilitating knowledge-based interaction and the sharing of tacit knowledge in a relationship-oriented learning transition. It should be noted that while trust and relationships can have substantial benefits over contractual control, building them is not without costs (Hendry, 1995). Not only is there a substantial amount of time required to foster this relationship, particularly at a distance, firms involved in these relationships need to invest in distance collaboration tools to facilitate regular collaboration, and may require regular travel for face-to-face interactions to take place.

A summary of these factors can be found in Table 1.

Table 1. Differences between Learning Transitions within Offshore Outsourcing.

Team Dynamic	Purpose	Relationship-Oriented Learning Transition	Task-Oriented Learning Transition
Communications	Internal coordination and feedback amongst team members	(a) Intensive and bi-directional due to multiple sources of challenge to previously held assumptions (b) High frequency (c) Deliverables are measured qualitatively and quantitatively (d) Can handle explicit and tacit knowledge	(a) Less intensive, knowledge flowing gradually from client sub-team to vendor sub-team (b) Low frequency (c) Deliverables are measured quantitatively (d) Best for explicit knowledge
Social linkages	Building trustworthy relationships between team members to enable knowledge flows	(a) High prevalence of face-to-face socialization (b) Trusting relationship (c) Quality of interactions is important	(a) Low prevalence of face-to-face socialization (b) Contractual relationship (c) Quality of interactions is less important

ORGANIZATIONAL DESIGN IMPLICATIONS FOR CLIENT AND VENDOR FIRMS

We argue above that task and relationship-oriented learning at team level will be associated with different organizational properties. Thinking more broadly about the client and vendor firms as multinational enterprises (MNEs), this logic will have implications for the wider organizational design of client and vendor firms as they internationalize through offshore outsourcing into each other's business domains and geographic territories. First and foremost, it is common that clients establish multiple teams across multiple vendors. The resulting network of teams and distribution of learning transitions have important organizational design implications.

Multiple client–vendor teams within the same client and vendor partnership may work on different projects across functional departments. Our working assumption has been that client–vendor teams are initiated in an offshore entry mode (see Fig. 3(a)). However, client–vendor teams may vary substantially in the learning transition adopted over time and the time it takes to move through transitions. Different teams may evolve in different ways: some through task-oriented learning and some through relationship-oriented learning (see Fig. 3(b)). Eventually, some of the teams move toward offshore-led innovation (see Fig. 3(c)). Thus we should not expect all teams to follow the same transitional path, and while the vendor may end up performing innovation for the client in some areas, this does not preclude the client from retaining control over governing variables in other areas.

Furthermore, if a client works with multiple vendors, there are likely to be a range of client–vendor teams across this network of partnerships. Initially, in offshore entry, the client maintains control and specification of the innovation process through continuing to set the governing variables through double-loop learning. The multiple vendors in this mode continue to carry out the actions set forth by the clients and maintain single-loop learning (Fig. 4(a) illustrates this for the case of two vendors). If the client chooses to retrench from innovation in certain projects with one vendor, while encouraging double-loop learning with another, a combination of task-oriented learning and relationship-oriented learning transitions will occur across various teams (Fig. 4(b)).

A potential issue arises when multiple teams involving multiple vendors attempt to adopt double-loop learning. This could result in multiple client–vendor teams involving multiple vendors in relationship-oriented learning transitions or attempts at an offshore-led innovation mode (Fig. 4(c)). A significant challenge here would be for the client to orchestrate

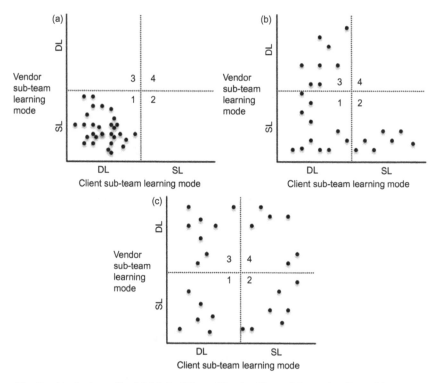

Fig. 3. Evolution of a Multiple Client–Vendor Teams' Learning Transitions over Time. A point on the figure represents one client–vendor team. This illustration shows 30 teams. (a) $t = 1$; (b) $t = 2$; and (c) $t = 3$.

several relationships that do not come into conflict because of simultaneous attempts to apply double-loop learning. The client may not have the ability to coordinate so many potentially turbulent relationships in their network. In this scenario, and variations of this scenario, client firms need to carefully consider how multiple teams can adopt *complementary* learning transitions that act in concert rather than conflict.

DISCUSSION AND LIMITATIONS

In this chapter, we contribute to both the offshore outsourcing and experiential learning literature by developing conceptual insights into the process

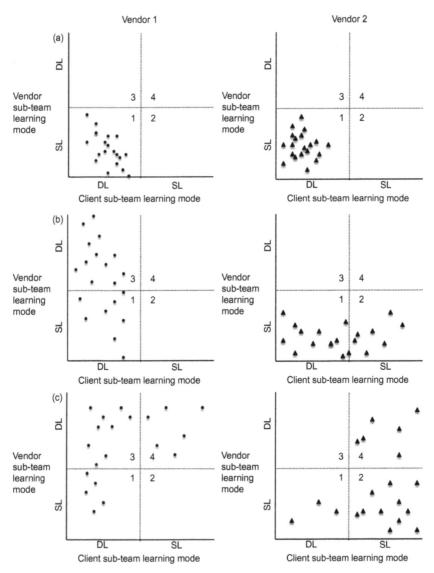

Fig. 4. Examples of Evolution of Multiple Client−Vendor Teams' Learning Transitions Over Time. (a) $t = 1$; (b) $t = 2$; and (c) $t = 3$.

by which firms engage in offshore outsourcing to source innovation. We apply experiential learning theory at a team level to understand how offshore vendors learn from direct on-the-job experience with clients, and the process by which these firms overcome liability of outsidership to become increasingly able to innovate in offshore outsourcing. We also consider implications for multiple teams within a network of vendors and draw attention to how a spectrum of learning among teams engaged in offshore outsourcing becomes a critical orchestration issue for modern MNEs (both clients and vendors).

Our contribution is to develop an argument that there are different learning transitions (relationship-oriented and task-oriented) that enable teams in offshore vendor firms to attain the capabilities needed to innovate on behalf of their remote clients. These transitions in turn are influenced by the intra-team dynamics within the international setting in which client and vendor teams are embedded. More specifically, a task-oriented learning transition is characterized by relatively low intensity of communication and an absence of socialization, while a relationship-oriented learning transition is characterized by intense communication and face-to-face socialization. We believe we are the first to take this approach.

In terms of theory, the model presented here raises fresh implications for the analysis of networked MNEs as embedded actors seeking collaborative advantage (Barkema et al., 1997; Dyer & Singh, 1998; Hamel, 1991; Jarillo, 1988; Simonin, 1997). Multiple learning transitions at team level are an integral part of the interorganizational network that arises within an offshore outsourcing arrangement. The experience of action and consequence by individuals engaged in offshore outsourcing means the principal locus of learning is at the team level. MNEs will learn as a result of embarking on an offshore outsourcing strategy, and the changes in the modes of learning between the teams involved will impact the type of learning transition adopted by those teams at any one time. Thus when a client seeks competitive advantage through an offshore outsourcing strategy, it is really seeking collaborative advantage in which an offshore vendor is able to learn about its business at a functional team level. This is of benefit to the vendor, who then becomes able to promote changes to governing variables and to adopt a proactive, innovative role in the client firm's project. Over time, this will enhance the vendor's credibility.

The experiential learning concept applied to offshore outsourcing also underlines the importance of the efficiency of learning as a result of networked inter-firm knowledge transfer (Cohen & Levinthal, 1990; Inkpen & Tsang, 2005; Kogut & Zander, 1992). It demonstrates how learning transitions at the team level are associated with internal team communication and social linkages between peers. Experiential learning is particularly important in an international setting as firms internationalize to gain access to knowledge and confront the challenges of various distances that arise from clients and vendors originating from different countries. As client firms gradually internationalize, grow, add new vendors and coevolve with them, each relationship can affect the network of an MNE. This therefore requires the firm to have flexibility and agility to adapt its network in response to diversity of operating in an international setting.

A client firm needs to recombine sources of value across expertise relocations as it seeks to enhance its competitive advantage through the offshore outsourcing of innovative activity. If some expertise relocations fail to provide value as intended, but others attempt to change governing variables where they are not needed, the firm may struggle to claim a competitive advantage. Thus, the aggregate effect of learning transitions across client and vendor sub-teams determines the success of the network of firms engaged in an offshore outsourcing strategy for a client.

We can also conceptualize the learning transition for an individual team as a discrete orchestration decision. The learning transition decision represents an important aspect of transition management that needs to be considered by both client and vendor firm managers. Client firms need to choose an ideal learning transition on a team-by-team basis, as well as consider the existing learning transitions of other teams, before embarking on an offshore outsourcing transition. Each team's contribution and innovative potential can be mapped and subsequently assessed in terms of the risks of knowledge leakage attached to the learning transition. If there were significant risks, and if the client wanted to remain in control of the governing variables surrounding the function in question, an "offshore entry" mode can be maintained. If there are no significant risks of proprietary knowledge leakage and the client wanted to adopt a cost- and performance-monitoring role only, then an "offshore-led innovation" mode can be pursued. However, our model suggests these risks will be distributed across the different learning transitions. While it is often assumed that vendor team members will understand clients by being transferred onshore to the client location, clients also need to better understand their remote vendors. As clients develop constellations of multiple teams with multiple vendors, they need to ensure that they have resources and attention appropriately distributed to assess risks across teams and to adjust learning transitions accordingly.

Our model sheds light on how vendors acquire and retain capabilities for innovation and capabilities to acquire and retain proactive behavior, deal with ambiguity, and to unlearn existing ideas and processes. In particular, the ability to learn from the client and to challenge previously held assumptions on behalf of the client needs to be nourished by offshore vendors aiming to collaborate in a more embedded way with their clients. This may also involve persuading clients to allow more rotations of staff from offshore to onshore locations as well as encouragement to use virtual communication technologies to provide opportunities for client–vendor teams to both formally and informally develop flexible, interpersonal connections, despite the large distances between them. This helps encourage communication, socialization and cross-cultural embedment development, and strengthens the client's beliefs of the long-term benefits to both firms of the onshore deployment of vendor staff who are then able to transfer tacit knowledge into vendor sub-teams.

Furthermore, as a client–vendor relationship develops, there is the potential for individuals from the vendor team to become so knowledgeable and capable in the client's business that they move to work for the client. Also, technologies change, and clients may change their innovation focus. This will change the client firm's need to maintain the original partnership with the vendor firm and start relationships with other vendors.

Whether a task-oriented or relationship-oriented learning transition is adopted varies depending on the situation. For example, in relationship-oriented learning, a client may be ready to share knowledge with the vendor, however wants to maintain some control. The client is likely to maintain double-loop learning while the vendor also adopts double-loop learning. Adopting a relationship-oriented learning transition may be beneficial in situations requiring a high-level of precision or regulation, such as the offshore outsourcing of pharmaceutical drug manufacturing and innovation, or in time-sensitive situations in which the learning curve needs to be shorter than a task-oriented learning transition allows for.

On the other hand, a task-oriented learning transition may be undertaken if risks of sharing knowledge are perceived to be low, if there is a lack of interest or available staff to partake communication and socialization processes, if the project task being outsourced is not time sensitive or considered a priority by the firm, or if organizational knowledge is already codified and easily accessible in manuals and other firm documents. For example, a task-oriented learning transition may be adopted when a client firm is downsizing and is losing employees. Tacit knowledge held by these employees is then lost on the client side. Furthermore, client employees may be unwilling to work with the offshore vendor firm, and therefore, take a back seat to the offshore outsourcing process by adopting

single-loop learning. The vendor sub-team, on the other hand, has relatively little knowledge, either due to having a non-communicative client or
being slower to engage in knowledge-intensive activities. This leads the
vendor to stay longer in the single-loop learning mode, as the learning
curve is steeper, before transitioning to double-loop learning.

This chapter has implications for researchers working within the topic of
offshore outsourcing and orchestration of a global MNE network.
Researchers could attempt to refine and develop the ideas presented here
by engaging with managers to better understand how client MNEs orchestrate their vendor networks and manage learning in multiple relationships
over time. Through detailed case studies (Yin, 1989), ethnographic techniques (Lofland, 1996), and by collecting and analyzing interview data,
researchers may be able to refine and extend the ideas developed here. The
case study approach has been extensively documented by Yin (1989) and,
as a phenomenological methodology, has the potential to extend or
uncover new variables of interest, can address issues of handling social constructs within learning, and is able to generate new theory. As an emerging
line of enquiry, an explorative and grounded approach to theory development could be appropriate.

Finally, as an explorative analytical exercise, our conceptual model has
a number of limitations. First, it does not treat the extent of knowledge-
intensity in the industry of the client firm in the development of the core
model. It is possible that relationship-oriented learning transitions are
more associated with high-velocity and rapidly changing environments
than task-oriented learning transitions. After all, knowledge-intensive work
often takes place in environments that are rapidly changing (Eisenhardt,
1989). Second, our model does not distinguish between near-shoring
(for example, the United States to Canada, or the United Kingdom to
Poland) and transcontinental offshore outsourcing (for example, Germany
to India). The psychic and cultural distances (Harrison, McKinnon, Wu, &
Chow, 2000; Swift, 1999; Walsham, Robey, & Sahay, 2007) that may arise
in newly formed interorganizational and transcontinental teams may con-
spire to limit the extent to which vendor double-loop learning transitions
can be adopted. Third, our paper does not focus on the issues that may
develop between client and vendor from proceeding with offshore-led innovation, such as control issues, appropriation issues, and changes in the
mode of outsourcing. We have addressed some of the concurrent changes
in organizational design that need to take place parallel to changes in innovation process, however there are likely additional organizational factors
that may play a role that need to be identified and addressed. Finally, we

have chosen to focus on offshore outsourcing context to study the learning process involved in transferring innovative tasks to a separate vendor firm, however different implications may exist in intra-firm learning. Future research may address these weaknesses and build on the arguments developed here in both theoretical and empirical contexts.

CONCLUDING REMARKS

In global offshore outsourcing, vendors learn how to innovate on behalf of their geographically and culturally distant clients through direct on-the-job experience. This, however, requires the transition of knowledge-intensive work from distinct teams within a client (normally in a high-cost developed country) to teams within a vendor (often located in a lower-cost developing or transition economy). We argue that both client and vendor sub-teams learn from their experiences with each other and adapt to changing conditions as a result of understanding the consequences of their actions in relation to each other. The multitude of client–vendor teams, including teams spread out across multiple vendors, becomes a critical issue in the orchestration of the global MNE as it seeks innovative capability in vendor firms around the world. We hope that future research can build on the approach we develop here to extend our understanding of inter-firm learning and coordination of distributed innovation in an increasingly globalized world.

NOTE

1. Experiential learning occurs when there is a "detection and a correction of errors" (Argyris, 1976, p. 365). In single-loop learning, organizational members are able to learn only within the constraints of governing variables (such as goals, plans, designs) imposed on them by others (Argyris, 1976) and the actor does not attempt to modify governing variables. In double-loop learning, an actor is able to detect errors and modify the governing variables. See also Argyris and Schön (1978).

REFERENCES

Ancona, D. G., & Caldwell, D. F. (1992). Bridging the boundary: External activity and performance in organizational teams. *Administrative Science Quarterly, 37*, 634–665.

Argyris, C. (1976). Single-loop and double-loop models in research on decision making. *Administrative Science Quarterly, 21*, 363–375.

Argyris, C. (2000). *On organizational learning.* Malden, MA: Blackwell.

Argyris, C., & Schön, D. (1978). *Organizational learning: A theory of action perspective.* Reading, MA: Addison Wesley.

Armstrong, D. J., & Cole, P. (2002). Managing distances and differences in geographically distributed work groups. In P. Hinds & S. Kiesler (Eds.), *Distributed work* (pp. 167–189). Cambridge, MA: The MIT Press.

Aulakh, P. S., Kotabe, M., & Sahay, A. (1996). Trust and performance in cross-border marketing partnerships: A behavioral approach. *Journal of International Business Studies, 27*, 1005–1032.

Bardhan, A. D. (2006). Managing globalization of R&D: Organizing for offshoring innovation. *Human Systems Management, 25*, 103–114.

Barkema, H. G., Shenkar, O., Vermeulen, F., & Bell, J. H. J. (1997). Working abroad, working with others: How firms learn to operate international joint ventures. *Academy of Management Journal, 40*, 426–442.

Baumard, P. (1999). *Tacit knowledge in organizations.* London: Sage.

Benito, G. R. G., Dovgan, O., Petersen, B., & Welch, L. S. (2013). Offshore outsourcing: A dynamic, operation mode perspective. *Industrial Marketing Management, 42*, 211–222.

Beulen, E., Tiwari, V., & van Heck, E. (2011). Understanding transition performance during offshore IT outsourcing. *Strategic Outsourcing: An International Journal, 4*(3), 204–227.

Buckley, P. J., & Casson, M. (1976). *The future of the multinational enterprise* (Vol. 1). London: Macmillan.

Chen, J., McQueen, R. J., & Sun, P. Y. T. (2013). Knowledge transfer and knowledge building at offshored technical support centers. *Journal of International Management, 19*, 362–376.

Cohen, W. M., & Levinthal, D. A. (1990). Absorptive capacity: A new perspective on learning and innovation. *Administrative Science Quarterly, 35*, 128–152.

De Vries, R. E., Van den Hooff, B., & De Ridder, J. A. (2006). Explaining knowledge sharing: The role of team communication styles, job satisfaction, and performance beliefs. *Communication Research, 33*, 115–135.

Dewey, J. (1938). *Experience and Education.* New York: Collier and Kappa Delta Pi.

Dunning, J. H. (1981). Explaining the international direct investment position of countries: Towards a dynamic or developmental approach. *Review of World Economics, 117*(1), 30–64.

Dyer, J. H., & Singh, H. (1998). The relational view: Cooperative strategy and sources of interorganizational competitive advantage. *Academy of Management Review, 23*, 660–679.

Eby, L. T., & Dobbins, G. H. (1997). Collectivistic orientation in teams: An individual and group-level analysis. *Journal of Organizational Behavior, 18*, 275–295.

Eisenhardt, K. M. (1989). Making fast strategic decisions in high velocity environments. *Academy of Management Journal, 32*, 543–577.

Gooderham, P., Minbaeva, D., & Pedersen, T. (2011). Governance mechanisms for the promotion of social capital for knowledge transfer in multinational corporations. *Journal of Management Studies, 48*(1), 123–150.

Govindarajan, V., & Bagla, G. (2013, August 8). *Emerging-market engineers power global innovation.* Retrieved from http://blogs.hbr.org

Grote, M. H., & Täube, F. A. (2007). When outsourcing is not an option: International relocation of investment bank research — or isn't it? *Journal of International Management, 13*, 57–77.

Hallén, L., & Wiedersheim-Paul, F. (1984). The evolution of psychic distance in international business relationships. In I. Hagg & F. Wiedersheim-Paul (Eds.), *Between market and hierarchy* (pp. 15–27). Uppsala, Sweden: University of Uppsala.

Hamel, G. (1991). Competition for competence and inter-partner learning within international strategic alliances. *Strategic Management Journal, 12*(Special issue), 83–103.

Harrison, G. L., McKinnon, J. L., Wu, A., & Chow, C. W. (2000). Cultural influences on adaptation to fluid workgroups and teams. *Journal of International Business Studies, 31*, 489–505.

Hendry, J. (1995). Culture, community and networks: The hidden cost of outsourcing. *European Management Journal, 13*(2), 193–200.

Hutzschenreuter, T., Lewin, A. Y., & Dresel, S. (2011). Governance modes for offshoring activities: A comparison of US and German firms. *International Business Review, 20*, 291–313.

IAOP. (2013). *The 2013 Global Outsourcing 100*. International Association of Outsourcing Professionals. Retrieved from http://www.iaop.org/Content/19/165/3612

Inkpen, A. C., & Tsang, E. W. K. (2005). Social capital, networks and knowledge transfer. *Academy of Management Review, 30*, 146–165.

Jarillo, J. C. (1988). On strategic networks. *Strategic Management Journal, 9*, 31–41.

Jarvenpaa, S. L., & Leidner, D. E. (1999). Communication and trust in global virtual teams. *Organization Science, 10*, 791–815.

Johanson, J., & Vahlne, J. E. (1977). The internationalization process of the firm – A model of knowledge development and increasing foreign market commitments. *Journal of International Business Studies, 8*(1), 23–32.

Johanson, J., & Vahlne, J. E. (2009). The Uppsala internationalization process model revisited: From liability of foreignness to liability of outsidership. *Journal of International Business Studies, 40*(9), 1411–1431.

Johnson, J. P., Lenartowicz, T., & Apud, S. (2006). Cross-cultural competence in international business: Toward a definition and a model. *Journal of International Business Studies, 37*, 525–543.

Kalman, M. E., Monge, P., Fulk, J., & Heino, R. (2002). Motivations to resolve communication dilemmas in database-mediated collaboration. *Communication Research, 29*, 125–154.

Katz, R., & Allen, T. J. (1982). Investigating the not invented here (NIH) syndrome: A look at the performance, tenure and communication patterns of 50 R&D project groups. *R&D Management, 12*, 7–19.

Katzenbach, J. R., & Smith, D. K. (1998). The discipline of teams. In J. R. Katzenbach (Ed.), *The work of teams* (pp. 35–49). Boston, MA: Harvard Business School Publishing.

Kogut, B., & Singh, H. (1988). The effect of national culture on the choice of entry mode. *Journal of International Business Studies, 19*, 411–432.

Kogut, B., & Zander, U. (1992). Knowledge of the firm, combinative capabilities, and the replication of technology. *Organization Science, 3*, 383–397.

Kolb, D. A. (1980). *Experiential learning. Experience as the source of learning and development.* Englewood Cliffs, NJ: Prentice-Hall.

Kuemmerle, W. (1999). The drivers of foreign direct investment into research and development: An empirical investigation. *Journal of International Business Studies, 30*(1), 1–24.

Kumar, K., & Becerra-Fernandez, I. (2007). Interaction technology: Speech act based information technology support for building collaborative relationships and trust. *Decision Support Systems, 43*(2), 584–606.

Kumar, K., van Fenema, P. C., & von Glinow, M. A. (2009). Offshoring and the global distribution of work: Implications for task interdependence theory and practice. *Journal of International Business Studies, 40*, 642–667.

Lahiri, S., & Kedia, B. L. (2011). Co-evolution of institutional and organizational factors in explaining offshore outsourcing. *International Business Review, 20*, 252–263.

Lane, P. J., & Lubatkin, M. (1998). Relative absorptive capacity and interorganizational learning. *Strategic Management Journal, 19*, 461–477.

Larson, A. (1992). Network dyads in entrepreneurial settings: A study of governance of exchange relationships. *Administrative Science Quarterly, 37*(1), 76–104.

Larsen, M. M., & Pedersen, T. (2011). *From in-house to joint R&D: The way forward for Nokia Denmark*. Richard Ivey School of Business Foundation.

Levy, D. L. (2005). Offshoring in the new global political economy. *Journal of Management Studies, 42*, 685–693.

Lewin, A., Lin, N., Aird, C., & Sappenfield, D. (2011). *The ever-changing global service-provider industry: Key findings for 2010*. Offshoring Research Network, Duke University's Fuqua School of Business & PricewaterhouseCoopers.

Lewin, A. Y., & Couto, V. (2006). *Next generation offshoring: The globalization of innovation*. 2006 Offshoring Research Network Report, Duke University/Booz Allen Hamilton, NC: Cary Printing Company.

Lewin, A. Y., Massini, S., & Peeters, C. (2009). Why are companies offshoring innovation? The emerging global race for talent. *Journal of International Business Studies, 40*, 901–925.

Lewin, K. (1942). Field theory and learning. In N. B. Henry (Ed.), *The forty-first yearbook of the National Society for the Study of Education: Part II. The psychology of learning* (pp. 215–242). Chicago, IL: University of Chicago Press.

Lofland, J. (1996). Analytic ethnography: Features, failings, and futures. *Journal of Contemporary Ethnography, 24*, 30–67.

Majchrzak, A., Rice, R. E., Malhotra, A., King, N., & Ba, S. (2000). Technology adaptation: The case of a computer-supported inter-organizational virtual team. *MIS Quarterly, 24*, 569–600.

Maskell, P., Pedersen, T., Petersen, B., & Dick-Nielsen, J. (2007). Learning paths to offshore outsourcing – From cost reduction to knowledge seeking. *Industry and Innovation, 14*(3), 239–257.

Maurer, I., Bartsch, V., & Ebers, M. (2011). The value of intra-organizational social capital: How it fosters knowledge transfer, innovation performance, and growth. *Organization Studies, 32*, 157–185.

Maznevski, M. L., & Chudoba, K. M. (2000). Bridging space over time: Global virtual team dynamics and effectiveness. *Organization Science, 11*, 473–492.

Mehrotra, K., & Agrawal, A. (2013, October 15). Tata consultancy net beats estimates as outsourcing orders climb. *Bloomberg Businessweek*. Retrieved from http://www.businessweek.com/news/2013-10-15/tata-consultancy-net-beats-estimates-as-outsourcing-orders-climb

Minbaeva, D., & Pedersen, T. (2010). What drives knowledge sharing behavior of individuals? *International Journal of Strategic Change Management, 2*(2/3), 200–222.

Nardi, B. A., & Whittaker, S. (2002). The place of face-to-face communication in distributed work. In P. Hinds & S. Kiesler (Eds.), *Distributed work* (pp. 83–110). Cambridge, MA: The MIT Press.

Noorderhaven, N., & Harzing, A.-W. (2009). Knowledge-sharing and social interaction within MNEs. *Journal of International Business Studies, 40*, 719–741.

Oshri, I., Kotlarsky, J., & Willcocks, L. (2007). Managing dispersed expertise in IT offshore outsourcing, lessons from Tata consultancy services. *MIS Quarterly Executive, 6*(2), 53–65.

Osterloh, M., & Frey, B. S. (2000). Motivation, knowledge transfer, and organizational forms. *Organization Science, 11*, 538–550.

Pavitt, C., & Johnson, K. K. (1999). An examination of the coherence of group discussions. *Communication Research, 26*, 303–321.

Penley, L. E., & Hawkins, B. (1985). Studying interpersonal communication in organizations: A leadership application. *Academy of Management Journal, 28*, 309–326.

Piaget, J. (1964). Part I: Cognitive development in children: Piaget development and learning. *Journal of research in science teaching, 2*(3), 176–186.

Polanyi, M. (1966). *The tacit dimension.* New York, NY: Doubleday.

Ramchurn, S. D., Huynh, D., & Jennings, N. R. (2004). Trust in multi-agent systems. *The Knowledge Engineering Review, 19*(1), 1–25.

Ring, P. S., & Van de Ven, A. H. (1994). Development processes of cooperative interorganizational relationships. *Academy of Management Review, 19*(1), 90–118.

Sidhu, J. S., & Volberda, H. W. (2011). Coordination of globally distributed teams: A co-evolution perspective on offshoring. *International Business Review, 20*, 278–290.

Simonin, B. L. (1997). The importance of collaborative know-how: An empirical test of the learning organization. *Academy of Management Journal, 40*, 1150–1174.

Srikanth, K., & Puranam, P. (2011). Integrating distributed work: Comparing task design, communication, and tacit coordination mechanisms. *Strategic Management Journal, 32*, 849–875.

Swift, J. S. (1999). Cultural closeness as a facet of cultural affinity: A contribution to the theory of psychic distance. *International Marketing Review, 16*, 182–201.

Tsai, W., & Ghoshal, S. (1998). Social capital and value creation: The role of intrafirm networks. *Academy of Management Journal, 41*, 464–476.

Walsham, G., Robey, D., & Sahay, S. (2007). Foreword: Special issue on information systems in developing countries. *MIS Quarterly, 31*, 317–326.

Williams, C. (2011). Client–vendor knowledge transfer in IS offshore outsourcing: Insights from a survey of Indian software engineers. *Information Systems Journal, 21*(4), 335–356.

Yin, R. (1989). *Case study research.* Newbury Park, CA: Sage.

Zand, D. E. (1972). Trust and managerial problem solving. *Administrative Science Quarterly, 17*, 229–239.

MULTINATIONAL FIRMS AND THE MANAGEMENT OF GLOBAL NETWORKS: INSIGHTS FROM GLOBAL VALUE CHAIN STUDIES

Valentina De Marchi, Eleonora Di Maria and Stefano Ponte

ABSTRACT

This paper aims at enriching the literature on international business (IB) studies to include insights from Global Value Chain (GVC) analysis to better explain how MNCs can orchestrate a global network organization. A first important contribution of the GVC literature is that it shifts the focus from single firms to their value chains, providing instruments to study how activities are split and organized among different firms at the industry level, and how MNCs can implement different governing mechanisms within a network-based setting. The GVC literature also highlights that retailers (as global buyers) often act as 'lead firms' in shaping the trajectories of global industries, while IB studies have so far focused predominantly on manufacturing firms. A fine-grained analysis of alternative forms of governance characterizing value chains can offer additional elements in explaining how MNCs can manage their

Orchestration of the Global Network Organization
Advances in International Management, Volume 27, 463–486
Copyright © 2014 by Emerald Group Publishing Limited
ISSN: 1571-5027/doi:10.1108/S1571-502720140000027009

network relationships in a global scenario. Finally, through their focus on upgrading, GVC studies suggest that knowledge flows and innovation dynamics taking place within value chains are as important as those taking place within the MNC's organizational border. We conclude by arguing that these insights can help the IB literature to examine the challenges and opportunities MNCs face in engaging with suppliers and to explain the dynamic evolution of orchestrating global activities at the global level.

Keywords: MNCs; network orchestrators; global value chains; governance; upgrading; global buyers

INTRODUCTION

The rapid transformation of the global economic and institutional scenario that occurred in the past few decades — with the emergence of new competitive firms and countries (especially in Asia) — has deeply transformed the way MNCs structure and manage productive and commercial activities at a global scale. Especially in the 1980s and 1990s, scholars of international business discussed *ad libitum* the differences in the forms MNCs can assume according to the degree of control over increasingly dispersed activities. Many scholars focused specifically on the hierarchical dimension of coordination and its consequences in terms of learning. They did so by comparing alternative forms of corporation — from international to multi-national, and from global to transnational (Bartlett & Ghosal, 1989; Doz & Prahalad, 1984; Porter, 1986). More recently, several studies expanded the initial idea of a transnational corporation proposed by Bartlett and Ghosal (1989) and applied network theory to describe the MNC as a "network orchestrator" (Parkhe & Dhanaraj, 2003), where key orchestration processes include managing resource mobility, value appropriability, and network stability in a global framework.

The increasing offshoring dynamics in MNCs have been coupled with intense outsourcing strategies for both manufacturing and marketing activities, also facilitated by modularization (standardization and computerization) (e.g., Berger, 2005). These processes have augmented the level of interdependence between MNCs and other actors along the value chain and thus the need for better understanding the global reconfiguration of economic activities. The concurrent international fragmentation of economic activities and their functional integration (Feenstra, 1998), and the growing role of emerging economy firms in the process of value creation, call for a broader and interdisciplinary analysis of the architects, orchestrators and drivers of global industries, and of how MNCs compete. Some theoretical contributions have started to explore the consequences of these trends on the organizational form of MNCs (e.g., Buckley, 2004, 2009). However, additional contributions are needed, specifically on how MNC orchestrate global networks. The literature on international business that focuses on foreign direct investment (FDI), as discussed in the eclectic paradigm (Dunning, 1993), needs to be further enriched (Vahlne & Johanson, 2013) to also include a deeper analysis of non-equity forms of MNC's internationalization processes to understand how value chain activities are managed, and how value is produced and retained.

This paper aims at providing key insights from Global Value Chain (GVC) analysis that can be helpful to the literature on international business (IB) studies that focuses on how MNCs orchestrate a global network organization. We do so by highlighting: (i) the role of MNCs as lead firms within industries; (ii) different forms of governance of economic activities within global industries; and (iii) the knowledge management implications for both MNCs and suppliers. The baseline of this discussion is that, in a context of increasing "disintegration of production and integration of trade" (Feenstra, 1998, p. 1), decisions on how to manage the value chain the MNC is embedded in are becoming as strategic as those concerning the internal configuration of the MNC, between HQ and subunits.

While the focus of the IB literature has been on understanding how businesses internationalize and why, the GVC literature takes externalization for granted and could be defined as a theory managing externalization in a global context. It provides a framework to understand how value chains are governed by a group of firms that operate at specific functional positions in a value chain through non-equity forms (see Bair, 2009b; Gereffi, Humphrey, & Sturgeon, 2005; Ponte & Sturgeon, 2014). GVC scholars have emphasized specifically how the value chain is increasingly structured in inter-firm networks on a global scale, identifying specific forms of networks, the conditions that lead to their occurrence and the different roles played by lead firms, depending on whether they are buyers – such as large retailers or brand vendors – or producers (Gereffi, 1994).

The literature on international management has widely explored how firms expand their activities upstream and downstream at the global level, discussing from multiple angles the drivers of internationalization and the organizational and economic outcomes of such processes (e.g., Buckley & Lessard, 2005). At the same time, the GVC approach has generated a stream of literature that explores the international organization of economic activities, focusing specifically on global sourcing rather than on internationalization via hierarchy (FDI). Since the mid-1990s, the GVC framework has been used by a growing number of scholars from multiple disciplines to describe and analyze the global spread of industries and study their "implications for both corporations and countries. By focusing on the sequences of value-added activities provided to bring a specific product, from conception and production to end use, GVC analysis provides a holistic view of global industries — both from the top down [...] and from the bottom up" (Cattaneo, Gereffi, & Staritz, 2010, p. 4). The GVC approach specifically examines how value is generated, (re)distributed, appropriated, and destroyed along functionally integrated but internationally dispersed activities (Bair, 2009a; Ponte & Gibbon, 2005).

GVC analysis has been widely deployed in international political economy, economic geography and in an increasing number of managerial studies (e.g., De Marchi, Di Maria, & Micelli, 2013a; Gereffi & Lee, 2012), but has made only limited inroads in the IB literature (for notable exceptions, see Beugelsdijk, Pedersen, & Petersen, 2009). We argue that GVC analysis can theoretically and methodologically enrich the field of IB studies concerned with MNCs by providing additional guidance on identifying how value is produced and distributed among economic players and at different geographical scales, with implications for how MNCs compete and are structured and how they evolve and cope with new global competitive contexts.

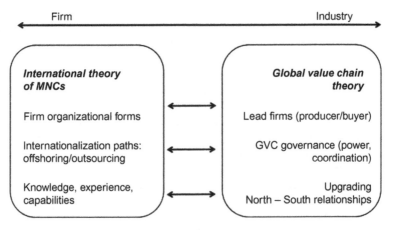

Fig. 1.   Orchestrating Global Networks: Three Levels of Analysis to Understand the Contributions of the GVC Framework to the IB Studies. *Source*: Authors' own elaboration.

In the next three sections we provide a series of key insights of the GVC approach that are relevant to three key levels of analysis of MNCs' internationalization that were developed in IB studies (see Fig. 1): (1) the organizational form of international firms; (2) internationalization paths (ownership, offshoring and outsourcing strategies); and (3) knowledge management in an international setting and its relationship with local contexts. This discussion is followed by a brief conclusion and a reflection on further research needs.

THE ORGANIZATIONAL FORM OF INTERNATIONAL FIRMS

Extending the Boundaries of Analysis

A main focus of the IB literature is the study of the forms that the internationalized firm can assume, considering for different degrees of decentralization and the relationship between disaggregation of activities and the integration among them (e.g., Buckley & Lessard, 2005; Devinney, Midgley, & Venaik, 2000). In their seminal contributions, Bartlett and Ghoshal (1987, 1989) compared alternative organizational solutions and concluded that the transnational form was the best option for firms to manage efficiency, responsiveness, and learning simultaneously on a worldwide basis. While the traditional focus has been on managing relationships between different units of the same firm, more recent perspectives opened up for the possibility of understanding how the firm structures its activities and resources globally, overcoming proprietary boundaries. As outsourcing becomes more widespread, the management of relations with suppliers becomes a key capability for MNCs.

A first set of important contributions are the studies that have explained the evolution of MNCs on the basis of a "global orchestrator" model, considering that MNCs increasingly "work more like a loosely coupled interfirm network than like a tightly knit single enterprise under hierarchical control" (Parkhe & Dhanaraj, 2003, p. 198). Through network studies, these scholars explain how headquarters (HQs) structure activities and coordinate resources globally. They take into account three fundamental network design processes: network range (the size of the network and its geographical configuration), structure (density of the network and autonomy of the nodes), and position (centrality and status of the nodes). Based on the decisions concerning those three aspects, HQ develops specific orchestration processes in order to improve MNC efficiency, flexibility, and learning. They conclude that, by managing resource mobility, appropriating value, and guaranteeing network stability, the MNC can achieve superior economic performance through internationalization.

Parkhe and Dhanaraj (2003) discuss the MNC as a global network orchestrator by considering the internal boundaries of the multinational firm. In their recent discussion of their revised Uppsala model, Vahlne and Johanson (2013) present instead the evolution of the MNC towards a network-based model, highlighting that "the MNE, or rather the multinational business enterprise (MBE), is a firm building and developing value-creating business networks in and between foreign countries both inside and outside the boundaries of the firm" (Vahlne & Johanson, 2013, p. 194). Contractor (1990) and Contractor and Lorange (2002) also point to the existence of different modes for the MNCs to manage activities, in addition to the contractual and fully-owned modes – suggesting that cooperative forms in international relations among firms are also important. As recently suggested by Hada, Grewal, and Chandrashekaran (2013), MNC's network partners may be considered as *extended links* of the MNC and through an appropriate management of relationships with those partner the subsidiary can achieve the MNC's objectives; in this sense, "the legal boundary of the subsidiary does not define its limits" (Holm, Holmström, & Sharma, 2005, p. 203). In his studies on "the global factory," Buckley (2004, 2009) describes MNC as a "structure through which multinational enterprises integrate their global strategies through a combination of innovation, distribution and production of both goods and services (Buckley, 2009, p. 131). Based on transaction cost theory, Buckley discusses how MNC can coordinate their value chains at the international level by exploiting their market power toward suppliers. From this point of view, the MNC moves beyond internationalization managed through ownership (FDI) to prefer non-equity forms for international management of business activities (from internalization to outsourcing in a global setting).

As Buckley (2009) also highlighted, the GVC approach can help develop these insights further, since it provides an integrated and network-based framework to understand how activities are split and organized among different firms. Contrary to IB studies, the focus of GVC research is on inter-firm linkages and global industries rather than on single firms. From this viewpoint, the GVC approach develops within a framework of established externalization of economic activities across economic players and adds further knowledge to understand the ongoing network-based processes of internationalization − beyond market and hierarchy. Actually, GVC analysis is focused exactly on understanding the nature and content of inter-firm linkages that span international borders, based on the recognition of a progressive disintegration of production − which became intensively evident from the 1980s and then in the 1990s, with particular emphasis in the US context − and the general passage from a model of vertically integrated firms to complex forms of coordination between independent actors that are geographically dispersed but functionally integrated (Gereffi & Korzeniewicz, 1994; Gereffi et al., 2005). An important theoretical contribution of GVC studies is specifically related to understanding how value chain activities are structured and governed among multiple firms at the international level. In this context, the concept of GVC governance refers to "both the process by which particular players in the chain exert control over other participants and how these lead firms (or 'chain drivers') appropriate or distribute the value that is created along the chain." (Bair, 2009b, p. 9). For GVC analysis, these "lead firms" play a critical role by defining the terms of supply chain membership, by incorporating or excluding other actors, and by shaping how, where, when, and by whom value is added (Gereffi, 1994; Ponte & Gibbon, 2005; Ponte & Sturgeon, 2014). It posits that governing tools in global industries often include both the exercise of "buyer-power" (the setting of product specifications, standards, logistics, volume, etc.) and of "normative power" (e.g., the shaping of expectations of how business should be organized or how quality should be assessed).

On the basis of these observations, a first key contribution of GVC studies in helping to understand global network orchestration refers to the boundaries to be considered in the analysis. These need to go beyond proprietary activities (at headquarter or at subunits) to also include the orchestration of activities of independent actors (various layers of buyers and suppliers).

Global Buyers as Network Orchestrators

A second insight related to organizational forms has to do with the nature of lead firms. In its initial articulation, governance within GVCs was described as dyadic, distinguishing between producer-driven and buyer-driven value chains (Gereffi, 1994). The first was said to be occurring mainly in the consumer durables and capital goods industries (e.g., the aircraft and automobile industries), while the second was observed in non-durable consumer goods (e.g., apparel, food). These two ways of organizing activities beyond market and hierarchy differ in terms of power dynamics and different competences of lead firms. Lead firms in producer-driven value chains are (large) manufacturers in capital-intensive sectors, governing a value chain based on their key competences on production and technology and acting as MNCs that transfer capabilities, usually toward developing countries (both through FDI and global outsourcing).

In buyer-driven value chains, large retailers (e.g., Wal-Mart) and "brand vendors" or "brand marketers" (e.g., The Gap) play a key role in governing global production and distribution. These firms sometime invest directly abroad, but they usually rely on non-equity forms of upstream internationalization to govern the value chain or use their market power to gain efficiency for global sourcing by relying on commercial competences rather than manufacturing ones. Hence, the organizational form of the international firm in GVC analysis has been explored similarly to Buckley's global factory approach, but with a radical new addition related to the role of retailers as firms able to lead global value chain and impose specific divisions of labor within industries and countries.

Thus, a second key contribution of GVC studies in explaining orchestration of economic activities at the global scale refers to a more complex picture of the players that can act as network orchestrators. IB studies have mainly approached the internationalization of manufacturing firms, with limited interests towards the service sector (Merchant & Gaur, 2008), agriculture and the extraction of natural resources. While the analysis of offshoring and the degree of fragmentation of value chains may be connected to the transformation of a firm into a "brand vendor," the role of large retailers in shaping upstream value chains globally has not been taken into proper account in IB studies, even those looking at the MNC as global network orchestrator. GVC studies have explicitly recognized the presence of buyer-driven chains and have highlighted the different set of competences and resources that these lead firms have, compared to firms mainly focused on productive activities. They have highlighted the role of "marketers" — who exploit specific commercial competences — as crucial in understanding how economic activities are dispersed among players and geographical contexts. Retailers, and not only manufacturing firms, are thus considered 'lead firms' that are able to structure GVCs (Coe & Hess, 2005; Gereffi & Christian, 2009; Gereffi & Lee, 2012). While the IB literature has approached international configuration from the perspective of MNCs, thus taking an internal/firm perspective, the GVC approach has instead focused on the role of buyers (and especially retailers), thus taking an external/industry perspective. Wal-Mart is a clear example here: in 2012, it had over $443 trillion USD in turnover, almost 30% in non-US markets that represented the growth engine of the company, and managed more than 100,000 suppliers located all over the world (company annual report data). As suggested by Gereffi and Christian (2009), the power of the company goes beyond the organizational confines of its retail empire. Thus, it is not possible to understand growth dynamics, labor relations within suppliers and competitors, and industry development trajectories without examining Wal-Mart's strategies. Another interesting case is Tesco, the UK leading retail chain that has expanded internationally with diverging experiences in different markets, including a problematic inroad in the US market (Ramasastry & Williams, 2013).

Enlarging the analysis of MNCs to include "buyers," whether we consider marketers (such as Nike, IKEA, and The Gap) or retailers (such as JC Penney and Wal-Mart), is a key contribution of the GVC perspective. These firms account for the lion's share of global sales in most labor-intensive industries (Gereffi, 1999) and should therefore be a key object of analysis. Hence, we maintain that global network orchestrators (Parkhe & Dhanaraj, 2003) can not only be MNCs – classified as manufacturing firms – but also large retailers that can impact on how value chain activities within specific industries are structured. Even though recent studies have progressively shown the blurring distinction of lead firms between buyers and producers (Bair, 2009a; Sturgeon & Kawakami, 2011), the adoption of a buyer perspective in analyzing the internationalization paths of MNCs is crucial to understanding their choices concerning internalization/outsourcing options. Depending on the strategic intent of MNCs (Hamel & Prahalad, 1989), alternative levels of outsourcing can emerge. As far as its manufacturing processes are concerned, the degree of outsourcing concerning production activities and its international expansion depends on the adoption of a buyer or a producer perspective. By drawing on the insights of GVC governance, we can better understand which are the most critical resources and competences the MNC relies on in order to build and maintain its competitive advantage and, consequently, the value-added activities the firm is interested in internalizing.

INTERNATIONALIZATION PATHS BETWEEN OUTSOURCING AND OFFSHORING

In addition to insights related to the organizational form of international firms, GVC analysis can provide additional tools to help explaining the ongoing and massive process of outsourcing and offshoring of

manufacturing as well as marketing and other service activities, supported
by decreasing costs of logistics and trade and by a new political economic
scenario at the global level (with the increasing economic and political
significance of China and other emerging economies) (e.g., Elms & Low,
2013; Steinfeld, 2010). From an IB perspective, Contractor, Kumar,
Kundu, and Pedersen (2010) analyze the strategies of outsourcing (make
vs. buy decisions) and offshoring (location of activities, domestic vs. international options) and propose a framework for interpreting these options
simultaneously. They argue that the degrees of disaggregation and dispersion of firm activities are interrelated, and that there is a trade-off between
alternative management solutions − from cost to control, from in-house to
cooperative and market-based forms of coordination. In other words, the
authors suggest that a firm's international dimension depends on how it is
able to dynamically combine the fragmentation of its value chain and its
form of organization between equity and non-equity modes. However,
further knowledge is required to explore the non-equity (cooperative)
modes of internationalization and how MNC can find a profitable balance
between alternative options in the coordination of its international activities in different locations.

The remarkable process of coupled outsourcing − offshoring that
characterizes 'lead firms' within industries has been the starting point for
the GVC literature, which has developed an interpretive framework of
organizational settings of industries at the global level that can be useful
for framing the way MNCs organize their networks. The GVC approach
can map simultaneously:

(a) how the value chain activities are split across firms (based on lead
    firm's outsourcing strategies) in specific industries;
(b) the mechanisms adopted by the lead firm (being retailers or manufac-
    turers) to coordinate its suppliers (i.e., governance); and
(c) the international location of those activities and players (offshoring/
    global sourcing setting).

A key contribution of the GVC approach to IB debates in this field is
that it explains the different options available for a lead firm to govern
value chains through non-equity mechanisms, and that identifies under
which conditions different forms of coordination are likely to occur. It
goes beyond Buckley's (2009) approach to power in outlining the global
factory structure, to not only acknowledge the role of power dynamics
spanning proprietary borders, but also identify specific governing options
and their determinants. While the focus of analysis in IB studies is on the

structure of value chain activities at the international level within the firm's boundaries – the multifaceted international corporation – the GVC approach examines lead firm's outsourcing strategies in an international setting beyond hierarchy. Lead firms select suppliers and organize GVCs dynamically and evaluate the level of suppliers' specialization and competences to govern more effectively.

More specifically, Gereffi et al. (2005) identify five possible forms of coordination, according to the value assumed by three variables: (1) the complexity of information required in the transaction; (2) the level of codification of the information exchanged; and (3) the level of suppliers' capabilities in relation to the requirements of a transaction. With high complexity of information, and low levels of codification and supplier capabilities, there is a high need for internal management of international activities (*hierarchy*). When the complexity of transactions is low, coupled with high codification and high capabilities by suppliers, we tend to observe *market* coordination. Between these two extremes, three non-equity forms are identified, all characterized by high complexity of transaction:

- *Captive* forms of organization tend to emerge when the ability to codify transactions is high, but supplier capabilities are low;
- *Relational* forms of coordination are observed, on the contrary, when the ability to codify transactions are low, but suppliers capabilities are high;
- *Modular* forms of coordination tend to take place when both the ability to codify transactions and supplier capabilities are high.

Broadly speaking, different approaches to GVC governance can be grouped in three perspectives: "governance as driving," "governance as linking," and governance as "normalizing" (Gibbon, Bair, & Ponte, 2008; Ponte & Sturgeon, 2014). In the first perspective, emphasis is on lead firms and their (producer/buyer) power in shaping the division of labor within the value chain at the international level. The second approach is based on the five alternative forms of linking (or coordination) explained above, and is focused on examining how lead firms and their first-tier suppliers (and/or buyers) are connected. The third perspective (not discussed in detail here, but see Gibbon et al., 2008) aims at describing governance as a way through which lead firm "normalize" the activities within the chain through "a project of re-aligning a given practice so that it mirrors or materializes a standard or norm" (*ibid*, p. 324). A recent contribution by Ponte and Sturgeon (2014) offers an integrative GVC governance framework that is built on three scalar dimensions: (1) a micro level – on the determinants and dynamics of exchange at individual value chain nodes; (2) a mesolevel — on how and to what extent linkage characteristics "travel" up- and down-stream in the value chain; and (3) a macro level — looking at 'overall' GVC governance.

The concept of governance and the different forms in which coordination can take place can inform IB scholars, even though GVC studies have mostly focused on the evolution of industries rather than on individual firm strategies. Our approach here supports the idea that a MNC orchestrates its activities by leveraging on different network-based forms (captive, relational, or modular), in addition to pure hierarchical forms of internationalization. More specifically, different types of linkages — such as modular, relational, and captive — imply different levels of effort in terms of explicit coordination for the MNC, and different factors that determine their occurrence. The specific typology of network is therefore strictly linked with the position the lead firm plays in its value chain: while buyer-driven value chains are almost always structured as network, this is not the case for producer-driven value chains, where the lead firm can also develop hierarchical presence abroad (such as in the automotive industry, see Sturgeon, 2009; or in the mobile communication industry, see Mudambi, 2008, discussed below). To conclude, even though the linkages between lead firms and their first-tier suppliers (or buyers) are said to be most influential (see, e.g., De Marchi, Di Maria, & Ponte, 2013b), governance characteristics may change along the chain (Ponte & Sturgeon, 2014). Hence, the GVC framework becomes useful to explore the forms of governance adopted within the global networks orchestrated by lead firms, with clear consequences on knowledge flows and innovation dynamics across organizations and locations.

KNOWLEDGE MANAGEMENT

Knowledge Flows Beyond Proprietary Boundaries

One of the key observations emerging in the IB literature is that the adoption of a transnational form allows the internationalized firm to benefit from flexibility and the opportunity to capture and exploit knowledge from multiple contexts, leading to the conceptualization of the MNC as an "integrated network" (Bartlett & Ghoshal, 1989, p. 61). From this point of view, MNCs are not only investigated as networks (with focus on business relationships), but also as "knowing MNCs," where the role of knowledge creation and distribution is crucial for value creation (Kogut, 2000). As Mudambi and Swift (2011) point out, MNCs have to integrate knowledge from different locations by exploiting their embeddedness into a variety of contexts to enhance their competences and strengthen their innovation processes. The distributed and open form that characterizes innovation processes (Chesbrough, 2003) challenges MNCs to source knowledge from actors external to its boundaries (suppliers, customers, or consumers), who are often also geographically dispersed.

While the IB literature focuses mainly on knowledge flows between the HQ and its subsidiaries (for a notable exception, see Contractor & Lorange, 2002), GVC analysis covers flows that take place between the lead firm and its value chain suppliers, and how they impact local producers and the MNC's ability to compete. This investigation is strictly related to the forms of governance adopted by lead firms within an industry and specifically to the three network-based forms (captive, relational, and modular). In fact, different levels of suppliers' capabilities impact on the coordination form adopted and on the knowledge flows that occur within the global value chain (across firms and countries). From this point of view, the attention in GVC analysis is not only on the MNC as focal node of the global network, but also on suppliers and how they can modify their position within the network in relation to the MNC, with consequences on how the MNC orchestrates its global network (and responds to and exploits different contexts). This way, we can better describe and explain knowledge flows that occur between MNCs and other external firms (the learning dynamics mentioned, e.g., by Bartlett & Ghosal, 1989; Vahlne & Johanson, 2013), and not only between the MNC's HQ and its subsidiaries.

In GVC analysis, knowledge dynamics are usually examined in relation to the process of "upgrading," a term often used to highlight paths for developing country producers to "move up the value chain" and to understand how knowledge and information flow within value chains from "lead firms" to their suppliers (or buyers) (Gereffi, 1999). From a GVC perspective, upgrading is about acquiring capabilities and accessing new market segments through participating in particular chains. The main GVC argument is that upgrading in various forms can be effectively stimulated through learning from lead firms rather than through (or in complementarity with) interactions between firms in the same functional position (horizontal transfer in clusters) or within the frameworks of common business systems or national systems of innovation (see, inter alia, Giuliani, Pietrobelli, & Rabellotti, 2005; Humphrey & Schmitz, 2002).

The GVC literature provides a classification of four ways in which suppliers may upgrade (Humphrey & Schmitz, 2002; Schmitz, 2006):

(1) *product upgrading*: moving into more sophisticated products with increased unit value;
(2) *process upgrading*: achieving a more efficient transformation of inputs into outputs through the reorganization of productive activities;
(3) *functional upgrading*: acquiring new functions (or abandoning old ones) that increase the skill content of activities; and
(4) *inter-chain upgrading*: applying competences acquired in one function of a chain and using them in a different sector/chain.

Initially, the normative expectation in the GVC literature was that developing country firms should follow a "high road" to upgrading, one eventually leading to performing functions in a value chain that have more skill and knowledge content (functional upgrading) (Gereffi, 1999). But much of the literature that followed highlighted a more complex set of upgrading (and downgrading) trajectories (Gibbon, 2001; Giuliani et al., 2005; Mitchell & Coles, 2011; Ponte & Ewert, 2009). In addition to economic upgrading, a number of studies in the GVC literature have analyzed the social and environmental dimensions of upgrading, providing insights on how they may (or may not) be combined (e.g., Barrientos, Gereffi, & Rossi, 2011; De Marchi et al., 2013a). While IB studies have focused on MNC strategies that include social and environmental aspects (e.g., through Corporate Social Responsibility), GVC studies take this analysis a step further by studying the impact and effectiveness of these decisions on suppliers.

By explaining how suppliers can upgrade, GVC analysis offers further elements to understand how MNC can structure and manage their global networks over time, in relation to the suppliers' characteristics and dynamics. The analysis of global sourcing is in fact becoming crucial in understanding MNCs' offshoring strategies and their organizational implications (Lewin & Volberda, 2011; Trent & Monczka, 2005). GVC studies have helped linking the global dispersion of value chain activities to lead firms' outsourcing strategies, through an analysis of suppliers' specializations, competences and governance forms in different countries and industries, such as the blue jeans industries in Mexico (Bair & Gereffi, 2001) and Turkey (Tokatli, 2007); the textile and clothing industry in Turkey and Bulgaria (Evgeniev, 2008); the footwear industry in Latin America (Pietrobelli & Rabellotti, 2007); the automotive industry in developing countries (Sturgeon & Van Biesebroeck, 2011); and the 'Made in Italy' industries (Chiarvesio, Di Maria, & Micelli, 2013). In dialogue with the discipline of development studies, GVC analysis has paid specific attention to the intensification process of lead firms' outsourcing towards suppliers located in low-income (and lower cost) countries, and has examined supplier competences and their geographical location as one of the key factors in understanding governance. They have also linked the 'smile of value creation' to specific geographical locations (Mudambi, 2007, 2008). A study by Dedrick, Kraemer, and Linden (2009) is a useful case in point. Through GVC analysis, they provide a detailed breakdown of how financial value is distributed along the value chain of Apple's iPods and notebooks, highlighting opportunities and constraints facing firms in the electronics industry, and concerns with value appropriation. Using data on bilateral trade balance regarding the iPhone4 generated by the OECD (2011), Gereffi (2013) also demonstrates that value chain actors in producer countries like China, "do not capture most of the value generated through its value chain export" (p. 12). All these inputs help understanding the dynamics of value creation and appropriation in relation to different MNC organizational forms, and highlight that the MNC as global network orchestrator manages knowledge flows beyond the hierarchical boundaries (HQ and subsidiaries) to also include suppliers.

Governance Mechanisms and Dynamic Upgrading Possibilities

In addition to the importance of considering knowledge flows across lead firms and suppliers and the impact these flows have on improving supplier competences, a key insight that can be learnt from the GVC literature is that the possibility for suppliers to upgrade through their relationships with the lead firm (MNC) depends on the specific mode of governance that configures a value chain. The GVC literature suggests that in chains characterized by "captive" relationships, significant product and process upgrading by local producers is likely to take place (often with the active support of buyers) (Schmitz, 2006). At the same time, functional upgrading is either discouraged or limited to some functions but not others (Bair & Gereffi, 2001; Gibbon, 2001; Gibbon et al., 2008; Giuliani et al., 2005; Mitchell & Coles, 2011; Ponte & Ewert, 2009; Schmitz, 2006; Schmitz & Knorriga, 2000). Thus, the "high road" to upgrading (eventually leading to functional upgrading) is either not followed or is taken only part of the way. When it is followed, its rewards may be unevenly distributed and/or have a limited timeframe (see Bair & Gereffi, 2003; for a successful example, however, see Tokatli, 2007). In chains characterized by market-type transactions, functional upgrading is more likely to take place, together with the transfer of new capabilities to different value chains

(Bazan & Navas-Alemán, 2004; Schmitz, 2006; Tewari, 1999). The knowledge for this to happen (market, customer preferences, design, etc.) seems to accrue in relationships with smaller buyers and/or domestic markets. However, the kind of investment needed in design, branding and marketing is more likely to be available to firms based in advanced or emerging economies than in low-income countries.

The GVC approach also sheds further light on the geographical and economic impact of the value produced by different GVC actors, addressing the links between the North and South in lead firms' sourcing strategies. In this sense, the GVC framework is also useful to support policy interventions aimed at re-positioning a country (or region) within GVCs (Cattaneo et al., 2010; Elms & Low, 2013). While MNCs can indeed seek opportunities to exploit the cost advantages of establishing relationships with low-skilled suppliers, suppliers can also threaten some of the core competences of MNCs if they manage to move "up" in the value chain (Sturgeon & Kawakami, 2011).

The relationship between MNCs, the location of activities and its governance also has implications for innovation and learning processes (Meyer, Mudambi, & Narula, 2010; Pietrobelli & Rabellotti, 2011; Saliola & Zanfei, 2009). Whenever the MNC orchestrates a global network the knowledge flows may be different according to the level of supplier competence. When lead firms/MNCs are buyers and concentrate on pre-production and post-production activities within the value chain, with manufacturing perceived as low value-added and related to standard processes, the learning dynamic can be described as mainly unidirectional (from the MNC to its suppliers, usually located in the South). But when suppliers are able to develop new knowledge autonomously, learning processes tend to be more bidirectional − not only between the HQs and subsidiaries (Pedersen, Petersen, & Sharma, 2003), but also between MNC (producer) and its suppliers.

Thus, GVC upgrading provides IB with a dynamic view of internationalization and organizational paths, as it highlights how learning processes (acquisition and exploitation of new knowledge) impact on the degree of disaggregation of the value chain in time, and how supplier competences are a key determinant for control and coordination decisions. From this perspective, suppliers can in fact either evolve autonomously, on the basis of their own strategies, or though the explicit investment of lead firms (e.g., De Marchi et al., 2013b; Ivarsson & Alvstam, 2010; Pietrobelli & Rabellotti, 2011).

Mudambi's (2008) analysis of MNC strategies in the mobile communication industry provides a case in point. From an IB/economic geography perspective, he describes the alternative strategies of offshoring and outsourcing decisions of MNCs and their implications in terms of geographical sourcing and innovation opportunities for such lead firms. The MNCs in this industry developed different strategies according to the relevance of manufacturing activities and the internal competences of the firm (higher in the case of Nokia and lower in the case of Apple), and with different forms of internationalization (vertically integrated for Nokia, network-based for Apple). While insightful, the main focus of Mudambi's (2008) study is on the strategies of individual MNCs. Wen and Yang (2010) examined the same industry through the lenses of GVC analysis. They highlighted not only the role played by technological advancement and by changes in supplier capabilities, but also explained how the development of new standards and supplier upgrading reshaped value chain governance and value creation and appropriation.

In sum, the large GVC literature on upgrading and its different interpretations (e.g., Morrison, Pietrobelli, & Rabellotti, 2008; Ponte & Ewert, 2009) highlights a dynamic vision of the disaggregation of economic activities among multiple firms along the chain that is rooted in suppliers' learning processes. From this point of view, the GVC approach can help in further understanding how learning takes place within international networks beyond the discussion on knowledge management processes within MNC organizational boundaries (Hutzschenreuter, Pedersen, & Volberda, 2007), to also include an analysis of how buyer-supplier relationships at the international level affects functional divisions of labor and value creation globally (Camuffo, Furla, Romano, & Vinelli, 2007; Gereffi & Lee, 2012). Recent GVC studies have in fact highlighted the rise of large suppliers, especially in developing countries, and how they have reshaped power dynamics and reconfigured entire value chains (Baldwin, 2013; Gereffi, 2014). Hence, from the MNC' point of view, supplier upgrading dynamically modifies how MNCs orchestrate their global networks, with impacts on value appropriability, network stability, and strategic alignment between MNCs and other network actors. Through their decisions on how to organize value chains at the global level, lead firms generate multiple socio-economic impacts in the countries where they invest (both directly and through outsourcing strategies). They also reshape opportunities and hurdles for suppliers to upgrade, while also facing the risk that successful functional upgrading turns suppliers into potential competitors.

CONCLUSIONS

The progressive disintegration of production, and the general passage from a model of vertically integrated firms to complex forms of coordination between independent actors that are geographically dispersed but functionally integrated, challenges the traditional IB literature, which had the single multinational firm as its primary focus. In addition to studying how HQ manages activities and knowledge flows across subsidiaries, it is therefore increasingly important to understand how MNCs manage the network in which they are embedded in, and how they orchestrate production activities, resource mobility and value creation and appropriation through non-equity linkages with network partners.

In this paper, we argued that GVC analysis can provide key insights to three main debates on how MNCs evolve and are able to cope in a new globally competitive context: the organizational form of international firms; internationalization paths between outsourcing and offshoring; and knowledge management in international organizations and networks (see Table 1).

A first important contribution of the GVC literature is that it helps shifting the focus from single firms to their value chains, providing instruments to study how activities are split and organized among different firms at the industry level and how MNCs can govern value chains through network-based modes of coordination. Moreover, the GVC literature highlights that retailers (global buyers) can also act as lead firms and are able to shape the trajectories of global industries. A fine-grained analysis of alternative forms of governance characterizing the relationships between lead firms and other value chain actors offers additional elements to explain how MNCs can manage their network relationships in a global scenario.

Through their focus on upgrading, GVC studies also suggest that knowledge flows and innovation dynamics taking place within the value chain are as important as those taking place within the MNC's organizational border. They need to be taken into account to understand the challenges and opportunities of engaging with (lower-skilled) suppliers and the dynamic evolution of the division of labor between MNCs and suppliers at the global level. Through the lenses of upgrading it is also possible to capture how suppliers change their position in the network, not only as a consequence of the knowledge acquired from lead firms, but also due to autonomous learning processes that can transform them in global suppliers or platform leaders (see Sturgeon & Kawakami, 2011 for the experience of the electronics industry).

Table 1. Orchestrating Global Networks: A Summary of GVC Insights on Key IB Debates.

Key IB Debate	GVC Insights
The organizational form of international firms: MNCs as networks	• In addition to proprietary activities (at headquarter or at subunits), the MNC can also orchestrate the activities of independent actors (e.g., suppliers) • In addition to manufacturing firms, retailers (global buyers) can also act as global network orchestrators
Internationalization paths: outsourcing and offshoring decisions	• The MNC orchestrates its activities by leveraging on different network forms of coordination (captive, relational, modular), in addition to pure hierarchy (governance)
Knowledge management in international organizations/ networks	• The MNC as global network orchestrator manages knowledge flows beyond the hierarchical boundaries (HQ and subsidiaries) to also include suppliers • When the MNC orchestrates a global network, the knowledge flows between the MNC and its suppliers can be unidirectional (from MNC to suppliers) or bidirectional, depending on the level of competence of suppliers • Suppliers upgrading processes dynamically modify how the MNC orchestrate its global network, with consequences on value creation and appropriability, and on network stability

Source: Authors' own elaboration.

In this paper, we proposed that the inclusion of such elements in IB analysis will improve the ability to understand how MNCs can remain competitive in a changing global arena by governing activities and resources that are not necessarily controlled hierarchically. On the one hand, the network organization form of MNCs has been progressively tackled in IB studies, within the assumption of increasing degree of fragmentation of economic activities accelerated by modularity and network technologies (e.g., McDermott, Mudambi, & Parente, 2013). On the other hand, GVC can offer a simultaneous and comprehensive view of the geographical elements of internationalization processes as well as of the competitive opportunities of the actors (retailers, producers, suppliers) and the economic systems and territorial contexts (clusters, regions, countries) involved.

We hope that our contribution will generate further debate between the GVC and IB fields, leading beyond the current "firm vs. industry" dichotomy and towards a "firm *and* industry" research agenda. We also welcome future contributions that tackle industry-specific settings and that take into consideration technological and market differences. Additional theoretical elaboration is also required in order to explain how the rise of "powerful" suppliers (Gereffi, 2014) impacts on MNC strategies, organizational solutions, and international configurations.

ACKNOWLEDGMENT

The authors are grateful to the Editors and to the participants of the Workshop on the Special Issue of Advances in International Management held in Milan, 22–23 November 2013, to Timothy J. Sturgeon and Maria Chiarvesio for useful comments on previous versions of this paper. The usual disclaimer applies.

REFERENCES

Bair, J. (Eds.). (2009a). *Frontiers of Commodity Chain Research.* Berlin: Stanford University Press.

Bair, J. (Eds.). (2009b). Global commodity chains: Genealogy and review. In *Frontiers of Commodity Chain Research.* Berlin: Stanford University Press.

Bair, J., & Gereffi, G. (2001). Local clusters in global chains: The causes and consequences of export dynamism in Torreon's blue jeans industry. *World Development, 29*(11), 1885–1903.

Bair, J., & Gereffi, G. (2003). Upgrading, uneven development, and jobs in the North American apparel industry. *Global Networks, 3*(2), 143–169.

Baldwin, E. (2013). Global supply chains: Why they emerged, why they matter, and where they are going. In D. K. Elms & P. Low (Eds.), *Global Value Chains in a Changing World* (pp. 11–82). Geneva: WTO Publications.

Barrientos, S., Gereffi, G., & Rossi, A. (2011). Economic and social upgrading in global production networks: A new paradigm for a changing world. *International Labour Review, 150*(3–4), 319–340. doi:10.1111/j.1564-913X.2011.00119.x

Bartlett, C. A., & Ghoshal, S. (1987). Managing across borders: New organizational responses. *Sloan Management Review, 29*(1), 43–53.

Bartlett, C. A., & Ghoshal, S. (1989). *Managing across borders. the transnational solution.* Boston, MA: Harvard Business School Press.

Bazan, L., & Navas-Alemán, L. (2004). The underground revolution in the Sinos Valley: A comparison of upgrading in global and national value chains. In H. Schmitz (Ed.), *Local enterprises in the global economy: Issues of governance and upgrading* (pp. 110–139). Cheltenham: Edward Elgar.

Berger, S. (2005). *How we compete: What Companies around the world are doing to make it in the today's global economy.* New York, NY: Random House.

Beugelsdijk, S., Pedersen., T., & Petersen, B. (2009). Is there a trend towards global value chain specialization? – An examination of cross border sales of US foreign affiliates. *Journal of International Management, 15*(2), 126–141.

Buckley, P. J. (2004). Government policy responses to strategic rent-seeking transnational firms. *Transnational Corporations, 5*(2), 1–17.

Buckley, P. J. (2009). The impact of the global factory on economic development. *Journal of World Business, 44*(2), 131–143. doi:10.1016/j.jwb.2008.05.003

Buckley, P. J., & Lessard, D. R. (2005). Regaining the edge for international business research. *Journal of International Business Studies, 36*(6), 595–599.

Camuffo, A., Furlan, A., Romano, P., & Vinelli, A. (2007). Routes towards supplier and production network internationalisation. *International Journal of Operations & Production Management, 27*(4), 371–387. doi:10.1108/01443570710736967

Cattaneo, O., Gereffi, G., & Staritz, C. (2010). Global value chains in a postcrisis world: Resilience, consolidation, and shifting end markets. In O. Cattaneo, G. Gereffi, & C. Staritz (Eds.), *Global value chains in a postcrisis world: A development perspective* (pp. 3–20). Washington, DC: The World Bank.

Chesbrough, H. (2003). *Open innovation: The new imperative for creating and profiting from technology.* Boston, MA: Harvard Business School Press.

Chiarvesio, M., Di Maria, E., & Micelli, S. (2013). Sourcing from northern and southern countries: The global value chain approach applied to Italian SMEs. *Transnational Studies Review, 20*(3), 389–404. doi:10.1007/s11300-013-0287-1

Coe, N. M., & Hess, M. (2005). The internationalization of retailing: Implications for supply network restructuring in East Asia and Eastern Europe. *Journal of Economic Geography, 5*(4), 449–473. doi:10.1093/jeg/lbh068

Contractor, F., & Lorange, P. (Eds.). (2002). *Cooperative strategies and alliances.* Oxford: Elsevier Science.

Contractor, F. J. (1990). Contractual and cooperative forms of international business: Towards a unified theory of modal choice. *Management International Review, 30*(1), 31–54.

Contractor, F. J., Kumar, V., Kundu, S. K., & Pedersen, T. (2010). Reconceptualizing the firm in a world of outsourcing and offshoring: The organizational and geographical relocation of high-value company functions. *Journal of Management Studies, 47*(8), 1417–1433. doi:10.1111/j.1467-6486.2010.00945.x

De Marchi, V., Di Maria, E., & Micelli, S. (2013a). Environmental strategies, upgrading and competitive advantage in global value chains. *Business Strategy & the Environment, 22*(1), 62–72. doi:10.1002/bse.1738

De Marchi, V., Di Maria, E., & Ponte, S. (2013b). The greening of global value chains: Insights from the furniture industry. *Competition & Change, 17*(4), 299–318. doi:10.1179/1024529413Z.00000000040

Dedrick, J., Kraemer, K. L., & Linden, G. (2009). Who profits from innovation in global value chains? A study of the iPod and notebook PCs. *Industrial and Corporate Change, 19*(1), 81–116. doi:10.1093/icc/dtp032

Devinney, T. M., Midgley, D. F., & Venaik, S. (2000). The optimal performance of the global firm: Formalizing and extending the framework responsiveness. *Organization Science, 11*(6), 674–695.

Doz, Y. L., & Prahalad, C. K. (1984). Patterns of strategic control within multinational corporations. *Journal of International Business Studies, 15*(2), 55–72.

Dunning, J. H. (1993). *Multinational enterprises and the global economy.* Reading, MA: Addison-Wesley.

Elms, D. K., & Low, P. (Eds.). (2013). *Global value chains in a changing world.* Geneva: WTO Publications. Retrieved from: http://www.cggc.duke.edu/pdfs/2013-07_Elms&Low_ eds_GlobalValueChains_in_a_ChangingWorld_WTO.pdf

Evgeniev, E. (2008). *Industrial and firm upgrading in the European periphery: The textile and clothing industry in Turkey and Bulgaria.* Sofia: Professor Marin Drinov Academic Publishing House.

Feenstra, R. (1998). Integration of trade and disintegration of production in the global economy. *The Journal of Economic Perspectives, 12*(4), 31–50. doi:10.1257/jep.12.4.31

Gereffi, G. (1994). The organization of buyer-driven global commodity chains: How U.S. retailers shape overseas production networks. In G. Gereffi & M. Korzeniewicz (Eds.), *Commodity chains and global capitalism.* Westport, CT: Praeger Publishers.

Gereffi, G. (1999). International trade and industrial upgrading in the apparel commodity chain. *Journal of International Economics, 48*(1), 37–70.

Gereffi, G. (2014). Global value chains in a post-Washington Consensus world. *Review of International Political Economy, 21*(1), 9–37.

Gereffi, G., & Christian, M. (2009). The impacts of Wal-Mart: The rise and consequences of the world's dominant retailer. *Annual Review of Sociology, 35*, 573–591. doi:10.1146/ annurev-soc-070308-115947

Gereffi, G., Humphrey, J., & Sturgeon, T. (2005). The governance of global value chains. *Review of International Political Economy, 12*(1), 78–104.

Gereffi, G., & Korzeniewicz, M. (1994). *Commodity chains and global capitalism.* Westport, CT: Praeger Publishers.

Gereffi, G., & Lee, J. (2012). Why the world suddenly cares about global supply chains. *Journal of Supply Chain Management, 48*(3), 24–32. doi:10.1111/j.1745-493X.2012. 03271.x

Gibbon, P. (2001). *At the cutting edge: UK clothing retailers and global sourcing.* Copenhagen: Centre for Development Research.

Gibbon, P., Bair, J., & Ponte, S. (2008). Governing global value chains: An introduction. *Economy and Society, 37*(3), 315–338.

Giuliani, E., Pietrobelli, C., & Rabellotti, R. (2005). Upgrading in global value chains: Lessons from Latin American clusters. *World Development, 33*(4), 549–573.

Hada, M., Grewal, R., & Chandrashekaran, M. (2013). MNC subsidiary channel relationships as extended links: Implications of global strategies. *Journal of International Business Studies, 44*(8), 787–812.

Hamel, G., & Prahalad, C. K. (1989). Strategic Intent. *Harvard Business Review, 67*(3), 63–76.

Holm, U., Holmström, C., & Sharma, D. (2005). Competence development through business relationships or competitive environment? Subsidiary impact on MNC competitive advantage. *Management International Review, 45*(2), 197–218.

Humphrey, J., & Schmitz, H. (2002). How does insertion in global value chains affect upgrading in industrial clusters? *Regional studies, 36*(9), 1017–1027.

Hutzschenreuter, T., Pedersen, T., & Volberda, H. W. (2007). The role of path dependency and managerial intentionality: A perspective on international business research. *Journal of International Business Studies, 38*(7), 1055–1068.

Ivarsson, I., & Alvstam, C. G. (2010). Supplier upgrading in the home-furnishing value chain: An empirical study of IKEA's sourcing in China and South East Asia. *World Development*, *38*(11), 1575–1587. doi:10.1016/j.worlddev.2010.04.007

Kogut, B. (2000). The network as knowledge: Generative rules and the emergence of structure. *Strategic Management Journal*, *21*(3), 405–425.

Lewin, A. Y., & Volberda, H. W. (2011). Co-evolution of global sourcing: The need to understand the underlying mechanisms of firm-decisions to offshore. *International Business Review*, *20*(3), 241–251. doi:10.1016/j.ibusrev.2011.02.008

McDermott, G., Mudambi, R., & Parente, R. (2013). Strategic modularity and the architecture of multinational firm. *Global Strategy Journal*, *3*(1), 1–7. doi:10.1111/j.2042-5805.2012.01051.x

Merchant, H., & Gaur, A. (2008). Opening the non-manufacturing envelope: The next big enterprise for international business research. *Management International Review*, *48*(4), 379–396.

Meyer, K. E., Mudambi, R., & Narula, R. (2010). Multinational enterprises and local contexts: The opportunities and challenges of multiple-embeddedness. *Journal of Management Studies*, *48*(2), 235–252. doi:10.1111/j.1467-6486.2010.00968.x

Mitchell, J., & Coles, C. (Eds.). (2011). *Markets and rural poverty: Upgrading in value chains*. Ottawa: IDRC.

Morrison, A., Pietrobelli, C., & Rabellotti, R. (2008). Global value chains and technological capabilities: A framework to study learning and innovation in developing countries. *Oxford Development Studies*, *36*(1), 39–58. doi:10.1080/13600810701848144

Mudambi, R. (2007). Offshoring: Economic geography and the multinational firm. *Journal of International Business Studies*, *38*, 206–210.

Mudambi, R. (2008). Location, control and innovation in knowledge-intensive industries. *Journal of Economic Geography*, *8*(5), 699–725. doi:10.1093/jeg/lbn024

Mudambi, R., & Swift, T. (2011). Leveraging knowledge and competencies across space: The next frontier in international business. *Journal of International Management*, *17*(3), 186–189. doi:10.1016/j.intman.2011.05.001

OECD. (2011). Global value chains: Preliminary evidence and policy issues. Paris: OECD. Retrieved from: http://www.oecd.org/dataoecd/18/43/47945400.pdf

Parkhe, A., & Dhanaraj, C. (2003). Orchestrating globally: Managing the multinational enterprise as a network. *Research in Global Strategic Management*, *8*, 197–214.

Pedersen, T., Petersen, B., & Sharma, D. (2003). Knowledge transfer performance of multinational companies. *MIR Management International Review*, *43*(3), 69–90.

Pietrobelli, C., & Rabellotti, R. (2007). Upgrading to compete. Global value chains, clusters, and SMEs in Latin America. Boston, MA: Harvard University Press.

Pietrobelli, C., & Rabellotti, R. (2011). Global value chains meet innovation systems: Are there learning opportunities for developing countries? *World Development*, *39*(7), 1261–1269. doi:10.1016/j.worlddev.2010.05.013

Ponte, S., & Ewert, J. (2009). Which way is up in upgrading? Trajectories of change in the value chain for South African wine. *World Development*, *37*(10), 1637–1650. doi:10.1016/j.worlddev.2009.03.008

Ponte, S., & Gibbon, P. (2005). Quality standards, conventions and the governance of global value chains. *Economy and society*, *34*(1), 1–31.

Ponte, S., & Sturgeon, T. (2014). Explaining governance in global value chains: A modular theory-building effort. *Review of International Political Economy*, *21*(1), 195–223.

Porter, M. E. (1986). Competition in global industries: A conceptual framework. In M. E. Porter (Ed.), *Competition in global industries*. Boston, MA: Harvard Business School Press.

Ramasastry, C., & Williams, C. (2013). *Tesco's fresh & easy: Learning from the U.S. exit*. London, Canada: Ivey Publishing (product ID: 9B13M126).

Saliola, F., & Zanfei, A. (2009). Multinational firms, global value chains and the organization of knowledge transfer. *Research Policy, 38*(2), 369–381. doi:10.1016/j.respol. 2008.11.003

Schmitz, H. (2006). Learning and earning in global garment and footwear chains. *European Journal of Development Research, 18*(4), 546–571.

Schmitz, H., & Knorriga, P. (2000). Learning from global buyers. *Journal of Development Studies, 37*(2), 177–205.

Steinfeld, E. S. (2010). *Playing our game, why china's rise doesn't threaten the west*. Oxford: Oxford University Press.

Sturgeon, T. (2009). From commodity chains to value chains: Interdisciplinary theory building in an age of globalization. In J. Bair (Ed.), *Frontiers of commodity chains* (pp. 110–135). Stanford, CA: Stanford University Press.

Sturgeon, T. J., & Kawakami, M. (2011). Global value chains in the electronics industry: Characteristics, crisis, and upgrading opportunities for firms from developing countries. *International Journal of Technological Learning, Innovation and Development, 4*(1–3), 120–147. doi:10.1504/IJTLID.2011.041902

Sturgeon, T. J., & Van Biesebroeck, J. (2011). Global value chains in the automotive industry: An enhanced role for developing countries? *International Journal of Technological Learning, Innovation and Development, 4*(1–3), 181–205.

Tewari, M. (1999). Successful adjustment in Indian industry: The case of Ludhiana's woolen knitwear cluster. *World Development, 27*(9), 1651–1671.

Tokatli, N. (2007). Networks, firms and upgrading within the blue-jeans industry: Evidence from Turkey. *Global networks, 7*(1), 51–68.

Trent, R. J., & Monczka, R. M. (2005). Achieving excellence in global sourcing. *MIT Sloan Management Review, 47*(1), 24–32.

Vahlne, J. E., & Johanson, J. (2013). The Uppsala model on evolution of the multinational business enterprise – From internalization to coordination of networks. *International Marketing Review, 30*(3), 189–210. doi:10.1108/02651331311321963

Wen, H., & Yang, D. Y. R. (2010). The missing link between technological standards and value-chain governance: The case of patent-distribution strategies in the mobile-communication industry. *Environment and Planning A, 42*(9), 2109–2130. doi:10.1068/a41203

DISINTEGRATION AND DE-INTERNATIONALIZATION: CHANGING VERTICAL AND INTERNATIONAL SCOPE AND THE CASE OF THE OIL AND GAS INDUSTRY

Colin Dale, Thomas Osegowitsch and Simon Collinson

ABSTRACT

Global trading of oil and gas means international markets are more open than at any previous time. As a result, the oil industry oligopoly is being deconstructed and vertically integrated MNCs are being reconstituted to address this fact. In parallel, emergent MNCs in the form of National Oil Companies are now entering the competitive arena. Traditionally dominant MNCs are adopting new operating models focused on techno-logical and financial strength. We examine changes in the once-dominant industry paradigm of vertical integration using several theoretical lenses. These include transaction-cost economics, the resource-based view and

Orchestration of the Global Network Organization
Advances in International Management, Volume 27, 487–516
ISSN: 1571-5027/doi:10.1108/S1571-502720140000027016

institution theory. The giant MNCs operated globally for decades and are an important variant of the MNCs studied in strategic management literature. We suggest the current theoretical models do not explain sufficiently how these MNCs respond to current changes and by using industry observation we contribute to modernization of this literature.

Keywords: Globalization; oil and gas industry; competition; multinational corporations

INTRODUCTION

In this volume, Pedersen, Venzin, Devinney, and Tihanyi (2014) and our fellow authors address a key question as to how the twin forces of global integration and local market responsiveness (Bartlett & Ghoshal, 1989; Prahalad & Doz, 1987) can determine the optimal configuration of MNCs. Sub-division of the organizational value chain (Copeland, Koller, & Murrin, 1980; Porter, 1985) has been discussed within the strategic management literature for thirty years. In this chapter, we contribute a new perspective with our analysis of changing organizational strategies in the oil and gas industry.

This chapter is intended to restore the focus of international business (IB) literature onto what is one of the most interesting but complicated industrial sectors. While this industry and its key players, the largest oil and gas MNCs, featured prominently in early strategic literature (Hymer, 1976; Penrose, 1959; Vernon, 1971) it has recently fallen out of favour for academic researchers. However, this core industry has experienced significant changes during its recent history, which are not being discussed.

We discuss the multiple forces driving these changes. These include rapid advances in technologies, increased stakeholder awareness of environmental impacts; discovery and impact of new resources such as shale oil and gas; the shifts in economic geography around patterns of demand; institutional effects such as the growing role of NGOs (e.g. Greenpeace) and an emergence of the global markets for trading intermediate and finished goods. We discuss the implications of these changes on the modern industrial architecture (Jacobides, 2005) and review the impacts on MNC strategies.

In particular, we focus on two strategic phenomena, vertical integration and internationalization. We explore a number of related organizational issues that link to these two concepts. The majority of our analysis and discussion centres on the comparatively recent shift in strategy away from vertical integration and a corresponding but selective de-internationalization that seems to occur as a result.

In this chapter, we operate primarily in deductive mode (Blaikie, 2003). We start with our detailed description of the evolution of the industry. We use quantitative industry data to substantiate and augment the more qualitative aspects of this discussion. We engage with a number of strategic and institutional theories before interpreting their explanatory power in light of our empirical evidence. Finally we discuss the implications of our work for the wider IB and strategic management literature.

INDUSTRY PROFILE

Positioning the Oil and Gas Industry

The oil and gas firms have been amongst the world's largest MNCs for over a century (Vernon, 1971; Yergin, 1991). They are some of the most global MNCs and some of these MNCs have a presence in over 100 countries. These organizations were once keenly studied by business scholars in general and by IB scholars in particular. Today they rarely feature in the literature despite a responsibility for a large share of global FDI and undiminished importance of the industry. It continues to account for a significant proportion of total world GDP, it supplies the dominant resources for power generation in many countries; its primary outputs are essential for most forms of modern transportation and it provides several products used in other industries, for example the petrochemicals used for plastics.

Our chosen industry contains two distinct segments: oil and gas. In this chapter we consolidate them to a single hydrocarbon industry as almost all the MNCs we address are operating in both segments. While the segments have differences − for example in terms of product distribution − they also share great similarities. In terms of our research focus, more of the empirical discussion focuses on the oil firms simply for the reason of greater longevity and the wider extent of historical literature. We note however gas is increasingly the direct substitute for oil in many uses, for example energy generation.

For the purposes of our investigation, we will define additional boundaries for our chosen industry. Like several other industries, it disaggregates into a series of discrete activities. Our convention is to split it between *upstream*, which encompasses the exploration, development and extraction of oil and gas reserves and *downstream*, which we treat as running from through refining and processing stages to distribution and marketing to end consumers. Trading and other activities such as storage and transportation are sometimes treated as a separate midstream segment but we elect not make that distinction here and henceforth these activities are subsumed within the downstream business.

The industry features two main groupings: the privately-owned, Independent Oil Companies (IOCs), including corporate giants such as Shell, Exxon, BP, Chevron, and ENI and fully or part state-owned National Oil Companies (NOCs) including very large MNCs such as Sinopec, Petronas, and Petrobras. Both groupings contain entities of disparate sizes but we suggest almost all are multinational rather than domestic firms in their geographic scope. They do, however, also pursue disparate strategies.

The industry has undergone a recent and pronounced change in its industrial architecture, defined as '… the templates that emerge in a sector and circumscribe the division of labor among a set of co-specialized firms …' (Jacobides, Knudsen, & Augier, 2006, p. 1201) Until recently, vertical integration was the industry dominant paradigm. However, the changes in the wider environment listed above and a contemporaneous rise of the NOCs have resulted in the recent reappraisal of this perspective.

The IOCs are rapidly decoupling their upstream and downstream operations and are implementing highly divergent strategies in these two heterogeneous businesses. While the upstream business in the IOCs is becoming increasingly global, there is significant and parallel evidence of widespread de-internationalization in the IOCs (Turcan, 2013), although this withdrawal is largely confined to the downstream business. In stark contrast, the NOCs, who have now grown into formidable challengers to these once-dominant IOCs, are continuing to expand both their vertical and international scope.

Chronological Overview

In this section, we chronicle the developments in the oil and gas industry over the last sixty years and document corresponding changes in industry architecture. We will build upon Baaij, de Jong, and van Dalen (2011) in identification of competitive regimes and augment this with our own contemporary analysis. We extend the Baaij et al. (2011) description of the oil and gas industry forwards to the present time and analyze the changes being experienced in the industry following the 2008 Financial Crisis.

As shown in Fig. 1, Baaij et al. (2011) distinguish between four separate regimes in the period 1954 to 2008. We contend in this chapter that this industry is entering a fifth regime with the balance of power shifting even further away from the IOCs. Competition in the industry now seems to play out more at a global level with this emergence of powerful and internationally diverse NOCs.

The history of the industry provided by Baaij et al. (2011) starts in 1954 with the *concessions-based* regime. The industry had already been in existence for over a century by then, albeit that it focused largely on oil. Gas was then unwanted by-product of the extraction processes, often flared off into the atmosphere. The first century of the industry culminated in the emergence of a group of IOCs, the so-called 'Seven Sisters' (Sampson, 1975),[1] who dominated the world's oil supplies at this time.

The regime reflects the production concessions that were granted by nations with oil deposits to the Seven Sisters. This loose cartel of IOCs was both vertically integrated, with every firm owning assets in every stage of

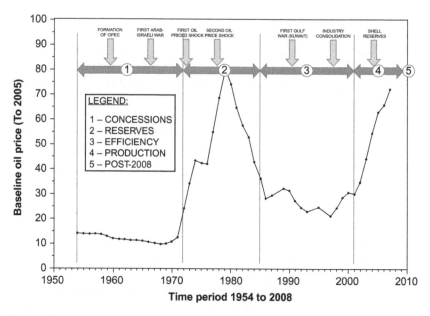

Fig. 1. The Regimes Model. *Source*: Adapted from Baaij et al. (2011, pp. 793–794).

the industry value chain and equally it was horizontally integrated, with production licenses being shared extensively between these firms. This implicit oligopoly controlled the industry and the role of the resource-owning nations was largely restricted to levying taxes on oil production.

The IOCs were adept at manipulating internal transfer prices to reduce their tax liabilities and boost profits (Penrose, 1971). By way of an institutional response, a small number of oil-producing nations formed Organization of Producing and Exporting Countries (OPEC) in 1960 to break the stranglehold that the Seven Sisters had placed on the industry. Emboldened by their OPEC membership, several OPEC nations nationalized or expropriated IOC assets on their territory, actions which fundamentally changed the industry architecture. Specifically this altered the role of the IOCs who had to relinquish ownership of the oil extracted in OPEC countries and they were effectively reduced to the status of contractors (Sampson, 1975). Further, this loss of control over OPEC supplies led in turn to the IOCs losing control of the pricing of crude-oil inputs into downstream operations (Cibin & Grant, 1996).

The other important effect was the emergence of the national oil companies (NOCs). Nationalization of IOC assets necessitated the creation of NOCs to hold these national oil reserves. For oil-producing nations however, the creation of the NOCs was primarily a means of (re)-establishing economic and political sovereignty. The NOCs were seen as '... an indispensable tool for mobilizing state policy ... (to ensure) ... a national mobilization of resources ...' (Khan, 1987, p. 185) While NOCs were then, and remain today, a varied and disparate group, almost all of them had objectives that extended far beyond just commercial success. In part, they were arms of the state. NOCs were also created by the oil-importing countries and these alternative forms of the NOC were granted significant downstream monopolies and were therefore tasked with the objective of securing supplies for domestic markets.

The concession-based regime gave way to the *reserves access* regime (Baaij et al., 2011) in 1973 when the OPEC nations drastically reduced crude supplies. The resulting first world oil crisis sent oil prices (and hence the tax revenues of oil-producing countries) sky-high. Due to the structure of their profit-sharing agreements (Vernon, 1976), the IOCs enjoyed exceptional profits during the crisis but now found themselves politically estranged from home- and host-governments (Stobaugh, 1976).

Having lost their valuable concessions, the Seven Sisters now became preoccupied with gaining control of new oil reserves. They invested their significant financial surpluses into the North Sea, Alaska, the Gulf of

Mexico and other non-OPEC territories in a bid to generate new reserves. These more challenging locations required development of considerable technical expertise in exploring for and developing complex hydrocarbon assets. Given the uncertainty over their futures, they invested in several unrelated industries, including newspapers, food processing, and retailing (Grant & Cibin, 1996; Lamont, 1997; Ollinger, 1994). Ultimately, few of these lateral diversifications succeeded and the ailing IOCs sought refuge in a first wave of mergers and consolidations between 1979 and 1984.

The reserves access regime brought with it another key development: the gradual emergence of the open market for crude. OPEC had further broken the stranglehold of the Seven Sisters when it began selling crude on the open market. This emerging new marketplace took the form of spot contracts for specific crudes (Brent in the North Sea, West Texas Intermediate in the United States) and these began to be traded in futures markets (e.g. NYMEX in New York) or on an offshore basis (the Brent crude forward market). This trading meant that producers could sell their crudes to any purchaser, rather than just being confined to their own, integrated and internal markets. Both the futures and forward markets allowed companies to secure crude supply in a more cost efficient and controlled manner and it also allowed the producers to lock in considerable future profits (Davis, 2006, p. 5).

In response to the emerging new trading markets, the Seven Sisters began to decouple the upstream and downstream businesses by moving to 'financial integration' rather than 'operational integration' (Stevens, 2005). In other words, while the IOCs continued to be present in all stages of the industry, they no longer refined their own crudes and they left it to the upstream and downstream businesses to sell and source their own oil (Stevens, 2003). Shell was the first organization to free its refineries from this requirement to purchase oil solely from inside the group. Between 1982 and 1988, all the majors granted operational autonomy to the upstream and downstream businesses, placing internal transactions on an arms-length basis. Upstream units were encouraged to sell to customers offering the best price while downstream units were encouraged to buy crude from the lowest cost supplier.

Operational de-integration also caused a fundamental change in the role of downstream operations. Rather than existing mainly to provide secure capacity outlets for production, refining and marketing became individual profit centres in their own right, expected to cover their cost of capital. With the availability of more granular performance data — enabled by advances in information technology and better international communications networks – the IOCs could manage their overseas operations in greater detail and from a distance. This allowed the centralization of management resources and the dismantling of country-based operations that previously defined the structure of IOCs (Grant, 2005). Exxon led the way in implementing this process of standardization but almost all the IOCs followed a similar strategy. The change is evident in this extract from the 1983 British Petroleum Annual Report:

> A significant feature of the oil industry in recent years has been the trend towards deintegration, or separation of upstream crude production from downstream refining and marketing. Each part of the oil business then stands on its own so allowing its performance to be measured against the value of its products in the international market. One consequence of this has been the development within the industry of a clearer picture of the true costs and profitability of the downstream oil operations.

By the mid-1980s, almost all the majors had emerged as significant players in the fledgling spot and futures markets for crude and refined product. They established trading businesses whose functions were to serve the needs of the production and manufacturing divisions but also to trade for profit in the global markets. Thanks to their financial strength and intimate knowledge of production levels, the oil majors would establish a dominant position in the markets for crude oil and refined products. The appeal of this new source of revenues was high. Its margins were slight but the volume churn in the times of uncertainty over supply (generated, e.g. by the fall of the Shah of Iran in 1979) yielded impressive returns with little or no capital expenditure accruing onto their balance sheets.[2]

The subsequent *efficiency focus* regime (Baaij et al., 2011) that began in 1986 was heralded by the plummeting oil price in the wake of an economic recession and parallel over-production following the failure of the OPEC quota system. To an increasing extent, oil prices and production levels were now determined by supply and demand. In response to this dramatic deterioration in the oil price, exploration activity was halted and IOCs scrambled to contain their operating costs (Grant, 2003).

The newfound efficiency drive was reinforced by the shareholder value philosophies taking hold during the mid-1980s. Unrelated assets in the IOCs were released as were some downstream oil and gas assets. Many of these downstream assets were eagerly snapped up by the NOCs, who wanted to integrate forwards into refining, marketing, and distribution and more generally to deepen their position and relative scale in the industry. This divestment of downstream assets by the IOCs also afforded the more pioneering NOCs their first opportunities for significant international expansion.

As oil prices continued to fall, the IOCs suffered significant losses. And again they sought refuge in consolidation, initiating the second wave of merger activities between 1998 and 2002. Weaker IOCs were taken over and what remained of the original Seven Sisters were consolidated into five 'super-majors' (Antill & Arnott, 2004) as Exxon bought Mobil; Chevron acquired Texaco and BP mounted a very aggressive acquisition strategy to buy out US oil firms. Only Shell refrained from similar large-scale acquisitions, due in part to its rather complicated dual nationality structure although it was an active acquirer in the downstream. Consolidation continued in the next tier, with Conoco and Phillips merging and the formation of the fifth super-major when Total acquired Elf and Aquitaine and Petrofina.

The *production focus* regime (Baaij et al., 2011) commenced in 2002 and is marked by rising demand from emerging markets coupled with increasingly tight global supplies. The corresponding rise in oil prices boosted profitability for both IOCs and NOCs. Even the downstream businesses enjoyed a few years of respite as refinery margins recovered due to capacity constraints. Extremely high oil prices[3] saw participants concentrate on expanding production. However few alternative sources of supply were emerging, triggering concerns over 'peak oil'. The Canadian heavy tar sands began production during this period but the very high extraction costs coupled with the lesser quality of crude meant they could not offset these sudden demand spikes in the booming world economy. As a result, the IOCs and many NOCs started a series of competitive bidding wars for increasingly scarce exploration rights based on the logical assumption that this new era of high prices and demand was here to stay.

The Fifth Regime

To these four regimes, we suggest addition of a fifth regime resulting from the 2008 Financial Crisis. This latest turning point for the industry triggered a massive slowdown in overall demand for energy and halted the rapid rise of the oil price, warranting our perception this new regime beginning. More significantly, this slowdown in demand coincides with the emergence a new source of hydrocarbons and especially technological developments that are associated with the nascent 'fracking' revolution.

Potentially the biggest industry level change for many years, unconventional hydrocarbons (shale oil and gas) are again redefining the industry architecture. The United States will soon shift from being a (net) importer of hydrocarbons to a (net) exporter (EIA, 2013).[4] Shale oil and gas, along with tar sands and drilling in sensitive regions such as Alaska, trigger the widespread debate over the environmental impact of this industry (Levy & Kolk, 2002). This debate magnifies the importance of non-governmental and stateless organizations (NGOs), for example Greenpeace, and gives rise to increasingly complex policies to control hydrocarbon extraction in sensitive regions.

The effects of these developments are wide-ranging. We extend our discussion of these changes by looking firstly at their impacts on IOCs. To maintain high dividend payouts to shareholders (Stevens, 2008) and to free investment capital for modern large-scale, complex, and risky exploration projects, the IOCs are assessing individual business on a standalone basis and are rationalizing their portfolios. Increasing divides between the upstream and downstream businesses are replicated and evident in the organizational structures adopted across the industry. Fig. 2 shows organizational structures for Exxon and Shell. Both subsume gas into their upstream business, in line with a view of similarity. Commonality of business structure in the two models is clear from the duplication of reporting lines.

The IOCS have culled less profitable operations, chiefly by network sales and exit from refining sites.[5] The IOC upstream businesses are continuing to expand post-2008 whilst the downstream business de-internationalizes, as evidenced by IOC withdrawals from multiple geographies including southern Europe, South America and parts of south-east Asia. This statement from Exxon illustrates this point:

> We divested our Downstream and Chemical assets in Argentina, Uruguay, Paraguay, Central America, Malaysia, and Switzerland, and restructured and reduced our holdings in Japan. The transition of our U.S. retail fuel business to a more capital-efficient branded wholesaler model is also nearly complete. Over the last 10 years, we have divested or restructured downstream interests in 19 refineries, 6,000 miles of pipeline, 191 product terminals, 37 lube oil blend plants, and more than 22,000 retail service stations. These Downstream portfolio improvements resulted in a nearly 4-percentage-point improvement in return on capital employed. (Exxon, Annual Report, 2012, p. 07)

These different strategies are driven solely by differences between business models. The upstream business remains exceptionally profitable and arguably is central to IOC survival as long as oil prices remain high. The downstream business is by far the larger business in terms of gross revenues

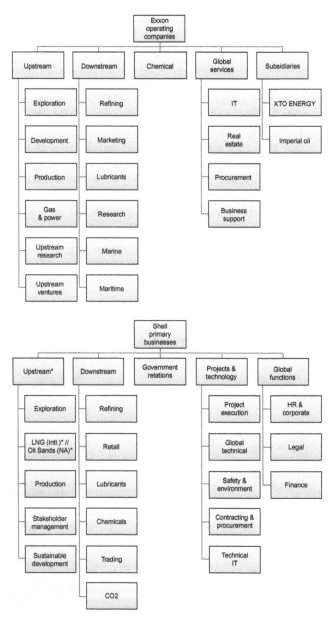

*UPSTREAM DIVIDED GEOGRAPHICALLY INTO PARALLEL INTERNATIONAL AND NORTH AMERICAN ORGANIZATIONS

Fig. 2. Typical IOC Organization Models. *Source*: All Data from Annual Reports.

but its profit level is highly marginal. Fig. 3 demonstrates this significant (and growing) disparity for some of the large IOCs. These findings are representative of the overall industry and this 'Pareto-esque' differential is evident in the data from the NOCs. In its 2012 annual report, Thailand's PTT reported exploration profit accounting for 90% of total earnings. The downstream and trading profit accounts for only 10% of this total, despite being responsible for close to 80% of group revenues (PTT, 2013).

Many of the downstream assets divested by IOCs were acquired by NOCs,[6] who are emerging after the 2008 Financial Crisis as fully-fledged rivals to IOCs. State-based capitalism, especially in emerging markets, has been in the ascendency in recent years. Guided by government backers, emboldened by access to cheap investment capital and reflecting the general economic malaise in the developed world, government-owned firms from

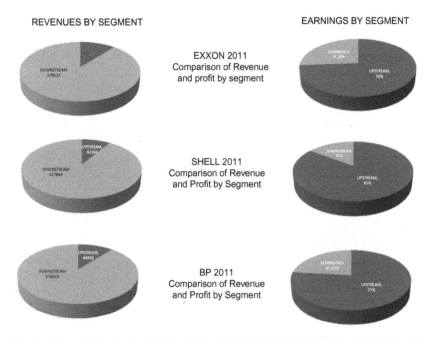

Fig. 3. Segment Analysis of Major Oil and Gas MNEs (US$ Millions). *Source*: All Data from Annual Reports.

the emerging markets are taking over increasing swathes of the global economic landscape (Economist, 2012a). These same organizations have been particularly active in the energy industry, which, according to a recent Economist survey, has the highest share of state-controlled companies in the MSCI index of emerging markets (Economist, 2012a).

Another Economist article (2011,) details more precisely the extent of this state involvement in this industry. Exxon and Shell may be vying for the title of world's biggest company by annual revenues, but their oil and gas reserves represent only a fraction of those controlled by organizations such as the National Iranian Oil Company (NIOC) or Saudi Aramco. Reserves data must be interpreted with caution, especially for NOCs, but one estimate suggests the reserves of NIOC are ten times greater than for Exxon and for production, Exxon produces less than a third the oil that Saudi Aramco does. Overall, it is estimated the NOCs now control around 90% of the world's total oil (Economist, 2013).

While the NOCs have also existed for several decades and played key roles in earlier regimes, their role today has changed fundamentally. Encouraged by home governments, the NOCs are continuing to expand their vertical and geographic scope. Stevens (2008) notes how many of these NOCS have followed in their privately-owned competitors' footsteps and have integrated vertically, perhaps as much as mimetic strategy (DiMaggio & Powell, 1983) rather than in competition. Increasingly they operate in all the segments of the industry value chain. Not content being only domestic champions, they are also internationalizing aggressively. As a consequence, several of these emergent NOCs are at the forefront of foreign direct investment programmes on behalf of their respective governments.

The NOCs have not only grown in size and scope. Some of them have also grown significant technical expertise. For instance, Brazil's Petrobras is thought to be second to none in terms of its capability in ultra-deepwater technologies (Economist, 2013). Malaysia's Petronas, Saudi Aramco and Norway's Statoil are similarly effective players. According to an analysis by Bain & Company, the super-majors invested US$ 4.4 billion in R&D in 2011. In comparison, the biggest NOCs invested US$ 5.3 billion and their R&D budgets are now growing twice as fast as those of the super-majors (Economist, 2013). Combining the two FSAs (Hymer, 1976) of low-cost investment capital and their growing capabilities in large-scale project management, several NOCs are now well equipped to bid for licenses that once would have been the sole preserve of the super-majors. Increasingly, the IOCs must hence present themselves less as 'owners' of assets and more as the 'partners' for dominant NOCs (Grant, 2012).

This industry's post-2008 regime also sees emergence of new actors, several of whom are focused on shale oil and gas technologies. In addition, traditional suppliers of oil field services are expanding both their range and scale (Bower, 2010). The market capitalization of large services suppliers, for example Schlumberger and Halliburton, is now comparable to the mid-size IOCs (Economist, 2012b). Increasingly these MNCs can offer 'full-service' contracts, taking project management roles and even some financial risk. A select few cases, for example Petrofac, take stakes in fields (Economist, 2012b). As a result, boundaries between suppliers and the IOCs are increasingly blurred, echoing the ideas of the global value chain as debated elsewhere in this volume (De Marchi, Di Maria, & Ponte, 2014).

These developments are reflected in Fig. 4, showing permanent employee headcounts for the industry for the last 20 years. The long-term trend for the IOCs seems to be one of on-going cost reduction, often achieved through outsourcing services. Fig. 4 suggests the averaged headcount of the super-majors (Shell, Exxon, BP, Chevron, and Total) is declining consistently while the opposite effect is seen in the oil services firms, here shown as Schlumberger. For the sake of this comparison we also show another former NOC now turned IOC, ENI, which was originally much smaller

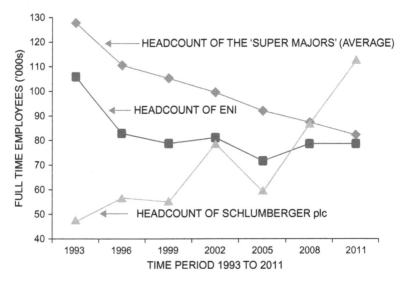

Fig. 4. Comparative Trend in Headcounts ('000s Employees). *Source*: All Data from Annual Reports.

than the super-majors but today is following very similar vertical and geographic strategies (Grant, 2012).

THEORETICAL ANALYSIS

We feel the complexity of these observed phenomena is such that any explanation necessitates use of multiple theories (Allison, 1969). Any singular theoretical perspective or model will most likely be inadequate when dealing with evolution across many decades, such as that represented here in the vertical and international scope of MNCs (see, e.g. Rosenbloom, 2000). In response to this shortfall we add institutional theories alongside more traditional economics and management based perspectives to explain these principles of vertical integration. For each of the theories, we present a brief overview before providing a focused assessment against the context of the oil and gas industry.

Transaction-Cost Economics Theory

Transaction-Cost Economics (TCE) theory sees firms as agents seeking to maximize profits in a world of imperfect markets. As such, firms have incentives to bypass less-than-perfect markets by bringing activities in-house. When the markets being bypassed extend across international boundaries MNCs will be created as the result (Buckley & Casson, 1976). This avoidance of market imperfections and the transaction costs associated with market imperfections is at the centre of this school of thought. The optimum scope of the firm (or here in the scope of the oil and gas MNCs) will be achieved at the point when the costs and benefits of further internalization are equalized at the margin.

There are various sources of transaction costs including asset specificity (Williamson, 1985); threat of intellectual property appropriation (Teece, 1986) and the challenges of coordinating interdependent investments (Chandler, 1977). The first of these costs is frequently applied in this context of the oil and gas industry. In line with the thinking of Williamson (1981, 1985), market imperfections may occur ex post in the case of transactions involving dedicated assets. When deciding to engage in a market transaction the industry may be competitive, but once specific investments in support of that transaction have been made, one or both parties may be locked-in. This may then lead to extensive bargaining, which in turn results in significant transaction costs.

In his assessment of the oil and gas industry in the 1970s, Teece (1976) identifies that considerable asset specificity existed in the industry. He elaborates that '... the design of any given refiner will depend, among other things, on the specific characteristics of the crude oil and other raw material to be processed, and the product mix that is desired from the refinery. There are many different grades of crude oil, and there will be differences in the yields of products obtained from them. "Sour" crudes contain significant amounts of sulphur, and refineries must be designed to remove the sulfuret compounds. ... Accordingly, it is quite difficult to switch a refinery to alternative crude streams, at least in the short run ...'.[7] The resulting small numbers problem (Williamson, 1985) opens up a several possibilities for opportunistic behaviour by one or both parties, thus rendering vertical integration the more efficient option.

Subsequent to Teece's original assessment, significant innovations are changing this aspect of the industry. An example is seen in more flexible refineries due to use of sophisticated catalytic cracking technologies introduced during the 1980s. According to Grant and Cibin (1996, p. 177) '... these investments were primarily at the refinery level with the objective of increasing the range of crude oils which could be refined and increasing flexibility in the output of different distillates. The major emphasis was on extending refineries' ability to refine heavier, higher sulfur crudes, and increasing the output of higher margin products such as unleaded gasoline'. The vertical disintegration noted above may be explained by these investments in operational flexibility, diminishing asset specificity.

Power Theory

The exercise of market power in this industry has been axiomatic for many authors (Yarrow, 1991) and regulatory agencies such as the US Federal Trade Commission (Barrera-Rey, 1995). A loosely defined power-based theory can be derived from combining resource dependency theories (Pfeffer & Salancik, 1978) with industrial organization theories (Bain, 1956).

Organizations are viewed as entities that attempt to boost their overall performance by reducing uncertainty and exercising power. According to Santos and Eisenhardt (2005, p. 495), '... reducing dependence and increasing power may be two sides of the same coin ...'. The implication is that organizational boundaries must be set so as to maximize control over crucial external forces or else '... if an organization does not increase power over external forces, it may forego opportunities to raise prices, gain scale, and thus enhance performance' (Santos & Eisenhardt, 2005).

MNCs expand vertically in response to uncertainty surrounding the supply of inputs, or to guarantee access to distribution and customers (Santos & Eisenhardt, 2005). Cacciatori and Jacobides (2005) find for instance that European contractors integrated previously distinct value-chain elements (design and construction activities) primarily to gain greater power and dominance over their customers and thus enhance profitability.

Industrial organization theories provide another set of power arguments. Companies may resort to vertical integration so as to make it more difficult for focused potential entrants to come into the industry (Bain, 1956). This assumes that most or even all competitors in an industry occupy several stages of the industry value chain. In that case, any potential entrant faces the prospect of having to enter not only the focal industry but also neighbouring stages (e.g. to secure the necessary supplies of crude or marketing outlets for their refined products). This makes for a more daunting financial and operational challenge and may as a direct result deter potential entrants.

As reported prior to the start of the reserves access regime, IOCs were overwhelmingly operationally integrated. In other words, they refined (and stored, distributed and marketed) their own products. There were few players in the fledgling spot market. Market transparency was poor and uncertainty was correspondingly high. The means to ensure profitability was in use of operational integration to ensure the supply of crude and distribution of refined output (Stevens, 2003, p. 97). We note that all these arguments might also be cast in transaction-cost terms. Thin and opaque markets will give rise to threats of opportunism and constitute a potential source of structural market failure.

Teece (1976, p. 115) suggests compelling advantages from vertical integration in the industry during the 1970s. Among other things, he notes that '... the large capital cost of refineries and the long-lived nature of the investment ... means an uninterrupted "throughput" through the life of the equipment contributes significantly to the profitable operation of the facility. Furthermore, a refinery can make only limited use of crude-oil inventories to guard against temporary shortages in supply ... All these considerations point to the vital importance of crude-oil supply dependability at a competitive price'. Coupled with the earlier points concerning asset specificity, this argument strongly supports the original IOC strategies of bringing upstream and downstream together under common ownership.

Operational integration also had the benefit of stymieing potential competitors. Vertical Integration at the time acted as '... a significant constraint to competition due to the creation of major barriers-to−entry ...' (Stevens, 2003, p. 97). Crucially, as both the spot and futures markets developed during the 1980s, these power rationales largely lost their relevance which may explain the decision of the IOCs to abandon operational integration and replace it with financial integration.

The Resource-Based View

The resources and capabilities lens (Barney, 1991) is another credible theory with which to explain developments in the industry. Several pioneering business analyses are broadly consistent with the resource-based view ('RBV') of the firm and make use of its theoretical arguments (Chandler, 1962; Nelson & Winter, 1982; Penrose, 1959). It is also relevant to note how some of these analyses specifically address the operation of the oil industry, usually from the perspective of the US IOCs.

In its simplest form, the RBV suggests that a firm's vertical scope should be set based on its relative competencies. Unless it holds distinctive resources and capabilities in particular stages of the industry value chain, the firm should source from independent suppliers or sell to independent buyers who excel at what they do. Beyond this simple maxim, there are also resource-based coordination arguments.

The production and distribution of complex products may impose significant coordination demands on firms. Consequently, vertical integration of the stages of production might be necessary to create the required level of coordination and to exploit the economies of scope and scale from managerial resources (Chandler, 1977). Again there is a corresponding transaction-cost economics argument, which arrives at similar conclusions (e.g. Chesbrough & Teece, 1996; Teece, 1986). Finally, arguments concerning technological trajectories of firms and the relevance of expenditures on research and development (Dosi, 1982) may also be considered as resource-based explanations.

In our analysis of the industry, some decades ago the resources and capabilities of the Seven Sisters were comparatively rare and inimitable. Only a few companies worldwide had the sufficient skills in project management, extraction and refining as well as the necessary financial resources to develop large projects. Correspondingly, it made sense for the IOCs to occupy all the stages of the industry value chain. Since then, circumstances have changed and more players (the NOCs, oil services firms and so forth) have entered particular stages of the industry. Several of these aggressively expanded their internal technical skills and resources, as we describe above, especially during our fifth regime.

The reversal of strategic vertical integration undertaken by IOCs can also be explained in terms of resource-based coordination arguments. In the distant past, the interfaces between production and refinery and between refinery and distribution were largely interdependent, requiring on-going and repeated adjustments, so favouring vertical integration. Over time, the emergence of global markets led to greater standardization of crude supplies and homogenization of the particular categories of refinery outputs, again as outlined above. This allows for 'structured dialogue' (Monteverde, 1995) between supplying and procuring stages to take place and vertical integration becomes redundant.

We arrive at the same conclusions when applying the lens of technological trajectories (Dosi, 1982). Given supply constraints, exploration and extraction have been forced into ever more challenging places as the easy reserves have already been exploited or are occupied by NOCs. This has triggered on-going upstream innovations such as the use of 3D seismic data, directional and horizontal drilling technologies and other new recovery techniques. The correspondingly steep technological trajectory has allowed individual companies to excel in particular niches, thus preserving the distinctiveness and economic rent potential of their upstream resources and capabilities.

While refining has seen some innovation – such as the introduction of catalytic cracking – it is seen as employing comparatively mature and established technology that is freely available 'off the shelf'. A flatter technological trajectory renders any downstream competence less rare and inimitable. This view is confirmed by the IOC investment data. During the 1970s and 1980s, investment levels in the downstream segment stayed remarkably constant, while exploration and production investment grew quite dramatically (Grant & Cibin, 1996, p. 171). Since then, investment in upstream research and development – by the IOCs, by the NOCs and even oil services companies in certain areas – has increased dramatically (Economist, 2013). As a response, the IOCs are abandoning their downstream assets and concentrating on exploration and extraction activities.

Institutional Theory

In this last part of the theoretical investigation, we will heed Santos and Eisenhardt's (2005) call for broader research perspectives when investigating organizational boundaries. By incorporating aspects beyond the mainstream management and economic theories, more effective research may result (Santos & Eisenhardt, 2005). Given the nature of the industry and the powerful institutions identified earlier (host governments, OPEC and increasingly non-governmental organizations such as Greenpeace), the institutional perspective would seem a logical complement to the above theories.

According to Santos and Eisenhardt (2005), the effect of institutions is germane to situations 'with well-identified and influential players', for example in oligopolies and regulated environments. Here, external relationships with specific organizations have a significant effect on performance (Santos & Eisenhardt, 2005). Institutional theory emerged in the strategic literature following the rise of emerging markets as both hosts — and increasingly now as homes — for MNCs. As strategy researchers turned their gaze to these markets, they noticed the conspicuous absence of functioning markets (Khanna & Palepu, 1999). In response, academic researchers increasingly adopted an institutional view to understand these emerging economies and their MNCs (Peng, Wang, & Jiang, 2008).

Institutional theory holds that firm choices are driven by the formal and informal constraints of the particular institutional context(s) (Jarzabkowski, 2008). Specifically, institutions reduce uncertainty by conditioning the norms of behaviour in an industry. An actor's strategic choices are informed and shaped by its given institutional context. Conventionally, theorists recognize three institutional pillars, ensuring compliance or legitimacy through expedience (the regulative pillar), through social obligation (normative pillar), or on a taken-for-granted basis (cognitive pillar) (Scott, 1995, p. 35).

The empirical profile of this industry suggests it is characterized by unique and powerful institutional frameworks. The regulatory pillar (Scott, 1995) seems particularly important, both in the form of significant state interventions and increasingly from third-party organizations — for example in terms of the sanctions placed on exports from a number of countries. Security of supply has been a matter of national security for many decades — Yergin (1991) suggests since the start of the First World War a century ago — and the term petro-politics attests to the highly geopolitical nature of this industry.

The growing role of the NOCs, as well as their growing vertical and international scope and scale, can be explained with reference to powerful institutional forces. The earlier strategic management and economics theories tend to assume that profit maximization will be the primary directive of MNCs.

Instead, profit maximization is only one of several objectives for these mainly state-backed entities. One example of this is in the local employment practices of the NOCs, such that in the Middle East preference and indeed protection is given to local staff over and above commercial considerations. Equally, Fig. 4 above shows headcount for the super-majors. We did not include data from the largest (Chinese) NOCs as it was almost an order of magnitude larger and so distorted the diagram and its message. Several of these NOCs now have individually more employees than the combined headcount in the super-majors yet only generate broadly similar levels of annual profit and revenue.

The increasingly aggressive stance by of emerging market governments regarding energy security is also manifested in the rise of the NOCs. These state-backed organizations are increasingly contesting the traditional domain of IOCs. NOCs are less beholden to corporate financial pressures and hence their strategies are motivated by the 'resource nationalism' (Stevens, 2003, 2008) of oil-producing nations leading them to expand into all stages of the industry, domestically as well as internationally.

Apart from the favoured treatment of NOCs, IOCs are also constrained by complex home- and host- country regulation and environmental concerns articulated by increasingly vocal and powerful NGOs (Levy & Kolk, 2002). The IOCs dedicate increasingly large resources to try and shape public policy and sentiment. One view is that the NOCs, coming from non-Westernized economies, place a lower emphasis on these aspects due to their different host political regimes. Regardless, long-term costs of failure are enormous, as impacts on Exxon of the Exxon Valdez spillage, Shell and the Brent Spar debacle and BP and the Deepwater Horizon explosion demonstrate many times over (Bower, 2010).

DISCUSSION AND CONCLUSION

For early business scholars (e.g. Chandler, 1977) vertically integrated firms represented the dominant business model inside most industries. The competitive advantage of industry champions such as Standard Oil, Ford, and

IBM was attributed to their extensive vertical scope. But history also reveals that industries undergo repeated cycles, alternately privileging both the integrated and non-integrated actors. The conclusion is that the decision whether to vertically integrate or disintegrate should be contingent on prevailing circumstances (Christensen, Verlinden, & Westerman, 2002).

Following this case analysis of the oil and gas industry across more than sixty years, we have arrived at a series of stylized facts. Key among these was, amongst the IOCs, a shift away from the vertically integrated models of the past. This shift goes hand in hand with a selective withdrawal from certain geographic markets. For the other key industry actors, the NOCs, the opposite was observed. These firms have continued to deepen their vertical integration as well as their international engagement.

We then confronted these facts with a number of key theories explaining vertical integration. The anecdotal nature of this data only allows preliminary testing of these theories. But clearly, strategic shifts in the industry are broadly convergent with the theories we sketched. All of them can credibly claim some support for their arguments. Given the 'big picture' nature of these shifts, it would not be surprising to find multiple causal mechanisms simultaneously driving outcomes for the industry.

With regard to the IOCs, Williamson and the transaction-cost theorists would argue that the industry evolution has led to relative increases in the cost of hierarchical governance versus transaction costs of markets, explaining the withdrawal of IOCs from downstream. Theorists in the school of industrial organization might make a counter claim, with some validity, that vertical integration in domestic and international markets was abandoned when it no longer held prospects of barring new entrants. Resource-based scholars would point out that the previously distinct capabilities in oil refining and marketing were rendered imitable over time, paving the way for the divestment of these stages.

Finally, institutional scholars can credibly suggest the change in institutional conditions on account of resurgent resource nationalism has drastically reshaped the environment of the IOCs and led to a corresponding change in strategic decisions regarding their vertical, and also international, scope.

In line with our contingency stance, in the past there were compelling reasons (TCE, RBV, power-based or institutional) for the IOCs to be vertically integrated. Many of these rationales have since disappeared as technologies developed, global markets and standards for the various oil- and gas-related products emerged, institutional norms changed and new players appeared. As a result, the industry architecture became temporarily misaligned (Cacciatori & Jacobides, 2005). The long periods of time between changes in some conditions and the efforts of the IOCs in unravelling their vertical integration are explained by the reputation this industry has developed for significant inertia (Grant & Cibin, 1996). The IOCs are perceived to make strategic changes only when environmental changes have sustained and deleterious effects on their overall profitability (Grant & Cibin, 1996).

In comparison, NOCs have developed in a more linear fashion, steadily building their degree of vertical integration and internationalization over time. This defiance of the new reality in the wider industry tells us something about the strength of institutional forces in this industry. Strong demand in emerging markets, coupled with limited global supplies further increased resource nationalism, eclipsing all other concerns. As a result, the NOCs were given even stronger incentives to continue with their existing strategic roadmaps.

This also tells us something about the privileged position these entities occupy. Unlike privately-owned oil and gas MNCs, they are the extension of the dominant institutions in this industry, the nation states. The close links between NOCs and their home governments are clearly evident even in the governance of the NOCs. For instance, a former Chairman of Gazprom, Dmitry Medvedev, is the current President of Russia. As a result of this ownership and other ties, the NOCs enjoy powerful advantages. They are heavily favoured by their owners in terms of access to new natural resources, as well as having access to lower cost capital funding. Most importantly, to varying degrees, the NOCs are free from many commercial pressures due to their objective of ensuring a national supply of oil and gas and its derivatives. These institutional arguments adequately explain why NOCs have been able to maintain strategies of vertical integration alongside increasing international expansion.

Given the limits in our approach and data, it is impossible to tell which of these theories achieves the highest explanatory power. Our own, somewhat speculative, belief is that institutional forces in this industry have become the dominant factor, giving institutional theories the upper hand. Equally, the economic and strategic management theories explaining vertical integration seem more pertinent to understand the development pathway of the IOCs. Since these theories assume profit maximization motives they cannot be expected to be good predictors of NOC behaviour. By contrast, institutional theory has relevance for both IOCs and NOCs. These institutional, economic and strategic arguments are intertwined. As Peng et al. (2008) remind us, business theories all too often take the institutional framework as given. In reality, resource-based, transaction-based and other arguments are heavily influenced by the prevailing institutional forces. Any particular strategy or type of behaviour may be appropriate and lucrative under one set of rules but illegitimate and deleterious under another set.

The change in vertical scope inside IOCs also impacts on their international diversity. While others point out the interconnectedness of diversification and internationalization (Meyer, 2006), our investigation highlights the nexus between MNC vertical integration and de-internationalization.

Beyond confirming certain theories, our investigation of the industry yields other insights for both the IB and strategic literature. Our analysis indicates de-internationalization may be more common than is acknowledged in the literature. Research on de-internationalization is sparse (Turcan, 2013), perhaps due to the connotations of failure associated with it (Benito & Welch, 1997).

Alternative perspectives place de-internationalization as a worthwhile exercise in error correction (Casson, 1986) or as an astute reaction to a changed set of circumstances. In the case of the oil and gas IOCs, de-internationalization theories seem to fit with best with this last description. Our findings highlight how both strategic de-internationalization and internationalization are specific to individual stages of the industry value chain and can occur in a variety of ways inside the IOCs. We are thus empirically reinforcing the arguments of Zander and Zander (1996) that internationalization (and by implication de-internationalization) should be studied at the business unit, rather than MNC, level.

Turcan (2011, p. 7) suggests that de-internationalization is best conceptualized as the spectrum of strategic decisions that equate to degrees of either partial, or complete, withdrawal from markets. De-internationalization has both mode and process elements. The former represent the reversal of market-entry strategies, which means to '... de-invest, de-franchise and de-export ...'. The process element of de-internationalization is frequently driven by shocks in the external environment that require strategic intervention. This seems to align well with our observations of oil and gas MNCs. The four regimes of Baaij et al. (2011) are book-ended by major shocks to the industry, although it is only following the 2008 Financial Crisis, the trigger for this suggestion of the fifth regime, that the IOCs commenced a large-scale effort to de-internationalize, overwhelmingly in their downstream.

Turcan (2011, p. 8) cites Ansic and Pugh (1999) who suggest that sunk cost is the main determinant of effectiveness in de-internationalization and this study supports this position. Upstream requires large upfront expenditures as sunk costs but generates huge profit with no potential for subsequent financial loss. There are therefore no reasons to de-internationalize in the upstream. Downstream is the opposite case: refineries are also very costly but the on-going profitability is extremely marginal. The possibility of incurring a loss is a fact of life and given that these downstream assets are often depreciated over a much longer period (Teece, 1976) it has, in accounting terms, fewer sunk costs and a higher capital value. This means disposal strategies are effective as long as purchasers exist and a removal of these assets from the balance sheet has little effect on overall firm profitability.

To further illustrate merits of in-depth analysis of industries and firms, we look at the body of work concerning the real benefits of internationalization. Research on the multinationality – performance relationship has produced notoriously varied results, which are attributed to many sources, including conceptual misspecification, measurement error, inappropriate analytical techniques and idiosyncratic sample characteristics (Hennart, 2011; Hult, 2011; Osegowitsch & Zalan, 2005).

Our profile of this industry highlights high heterogeneity between the businesses and underscores the difficulty in conducting aggregated analysis that involves any large or complex organizations. Our investigation has revealed a simultaneous adoption of two opposite strategies. The growing internationalization of the upstream is coupled with de-internationalization in the downstream, which would defy all but the most granular analyses of both multinationality and performance.

We suggest the empirical dichotomy also occurs in other industries. De-internationalization has been seen widely in financial services: several large investment banks have withdrawn from many of their international markets. This represents another case of divergent line-of-business strategies, as retail banking operations have been affected far less after the 2008 Financial Crisis. Another example is in technology, when the hardware manufacturers such as IBM and HP moved into services. These two segments are very different – hardware is high cost whilst services offer steady state revenues – but their vertical integration was vital to firm survival at the time. Tension between these businesses has now emerged however, as services revenues are harder to protect and the segment is changing due to the entry of low-cost competitors from emerging nations. The parallels to the oil and gas industry are clear just by comparing Essar (an Indian refiner) with Wipro (an Indian IT firm) and in terms of the removal of benefits from vertical integration of disparate businesses these entrants have caused.

The summary insight of our investigation is that the underlying practicalities of strategic models such as vertical integration need to be better understood by academic researchers. The subtle shift from operational integration to financial integration identified in this industry is a case in point. While on the surface, vertical integration remained unchanged during the 1970s and 1980s, the real strategic shift has had fundamental implications for the IOCs, especially for their profitability. These points all culminate in this call for longer-term, whole-of-industry focused research so as to afford the scholar a genuine understanding of the subject area and its context and ultimately allow accurate analysis.

NOTES

1. The 'Seven Sisters' were Royal Dutch Shell, Anglo-Iranian (later renamed British Petroleum and now BP), Gulf Oil, the Texas Corporation (later renamed Texaco) and three direct descendants of the original Standard Oil Trust: Standard Oil of New Jersey (later renamed Exxon), Socony-Vacuum (a merger consisting of Standard Oil of New York (Socony) and Vacuum Oil; this merged entity was then later renamed Mobil) and Standard Oil of California (Socal, later renamed Chevron).

2. PTT of Thailand is one of the few MNCs in the industry that provides detail on trading volume and revenues. In 2011, trading volume accounted for some 54% of this NOC's US$86b annual revenue. However, the trading profit accounts for less than 1% of annual earnings. Bower (2010) notes none of the large IOCs provide details on the extents of their trading businesses, all of which are subsumed into the overall downstream businesses.

3. When adjusted for inflation, oil prices were still below the levels reached in the world oil crises of the 1970s.

4. Advances in shale oil recovery technology drove a 39% jump in U.S. oil production since 2011, the steepest rise in its history, and will boost output to a 28-year high in 2014 (Loder, 2014).

5. This is done in tandem with occasional asset sales in the upstream segment. For example, the super-majors are gradually exiting their mature North Sea fields as returns on capital no longer meet internal benchmarks.

6. Not only are these downstream assets sold to NOCs, many of them are simply closed. According to the International Energy Agency, 15 European refineries have closed in the past five years, with a 16th due to shut later this year (Loder, 2014) and in the United States, large parts of the US East Coast refining capacity lies mothballed.

7. Asset specificity in the case of this industry also arises from the site-specificity (Williamson, 1985) of buyers and sellers. Teece (1976) highlights how the typical refiner at the time could only draw crude from areas to which they had access by pipeline or deep-water port. Given that a more limited pipeline and infrastructure

network existed during this time, site-specificity would also seem to have been a significant industry factor.

ACKNOWLEDGEMENTS

The authors are grateful to Dr. Carmel de Nahlik and Dr. Peter Miskell for comments on the original chapter and our peers among the editors and fellow authors of this volume during the workshop in Bocconi University in November 2013 for their assistance in enhancing the contents of this chapter.

REFERENCES

Allison, G. (1969). Conceptual models and the Cuban missile crisis. *The American Political Science Review, 63*(3), 689–718.

Ansic, D., & Pugh, G. (1999). An experimental test of trade hysteresis: Market exit and entry decisions in the presence of sunk costs and exchange rate uncertainty. *Applied Economics, 31*(4), 427–436.

Antill, N., & Arnott, R. (2004). Creating value in the oil industry. *Journal of Applied Corporate Finance, 16*(1), 18–32.

Baaij, M., de Jong, A., & van Dalen, J. (2011). The dynamics of superior performance among the largest firms in the global oil industry, 1954–2008. *Industrial and Corporate Change, 20*(3), 789–824.

Bain, J. (1956). *Barriers to new competition.* Cambridge, MA: Harvard University Press.

Barney, J. (1991). Firm resources and sustained competitive advantage. *Journal of Management, 17*(1), 99–120.

Barrera-Rey, F. (1995). *The effects of vertical integration on oil company performance.* Oxford Institute for Energy Studies, WPM, 21.

Bartlett, C., & Ghoshal, S. (1989). *Managing across borders: The transnational solution.* London: Taylor and Francis.

Benito, G., & Welch, L. (1997). De-internationalization. *Management International Review, 37*(2), 7–25.

Blaikie, N. (2003). *Analyzing quantitative data: From description to explanation.* London: Sage.

Bower, T. (2010). *Oil: Money, politics, and power in the 21st century.* Manchester: Grand Central Publishing.

Buckley, P., & Casson, M. (1976). *The future of the multinational enterprise.* Basingstoke: Macmillan.

Cacciatori, E., & Jacobides, M. (2005). The dynamic limits of specialization: Vertical integration reconsidered. *Organization Studies, 26*(12), 1851–1883.

Casson, M. (1986). *Multinationals and world trade: Vertical integration and the division of labour in world industries.* London: Allen and Unwin.

Chandler, A. (1962). *Strategy and structure: Chapters in the history of the industrial enterprise.* Cambridge, MA: MIT Press.

Chandler, A. (1977). *The visible hand: The managerial revolution in American business.* Cambridge, MA: Harvard University Press.

Chesbrough, H., & Teece, D. (1996). When is virtual virtuous: Organizing for innovation. *Harvard Business Review, 74,* 1.

Christensen, C., Verlinden, M., & Westerman, G. (2002). Disruption, disintegration and the dissipation of differentiability. *Industrial and Corporate Change, 11*(5), 955–993.

Cibin, R., & Grant, R. (1996). Restructuring among the world's leading oil companies, 1980–92. *British Journal of Management, 7,* 283–307.

Copeland, T., Koller, T., & Murrin, J. (1980). *Valuation: Measuring and managing the value of companies.* New York, NY: Wiley.

Davis, J. (2006). And then there were four … ' A thumbnail history of oil industry restructuring, 1971–2005, Chapter 1. In Davis, J. (Ed.). *The changing world of oil: An Analysis of Corporate Change and Adaptation.* Canada: Dalhousie University.

De Marchi, V., Di Maria, E., & Ponte, S. (2014). Multinational firms and the management of global networks: Insights from global value chain studies. In T. Pedersen, M. Venzin, T. M. Devinney, & L. Tihanyi (Eds.), *Orchestration of the Global Network Organisation* (Vol. 27). Advances in International Management. Bingley, UK: Emerald Publishing Group.

DiMaggio, P., & Powell, W. (1983). The iron cage revisited: Institutional isomorphism and collective rationality in organizational fields. *American Sociological Review, 48*(2), 147–160.

Dosi, G. (1982). Technological paradigms and technological trajectories: A suggested interpretation of the determinants and directions of technical change. *Research Policy, 11,* 147–162.

Economist. (2011). Big Oil's bigger brothers, October 29, 2011.

Economist. (2012a). Special Report on State Capitalism, January 21, 2012.

Economist. (2012b). The unsung masters of the oil industry, July 21, 2012.

Economist. (2013). Supermajordämmerung, August 3, 2013.

EIA. (2013). Retrieved from http://www.eia.gov/

Exxon. (2012). Financial & Operating Review. Retrieved from http://exxonmobil.com/ Corporate/Files/news_pub_fo_2012.pdf. Accessed on January 20, 2014.

Grant, R. (2003). Strategic planning in a turbulent environment: Evidence from the oil majors. *Strategic Management Journal, 24*(6), 491–517.

Grant, R. (2005). *Contemporary strategy analysis and cases: Text and cases.* (7th ed.). Oxford: Blackwells.

Grant, R. (2012). *Contemporary strategy analysis and cases: Text and cases.* (8th ed.). Oxford: John Wiley & Sons.

Grant, R., & Cibin, R. (1996). Strategy, structure and market turbulence: The international oil majors, 1970–1991. *Scandinavian Journal of Management, 12*(2), 165–188.

Hennart, J.-F. (2011). A theoretical assessment of the empirical literature on the impact of multinationality on performance. *Global Strategy Journal, 1,* 135–151.

Hult, G. (2011). A strategic focus on multinationality and firm performance. *Global Strategy Journal, 1,* 171–174.

Hymer, S. (1976). *The international operations of national firms: A study of direct foreign investment.* Cambridge, MA: MIT Press.

Jacobides, M. (2005). Industry change through vertical disintegration: How and why markets emerged in mortgage banking. *Academy of Management Journal, 48*, 465–498.

Jacobides, M., Knudsen, T., & Augier, M. (2006). Benefiting from innovation: Value creation, value appropriation and the role of industry architectures. *Research Policy, 35*, 1200–1221.

Jarzabkowski, P. (2008). Shaping strategy as a structuration process. *Academy of Management Journal, 51*(4), 621–650.

Khan, K. (1987). National oil companies: Form, structure, accountability and control. In K. I. F. Khan (Ed.), *Petroleum resources and development: Economic, legal and policy issues for developing countries*. London: Belhaven Press.

Khanna, T., & Palepu, K. (1999). The right way to restructure conglomerates in emerging markets. *Harvard Business Review*, (4), 125–134.

Lamont, O. (1997). Cash flow and investment: Evidence from internal capital markets. *The Journal of Finance, 52*, 83–109.

Levy, D., & Kolk, A. (2002). Strategic responses to global climate change: Conflicting pressures on multinationals in the oil industry. *Business and Politics, 4*, 275–300.

Loder, A. (2014). Unforeseen U.S. Oil Boom Upends Markets as Drilling Spreads. *Washington Post*, January 08. Retrieved from http://washpost.bloomberg.com/Story?docId=1376-MZ01366VDKHY01-5UAQ7ALIIUEHM5GK75KB1HT9IQ. Accessed on January 20, 2014.

Meyer, K. (2006). Global focusing: From domestic conglomerates to global specialists. *Journal of Management Studies, 43*(5), 1109–1144.

Monteverde, K. (1995). Technical dialog as an incentive for vertical integration in the semiconductor industry. *Management Science, 41*(10), 1624–1638.

Nelson, R., & Winter, S. (1982). The schumpeterian trade-off revisited. *The American Economic Review, 72*(1), 114–132.

Ollinger, M. (1994). The limits of growth of the multidivisional firm: A case study of the US oil industry from 1930–90. *Strategic Management Journal, 15*(7), 503–520.

Osegowitsch, T., & Zalan, T. (2005). *Two decades of multinationality-performance research: The persistent problem of under-specification, Australian centre for international business*. Australia: University of Melbourne.

Pedersen, T., Venzin, M., Devinney, T., & Tihanyi, L. (2014). Introduction to part II: Orchestration of the Global Network Organisation. In T. Pedersen, M. Venzin, T. M. Devinney, & L. Tihanyi (Eds.), *Orchestration of the Global Network Organisation* (Vol. 27). Advances in International Management. Bingley, UK: Emerald Publishing Group.

Peng, M., Wang, D., & Jiang, Y. (2008). An institution-based view of international business strategy: A focus on emerging economies. *Journal of International Business Studies, 39*, 920–936.

Penrose, E. (1959). *The theory of the growth of the firm*. Oxford: Oxford University Press.

Penrose, E. (1971). *The growth of firms: Middle east oil, and other essays*. London: Cass.

Pfeffer, J., & Salancik, G. (1978). *The external control of organizations: A resource dependence perspective*. New York, NY: Harper & Row Publishers.

Porter, M. (1985). *Competitive advantage*. New York, NY: Free Press.

Prahalad, C., & Doz, Y. (1987). *The multinational mission: Balancing local demands and global vision*. New York, NY: Free Press.

PTT. (2013). 2012 Annual Report. Retrieved from http://ptt.listedcompany.com/ar.html. Accessed on January 20, 2014.

Rosenbloom, R. (2000). Leadership, capabilities, and technological change: The transformation of NCR in the electronic era. *Strategic Management Journal, 21*(10–11), 1083–1103.

Sampson, A. (1975). *The seven sisters: The great oil companies and the world they shaped.* New York, NY: Viking Press.

Santos, F., & Eisenhardt, K. (2005). Organizational boundaries and theories of organization. *Organization Science, 16*, 491–508.

Scott, R. (1995). *Institutions and organizations.* Thousand Oaks, CA: Sage.

Stevens, P. (2003). Economist and the oil industry: Facts versus analysis, the case of vertical integration. In L. C. Hunt & C. Robinson (Eds.), *Energy in a competitive market: Essays in honour of Colin Robinson.* Philadelphia, PA: University of Pennsylvania Press.

Stevens, P. (2005). Oil markets. *Oxford Review of Economic Policy, 21*, 1.

Stevens, P. (2008). National oil companies and international oil companies in the ME: Under the shadow of government and the resource nationalism cycle. *The Journal of World Energy Law & Business, 1*, 5–30.

Stobaugh, R. (1976). The oil companies in the crisis. In R. Vernon (Ed.), *The oil crisis.* Toronto, ON: McLeod Limited.

Teece, D. (1976). *Vertical integration and vertical divestiture in the U.S. Oil industry: Economic analysis and policy implications.* Stanford, CA: Institute for Energy Studies.

Teece, D. (1986). Profiting from technological innovation: Implications for integration, collaboration, licensing and public policy. *Research Policy, 15*(6), 285–305.

Turcan, R. (2011). De-internationalization: A conceptualization. In AIB-UK & Ireland Chapter Conference' *International Business: New Challenges, New Forms, New Practices.*

Turcan, R. (2013). The philosophy of turning points: A case of de-internationalization. *Advances in International Management, 26*, 219–235.

Vernon, R. (1971). *Sovereignty at bay: The multinational spread of US enterprises.* New York, NY: Basic Books.

Vernon, R. (1976). An Interpretation. In R. Vernon (Ed.), *The oil crisis.* Toronto, ON: McLeod Limited.

Williamson, O. (1981). The economics of organizations: The transaction cost approach. *American Journal of Sociology, 87*, 548–577.

Williamson, O. (1985). *The economic institutions of capitalism.* New York, NY: Free Press.

Yarrow, G. (1991). Vertical supply arrangements: Issues arid applications in the energy industries. *Oxford Review of Economic Policy, 7*, 35–53.

Yergin, D. (1991). *The prize – The epic quest for oil, money and power.* London: Simon and Schuster.

Zander, I., & Zander, U. (1996). The oscillating multinational firm: Alfa laval in the period 1890–1990. In I. Björkman & M. Forsgren (Eds.), *The nature of the international firm: Nordic contributions to international business research.* Copenhagen: Business School.

AUTHORS' BIOGRAPHIES

Sergey Anokhin is Associate Professor of Entrepreneurship and Director of the Center for Entrepreneurship and Business Innovation at Kent State University. At the time of the study, he also was a visiting professor at Voronezh State University. His research interests include entrepreneurship and innovation management in a variety of contexts. His teaching portfolio includes doctoral, MBA, and undergraduate courses in strategy, global management, and entrepreneurship delivered in traditional, online, and blended formats.

Kazuhiro Asakawa is Mitsubishi Chaired Professor of Management and a Professor of multinational organizations and strategy at Graduate School of Business Administration, Keio University, Japan. He received his PhD from INSEAD and his MBA from Harvard University. His research interests are focused on innovation and R&D management of multinational corporations, cross-border knowledge sourcing and leveraging, subsidiary evolution, and autonomy-control dynamics. He is an Associate Editor of Global Strategy Journal and serves on the editorial boards of Journal of International Management, Journal of International Business Studies, and Academy of Management Perspectives. He was also a Senior Editor of Asia Pacific Journal of Management. He was a Visiting Scholar at MIT Sloan School of Management, and he also taught at many overseas universities, including Yonsei University, Johannes Kepler University Linz, WU-Vienna Doctoral Workshop, and McGill MBA Japan Program. He currently chairs the Japan Chapter of the Academy of International Business.

Gabriel R. G. Benito (PhD, Norwegian School of Economics) is Professor at BI Norwegian Business School, where he currently also serves as Dean of Doctoral and Masters Programs. He is a Consulting Editor of Journal of International Business Studies and member of the Editorial Boards of Academy of Management Perspectives, Global Strategy Journal, International Business Review, Management International Review, and Management and Organization Review. Recent books include Foreign Operation Methods (with L. S. Welch and B. Petersen, 2007, Edward

Elgar), and Multinationals on the Periphery (with R. Narula, 2007, Palgrave). His research agenda currently concentrates on strategies and structures of multinational enterprises. His research has appeared in many books and journals, including Journal of International Business Studies, Journal of Management Studies, Journal of Economic Geography, Applied Economics, Managerial and Decision Economics, Management International Review, Journal of Business Research, and International Business Review.

Arnaldo Camuffo is Professor of Business Organization at the Bocconi University, Milan, Italy, where he is also Director of the PhD Program in Business Administration and Management and Director of CRIOS – Center for Research in Innovation, Organization, Strategy & Entrepreneurship.

After getting an MBA from the Sloan School of Management at M.I.T. and a PhD in Management from the Ca'Foscari University of Venice, Italy, he taught at the Ca' Foscari University of Venice and at the University of Padova, Italy, and held visiting positions at the University of Deusto, at the Massachusetts Institute of Technology and at the University of Michigan, Dearborn. His research appeared in Strategic Management Journal, Organization Science, Research Policy, MIT Sloan Management Review, Industrial and Corporate Change, Industrial Relations, International Journal of Management Reviews, Industry and Innovation, International Journal of Human Resource Management, International Journal of Operations and Production Management, Entrepreneurship and Regional Development, Cross Cultural Management, and Journal of Management Development.

Simon Collinson is Dean of Birmingham Business School and a Professor of International Business and Innovation at the University of Birmingham. He is a Visiting Professor at Zhejiang University, a member of the council of the UK Economic and Social Research Council (ESRC), the British Academy of Management council and the Executive Board of the Association of Business Schools. Simon has published numerous articles and books on the management of innovation, international business strategy, and organizational complexity. His research features on BBC Radio 4 and in the Times, the Sunday Times, the New Statesman, Management Today and US News & World Report.

Colin Dale is a former management consultant with a leading strategy firm. He is now a doctoral candidate at the Henley Business School, University of Reading and is conducting empirical research in the oil and gas industry. He is the 2014 recipient of the AIBUKI/Michael Z. Brooke prize.

Valentina De Marchi is Senior Post Doc at the University of Padova, Italy, Department of Economics and Management "Marco Fanno." Her main research focus is the study of environmental innovations and sustainability strategies and she is also interested in and published on internationalization and global value chains, on the evolution of Italian industrial districts and on the role of Knowledge Intensive Business Services (KIBS) within regional innovation systems. Her studies have been published in journals such as Research Policy, European Planning Studies, Business Strategy and the Environment, Economia Politica: Journal of Analytical and Institutional Economics, Journal of Knowledge Management, Competition & Change.

Eleonora Di Maria is Associate Professor of Business Management at the University of Padova, Italy, Department of Economics and Management "Marco Fanno." Her research focuses on internationalization strategies of firms and local economic systems, global value chains, as well as on Knowledge Intensive Business Services (KIBS) and innovation processes related to environmental sustainability. She has edited several books and her studies have been published in international books and journals such as Research Policy, Journal of Knowledge Management, International Journal of Operations and Production Management, Industry and Innovation, Knowledge Management Research & Practice, European Planning Studies, Business Strategy and the Environment, Competition & Change.

Frank Elter holds a doctorate in strategy and organization from the BI Norwegian Business School. He is currently Vice-President in Telenor Research and heads Telenor's research strategy. In addition he is doing active research with special interest in strategy, organization, and international management. He has held several positions in Telenor since he joined the company in 1995: Headed organizational change programs; advised executives on implications of future technology trends; Head of Strategy in Telenor Nordic Mobile; and Vice-President in Group Strategy.

Igor Filatotchev is Associate Dean and Professor of corporate governance and strategy at Cass Business School, City University London, and Visiting Professor in Vienna University of Economics and Business. He earned his PhD in economics from the Institute of World Economy and International relations (Moscow, the Russian Federation). His research interests are focused on corporate governance effects on entrepreneurship development, strategic decisions, and organizational change. Key research programmes currently in progress include analysis of resource and strategy roles of corporate governance; corporate governance life cycle; and a knowledge-based view on governance development in entrepreneurial firms and IPOs.

Paul N. Gooderham is Professor of International Management and Head of the Department of Strategy & Management at NHH: Norwegian School of Economics, Bergen. Among his books are a co-authored text book, International Management: Theory and Practice (Edward Elgar) published in 2013. His research interests are concentrated on international and comparative management. Since 1994, he has been a member of Cranet the largest comparative HRM research network in the world. He has published numerous articles in journals such as Journal of Management Studies, Journal of International Business Studies, Strategic Management Journal, Human Relations, Management International Review, International Journal of Human Resource Management, European Journal of Industrial Relations, and Administrative Science Quarterly.

Stefan Heidenreich is Account Manager at GfK Austria. In his previous position as a Research Associate at the Institute for International Business, he earned a PhD from WU Vienna University of Economics and Business. His research focused on antecedents and consequences of political strategies in emerging markets and investments in high-risk countries. He presented his research across the globe and is published in several book chapters.

Jasper J. Hotho is Associate Professor of International Business at the Department of International Economics and Management at Copenhagen Business School. His research focuses on how societal institutions affect learning and decision-making processes in multinational organizations, and on how individuals and organizations handle conflicting institutional demands. In addition, he is interested in the study of capitalism and its varieties, and the use of set-theoretic methods for socio-economic analyses. His work on these topics has been published in journals such as *Organization Studies, Management Learning*, and the *British Journal of Management*. He sits on the editorial review boards of the *Journal of Management* and the *Journal of International Business Studies*.

Christopher J. Ibbott is a strategic business advisor in private practice, a Visiting Professor in the Surrey Business School at the University of Surrey, UK, and a published author. Ibbott is an internationally experienced Senior Executive with significant business accomplishments in the

Information Technology and Telecommunication industries. At Vodafone Group Plc., he was Director, Network Supply Chain Management in Group Technology and prior positions included Director, Global Supply Chain Management and Director, IT and Project Management in the UK mobile operating company. Prior company positions included Consultant Director, Terminals at Orbitel Mobile Communications Limited; Managing Director & Regional VP at Memorex Telex (UK) Limited; Senior VP & GM European Operations at System Industries, Inc. of California. He has Master of Technology and Doctor of Business Administration degrees awarded from Brunel University, UK, and is a CEDR (London) Accredited Mediator.

Amit Karna is Assistant Professor at the Department of Strategy, Organization and Leadership at the EBS Universität für Wirtschaft u. Recht's EBS Business School. He was also Visiting Scholar at University of California Berkeley's Haas School of Business in 2011. He obtained his doctoral degree in Strategy from Indian Institute of Management Ahmedabad. Prior to academics, he worked in the industry for five years with an Indian multinational business group.

Amit's research interests include Dynamic capabilities, Capability building, Internationalization, Emerging Market Firms, and Agglomerations. He serves on the Editorial Review Board of Journal of Management, and as an ad hoc reviewer for Strategic Management Journal, Research Policy and Journal of Management Studies among others.

Andrey Kretinin is a doctoral candidate in the Department of Marketing and Entrepreneurship at Kent State University. His primary research envelops the domains of strategic management, entrepreneurship, family business, and international business, with focus on franchising, its structure, governance, internationalization, and expansion. He currently teaches case-based undergraduate courses, such as marketing research, marketing management, and international marketing both in-class and online.

Maya Kumar (MBA) is a PhD Candidate in General Management and International Business at the Richard Ivey School of Business in Canada. She has lived in the United States, the Netherlands, Hong Kong, and Singapore and worked in the fields of logistics and supply chain management and biotechnology. Her research interests include management of global innovation, knowledge sharing and virtual teams, and offshore outsourcing in high-tech sectors. She has published teaching cases on international firms with the Asia Case Research Centre.

Vikas Kumar is Associate Professor of International Business and Strategy in the Discipline of International Business at the University of Sydney Business School. His previous appointments were at Bocconi University (2004–2009), and as Visiting Scholars at Stanford University (2008–2009) and University of Reading (2012–2013). He has been elected as the Representative-at-large (2013–2014) for the Global Strategy Interest Group in the Strategic Management Society. He obtained his doctoral degree in International Business in 2004 from Saint Louis University.

Vikas's research interests include Internationalization, Emerging Market Firms, Emerging Markets, Business Groups, and Outsourcing/Offshoring. He has been co-guest editor of the special issues in Journal of Management Studies (2010), Journal of International Management (2013), Management International Review (2014). Vikas serves on the Editorial Review Board of JMS, MIR, TIBR, and the Global Strategy Journal (GSJ). He is the director of the Emerging Market Internationalization Research Group (EMIRG) at the University of Sydney Business School.

Marcus M. Larsen is Assistant Professor at Department of Strategic Management and Globalization, Copenhagen Business School. His research interests are related to the organizational design of offshoring, and particularly on how the relationship between complexity and learning influences decision making and performance. His research is published in journal such as Strategic Management Journal, Global Strategy Journal, and Journal of International Management. He has also published a number of teaching cases.

Gabriella Lojacono is Associate Professor of Strategy and Director of the M.Sc. in Management at Bocconi University and Senior Professor at SDA Bocconi School of Management. Her research focuses on International Business and Design Management. She has published numerous articles and chapters in scholarly and applied publications including Sloan Management Review and Long Range Planning. She teaches corporate executive programs and gives lectures on international strategies at Master and undergraduate programs. Gabriella Lojacono received her PhD from the Bocconi University's School of Management. During her Ph.D, she spent a period at Copenhagen Business School as Visiting Scholar. She received her B.S. in Bocconi University's General Management Program, specialization in Finance. She worked with range of clients, including Alessi, B&B, Poliform, Scavolini, Boffi, Ikea, Flos (furniture and lighting industry). Thanks to such an industry experience, she wrote two book for entrepreneurs and managers on the furniture industry titled "Le imprese del sistema arredamento: strategie di design, prodotto e distribution" ("The firms of the furniture system: product and distribution strategy") edited by ETAS/RCS, 2003 and "Competitività e crescita internazionale delle imprese del sistema arredamento" ("Competitiveness and International Growth of Furniture Companies") ETAS/RCS, 2007.

Randi Lunnan (PhD, Norwegian School of Economics) is Department Chair and Professor at the Department of Strategy and Logistics, BI Norwegian Business School. Her research interests include strategic alliances as well as the structuring of multinational enterprises. She is on the editorial board of Global Strategy Journal. Her research has appeared in many books and journals, including Strategic Management Journal, Journal of Management, Journal of Management Studies, Journal of World Business, Journal of International Management, Scandinavian Journal of Management, and Academy of Management Executive.

Tuija Mainela is a Professor of International Business at the Oulu Business School, University of Oulu, Finland. Her main research interests are international networks and their dynamics, networking behaviours in international operations, social relationships in business, and international entrepreneurship. On these topics, she has published in journals, such as International Journal of Management Reviews, Industrial Marketing Management, Scandinavian Journal of Management, Management Decision, Journal of Service Management and Journal of International Entrepreneurship.

Elizabeth Maitland is a Senior Lecturer in Strategy and International Business in the School of Management, University of New South Wales, Australia. Her research focuses on the decision-making and activities of multinational enterprises (MNEs) in diverse regulatory, economic and social contexts; the nature of state-MNE relations; and corruption. Elizabeth's work has been published in leading journals, including *Journal of International Business Studies, California Management Review, Management International Review* and *Advances in International Management*. She is on the editorial boards of the *Journal of International Business Studies* and *Human Relations.*

Snejina Michailova (PhD from Copenhagen Business School, Denmark) is Professor of International Business at The University of Auckland Business School, New Zealand. Her research interests include organizational behavior issues in a cross-border context, knowledge based perspectives on organizations, and methodological issues in management and international management research. Her work has appeared in *Academy of Management Review*, *Academy of Management Executive*, *Journal of Management Studies*, *Journal of International Business Studies*, *Journal of World Business*, *Management International Review*, *International Business Review*, *International Journal of Human Resource Management*, *Journal of International Management*, *Critical Perspectives on International Business*, *California Management Review*, *Long Range Planning*, *Management Learning*, *Journal of Knowledge Management*, *Organizational Dynamics*, *Employee Relations*, *European Management Journal*, *Business Strategy Review*, and other journals. Snejina has co-edited books on knowledge governance (Oxford University Press), Women in international management (Edward Elgar), HRM in Central and Eastern Europe (Routledge) and research methodologies in non-Western contexts (Palgrave Macmillan). She serves on the editorial boards of several academic journals.

Todd Morgan is a doctoral candidate in the Department of Marketing and Entrepreneurship at Kent State University. His research concerns strategic orientations of the firm and organizational reputation and how they impact competitive advantage. He also focuses on new product development processes and resource alignment of partnering firms and how they affect innovation outcomes.

Phillip C. Nell is an Associate Professor at the Department of Strategic Management and Globalization at Copenhagen Business School. Phillip received his doctorate and his habilitation from WU Wien (Vienna University of Economics and Business).

Before joining academia, Phillip gained considerable industry experience as a consultant with Roland Berger Strategy Consultants. He has conducted projects and research in cooperation with firms such as Gerresheimer, Kone, Puma, Boehringer Ingelheim, and T-Systems as well as non-profit organizations such as Diakonie, giving him lots of insights into management practice. Phillip is widely experienced both in degree-course and executive education. His research interests are centered on the organization of the multinational corporation, the management of subsidiaries, and the role headquarters play in large and complex organizations. His research has been accepted for publication in Strategic Management Journal, Long Range Planning, Journal of International Management, Journal of World Business, and Research Policy among others.

Thomas Osegowitsch is a Lecturer in the Department of Management and Marketing at the University of Melbourne in Australia. His research works focus on the strategies of Multinational Corporations. His work has been published in a variety of academic journals and books including Journal of International Business Studies and Business Horizons.

Chiara Paolino is Assistant Professor of Organization theory at Università Cattolica del Sacro Cuore, Milan. Her area of expertise revolves around lean management, organizational and individual learning, and organizational climate. She teaches Organization Theory and Behavior at undergraduate, master, graduate and PhD level.

Smita Paul is a PhD student in the field of International Business at The University of Auckland Business School, New Zealand. Her PhD thesis examines the dynamic nature of multinational enterprise relationships, specifically the structure and configuration of intra-firm relationships. Her research interests include the business network perspective of organizations and inter- and intra-organizational knowledge sharing in multinational enterprises. Her previous experience has included teaching courses on management, sustainable business and international business.

Alexander Paulsson is holding master degrees in History, Political Science and Business Administration and is currently completing a PhD at Lund University School of Economics and Management, Sweden. His research interests include bureaucracy, informal economy, the role of commodities in political theory, and the cultural history of market society.

Elina Pernu is a Postdoctoral researcher at the Oulu Business School, University of Oulu, Finland. Her main research interests include multinational corporations, internal networks, sense-making in organizations and management of global customer relationships.

Rebecca Piekkari is Professor of International Business at Aalto University, School of Business (formerly known as Helsinki School of Economics). Her research focuses on the challenges of managing multinational corporations. More specifically, she has contributed to two main research streams: language in international business and the use of qualitative methods in international business and management research. She has also participated in a discussion about language as a methodological question in management and organization studies. Her work has been published in journals such as the Academy of Management Review, Journal of

Management Studies, and Journal of International Business Studies as well as in several handbooks in the area.

Håkan Pihl is PhD and Senior Lecturer in Business Administration at Lund University School of Economics and Management, Sweden. He is also associated to Kristianstad University, Sweden. Håkan Pihl has published research in areas such as international business, the theory of the firm and environmental economics. He is interested in new institutional economics related to coordination and control and has written textbooks in economics and environmental economics. Håkan Pihl is currently the Director of Education at Lund University School of Economics and Management and responsible for a Master of Science program in Management.

Stefano Ponte is Professor of International Political Economy at the Department of Business and Politics, Copenhagen Business School. His research deals with how the global economy is governed and how developing countries and emerging economies fare in it. Stefano's work is informed by global value chain analysis and convention theory and explores the overlaps and tensions between private governance and public regulation, especially in relation to sustainability issues. He has published several books on these topics and his articles have appeared in journals such as Economy & Society, World Development, Global Networks, and Competition & Change.

Jonas F. Puck is Head of the Institute for International Business and Full Professor at the WU Vienna University of Economics and Business. His current research interests are strategies in emerging markets, investments in high risk countries, non-market strategies, and migrants as facilitators of internationalization. Jonas serves on the Editorial Boards of the Journal of International Business Studies, Long Range Planning, European Management Journal and the Journal of World Business. His research has been published in journals such as the Journal of International Business Studies, Journal of International Management, Long Range Planning, International Business Review, Management International Review, Human Resource Management (US) and the International Journal of Human Resource Management, among others. In addition, he is editor or author of five books and numerous book chapters.

Vesa Puhakka is a Professor of Management at the Oulu Business School, University of Oulu, Finland. His main research interests are international entrepreneurship, opportunity creation processes, growth generating mechanisms of regions and strategy practices of organizations. His latest research on international entrepreneurship has been published in International Journal of Management Reviews. The Academy of Management and the NFIB Education Foundation awarded his doctoral dissertation for outstanding research in the fields of entrepreneurship and independent business in 2003.

Ayse Saka-Helmhout is an Associate Professor of Strategic Management at Nijmegen School of Management, Radboud University in the Netherlands. Her research focuses on the nature of the relationship between MNEs and their institutional environments to advance debates on institutional change. Her work highlights how MNEs respond to multiple institutional pressures from a comparative perspective and through processes of translation and situated practice-based learning. Her more recent work is focused on inclusive innovation for socio-economic development in emerging markets. Her work has appeared or is forthcoming in journals such as *Organization Studies, Journal of International Business Studies, Journal of Management Studies, Journal of World Business*, and *Management International Review*. She serves as a Senior Editor for Organization Studies.

André Sammartino is a Senior Lecturer in Strategy and International Business in the Department of Management & Marketing, University of Melbourne, Australia. He received his PhD from the University of Melbourne. His research focuses on (i) the internationalization choices of MNCs, specifically the role of cognition within decision processes, and the portfolio outcomes in terms of geographic distribution; and (ii) the reconfiguration of MNC footprints, especially with regard to specificity and cognitive constraints. André's work has appeared in such journals as *Journal of International Business Studies, California Management Review, Advances in International Management, Multinational Business Review* and *Australian Economic History Review*.

Raffaele Secchi is Assistant Professor of Operations at the Bocconi University, Milan. He is also Head of Operations and Technology Management Unit at SDA Bocconi School of Management. He taught at the Bocconi University, LIUC Università Cattaneo, and USI (Università della Svizzera Italiana). He was Visiting Fellow at Warvick Business School. He has authored or co-authored several articles, book chapters, and four books on operations and supply chain management. His research appeared in Industrial Marketing Management and Production Planning & Control.

Marianne Storgaard is postdoc at the University of Southern Denmark, Department of Entrepreneurship and Relationship Management. Her research and teaching interests focus on cross cultural management, change management and particularly challenges in the headquarter-subsidiary collaboration. Currently, she is involved in a large research project focusing on the intersection between the fields of change management and design.

Janne Tienari is Professor of Organizations and Management at Aalto University, School of Business, Finland. He also works as Guest Professor at Stockholm University, School of Business, Sweden. Tienari's research and teaching interests include gender and diversity, managing multinational corporations, strategy work, and cross-cultural management and communication. His latest passion is to understand management, new generations and the future. He has published in journals such as the Academy of Management Review, Organization Science, Organization Studies, Journal of Management Studies, Human Relations, British Journal of Management, Organization, and Journal of Management Inquiry.

Sverre Tomassen (PhD, BI Norwegian School of Management) is an Associate Professor in international strategy at BI Norwegian Business School. He is currently on sabbatical at School of Business, the University of Hong Kong. His current research interests include international management, and strategies and structures of multinational enterprises. He serves on the editorial board of Management and Organization Review. His research has appeared in several books and journals, including Journal of Management Studies, Journal of International Management, Scandinavian Journal of Management, and International Business Review.

Svein Ulset is Professor of International Strategy at NHH – Norwegian School of Economics, Bergen. His research interests include corporate strategy, organizational economics, international business and telecommunications economics. He has published in journals such as Journal of Economic Behaviour & Organization; Telecommunication Policy; International Journal of the Economics of Business; Industrial and Corporate Change.

Rajesh Upadhyayula is an Associate Professor of Strategy at the Indian Institute of Management Kozhikode Kerala. He brings in a wide and rich experience of working with large Indian Multinational corporations and social sector organizations. He has a doctoral degree from Indian Institute of Management, Ahmedabad. He was also a visiting PhD scholar at UNU-MERIT, Netherlands.

Rajesh's current research interests include a study of agglomerations, diversification, offshoring and emerging market firms.

Alfredo Valentino received his PhD in Management from Luiss Guido Carli University in Rome, for which he got a 3 year scholarship. Actually, he is Adjunct Professor of general management at Cà Foscari University in Venice and he works as teaching assistant in International Management at Luiss Guido Carli. His primary research interests focus on International Business and in particular on the HQ-system design, HQ-subsidiaries relations and HQ location decision. In addition, he is interested in the study of how institutional and environmental factors can influence organizational design and decision-making process in multinational corporations.

D. Eleanor Westney is Professor of Organization Studies at the Schulich School of Business in Toronto, Canada, a Visiting Professor at the School of Business at Aalto University in Helsinki, Finland, and Professor Emerita of the M.I.T. Sloan School of Management. She holds a PhD in Sociology from Princeton University, and her research focuses on organization theory and multinational corporations, Japanese organizations, the internationalization of R&D, and cross-border learning. She is a former Dean of the Academy of International Business Fellows, and in 2013 received the Booz & Company Eminent Scholar award from the International Management Division of the Academy of Management.

Christopher Williams (PhD, Birkbeck College, University of London) is Assistant Professor of International Business at the Richard Ivey School of Business in Canada. He has lived and worked in the UK, Germany, and The Netherlands and spent two decades in industry before entering academia. His research interests include entrepreneurship in international firms, knowledge creation and transfer, offshore outsourcing, and national systems of innovation. Dr. Williams' studies have been published in Journal of Management, Journal of Management Studies, Journal of World Business and Research Policy. He has also published a number of teaching cases on international firms with Ivey Publishing.